MODELS FOR CHRISTIAN HIGHER EDUCATION

Models for Christian Higher Education

Strategies for Survival and Success in the Twenty-First Century

Edited by

Richard T. Hughes
and
William B. Adrian

WILLIAM B. EERDMANS PUBLISHING COMPANY
GRAND RAPIDS, MICHIGAN / CAMBRIDGE, U.K.

© 1997 Wm. B. Eerdmans Publishing Co.
255 Jefferson Ave. S.E., Grand Rapids, Michigan 49503 /
P.O. Box 163, Cambridge CB3 9PU U.K.

Printed in the United States of America

02 01 00 99 98   7 6 5 4 3 2

Library of Congress Cataloging-in-Publication Data

Models for Christian higher education: strategies for survival and success in
the twenty-first century / edited by Richard T. Hughes and William B. Adrian.
            p.   cm.
Includes bibliographical references.
ISBN 0-8028-4121-X (pbk.)
1. Church colleges — United States — Case studies.
2. Church and college — United States — Case studies.
3. Christian education — United States — Case studies.
I. Hughes, Richard T. (Richard Thomas), 1943-   . II. Adrian, William B.
            LC427.M63 1997

371.071 — dc21   96-37653
                                                     CIP

Contents

CONTENTS

The Reformed Tradition

The Mennonite Tradition

The Evangelical/Interdenominational Tradition

Contents

The Wesleyan/Holiness Tradition

The Baptist and Restorationist Traditions

Conclusion

Acknowledgments

The editors of this volume would like to express their gratitude to the Lilly Endowment, Inc., without whose generous fiscal support the project that resulted in this book would never have been possible. We are grateful as well to the presidents of the colleges and universities that participated in this project for their encouragement and support. We also thank Kindy De Long, project assistant, for the extremely competent and professional way in which she handled the details and logistics of the project over a period of many months, and Pepperdine University graduate students Karl Nichols and Bob Cargill for their assistance in preparing the final manuscript for publication.

Finally, we wish to thank several consultants who, under the auspices of a Lilly Endowment planning grant, helped us to conceptualize this project when we were still unclear regarding how best to proceed. Those consultants included Catherine Albanese, Diana Hochstedt Butler, Conrad Cherry, Burton Clark, Lawrence Cunningham, Dan G. Danner, Sally M. Furay, Philip Gleason, Nathan Hatch, George Marsden, Albert Meyer, Arlin Meyer, Wilson Miscamble, Gordon Melton, John Orr, Stephen A. Privett, Sheldon Rothblatt, Mark R. Schwehn, Timothy Scully, Victor Stoltzfus, and Mary Stewart Van Leeuwen.

Introduction

Richard T. Hughes

How is it possible for Christian institutions of higher learning to develop into academic institutions of the first order and, at the same time, to nurture in creative ways the faith commitments that called these institutions into existence in the first place? More than this, how is it possible for Christian colleges and universities to weave first-class academic programs from the very fabric of their faith commitments? These are the questions with which this book begins.

Such questions are hardly academic. Instead, they speak to an immensely practical problem with enormous implications for the success or failure of Christian higher education in the United States. It is, indeed, the single problem that, time and again, has bedeviled attempts to create within the American context substantive Christian universities of the first order. As George Marsden and James Burtchaell have explained, Christian educators in America have established numerous Christian colleges and universities, only to see those institutions eventually abandon their Christian orientations in the interest of a purely Enlightenment-based search for truth.[1]

On the other hand, many Christian colleges — and this is a story that Marsden and Burtchaell did not trace — cling so tightly to a particularistic, *a priori*, Christian worldview that they place limits on the search for truth, largely abandon the Enlightenment-based presuppositions of higher education, and thwart any possibility that they might eventually take their place in the larger American culture as serious colleges or universities of the highest

---

1. See James Tunstead Burtchaell, "The Decline and Fall of the Christian College," *First Things* (April 1991): 16-29, and "The Decline and Fall of the Christian College (II)," *First Things* (May 1991): 30-38; and George Marsden, *The Soul of the American University* (New York: Oxford University Press, 1994), and "The Soul of the American University," *First Things* (January 1991): 34-47. See also Marsden and Bradley Longfield, eds., *The Secularization of the Academy* (New York: Oxford University Press, 1992).

1

order. If Christian higher education is to make a significant mark on the larger culture, Christian educators must find some way to address this problem successfully.

In order to gain perspective on this question, William B. Adrian, at that time the provost of Pepperdine University, asked me in 1990 to work with him in a comprehensive assessment of Christian institutions of higher learning in the United States. In consultation with the Lilly Endowment, however, we determined to pursue a project much more modest in scope.

Accordingly, we identified seven faith traditions ranging from Roman Catholic to Southern Baptist, and then identified within each of those faith traditions two institutions — fourteen in all. Again, in consultation with the Lilly Endowment, we determined to focus the project on historical narrative. We hoped that the fourteen participating institutions would be willing to have their stories told — candidly and forthrightly — by scholars within those institutions who are known and respected by their own faculty colleagues and the larger academic guild for the quality of their work.

We therefore asked one or two scholars at each of these institutions to write a historical narrative, describing how his or her institution has sought to address the relation between faith and learning from the founding of the institution to the present. For the most part, we engaged senior scholars who were not only competent but secure with the kind of charge we gave them. We are grateful to the presidents of each participating institution for their willingness to allow their institutions to be a part of this project.

Because we wished to ask not about the decline of Christian institutions of higher learning, nor about institutions that have divorced themselves from their founding faith commitments, we deliberately selected institutions for this project that have strong academic reputations and that continue to work within the context of their historic faith commitments. This means that from the perspective of this book, each institution whose narrative appears in this volume is, in a fundamental sense, a success story.

Nonetheless, we emphasized to each of the scholars selected to participate in this project that the narrative should not be a public relations piece, but should tell the story of the institution candidly and forthrightly, warts and all. The narrative should take account of key turning points not only in the life of the institution but in the broader American culture — World War II or the cultural upheavals of the 1960s, for example — and should explore how key events in the larger culture helped shape the relation between faith and learning at that institution.

The narrative, we also urged, should explore how the relationship between faith and learning helped determine faculty hiring, student recruitment, student life, allocation of scholarship funds, classroom instruction, the nature and quality of faculty scholarship, and the selection of trustees and senior administrators. Narratives also should ask how all those factors, in turn, impacted the relation between faith and learning. Not every essay in this book addresses all of the questions listed here, but all address at least some of these seminal issues. With these kinds of questions, and with the candor and forthrightness which we encouraged each of the writers to embrace, we anticipated that this book might prove useful to a wide assortment of people — trustees, presidents, deans, and faculties — who live and work in the world of Christian higher education.

For the sake of geographical comparison, we determined that within each of the seven faith traditions, one participating institution should be on the West Coast and one should be located in a more traditional region of the United States — the Midwest, the East, or the South. It was our sense that institutions situated in those regions with a longer and more settled history typically rely for funding and for students on church constituencies that on the West Coast are often too few and too weak to provide substantial support, and we wished to see how that difference played out in actual fact. The faith traditions and institutions invited to participate in the project are as follows.

Faith Tradition	Institution
Roman Catholic	University of Portland, Oregon
	St. John's University/College of St. Benedict, Minnesota
Lutheran	California Lutheran University, California
	Saint Olaf College, Minnesota
Reformed	Whitworth College, Washington
	Calvin College, Michigan
Mennonite	Fresno Pacific College, California
	Goshen College, Indiana
Evangelical/ Interdenominational	Seattle Pacific University, Washington
	Wheaton College, Illinois
Wesleyan/Holiness	Point Loma Nazarene College, California
	Messiah College, Pennsylvania
Baptistic/Restorationist	Pepperdine University, California
	Samford University, Alabama

Several colleagues who read the original proposal for this project questioned the wisdom of structuring the project along denominational lines. However, this has been in our judgment one of the project's greatest strengths since, as this project has reminded us time and again, there is no such thing as generic Christian higher education. This may sound surprising in the face of much contemporary scholarship, not to mention conventional wisdom, that suggests that denominational distinctives are growing less and less important in the United States.[2] While that may be true, it is nonetheless the case that Catholic institutions, for example, often live out of a distinctly Catholic worldview, Lutheran institutions out of a Lutheran worldview, and Mennonite institutions out of a Mennonite worldview. Indeed, one even sometimes finds that colleges and universities related to the same denominational family may differ from one another in their approach to Christian higher education, depending for example on which branch of the Mennonite church one has in mind or which Catholic order sponsors a given Catholic institution.

Further, to the extent that these institutions seek to structure their work around a Christian mission at all, they inevitably must draw upon their own historic Christian identities or church connections. They really have little other choice since institutions cannot convert from one tradition to another as an individual might. A Catholic institution cannot transform itself into a Lutheran institution, nor can a Reformed institution, for example, live out of the kind of restorationist heritage that informs institutions related to the Churches of Christ.

It is true that some Protestant institutions — Wheaton College is a notable case in point — eventually shed denominational allegiances in favor of a broad evangelical consensus. Yet one cannot understand even these institutions apart from specific denominational perspectives. Wheaton, for example, first emerged as a distinctly Wesleyan institution, a perspective that continued to exert a substantial influence on the college long after Wheaton became the flagship institution of American fundamentalism in the early twentieth century. In more recent years, key members of the Wheaton faculty, most notably Arthur Holmes and Mark Noll,[3] have contributed to Wheaton a distinctly Reformed understanding of the task of Christian higher education.

One can make a similar judgment regarding Seattle Pacific University, the institution paired with Wheaton in this volume under the category "evangelical/interdenominational." Seattle Pacific University has not yet become as broadly evangelical as Wheaton has been for many years, but it clearly has embarked on that transition. Like Wheaton in its early years, Seattle Pacific still maintains a strong Wesleyan orientation that complements its more broadly evangelical commitments. For that reason, Seattle Pacific makes an especially fascinating comparison with Wheaton.

Because denominational distinctives and particularistic theological perspectives are so important to Christian institutions of higher learning, we have prefaced each pairing of institutional narratives in this volume with a "world-

2. See, e.g., Robert Wuthnow, *The Restructuring of American Religion: Society and Faith Since World War II* (Princeton: Princeton University Press, 1988).

3. See Arthur Holmes, *The Idea of a Christian College* (Grand Rapids: Eerdmans, 1975), and Mark Noll, *The Scandal of the Evangelical Mind* (Grand Rapids: Eerdmans, 1994).

view" or "theological" essay in which a respected representative of a given tradition defines the substance of that tradition and then asks what that tradition can contribute to the task of Christian higher education. In order to whet the reader's appetite for these explorations, it is perhaps worth generalizing even here in the volume's introduction about the difference it makes that a given college or university is related to a particular denominational heritage. Since extensive essays are provided for each denominational tradition later in this book, we will limit our remarks here to the Catholic tradition and to the three Reformation traditions represented in this volume: Reformed, Lutheran, and Mennonite.

If one wishes to go to the heart of the Reformed heritage, one must recall that this tradition has exalted the sovereignty of God over all creation for more than four hundred and fifty years, ever since John Calvin sought to transform the city of Geneva into a model kingdom of Christ. It is little wonder, then, that Calvinist scholars who think and write about the issue of Christian higher education speak often of developing within the academy a "Christian worldview." By this, they mean that Christian scholars must place their scholarship squarely under the sovereignty of God and in the service of Christ, and approach every discipline from a distinctly Christian perspective.

In this context, notions like "secular" and "secularization" make a great deal of sense: secularization occurs when any dimension of human activity escapes the sovereignty of Jesus Christ. From this perspective, Christian colleges or universities that fail to subordinate learning to a Christian worldview may fall victim to the process of secularization. The creation of a distinctly Christian worldview that governs both teaching and learning is therefore a task that requires both dedication and vigilance. This is the spiritual heritage that informs Calvin College and, perhaps to a lesser degree, many other Reformed institutions as well.

Several scholars from the Reformed tradition currently stand at the cutting edge of discussions regarding Christian higher education and urge the rest of us to employ a "Christian worldview" in our work as well. One thinks here, for example, of George Marsden, Nathan Hatch, Nicholas Wolterstorff, Ronald Wells, and Arthur Holmes.[4] Because the work of these scholars is so visible and so compelling, it is easy to imagine that the Calvinist model for Christian higher education is the only available model.

4. See Marsden and Longfield, eds., *The Secularization of the Academy;* Marsden, *The Soul of the American University;* Nathan O. Hatch, "Evangelical Colleges and the Challenge of Christian Thinking" in Joel Carpenter and Kenneth W. Shipps, eds., *Making Higher Education Christian* (Grand Rapids: Christian University Press, 1987); Nicholas Wolterstorff, *Reason within the Bounds of Religion* (Grand Rapids: Eerdmans, 1976); Ronald A. Wells, *History through the Eyes of Faith* (San Francisco: HarperSanFrancisco, 1989); and Holmes, *The Idea of a Christian College.*

But one must remember that Calvinism is only one among several theological traditions in the Christian family. The Mennonite model, for example, is a model fundamentally different from that offered by the Calvinist heritage. For Mennonites, the driving force for Christian higher education is not the sovereignty of God over all creation, but a vision of radical discipleship. This vision dramatically transforms the traditional, Enlightenment-based task of learning at places like Fresno Pacific College, a Mennonite Brethren school in California, or Goshen College, a Mennonite institution in Indiana. At Goshen, for example, every student spends at least one semester abroad, but not to study at one of the more chic locations in Europe or Asia. Rather, that student will study in a third-world country, combining scholarship with intentional service to the poor and the dispossessed. Likewise, Fresno Pacific, located in a city where poverty and human need abounds, makes service to the dispossessed a central dimension of the overall curriculum.

In the course of one of my visits to Goshen College, a Mennonite scholar insightfully commented on the difference between the Mennonite and the Reformed models for Christian higher education. The Reformed model, she observed, tends to be cerebral and therefore transforms living by thinking. The Mennonite model, on the other hand, transforms thinking by living and by one's commitment to a radically Christocentric lifestyle. For this reason, she suggested, the Reformed model may be particularly suitable to graduate education, while the Mennonite model may be especially appropriate for undergraduate learning.

The Lutheran tradition approaches education from a perspective very different from that offered by either the Reformed or the Mennonite models. In the first place, with their strong sense of justification by grace through faith, Lutherans have never made radical discipleship, as embraced by Mennonites, a distinguishing feature of their heritage. Likewise, Lutherans have never been anxious to bring all creation under the sovereign sway of God, at least not on this side of the second coming. Instead, Lutherans insist that the Christian lives simultaneously and inevitably in two kingdoms — the kingdom of this world (nature) and the kingdom of God (grace).

On the one hand, Lutherans acknowledge that the world as it is — deformed and estranged from God — is nonetheless God's creation and therefore worthy of study and understanding on its own terms. This is precisely why many Lutherans resist the notion of secularization. At the same time, they also revel in the promise of God's transforming grace. In this present world, however, the Kingdom of grace never triumphs over the kingdom of nature. Instead, these two dimensions always coexist in dialectical tension. The task of the Christian scholar, therefore, is not to impose on the world — or on the material that he or she studies — a distinctly "Christian worldview." Rather, the Christian scholar's task is to study the world as it is and then to bring that world into dialogue with the Christian vision of redemption and grace. This theological vision is the great strength of Lutheran higher education for it enables Lutherans to take religious and cultural pluralism with a seriousness that often escapes other Christian traditions. A recent and especially insightful book by Mark R. Schwenn, dean of Christ College (the honors college) at Valparaiso University in Indiana, explores this uniquely Lutheran, dialectical understanding of Christian higher education in considerable detail.[5] Unfortunately, Schwenn nowhere acknowledges in his book the distinctly Lutheran sources for his vision.

In Catholic institutions, the discussion regarding the nature of Christian higher education takes on still other characteristics. Roman Catholic theology is fundamentally incarnational and sacramental. The vision of Christian higher education at a Catholic institution, therefore, often asks how Christian scholars — and graduates of Catholic institutions — can bring the presence of Christ into a world filled with suffering, poverty, and injustice.

If we were to compare the Catholic tradition on this score with its various Protestant counterparts, we would have to conclude that it looks very much like the Mennonite tradition, on the one hand, and the Lutheran, on the other. The Catholic heritage shares with the Mennonite tradition an intense concern for ethics and social justice. But Catholics share with Lutherans their motivation for that concern — the conviction that the world is God's creation and the object of God's love and grace. For this reason, Catholics, like Lutherans, often resist theories of secularization and find the grace of God displayed in actions and events that a variety of Protestants, especially in the Reformed tradition, might find altogether secular. While Catholic higher education, therefore, is compatible in many ways with a Lutheran worldview, it typically stands worlds apart from the kinds of concerns that govern higher education in the Reformed context.

For all of this, it must be said that there is no such thing as a stereotypical Catholic institution of higher learning, simply because the orders that sponsor so many Catholic institutions differ dramatically from one another in their historic emphases. This will become apparent from the Catholic essays in this book. While one essay focuses on two Benedictine institutions, St. John's University and the College of St. Benedict in Minnesota, the other explores the faith/learning nexus at the University of Portland, an institution sponsored by the Order of the Holy Cross.

While the rationale for the pairing of institutions in this volume is for the most part self-evident, a word of explanation is in order regarding two denominational categories: Wesleyan/Holiness and Baptistic/Restorationist.

5. Mark R. Schwenn, *Exiles from Eden: Religion and the Academic Vocation in America* (New York: Oxford University Press, 1993).

INTRODUCTION

While California's Point Loma Nazarene College stands unequivocally in the Wesleyan/Holiness tradition, one cannot make so categorical a judgment regarding its counterpart institution, Messiah College in Pennsylvania. Messiah is a hybrid institution, shaped by four distinct theological traditions: Anabaptism, Pietism, Wesleyanism, and broad evangelicalism. Founded by the Brethren in Christ, a small church that embraces all these strands, Messiah College is hardly Wesleyan to the same degree that Point Loma Nazarene College is. We nonetheless included Messiah College in the Wesleyan/Holiness category for two reasons. First, since Messiah is rapidly emerging as one of the strongest of the conservative Protestant colleges nationwide, it was important to include Messiah in this project. And second, while we might easily have categorized Messiah as a Mennonite institution or as an evangelical/interdenominational institution, it is not improper — as Douglas Jacobsen notes in his narrative — to describe Messiah in Wesleyan terms.

The Baptistic/Restorationist category will be perhaps most puzzling to many readers. Restorationist in this context refers to the spiritual descendants of Alexander Campbell and Barton W. Stone, two religious leaders in the first half of the nineteenth century who sought to restore primitive Christianity in an effort to provide a foundation upon which all Christians might unite. Ironically, in the late nineteenth century, that movement divided into two separate denominations: the Disciples of Christ who carried the banner of ecumenism, and the Churches of Christ who stoutly maintained the vision of the restoration of the ancient faith. Pepperdine University is one of several colleges and universities related to Churches of Christ and therefore falls squarely in the "restorationist" category.

But how does "restorationist" correlate with "Baptistic"? First, the "restoration movement" led by Campbell and Stone in the early nineteenth century had deep roots in the Baptist tradition. Campbell himself identified with the Baptist tradition for a time, and thousands of converts to this movement came from the ranks of Baptists. Second, the Baptist tradition has a strong restorationist strand in its own history and has produced a variety of splinter movements — like the Landmark Baptists of the nineteenth century, for example — who have sought to recover the purity and simplicity of the ancient Christian faith. And third, Churches of Christ and Southern Baptists in particular share a common cultural heritage, that of the American South.

Still, the reader might well ask why we did not compare Pepperdine University with another Church of Christ-related institution. The answer to that question can be found in three words: lack of money. Because funding for this project was limited, had we compared Pepperdine with another Church of Christ-related institution, we could not have included an essay on a Baptist institution, and vice versa. Because the Church of Christ and the Baptists share much in common, therefore, we decided to compare Pepperdine with Samford University, a Southern Baptist institution in Birmingham, Alabama.

Still, Churches of Christ and Southern Baptists are sufficiently dissimilar that we thought it important to include in this book a separate worldview essay for each of these traditions — something the reader will notice in the final section of the book.

Finally, we regret that a limited budget virtually dictated that we could not include in this project as many denominational traditions as we had hoped to consider. There are numerous traditions missing from this book, most notably mainline Methodism. Still, we hope that the institutions and denominational traditions represented here are sufficiently diverse that this book will be challenging and beneficial to the broad cross-section of people who care deeply about the future of Christian higher education in the United States.

THE ROMAN CATHOLIC TRADITION

What Can the Roman Catholic Tradition Contribute to Christian Higher Education?

Monika K. Hellwig

Any venture or community that claims to be Catholic must, of course, first of all be Christian. That means that before consideration of specifically Catholic traditions and perspectives, one must look at what is common to Christians.

The common identity of Christians certainly involves taking our relationship to God our creator and redeemer with ultimate seriousness, both in our search to know and understand anything whatsoever and also in the practical dimensions of our relationships and the apportionment of time, talent, and resources.

Second, this common identity also includes faith in and discipleship of Jesus Christ. While there may be varying emphases in this respect, Christians make a serious effort to understand as fully as possible the outlook, concerns, and goals of Jesus in his own time and their application in our time. Such an effort is progressive and draws upon all the resources at one's disposal. The resources at the disposal of institutions of higher education are considerable when they are really harnessed to this purpose.

Third, the common identity of Christians includes acknowledgment of and gratitude for empowerment by the Holy Spirit bequeathed to His followers by Jesus. This empowerment (or grace, or justification) makes countercultural perceptions and initiatives possible. It provides a context in which scholarship, technology, civic responsibilities, and the sifting and handing on of culture are assessed and practiced in characteristic ways.

A Catholic Way of Being Christian

Within the broad context of what it means to be Christian, there are certain distinctive characteristics that make the specific difference of Catholicism. Among these one might identify an emphasis on the continuity of faith and reason, respect for the cumulative wisdom of past generations in the tradition, an effort to be inclusive in membership and values, acknowledgment of the communitarian aspect of the redemption, and the pervasive appreciation of the sacramental principle.[1]

Among these characteristics, the conviction about the continuity of faith and reason is most obviously and immediately pertinent to the conduct of higher education; this will be spelled out in the next section of this essay. It is important, first, to understand this characteristic correctly and to differentiate it from the perspective of the rational supernaturalists of the Enlightenment. Although there were some ill-conceived efforts in the eighteenth century to counter the Enlightenment in its own terms with an apologetic that seemed to proceed rationally from data of experience to the apparently necessary conclusion that the Catholic Church held the ultimate truth, this notion was patently out of touch with central tenets of the faith.

The continuity of faith and reason as understood in Catholicism does not claim that reason can arrive at either the act of faith or the content of faith. What is claimed is threefold. First, faith is not a sub-rational but a supra-rational quality, so that the leap of faith, if authentic, takes off, so to speak, from grounds of credibility. If it were not so, one could not hold people responsible for such appalling folly as the Jonestown mass suicide, the deeds of the Manson crowd, or re-emergent Satan worship. Catholic understanding of faith as gift and virtue, therefore, sees a role for reason that is prior to faith and involves discernment whether the invitation to faith is authentic. Second, the continuity of faith and reason is claimed in relation to understanding the faith that is embraced and building a coherent worldview and a coherent way of life consonant with that faith. Third, reason is to be used to apply the faith to worldly challenges, whether in interpreting what is going on in the world in our time, or in establishing a strategy of response. It would be foolish, of course, to suppose that only Catholic Christians are concerned with these three ways of employing reason in service of faith. They have no monopoly here, but it must be said that Catholic tradition has placed special emphasis on the role of reason, so that it has become a constitutive element of Catholicism.

1. For other approaches see James Provost and Knut Walf, eds., *Catholic Identity* (Maryknoll: Orbis, 1994), especially David Tracy, "Roman Catholic Identity amid the Ecumenical Dialogues," pp. 109-117; and Norbert Greinacher, "Catholic Identity in the Third Epoch of Church History," pp. 3-14.

Monika K. Hellwig

A second constitutive trait of Catholicism is a great respect for the cumulative wisdom of the Christian generations that have gone before us. This includes the constant remembrance and reverencing of those we consider role models or heroes of the tradition — the martyrs; those whose lives were profoundly marked by practical compassion for the suffering, the poor, and the disadvantaged; those who were notable persons of deep and constant prayer, and so forth. The treasuring of the wisdom of the generations also includes the gathering, recording, and passing on of spirituality traditions and devotional customs. Last but not least, it includes the theological traditions and the past efforts to formulate doctrine, not to mention the building of philosophical systems apt for expressing our theological traditions.

This Catholic trait particularly marked the parting of the ways in the sixteenth century between the Reformers and the Roman party. Today no educated Catholic will dispute the claim of the Reformers that the Christian message and Christian life had become appallingly corrupted and that a return to sources was urgently needed. In fact the Catholic Church officially echoed and endorsed this claim in the Second Vatican Council.

But the characteristically Catholic element is the desire, while putting everything under the scrutiny of Scripture, to save and treasure and keep alive for future generations whatever was good and fruitful in the experience, thought, and action of the faithful in the course of the centuries. This implies a way of doing theology which takes the whole historical development into account and places a positive value on knowing the history and literature of the tradition.[2]

A third trait is the effort to be inclusive. This effort extends even to those only marginally committed. While this characteristic has its "downside," it also is an expression of hope and of evangelical outreach. It is exemplified in the very existence of an official sacrament of repentance and conversion in the Church, offered routinely to all the faithful with the understanding that conversion to Christ is a lifetime enterprise, and that therefore the Church exists not only for the devout and morally upright but for all who will come. The effort to be inclusive also applies across economic and social lines; a community of worship ideally welcomes people of all classes in society, none of whom should be afraid or ashamed to mingle on a basis of equality and fellowship. Nor should ethnic, cultural, and linguistic difference exclude anyone from the community of worship.

One reason for the former insistence on a Latin liturgy was that, although many did not understand the precise Latin formulations (or indeed, the symbolism) used in the Mass, they found it familiar from lifelong usage, and

2. For a longer and fuller account, see Monika K. Hellwig, *Tradition: The Catholic Story Today* (Cincinnati: Pfaum, 1974).

therefore could feel at home in a Catholic Church anywhere in the world. Another reason was the sense that this liturgy, although obscure in symbolism and language, had classic, emotionally austere characteristics in its Gregorian chant along with unchanging formulations in a dead language with hieratic connotations.

The inclusivist tendency inherent in Catholicism has also an ecumenical dimension, one which has been greatly enhanced since the Second Vatican Council — an affirmation that the universal salvific will of God must somehow have provided the opportunity of salvation for all persons of good faith, even those who may never have become believers in Jesus Christ.[3]

A fourth characteristic of Catholicism is the acknowledgment of the communitarian nature of the redemption. This has had many manifestations, not all of them helpful. Its roots lie in the Acts of the Apostles and the Sermon on the Mount. The original meaning of baptism had a strongly communitarian character, namely, rebirth into a people of God reshaping history by the power of the Spirit, transforming not only relationship with God but also all relationships among people as well as the structures of society which give predictability and stability to those relationships.

As is now widely recognized among Catholics and Protestants alike, a thoroughly unhelpful development of this sense of the communitarian character of the redemption emerged with the Constantinian establishment, leading ultimately to such travesties as the crusades, the arrest and execution of dissidents, and religious wars among Christians. While the Catholic Church has tended to cling to this misguided understanding of the communitarian character of redemption, there has been a radical retrieval of a more defensible sense, beginning with the encyclical letter of Pope Leo XIII, *Rerum novarum*,[4] and coming to a clear synthesis and new focus with the constitution, *Gaudium et spes*,[5] of the Second Vatican Council.

The communitarian emphasis accounts for the new impetus in Catholicism worldwide towards both a doctrinal and practical concern for peace and social justice. It also accounts for the radical transformations in the official liturgy and in the life of many parishes and grass-roots groups. One sees in the Third World base ecclesial communities engaging in biblically based communal reflection and solidarity in the struggle for survival. In the wealthy nations of the world one sees increasingly active lay participation in church

---

3. See *Nostra aetate* in Austin Flannery, ed., *Vatican Council II* (Wilmington: Scholarly Resources, 1975), pp. 738-742.

4. 1891, now outdated. A good contextualized summary is available in Donal Dorr, *Option for the Poor: a Hundred Years of Vatican Social Teaching* (Maryknoll: Orbis, 1985), ch. 1.

5. See Flannery, *Vatican Council II*, pp. 903-1001.

planning and concerns, and also an increasing share of attention, time, and resources given to global problems.

The final defining characteristic, and perhaps the most significant, is the pervasive appreciation of the sacramental principle. This has come to be a code term for the conviction underlying the phenomena that Protestants most readily notice about Catholic life and worship — an exuberant wealth of symbolic expression in the prevalence of statues and images of all kinds, a plurality of devotional practices involving shrines, pilgrimages, saints' stories, canonization procedures, rumors of miracles, elaboration of ceremony and vestments, incense and candles and (formerly) bells, and of course seven sacraments instead of the New Testament two.

What is behind all this is simple: the realization that in a confused and sin-laden history our access to God is in double need of mediation. As creatures, corporeal beings in space, time, and cultural context, we relate to God through created things — speech, analogies, images, expression in gesture and song, and so forth. Moreover, situated within a sin-distorted history and culture, we do not find this mediation of created things spontaneously in our everyday existence. We need to seize the moments of clarity, the revelatory memories, the acquaintance with inspirational persons, the stories and images that carry insight and inspiration. The sacramental principle is the understanding that it is important to build on all these, fashioning a way of life, thought, and worship that can be handed on, making the presence and claims of God as nearly as possible a pervasive, felt experience.

The church has, of course, suffered repeatedly from the problem that Martin Luther pointed out so poignantly — that the sacramental has an inbuilt tendency to degenerate into the superstitious, if not the downright magical. While the Reformers so rightly protested against this as a perversion of the deeply personal and spiritual nature of faith and justification, it has been the Catholic contribution to struggle, time and again, to rescue the authentically sacramental and to preserve it. The present time finds the Catholic Church again in a promethean effort to do this, springing from biblical, liturgical, and patristic scholarship that produced the document, *Sacrosanctum concilium*[6] of the Second Vatican Council, and numerous post-conciliar implementation documents.

Clearly, it cannot be claimed that any one of these five characteristics is uniquely Catholic. Each is shared with some or almost all of the other Christian communities. Yet, if we are to look for the specific difference of Catholicism among the Christian churches, we shall find it in the combination of these attributes and the considerable emphasis given to each of them.

---

6. See Flannery, *Vatican Council II*, pp. 1-40.

Continuity of Faith and Reason in Higher Education

It has often been pointed out that the medieval origins of our universities, and indirectly of the American liberal arts college, point to the role that institutions of higher education can play in the intellectual outreach and consolidation of the religious tradition. That this is a central function of the contemporary Catholic institution of higher education is certainly assumed in recent documents of the Holy See. The 1983 Code of Canon Law prescribes:

> The competent ecclesiastical authority is to provide that at Catholic universities there be erected a faculty of theology, an institute of theology, or at least a chair of theology so that classes may be given for lay students.

> In the individual Catholic universities classes should be given which treat in a special way those theological questions which are connected with the disciplines of their faculties. (*C.I.C.* 811, nos. 1 & 2)[7]

The second paragraph holds special interest because it is concerned to provide a continuous theological reflection on issues raised by other disciplines, such as the natural and social sciences, implying that students are not to be left without professorial help in trying to integrate their secular learning with the understanding of their faith tradition. This becomes a dominant theme in the 1990 apostolic Constitution, *Ex corde ecclesiae*,[8] of Pope John Paul II, himself formerly a university professor of philosophy in Poland.

> A Catholic university's privileged task is "to unite existentially by intellectual effort two orders of reality that too frequently tend to be placed in opposition as though they were antithetical: the search for truth and the certainty of already knowing the fount of truth." (*ECE*, 1, quoting a previous papal discourse)

> . . . a Catholic University is distinguished by its free search for the whole truth about nature, man and God. (*ECE*, 4)

> . . . rapid developments in science and technology . . . enormous economic and industrial growth . . . require the correspondingly necessary *search for meaning* in order to guarantee . . . the authentic good of individuals and of society as a whole. (*ECE*, 7)

---

7. *Code of Canon Law. Latin-English Edition* (Washington: Canon Law Society of America, 1983), pp. 304-305.

8. For the full text of the document in English, see John P. Langan, ed., *Catholic Universities in Church and Society* (Washington: Georgetown University Press, 1993), pp. 229-254.

The document goes on to describe four characteristics that must be realized if the Catholic institution of higher education is to fulfill its critical mission: Christian inspiration of the university as a community, not only of isolated individuals within it; reflection upon the "treasury of human knowledge" in its continuing growth, carried out by the light of the Catholic faith; an institutional fidelity to the Christian message as handed on in the Church; and an institutional commitment to the service of the people of God and the whole human family in their pilgrimage to their true, transcendent goal (*ECE*, 13). Furthermore,

> In a Catholic University research necessarily includes (a) the search for an integration of knowledge, (b) a dialogue between faith and reason, (c) an ethical concern, and (d) a theological perspective. (*ECE*, 15)

This theme is pursued at length in the following sections of the document. Theology is given a special role here. Besides its obvious function of giving intelligibility to faith in changing cultural settings, the document looks to theology to play a role (in partnership with philosophy) in the integration of disciplines and the fostering of interdisciplinary studies, bringing to the various disciplines "a perspective and an orientation not contained within their own methodologies" (*ECE*, 19, 20).

This understanding is strongly countercultural for three reasons. It challenges the prevailing patterns of recognition and promotion for professors, which are linked to sharp specialization of disciplines and even within disciplines. Further, it challenges the prevailing assumption of the radical, intrinsic secularity of the disciplines. Finally, it challenges some contemporary interpretations of tenure and academic freedom, in which scholars acknowledge accountability to the academy according to certain canons of competent scholarship in their own fields and reject any accountability beyond that. If the norms of *Ex corde ecclesiae* were realized in a university or college, they would significantly advance a characteristically Catholic contribution to higher education.[9]

The Cumulative Wisdom and Higher Education

The second characteristic of Catholicism as it applies to higher education can be dealt with rather briefly because it is readily explained and understood. There is a great wealth of literature, art in all its forms, ethical and political

9. An interesting exercise in envisaging this has been published in Theodore Hesburgh, ed., *The Challenge and Promise of a Catholic University* (Notre Dame: Notre Dame University Press, 1994), especially "What Is a Catholic University?" by Richard McBrien, pp. 153-164.

philosophy, ritual and devotional forms, and so forth, which the Catholic community has passed on through the ages. There is also a danger that the demands of multi-disciplinary advances in research, theory, and technical expertise will crowd out the passing on of this heritage. There is a tendency for courses in computer science and statistics to take up curriculum space that was traditionally available for classical languages and philosophy. Likewise, modish or highly specialized courses in literature tend to crowd out the great classics of western Christianity. There is a rush to "instant culture," "instant symbols," and "instant wisdom." In all of this it is clear that a fully Catholic higher education must cling to the liberal arts tradition of historical, philo-sophical, and artistic depth, in a calmer search for meaning from the wisdom of the past than is generally envisioned in contemporary curricula. It is easy to understand in theory, difficult to accomplish in practice, and certainly countercultural at every step.

Inclusivity and Higher Education

In the decades since the Second Vatican Council there has in fact been a great deal of reflection by faculty and administration of Catholic universities and colleges on the implications of inclusivity. This has concerned in the first place the question whether the Catholic institutions of higher education have be-come too elitist in their recruiting. While the founders of the major religious congregations involved in higher education almost always envisaged an open-ing of educational opportunities to needy students, the exigence of keeping the institutions afloat financially have tended to exert pressure away from this ideal. This is particularly so because institutions that began by educating the needy and financing themselves by the contributed services of vowed religious had little opportunity to build up endowments and were sometimes the vic-tims of their own success. The need to reexamine this history has already received considerable attention, as indeed it should.

The aspects of inclusivity that are most sharply challenging Catholic higher education now are the ecumenical and the cultural. As a world church the Catholic community includes within itself a great variety of cultures, though Catholic missions have not always been very attentive to issues of incultura-tion, and have often been conducted on the basis of outright cultural impe-rialism. The challenge this presents in our times affects higher education in a special way. One of the aims of a liberal education such as Catholic institutions claim to offer is certainly to develop an open-mindedness and discernment that can transcend popular prejudices. It is highly desirable in today's world with its many ethnic wars and oppressions that such openness be recognized as an obligation of believers before God. Because of the worldwide diffusion of the Catholic Church, Catholic colleges have special opportunities along these lines in offering a year of overseas study as part of a degree granted by the home institution, and by attracting students from other cultures as exchange students in the home institution.

Acknowledgment of the ecumenical dimension of inclusivity requires in our time not only knowledge and appreciation of the other Christian churches and their traditions and values but, beyond this, knowledge and appreciation of non-Christian traditions and respect for their spiritual insights. The documents *Lumen gentium*[10] and *Nostra aetate*[11] of Vatican II seem to have gone further in acknowledging the positive and salvific aspects of the non-Christian religions than most Protestant churches are prepared to go. This should certainly be reflected in curricula and in the ways in which theology is taught.

The Communitarian Aspect of Redemption and Higher Education

The Catholic emphasis on the communitarian character of the redemption is reflected in the expectations of the Catholic university as expressed in *Ex corde ecclesiae*:

> A Catholic university pursues its objectives through its formation of an authentic human community animated by the spirit of Christ. The source of its unity springs from a common dedication to the truth, a common vision of the dignity of the human person, and, ultimately, the person and message of Christ, which gives the institution its distinctive character. (*ECE*, 21)

This stress on the need to form community around deeply held Christian convictions and values has been expressed in the traditional wisdom in terms of *cura personalis*, the concern for the whole person of the student and of all who are involved in the institution. Genuine human bonds of friendship and mutual respect and support are envisaged as the core of the educational enterprise, because not only book learning but human formation for leadership and responsibility in all walks of life are sought through the community experience of higher education.

The emphasis on community within the institution extends also to its relationship with its sponsoring church:

10. See Flannery, *Vatican Council II*, pp. 350-426.
11. See Flannery, *Vatican Council II*, pp. 738-743.

> Every Catholic university, without ceasing to be a university, has a rela-
> tionship to the Church that is essential to its institutional identity. As such
> it participates most directly in the life of the local church in which it is
> situated; at the same time, because it is an academic institution and there-
> fore part of the international community of scholarship and inquiry, each
> institution participates in and contributes to the life and the mission of
> the universal church. . . . (*ECE*, 27)

This poses a particular challenge in our times, setting up a tension between
the claims of loyalty not only to the tradition of the centuries but to the
hierarchic authorities of the present and the claims of independence of
scholarship as understood, for instance, by the American Association of University Professors.[12]

The communitarian dimension impinges further upon the goals and policies to be set by Catholic universities and colleges in the demand to take
seriously the unity of the human race, and the consequent demands that
scholarship, teaching, and study serve the interests of justice and peace and
participation by all in the goods and opportunities of the world. As has been
widely recognized, there is a strong exigence that the scholarly activities of the
Catholic institutions of higher education should serve to relieve suffering and
foster true good, not for one country or one class or race, but for the whole
human community.

The Sacramental Principle and Higher Education

Catholic commitment to implement the sacramental principle as fully as
possible also makes certain demands on the conduct of higher education. To
be fully Catholic the institutions ought to be different in a sensible, tangible
way that strikes all who step onto the campus. The identity of the institution
should be evident in the calendar of events, the central location of campus
ministry and privileged placement of chapels, the privileged place given to
library holdings in theology, religious studies, ethics, etc., the unashamed use
of religious motifs and images in the adornment of buildings, and most of all
in the easy inclusion of religious topics and themes in conversations of faculty
and administrators on campus, allowing students to realize that this is the
integrating factor of scholarship on the campus.

Although universally observed, it should be mentioned that the Catholic
character of a college or university requires regular availability of Catholic

---

12. These tensions are fully discussed in Langan, ed., *Catholic Universities in Church
and Society.*

worship, especially Eucharist, on campus in ways that give it pride of place and do not suggest that the worshippers should act as an apologetic minority. Here also, the effect of Vatican II is to raise consciousness of the need to provide appropriate worship opportunities for students from other traditions. There is a strong sense of the need to honor the spiritual dimension of everyone's life and tradition. This requires a certain countercultural thrust against the privatization and marginalization of the spiritual that suggest that a modern post-Enlightenment society keeps its deepest convictions out of public view.

Conclusions

What then can Roman Catholic tradition contribute specifically to higher education? Much, if it is shaped according to the characteristic attributes that specify Catholicism among the church traditions, but not much if it loses its specificity in the attempt to approximate more nearly to the style and patterns of secular education. The five attributes enumerated above are certainly not the only means of describing what the particular contribution might involve, but they seem to be well attested as central elements.[13]

13. For alternative and thoughtful approaches see Michael Buckley, "The Catholic University and the Promise Inherent in its Identity" in Langan, ed., *Catholic Universities,* pp. 74-89; Tracy, "Roman Catholic Identity amid the Ecumenical Dialogues" in Langan, ed., *Catholic Universities,* pp. 109-117; Greinacher, "Catholic Identity in the Third Epoch of Church History" in Langan, ed., *Catholic Universities,* pp. 3-14; and Harold Attridge, "Reflections on the Mission of a Catholic University," in Hesburgh, ed., *The Challenge and Promise of a Catholic University,* pp. 13-25.

Faith and Learning at the College of Saint Benedict and Saint John's University

Emmanuel Renner, O.S.B.,
and Hilary Thimmesh, O.S.B.

Saint John's University and the College of Saint Benedict are located five miles apart in central Minnesota. Saint John's was founded by monks of the Benedictine order and chartered under frontier conditions in 1857. Initially Saint John's probably resembled a rudimentary German gymnasium more than an American college. The first catalog was published and the first bachelors degrees conferred in 1870. The College of Saint Benedict was founded in 1913 by the Convent of Saint Benedict in St. Joseph, Minnesota, as a college for women. In the last thirty years the colleges have gradually combined their academic programs and many administrative and support services, but they continue as separate corporations in a coordinate relationship which maintains Saint John's as a men's college, Saint Benedict's as a women's college, each appointing its own faculty and conferring its own degrees.

Saint John's University to 1968

Saint John's University dates its founding to 1857 when the Territorial Legislature of Minnesota granted the Order of Saint Benedict a charter to establish Saint John's Seminary. "Seminary" was used as a general term and the charter expressly provided that "no student shall be required to attend the religious worship of any particular denomination." In the minds of the founders, however, Saint John's was part of a frontier missionary effort to meet the needs of German-speaking Catholics immigrating to Minnesota, and in the following decades Saint John's was undoubtedly influential, along with the Benedictine sisters in nearby St. Joseph, in attracting a preponderantly Catholic population to the surrounding area. To this day finding a church of any other denomination in many of the villages and hamlets that dot the region comes as a mild surprise.

Classes commenced for five local boys at "Saint John's Seminary" in November 1857, but the next nine years were precarious for the fledgling school as the founders moved from one pioneer dwelling to another and finally carved out a place for themselves and their students in the forest a dozen miles west of Sauk Rapids, the northernmost stop for riverboats on the Mississippi. In 1866 Saint John's College, as it was popularly known, settled in its present location, a six-piece band was formed, and the school began to take on its permanent shape. A three-year theological seminary, distinct from the collegiate classical course and the preparatory course for high school students, was organized in 1868. The following year the state legislature authorized Saint John's to confer such degrees and diplomas "as are usual in colleges and universities." In 1872 the college introduced a commercial course which offered the equivalent of business college training augmented by courses in religion. This commercial program supplied many neighboring communities with pioneer bankers and businessmen in the years to come, while the classical course leading to the bachelors degree prepared young men for the seminary and the professions.

This organization of the college continued for fifty years. In 1922 the commercial course was discontinued and the college became exclusively a four-year liberal arts institution offering bachelor of arts and bachelor of science degrees.[1] Latin and Greek became electives except in the pre-divinity program, but a two-credit course in religion continued to be required each semester as well as a three-credit course in ethics in the senior year. In addition, sixteen credits in philosophy were required in the junior and senior years, four hours a week for two years.

That this curriculum of some seventy-odd years ago was heavily religious is apparent. That it was academically distinguished is not so clear. In 1922 the college was very small and shared faculty and premises with students in the

---

1. Until 1922 Saint John's University, so named by amendment of the charter in 1883, functioned under a rector appointed by the president to oversee all levels of instruction. These were called "courses" as in *cursus theologiae* or *cursus classicus,* or in English, "a course of study." A European notion of university structure was evident. In 1922 the new president, Abbot Alcuin Deutsch, abolished the office of rector and Saint John's particular use of the term "course" by appointing deans of the seminary, the college, and the preparatory school.

newly-named preparatory school. Several of the 22 members of the faculty taught prep classes as well as college classes, yet the catalog listed 132 college courses in 25 disciplines ranging from astronomy to speech education. Even though students typically registered for six courses a semester, classes must have been very small and the professors greatly extended if all or even most of the advertised offerings were actually taught, but the college was now on track for its surprising development in the next decade.

In 1933 Father Virgil Michel was appointed dean of the college by Abbot Alcuin Deutsch, head of the Benedictine community since 1921 and president of the college. Abbot Deutsch held a doctorate in theology and took a keen interest in the college. With his encouragement several Benedictine monks pursued advanced studies in theology and philosophy at European universities and became familiar with new directions in European Catholicism stemming from revitalized understanding of liturgical worship. Virgil Michel was part of this group, having completed a doctorate in English at Catholic University; he was a thinker and a writer who saw the social and economic implications of the liturgical movement. It was through his influence that persons with interests as diverse as racial justice, the cooperative movement, and the Catholic Worker became interested in Saint John's in the 1930s. He entered into serious correspondence with Robert Hutchins about adopting the Chicago Great Books program, and he was responsible for a range of intellectually stimulating developments at Saint John's which continued after his untimely death in 1938.[2] On the eve of American entry into World War II college enrollment had grown to 450 and the faculty to 55, including ten laymen. Saint John's had become an exciting place to work and study.

Did academic development come at the expense of religious emphasis? Not if one can judge by the curriculum and by parietal rules. A two-credit course in religion each semester continued to be a bedrock requirement. Twelve credits were required in philosophy. Catholic emphasis was evident in other courses: Newman and the Catholic Literary Revival; Catholic Backgrounds and Current Social Theory. This was a time when thinkers like Etienne Gilson and Jacques Maritain, historians like Christopher Dawson, novelists like Graham Greene, Georges Bernanos and François Mauriac were giving a new luster to Catholic learning and letters, and a new cachet to piety. A crucifix hung above the blackboard in every classroom and classes began with prayer. Outside of class

2. See Abigail McCarthy, *Private Faces/Public Places* (New York: Doubleday, 1972) for an assessment of Virgil Michel's impact at Saint John's and the broad significance of the liturgical movement: "Virgil Michel, like other Christian thinkers, looked on a twentieth century where men lived in despair and upheaval and where pessimism prevailed. . . . His answer was the re-Christianization of society, a reordering, a re-creation of the [social and economic] interdependence of the 'age of faith.'" Pp. 70-71.

religious discipline channeled student life: required daily attendance at mass by all students (despite the charter), an annual three-day closed retreat between semesters, highly restrictive rules about leaving campus or receiving visitors, and prescribed evening study hours and evening prayer — a simplified form of monastic compline — in the dorm corridors before bedtime.

The rationale for this approach to college education was stated in every catalog from 1922 to 1945. Saint John's aimed to produce

> personalities fully imbued with the ideals of American life and of Chris-
> tianity, whose impact on society will help in the creation of a better social
> order. . . . The discipline is mild but firm and aims to produce men of
> character and high-minded citizens. . . . Discipline is enforced rather by
> appealing to the students' sense of honor, to moral and religious motives
> than by the use of severe methods.

This was the explicitly religious context in which young men "of good moral character" were accepted as students and lived out their college career at pre-war Saint John's.

For purposes of this study, the close of the post-war period at Saint John's can conveniently be dated to July 1968, when Saint John's University and the College of Saint Benedict formally considered and rejected a recommendation that they merge after jointly adopting a 4-1-4 calendar and a sweeping curriculum revision in the preceding year.[3] This period of twenty-three years saw major changes and developments in the college within a pattern of overall continuity.

The most obvious change was growth in enrollment. In 1945 college enrollment stood at 434 students, half of whom were freshmen. In 1968 college enrollment was 1443. After the wave of ex-GIs in 1945 and 1946 doubled enrollment in two years, the college grew slowly but steadily. The increase in enrollment had two effects on the religious climate of the campus. One was that Saint John's began to have a significant number of non-Catholic students. The other was that the number of off-campus students increased. As a result of these two developments, taking a course in religion each semester was now described as obligatory only for Catholics — others could take a Saint John's degree without any study of religion — and attending mass daily became optional, although recommended, for students who did not live on campus.

The faculty grew as enrollment grew, and this too gradually affected the

---

3. The recommendation resulted from a co-institutional study chaired by Lewis B. Mayhew, whose report said in part: "to delay more than two years would so irreparably damage either or both institutions that ultimate merger or cooperation would no longer be possible." The colleges gave this dire warning serious thought but decided that intensified cooperation while retaining their separate identity was the wiser course.

religious climate. In 1945 the faculty numbered 52: 44 monks (i.e., members of Saint John's Abbey) and eight laymen. In 1968 the faculty numbered 133: 73 monks, 57 laymen, one laywoman, one sister from the College of Saint Benedict, and one diocesan priest. Most of the lay faculty were Catholic, some of them particularly committed Catholics who sought out Saint John's for its leadership in some areas of Catholic thought. Still the gradual shift to a sizable presence of lay people on the faculty meant a certain secularization of the campus. Personal ties and professional contacts with other colleges, most of them not Catholic, many of them not church-affiliated, became more common. Faculty meetings were devoted less to regulating student life; concern about how the students lived became detached from the educational program per se. Catholic devotional practices waned. Religious clubs like the St. John Berchmans Society, the Catholic Youth Organization, and the Knights of Columbus gradually assumed a lower profile in student life. Professors who had taught elsewhere or were fresh from graduate school were not accustomed to saying a prayer before class and no one insisted they should. Old classrooms were refurbished, new ones carved out of existing space, a new library and a new science building went up, and crucifixes were omitted. Thus in a variety of ways the college was becoming less explicitly religious, less exclusively Catholic.

This gradual change is discernible in official statements from that era. In 1946 the catalogue forthrightly proclaimed that "the University has for its chief aim a liberal education for a way of life guided by Catholic truth." Ten years later this statement had been modified to say that "Saint John's University seeks to impart a broad liberal culture permeated with Christian ideals and a Christian sense of values." By 1964 this gave way to the stated aim of preparing students for roles of leadership in contemporary society, which "the University believes . . . can best be done by aiding the student to inquire into the Christian conception of man and into the expanding frontiers of knowledge and human accomplishment." The shift from *truth* to *values* to *inquiry* as educational goals suggests how the attitude of the institution itself had changed.

This shift in emphasis is apparent in the replacement of religion courses by theology courses between 1953 and 1961. A two-credit religion course each semester had been a standing requirement since the college began. The purpose of the requirement was frankly catechetical as the aim of the department of religion, reprinted year by year in the course bulletin, made clear:

> The Department of Religion seeks to present the divine plan of redemption and the part which the members of the Church are privileged to play in the unfolding of that plan. Courses are designed to deepen the student's under- standing of the truths of faith and to motivate him to conscious participa- tion in the life of the Mystical Body through personal sanctification and through alertness to social obligations in home, parish and community.

Under this rubric were offered such courses as "Survey of the Christian Life," "Bible Study," and "Life Problems and Marriage." Academic quality varied with the qualifications of the teachers, some of them theologians or Scripture scholars, while others in a given year might come from fields as disparate as English, history, classical languages, political science, and archaeology. What they had in common was four years of seminary training and ordination to the priesthood, which was in practice the primary qualification.

It is against this background that the shift to a requirement in theology must be understood. In 1946 a list of three-credit theology courses for under-graduates appeared in the course bulletin in response, as the bulletin said, to "the growing need on the part of the laity for a deeper grasp of Catholic truth." All of these courses were taught by theologians and met the same academic standards as courses in other disciplines. In 1953 it became permissible for upperclassmen to substitute theology courses for the religion courses obliga-tory for Catholic students each semester. In 1961 courses in religion disap-peared from departmental listings and the religion requirement was changed to one theology course each year, thus 12 credits in four years — four credits less than the old religion requirement — and there it stayed until the cur-riculum revision of 1967.

In a further development of theology on campus, it was during this period that the Benedictine Institute in Sacred Theology came into being. Its aim was to offer graduate theological education for women in Catholic religious orders at a time when few Catholic schools of theology admitted women. Initiated in 1957 by the College of Saint Benedict, this program was moved to Saint John's to take advantage of the resources of the School of Theology and accredited as a masters program in 1963. It was eventually incorporated into the School of Theology.

Among other things the change from religion to theology in the college requirements recognized the higher intellectual reach of students. Under pres-sure of growing enrollment, admissions standards became more selective in this period, and it is paradigmatic for this study that by 1960 Saint John's had become more demanding academically and less demanding — or at least less prescriptive — about religious values and practices. Under "Student Life" the catalogue still declared that:

> Saint John's University endeavors to make the study of religion and the spiritual formation of the student the heart of its entire educational pro-gram.

To newcomers and visitors Saint John's must still have seemed a pervasively Catholic campus with a new church large enough to accommodate the entire student body and with a faculty two-thirds of whom wore the Benedictine habit. But relative to its past the college was now both more permissive about student life and religious practice and more professional about teaching and the conduct of its affairs.

The trend toward greater professionalism is evident in administrative initiatives of the period. From 1875 until 1958, Saint John's University operated under the abbot as president. In that year Abbot Baldwin Dworshak appointed Father Arno Gustin, O.S.B., as president, creating the title of chancellor for the abbot. One of the new president's first acts was to form a Board of Lay Trustees, essentially advisory in character, which nonetheless brought lay persons into the councils of the monastic sponsors of the school for the first time, and under successive presidents was to develop into the Board of Regents established in 1982.

Father Colman Barry, O.S.B., president from 1964 to 1971, advanced Saint John's on several fronts. Father Barry was a historian with a strong ecumenical — some would also say entrepreneurial — bent, whose talents matched the expansionist mood of higher education in the 1960s. He is best known for three flourishing enterprises inaugurated during his administration: the Institute for Ecumenical and Cultural Research; the Hill Monastic Manuscript Library; and Minnesota Educational Radio, eventually spun off from Saint John's as Minnesota Public Radio. None of these was directly linked to the academic program but each in its own way broadened the scope of the institution. Less noted among Colman Barry's achievements but more central to the vitality of the academic enterprise was his introduction of tenure, a standard budgeting procedure, and a quantum leap in faculty salaries to meet AAUP standards. Toward the end his administration was shaken by Saint John's version of the student uprisings of the late 1960s. These tumultuous years, during which an alumnus, Eugene McCarthy, became a student hero, paradoxically demonstrated the vitality of the institution and the disappearance of the Catholic ghetto once and for all. In retrospect the post-war period seems a time of healthy balance between a clear-cut Christian identity and a well-integrated intellectual climate.

The College of Saint Benedict to 1968

The College of Saint Benedict (CSB) grew out of Saint Benedict's academy, a Catholic boarding school for girls founded in 1880 by Benedictine sisters who came to Minnesota in 1857. As early as 1905 the Benedictine community began to plan for the establishment of a college, to educate the sisters in their own fast-growing community and Catholic girls.

The college opened in 1913 with six students in a lower division program. In 1918 it offered its first bachelors degrees. By 1932 the bulletin listed an impressive number of courses in the departments of religion, philosophy, history and the social sciences, English language and literature, psychology and education, Latin, French, and German, biology, chemistry and physics, mathematics, and music. That year, with 166 students and 40 faculty, the college applied to North Central Association for accreditation and received it. The NCA report praised Saint Benedict's for its standards of scholarship and its atmosphere of culture and refinement.

Because the Benedictine community sponsored the college, it assumed the responsibility for articulating and preserving the mission of the college and for ensuring its financial viability. Until 1932 the annual bulletin noted that the college was under the patronage of the bishop of Saint Cloud, but there is no evidence of regular involvement by the bishop or diocesan priests in the administration or in overseeing the curriculum. Since the beginning the college has generally enjoyed a good relationship with the bishop, but that is not to say that there haven't been letters or telephone calls between the bishop and the president from time to time about such issues as controversial campus speakers.

Sister Claire Lynch, the academic dean from 1932-1940, established a Board of Lay Advisors in 1934 which continued until 1961, when the college was separately incorporated under a predominantly lay Board of Trustees. In addition, she was influential in founding, in 1940, an Omega Chapter of Delta Epsilon Sigma, a national scholastic honor society for students of Catholic colleges, established at a time when Phi Beta Kappa excluded Catholic colleges from membership.

The faculty understood the educational importance of nonacademic experiences and encouraged students to become active in campus clubs, including the Minnesota League of Women Voters and the International Relations Club, through which students cooperated with those clubs on other Minnesota campuses. Regular convocations included such nationally-known speakers as Mortimer Adler, Carl Sandberg, Dorothy Day, Helen C. White, and Christopher Hollis.

As members of a Catholic college, the faculty accepted the responsibility of providing instruction in religion to enable students to obtain a thorough knowledge of Christian doctrine and develop intelligent Catholic leadership. All Catholic students were obliged to take religion courses every semester. By 1935 the bulletin listed the following religion courses: Liturgical Worship, Catholic Moral Ideal of Life, Dogmas and Life-Motives, Grace and the Sacraments, The Church of Christ, Church History, and Sacred Scripture.

The college also made use of noncurricular means to carry out its religious mission. The Benedictine sisters, who comprised the large majority of the faculty, encouraged students to attend morning mass in chapel and to pray compline, a liturgical form of evening prayer, together in the dormitories in the evenings. Many students also participated in the Sodality of the Blessed Virgin Mary. Until 1931 students of all denominations were required to be present at public religious exercises for the sake of uniformity and preservation of discipline.

Faculty also encouraged students to became actively involved in social justice issues and volunteer services. At first they assisted poor families and taught catechism in rural parishes in central Minnesota and in the Indian missions where the Benedictine sisters staffed grade schools. In the 1930s two convocation speakers, Dorothy Day and Baroness Catherine de Hueck, inspired the young women to volunteer at Catholic Worker House and at Friendship House. While participating in this enriching experience in New York in 1938, some CSB students recruited two black students, and thus the College of Saint Benedict became one of the first Catholic women's colleges to accept African-American students. When a few alumnae objected to accepting "colored" students, Sister Claire Lynch reminded them in a letter that the college had a policy of accepting students of any race, and the college already had Chinese, American Indian, and Filipino students. Sister Claire then reminded the alumnae of the college's responsibility "to inculcate and live the teachings of the Church, which condemn racial discrimination as unjust, immoral, and unChristian."[4]

When CSB refers to its mission as a Benedictine college, the emphasis has often been on the Benedictine values of respect for thorough scholarship, a spirit of moderation, and a sense of community. In 1935, Saint Benedict's began producing an annual initiation pageant, "So Let Your Light Shine," celebrating the spiritual and cultural achievement of Benedictines since the sixth century. The whole student body was involved in this ritual celebration through choral reading, song, and interpretive dance. At the culmination of the pageant, ranks of first-year students, wearing cap and gown, marched across the dark campus to receive flaming torches of learning from Benedictine saints of the past fourteen centuries and to accept their responsibility to pass on learning to others in the future. While the pageant romanticized the role played by Benedictines in the civilization of Europe, the ritual nevertheless played an important formative role by presenting the Benedictine heritage and inspiring students to value both learning and culture. In the late 1960s joint classes with Saint John's University no longer allowed the shortening of classes for rehearsal at the beginning of the fall semester and the pageant was discontinued. Since then a variety of means have been used to promote Benedictine values.

From the beginning the college has remained faithful to its mission as a college for women, although the way in which it has understood how to fulfill

4. Lynch correspondence, September 27, 1938, Convent of Saint Benedict Archives.

that mission has changed since the women's movement in the 1960s. For years CSB stated that one of its functions was to prepare its students for motherhood and homemaking, service to their community, and a career. The 1934 Bulletin spelled out the qualities of such an ideal Catholic graduate:

> [She] has a reasonable faith — that is, she knows Bible history, Church history, philosophy, and ethics well enough to make her religious practice really intelligent. She has a strong moral fibre. She has the intellectual culture that comes with the best that a liberal arts college can offer. As a social leader she contributes to the happiness and advancement of the community in which she lives. Christian home-building is to her not only a most desirable vocation but also an art deserving the fullest attention of a cultured woman. To it she brings intelligent planning, clear sighted appreciation of its beauty and difficulties, enthusiasm, and a gracious spirit. . . . Her philosophy of life is based upon the blessedness of giving and helping.[5]

As this passage suggests, while the faculty promoted the value of homemaking, they also hoped to instill the value of leadership and responsibility in the larger community. In addition, the faculty understood the practical need for careers other than homemaking and offered courses in home economics, education, and social work. Later, with the full tide of the women's movement, the college added majors for careers in professions that had been traditionally male-dominated. It also ceased to assume that motherhood and homemaking were the immediate goals of its alumnae. As the relationship with SJU continued to develop the college intentionally sought to preserve the advantages of a women's college in having women faculty as role models of leadership and scholarship and in offering numerous opportunities for students to practice leadership in service.

These excerpts from historical records affirm the college's intention to solidify its purpose as a Catholic, Benedictine liberal arts college for women. It was like other Catholic colleges of the 1930s and 1940s in its commitment to liberal education and to the spiritual development of its students. Catholic identity was manifested by scholastic philosophy and theology, which served an integrating function, courses on marriage and the family, and literature courses on contemporary Catholic authors. Faculty, still predominantly members of the Benedictine community, joined the several national Catholic scholarly societies. In addition, by the 1940s students were actively involved in the National Federation of Catholic Colleges as well as in organizations that emphasized Catholic action.

Philip Gleason's essay, "American Catholic Higher Education, 1940-1990:

5. 1934 Bulletin, 18-19.

The Ideological Context,"[6] presents a clear description of the evolution of Catholic colleges from this "Catholic Renaissance" subculture of the 1930s and 1940s. By the 1950s, he points out, Protestants and secular liberals challenged what they called the cultural ghetto of the Catholic Church, and they were soon joined by Catholic intellectuals who were more interested in Catholics becoming part of mainstream America than in promoting a separate Catholic culture. This growing criticism, combined with the effects of Vatican Council II, encouraged Catholic colleges to rethink how they might best fulfill their mission. Other societal influences promoted further change. For most colleges the GI Bill at the end of World War II drastically increased the student population. Although only a few women veterans enrolled at CSB, the college was affected indirectly by the influx of GIs at Saint John's. Their unwillingness to accept authoritarian student rules proved contagious. Predictably, CSB students who related socially with SJU students gradually began to demand greater freedom from restrictive regulations.

Saint Benedict's did not experience significant curricular changes until 1967, when it changed its graduation requirements. Philosophy and theology were no longer required as separate courses each year but were integrated into nine four-credit interdisciplinary core courses using the theme "The Search for Meaning." This general education program continued until 1988, when the two colleges instituted a new core curriculum.

The CSB student population did not increase significantly until the college, with the help of low-interest government loans, was able to build several new dormitories, beginning in 1956. The greatest growth occurred in the decade of the 1970s. In 1969-1970 the student population was 782, with 94 percent of students Catholic; that year 35 out of 52 faculty were Benedictine sisters. By 1979-80 there were 1635 full-time students, with an estimated 91 percent of them Catholic, and 33 out of 123 faculty were Benedictine sisters. There is a certain irony in the fact that in 1971 the college reaffirmed its intention to remain small — not over 1000 students — in order to fulfill its purpose as a Benedictine college.[7] Within eight years it was no longer small and its proportion of Benedictines had decreased considerably.

This rapid growth created other serious growing pains: more faculty had to be hired and more classrooms, a new library, science building and sports facilities were needed. It took years to meet the physical plant needs, but one distinct advantage at the present time is that the campus buildings are relatively new and require minimal repair and replacement.

Dr. Stanley Idzerda, the first lay president of the college from 1968-1974,

---

6. In George M. Marsden and Bradley J. Longfield, eds., *The Secularization of the Academy* (New York: Oxford University Press, 1992).

7. *Directions for the Future*, 1970-1971.

made several significant improvements. During his presidency, a faculty handbook was developed, faculty became more involved in governance, and a comprehensive planning process was established to improve decision-making. In addition, the college began its first study abroad program in cooperation with five other colleges. Several academic programs were established including the nursing department and the continuing education program. Dr. Idzerda was also very active in working with SJU to build on the relationship between the two colleges.

While cooperation between the College of Saint Benedict and Saint John's University began as early as 1953 in some teacher exchanges, it evolved in the 1960s and 1970s with more formal but piecemeal changes. This cooperative venture occurred at a time when numerous men's colleges were becoming co-ed or were merging with women's colleges, often to the detriment of the women's education. The CSB/SJU partnership has resisted such a development, a fact which has had a profound impact on both colleges.

The College of Saint Benedict and
Saint John's University Since 1968

In 1968 the College of Saint Benedict installed its first lay president, Dr. Stanley Idzerda, and the two colleges set about systematically drawing their programs and operations closer together in accordance with the Mayhew report noted above. Dr. Sylvester Theisen, professor of sociology, was named to chair a joint faculty committee on cooperation and given the function of coordinator of cooperation. He was an excellent choice — respected on both campuses, experienced, resourceful, and incorrigibly optimistic. Four years into the job, he described cooperation between the colleges as a process of "coordination without corporate merger."[8] He reported:

> The growth of cooperation between CSB and SJU has been a series of responses to needs arising from experience, rather than a fulfillment of an ideology imposed from above. This pragmatic approach, staying close to our experience, seems very slow to some persons and highly ambiguous to many, but we believe that it is organic and healthy.[9]

This pragmatic approach to cooperation has continued to the present. Each college continues to operate under its own governing board, at CSB the Board of Trustees referred to earlier, at SJU the Board of Regents established in 1982, which functions within limits set by the monastic chapter and includes the

8. Report to the Board of Trustees, College of Saint Benedict, January 6, 1972.
9. Report of the Joint Faculty Committee on Cooperation, February 10, 1972.

three officers of the monastic corporation and eight representatives of the chapter among its 44 members. Systematic collaboration over the past quarter century has integrated the academic life of the two campuses. Today their 325 faculty members teach in combined departments, share the same facilities, and guide a combined enrollment of about 3400 undergraduates — now slightly more women than men — through the same curricula. By the usual criteria — faculty credentials, admissions standards, learning resources, placement of graduates — CSB/SJU offers a good liberal arts education across the board. Each college has had a Rhodes scholar since collaboration began. Some sixty graduating seniors have received Fulbright awards. The faculty ranks teaching as its most important role, according to the survey conducted for this study, but it also engages in extensive scholarly research.

The faculty continues to be predominantly Christian and enrollment predominantly Catholic, but has academic quality been achieved at the cost of watering down the religious character of the two colleges? On a quick reading one might say so, for many of the historic evidences of religion on campus have disappeared. One would look in vain for references to "Catholic leadership" or "Christian homemaking" or "a liberal education for a way of life guided by Catholic truth" in the publications of either college today. Most faculty members are lay and their religious commitments, as distinct from their moral and ethical principles, are frequently unknown. No religious observance is required of students. Graduation requirements include a single four-credit course in theology and a cross-disciplinary course in the Judeo-Christian heritage. Aside from the impressive chapels on both campuses and occasional displays of sacred art in the campus galleries, there are few public symbols of religion. Even Benedictine religious garb is less common than it used to be since Benedictines on both campuses often prefer to dress like their lay colleagues.

But inquiry into the present condition of religion on the campuses needs to go deeper than merely noting how religious observance differs from that in the past. To assess the vitality of religion on campus today one must look to the shape of contemporary religious thought and practice in society at large. David O'Brien is surely right when he points to one of the major documents of Vatican Council II, *The Church in the Modern World* (1965), as a magna carta for Catholic colleges, affirming as it does the study of human sciences, the worth of secular culture, the importance of dialogue with those beyond the church, and the Christian dimension of service to society.[10] This authoritative document summarized and sanctioned movements already afoot on Catholic campuses as the American church moved out of its immigrant status

10. David O'Brien, *From the Heart of the American Church* (Maryknoll: Orbis, 1994), p. 49.

to full participation in a pluralist society. More important, it pointed to the possibility that secularization could very well mean sacramentalization to those who recognized the presence of God in the world.

In this view the world is a sacrament of God's presence in the sense that the divine reaches us through the finite. Many authors could be cited on this point. Richard McBrien speaks of a Catholic vision which sees God in and through all things — people, events, places, the world at large.[11] Alexander Schmemann describes the sacramental approach as a basic intuition that the world is an epiphany of God, a means of God's revelation, presence, and power.[12] Andrew Greeley draws out the implications of an imagination that views creatures as metaphors for God, as hints of what God is like, and therefore takes a positive view of human potential and social change.[13] In the sacramental view Christianity is established in the world in order to come to fulfillment there, and the role of the church is not to maintain a separate domain of the sacred but to discover and realize God's grace in the secular milieu, where "God continues to speak to us and summon us to respond for the sake of the Kingdom, which is the reign of God's love and justice throughout the whole of creation."[14]

This of course is not an exclusively Catholic perspective as applied to higher education,[15] nor is it an orientation unknown before 1965, but its reaffirmation and development in contemporary Catholic thought has led to a profound reassessment of the role of the church in higher education. To act on this refreshingly positive view Catholic colleges needed to shed their old defensiveness, their sense of ministering to an embattled minority in a Protestant culture, and to address the minds and hearts of young adults who were already thoroughly acculturated to the modern world. Merely catechizing them along neoscholastic lines would not do. Nor, for that matter, would the study of theology alone be sufficient, although it is noteworthy that writers as diverse

11. Richard McBrien, *Catholicism* (Minneapolis: Winston Press, 1980), p. 1180.

12. Alexander Schmemann, *For the Life of the World* (Crestwood: St. Vladimir's Seminary Press, 1973), p. 120.

13. Andrew Greeley, "Sacraments Keep Catholics High on the Church," *National Catholic Reporter* (April 12, 1991): 12-13.

14. McBrien, *Catholicism*, p. 97.

15. See for example Harry Smith, *Secularization and the University* (Richmond: John Knox Press, 1968). Smith distinguishes between *secularization* and *secularism*. Citing Friedrich Gogarten and Dietrich Bonhoeffer on the mode of God's presence in the world, he says: "The development of secularization in higher education is not to be deplored, therefore, but welcomed as an integral part of the process in which modern man has 'come of age'. Christians are called to full participation in the life of the secular university not because they want to infiltrate, restore, or dominate it, but because it is part of the created world, the inheritance turned over to them." P. 134.

as Pope John Paul II[16] and Robert T. Sandin[17] have argued for the centrality of theology as an integrating discipline.

In the aftermath of Vatican II, in fact, modern psychology, generally kept at arms length by the church until then, suddenly seemed a more potent religious force than theology as Catholics discovered that psychoanalytical theory and psychotherapy were not incompatible with religious belief. At Saint John's the alliance between these previously hostile forces was symbolized for twenty years, 1953-1973, by the Mental Health Institute, an ecumenical summer program which included some of the most distinguished psychiatrists and psychotherapists in the country. Men like Dana Farnsworth and Gregory Zilboorg, Francis Braceland and Howard Rome, addressed the pastoral needs of ministers of all faiths, and they made it impossible to think of Christian life and practice as if Freud, Jung, and the like had never existed. Their effect over two decades of friendship with many members of the Benedictine community and the faculty was gradual but profound, and has yet to be adequately analyzed.

To preface the description of present religious emphasis and attitudes at CSB/SJU with these observations is not to imply that at some moment in the late 1960s or early 1970s the two colleges understood and adopted a radically revised notion of what it means to be Catholic in contemporary society, but it is to suggest that a revitalized theology has led them to view the life of faith as altogether broader and more entwined in the diversity of experience than an earlier generation assumed. Neither is it to claim entire satisfaction with the present state of religious emphasis on the two campuses. Rather it is to make the more modest claim that education at Saint Benedict's and Saint John's retains a distinctly religious and indeed Christian character.

To begin with official statements, the introduction to the current course catalogue advises students:

16. See "Ex Ecclesiae Corde," Apostolic Constitution on Catholic Universities, 1990. John Paul II sees an important role for theology in the synthesis of knowledge, but also sees a gain for theology in its interaction with other disciplines (Par. 19). This important document, strongly positive in tone, addresses universities properly so called, but its general principles are equally applicable to undergraduate institutions. Recognition of the role of non-Catholics in Catholic institutions and emphasis on formation of "an authentic human community animated by the spirit of Christ" (Par. 21) are particularly noteworthy.

17. See Robert T. Sandin, *The Search for Excellence* (Macon: Mercer University Press, 1982), p. 118: "The foundation of a unified program of Christian higher education is a theological understanding which permits the integration of Christian faith with advanced scholarship, the permeation of the educational process by a Christian interpretation, and the penetration of the life of the campus by the central ethical and theological convictions of the Christian church."

The liberal arts education provided by the College of Saint Benedict and Saint John's University is rooted in Catholic and Christian tradition and guided by the Benedictine principles of the colleges' founders and sponsoring religious communities.

Extended commentary refers repeatedly to the Benedictine influence on both campuses and the resulting emphasis on human concern, social justice, community values, and commitment to service.

Admissions materials reflect this emphasis. The current flyer sent as a first response to potential applicants highlights the partnership of the colleges and describes CSB/SJU as "Catholic, Benedictine colleges where scholarship and spirituality flourish." It adds that

> the Benedictine men who live at Saint John's University and the Benedictine women who live at the College of Saint Benedict embody the centuries-old traditions of *community* [and] the Benedictine focus on the balance of mind, body, and spirit.

Saying it doesn't make it so, of course, but emphasis on living in community as a time-tested Benedictine formula for mutual sharing and service echoes through the admissions materials and carries over into descriptions of residential life. Thus the guide for student life at the College of Saint Benedict says:

> The goal of CSB residence life is to make the residence area a home . . . where you learn to build interpersonal relationships: sharing, working and playing together. It's a place to be challenged and make mistakes, yet be supported and accepted as you change and grow. It's a place to discover who you are in relationship to others . . . [and] can become a community of people who support and value one another as unique and worthwhile individuals.

Similar language is used in SJU documents to describe the effect of the residential philosophy at Saint John's, where more than twenty Benedictine members of the faculty and staff live with the students, continuing a practice that dates from the school's founding. It is perhaps particularly in the residential setting that the language of the admissions flyer comes to life.

> This [Benedictine] approach to living is never preached but, rather, uniquely conveyed through quiet and powerful examples.

All of this is summed up in the recently adopted "Coordinate Mission and Values," which commits CSB/SJU to provide "an experience of Benedictine values which fosters attentive listening to the voice of God, awareness of the meaning of one's existence, and the formation of community built on respect for individual persons."[18]

These references to the Benedictine way of life perhaps need some explanation. Historically, Benedictines have deep roots in European culture. They derive their inspiration from the *Rule of Benedict*, a sixth-century guide for religious life in community, which for nearly a thousand years provided the dominant model for monasteries of men and women from the Mediterranean to the Baltic and has blossomed out into a worldwide religious family in modern times. The Benedictines were not a centralized order but formed autonomous communities defined as Benedictine by adherence to the *Rule*. Their purpose was simply to seek God in obedience to a spiritual teacher, an abbot or an abbess, chosen by them from among their ranks. Their commitment was to a disciplined way of life, austere but not starkly ascetical, steeped in Sacred Scripture and supported by mutual charity. Since sacred reading claimed much of their time, Benedictines were necessarily advocates of literacy, and they frequently conducted schools for their own aspirants and other local youth. Since they aimed to be self-sufficient they also farmed or engaged in crafts from which they could earn a living; the *Rule* cautioned them to esteem manual labor. It also cautioned them to receive each guest as Christ himself and to practice hospitality accordingly. Modern Benedictine communities continue to be guided by the *Rule of Benedict*. This short summary may suggest what is meant by Benedictine values and why people of different religious backgrounds — Christian and non-Christian — can find common ground in them. It perhaps also explains why faculty response to the survey conducted for this study indicated wider acceptance of Benedictine values than of Catholic belief and practice.[19]

Religious practice by the students is of course an important indicator of the religious character of the colleges today. A summary can only indicate kinds of activity. Both colleges have an active campus ministry with students involved in planning and carrying out liturgies for Sunday and other special occasions. Small group retreats off campus are scheduled periodically during the year. Students are invited to join Bible study groups and to take part in

18. The full statement, adopted by both boards in May 1995, refers in addition to the liberal arts curriculum, the learning environment, the significance of gender in personal development, and service to the common good.

19. Respondents were asked to indicate their judgment about whether greater emphasis on Catholic belief and practice or greater emphasis on Benedictine values would have an inhibiting effect on achieving academic distinction. Half of the respondents (50.8 percent) saw no problem with greater Catholic emphasis; the proportion rose to three-fifths (59.9 percent) when "Benedictine" was substituted for "Catholic." On the negative side, about twice as many (29 percent to 15.6 percent) questioned greater Catholic emphasis as questioned greater Benedictine emphasis.

Lenten prayer services. The chaplains provide spiritual counsel for individual students. In all, the range of opportunities for religious practice is extensive and includes a standing invitation from the Benedictine communities to join in their daily hours of prayer and Eucharist.

To get a full view of the religious character of the colleges, however, one must look beyond formal religious activities to the corollaries of faith lived out in community. For example, nearly a thousand students each year participate in VISTO (Volunteers in Service to Others) by engaging in local service to the needy, the elderly, and children, and by going further afield during vacations to join in service to the urban homeless, migrant workers, and impoverished people in Appalachia and Central America. Sponsoring such service is one of the functions of campus ministry on both campuses. This sort of social action has antecedents. Along with Saint John's and most other college campuses in the early 1970s, many of Saint Benedict's students and faculty protested the Vietnam War. The protests were moderate, avoiding classroom disruption and focusing on educational experience. Chaplains in campus ministry played a predominant role in encouraging student activism in social justice issues. For example, several students and faculty participated in the boycotts organized by Cesar Chavez, and some students spent January and the summer months working with Chavez in California.

Students today also enlist in programs of service to other students such as the Peer Resource Program, whose members do everything from running the challenge course in the woods at Saint John's to presenting January Term seminars on drug and alcohol abuse for the freshman class, and the Career Advisors, students who assist their peers with career exploration and choice. The orientation to service implied in such programs flows quite naturally from the religious values advocated by the colleges, but it has not come about accidentally. Professionally trained staff have been involved in planning ways to call students to personal responsibility for their actions and to reflect on their nonacademic experiences as part of the process of encouraging moral development. Some students build a portfolio which includes written reflection on their personal growth. Faculty, student development staff, and students are working together in a collaborative leadership project which has as one of its focuses examination of behaviors on campus which nurture ethical commitment to service and behaviors which act as obstacles to such commitment. One of the goals is to seek ways to shape the environment so as to enable everyone to become an ethical leader engaged in service to others.

Attention to community building leads to a spiritual outlook on the natural environment as well. The colleges are located in a relatively unspoiled small town, rural setting. Saint John's lies in a large tract of woods and lakes. The academic program in environmental studies grows out of the Christian belief that God is the ultimate creative energy in the universe and out of the Benedictine ethos of responsible stewardship. Again, integration of academic and religious components is the guiding principle. Biology and chemistry, modeling in mathematics and computer science, politics and economics, theological and ethical reflection all have a part. As one faculty member remarks, "As searchers for God, we strive to hand on a lively sense of the presence of God in nature to our students."

Beyond the campuses the two colleges have made a commitment with others in the greater St. Cloud area to collaborate in building a multicultural community. Through a joint Office of Cultural Enrichment, the two colleges have played a role in establishing multicultural summits whose purpose is to promote community transformation through multiculturalism. Three multicultural summits have been held, the most recent in April 1995. In between these conferences, several working groups meet to draft action plans as agenda items for the summits. This process of partnerships building community is not perceived as a fad but rather as part of the colleges' continuing commitment to social justice, based on the principle of respect for every person.

In a separate area which also has implications for community, the colleges have faced the challenge of ensuring equal education for women in the coeducational classrooms that have resulted from the collaborative relationship. The women's movement has influenced many of the faculty from both colleges to study the role of women in history and culture. A minor in Gender and Women's Studies has been introduced to provide an inter-disciplinary and multi-disciplinary framework within which to explore the social construction of gender and sexuality. In addition to the study of gender, the coordinate faculty and student development staff are currently developing a multicultural framework for providing a study of the cultures of our nation and world.

Under the heading of community one can also look at the religious profile of the faculty as a whole. It has frequently been asserted that a Christian college can only retain its religious character by assuring that the majority of the faculty share the same religious commitment. As the colleges have increased in size, the proportion of Benedictines on the faculty has continued to decrease; they now constitute about one-fifth of the faculty and with few exceptions are concentrated in theology and the humanities. Neither college has sought to maintain a critical mass of Catholic faculty. Both have sought persons who support the spiritual dimension of their mission, and both have tried to find ways to assure that lay members of the faculty understand and appreciate the Benedictine heritage. For example, both Benedictine sisters and monks have invited the faculty to participate in a series of conversations on incorporating Benedictine values into the educational experience of students. A separate group of faculty members support a continuing conversation on spirituality.

To this point we have noted that the religious character of Saint John's University and the College of Saint Benedict has changed since the 1960s. We have suggested that religion on campus today needs to be understood in the light of changes in the church since Vatican Council II and the social upheaval of the late 1960s. We have described a number of campus programs that take their inspiration from a sense of Christian community.

But statements of religious purpose and descriptions of programs that draw on a sense of community do not of course reveal how faculty and students view the relation of faith and learning on these two campuses. To learn how religion affects present-day faculty and students, the results of surveys conducted in February and March 1995 are instructive. One survey was addressed to the faculty; two-thirds of them responded. The other went to a statistically valid random sample of the senior class. What follows is a summary of main points.

We have already noted that the colleges do not have a policy of maintaining a critical mass of Catholic faculty. They do not in fact inquire about the religious affiliation of prospective faculty members except for positions in theology. The survey suggests that most faculty believe that this is the right approach and that it would be alien to the character of the colleges to require evidence of religious commitment from them. Yet eight out of ten indicate that they are Christian, the majority of them Catholic, and many of them, a good half, regard their religious beliefs as relevant to the way they teach.

From the students' point of view the faculty are good role models. There is large agreement on this point, and many students, well over half, say that some of their teachers have helped them appreciate their faith. Apparently this does not depend on knowing the religious affiliation of their teachers since almost all of the students say they do not know which of their teachers are Catholic.

On broad questions of ethical, moral, and religious values, faculty and students appear to be in accord. The faculty gives great importance to creating an atmosphere of open inquiry, discussion, and debate, and almost unanimously endorses this principle in regard to its own freedom in the classroom and in scholarly research, even if Christian and Catholic beliefs come into question as a result. Yet in almost equal numbers they endorse encouraging the students' moral development and sense of social responsibility. Not as many of them, although still a good two-thirds, regard it as important to encourage growth in faith.

A majority of the students in turn think that their college experience has strengthened their faith and that specifically they have grown in their knowledge of the gospel. That this is not an abstract knowledge appears from their very high rating of social responsibility and concern for human rights as practical applications of the gospel to life. On an even broader scale, two-thirds of them view the world as sacred because God created it and redeemed it. Quite consistently with this view, they see spiritual value in care for the natural environment. Pressed further on their understanding of a Christian outlook on life, by more than two to one they reject the proposition that one's morality should be no concern of others as long as others are not harmed by one's conduct. Nine to one they reject the notion that the individual can do little to bring about social change. They appear to have a sense of community values and by about two to one credit the Benedictine environment on this score.

When it comes to theology and to religious practice, however, it is perhaps fair to say that both faculty and students are chary of requirements. By a large majority students reject the proposal that more than one theology course should be required. Many of them point to the religious value they found in the required course on Judeo-Christian heritage, and a majority say that the required Senior Seminar provided them with ethical guidance as it is intended to do.

The faculty, for their part, are about equally divided on whether growth in faith should be an objective of the academic program. About half favor requiring study of the Bible. Slightly more than half would approve a course in the Catholic intellectual tradition, not a current requirement. Slightly less than half approve presenting a Christian perspective in core courses other than theology. The number opposed or neutral on these questions is significant and perhaps surprising in view of the religious composition of the faculty. What is not surprising in light of this response is that about six out of ten faculty members would not lead their class in prayer or discuss their religious experience in class, even though they would do so with students outside of class.

As for churchgoing, the students are about equally divided on whether this is a regular student practice or not, and while a slight majority of faculty would encourage student participation in campus worship services, this number shrinks to about a third when the question is whether faculty should be given the same encouragement. Student response to another question perhaps sheds some light on the importance they do or do not see in liturgical worship. Queried about the pioneer role of St. John's in liturgical reform, the majority simply indicate unawareness. As to their actual practice, the same number say that they value the campus opportunity to take part in the Eucharist regularly, and a very large majority agree that students are encouraged to grow closer to God in prayer.

All in all, one has the impression of religion by osmosis rather than infusion. Faculty are for completely open inquiry and discussion but also for moral, ethical, and religious values. Over half of the students think that the colleges instill moral values by maintaining a Christian environment. Two-thirds of them think that they have learned about Benedictine values by associating with Benedictines. A sizable majority of them have taken part in volunteer service while in college and a sizable majority say that their college studies have had an ecumenical effect, leading them to a greater appreciation of other religions. And in about the same proportions they are happy that during their four years here the colleges did not hassle them about religion!

If the composite picture that emerges from this review of faith and learning on the two campuses looks something like the mixture of faith and doubt, secular and sacred in society at large, that may be because open conversation is the paradigm for much of our pedagogy. A visitor from a distinguished New England college a few years ago noted here "the generosity of mind which can entertain any intellectual posture brought to a conversation for examination, exploration, evaluation."[20] The presence of the two monastic communities undoubtedly contributes to the conversation by providing both a sense of history and a contemplative background against which the complexities of individual experience and urgent contemporary issues can be viewed in a larger, longer perspective. The School of Theology at Saint John's, now made up principally of lay students, male and female, Catholic and Protestant, is a strongly Christian and ecumenical influence. So is the Institute for Ecumenical and Cultural Research, located at Saint John's but not a part of either college, yet a partner in the conversation which links the colleges and enriches both learning and faith.

The comments of some graduating seniors may provide a fitting conclusion. One says, "My work at St. John's and St. Ben's has strengthened my faith as a Lutheran, and enforced my decision to stay Lutheran." Another says, "I think faith is a personal thing and I believe St. John's and St. Ben's really encourage and offer programs to strengthen your faith, but don't insist and don't invade, which makes me very happy." A third comments, "[My education here] has helped me take a look at who I am and what I believe in. It gave me a chance to step away from the church and my going to church every week simply because that's what I did with my parents. Now I genuinely have developed my own faith. I can truly and proudly walk in the light of the Lord." A sobering comment comes from another student who to the question, How has your education here strengthened your faith? simply responds: "It hasn't."

In the midst of the hectic pace of campus life, administrators and faculty continue asking the question, "Are SJU and CSB becoming secular colleges?" — the title of a faculty panel in 1993. One panelist's response to that question resonated with many participants when he said, "Our colleges are not becoming more 'secular'; I am not afraid of the world or of the present age. The danger is more subtle and far more corrosive: the danger is that in our effort to take our place among our colleagues in academe, to keep up with the latest in higher education . . . we are starving our souls."[21]

20. Penny Gill, *A Sense of Place: Saint John's of Collegeville* (Collegeville: Saint John's University Press, 1987), p. 72.
21. Columba Stewart, O.S.B., associate professor of theology, November 18, 1993.

This is not a new concern for any church-related college nor a concern likely ever to be ended. We continue to yearn for, and to work toward, the ideal described by that same panelist:

> I see another kind of place, where the centrality of prayer is not proven by uniformity of rite but by privilege of opportunity. Where prayer itself is not measured by conformity to approved words but by reality of reflective experience whether explicitly directed to God or not. Where the Bible and liturgy at the heart of the Catholic tradition live at the center of the university in a way which neither judges nor excludes but simply is. . . . Where everyone has to reckon with traditions and experiences which assert that thinking is not enough to make us worthy of our humanity.

Throughout the history of our two Catholic colleges we have taken seriously our commitment to a liberal education which nurtures a fruitful dialogue between our faith and our culture. And we have maintained our commitment to remain authentic Catholic colleges, building a faith community dedicated to the search for truth, a respect for the dignity of all persons, and a love of God and one another. We continue, with hope and faith, on our journey to "another kind of place."

The University of Portland:
Center of Christian Humanism

Dan G. Danner

The University of Portland is affiliated with the Roman Catholic Church, having been purchased in 1901 by Archbishop Alexander Christie from the Methodist Episcopal Church. Originally known as Columbia University, it was fashioned on the hope that it would become the "Notre Dame of the Pacific Northwest." Its driving presence is inspired by the priests and brothers of the Congregation of Holy Cross who divested ownership and governance to a lay board of trustees in 1961. The University of Portland has a College of Arts and Sciences, College of Business Administration, School of Education, School of Nursing, The Multnomah School of Engineering, and a Graduate School.

In an address to celebrate 150 years in America and 90 years at the University of Portland of the Congregation of Holy Cross, James Lackenmier, C.S.C., President of King's College, reflected on what the Holy Cross experience in Catholic higher education has come to be. That experience is not inspired by the particular spirituality of a dominant founder such as Ignatius Loyola or Benedict; in fact, it has been referred to as a more "vernacular" than "classical" experience. Often the Holy Cross experience is expressed by what it is not — not Jesuit, not Dominican, not Franciscan, not Benedictine. But Lackenmier attempted to put the matter in a positive light: it is a commitment to excellence, a concern for the personal formation of students, and an experience of collaboration, equality, and mutuality among all those who participate in the mission of a Holy Cross university.[1]

1. James Lackenmier, C.S.C., "American Catholic Higher Education and the Holy Cross Tradition," October 14, 1992, University of Portland, Portland, Oregon.

At the heart of the Holy Cross mission in higher education is the study of theology, philosophy, and the liberal arts, seen as fully consistent with pre-professional programs in business, engineering, nursing, mass communications, and criminal justice. As this mission is etched out in the lives of individual students, Holy Cross believes it will bear fruit by contributing to aesthetic sensitivities, passion for justice, and compassion for the poor. Students' privacy and autonomy are to be respected, and student development programs such as campus ministry and residence life are designed to make known Holy Cross' concern for the welfare of students.

The history of the Congregation of Holy Cross is that of a distinctive religious order. Father Basil Moreau, founder of Holy Cross, revitalized parishes in France during the early nineteenth century in the wake of the anticlerical and anti-ecclesiastical turmoil of the French Revolution. Father Moreau was a priest of the diocese of Le Mans and a seminary faculty member when he was asked to assume the direction of the Brothers of St. Joseph. At the time Father Moreau assumed this role, he was in the process of organizing a band of diocesan priests who had a special gift for preaching and who would be headquartered at the seminary. They would become known as "auxiliary priests," conducting preaching missions and renewal programs in parishes all over the diocese of Le Mans. These priests and brothers would form a new congregation, a congregation of Priests and Brothers of Holy Cross composed of clerics and canonical laymen. A third society of religious women soon would join them to form a single congregation comprised of three equal societies.

Moreau's legacy was a realization of the ideal of equality and mutuality among clerical and lay religious. This legacy would find fertile ground in the American context and particularly in American Catholic higher education. In the late nineteenth century and well into the twentieth, Holy Cross schools, mainly secondary schools with fledging collegiate programs, were staffed predominantly by Holy Cross religious, although some laymen contributed heartily. Ownership and governance of schools were in the hands of the congregation. Before World War II, expansion and sophistication of Holy Cross collegiate programs paved the way for the large numbers of post-war students who took advantage of the GI Bill to attend Holy Cross colleges and universities, thereby necessitating increased numbers of lay faculty and administrators. The result was increasing professionalism, specialization, and academic sophistication as well as diversity of educational, cultural, and religious backgrounds.

The 1960s saw no increase in Holy Cross religious but rather the further expansion of lay faculty members, administrators, and professional staff. It was during this crucial time in Catholic higher education, in the wake of the renewal ethos of Vatican II, that Holy Cross schools modified the fundamental ownership and governance of their schools, colleges, and universities, transferring them to predominantly lay governing boards. In this significant way, the nature of the church and the role of the laity, as inspired by Vatican II, was given support and vindication in Catholic higher education. What could not be compromised, however, during the transition, was the stamp of identity and mission of the Holy Cross vision. This quality of adaptability has been called "the principal charism of Holy Cross."[2]

The University of Portland and Holy Cross Beginnings

The specific engagement of the Congregation of Holy Cross with the University of Portland dates from the beginning of the twentieth century.[3] Archbishop Alexander Christie purchased the property of the defunct Portland University, founded in 1891 by the Methodist Episcopal Church, in 1901. It was renamed Columbia University, and the Holy Cross vision for its new academic venture was to "promote Christian humanists trained for the active life."[4] It was fashioned on the hope of becoming the "Notre Dame of the Pacific Northwest," and the congregation moved west to Portland in the summer of 1902 to assume the roles of faculty and administrators. Functioning mainly as a preparatory school for boys during its early days, Columbia University required religion courses (no academic credit was given), and in 1922 Archbishop Christie and Cornelius Haggerty, C.S.C., were able to establish a traditional curriculum of Latin, Greek, and philosophy. Strict rules of discipline were enforced, and although students from all denominational backgrounds were permitted to attend the university, all students were required to attend "divine service in the University chapel at stated times." Columbia University avowed being a "strictly Catholic institution."[5] James T. Covert believes that "because of the stress on devotional observances and ethical influence of the priests and brothers, the Christian environment must have profoundly affected students. . . ."[6]

After World War I, Columbia University began to change from a preparatory school to an accredited junior college, but the curricular vision remained the same: the "sanest thought of the great Greeks, shot through with the illumination of Christ."[7] In 1922, in the aftermath of the School Bill Con-

2. Lackenmier, "American Catholic Higher Education and the Holy Cross Tradition."
3. The chronicle of the University of Portland has been comprehensively written by University of Portland alumnus and history professor, James T. Covert in *A Point of Pride: The University of Portland Story* (Portland: University of Portland Press, 1976).
4. Covert, *A Point of Pride*, p. 10.
5. See Covert, *A Point of Pride*, p. 45.
6. Covert, *A Point of Pride*, p. 53.
7. See Covert, *A Point of Pride*, p. 55.

troversy in Oregon, Columbia University pushed forward its staunch Catholic identity "whose primary purpose is the inculcating of Catholic ideals, thought and practice during the period that the student is acquiring that secular knowledge which will prepare him to take his proper place in the world."[8] In 1933-34, however, in order to attract more students, requirement of religion courses for non-Catholics was softened. Eventually the junior college separated from the preparatory school in 1927, and the institution moved on to become an accredited four-year liberal arts college in 1934. The next year the school was renamed "The University of Portland."

Change of Name and Vision

During this pre–World War II era, most of the faculty and staff were members of the Congregation of Holy Cross. Classes commenced with prayer and a religious atmosphere was evident everywhere. Greek and Latin continued to form the basis of the liberal arts curriculum and required courses in religion, philosophy, English, speech, foreign language, history, social science, and biology dominated lower-division study. In fact, eighteen hours in both philosophy and theology were required of Catholic students as the university began to expand its curriculum to include pre-professional programs such as business administration. Student organizations, such as the Holy Name Society and Holy Communion League, enhanced the religious climate (the former to mitigate profanity, the latter to encourage reception of communion). Chapels were present in each boarding area and daily communion encouraged. By 1924, the Purgatorial Society had been formed to pray for the souls of the departed. A "genuinely Catholic culture," in the words of Joseph J. Boyle, C.S.C., president in 1935, would be maintained despite the change of the name of the university.[9]

The next decade, from 1935 to 1945, was a decade of "weird cacophony."[10] The outbreak of the war brought on a depressed economy and fewer students. The Sisters of the Presentation departed the university in 1940 for the motherhouse in Illinois; they were replaced by the Sisters of Notre Dame de Namur who stayed until 1944. The university *Bulletin* of 1945 recorded that the supreme objective of education was the "formation of the Christian scholar": the man with the "Christian outlook on life and of genuinely scholarly habits."[11] Consequently, four-year programs continued to require the study of

8. See Covert, *A Point of Pride*, p. 64.
9. See Covert, *A Point of Pride*, p. 88.
10. Covert, *A Point of Pride*, p. 97.
11. See Covert, *A Point of Pride*, p. 102.

philosophy and theology, with the higher number of hours devoted to philosophy. The only exception was the School of Nursing. The decade witnessed greater numbers of lay faculty, particularly in the School of Nursing, and added professionalism as evidenced by advanced study and degrees.

During the war years, the Catholic identity of the university was enhanced by its assistance in the centennial celebrations of the archdiocese in 1939. Priests who taught in university lecture halls during the week and who conducted mass in residence halls also assisted in local parishes and missions. At the same time, the university was achieving greater recognition in the city of Portland in such activities as the Boy Scout movement and labor arbitration. Additional campus groups such as the St. Vincent de Paul Society and the Catholic Youth Federation stimulated the religious climate of the campus.

The post–World War II years brought sprawling enrollments and record numbers of baccalaureate degrees. But in the 1950s a different trend began. The university became coeducational in 1951 and the Reserve Officers Training Corps was allowed on campus the same year. Beginning in 1950, 36 percent of the student body was Catholic from the city of Portland, eight percent Catholic from Oregon outside Portland and another eight percent Catholic from outside Oregon — a total Catholic population of 52 percent. By 1954-55, the Catholic population had increased steadily to 73 percent.[12] But economic times were difficult for private colleges and universities, and the University of Portland faced rising student tuition and uncertain enrollment. During the presidency of Theodore Mehling, C.S.C. (1946-50), an Associate Board of Lay Trustees was created to act in an advisory capacity. In 1952, the Oregon Colleges Foundation helped by making funds available for private institutions.

From 1946 through the early 1950s, most students were majoring in professional programs. "Religion" was still part of the liberal arts curriculum and was required of Catholic students only; all students were required to take philosophy (fifteen semester hours in 1955). In 1946-47, 36 clergy and 51 lay people made up the faculty, and in 1954-55 the percentage of clergy and lay people remained about the same with a slight decrease in the total number of faculty. Lay members now included many women faculty; earned doctorates among the faculty had increased, and the living endowment given by the Congregation of Holy Cross for the financial needs of the university contributed immeasurably to the institution's survival and well-being.

During the 1950s, student life was still a focus for the disciplined "high-minded devotion to the noblest ideals of college life."[13] Religious groups and Catholic confraternities continued to influence student culture; the Marians, for example, devoted to Mary, the Mother of Jesus, established "The Living

12. Covert, *A Point of Pride*, p. 133.
13. Covert, *A Point of Pride*, p. 155.

Rosary" that became a May tradition at the campus grotto. Young Christian Students and the Blanchet Club were Catholic action groups; the latter established a house for the poor in the heart of Portland's skid-row district in order "to try to see Christ through them."[14] The vision of Holy Cross and its apostolate in Catholic higher education seemed secure at the University of Portland during the post-war years of the early 1950s.

The Waldschmidt Legacy

Paul E. Waldschmidt, C.S.C., became president in 1962. He brought a new and unique presence to the university. Covert calls him "the architect of the University of Portland in its present form."[15] Campus ministry became a focus of university life. The position of university chaplain replaced that of prefect of religion and diversification of spiritual programs was the result. New buildings were erected; a new women's dormitory, Villa Maria, was constructed at the point farthest removed from men's residence halls. When a new commons was built in 1959, the old commons was renamed St. Mary's and used as a chapel, with discussion and reading rooms and a chaplain's office. In a convocation in January of 1963, Mortimer J. Adler gave an inaugural lecture in honor of Waldschmidt in which he praised the university's commitment to a core curriculum with the heavy emphasis on theology and philosophy, particularly the former, which he regarded as the "fountainhead of all truly humane learning."[16] This kind of vindication of the Holy Cross vision gave credence to the university's concept of a "core curriculum" which in 1966-67 consisted of 48 semester hours, including nine hours required in theology and philosophy, although non-Catholic students could substitute humanities courses for theology if they desired.

In 1966-67, 32 of 144 faculty were members of the Congregation of Holy Cross. Priests and brothers wore Roman collars with black cassocks. There was a crucifix in each classroom and classes began and often ended with prayer. But the late 1960s and early 1970s would see a change; many priests wore the Roman collar with dark suits and some wore ordinary attire. Student dress codes were abandoned in 1968. The Second Vatican Council brought a new religious dimension to campus life wherein religion was exercised in more personal and less institutional fashion. Daily masses continued but religious clubs waned and other religious festivities disappeared. In their place came the "Antioch Weekend," the legacy of Charles Harris, C.S.C., when students

14. See Covert, *A Point of Pride*, p. 159.
15. Covert, *A Point of Pride*, p. 174.
16. See Covert, *A Point of Pride*, p. 188.

and faculty could explore practical aspects of Christian faith in settings away from campus. The University of Portland Community Action Program (UPCAP), a federally-funded enterprise, was implemented to "stimulate community participation for improving urban conditions throughout Portland."[17] Increasing numbers of international students fostered global awareness and cross-cultural symposia. The University of Portland had one of the highest percentages of international students per capita of all Oregon colleges in 1970.

The year 1967 was pivotal for the University of Portland, for it was during January of that year that the Holy Cross Provincial Chapter met at Notre Dame to decide the future of both Notre Dame and the University of Portland. Howard Kenna, C.S.C., Provincial Superior, reported that a new mood brought about in the spirit of Vatican II should foster lay participation, ownership, and management of Catholic colleges and universities. This would not dislodge Holy Cross priests and brothers from their distinctive vision and roles in providing academic, administrative, and pastoral leadership, nor would it mean that the nature of Holy Cross schools would be any less Catholic.[18]

In 1967, the assets of the University of Portland were thus given to a lay board comprised of 40 laymen from the Portland area with a Deed in Trust Agreement which stipulated that there would "always be an integral and pastoral program of Catholic thought and culture" at the university. If the Deed in Trust were violated, the transfer would become null and void. The campus newspaper, *The Beacon,* reported that this "stipulation of course leaves room for the eventual hope of an ecumenical university that would offer other theology and philosophy courses besides Roman Catholic ones."[19]

Waldschmidt courageously and forthrightly led the transition. He indicated that 326 of the 339 Roman Catholic colleges in the United States were operated by religious communities, a situation that required of these communities reassessment of a variety of assumptions. For example, many communities had taken for granted the necessity of financial resourcefulness in light of members' vow of poverty; many had felt, as well, a certain possessiveness toward the institutions they sponsored. With the change Waldschmidt initiated, however, "all offices from the president on down [would] be open to all qualified applicants whether clergy or lay."[20] Only five members of the new board would be members of the Congregation of Holy Cross. Waldschmidt reported to the Portland press that the university would clarify "church-state issues" since under the new reorganization the church would no longer operate or control the university even though a strong Catholic academic, theological, and pastoral presence was ensured. Waldschmidt

17. Covert, *A Point of Pride,* p. 211.
18. *Provincial Review,* vol. 15, no. 1 (February 1967).
19. *The Beacon,* January 13, 1967.
20. *The Beacon,* January 13, 1967.

promised that a "variety of faiths" would be represented on the board. When probed about whether the move was made to qualify for federal aid, the president said that the change had been in the making long "before the federal aid to parochial and church-related schools was in question," and that current changes created no reason to expect more federal aid.[21]

Over a decade later, Father Waldschmidt reflected on this historic move. In May of 1979, looking back on the successful transition, he noted how Protestants had been making similar moves, yet continued to run institutions and maintain the religious character of their schools. Waldschmidt worked out a system whereby religious and lay people would be salaried at the same level except, of course, salaries for religious would be sent to the religious house. In turn, priests and brothers could give back to the university not just contributed services but actual dollars. He confessed that his greatest challenge was guaranteeing that the university would remain Catholic. The danger of losing "Christian contact," a danger to which Yale and Harvard had succumbed, was ever-present; the Deed in Trust, however, would ensure that the University of Portland would always have a vital program of philosophy and theology along with religious counseling and guidance. The Congregation of Holy Cross would thus be guaranteed the implementation of its historic vision and apostolate. Interestingly, Waldschmidt seemed a bit miffed that Notre Dame got the "lion's share" of publicity for the same venture when that institution was not as prepared as the principals in the University of Portland transition. Waldschmidt observed: "I really feel that the University of Portland was the first one in the nation among the College Catholic Houses to really work this thing out."[22]

Waldschmidt was not spared criticism in taking this step, particularly from members of his own community and alumni: they "always were talking about how we were destroying the Liberal Arts and the religious emphasis on it, the religious traditions." But "we tried to strengthen the religious program" by not wavering on theology and philosophy requirements in the core curriculum and by insisting that "the priests would have primarily [sic] responsibility for the chaplaincy at the University." If anyone else, such as Protestant groups, wanted to provide chaplains, they could do so, but the university would not support such efforts financially. The "flak" that the ebullient president endured would take its toll, but he stayed his course and was unwavering in his belief that this was the wave of the future for Catholic higher education in America.[23]

The statutes of the university would later provide that the president be a member of Holy Cross. The only lay president was Arthur A. Schulte Jr., who was selected interim president in 1981-82; three years before, in 1978, Wald-

---

21. *The Beacon*, April 28, 1967.
22. University of Portland Archives, Oral History Program II, p. 109.
23. University of Portland Archives, Oral History Program II, p. 117.

schmidt had been appointed Auxiliary Bishop of the Archdiocese of Oregon. Earlier fears of the loss of Catholic identity proved unfounded, and rather than playing a diminished role, Holy Cross, in the language of a former student, "has a presence today that is as vital as ever."[24]

In its self-study report to the Northwest Association of Secondary and Higher Schools in December 1969, the university stipulated how the Deed in Trust would be implemented. The report indicated that theology was held to be a "valid academic discipline," and the study of theology would be "an integral part of the basic or core curriculum required of all its students." In addition, the university would offer "a comprehensive curriculum ... of academic, non-polemical quality in the philosophical, theological and cultural aspects and tenets of the traditional and contemporary Roman Catholic Religion" which would be required of all Catholic students. The importance of the "examined life" and a "scale of values" with the necessity of moral, ethical, and spiritual commitment were likewise highlighted, and the university made a commitment to cooperate with other Christian and non-Christian religions to provide counseling and guidance. The Congregation of Holy Cross would continue its vital role and would be given preferential treatment in hiring; in turn, the congregation would "make an annual contribution to the university for unrestricted purposes."[25]

In the mid 1970s, in a report entitled, "Profile of a University," the Development Committee of the Board of Regents gave the board's sense of what the Deed in Trust represented. The report, whose primary purpose was to market the University of Portland for community and financial support, indicated that the university was a private institution of higher learning, "Christian in orientation, Catholic in tradition." Non-polemical courses in theology and philosophy were designed to foster moral and ethical values for personal conduct. Special mention was made in the report that the university was able to escape the problems of the turbulent 1960s experienced at other schools because of the undergirding principles of the university "where mutual respect and trust prevailed." The report also focused on the university's attention to the individual student and the breadth rather than the narrow specialization of its curricula. The university strives to "educate the whole person" with a pedagogy "rooted in the JudeoChristian heritage" whose main goal is the provision of an environment that "encourages and facilitates the intellectual, spiritual, cultural and social growth of its students."[26]

24. Teri Van House, "When the Guard was Changed," *Portland Magazine* (Summer 1987): 6-7.

25. Preliminary Self-Study Report of the University of Portland, Northwest Association of Secondary and Higher Schools, December 1969.

26. "Profile of a University, 1975-76," Report of the Development Committee of the Board of Regents, University of Portland, 1975.

Christian Humanism at the University

The term "Christian humanism" has become a sub-theme in the university's attempt to depict the Catholic nature of the institution. Professor Covert uses the term liberally in his history of the university. To Covert, Christian humanism "is a balanced philosophy of human living, a proper, dutiful appreciation and use of the human potential actualized in accordance with God's precepts." Its historic zenith, for Covert, was the Renaissance and was epitomized by Erasmus and Thomas More, but its contemporary application in the context of higher education is "rooted in the academic curricula whence it came." This means that to be Catholic the University of Portland must vouchsafe its identity by providing the classical "core curriculum of theology, philosophy, and the humanities to all its students."[27]

In September of 1964, Father Waldschmidt reflected on the same theme at the annual faculty orientation meeting. He characterized the University of Portland as a "Center of Christian Humanism." Waldschmidt saw Christian humanism more in the classical Greek tradition, but its application to the American Catholic university was clear: excellence according to the standards by which secular institutions are judged, and "excelling in that which is the proper sphere and reason for being a Catholic institution." This vision entailed for Waldschmidt a knowledge of "man as man" in all relationships — to God, to society, to self. It demanded a "thorough understanding of Catholic theology, both dogmatic and moral." It required habits of intellectual curiosity, discriminating inquiry and precision, and a "systematic, orderly approach to truth." It included speaking and writing intelligently, an appreciation for art, literature, music, and "all that makes up our cultural heritage." As a "truly philosophical mind" it presupposed developed, examined attitudes and principles "relative to man as a social and political being," and it required a knowledge of the physical universe and the principles which govern it. This vision was not without its liberalizing component, for it entailed civic and professional service within a larger community, yet was also apparent in personal contact between faculty and student and the interdisciplinary challenges of learning.[28]

The years 1967 to 1976 were thus critical to the University of Portland's etching out its Catholic identity in a modern, post–Vatican II form. There would be financial crises and dwindling enrollments ahead, and more students would look for professional or pre-professional programs of study. The number of faculty would decrease by a third and several graduate programs would

27. Covert, "Christian Humanism," *Delta Epsilon Sigma Journal* 33 (March 1989): 14-19.

28. Paul E. Waldschmidt, C.S.C., "The University of Portland: Center of Christian Humanism," Faculty Orientation, September 14, 1964, in *University of Portland Development Report*, vol. 1 (Summer 1964).

be eliminated. Still, what Covert calls the "economic miracle" saved the institution and prepared it for a successful venture into the 1980s and 1990s.

Subtle changes have painted the university in different colors, however. After resisting coeducation dormitory living, the university is currently experimenting with student demands for a more realistic social structure in which to live and learn. The university ended its mandatory student-housing requirement although it continues a very rigorous student life program. The erection of Holy Cross Court for priests and brothers provides many religious a semi-cloistered, private environment in which to live, and some priests still prefer to live in residence halls among students.

One of the most significant changes during the decade of the 1970s was the requirement that all students, whether Catholic or not, take courses of study in theology. "Theology" clearly had replaced "Religion," for the teaching of Christian faith had become a self-conscious model within the religious studies discipline. Nine hours of theology within the university core, required of all the students in the university, and twelve hours of theology required of students majoring in the College of Arts and Sciences brought about what Covert calls "a silent revolution that went largely unnoticed."[29] The Department of Theology hired the first Protestant theologian in the fall of 1969, and the department began to take on an ecumenical character. All students, again whether Catholic or non-Catholic, were required to study world religions and the Judeo-Christian scriptures, and the Department of Theology began offering a baccalaureate major for the first time in its history.

It was during this same period, however, that the School of Engineering attempted to skirt theology requirements in a number of creative if clandestine ways. The university *Bulletin* exempted the School of Engineering from following the university core requirements of nine hours in favor of a reduction to six hours, and the wording of the *Bulletin* of 1973 (for programs through 1975) indicated: "Temporary exemptions to the University Core will be allowed and will be reviewed annually for their validity." This exemption, however, continued throughout the 1980s and the early 1990s and is still part of the *Bulletin* today.

In 1975, the university employed 101 full-time faculty; all faculty categories taken together pushed that number to 172. Twenty-two percent were clergy, 78 percent lay, with 29 percent of faculty members being female. In 1967, two-thirds of the student body was Catholic, but ten years later the Catholic population had decreased to about one-third of the student body. A survey conducted by the Department of Psychology in 1970 to test whether a Catholic institution such as the University of Portland produced "graduates who have the characteristics of a person educated in a quality liberal arts college" re-

29. Covert, *A Point of Pride*, p. 249.

ported that the university was very much in the mainstream of liberal arts colleges, and that intellectual and social conservatism, often associated with private, church-related institutions, was not the case at the University of Portland. The surveyors added that the university "appears to offer a balanced emphasis between individuality and social good, and at the same time minimizing conventionality just for the sake of social acceptance."[30]

The Challenge of the Post-1960s Era

The decade of the 1970s was for the University of Portland a time for growth and experimentation in a new mode. There were diminishing numbers of priests and brothers; there was the excitement and challenge — perhaps even the intimidation — of Vatican II; there were tough economic conditions, and there was a social upheaval which would variously be labeled "future shock," the "greening of America," and the "making of a counter-culture." New, more ecumenical forms of spirituality were witnessed on campus. Some external forms of Catholic identity vanished, but in their place came what Covert calls "a kind of *devotio moderna,* as evidenced by folk masses, intensive "Antioch Weekends," and a charismatic movement which often comprised close to two hundred persons attending Saturday night meetings. Was this the essence of adaptability, that "charism of Holy Cross"?

In contemporary Catholic discussions of what it means to be a Catholic university, "adaptability" may be understood by some as acquiesence to secularization. James T. Burtchaell, C.S.C., formerly of Notre Dame, believes modern Catholic colleges and universities tend to adopt language to describe and identify themselves which is too "generalizing." In his view, references to Catholic institutions as "Judeo-Christian," to the Catholic faith as a "heritage," and to Catholic values as "humanizing values" represent a loss of Catholic nerve. In Burtchaell's words, "[w]hat was first intended unreflectively as an act of denominational ecumenism devolves into interdenominational vagueness and then into nondenominational secularism."[31]

Burtchaell sees as imperative and mandatory for a university which lives in the spirit of a particular religious faith-community and partakes of that community's nomenclature and institutional character, five criteria: (1) the college must function as a specific Christian community in active communion within a church; (2) in all its constituencies there must be a predominance of committed and articulate communicants "of its mother church"; (3) noncon-

30. See Covert, *A Point of Pride,* p. 260.
31. James T. Burtchaell, C.S.C., "The Decline and Fall of the Christian College (II)," *First Things* (May 1991): 30-38.

58

formists should feel welcome but should also be aware of the university's institutional commitment and how it transcends commitments to individual members; (4) the institution can expect distrust and suspicion from intellectual elites, but it should nonetheless invigorate the practice of Christian faith by exploring far-reaching insights and judgments; and, (5) all this must be done "out-loud" and "honestly."[32]

Burtchaell doubtless would be somewhat chagrined at Thomas C. Oddo, C.S.C., president of the University of Portland from 1982 until his tragic death in 1989. Oddo appeared reluctant to speak or write explicitly about the university's Catholic character and the legacy of Archbishop Christie other than to refer to it as "a rich mix of people, vibrant and caring and working together," a place "where youths can explore and prepare lives under scholarly guidance" and "where moral and ethical concerns are always paramount."[33] In an important reflection on the balance needed in a church-related university between responsibility and academic freedom, published by the university in 1986, Oddo expressed his concern about "recent interventions of Church authorities in the lives of some Catholic institutions and Catholic scholars." He did not want to see either "Catholic" or "University" lost in the mission of the university; "we can and must . . . stand for a Catholic tradition, teach and promote a way of life and Christian values within our Catholic university," and yet make certain that every idea will be pursued with vigor in the search for truth. For Oddo, this meant on the one hand that one needed "to let our institutions pass on the values and grapple with the moral dilemmas" we face as moderns, but on the other hand, to allow all ideas free recourse of consideration and respect. This does not mean we stand for nothing, to be sure, but as a reflection of the university's core curriculum, Oddo confessed, "I'd like to think that our teachers would find a way to stand for answers, to hold out rights and wrongs and to avoid total moral relativity, while still respecting — and even raising — alternative viewpoints."[34]

What does being a Catholic university entail and wherein does its Catholic character take visible or empirical form? For many University of Portland alumni, the answer is in the Holy Cross presence at the university throughout its history, both in teaching and providing pastoral ministry. For others, Catholicity is not defined by the presence of a religious order necessarily, or even with required theology curricula, but in a kind of orthopraxis of Catholic social action and voluntarism, defining "Catholic education beyond books,

32. Burtchaell, "The Decline and Fall of the Christian College (II)," 30-38.

33. Thomas C. Oddo, C.S.C., "The Challenge of Excellence," *Portland Magazine,* August 1983.

34. Thomas C. Oddo, C.S.C., "Value-Centered Education and Freedom of Inquiry: Some Perspectives on the Delicate Balance," University of Portland, 1986.

departments and mission statements."[35] Still others are convinced of the necessity of guaranteeing a critical mass of Catholics, especially among the faculty, who are in tune with the vision and mission of the institution, believing in the dictum, "as goes the faculty so goes the university."[36]

The discussions will continue. Philip Gleason, Notre Dame historian, believes that "Catholic colleges and universities have yet to solve their identity problem."[37] This identity crisis doubtless gave rise to the American Bishops' Pastoral Letter, "Catholic Higher Education and the Pastoral Mission of the Church," in 1981, and clearly was the impetus for *Ex corde Ecclesiae,* the Vatican's declaration on the fundamental characteristics of a Catholic college or university. The document, *Ex corde Ecclesiae,* today represents the official Roman Catholic understanding of what constitutes a Catholic identity in the context of higher education. Issued in August 1990, it mandates a Catholic institution of higher learning where there is Christian inspiration of individuals and the whole community, where there is Catholic reflection upon the ongoing treasury of human knowledge, and where fidelity to the Christian message mediated through the church is complemented by an institutional commitment to the service of the people of God and to the human family "in their pilgrimage to their transcendent goal which gives meaning to life."[38]

The University of Portland Today: What Makes It Catholic?

So where does the University of Portland stand today? David C. Tyson, C.S.C., the university's current president, wants the University of Portland to become the "premiere Catholic teaching university in the west in the next century." Not a few current faculty members believe that Father Tyson has systematically championed a more positive and unequivocal Catholic identity at the University of Portland since he began serving as president in July 1990. Supporters of Father Tyson's emphasis often point to an apparent reluctance

---

35. Lawrence S. Cunningham, "Gladly Wolde He Lerne and Gladly Teche: The Catholic Scholar in the New Millennium," *The Cresset* (June 1992): 4-10.

36. See Cunningham, "Gladly Wolde He Lerne," 4-10.

37. Philip Gleason, "American Catholic Higher Education, 1940-1990: The Ideological Context," in George M. Marsden and Bradley J. Longfield, eds., *The Secularization of the Academy* (New York and Oxford: Oxford University Press, 1992), p. 251.

38. See Cunningham, "Gladly Wolde He Lerne," 4-10; and J. Patrick Murphy, C.M., *Visions and Values in Catholic Higher Education* (Kansas City: Sheed and Ward, 1991), especially Sally M. Furay's introduction, "The Context: American Catholic Higher Education and the Transmission of Values," pp. xv-xviii. Also helpful and exceedingly insightful is John P. Langan, S.J., ed., *Catholic Universities in Church and Society: A Dialogue on* Ex corde Ecclesiae (Washington, D.C.: Georgetown University Press, 1993).

on the part of previous administrations to be proud of the university's Catholic identity.

Today, as we have suggested, Catholic identity may take several forms. The spectrum of possibilities begins with a conservative emphasis on a critical mass of Catholic faculty and students and required courses in theology and philosophy and reaches to the more liberal concern with academic excellence and the teaching and practice of social justice. In order to understand the theological underpinnings which define the University of Portland and its Catholicity today, however, it is important to recall the conditions of the huge wave of Catholic immigrants who came to America in the nineteenth and early part of the twentieth centuries. Before World War II, American Catholics were outsiders looking in at a cultural mainstream which defined them as sub-culture immigrants. Students of the history of Christianity know, however, that Catholicism is historically non-sectarian. Only rarely has it stood over against culture. Since the conversion of Constantine, the Catholic tradition has attempted to imbue the world with the spirit of Christ because it understands the incarnation of God in Jesus Christ to be a sacramental affirmation of the world. In the words of J. Bryan Hehir of Harvard, Catholics "are at home in the world, but not too at home."[39]

After World War II, liberal arts were championed on many college and university fronts and traditional values surfaced again in post-war America. The Catholic legacy of probing the great ideas of Western civilization in the context of philosophical and theological foundations gave Catholics the opportunity to prove Paul Blanchard wrong in his charge that "Catholic power" was a threat to American freedom. *Commonweal*, the Catholic weekly magazine, pushed for Catholics to come out of their self-imposed isolation as an immigrant culture, accept the reality of American pluralism, and plunge into the mainstream of American religious culture with an ecumenical spirit. Monsignor John Tracy Ellis castigated Catholic ghetto mentality in 1955 and challenged Catholic intellectuals to prove to America that Catholics were adroit enough to present their distinctive religious convictions with coherence and effectiveness.[40]

In the 1960s John Kennedy was elected President and the pontificate of John XXIII "gave promise of the dawn of a new era in American Catholicism."[41] Catholics became more upwardly mobile and assimilated into the American social and political mainstream. The Second Vatican Council gave impetus to this transition, ironically providing Catholics with an ethos more

---

39. J. Bryan Hehir, *Current Issues in Catholic Higher Education* 15 (Summer 1994): 37-44.

40. Gleason, "American Catholic Higher Education, 1940-1990," pp. 235-44.

41. Gleason, "American Catholic Higher Education, 1940-1990," p. 244.

consistent with American cultural values. When the Council emphasized collegiality, the ideology of self-government could more easily be appropriated. The church's people-of-God ecclesiology rang true to the notion of American equality. The right of conscience seemed consonant with American individualism. The pastoral orientation of the documents of Vatican II fit well with the American predilection for the practical, and Catholic social justice teachings resonated with American social action. In short, the church's opening up to the modern world was a Catholic way of relating to American this-worldliness. Vatican II pushed Catholics amazingly into the mainstream. As Notre Dame historian Philip Gleason observes, the "council . . . summoned American Catholics to move in the direction they were already going."[42]

The era since the 1960s has therefore presented an unprecedented challenge for American Catholics and particularly for American Catholic higher education. The University of Portland shared the openness within American Catholicism to self-criticism, diversity, a search for excellence, and a return to theological studies within the framework of a university. The conciliar emphases on religious freedom and lay autonomy raised new issues of academic freedom for Catholics, and the 1970s saw entangled conflicts between the academy and papal and episcopal authority. The question of what constituted the Catholic identity of a Catholic university became the key question as the University of Portland wrestled with its mission.

Was the university's mission statement adequate to define Catholicity? One problem with mission statements is not what they state but what they fail to state. Many statements of Catholic institutions have been vague and generic, quite like those of other private, religiously affiliated colleges and universities. Even "a good secular university could . . . locate itself comfortably within [their] rubrics."[43] James Burtchaell's warning, noted above, that Catholic colleges and universities might well fall into the same trap as Harvard, Yale, and Vanderbilt could be understood as a protest against absorption of Catholic identity into the lowest common denominator, "offending no one and subsuming the Catholic commitments . . . under general phrases about tradition and slogans that have become almost politically correct."[44]

The University of Portland's mission statement emphasizes that it is "an independently governed Catholic university" which is composed of diverse races, ages, nationalities, and religions. It maintains its tie and commitment to the liberal arts as the foundation of learning; it provides excellent teaching

42. Gleason, "American Catholic Higher Education, 1940-1990," p. 245.
43. Michael J. Buckley, S.J., "The Catholic University and the Promise Inherent in its Identity" in John P. Langan, S.J., ed., *Catholic Universities in Church and Society,* p. 77.
44. Buckley, "The Catholic University," p. 78.

and individual attention "in an environment that fosters development of the whole person." Central to the daily life of the university is a "concern with issues of justice and ethical behavior," enabling the university community to encourage service to God and neighbor. Yet, is this enough to vouchsafe the Catholic identity of the University of Portland?

For many Catholics, more important than mission statements is a critical mass of faculty who have a common vision of what Catholic education is all about. This, they argue, will ensure the perpetuation of a certain culture and climate necessary to give both empirical and spiritual witness to the Catholic character of the institution. This witness will not be fostered by moralism, sectarianism, or tests of orthodoxy but by a kind of faith which requires a commitment "that keeps consciously alive the Catholic intellectual tradition as a central fabric" of the institution.[45]

In the case of the University of Portland, this critical mass is provided by the Congregation of Holy Cross. Since the mid-1960s, however, serious problems have surfaced to change the way Catholicity is defined and reflected in those Catholic colleges and universities bearing the stamp of religious houses. There have been fewer priests, sisters, and brothers. In 1964-65, for example, 73 percent of all full-time faculty in Catholic institutions of higher learning were lay persons. We have seen that this was the case at the University of Portland. The change of ownership and governance in 1967 amounted to a distancing of the institution from ecclesiastical control while attempting to maintain its Catholic mission and programs. Perhaps of even greater impact was the way the Second Vatican Council affected the self-understanding of religious communities and likewise how this trickled down into the life of their academic institutions.[46]

Thus on one side of the spectrum of Catholic higher education are those who desire the guarantee of a central culture of persons who promulgate the mission of the institution. They see the importance, even the mandate, of requiring traditional Catholic teachings which are an integral part of the curriculum. Laurence Cunningham, lay professor of theology at Notre Dame, does not define the religious character of an institution by the mere presence of a theology department. He insists, however, that a "Theology" department is preferable to a "Religious Studies" department because it depicts in nomenclature what in fact the reality is: a Catholic university where Christian faith is reflected within a historic intellectual tradition. For a Catholic college or university to fail to require the study of theology as an academic discipline, Cunningham argues, is an "abdication of responsibility." The department

45. Hehir, *Current Issues,* 37-44.
46. Philip Gleason, "The American Background of *Ex corde Ecclesiae:* A Historical Perspective" in Langan, ed., *Catholic Universities in Church and Society,* pp. 5-6.

should be dedicated to the Christian tradition in general and "serious about its own" Catholic heritage in particular.[47]

Theology departments are not necessarily (and restrictively) the locus of Catholic teachings, however. In a broader sense, as Father Theodore Hesburgh, long-time president of Notre Dame, was fond of saying, the Catholic university is the place where the church does its thinking. The Catholic intellectual life, conservatives argue, is the business of all departments, colleges, and schools within the university. The essence of Catholicism has been the marriage of faith to reason, of grace to nature, of Jerusalem to Athens. Catholics are committed *because they are Catholic* to an exploration of truth, and therefore regard the "world as an appropriate locus of both anthropological and theological reflection and action." As Jesus was the "man for others," the Catholic university seeks to be an intellectual "community for others."[48] As a consequence, David O'Brien of the College of Holy Cross argues that we "need to develop Catholic Studies programs to provide the institutional base for Catholic scholarship and teaching."[49]

Today, the University of Portland would please some conservatives. The guarantee of Holy Cross presence, the required theology courses in all schools and colleges as part of the university core curriculum, the Theology Department which self-consciously offers courses in the Christian tradition as well as specifically Catholic courses, and the mandate of campus ministry ensure a Catholic presence. The question remains, however, of the extent to which the Catholic intellectual tradition is reflected in curricula outside philosophical and theological frameworks. Future self-study, imposed from within the academic leadership of the University, will be necessary to weigh this important dimension of Catholic identity at the University of Portland.

What about liberal criteria for defining what is Catholic about a Catholic university? While conservatives fear the loss of Catholic identity, liberals fear oppression and interference by the institutional church in the domain of academic freedom. As a consequence, many liberal Catholics have found a place of refuge for their academic pursuits and teaching in the modern Catholic university; it is here where they find Catholic identity in an atmosphere of free exchange. With the pressure to pursue solid academic standards and the invitation to outside accreditation agencies to vindicate and challenge such standards, Catholic institutions of higher learning began

47. Cunningham, "Gladly Wolde He Lerne," 4-10.
48. Timothy R. Scully, C.S.C., "What is Catholic about a Catholic University?" in Theodore Hesburgh, C.S.C., ed., *The Challenge and Promise of a Catholic University* (Notre Dame: University of Notre Dame Press, 1994), pp. 318-319.
49. David J. O'Brien, "Conversations on Jesuit (And Catholic?) Higher Education: Jesuit Si Catholic . . . Not So Sure," *Conversations* (Fall 1994): 4-12, 14, 30.

playing a new game. Emerging as ghetto immigrants into the mainstream of American pluralism, Catholics surprised even themselves at how well they could acculturate. Now that they were in the business of education, Catholics should continue their successful search for "truth about the world and the place of the human person within the world."[50] What could be more Catholic?

With Vatican II paving the way for a new form of Catholic consciousness, Catholic colleges and universities shifted from Catholic to more pluralistic constituencies, in the case of both students and faculty. It became the essence of Catholic identity to achieve solid academic standards. Obviously a major feat, such achievement came at a price: as faculty became better scholars and professionals, were they still good Catholics? So the confrontations and entanglements between Catholic officialdom and the academy brought public attention to the difficulty of being a "Catholic university," an oxymoron in the view of Catholic critics.

This set the stage for more liberal responses. Diversity became an important slogan; after all, the word "catholic" does carry with it a sense of recognized diversity within universality. Sally M. Furay, R.S.C.J., believes that Catholics cannot be a "tidy, neat and submissive people," but a people who cultivate a truly appreciative attitude toward differences which do not divide but enrich the whole.[51] Sister Furay is aware that Catholic colleges and universities are educating huge numbers of non-Catholics; in her view, the goal of Catholic pedagogy is not the training of Catholic leaders but helping students to develop a sense of responsibility for their moral behavior. "Unless the dual goals of academic excellence and value-centeredness are operationalized in the education we offer, our catalog rhetoric is not only meaningless, but worse, misleading."[52]

Liberals speak of "value-oriented education" as a euphemism for Catholic identity; to many liberals this is what it means to be Catholic in the pluralistic and professional environs of the American academy today. Liberal Catholics believe that endemic to Catholic tradition is an ethos which fosters academic freedom, a passionate quest for truth, and respect for the human person. These values often emerge in Catholic social action or even in art and architecture. Since Vatican II, Catholicism has seen the departure of symbols, rituals, and practices which once identified people and institutions as Roman Catholic. Now, for some liberal Catholics such as Ann O'Hara Graff of Loyola

50. Scully, "What is Catholic about a Catholic University?" p. 317.
51. Sally M. Furay, R.S.C.J., "The Context: American Catholic Higher Education and the Transmission of Values," in Murphy, *Visions and Values in Catholic Higher Education,* pp. xvi-xvii.
52. Furay, "The Context," p. xviii.

University in Chicago, the "stories" of Catholic colleges and universities have become the salient features of contemporary Catholicism. For Professor Graff, the locus of Catholic identity is in the sense of community, the respect for the dignity of all persons, especially women in their oppression, and the work of peace and justice — "these are readily grounded in the gospel and hallmarks of the best of Catholic tradition." Because "we believe that all things are created through the word and wisdom of God, to seek truth is to seek God."[53]

Thus progressive Catholics define Catholic identity of Catholic institutions of higher learning with peace and justice education. In 1975, the Association of Catholic Colleges and Universities appointed a Task Force on Education for Justice and Peace, and during the 1980s a number of programs, including those implemented at the University of Portland, both curricular and cocurricular, multiplied rapidly. These educational ventures were not attempts merely to define what was Catholic about Catholic higher education, but realizations and implementations of Catholic incarnational theology as outreach into the world. But, in fact, the theme of peace and justice became the common ground where both the Vatican and American Catholic academics could meet, notwithstanding the tensions which had developed between them. The Catholic college or university now had the opportunity to stand at the forefront of a new stage for American Catholics, a place of mixing together discipleship and citizenship, where society itself becomes "an object and horizon" of apostolic outreach.[54]

Within what might be called this liberal tradition, it is instructive to read an article by Cecilia Wanner, a current student at the University of Portland. The article appeared in *The Beacon*, the campus newspaper, and contained information about service opportunities open to University of Portland graduates. She began her article with a short paragraph:

They began a mission to help others.

Along the way, they themselves were helped.

Ms. Wanner then went on to highlight the experiences of several Holy Cross Associates who began a year in Portland "to live out their vows of service, community, spirituality and simple living." One member of the group became a Holy Cross Associate because he wanted "to learn about relationships, people on the margins of society and himself as well." He works as an activities director at an HIV day center. Another member works as a case manager with Hispanic immigrants. Still another is an outreach coordinator at West Women's and

53. See Murphy, *Visions and Values in Catholic Higher Education*, p. 216.

54. See David O'Brien's untitled response to Philip Gleason's lead article, "The American Background of *Ex corde Ecclesiae*: A Historical Perspective" in Langan, ed., *Catholic Universities in Church and Society*, pp. 25-26.

Children's Shelter in Portland. The Office of Volunteer Services at the university provides and encourages a host of service opportunities for students (and faculty) both while they are engaged in study and upon graduation. Hundreds of students, as a consequence, have taken part in urban and rural "plunges" in order to relate their learning and service commitments to social activism.[55] It is clear that the University of Portland today shares much of the liberal sentiment in defining its Catholic identity.

There are other ways in which the University of Portland is attempting to define its Catholicity today. A recent example can be seen in a memorandum which Charles D. Sherrer, C.S.C., academic vice president, sent to the university community. Dated January 4, 1995, it reminded the university community of Holy Week and how the custom of closing the university on Good Friday was restored "several years ago in acknowledgment of the special religious character of the day and to give members of the University community full opportunity to participate in religious services on campus, in their home parishes, or in other churches." The attempt to be more forthright about its Catholic heritage and identity is also exemplified in new nomenclature: on documents emanating from the public relations office, the university has now adopted the epithet, "Oregon's Catholic University."

Conclusion

It is easy to see evidence of the University of Portland's conscious attempt to define itself in Catholic terms as it struggles with the ethos of the post-Vatican II church, the necessity to pursue excellence in academic programs, and the challenges of religious pluralism in America. The best self-definition of the university is that which Father Waldschmidt gave it in 1964: "a center of Christian humanism." Father Lackenmier's reference to the Holy Cross legacy in higher education as a commitment to excellence, a concern for the personal formation of students, and the experience of collaboration in the Holy Cross vision — a theme with which we began this essay — is merely an exegesis of what many at the University of Portland understand Christian humanism to be. There will be ongoing discussions concerning the extent to which this is Catholic enough. But if it is the "fundamental proposition of a Catholic university" to link together the religious and the academic, and if it is the nature of Catholicism to be at home in the world of ideas and social institutions with its essentially non-sectarian, the-world-as-sacrament theology — a theology Charles Curran has called the idea of

55. Cecilia Wanner, "Associates Dedicate Year to Serve," *The Beacon*, (November 3, 1994).

"Catholic 'and' " — then the University of Portland may gradually become what it already is, for in the *promise* to become such an institution lies its identity.[56]

56. See the stirring comments of Michael J. Buckley, S.J., "The Catholic University and the Promise Inherent in its Identity" in Langan, *Catholic Universities in Church and Society,* pp. 76-87.

THE LUTHERAN TRADITION

What Can the Lutheran Tradition Contribute to Christian Higher Education?

Richard W. Solberg

"What has Jerusalem to do with Athens, the Church with the Academy?" Ever since the second century, when Tertullian first posed his celebrated rhetorical question, persons of scholarly bent have engaged it in spirited debate. Answers have varied from that of Tertullian himself who, having met Jesus Christ, saw no further need for speculation or research, to that of some twentieth-century children of the Enlightenment who, having met the goddess of science, see no further need for religious faith. Some of the liveliest intellectual discussions, however, have taken place between these two extremes, as people grappled to define a proper relationship. That the question is still stimulating discussion in both the church and the academy is evident in this present project.

Reformation Roots

The Lutheran Reformers of the sixteenth century affirmed a vital connection between Jerusalem and Athens.[1] Luther and Melanchthon and their colleagues were Christian intellectuals who were committed both to the eternal truth revealed in the Scriptures and to the role of reason in the life of the mind. As university professors, theologians, and philosophers, they spon-

1. David W. Lotz., "Education for Citizenship in the Two Kingdoms: Reflections on the Theological Foundations of Lutheran Higher Education" in *Papers and Proceedings of the 65th Annual Convention* (Washington, DC: Lutheran Educational Conference of North America, 1979), p. 7.

sored religious reforms that found counterparts in both the universities and the schools of Germany. Luther himself advocated universal education for children under the direction of civil authorities, as well as co-education, public scholarships, and municipal libraries offering the best books from both pagan and Christian sources. He brought curricular reform to the universities, introducing Greek, Hebrew, and humanistic studies. Melanchthon, known as *Praeceptor Germaniae*, the "schoolmaster of Germany," established the *Gymnasium* to prepare Latin school graduates for university entrance. He led in reorganizing the universities of Leipzig, Tübingen, and Heidelberg, and helped establish new universities at Jena, Marburg, and Königsberg. Since the Reformation, therefore, higher education in a Christian context has been a Lutheran priority.[2]

A Continuing Tradition

In reflecting on the continuing Lutheran tradition in the German university, the late Sydney Ahlstrom cited three sub-traditions that have flavored European intellectual history and have claimed rootage in Luther's thought: the scholastic, the pietistic, and the critical. The scholastic arose during the tumultuous years of the early seventeenth century, a period fraught with religious wars and confessional controversy, as Lutherans debated and fought with the Counter Reformation on one hand and Reformed theologies on the other. The rigid formalism of scholasticism, intended to preserve and defend the gains of the Reformation, was countered in the late seventeenth and eighteenth centuries by Pietism, which also had Lutheran roots, emphasizing the inner spiritual life and engagement in mission work and deeds of mercy.

The critical tradition that emerged in the eighteenth and dominated the nineteenth century was a response to the rise of modern science and the impact of the Enlightenment. It was marked by an investigative spirit — a willingness to ask deep questions and to query accepted assumptions, even in relation to the study of Scripture and both Hebrew and Christian history. Lutheran scholars were in the forefront in these ventures, often pioneering into unexamined fields in both historical and scientific inquiry. This tradition includes such philosophers as Kant and Hegel and biblical scholars and theologians from Semler to Ritschl and Bultmann. These thinkers seldom agreed with each other, and found critics in both religious and non-religious circles. But criticism and controversy are at home in any tradition that

2. Richard W. Solberg. *Lutheran Higher Education in North America* (Minneapolis: Augsburg, 1985), pp. 15-19.

encourages freedom and creativity, qualities that were very much a part of the Wittenberg heritage.[3]

In the migration of Lutherans from Europe to America, however, the "critical tradition" was largely left behind. Most German immigrants in the eighteenth century were peasants and came to a country still in the frontier stage. The few university-trained clergy who came to care for their spiritual needs had been trained in centers of German Pietism. As the supply of European clergy dwindled, the earliest Lutheran ventures into higher education were primarily directed to the preparation of more pastors. Colleges were founded to provide the basic classical languages necessary for theological study.[4] Thus, a tradition that had been broadly involved in the intellectual milieu of European thought was narrowed to a concern for preparing frontier pastors in an institutional climate strongly flavored by American evangelical revivalism.

Unfortunately, when the modern American university came into being in the late nineteenth century, Lutheran higher education did not re-enter the field of university education, even though the American university was modeled after the German pattern that had been the cradle of the Lutheran Reformation. Significant contributions have been made by individual Lutheran theologians and scientists, both in the secular universities of America and in some Lutheran colleges, but Lutheran higher education has not been able to provide a serious institutional challenge to the dominant influence of the "Enlightenment culture" of American higher education.

Nonetheless, there are rich resources within the Lutheran tradition that, if properly utilized, can illumine the continuing debate between faith and learning. The following brief review of several of Luther's doctrines in their relation to education may be especially useful to church-related colleges as they re-examine their particular role in present-day American higher education.

Luther's Worldview

Luther's theology incorporates a realistic view of human nature and of world history. Sin — the deep corruption that has infected the whole of God's creation, both the human heart and the natural order — was very real to Luther. All human efforts to "Christianize" society, he asserted, or to impose a "Christian worldview" fail to grasp the depth of the corruption and the perversity

3. Sydney E. Ahlstrom, "What's Lutheran about Higher Education? — A Critique," *Papers and Proceedings of the 60th Annual Convention* (Washington, DC: Lutheran Educational Conference of North America, 1974), pp. 8-16.

4. Solberg, *Lutheran Higher Education*, pp. 52-57.

of human nature. Yet, in spite of human pride and rebellion, God the Creator so loved the world that He sent His Son Jesus Christ to redeem the human family. Nor has He forsaken His created world. Until He is ready to restore the natural order in the "end-time," God benevolently upholds, governs, and restrains it from self-destruction.

Such a view of the world and society was rejected out of hand by the philosophers of the eighteenth-century Enlightenment for whom humanity was the measure of all things, and who on occasion drew up plans to construct the best of all possible worlds in accord with immutable laws of nature. This latter, more optimistic view was current among the founders of the American Republic. It persisted throughout the nineteenth century in Jacksonian democracy, spawning a variety of utopian experiments, and eventually found expression in the Social Gospel.

In the midst of all these progress-oriented models, Lutheran theology represented a countervailing position.[5] While rejecting the optimism of the Social Gospel, it offered a plausible explanation of human selfishness and greed. But Lutherans were not doom-sayers, sounding either the imminent self-destruction or the divine destruction of a sinful world. They shared Luther's faith in a God of grace who mercifully restrains evil and who has endowed his creatures with a reasonable degree of common sense and civic responsibility. Students of history and the social sciences might find in this view of the world and human nature a safeguard against both the extremes of triumphalism and despair and a healthy incentive to realistic constructive social action.

A Theology of Paradox

Luther's theology has often been described as a "theology of paradoxes," a description that is rooted in Luther's own struggle of faith. Through personal experience, he had discovered, like St. Paul, that even though by God's grace his sins were forgiven, he was constantly assailed by temptations and frequently failed. Finally, again like St. Paul, he found assurance in the paradox that, by the grace of God alone, he was a sinner and "forgiven" or "justified" at the same time: *"simul justus et peccator"* — the ultimate paradox![6]

This was for Luther both a liberation and a source of unending wonder, that a righteous and holy God could reach out to him, "dust and ashes and full of sin," and embrace him in love and forgiveness. The reality of his sinful

---

5. Sydney E. Ahlstrom, *A Religious History of the American People* (New Haven: Yale University Press, 1972), pp. 518-522.

6. Roland Bainton, *Here I Stand* (Nashville: Abingdon-Cokesbury Press, 1950), p. 65.

nature never allowed Luther the luxury of prideful self-esteem. Nevertheless, as a redeemed child of God, he dared to face the powers of Church and Empire, engage in disputes, and make affirmations that could have cost him his life.

Qualities such as these, rooted in Luther's personal experience, have a direct relation to Lutheran attitudes toward education in general and Christian higher education in particular. In all education, humility before God and the vastness of the unknown is the beginning of both wisdom and learning. Everyone, even the most sophisticated scholar, is a learner, subject to error and correction. But at the same time, by the creative grace of God, even the most unmotivated or disheartened undergraduates may receive a renewed sense of individual worth that can energize them for achievements far beyond their own expectations.

Christian Liberty

Yet another paradox found expression in Luther's exposition of Christian liberty. When, in preparing his lectures on St. Paul's letter to the Romans, he first discovered the life-changing reality of justification by grace through faith in Jesus Christ, Luther felt as if he had "gone through open doors into paradise." Like St. Paul, he had become a free man, no longer bound by the law but "free in Christ." No master, pope, or emperor could any longer bind his conscience. In a tract published in 1520 entitled "The Freedom of the Christian Man," he declared the end of legalistic religion and the liberation of the Christian conscience. "A Christian," he wrote, "is a perfectly free lord of all, subject to none!"

The implications of this doctrine for both intellectual and spiritual freedom were far-reaching, not only for Luther himself but for the tradition he generated. Neither the personal conduct of the Christian nor his religious or intellectual inquiry is subject to any human judgment. In Luther's thought, the descriptive use of the term "Christian" implied "freedom" rather than "restriction." Luther's daring affirmation, based on his understanding of the grace of God, might help to erase the popular image of the Christian college in America as restrictive in both thought and conduct.

But the same overwhelming grace of God that freed Luther's mind and spirit from legalistic shackles paradoxically bound him in thankfulness to love and serve his neighbor. Hence, he wrote, the Christian is not only the "perfectly free lord of all, subject to none," but according to the law of love, he is also "a perfectly dutiful servant of all, subject to all!"[7] The implementation of such

7. Harold J. Grimm, ed., *Luther's Works* (Philadelphia: Muhlenberg Press, 1957), vol. 31, p. 344.

an ethic on the campuses of Christian colleges would strengthen the sense of community among students, encourage projects and careers of social outreach, and ultimately contribute to a more humane social climate in America.

The Two Kingdoms

One of Luther's most creative doctrines, especially useful in dealing with the issues of faith and reason, was his concept of "two kingdoms."[8] Basing his position on the first article of the Apostles' Creed, he declared that God the Creator is the ruler of two "kingdoms" or "realms." The heavenly kingdom is a spiritual one, in which faith rules over reason and in which God reveals and fulfills His plan for the redemption of the human family. This kingdom is manifested in the holy catholic church, the body of believers redeemed by grace, through faith in Jesus Christ.

The earthly or secular kingdom is the created world, pronounced by God at the creation as "good," but since marred by sin and awaiting its ultimate redemption at the "end time" through the re-creating act of God. Meanwhile, God benevolently preserves and directs it through such agencies as governments, families, and schools — social and economic structures described by Luther as "orders of creation." For Luther, "secular" by no means connoted "God-forsaken." All people, both believers and unbelievers, are members of God's secular kingdom and serve as His agents in ordering and governing it. Both are ultimately responsible to God for their stewardship, whether they acknowledge it or not. This worldview is far removed from the Deism of the eighteenth century in which God may be recognized as a first cause but not as a loving Father who personally cares for His creation.

Christians, as members of both kingdoms, are called upon to love God with all their heart and soul and mind. Ideally, they see their service in the world as an expression of thanks to God for both spiritual and temporal blessings, and as an opportunity to serve their neighbor. In the fulfillment of their roles as citizens and servants, entrepreneurs, professionals, or peasants, they are free to join hands with anyone, Christian or not, who desires to improve and enrich the human condition.

Luther's philosophy of education grew directly out of his concept of the two kingdoms. He placed education squarely within the "orders of creation" or God's "secular realm." Its purpose, grounded in the Creed's first article, is to foster the capacity to learn, to enhance and enrich people's lives, and to equip students to make human society what God intends it to be. In his famous

8. William A. Lazareth, "The Christian in Society," introductory essay in James Atkinson, ed., *Luther's Works* (Philadelphia: Fortress Press, 1966), vol. 44, pp. xi-xvi.

sermon of 1530, "On Keeping Children in School,"[9] he urgently advocated the training of teachers who could lead a whole new generation into civic responsibility and assure good and orderly government. This task he laid directly on the civil magistrates as their Christian responsibility.

Institutions established by the church — colleges and universities in particular — offer faculty and students the opportunity to promote learning and justice and to sustain intellectual inquiry and conversation. They may explore the creation, ask questions, and seek answers, knowing always that they are at work within God's secular kingdom.[10]

Each academic discipline, whether theology, philosophy, or science, has an integrity of its own and is not subject to any other. The theologian and the scientist need not be in conflict. They may work independently or in concert, in a commonwealth of learning under God's benevolent rule and with His blessing. This Lutheran doctrine paved the way in the German university for the modern concept of academic freedom.[11]

The Priesthood of All Believers

Another significant doctrine that Luther affirmed was "the priesthood of all believers." This was the Lutheran response to the medieval practice of monasticism and the "higher righteousness" attributed to all churchly professions. In his "Address to the German Nobility" in 1520, Luther attacked the distinctions given to clergy and nobility by affirming that since all persons — whether rich or poor — were originally brought to God in baptism, their subsequent access to God should not be limited. There was no need of mediation by a priest; every believer could be his or her own priest.[12]

While the doctrine of the "priesthood of all believers" was primarily related to the "heavenly kingdom," namely, the relation of the Christian to God, it had significant implications for the believer's life in the secular realm as well. It enhanced the inherent dignity of all persons in all their relationships. If all could approach God directly, no person need feel of inferior worth among his or her fellow citizens. Using their God-given talents, all could seek to serve the community in ways best suited to their gifts.

9. Robert C. Schultz, ed., *Luther's Works* (Philadelphia: Fortress Press, 1967), vol. 46, pp. 237-240.

10. "The basis for Partnership Between Church and College: A Statement of the Lutheran Church in America" (New York: Division for Mission in North America, Lutheran Church in America, 1976), p. 3.

11. Solberg, *Lutheran Higher Education,* p. 19.

12. Atkinson, ed., *Luther's Works,* p. 127.

Christian Vocation

Just as each person possessed dignity as an individual, so every work or profession was a valued channel of service. Having been "called" by God in baptism, the Christian was obliged to give expression to that call by faithful service in some useful secular "calling" or "vocation." No hierarchy of services would distinguish one person's vocation from that of another. Faithfulness and integrity, not public honor or recognition, are the standards by which God judges a person's work. In the classic example cited by Luther, the faithful work of a scullery maid is as praiseworthy in God's economy as that of the learned scholar.

This liberating doctrine has helped to lift the aspirations and the self-esteem of Lutherans in all occupations, but it has given special impetus to the desire for education. The motivation to service as a productive member of God's earthly kingdom has energized the persistent Lutheran passion for learning. It has been the impulse that has impelled Lutherans, wherever they have been, to found schools and colleges.

Since Luther's day his followers have also been supportive of public education, and have participated freely as students and teachers in both public and private professional and graduate higher education of all kinds. In the preparation of clergy, European Lutherans have traditionally studied theology in state-supported universities. In 1860, before the emergence of the modern university in America, German Lutherans in Ohio even tried to establish a university on the European model, with the four classic faculties of letters, law, medicine, and theology.

In their ventures into higher education in America, Lutherans have never lacked a theological base for full participation in the intellectual or scientific marketplace. Without claiming a unique Lutheran approach to higher education, Lutheran theology would hold all of higher education, including its own, to the highest standards of openness and integrity. All investigation into the arts and sciences and all technology is good, if it is pursued with the well-being of the human family and of God's creation in mind. This stance is by no means exclusively Lutheran, perhaps not even exclusively Christian, but in the hands of courageous proponents, it can challenge any philosophy in the marketplace, whether deistic, mechanistic, or sectarian.[13]

An Unfulfilled Resource

Having this potential resource available in their own tradition, Lutherans must admit that their colleges have not always been prepared to use it effectively.

13. Robert W. Bertram, "What's Lutheran About Higher Education? — Theological Presuppositions" in *Papers and Proceedings of the 60th Annual Convention,* pp. 17-20.

Whether because of limited financial resources, the cultural immaturity of its immigrant populations, the contagious influence of sectarian American Protestantism, or a simple lack of courage, Lutheran educators have too often been unwilling to take the educational risks implicit in Lutheran theology. Instead, they have responded to the trends and movements in American higher education in much the same ways as other church-related colleges.

In order to provide theological training for pastors, Lutherans established classical colleges, very similar to hundreds of others begun by other Protestant denominations during the so-called "American College Movement" in the early and mid-nineteenth century. When Charles Eliot of Harvard led the assault on the classical curriculum after the Civil War, denominational colleges, including the Lutheran colleges, generally resisted. Few, however, were able to withstand the growing public demand for a wider variety of scientific and practical subjects. Meanwhile, in the 1870s, the American university emerged, offering specialized programs of advanced learning and scientific research that reflected the growing pragmatism and materialism of American culture.

Lutheran colleges continued to provide classical and biblical preparation for their clergy, but they also added the practical courses that would assist young Scandinavian and German immigrants to take their place in American society. In due time, like most church-related colleges, they also adopted co-education, fraternities, literary societies, and athletic programs. Insofar as controversial currents of intellectual and scientific debate over issues like evolution were concerned, most Lutheran colleges either ignored them or warned their students against them as threats to their religious faith.

One distinguishing feature of Lutheran colleges during the twentieth century has been that, unlike many other Protestant denominational schools, they have not typically chosen to disaffiliate from the church. The confessional character of the Lutheran church, its historic commitment to higher education, the loyalty of college leadership to the church, and the persistent concern over providing proper preparation for the clergy have kept the church relationship generally alive and strong.[14] A continuing commitment to the defense of the liberal arts and humanities as more hospitable to the spiritual and social development of students has also provided a unifying rallying point for Lutheran colleges as members of a distinctive community within American higher education.[15]

14. Richard W. Solberg and Merton Strommen, *How Church-Related Are Church-Related Colleges?* (Philadelphia: Board of Publication, Lutheran Church in America, 1980), pp. 73-90.

15. Harold Ditmanson, ed., *Christian Faith and the Liberal Arts* (Minneapolis: Augsburg, 1960). See also Mary Hull Mohr, "A Liberal Arts Perspective" in *The Mission of the ELC Colleges and Universities: The Joseph A. Sittler Symposium* (Chicago: Evangelical Lutheran Church in America, 1989), pp. 38-48.

The most serious critique one could level at Lutheran higher education in America is that it has failed to fulfill the educational challenges implicit in its own theology. However, there are also some aspects of Lutheran theology affecting higher education on which Lutherans themselves have differed sharply. Following Luther's doctrine of the two kingdoms, some have separated the two realms completely, denying the dual role of the Christian as a citizen of both kingdoms. This has resulted in quietism with respect to social action, and also the closing of certain areas of scientific research and teaching as "dangerous" to a student's faith.

Some segments of American Lutheranism have yielded to the temptation to codify their theology into absolute formulas and propositions. This has tended to limit the free inquiry and critical judgment that the Lutheran tradition at its best has encouraged. Its final result is sectarianism.

Luther's frequent use of paradox in dealing with doctrine and practice is persistently riddling to the logical mind. The sinner who is at the same time justified, the free man who is the servant of all, the mystery of Christ's real presence in the sacrament — all these Lutheran doctrines elude logic and may even cause offense to those who seek security in more legalistic religious formulations.

A View Toward the Future

Having dealt at length with the wealth of theological resources implicit within the Lutheran tradition, and some of its vulnerabilities, it remains to inquire how Lutheran colleges can make their best contribution to Christian higher education as representatives of their distinguished tradition. Lutherans should strive to make the best possible use of their own academic institutions — more than forty colleges and small universities and a dozen theological seminaries — as centers of thought and action. It would not be wise to discard the denominational identity of these schools, even though such labeling has contributed to a general sectarian image of all church-related colleges.

Lutheran colleges should boldly affirm their family identity, while at the same time seeking to embody the highest standards of academic performance by both faculty and students. They should seek to enroll students from Lutheran congregations, but remain open to qualified students from all sectors of society. Given the competitive conditions facing private higher education in America, the percentage of Lutheran students in attendance can no longer be regarded as the definitive measure of a Lutheran college. Moreover, Luther's emphasis upon Christian service in the secular kingdom should counteract any tendency to parochialism. Of much greater importance is the quality of the faculty and the commitment of significant leaders to a Christian understanding of the relation between faith and learning. Members of the religion faculty in particular should be able to interpret Lutheran theology as it relates to the entire curriculum. Finally, it is essential that there be strong presidential leadership, fully supported by a board of regents, committed to the shaping of an institutional policy that reflects Lutheran principles.

The accomplishment of these goals in Lutheran colleges will make equally heavy demands upon the sponsoring church. The church, too, must be willing to affirm the colleges as authentic cultural voices of the church, must abjure any sectarian spirit, and must seek to recover and express the universal understanding of the church that Martin Luther professed. It should expect a clear proclamation of the gospel on the college campus. Indeed, it is essential that there be a strong worshipping community on every Lutheran campus, open to all, and led by a pastor who also dares to accept the risks and the challenges implicit in Luther's theology. Colleges of the Lutheran tradition will contribute most to Christian higher education in America by making an honest and forthright effort to shape their programs in harmony with that tradition.

Religious Vision and Academic Quest at St. Olaf College

Mark Granquist

St. Olaf College was founded by Norwegian Lutheran immigrants as a coeducational school to educate their children. Since its founding 120 years ago, it has become a highly selective liberal arts college, enrolling nearly 3000 students a year. A college of the Evangelical Lutheran Church in America, St. Olaf has strong historical and institutional roots in the Lutheranism of the Upper Midwest.

During the latter part of the nineteenth century, Norwegian-Americans developed over 75 Lutheran "academies" in the United States and Canada.[1] These academies were, in effect, residential high schools operated under religious auspices, some of which offered college preparatory programs. The motivations for this movement were varied: a desire for religiously based education outside of the "common schools," the desire to preserve Lutheran and Norwegian identities, the need to prepare students for the ministry, and the lack of good schools, especially in rural areas. Many of these academies did not survive more than a few years; a few still remain in their original capacity; while others grew into full-fledged colleges. St. Olaf College is one of this latter group.

---

1. Richard W. Solberg, *Lutheran Higher Education in North America* (Minneapolis: Augsburg, 1985), p. 228.

The Early Years

Founded in 1874, St. Olaf's School (as it was originally called) was the vision of the Rev. Bernt Julius Muus and local supporters in Southeastern Minnesota.[2] Muus was a Norwegian Lutheran pastor and a staunch proponent of parochial schools (in opposition to the public schools). After initial attempts to found a school in his parsonage in Kenyon, Minnesota, Muus set up St. Olaf in Northfield in 1874 with the backing of local business leaders. As Muus advertised them, the purposes of the school were "1. To give the confirmed youth a higher education for practical life than the home schools can do; [and] 2. To direct the moral conduct of the students."[3] The articles of incorporation suggest a more definite agenda: "[to promote] the advancement in education of pupils, from fifteen years of age and upwards, as a college, [and to] preserve the pupils in the true Christian faith, as taught by the Evangelical Lutheran Church. . . ."[4]

Several early features of St. Olaf were important and noteworthy. It was, from the start, co-educational, and focused equally on men and women. It offered a broad educational agenda, not just the preparation of teachers and ministers for the church. And though the school was self-consciously Lutheran in orientation, it had no formal affiliation with any organized Lutheran body.

These early features of St. Olaf are important for understanding its position within the complicated world of Norwegian-American Lutheranism.[5] The largest denomination was the Norwegian Synod, of which Muus was a pastor. The synod's college, Luther College in Decorah, Iowa, was a school for men and focused primarily on pre-ministerial training and classical education. The pietist or "free church" wing of Norwegian-American Lutheranism had Augsburg College in Minneapolis. Though not hostile to the public schools, the founders of Augsburg envisioned a complete course of theological education in one institution — academy, college, and seminary. St. Olaf, founded after these two institutions, stood between these two positions, which often meant the young school was caught up in partisan church politics.

2. On the history of St. Olaf, see William C. Benson, *High On Manitou: A History of St. Olaf College 1874-1949* (Northfield: St. Olaf College Press, 1949), and Joseph M. Shaw, *History of St. Olaf College 1874-1974* (Northfield: St. Olaf College Press, 1974). On the general situation of the Norwegian-American colleges, see Einar Oscar Johnson, " 'Soli Deo Gloria': A Study of the Philosophy and Problems of Higher Education Among Norwegian Lutherans in the American Environment," Ph.D. dissertation, University of Washington, 1960.

3. Shaw, *History,* p. 45.

4. Articles of Incorporation, 1874, in Johnson, " 'Soli Deo Gloria,' " p. 489.

5. On this topic, see E. Clifford Nelson, *The Lutheran Church Among the Norwegian Americans,* 2 vols. (Minneapolis: Augsburg, 1960); see also Johnson, " 'Soli Deo Gloria.' "

During its first twenty-five years (1874-99), while St. Olaf remained independent of formal denominational ties, the fledgling school found itself at the center
of two major church controversies. A portion of Norwegian Synod clergy (including Muus and St. Olaf's first President, Rev. Thorbjorn Mohn) broke with the
synod during the 1880s over theological issues, and St. Olaf became the college of
this breakaway group. This group merged with other Norwegian groups in 1890
to form the United Norwegian Lutheran Church (UNLC), and St. Olaf was
designated the denomination's official college. However, the supporters of Augsburg College, also party to the merger, resisted this designation, fearing for their
own school, and battled for the disenfranchisement of St. Olaf, which occurred in
1893.[6] With the loss of church support, and the financial recessions of the 1890s,
St. Olaf struggled to survive. The Augsburg supporters, not content even with St.
Olaf's disenfranchisement, later withdrew from the UNLC, which reestablished
ties with St. Olaf in 1899. Since this date St. Olaf has remained legally bound to
the Lutheran denominations which succeeded the UNLC.

The complexion of St. Olaf in these early years was of a school based on three
principles: Lutheran Christianity, the Norwegian-American ethnic heritage, and
the model of the American college. The early founders of St. Olaf were sure that
these three principles were compatible, and they borrowed especially from
American educational models as the inspiration for their school. Co-educational
from the start, St. Olaf was intended to train young men and women in a broad
range of subjects, fitting them generally for life in the world. This was in pointed
contrast with other schools, especially Luther and Augsburg, which focused
mainly on the training of pastors and church teachers. St. Olaf added a college
course in 1886 and began to seek university-trained Ph.D.s for its faculty, the first
of whom arrived from Johns Hopkins in 1887.[7] Though severely hampered by
lack of resources, the goal of becoming a first-class educational institution
remained powerful for the first generation of St. Olaf's leaders.

There were many, from various corners of Norwegian-American Lutheranism, who were suspicious of this basic orientation. The leaders of Luther
College and the Norwegian Synod, educated in the classical models of old-world
education, were suspicious of the rigor and soundness of St. Olaf's Lutheran
orthodoxy.[8] The pietist supporters of the Augsburg model were doubtful of St.
Olaf's Christianity. In the heated exchange over the "school question" of the 1890s,

> the friends of Augsburg flayed St. Olaf for its humanism and rationalism,
> its "luxurious facilities, its doctors of philosophy, its masters of arts" and

6. See Nelson, *The Lutheran Church,* vol. 2, pp. 38-81, and Johnson, " 'Soli Deo Gloria,' "
pp. 197-237, for more details about this struggle.

7. Shaw, *History,* pp. 11, 86.

8. Benson, *High on Manitou,* pp. 76, 88-89.

its deficits, while St. Olaf's supporters attacked Augsburg for lack of scholarship and the dangers inherent in stressing theological over general education.[9]

St. Olaf would continue to stake out its own position within the crowded world of the Norwegian-American schools.

Development and Stabilization

The year 1899 was a turning point for the school. The selection that year of St. Olaf as the college of the UNLC stabilized the school's financial position, and the leadership of the school was passed from Thorbjorn Mohn to Rev. John Nathan Kildahl, who served as president from 1899 to 1914. Kildahl guided the college through a period of rapid development as the school expanded from 14 faculty and 184 students (46 in the college) in 1899 to 34 faculty and 518 students in 1914. In addition, seven new buildings were completed to complement the two already standing.

But there were other changes — less visible but equally important — that would show the openness of St. Olaf to the models of the American system of higher education. In 1900, a new course of study, the scientific course, was added to the existing English and classical courses. The elective system, championed by Harvard President Charles Eliot, was gradually introduced by 1914, with an attendant reorganization of the curriculum and the expansion of course offerings. Kildahl sought and obtained accreditation of the school by the North Central Association in 1915. A master's degree program was instituted in 1905, which was later dropped.[10] The academy program was eventually transferred to another institution in 1917. Many new professors were hired (a number with doctorates) who would serve as the core of the St. Olaf faculty for a generation. These new teachers included two who achieved national reputations, the novelist O. E. Rolvaag and the director of the St. Olaf Choir, F. Melius Christiansen.

Much of this growth was achieved through the efforts of President Kildahl or later developed out of his planning. However, Kildahl also sought to develop the Christian identity of the institution equally with the academic program, mainly through the personal example of his piety and preaching. In addition, Kildahl guided St. Olaf through the tricky waters of its new affiliation as the official college

9. Shaw, *History,* pp. 94-95. The "luxurious facilities" of the period consisted of a couple of brick buildings and other lesser structures.

10. A total of 18 masters' degrees were granted, many of which were earned by St. Olaf faculty. See Shaw, *History,* p. 178.

of the UNLC.[11] Though its first 25 years had been hard because of lack of funds and ecclesiastical politics, St. Olaf had not been under the burden of direct church control. When it became officially the church college, St. Olaf was subject to new institutional oversight. For example, new faculty members had to be ratified by action of the church convention. Kildahl and his successors, having close ties to the centers of power within the denomination and skilled in church politics, managed to shield the college from too much heavy-handed, outside interference.

Rev. Lauritz A. Vigness served as president of the college from 1914 to 1918, a period which saw the continuation of certain themes of the Kildahl administration — the push for accreditation and educational standardization and the expansion of faculty and facilities. Vigness represented St. Olaf in the formation of the American Association of Colleges in 1915, arranged the end of the academy course at St. Olaf in 1917, and reorganized the faculty, instituting traditional academic ranks. He also presided over the college during the Norwegian-American denominational merger of 1917, and the changes brought by the First World War.

Coming of Age Academically

The era of St. Olaf's fourth president, Rev. L. W. Boe (1918-1942) saw St. Olaf achieve its status as the premier Norwegian Lutheran college in the United States.[12] It was a period of rapid growth in both quantitative terms (students, faculty, buildings, and financial resources), and in the quality of the academic program. It was also the period when St. Olaf began to reach outside of itself and seek its place in the wider world of American higher education.[13]

Boe perpetuated his predecessors' aspiration for St. Olaf, yet sought a widening of the college's vision. Toward the end of his term as president he told the students,

We are frankly a Lutheran college. We have, thank God, many who do not belong to the Lutheran Church. If you want to come to St. Olaf, take St. Olaf as it is. We make no pretense of being anything but a Christian college. It isn't a type that is a series of dogmatic statements. We want to stand for Christianity as something that functions, something that is lived.[14]

11. Benson, *High on Manitou,* pp. 130-131.
12. On this conclusion see *Christian Education Through Twenty Years and the Annual Report* (Minneapolis: Board of Christian Education, Norwegian Lutheran Church in America, 1937), pp. 46-55; and Johnson, *History,* pp. 245-339, especially the comparative tables.
13. Shaw, *History,* pp. 337-338.
14. From a chapel talk, 1939, in Erik Hetle, *Lars Wilhelm Boe: A Biography* (Minneapolis: Augsburg, 1949), p. 101.

He had faith in his faculty and students; compulsory chapel attendance was eliminated in the early 1920s, but Boe expected the students to come to chapel anyway.[15]

The search for academic advancement was evidenced in many ways. Boe added in the 1920s many faculty who would become cornerstones of the institution for decades to come. When the North Central Association in 1922 substantially raised the standards for the college endowment for continued accreditation, a drive was launched that tripled the endowment. The prime goal toward which the college was working, though, was qualification for a chapter of Phi Beta Kappa on campus. This meant a substantial increase in buildings (especially the library), endowment, resources, and faculty salaries, among other things. The push for recognition was stalled somewhat by the depression and then the Second World War, but St. Olaf achieved Phi Beta Kappa status in 1949, far in advance of the other Norwegian Lutheran colleges.[16]

One important aspect of the drive for excellence in education along American lines is vividly symbolized by the buildings that were erected during the Boe administration. Substantial academic buildings and dorms were built in a "Norman Gothic" style, using local limestone. These buildings stood in marked contrast to the earlier brick structures, and were part of a comprehensive campus plan drawn up by a Chicago architectural firm.[17] The new style gave an air of respectability to the campus. Was it perhaps an attempt to imitate the Gothic revival style of other schools, most notably the University of Chicago?

Upon the death of Boe in 1942, Rev. Clemens Granskou was elected president, guiding St. Olaf through the upheavals of the war years and the college's rapid expansion during the 1950s. The student population and the faculty doubled in the 20 years between 1942 and 1962, and the campus saw another construction boom which added new academic buildings and dorms. During these years, too, there was an increased emphasis on reforming the curriculum and the academic calendar.

Increased size and complexity of the college meant that a new style of organization was necessary — one that shifted the day-to-day administration away from the president and toward other administrators and faculty. This

15. Shaw, *History*, p. 272. On this subject, Benson writes, "Chapel attendance was not required except in so far as it was left to the conscience of each student and faculty member to justify his absence on the same basis as he would excuse himself from a class exercise. As a result, chapel attendance was usually excellent." *High on Manitou*, p. 240.

16. On this push for Phi Beta Kappa, see Shaw, *History*, pp. 335-338. On comparison with other colleges, see Johnson, " 'Soli Deo Gloria," p. 288.

17. Shaw, *Dear Old Hill: The Story of Manitou Heights, The Campus of St. Olaf College* (Northfield: St. Olaf College Press, 1992), pp. 102-108.

was the thrust of a report delivered to Granskou in 1951 by an outside consultant, a report with which Granskou seemed to have great sympathy. One major change was the upgrading of the position of dean of the college, a post that now carried with it much more responsibility.[18]

During the 1950s, St. Olaf became more involved with other selective private colleges in the Midwest in the formation of the Associated Colleges of the Midwest (ACM) in 1951, of which St. Olaf was a charter member. In this association with schools such as Carleton, Lawrence, Knox, Grinnell, and others, St. Olaf was linked to a more traditionally American (and secularized) form of higher education than before. Of the ten schools in the ACM, St. Olaf was by far the most formally related to a religious denomination.[19] St. Olaf also worked in certain areas in cooperation with Carleton College, across town in Northfield.

The proximity of St. Olaf to Carleton deserves further examination. Although not significantly older than St. Olaf, Carleton was founded along the lines of the New England colleges, quickly becoming academically respectable and nationally known. Carleton, it seems, has long stood as an example for St. Olaf, a model either to emulate or avoid, given one's own educational philosophy. If St. Olaf developed with one eye on other Norwegian-Lutheran colleges, certainly the other eye was trained on the "American" colleges of which Carleton was a prime and omnipresent example.

Relations between the two schools have been uneven. On the one hand, they have cooperated in some areas — in joint faculty appointments and programs, in the ACM programs, and in other practical areas. When St. Olaf applied to join the American Association of Universities in 1930, its successful application came on the recommendation of the President of Carleton. On the other hand, cooperation has not been as obvious as the close proximity of the campuses might indicate. The two schools, for example, both adopted new academic calendars in the early 1960s, but the two calendars are incompatible, making it difficult for students to cross-register for courses.

Faith and Learning

During the postwar period, religious changes at St. Olaf were in the works. In 1951, the school created the position of full-time pastor, a post which has been continued to this day. Simultaneously, the St. Olaf Student Congregation was organized. Most important, a chapel was finally built on campus in the late 1950s. There had been a chapel at the turn of the century, but when it burned,

18. Shaw, *History,* pp. 453-454.
19. Shaw, *History,* p. 443.

the structure was not replaced.[20] A long-standing ban against dancing on campus was repealed in 1961.

During the 1950s, the faculty and administration began consciously to wrestle with issues of academic excellence and religious vision in the institution. These questions had been a part of the school ever since its founding, but from the 1950s onward has come the need to examine these issues in a regular and systematic way. The first such attempt was undertaken by a self-study committee in 1954-56. This committee organized a seminar of Lutheran faculty, investigated St. Olaf's own position, and issued a publication whose title indicated the scope and thrust of the study itself: *Integration in the Christian Liberal Arts College*.[21] In both theoretical and practical chapters, the authors sought a coherence and an integration of the educational experience, one in which academic excellence and a Christian outlook complement one another. Examining a number of models for such integration, it suggested a stance of "critical participation." This meant neither a Christian rejection of the world (world of secular learning), nor an accommodation to or immersion in that world, but a tension which would bridge the gaps. The study suggested that

> critical participation is properly a tension between Christian faith and human culture. . . . [It is] a tragic optimism. One with this view knows that the best of human efforts is far short of adequacy, and yet the Christian is to live out his time among men.[22]

Many of the specific academic recommendations of the committee were not, however, immediately instituted at St. Olaf. College historian Joseph Shaw suggests that the lack of immediate political support among the wider faculty led to inaction on the specific proposals. He comments,

> Some thought that the entire endeavor was too heavily weighted on the side of philosophy and theology. . . . Some feared that integration would mean a reduction of departmental autonomy, or remained unconvinced that fragmentation was any problem.[23]

20. Shaw, *Dear Old Hill*, pp. 76-79 and 167-178.

21. St. Olaf College Self Study Committee, *Integration in the Christian Liberal Arts College*, 2 vols. (Northfield: St. Olaf College Press, 1956). The conclusion to one section stated, "The Christian liberal arts colleges of our Church are a standing testimony to the Church's concern for the best culture of its members, a learning that is integrated within the context of the world-view which as Christians we believe to be the only true and valid framework of knowledge." p. 82.

22. Self Study Committee, *Integration in the Christian Liberal Arts College*, p. 66.

23. Shaw, *History*, p. 457.

Although the recommendations were not immediately implemented, the study did lay the groundwork for substantial institutional change in the late 1950s and early 1960s. One significant change came in 1964, with the adoption of a new 4-1-4 calendar and a corresponding new curriculum. Other currents during this time were the formalization of faculty governance, a sustained attempt to raise faculty salary levels, the institution of tenure, and the requirement that entering students take SAT tests for admission.

The St. Olaf self study, by virtue of its publication, gained some national attention for the college; if its recommendations were ignored at home, it became known within some educational circles as a model for church-related liberal arts colleges. One educator reviewed the work and suggested,

> The work of the St. Olaf committee is an unusually well-integrated approach to their problem. . . . Few studies of the kind have taken so comprehensive a view of their task. Whatever its shortcomings, it is a model for future study by any college engaged in a similar enterprise.[24]

Another generally positive article saw the study as a "very sincere effort" of a church-related college to provide for an integrated educational model, incorporating Christian theology. This study, however, noted that the plan was generally not implemented and criticized it as being too static and "intellectual."[25] Certainly St. Olaf gained from the notice and attention of the national educational community.

Sydney Rand became St. Olaf's sixth president in 1963 and served until 1980. From 1964 to 1984, the student population increased from 2000 to 3000, and the faculty doubled from 175 to 355. By 1974, an increasing diversity of students at St. Olaf was apparent. In a study of Lutheran colleges in the 1970s, St. Olaf was characterized as only one of three schools which fit the profile of a "national" institution, drawing at least 25 percent of students from outside its adjacent states.[26] Other academic innovations included the development of the paracollege, an alternative educational process based on the British tutorial system, and the great expansion of international study by students and faculty. Currently over 50 percent of students study abroad during their career at St. Olaf.

24. Russell Thomas, "Will the Liberal Arts Colleges Return to Liberal Education?" *Journal of General Education* 10 (January 1957): 36.
25. Lewis B. Mayhew, "Illustrative Courses and Programs in Colleges and Universities" in Henry Nelson, ed., *The Integration of Educational Experiences* (57th Yearbook of the National Society for the Study of Education, part III) (Chicago: National Society for the Study of Education, 1958), esp. pp. 235-240.
26. Gary A. Greinke, *Survival With a Purpose: A Master Plan Revisited* (n.p.: Lutheran Educational Conference of North America, 1977), p. 29.

The integration of the college's academic mission with its religious heritage was a continuing concern during the 1960s and 1970s. St. Olaf faculty participated in 1960, 1961, and 1977 (as well as in other years) in joint Lutheran college workshops, sponsored by the American Lutheran Church and dedicated to the exploration of this concern.[27] In addition, a series of lectures was held on campus in January 1973, under the title "A Teacher's Faith and Values," in which various St. Olaf faculty addressed this issue.[28]

Finally, a major restatement of the college's mission was undertaken and adopted in 1974 as a part of the celebration of St. Olaf's centennial year. The centennial statement, entitled "Identity and Mission in a Changing Context" and authored primarily by religion department chair Harold Ditmanson, speaks purposely of the "context" of education at St. Olaf.[29] After speaking of the academic aspects of this context, the document moves toward Christian faith, seeing this tradition as another context in which a St. Olaf education is based. Speaking of the intersection of the religious and academic contexts, the document states,

> We wish to say emphatically that St. Olaf College does not consider its commitment to a Christian context for education to be an academic liability. This commitment is quite compatible with the determination that the college will not be compromised by sectarian limits on what can be taught, studied and expressed. But it is also compatible with the conviction that no member of the community should be able to avoid being brought face to face with his own ultimate commitments and with the persistent problems of human life to which Christian faith speaks.[30]

It is also interesting that the study notes St. Olaf's changing profile, attracting students and faculty outside of its traditional constituency because of its academic reputation,[31] a trend that has continued during the 20 years since the study.

27. Publications include Harold Ditmanson, et al., eds., *Christian Faith and the Liberal Arts* (Minneapolis: Augsburg, 1960); "A Report and Findings, Higher Education Workshop, St. Olaf College, Northfield MN, June 19-24, 1961," (Minneapolis: Board of Christian Education, American Lutheran Church, 1961); Tom and Anne Mundahl, *Vision and Revision: Old Roots and New Routes for Lutheran Higher Education* (Minneapolis: Division for College and University Services, American Lutheran Church, 1977); see also the publications of the Association of Lutheran College Faculties, and the Lutheran Educational Conference of North America.

28. Eugene England and Erling Jorstad, eds., *A Teacher's Faith and Values: January Interim Lectures, 1973* (Northfield: St. Olaf College Press, 1973).

29. *Identity and Mission in a Changing Context,* "A Centennial Publication of St. Olaf College" (Northfield: St. Olaf College Press, 1974).

30. *Identity and Mission,* p. 19.

31. *Identity and Mission,* p. 4.

Rand was succeeded as president by Rev. Harlan Foss, chair of the religion department, who served from 1980 to 1985. In 1985 Foss was succeeded by Melvin George, the first lay president of the college, who served from 1985 to 1994. The current and ninth president is Mark U. Edwards who was installed in the fall of 1994.

The trends outlined in the 1974 Centennial report have continued to the present. The number of students has remained constant at around 3000, while the number of faculty has grown to over 400. The mix of students and faculty has become increasingly more diverse and more nationally oriented. The percentage of Lutheran students has dipped to about 50 percent, while the percentage of faculty who are alumni has dropped to 18 percent. The number of faculty who have undergraduate degrees from Lutheran institutions has decreased to 29 percent.

The Recent Past

Two major events of the 1980s and 1990s are notable. The first is the adoption of a new college mission statement by the faculty and the Board of Regents in 1987. The statement identifies three key elements of the institution: "an education committed to the liberal arts, rooted in the Christian Gospel, and incorporating a global perspective." The statement in its longer form describes "a distinctive environment that integrates teaching, scholarship, creative activity, and opportunities for encounter with the Christian Gospel and God's call to faith."[32] It should be noted that this statement employs more distinctively Christian language than the statement that preceded it.

The other major innovation of this last period was the adoption of a new general education curriculum in 1994. This new curriculum is an attempt to redesign the core educational program of the college with a focus on interdisciplinary studies. One change pertains to the religion requirement for all students. Formerly the requirement called for three courses, at least one of which would be in some area of the Christian tradition. The new core curriculum moves the requirement to two courses: a standardized first-year course and a second course focused on Christian theology. The former third religion course was dropped, but added to the new curriculum is a senior level course in ethical issues "in dialogue with aspects of the Christian tradition."[33]

It is clear from this sketch of St. Olaf's history that the institution has a long history of striving for academic excellence. Even though the institution's

32. St. Olaf College Mission statement, 1987, found in the 1994-95 *College Catalog,* p. 2.
33. For the details of the new curriculum, see *St. Olaf College Catalog, 1994-95,* pp. 15-17.

92

actual progress has not always lived up to its ideals (or its rhetoric), there has been a clear and purposeful progress toward achieving academic excellence at St. Olaf, especially in the twentieth century.

The question of the institution's religious vision is more complex, especially insofar as that vision relates to the push for academic quality. It is therefore necessary to understand the ways in which St. Olaf's religious heritage has been evident in the institution. The structural elements of St. Olaf's religious heritage are present, but not overwhelming. The college is legally tied to the Evangelical Lutheran Church in America, and receives some minimal financial support from this denomination. Seventy-five percent of the members of the Board of Regents must be Lutheran. The college itself supports a college pastor and a Lutheran Student Congregation which holds voluntary daily chapel and Sunday services.

There are, however, no forms of denominational subscription, quotas, or other requirements for students and faculty. There is no mandatory statement of faith; the college has students and faculty of other faiths outside of Christianity, and those who profess no particular faith at all. Almost from the beginning the college has allowed for this kind of diversity among both students and faculty.

Among the faculty, especially, it is clear that in the last 40 years the composition has become more diverse. With the growth of the institution especially of the faculty, and with the lessening of the direct role of the president in faculty hiring, more attention is now paid to academic credentials in hiring. Fewer faculty come out of traditional Lutheran colleges, although this does not necessarily mean that those from elsewhere are less religious. Obviously, there is some element of self-selection at work here, too: those who come and those who remain might be more inclined toward St. Olaf's religious heritage. Many departments experienced an entire generational shift in the 1980s, a shift also seen in the presidency: when Harlan Foss retired in 1985, he was succeeded by Melvin George, the first non-clergy president.

A very recent study (1995) of the St. Olaf faculty examined the relationship of religious commitment to academic excellence. In general, members of the faculty hoped to retain the Christian orientation of the school, but were suspicious of traditional means of attaining or verifying such an orientation. Respondents, for example, overwhelmingly endorsed the 1987 mission statement, even if some of the respondents qualified their endorsement in their written comments. Some suggested that the language in the statement was vague or problematic, or that they supported the statement with reservations. On balance, faculty respondents seemed optimistic that it was possible for the college to maintain a Lutheran and Christian identity *and* achieve academic excellence, and a majority were confident that the church-related character of St. Olaf was being maintained.

On the other hand, faculty respondents did not support more overt means of measuring or ensuring religious affiliation, especially on the part of students or faculty. A majority of respondents rejected the notion that faculty should be required to make public commitments of faith, and the faculty was evenly divided as to whether St. Olaf's identity required any particular number of Christians on the faculty. Required student or faculty attendance at college-sponsored worship was strongly rejected. A majority agreed that their religious beliefs were relevant to their teaching, but were divided on what sorts of religious practices they were comfortable with in their classrooms. The responses reflected some division between older faculty and those educated at Lutheran or Christian colleges, on the one hand, and those who were younger or not from a church-college background, on the other; the latter were less comfortable with traditional Christian language and practices.[34]

Students, too, are increasingly more diverse, an outcome which reflects an objective of the institution. Students must meet the curricular goals, including the religion requirement, and are subject to some moral restrictions, most obviously a ban on alcohol consumption or possession on campus, but beyond this are free to express their religious loyalties as they may wish. Many students have at least nominal connections with some religious organization, although in 1994-95, 259 out of nearly 3000 were listed as "no affiliation" or "no information."[35] Historically, a significant number of students have come from clergy families. In 1944, for example, 9.3 percent of the student body fit this description.[36] Alumni connections to the college are also strong, and many students come from alumni families. Yet in 1974 the centennial study recognized that this, too, was changing:

> Whereas about 90 percent of St. Olaf students once had a natural relation
> to the College through church or alumni relatives, nearly one out of every
> three students currently enrolled has no such special connection.[37]

These categories, however, are still fairly limited in their usefulness for measuring the religious connections of the student population.

Alumni of the college comprise another important factor in gauging its religious identity. Many alumni are very active participants in their congregations and in denominational matters. Although St. Olaf was not founded primarily to produce pastors, quite a number of graduates of the institution have gone into the ministry. In a 1934 survey of 3,296 alumni, for example,

---

34. "Results of a Survey of Attitudes of Faculty at St. Olaf College on the Issues of Church-related Status and Academic Excellence," unpublished survey results, compiled by the author, June 1995. This analysis, and the raw data of the survey itself, is located in the St. Olaf College Archives.

35. *St. Olaf College Catalog, 1994-95*, p. 155.

36. *St. Olaf College Bulletin* 10 (April 1944): 149.

37. *Identity and Mission*, p. 4.

508 were employed in "religious work."[38] Historically and currently, St. Olaf has contributed the largest number of ministerial candidates to Luther Seminary in St. Paul.[39] Of the 66 current bishops leading the ELCA, the largest single number, 11 in all, are St. Olaf alumni.[40] This aspect of the church connection goes beyond the clergy, however, to lay leaders and musicians. St. Olaf consistently ranks first, for example, in graduates working in the Lutheran Volunteer Corp, a social service and justice organization.

Though St. Olaf has a national reputation for its musical programs, this dimension is often overlooked as a source of its religious identity. St. Olaf produces many professional musicians for church work, and has a cooperative program with Luther Seminary for a joint M.A. in "Worship in Music." But the number of students who participate in musical organizations far exceeds the number of majors, and many of these participants continue their music in church congregations after graduation. The music and religion departments annually host a joint Summer Conference in Music and Theology.

Conclusions

There are many other aspects of St. Olaf's religious identity that could be identified here if space allowed. It seems clear, however, that outside of certain structural elements of church relation, the college's religious identity is dependent on the personal, voluntary commitments of faculty, students, and alumni. There is a definite cultural and social dimension to these commitments. Because the college has traditionally recruited Lutherans from the Upper Midwest, it has attracted individuals with these qualities. But as we have seen, this is a diminishing trend; already in 1954 the self study committee noted:

> The college was founded primarily to provide religious and educational leaders for "hyphenated" agrarian communities in the Upper Midwest. . . . Conditions have changed. . . . Pressures . . . have altered our institutions, including the college . . . to a degree which might have made it unrecognizable to St. Olaf founding fathers three short generations ago [not that they necessarily would have disapproved . . .]. The basic question is whether change has been the result of drift or the result of educational judgment and vision.[41]

38. *St. Olaf College Catalog, 1933-34*, p. 132.

39. This is seen in the annual catalog of the seminary. For 1993-94, 67 St. Olaf graduates enrolled in the school. See also the historical statistics in *Christian Education Through Twenty Years and the Annual Report*, p. 54.

40. *St. Olaf College Magazine*, 1994.

41. *Integration in the Christian Liberal Arts College*, vol. 2, pp. 36-37.

In the midst of such institutional change and with the diffuse means for achieving the college's religious vision, has the integration of Lutheran identity with the academic program of the school been misplaced?

One could read the history of the college in such a way, and suggest that all the post-war concern with a Christian view of higher education at St. Olaf is an attempt to "close the barn door before the horse gets out." But perhaps such a view loses sight of St. Olaf's vision of integration and superimposes on this community a model of religious and academic integration that does not fit its history and traditions.

As Richard Solberg notes in his essay in this book, there is in Lutheranism a paradoxical relationship between the worlds of faith and reason, between this world and the next. This means that Lutheran educational institutions have lived with a tension between these two elements, trying to resist a reductionism that pushes entirely toward either the sacred or the secular. The history of St. Olaf has shown that this tension has been present within the institution and its formulations since the beginning.

When St. Olaf Regent and religious historian Martin Marty addressed an opening convocation of the school on what it means to be "a college of the church" — as St. Olaf calls itself — he observed:

> Colleges of the church know a starting point, one which privileges the notion that we are going to treat sacred things sacredly. They recognize the transcendent as transcendent, the spiritual as spiritual, the religious as religious. . . . A college of the church engages in the enterprise of criticizing the whole enterprise of college and church, but it also poses questions about the surrounding culture.

Marty likened the whole process of education as a "conversation" involving college, church, and secular world, and observed of this conversation, "You never know where it will go."[42]

This sort of understanding of the dialectical processes of engagement between the religious and academic missions of the institution is, it seems, the integrating focus that has characterized St. Olaf (at its best) from the beginning. Such a conversation is difficult and sometimes frustrating to maintain, and reductionism is always a danger. The future will tell if St. Olaf as a community is able to maintain this as a means of integrating its religious vision and academic quest.

42. Martin Marty, "St. Olaf College Opening Convocation Address," September 9, 1992.

Faith and Learning at California Lutheran University

Byron R. Swanson
and Margaret Barth Wold

California Lutheran University was founded in 1959 in Thousand Oaks, California, and the first classes were offered in 1961. Located about 45 miles northwest of Los Angeles, the 290-acre campus is tucked into the rolling hills of the Conejo Valley. CLU — an independent, residential, comprehensive liberal arts university — is one of 28 colleges/universities of the Evangelical Lutheran Church in America (ELCA). The college became a University in 1986 and, in addition to its undergraduate degrees, offers master's degrees in business, public administration, education, and counseling as well as basic credential programs. In keeping with the focus of this volume, this essay will restrict itself to the undergraduate traditional program that has been the primary concern of CLC/CLU during its relatively brief life span.

In front of the Pearson Library at California Lutheran University is a statue of Martin Luther. To get to the building on campus that most prominently symbolizes CLU's *academic* mission, one must first walk by the representation of the person who most clearly symbolizes the school's *religious* heritage. These two symbols seem to provide a tidy introduction to an essay that deals with the integration of faith and learning.

In reality the symbolism is somewhat blurred and untidy because the art form of the statue is abstract. Entitled "The Enormous Luther,"[1] the 25-feet-tall

---

1. The statue was a gift of the first graduating class at CLC and the work of a renowned art professor emeritus, Sir Bernardus Weber, who attempted to portray the enormity and

and 12-feet-wide cast bronze monument is huge and impressive, but offers only vague suggestions of body and facial features. As a result the massive figure leaves some onlookers perplexed and bewildered. Though discomforting, confusion is actually a very appropriate response. As the introductory chapter by Richard Solberg points out, the Lutheran perspective on the relationship of faith and learning represents a "critical tradition" which prizes ambiguity, risk-taking, and controversy. It calls for thoughtfulness and reflection rather than an affirmation of clear-cut absolutes and simple answers. In the spirit of the gospel it seeks openness, integrity, and freedom from legalistic shackles. The Lutheran heritage encourages scholars to engage the academic world to the fullest, and all those who study and teach at Lutheran institutions need to realize that in doing so they can expect no easy answers. They must be prepared, therefore, to wrestle with complex and complicated questions without the assurance that they will ever come to uniform and harmonious conclusions.

With that in mind, one should not be surprised to find in the pages that follow numerous examples of the California Lutheran community sometimes accepting, sometimes avoiding, and sometimes rejecting their "critical" Lutheran academic heritage with all of its risks and uncertainties. This, then, is their story of what it means to be California Lutheran University.

Take My Farm and Build Your College

As far back as the turn of the century, when the first Norwegian Lutheran settlers came to farm the hospitable valleys of California, they brought with them the dream of a college of their own. Twice before, the dream had seemed about to become reality. The legendary Leland Stanford had once offered fifty acres of land near Palo Alto to some Swedish Lutherans, only to withdraw the offer when asked to fund buildings as well.

Again, in 1928, a group of developers in the Los Angeles area gave the Lutheran church a 100-acre site in the Del Rey Hills. Although 5,000 persons were present for the dedication of the land, according to a front-page article in the *Los Angeles Times*,[2] and building plans had already been drawn, the 1929 stock market crash postponed the scheduled ground-breaking indefinitely. Eventually, the prime piece of property was sold and all hopes for a college were put aside during the social upheavals of the Great Depression and World War II.

---

the profound strength of the contribution that he felt Luther had made to the life of the church and to society.

2. Mary Hekhuis, *California Lutheran College: The First Quarter Century* (Thousand Oaks, CA: California Lutheran University, 1984), p. 3.

When the War was over and the 1944 "GI Bill of Rights" made it financially possible for a million veterans to return to college, doubling or even quadrupling the size of some of the Lutheran colleges around the country,[3] it seemed the perfect time to act on the dream. A thousand people a day, it was reported, were moving into the San Fernando Valley alone. Post-war California boomed with the phenomenal growth of the aerospace and housing industries and the influx of young families eager to share the good life in the Southwest. One Lutheran church body in the United States reported starting a new congregation every 54 hours, many of them in California.[4]

At that time there were 16 Protestant and 12 Roman Catholic colleges in California, but Lutherans had no four-year college. For a people who valued a professional clergy and a literate, educated laity, this was not an acceptable situation. Some of the Lutheran newcomers to California were alumni of Lutheran colleges elsewhere in the country, but many regarded them as too far away for their children to attend.

If, later on, doubts about starting a college ever did arise, the founders and their supporters needed only to recall the gracious events that marked its beginnings to be reassured that the timing was right and that their commitment to a college in California was not misplaced. Looking back over these events, one member of a planning group called the "Committee of Twenty-Five" mused, "It seemed to me that we were all simply swept along by a conviction that the decisions we were making were being directed by the Holy Spirit."[5]

The Committee of Twenty-Five grew out of a meeting convened in North Hollywood, California, on Sept. 13, 1954, by Dr. Gaylerd Falde, president of the California District of the Evangelical Lutheran Church (ELC), a leader "guided by a vision of an institution that offered academic excellence and that was 'unashamedly Christian.'" In reply to those who questioned why the church should promote the liberal arts, his answer seems to reflect the "critical tradition" of Lutheran higher education discussed by Solberg. He quoted Martin Luther's conviction that the liberal arts, "invented and brought to light by learned and outstanding people — even though these people are heathen — are serviceable and useful to people of this life. They are the creation and noble, precious gifts of the Lord."[6]

At the committee's first meeting was Dr. Orville Dahl, executive secretary

3. Richard W. Solberg, *Lutheran Higher Education in North America* (Minneapolis: Augsburg, 1985), p. 309.

4. Solberg, *Lutheran Higher Education*, p. 315.

5. Excerpted from a conversation between two members of the Committee of Twenty-five, March 21, 1995.

6. Ansle T. Severtson, *Gaylerd Falde, a Bishop for His Time* (Thousand Oaks, CA: California Lutheran University, 1993), pp. 102-103.

of the Board of Higher Education of the ELC and an educational consultant. Dahl would become the creative force behind the college. Three years later in 1957, a charitable foundation, California Lutheran Educational Foundation (CLEF), was formed by cooperating Lutheran church bodies for the purpose of gathering funds and organizing a college. Dahl was elected director and Falde the chairman of its Board of Governors.

Dahl and members of the CLEF board visited over 50 sites in their search for a location for the proposed college but were unable to find one that was not too expensive to buy or too difficult to develop. Finally, Dahl told his wife, "If God wants a Lutheran college, he's going to have to build it." His wife reminded him that on his list was one more site to visit.

That last visit took him 45 miles northwest of Los Angeles to the scenic Conejo Valley where a Norwegian farmer, Lawrence Pederson, offered his land for sale, but Dahl felt that the price was too high. Disappointed, he was getting into his car to leave when he saw an approaching truck stirring up dust on the dirt road. Richard, Lawrence's brother, stepped out and handed Dahl a newspaper clipping that told of the Lutheran search for a college site. Then Richard made this simple comment: "I've been waiting for you."[7]

The next day Dahl returned and experienced, as he later said, "the greatest single moment of my life" when a weeping Richard Pederson handed him the deed to his 130-acre ranch in the then unincorporated area of Thousand Oaks, with the words, "Here, [take my farm and] build your college." Later, Mr. Pederson said he wanted his gift "to provide youth with the benefits of Christian education in a day when spiritual values can well decide the course of world history."[8]

In 1957, Dahl became president of CLC. "Like the director of a stage play, Dr. Dahl was busy in every facet of the production," wrote Mary Hekhuis, the former director of Public Information.[9] He was convinced that without a strong church connection, the college would never become a reality. He had an outdoor worship center constructed and a swimming pool built to entice congregations to come out to the future campus for Sunday worship and picnics. He organized a program of "Fellows" who would serve as "spiritual alumni" and pledge support on a regular basis. He helped with the harvesting of farm crops in the early years, edited Articles of Incorporation and, in a 1958 letter to "The Pastors and Lay Leaders of the Participating Church Bodies of CLEF," he challenged the confirmed members of the supporting Lutheran churches "to back up words with deeds."

7. Mary Hekhuis, *CLU Magazine* 2 (Winter 1995): 9.

8. Hekhuis, *CLU Magazine* 2 (Winter 1995): 9. Further purchases and gifts of land brought the campus to its present total of 290 acres.

9. Hekhuis, *California Lutheran College,* p. 17.

We go forward sure in the knowledge that God wills this college for ourselves, our children, and their children. We stand on the threshold of a new era and a new dimension in Kingdom work in the West. Let us move forward in prayer letting the spirit of Jesus Christ manifest itself in our planning and our giving. Let us be both bold and careful. Let us be both practical and visionary. Let us be both humble and courageous, changing crisis to victory, changing problems to opportunities, and contributions into investments. With such spirit we cannot fail . . . without such a spirit there is no point in succeeding.[10]

California Lutheran College opened its doors to its first students in the fall of 1961. Church contributions of $400,000, together with many individual gifts and loans, had made possible the completion of a campus "Centrum" of eight buildings. In addition to these new buildings, the old farmhouse and the chicken coops were remodeled and pressed into service as classrooms and offices. The new college was now planted in this fertile setting, rimmed by rolling hills, nourished by a running stream, and shaded by orange and walnut groves of the picturesque old Pederson Ranch.

Now, with its beautiful but modest physical campus functioning, there was a need for these pioneer educators to wrestle with what it meant to be a *Lutheran* college. A strong indication of their convictions was the day selected for the college's formal dedication — Reformation Sunday at the end of October. A highlight of the service was "a thunderous rendition" of Luther's "A Mighty Fortress Is Our God" performed by the newly formed choir and orchestra along with the 4,000 Lutherans who came to see a long standing dream turned into a reality.[11]

Of the 302 students who enrolled in that first year, almost all were Lutheran. The second year freshman class also reflected close ties to the Lutheran church with 92 percent of its members coming from Lutheran congregations.[12]

The first faculty members were all Lutheran, often recruited from other Lutheran colleges. Apparently there was an understanding during the first two years that only Lutherans should be hired, indicating that the young college was uncertain about that risk-taking part of its Lutheran heritage that called for openness and freedom even regarding those who would teach in its classrooms. One long-time faculty member is convinced that she was not hired the first time she applied because she was not Lutheran.[13] The policy was changed

10. Letter from Orville Dahl, Sept. 5, 1958, CLU Archives.

11. Hekhuis, *California Lutheran College,* p. 26.

12. *"What's the Profile?" A Guide for Counselors of College-Bound Students,* 1962. CLU Archives.

13. Interview with faculty member, Feb. 17, 1995.

after those first two years, however, revealing some soul searching and agonizing that must have gone on in the adoption of a policy that was open to faculty and students of all religious persuasions.

But there were other Lutheran (or Christian) identity issues that needed to be addressed. As one of the professors in those first years recalls, the "student body was dominated by . . . fundamentalist Lutherans."[14] And "several pastors of . . . supporting parishes . . . demanded that . . . CLU fire members of the philosophy, religion, and history departments who violated the inerrancy of scripture by speaking of 'myths' and historical criticism."[15] Those first contracts for new faculty listed the following requirement among the conditions for being hired: "As a member of the staff of this Lutheran educational institution, you are expected to show by precept and example that you are an evangelical Christian with a living faith in Jesus Christ as the Son of God and Savior of the world." Students at CLC were required to take four courses (12 credit units) in religion. Attendance at the daily chapel services was mandatory,[16] and the women's dormitory was strictly policed. In 1962, in the pamphlet that was distributed to prospective students, they were told (in the hyperbole so often typical of college admissions statements) that "the real meaning of CLC being a Christian college[17] is that Christ is unashamedly and without apology the central reality in all things. Through personal associations, classrooms, athletic field, dormitories, chapel and the entire program of the college, Christ is the Center."[18] As sincere and committed as the founders were, one former professor refers to the situation at CLC at this time as "enforced prevalent parochialism."[19] This observation offers food for thought inasmuch as in all of these quests for Lutheran identity nothing indicates the historical Lutheran understanding that faculty and students should be challenged to take risks, and if necessary, to be willing to involve themselves in controversy and critical reflection.

In order to maintain a close relationship with the church, the governance

---

14. These are Lutherans who had embraced a fundamentalistic outlook. They would be basically literalistic and absolutistic in their interpretation of Scripture.

15. Written questionnaire response from emeritus faculty member, Nov. 17, 1994.

16. Interview with alumna who said, "We went because chapel was a time for the whole student body to get together. Besides, most of us were Lutherans!" Feb. 16, 1995.

17. "What's the Profile?" Although CLC could certainly be described as a "Christian" college in the general sense in which that phrase is used to describe many institutions today, the term "church-related" is now preferred. If CLC were to locate itself in Merrimon Cunninggim's classification it would, along with other Lutheran Colleges, probably find itself among the "proclaiming colleges." See Robert R. Parsonage, ed., *Church Related Higher Education* (Valley Forge: Judson Press, 1978), p. 34.

18. "What's the Profile?"

19. Response from questionnaire, Nov. 17, 1994.

section of the CLC Articles of Incorporation included a unique provision for a "Convocation" of 80 persons to be elected at the annual conventions of supporting synods. These representatives of Lutheran congregations were to meet on campus once a year and, although their only legal responsibility would be the election of 20 of the 30 members of the Board of Regents, their influence was such that the administration and Board of Regents tended to listen carefully to their concerns and comments as valid expressions of the opinions and reactions of the church bodies they represented. On an organizational chart they were listed above the Regents.[20]

In its desire for academic respectability, the administration of the young college hired an able faculty, 40 percent of whom had doctoral degrees.[21] As Dahl reported to the Regents in 1959, the plans for the new college "stirred considerable enthusiasm among prospective teachers and students. More than one hundred inquiries have been received from teachers, many of high rank and long experience, who would like to join the faculty."[22]

So impressive was the faculty Dahl gathered that, even with the accrediting agency's concern over a library of only 10,000 volumes, the Western Association of Schools and Colleges (WASC) granted the school full regional accreditation in the unbelievably short period of six months after its opening.

It was inevitable that the leadership of a president as charismatic and forceful as Orville Dahl should soon come to an end. The skills that had made him such an effective planner and builder now drove a wedge between him and the very faculty members he had brought to the school. Their grievance was that responsibilities that they felt belonged to the academic dean and department heads were being assumed by the president and the regents. Soon the rift was so pronounced that, in the fall of 1962, Dahl wisely resigned as president. The dean of the college and several faculty members also resigned, and with their resignations an exciting era came to an end.

Out of a Troubled Decade — A Transforming Moment

The president called to guide the college through the tough years of the 1960s was the Rev. Raymond Olson. Few could have guessed when Olson took office that he would serve during the twentieth century's most turbulent decade. Before the first students were to receive their degrees, the United States would send money and arms to South Vietnam, an act that led eventually to an

20. The role of the Convocators at CLC has remained unchanged. Their voice, though indirect, continues to influence administrators and Regents.

21. Solberg, *Lutheran Higher Education*, p. 312.

22. Dahl's Report to the Board, 1959, p. 4. CLU Archives.

unpopular war and to campus protests across the country. In 1962 campus riots would erupt nationwide when a 29-year-old black Air Force veteran, James Meredith, attempted to enroll at the University of Mississippi.

The fledgling college would be given little opportunity for peaceful growth. In 1963, President John Kennedy would be shot to death, and five years later his brother, Robert, a U.S. Senator, would also die from an assassin's bullet. A few months later, Martin Luther King, renowned civil rights leader, would be gunned down.

Pressures to bring about social justice for women and people of color would upset the traditional norms of white American society, and mainline church establishments would reel from the impact of Vatican II, the rise of neo-pentecostalism in their ranks, and the defection from their membership rolls of thousands of young people disillusioned with established authority.

In these controversial, complex, and risk-filled times — so different from the quiet 1950s — the college was faced with the inevitable dilemma of how to react. Would it, as many in the decade of the 1960s did, seek easy answers, and with absolute certainty reject the ideas of those who called for change and justice for all? Or would it dare to join the controversy, take risks, and deal with the ambiguities and the complexities with critical reflection and thoughtfulness?

President Olson, as a Lutheran pastor, was equipped to bring a healing, pastoral presence to the campus. Although he was not primarily an educator, he would be forced to wrestle with the issues of what it meant to be a Lutheran college in the context of a troubled decade. For example, when several pastors of CLC's supporting parishes demanded that the president fire members of the faculty for using biblical criticism, Dr. Olson "staunchly backed the accused teachers citing Lutheran traditions of open scholarship."[23]

The social unrest that was smoldering on the nation's campuses brought another issue into focus. Although slow in coming to CLC, when this restlessness finally erupted, it compelled the president and the college community to move out of its sheltered and rather innocent isolation. The risk-taking critical tradition of Lutheran higher education was gaining a foothold. Two marches down a major thoroughfare in Thousand Oaks illustrated the growing willingness of members of this CLC community to dare to engage in controversy. Reflecting on these events 25 years later, one student explained,

The first [march] was in reaction to the assassination of Martin Luther King. The second was as part of the [National Vietnam] War Moratorium. Both events and the surrounding activities reflect the *zeitgeist* of the time,

23. Written questionnaire response, Nov. 17, 1994, from an emeritus professor who taught at CLC during the Olson years.

104

but for me . . . they also are part and parcel of events that shaped many of our attitudes and values about humanity, the value of people, our world view and many of our social and political views.[24]

This same student describes his memories as an indistinguishable "collage . . . of both civil rights activities and anti-war activities." What did it mean to him to participate in two marches from CLC to downtown Thousand Oaks? "I was not that involved in campus religious life," he writes, "but . . . an active campus pastor . . . who spoke actively on war issues in chapel . . . was probably as responsible as anyone for keeping me connected to some form of the organized church at a time when I doubted its relevancy."[25]

An alumna writes of her pride when President Olson marched with them and spoke out against the war, even at the risk of offending some of the more conservative church members. She suggests that even if the marchers didn't all agree on the issues, "we agreed on the importance of controversial debate, bringing in speakers from the outside world, the importance of philosophical discussion, and struggling with the issues of the day."[26] Still another alumna insightfully wrote that "choosing to oppose the war (which I had previously supported) was a major turning point for me, particularly in terms of questioning authority. . . . Choosing to take a public stand against the war . . . felt risky, but also right."[27]

These student marchers, whether they were aware of it or not, were part of a transforming moment in the history of their alma mater. One of the members of the philosophy department at that time looks back now and concurs. He recalls how events such as the Kent State Massacre caused the CLC students and faculty to debate more openly than ever before what it meant to be a Lutheran College. Through the classroom, through marches, through debates, and through a host of controversial speakers[28] who were invited to CLC during this decade, the institution was given an opportunity to demonstrate its commitment to academic freedom.

Dr. Olson's actions in support of the students did indeed offend some of the pastors and parishioners in the supporting congregations who then acted on their threats to withdraw financial support, compounding a fiscal crisis

24. Letter from Don Hossler to Gerald Swanson, October 11, 1994.
25. Letter from Don Hossler to Gerald Swanson, October 11, 1994.
26. Letter from Eloise Cohen to Gerald Swanson, October 13, 1994.
27. Letter from Jean M. Blomquist to Gerald Swanson, September 28, 1994.
28. Angela Davis, Adam Clayton Powell, Dick Gregory, and Bishop James Pike were some of the speakers who were considered "controversial." President Olson encouraged this practice, but insisted on objectivity by requiring, when possible, that "both sides" be represented during the same academic year. (Written questionnaire response from an emeritus professor, November 17, 1994.)

that had been impending for some time. In mid-decade, the WASC Accrediting Committee expressed concern over a plant indebtedness in excess of $1,731,000 and a deficit in current funds of over $350,000. Dr. Olson had inherited the debt without an endowment fund to support it, and a series of deficit budgets during his tenure added to the total indebtedness. Gifts and grants were insufficient to balance the budget, and the Board of Regents complained that they had difficulty getting exact readings on income versus expenditures. One faculty member confesses that "we took advantage of the fact that Dr. Olson gave us so much freedom. It was a temptation to overspend our departmental budgets by buying things we really needed but wouldn't have been permitted to buy if someone had held a firmer rein on the budget."[29]

In spite of the turmoil of those first years, the school grew in numbers and academic reputation and the student body and faculty revealed increasing diversity. In the fall of 1963 there were 550 students and in 1964 enrollment reached a total of 736 students from 24 states, the People's Republic of China, and Sweden. Students were now coming from a variety of church backgrounds and, although Lutherans still comprised about 78 percent of the student body, 17 other denominations were also represented. Remarkably, the percentage of Lutherans on the faculty and administration stayed the same, around 69 percent, while their total numbers grew from 51 to 82. Between the years 1963 and 1966, the full-time teaching faculty grew in numbers from 38 to 59. At that time Presbyterians and Methodists represented most of the non-Lutheran faculty.

Reflecting on his perceptions of CLC in those first years, one alumnus says that the students "represented three main areas of interest — one-third were involved in religious or cultural activities, one-third in academics and the other third in football, with some overlap, of course."[30] The fact that the Dallas Cowboys brought their summer training camp on to the CLC campus in 1963 and kept it there until 1984 probably contributed to his perception of the significance of football. Another alumnus recalls a campus dominated by music with tours by the college choir and the Kingsmen Quartet important as a means of student recruitment.[31] Certainly, by the mid-1970s, the choir's reputation was such that large audiences were attracted to its annual concerts at the Los Angeles Music Center. Bus loads of concert-goers came every year from Lutheran congregations in the Southern California area.

In spite of these evidences of growth in the student body and faculty, and other positive factors, the cloud of indebtedness had grown ever darker and by now had reached critical proportions.

29. Interview with faculty member, March 22, 1995.
30. Interview with 1964 graduate, January 13, 1995.
31. Interview with 1964 graduate, February 16, 1995.

Out of Financial Crisis — A Second Transforming Moment

For many persons affiliated with the college throughout its history, the year 1970, when the school's debt reached a staggering $3,600,000, can be identified as another of CLC's "transforming moments." Facing bankruptcy, the college and its supporting church bodies had to make a decision. Should the college be realistic and close its doors in light of the burden of a huge debt? Was the school worth saving? Should the Lutheran Church on both the national and local levels commit itself to the cost and sacrifices that would have to be made if the college had any hope of survival? The decision was made that the college *was* important and that every effort should be made to keep it alive.[32]

Maurice Knutson, a Lutheran layman who had experience in crisis management, was brought in by the national church as a financial troubleshooter. By applying extremely austere measures that included cutting the faculty from 70 to 63 persons, he managed to end the year with an $80,000 surplus in the budget and to reduce the debt by $800,000. The national church bodies made a guaranteed commitment for a loan of $1,000,000 as a demonstration of their faith in the school's mission. Richard Pederson's inspired gift and vision had been marvelously affirmed, and as Mary Hekhuis said, "When push comes to shove, the church is always there with its support!"[33]

In May of 1971, after eight arduous years as president, Dr. Olson resigned. During his tenure, in spite of the financial crisis and social upheaval, the school enrollment had tripled in size to 1,000 students. In addition, relationships with the now incorporated city of Thousand Oaks had been greatly strengthened.

When the search for a new president failed to produce a candidate from outside the campus, the Board of Regents, advised by Knutson, appointed Dr. Mark Mathews, chair of the Business Administration and Economics Department, as acting president in 1972. Because Mathews was a Presbyterian, the by-laws of the institution had to be changed to permit him to hold that office, an action that, though not theologically motivated, was consistent with the critical tradition in Lutheran higher education.

Under Mathews' fiscal management the college reversed its deficit trend and a period of financial stability and creative growth followed. A sense of optimism and commitment permeated the campus.

In 1971, the football team won the NAIA championship in its division. It

---

32. Interview with faculty member, June 14, 1995, who recalls that the acting dean at that time was convinced that the national church made the decision to support CLC because of its high regard for the faculty of the college. It was becoming more and more evident that this faculty was appreciated for its academic qualifications but also for its comprehension of the Lutheran perspective of higher education.

33. Interview with Mary Hekhuis, January 12, 1995.

was a feat never again achieved but it served at that time to give student and alumni morale a welcome boost. In fact, one recent graduate claims that that championship 20 years earlier had been a factor in his decision to come to California Lutheran. An excellent student and a religion major, he saw in this achievement evidence that the college was active in the world and not sheltering itself from secular and worldly endeavors.

Academic development became a primary concern in the 1970s. In the fall of 1971, the college instituted a 4-1-4 curriculum pattern of two semesters divided by a January interim month, a format which continued until 1989. The curriculum was also expanded to include a fifth year that enabled teachers to obtain California credentials. Graduate programs in education and business were started and efforts were made to increase minority student enrollment. In the spring of 1972, a long-time faculty member saw the need for and initiated an annual Colloquium of Scholars and Honors Day Convocation designed to stimulate and recognize student academic achievement. The library had now grown to include 89,474 volumes and 769 periodicals and the need for a larger building was obvious. Though urgent, the dream was not to be realized during Mathews' presidency, as he had hoped. CLC's graduate studies program was expanding steadily, with masters degrees offered in the areas of education, special education, business administration, administration of justice, and public administration.[34]

As one of the steps in its quest for financial stability, the college put a heavy emphasis on off-campus continuing education classes, and at one point 12,000 persons enrolled in these programs. This lucrative program featured short courses, seminars, and workshops aimed mostly at teachers who needed to upgrade their credentials. Unfortunately, the college failed to adequately supervise course "brokers" who in some cases "sold" credits by designing and filling classes that were never even taught, and in other cases failing to sufficiently control requirements and grading. As the former director of higher education for the Lutheran Church in America stated, it was an unconscionable lack of responsibility on the part of the college and represented a betrayal of the highest academic ideals. This action put the future of the college in jeopardy and was fully as damaging as the financial crisis had been.[35] For the most part, the college community was not even aware of this scandal, but when they learned of it many of the faculty were deeply embittered primarily because of the damage done to the academic reputation of the college. Not surprisingly, the college soon found itself on probation by WASC. Fortunately the college took severe steps to correct the situation and managed to get the

34. These degrees were considered terminal and not preparation for studies leading to a Ph.D.

35. Interview with Richard Solberg, June 26, 1995.

program back under its control, and the probation was lifted. The acting dean at that time is convinced today that the favorable response given by WASC (in spite of negative media coverage) was heavily influenced by the credibility that CLC had because of its affiliation with the network of Lutheran colleges throughout the country.[36]

Several examples of the college's willingness to ask tough questions took place in the 1970s. The campus pastor at that time developed an active community of faith that made a significant impact on the community of learning. In fact, Mathews envisioned the roles of campus pastor, academic dean, and dean of students as a troika with equal power in the administration. In the words of the campus pastor, this was the "golden age" of integration of faith and learning. With the encouragement and support of President Mathews, a student congregation — Lord of Life — was organized with its own student leaders. A weekly campus wide discussion series called "Christian Conversations" addressed diverse social concerns and controversial issues such as the unpopular war in Vietnam, abortion, homosexuality, sexism, poverty, racism, sanctuary for Central American refugees, and the World War II atomic bombing of Nagasaki and Hiroshima.

Another example centered around the establishment in the early 1970s of a research center to investigate pornographic materials. The center was brought on campus at the request of the National Legal Data Center (NLDC) which had as its aim the suppression and censorship of pornography through legal constraints. Supported by the Nixon administration and the FBI, the center was welcomed on campus for the income it provided and because the president, together with some of the faculty, felt that this gave the school an opportunity to address a basic question of Christian ethics, namely the need to treat people as valuable individuals and not as sex objects. When some of the faculty learned that the goal of the center was to sponsor legislation leading to government censorship of pornographic materials, a sharp debate broke out on the subject of First Amendment rights of freedom of speech and freedom of the press. Among those arguing against the center were members of the English and philosophy departments, other faculty, and some Lutheran pastors in the area.[37] These people cited Lutheran traditions of open scholarship, but were also motivated by their unhappiness with government attempts to suppress voices advocating an end to the Vietnam War. The debate created

36. Interview with faculty member, June 14, 1995.

37. Although the religion department did *not* provide any meaningful involvement in this debate, one of its members did support the presence of the NLDC on campus. A high administration member at that time suggests, however, that friction within the three-man department meant that the department "did not play any significant role in the campus in the 70s." Interview on December 2, 1994.

interest throughout the country and even the *New York Times* called to interview members of the faculty. The First Amendment rights position prevailed and three years after it opened, the center was removed from campus.

A third example of CLC's willingness to wrestle with controversial questions also deals with the issue of censorship. In the context of the free thinking and often unbridled 1960s, there was an understandable desire on the part of some faculty and administrators at CLC to control the various student publications such as the weekly newspaper, the *Echo,* and *Morning Glory,* the annual literary magazine, where students were eager to "tell it like it is." The concern of these faculty and administrators was that parents, church people, and other members of the community might be shocked by what they read and the college might lose valued support and financial backing. In the debate that followed, the supporters of free speech and free press had to stress again that First Amendment rights are consistent with the goals of Lutheran higher education. After all, they said, student publications were not to be public relations tools. On the contrary, as discomforting as it might be, their purpose was to encourage students to wrestle with complicated issues and engage the world to the fullest!

Another special opportunity for full engagement of students into the world of thought was the introduction of the Humanities Tutorial Program. "Hum Tut" was a one-year, team-taught course offered to highly qualified students by faculty members from the English, history, philosophy, and religion departments and was designed to provide a broad and general introduction to great books and writers. The Bible and Christian thinkers such as Kierkegaard and Bonhoeffer were studied. But students also read from the classics including Homer, Plato, and Aristotle as well as Christian antagonists, Nietzsche, Lenin, and Marx. For years this program made a meaningful impact on students as it encouraged them to broaden their "education, perspective and appreciation for life through the study of other disciplines and other paths of inquiry."[38]

Wishing to maintain close ties to CLC's historic church constituency, Mathews encouraged the creation of a new position, director of church relations. Through this office relationships with pastors and church people were fostered by means of personal contacts, regular newsletter mailings, and visits by teams of students and faculty who were sent to individual congregations and synodical gatherings.

One alumnus who was a student at CLC in the 1970s feels that, in spite of this outreach to congregations, there was a subtle shift in the way the college was presenting itself to the public. From its beginning, the CLC logo — an

38. *CLC Bulletin* 6 (May 1980): 49. The "Hum Tut" program continues to "prepare students to become informed, careful and independent thinkers" and encourages "critical and reflective interpretation." *CLU 1994-95 Undergraduate Catalog,* p. 30.

oval shield and a prominent cross with the words, "Love of Christ, Truth, Freedom" encircling the cross — had been used on college stationary, the catalog, and other publications. Slowly, over a period of half a dozen years, that logo was replaced by an oak tree encircled by a stylized cross and minus the motto. To this particular alumnus this change seemed to suggest "a minimizing of CLC's relationship both to the gospel and to the church," while to another alumnus the new logo indicated a meaningful engagement of the college with its community, the world of "a thousand oaks." For him the cross was always evident in the logo, even though in an abstract form. Their differing perceptions reveal the ambiguity that Lutheran thought not only fosters, but with which it struggles to live comfortably.

A growing diversity in the religious affiliation of faculty members took place in the 1970s. In the first year of the decade Lutherans represented 60 percent of the faculty but by the 1978-79 school year were only 45 percent. That year "other Christians," with 49 percent, outnumbered Lutherans on the faculty for the first time in the school's history. Three percent were Jewish, while two percent claimed no religious affiliation at all. The religion faculty, not yet ready to embrace total openness and diversity, and feeling the need to keep close ties to its Lutheran constituency, agreed that all members of that department not only had to be Lutheran but also ordained pastors.[39]

Under Dr. Mathews' leadership, CLC had weathered its financial crisis and its academic character had survived a severe challenge to its integrity. The school had taken some significant steps toward shaping its identity as an institution committed to both faith and learning. Working this out in the context of its Lutheran heritage would continue for some time to be a struggle for a college that was coming of age.

A Time Of Maturation — Transforming the Campus

Dr. Mathews resigned his presidency in 1980 in order to go back to his first love, the classroom, and in 1981 the Rev. Jerry Miller, a Harvard graduate and the executive director of the National Lutheran Campus Ministry, became the fourth president of CLC.

This new president brought a gift for aggressive fund raising to the college and moved quickly to hire a vice president for development, engaged a consulting service to develop a capital campaign and, through the restoration of

---

39. This effectively eliminated women as candidates for the religion faculty since it was not until 1970 that some of the Lutheran church bodies in the U.S. permitted women to be ordained, and it would take many more years of study before they could qualify for advanced degrees in the theological disciplines.

CLEF, emphasized the giving of deferred gifts. The fiscal year 1983-84 recorded contributions and grants totaling $3,250,000, including a $1 million gift, the largest single gift to that date.

With funds in hand, the college was now able to enter into a construction period during which three major buildings on campus were erected. In 1985 Pearson Library was occupied, in 1988 the Ahmanson Science Center was completed, and in 1990 the Samuelson Chapel was ready for use. Whether by intention or by accident, the library and science building were constructed before the chapel. One might suggest that this order reflects elements of Luther's doctrine of vocation, namely, that the calling of a Lutheran university is to be first and foremost a quality *academic* institution.

When Pearson Library and its adjoining 250-seat Preus-Brandt Forum were built, it was no surprise that the college stated in its 1988 report to WASC that the new "facility has had a significant positive impact on the academic environment at California Lutheran University."[40] As one student said, after participating in the all-campus "book moving" from the old to the new library, "Now I feel like we're really a college!"[41]

Building the Ahmanson Science Center meant that for the first time all of the sciences had adequate space and equipment to initiate significant research programs. It was taken for granted that in their research, no matter how controversial the subject might be, all theses from evolution to genetics were open to challenge and investigation.

Samuelson Chapel brought to the campus a towering cross-topped land-mark with beautiful stained glass windows and a majestic 39-rank, tracker-action pipe organ. In the pew racks the *Lutheran Book of Worship* shared space with *Gather,* a Roman Catholic book of worship. Chapel speakers included lay and ordained, women and men, Lutherans and other Protestants, Jewish rabbis and Roman Catholic priests, Hispanic Americans and African Americans, old and the very young members of the university preschool who led the community in worship once each semester. The preacher at the dedication put it well when she said that the chapel was to be "a place of grace" where all were welcomed.

The college community felt a sense of near completeness. The library, the science building, and the chapel! Faith and learning, it seemed, had both been affirmed even in the brick and concrete of campus structures.

The growth in the academic areas at this time was not as easy to measure or visualize as the erection of new buildings, but several signs of maturation can be noted. In 1983 the college was evaluated by the Western Association of

40. CLU *Fifth-Year Report* to WASC (August 1988), p. 86.
41. At that time, the library's book collection numbered over 100,000 volumes, supplemented by journals, microforms, and audiovisual software.

Schools and Colleges (WASC), and its accreditation was reaffirmed for ten years, the maximum time possible. Two years later, in 1985, a prestigious endowed lecture series was introduced[42] focusing on the relation of science and philosophy with the "search of truth" its stated goal. The English department had long recognized the need to improve students' writing skills and, under a National Endowment for the Humanities grant, many members of the humanities faculty were thoroughly instructed in the use of "writing across the curriculum."[43] The school established a writing center to support the program. By 1988, in only its 29th year, CLU's academic reputation was affirmed in a study of small comprehensive colleges conducted by *U.S. News & World Report.*

In the early 1980s the college committed itself to the creation of an environment supportive of ethnic and cultural pluralism. In 1981, the college developed a four-year working relationship with an international study group from Japan. With a peak enrollment of 40-45 Japanese students on campus, CLC gained some valued insights into both the joys and difficulties of developing a diverse student body. The 1983 WASC evaluation encouraged the college to be more multiculturally inclusive. For that reason and also at the insistence of some Regents and Convocators,[44] CLC's report to WASC five years later included a revised mission statement affirming its welcome to "students of all ages as well as all cultural, religious and ethnic backgrounds."[45] In 1986 a determined effort was made to recruit internationally in Scandinavia, and at one time there were approximately 70 Norwegian students on campus and a lesser number from Sweden and Denmark. A grant from the Irvine Foundation enabled the college to recruit and offer financial aid to minority students, and a successful effort was made to attract students from Ventura County's significant Latino population. An Office of Multicultural Services was established to support and facilitate various ethnic organizations and events. In a little over two decades the college that had opened its doors to a student body that was nearly all Lutheran, many of whom were blond and blue eyed, now included a growing number of students of color who brought a welcome diversity to the campus. The traditionally Scandinavian Santa Lucia was an African American woman one year. Indeed, multicultural growth was increasing the sensitivity of a previously rather homogeneous college community.

42. The Harold Stoner Clark Lectures.

43. It was also at this time that faculty professional development was significantly enhanced by a sizable grant from the Hewlett Foundation.

44. The university by-laws require that persons of color and/or persons whose first language is other than English constitute at least ten percent of the Convocation and the Board, a policy followed by other agencies and assemblies of the ELCA.

45. From the revised Statement of Mission in the CLU *Fifth-Year Report* to WASC (August 1988), p. 76.

In the fall of 1985, the Board of Regents concurred with the administration that CLC was ready to become a "university." Not everyone in the college community was in agreement. Those opposing the change felt that it would mean sacrificing the college's focus on liberal arts, with the result that the humanities might simply exist to serve the requirements of the professional schools. They also argued that the college was not ready, had inadequate library resources, and in all honesty, was seeking the prestige that would be associated with university status. Those favoring the change noted that the college already had graduate programs at the masters level in five distinct areas and that, even though CLC was the only four-year college in the county, the school was being compared with California's two-year community colleges. They were persuaded that becoming a university would force the college to take more seriously the scholarly quest for academic excellence. Most important for this study was the conviction of some that by becoming a university the college could no longer limit itself to serving primarily a Lutheran constituency, but would be forced to expand its scope, become a regional institution, and serve the varied academic and professional needs of the diverse population within its geographic area. On Jan. 1, 1986, California Lutheran College became California Lutheran University.

In 1989 CLU joined the Southern California Intercollegiate Athletic Conference (SCIAC), which held membership in the NCAA Division III. This division encourages *academic* scholarships, but does not allow financial aid to be granted on the basis of athletic ability. The decision to make this move created a controversy of volcanic proportions at the college, among the alumni, and in the local newspaper. Those who did not favor this action argued that CLU's eminently successful football program was bound to suffer because of the loss of athletic scholarships.[46] The school would also lose prestige, they said, because CLU would be "moving down" from Division II to Division III. Most significant, especially for this study, was the argument that if it joined the SCIAC conference, CLU would likely give up its church relatedness as other schools in the conference had done.[47] Those who favored the "athletic fit" of

---

46. Under the leadership of an articulate, committed, and charismatic coach who integrated his Christian principles into his coaching philosophy, the college, from its earliest years, had a dominant football program. They won a national championship in 1971, and several of their players went on to enjoy success as professionals in the NFL.

47. It is true that Whittier (Quaker), Occidental (Presbyterian), Pomona-Pitzer (Congregational), Redlands (American Baptist), and Claremont-Mudd-Scripps (Congregational) had over the years become independent and "free from ecclesiastical identity." The University of LaVerne, however, continues to have "ties" with the Church of the Brethren. Cal Tech never had any denominational affiliation. In contrast, the Golden State Athletic Conference, which CLU was leaving, consisted of eight schools, all of which were Christian colleges representing conservative theological perspectives. (All information taken from current college catalogs.)

SCIAC stressed financial savings, the close geographic proximity of the conference schools, and a reduction in the influence of football on the academic program which some felt had been like the tail wagging the dog. But the strongest argument favoring the move was the one based on scholarship. The schools in the conference excelled academically and, as the 1988 CLU report to WASC noted, "joining the SCIAC would allow us to increase our academic expectations." CLU, it said, "desires to welcome students who wish to enrich their education by participating in athletics, not athletes who merely agree to fulfill minimal requirements."[48] Strongly endorsed by President Miller, the athletic director, the Faculty Athletic Policy Committee, the faculty, and the Board of Regents, CLU joined the conference, thereby making its athletic program consistent with its educational objectives.

A curriculum revision called CORE 21, outlining the new general education requirements for graduation, went into effect in the fall of 1991. With a goal of preparing students for the challenges and uncertainties of the twenty-first century, this curriculum required that students take classes to develop critical understanding in areas such as gender and ethnic studies and skill in at least one foreign language. The revamped curriculum, it was hoped, would open student minds to thoughtful, probing, and intellectual reflection that would replace the quest for absolutes and simple answers.

The decade of the 1980s began with signs that the college was showing growth in its understanding of its Lutheran critical tradition. Several actions and/or events are illustrative. In 1982 President Miller, together with the dean, developed a statement regarding religious affiliation and faculty selection at CLC. The document affirmed that CLC's "commitment to Lutheran higher education does not demand Lutheran Church membership of every faculty member as a condition for service. . . . It is, however, expected that all faculty members actively support the College's ongoing effort to discern and fulfill its Christian, Lutheran commitment to higher education." While the assertion was made that "religious affiliation per se is not an adequate basis for refusing to consider a candidate," concern was expressed over "affiliation with some religious groups . . . [whose] beliefs, practices, or policies . . . appear to oppose the tradition within which the college functions."[49] The college was moving closer to the Lutheran understanding of what it means to be a church-related institution. Cal Lutheran had opened the door to diversity while at the same time defining certain limits.

Later in the decade, however, indications surfaced that some members of the college community and its constituencies were less appreciative of this

48. CLU *Fifth-Year Report* to WASC (August, 1988), pp. 54 and 57.
49. "A Statement Regarding Religious Affiliation and Faculty Selection at CLC," 1982. CLU Archives.

critical tradition. Solberg, in his introductory chapter, puts this in context. Throughout this essay the term "critical" has been used to refer to the understanding of the Lutheran tradition as it was conceived in sixteenth-century Germany under the leadership of Martin Luther. As Solberg (who quotes Sydney Ahlstrom) explains, however, by the seventeenth century Lutheran theology had become rigidly orthodox, dogmatic, and scholastic as it sought to defend its position against the Reformed tradition on one hand and the Counter Reformation on the other. By the eighteenth century another shift emerged when many Lutherans in Germany reacted against the formalism of scholasticism, developed a pietistic movement which focused on the heart rather than the head, and emphasized good works and deeds of mercy. All too often, however, the "good works" of pietism degenerated to prohibitions against activities like dancing, card playing, drinking, and sexual permissiveness. Both "scholasticism" and "pietism" surfaced frequently at CLC/CLU during the decade of the 1980s, challenging the "critical" tradition of the Lutheran heritage.

The "scholastic" tradition emerged especially when criticism was leveled at the CLU religion department for using biblical critical methods in the classroom.[50] In another instance a committee was formed in the late 1970s in order to establish a chair in confessional theology and was motivated in large part by the desire to preserve the Lutheran scholastic orthodox tradition as that committee understood it.[51] A further challenge to the Lutheran critical tradition surfaced in the 1970s and 1980s when a biology professor who did not agree with the theory of evolution rejected the critical approach and taught "scientific creationism."

The pietistic tradition also made itself felt on campus during this decade. President Miller recalls frequent demands to fire members of the Student Affairs staff for not adequately enforcing the ban on the consumption of alcohol on campus.[52] Two other examples of the pietistic tradition need a fuller development. In all of the interviews for the essay, the name of one professor was mentioned more than any other as the ideal example of faith and learning at CLC/CLU. Deeply religious, academically demanding, dynamic, outgoing, and charismatic, he lived life with gusto. He loved his students and they loved him as was evidenced by the fact that he was elected professor of the year four times. He had inherited, however, a pietistic understanding of the Lutheran heritage, and at the beginning of the decade actually

50. Interview with President Miller.
51. Further information about this chair (named after Dr. Gerhard Belgum) will be found later in this chapter.
52. Interview with President Miller. The ban on alcohol has been maintained primarily for legal and social reasons — *not* theological ones.

resigned from the college, in part because of his disapproval of some incidences of sexual activity and drinking that were taking place in the residence halls. He was persuaded to rescind his decision to retire and remained at CLU until his sudden and unexpected death in the late 1980s.

In the spring of 1990 another event occurred on campus that involved the Thousand Oaks community with the question of what it means to have a Lutheran University in its midst. Since the early 1980s the CLU Women's Resource Center (WRC) and the local branch of the American Association of University Women (AAUW) had collaborated to present "Creative Options: A Day For Women," an event that was unafraid to tackle current, and sometimes controversial, issues. Of the 66 workshops that were offered that year, topics included finances, environment, parenting, women's history, spirituality, athletics, and two — lesbianism and abortion — that brought a vigorous negative reaction from many in the community. In spite of the pressure from some nearby congregations and considerable unfavorable publicity from the community, President Miller issued a statement which, when published in the local newspapers, explained the critical Lutheran position.

> The university welcomes the expression of all points of view on . . . appropriate subjects related to education and our society. The administration of the university does not dictate, monitor or veto the subject matter of educational programs or workshops offered on the campus. We affirm academic freedom and the freedom of speech for all people while fully affirming the essential values for life inherent in the Christian faith and the Lutheran tradition in higher education.[53]

Under Miller's leadership, the college had experienced another transforming moment. Through the addition of major buildings, progress and recognition in academics, awareness of and improvement in becoming more multicultural, a move to university status, membership in a new academically oriented athletic conference, a major revision of its curriculum, and its continuing struggle with its Lutheran heritage, CLC/CLU showed definite signs of maturation, with all of the pain and joy that are a part of any growing experience.

The Mature University: Integrating Faith and Learning

Dr. Miller resigned the presidency in the spring of 1992 and Dr. Luther S. Luedtke, a Lutheran layman and professor of English and American studies, was inaugurated as president in the fall of 1992. A Phi Beta Kappa graduate

53. Letter to the Editor, Thousand Oaks *News Chronicle* (March 2, 1990).

of a Lutheran church-related college, he earned his Ph.D. at Brown University. Luedtke served 22 years on the faculty of the University of Southern California and is recognized internationally through his lectures and writings.

As an active Lutheran layman who has served as a congregational chair and a Sunday school teacher and has chaired various congregational committees, Luedtke embodies faith and learning in his own person.

Soon after taking office he became the catalyst for a reexamination of CLU's mission statement. With input from representatives of the many university constituencies, its three sentences define the nature of the institution, the significance of its heritage, and its central and distinctive purposes. An understanding of the Lutheran critical position is evident in the statement.

> California Lutheran University is a diverse scholarly community dedicated to excellence in the liberal arts and professional studies. Rooted in the Lutheran tradition of Christian faith, the University encourages critical inquiry into matters of both faith and reason. The mission of the University is to educate leaders for a global society who are strong in character and judgment, confident in their identity and vocation, and committed to service and justice. (Adopted 1995)

As the University emerges from its adolescence, it faces significant challenges in areas such as enrollment, SAT scores, sources of revenue, and the demand for student financial aid. It is hoped that the mission statement will provide a basis for fruitful strategic planning. Aggressive leadership is required and the president has gathered a new administrative team composed of four vice presidents, the registrar, and the chief financial officer.

The most significant change in the Luedtke administration has been the appointment of the first woman vice president of academic affairs. She inherits a faculty academically well qualified to move the university into a promising future. A student-faculty ratio of 14.5:1 fosters close relationships between students and a faculty of 112 members, 92 full-time and 15 on half to three-quarter contracts. Over all, 80 percent have a Ph.D., while 88 percent hold the terminal degree in their field. The percentage varies by disciplinary area. A total of 96 percent hold the doctorate in the humanities, 89 percent in the social sciences, 82 percent in natural sciences (100 percent in biology, chemistry, geology, and physics) and 75 percent in the School of Education.[54]

In addition to the percentage of faculty doctorates, high student SAT scores, and GPAs, academic quality is also measured by what happens to students when they come to the university. Are they introduced to multicultural diversity? Are they challenged to wrestle with questions of morality and to become

---

54. WASC *Self Study Report* (Spring 1995), ch. 6, p. 1.

involved in acts of service and justice? Are any questions off-limits, or are they encouraged to engage freely in research and classroom discussion?[55] As long as the university remains true to the Lutheran critical tradition in higher education, it should do well in these areas.

The creation of "CLUnet" (a universal fiber-optic telecommunications and data network installed in 1994) witnesses to the institution's emerging commitment to communications and technology as both a field of study and as a pedagogical resource.[56] The university also has a strong commitment to teaching, and to encourage the highest standards in the classroom, a new award for teaching was presented for the first time in the spring of 1995.

The report submitted to WASC in 1995 raised the question, "How shall CLU develop a model of excellence that is distinctive, credible and consistent with the best of its own traditions — one that positions CLU as an institution academically equal to the strong independent colleges and small comprehensive universities in Southern California? . . . We believe that the answer lies in strengthening the quality of our academic programs."[57]

Having drawn attention to scholarly concerns, the mission statement goes on to focus on the university's Lutheran heritage. Significantly, the percentage of Lutheran undergraduates at CLU dropped from nearly 100 percent in 1961 to 24.5 percent in 1994. This means that in all likelihood CLU has a student body largely ignorant of the historical heritage of their university and the meaning of its church relationship.

Also there is some concern that the faculty awareness of CLU's Lutheran tradition is deficient. In a recent survey of faculty, respondents were asked to estimate faculty understanding of the Lutheran heritage in higher education. Unfortunately, 34 percent rated it as "weak" and an additional 21 percent said they did not know. Only 8 percent said they had a "strong" understanding.[58]

In its 1995 WASC report, the university acknowledged "some concern that faculty . . . have not had many occasions to learn about the meaning and significance of CLU's Lutheran Heritage."[59] Therefore, the formulation of the new mission statement committed the university to define this tradition. Progress is being made.[60] For example, this issue was an important theme at the fall 1994 faculty retreat. The university's participation in the Lilly project that has given rise to this book has also encouraged further dialogue on this issue.

55. Interview with vice president of academic affairs.
56. WASC *Self Study Report* (Spring 1995), intro., p. 2.
57. WASC *Self Study Report* (Spring 1995), intro., p. 2.
58. WASC *Self Study Report* (Spring 1995), ch. 6, p. 20.
59. WASC *Self Study Report* (Spring 1995), ch. 6, p. 5.
60. The academic dean says that she now feels a mandate (even a calling) to discuss faith when hiring new faculty. She is committed to spend quality time talking about what it means to teach at a Lutheran university.

Deep questions still remain, however, about the desirability of maintaining a "critical mass" of Lutherans at CLU. The Board of Regents at present is 85 percent Lutheran and, according to the by-laws, must be at least 60 percent Lutheran.[61] The Convocators, who are almost all elected from supporting congregations, are nearly all Lutheran, but no requirements have ever been established for the administration, faculty, or student body. Currently the president and all of the vice presidents are Lutheran, but Lutherans among the faculty have dropped from 100 percent the first year to 35 percent in 1995. Finally, as noted above, the Lutheran student population has declined to 24.5 percent.[62]

This discussion of whether or not there ought to be a critical mass came to a head in the religion department in the spring of 1995. At present one of the department members is Jewish and one belongs to the Church of the Brethren. Both have made strong contributions to the university and both are highly appreciated. But in the process of searching for a new member of the department tension arose when the resume of another non-Lutheran candidate was seriously considered by the search committee. Those favoring a candidate who is not a Lutheran felt their preference would be consistent with the Lutheran critical tradition as long as the applicant had excellent academic and classroom credentials. Those favoring a Lutheran insisted that it was important for the university to be involved in the life of the church, but most of all it was essential to have a majority of Lutherans in this particular department (more so than any other department on campus) so that there would be persons qualified to interpret and share the Lutheran perspective with the rest of the CLU community. Because of the complexity of the issues the decision was postponed, and the discussion continues.

Among the many factors in the culture of Southern California that impact the religious mission of the university, two can be noted. The first is the significant Mexican-American population from which students are recruited by CLU. In its final issue in the spring of 1995, the student newspaper, *Echo*, reported that "Cal Lu is not just for Lutherans," and that for the first time Roman Catholics outnumbered Lutherans on campus. The growing number of Latinos in the student body contributed to this change. CLU feels comfortable with this situation and has indeed ministered to its Roman Catholic students throughout the years. Priests regularly celebrate the Mass, and faculty

61. WASC *Self Study Report* (Spring 1995), ch. 1, p. 7.
62. The WASC *Self Study Report* speaks to this issue when it says, "This sharp decline in the percentage of Lutheran students, while not surprising given the demography of California and the 'aging' of the Lutheran Church, is nevertheless cause for concern. Since CLU's identity, alumni, and donors are fairly closely tied to the church, it is important to recruit more aggressively in the churches and at the same time articulate the significance of CLU's Lutheran heritage to a more diverse constituency." Ch. 9, p. 3.

from St. John's Seminary occasionally teach courses on Roman Catholic thought at CLU.[63]

The second cultural factor impacting the religious climate at CLU is the conservative political nature of this area. A large number of students on campus have organized a Republican Club which they say has "gained national prominence" by having "the highest ratio of club members to number of students of any College Republican club in California."[64] Some of their goals include having an American flag in every classroom, having a Christian prayer at every student senate meeting, and banning homosexual groups or activities from the campus. When representatives of this club came to a student senate meeting prepared to push through a resolution aimed at condemning "any homosexual activities, groups or policies,"[65] it brought a vigorous and widespread negative reaction from a large number of students on campus. The responding group quoted CLU's new mission statement and went on to affirm that CLU "welcomes all people with open arms."[66] The Republican Club resolutions were defeated and the sponsoring senators recalled.

Conclusions

What does the future hold for the integration of faith and learning at California Lutheran University? After working for several years, the "Marketing Action Committee" produced, in the spring of 1995, a document entitled "Ten Main Messages." Without any input from this Lilly study, the "messages" remarkably address the thesis of this essay. At the top of the list the first two messages read as follows:

1. The Lutheran tradition cherishes education, faith and freedom of inquiry and encourages the noblest expression of Christian values. The University welcomes students of all beliefs and provides them the opportunity to explore religious issues as part of their formal education and to do so in the spirit of openness, reason and tolerance.
2. CLU offers personalized learning in a rigorous academic environment, utilizing the latest in technology and curriculum innovations.

63. Jewish rabbis are also invited to minister to students by speaking in chapel each semester.

64. From "Resolution Commending . . . the CLU College Republicans," May 3, 1995.

65. From "Resolution Supporting Christian Values," May 3, 1995.

66. From "Statement of Our TRUE Intent," May 3, 1995.

The university's commitment to both faith and learning was symbolically affirmed on January 25, 1995, at a moving ceremony in which the Gerhard and Olga Belgum Chair of Confessional Theology was named as the very first endowed chair at California Lutheran University. Dr. Gerhard Belgum, the founding director of the Center for Theological Studies at CLU, was a Lutheran pastor, a college professor, and a noted theologian. Olga Belgum served 12 years as executive secretary to President Miller.

Looking to the future, President Luedtke describes the integration of faith and learning at CLU with an architectural metaphor. Noting that the entrance to the library now faces away from the chapel, he envisions in the new campus plan that the library entrance will open on a plaza that will connect it to the entrance of the chapel. They will face each other — a place of faith and a place of learning — as a recognition of mutual interdependence.

Thus, California Lutheran University is challenged to make bold statements of faith and learning, both on paper and in brick and concrete, all the while acknowledging the difficulty of bringing them to reality in a region whose people are largely unacquainted with Lutheran tradition and practice. The task of the future will be to continue to make the name of the university synonymous with academic excellence and a living faith.

THE REFORMED TRADITION

What Can the Reformed Tradition Contribute to Christian Higher Education?

James D. Bratt

Calvinism[1] has shown consistent patterns of development wherever it has spread over the years, yet those patterns are grounded in tensions among some of its basic beliefs. No Christian tradition makes more emphatic claims about the sovereignty of God — or about the degree to which human beings defy the same. Reformed theology insists that the world belongs to God — but that "the world" is lost in sin and evil. Its soteriology maximizes human dependence, but its ethic maximizes human activism. Second to none in Protestantism, Calvinists teach salvation by grace — but then a life according to the law. They claim every domain on earth for Christ, would have every moment lived *coram Deo* (before the face of God), yet have also set loose one of the most efficient engines of secularization that the modern world has seen.

These beliefs and the antinomies between them deserve consideration here because they all have consequences for education. Their first consequence is a passion for education itself, a passion which Calvinists sometimes have exaggerated to the status of legend but which is still warranted in considerable fact. To begin with the founder, John Calvin counted highest among all the roles he played that of "teacher in the church," and of the reforms he inspired in Geneva he deemed the new Academy (1559) as perhaps of greatest con-

---

1. For reasons of style and efficiency I am using "Calvinism" and the "Reformed tradition" (and variants on both) synonymously in this essay. This practice ignores some of the variety in the tradition and the key role of figures besides the Reformer of Geneva in its beginnings and enduring definition, but these factors do not seem vital to our purposes here.

sequence.[2] His branch of the Reformation started twelve new colleges or universities in Europe (five French, five Dutch, two British), most famously that in Leiden which received a school as the prize for outlasting the Spanish siege in 1574. A like proclivity appeared in British North America. Reformed denominations built five of the nine colleges founded there before the American Revolution and almost a third (65 of 207) of the colleges founded in the United States prior to the Civil War, far above their proportion of the American population.[3]

These institutions bear a family resemblance but also show significant variation; that is, they grew from a common core of theological commitments and social aspirations but have played out their internal tensions in different ways. For that reason, and also because this essay is written by a historian and not by a theologian, we can best proceed by reviewing the ideas in the Reformed tradition most salient for education, then examine three institutional cases which show the divergent paths or recombinations these impulses can take in practice.

The Theological Heritage

In years past commentators carried on something of a quest for *the* key teaching of Calvinism.[4] Those critical of the system often nominated predesti-

2. Quoted phrase is from the 1559 edition of Calvin's *Institutes*, 1.25, cited in T. M. Moore, "Some Observations Concerning the Educational Philosophy of John Calvin," *Westminster Theological Journal* 46 (Spring 1984): 140. On the Geneva Academy, see William J. Bouwsma, *John Calvin: A Sixteenth-Century Portrait* (New York: Oxford, 1988), p. 14; also John T. McNeill, *The History and Character of Calvinism* (New York: Oxford, 1954), pp. 191-196.

3. E. Digby Baltzell, *Puritan Boston and Quaker Philadelphia* (Boston: Beacon, 1979), p. 248. By another calculation, that of Donald Tewksbury, in 1850 "two-thirds of the colleges in the land were directly or indirectly under the control of the Presbyterian Church." Cited in Baltzell, *Puritan Boston and Quaker Philadelphia*, p. 248.

4. A review of this "search" is found in Alister E. McGrath, *A Life of John Calvin: A Study in the Shaping of Western Culture* (Oxford: Basil Blackwell, 1990), pp. 147-151; also in Susan E. Schreiner, *The Theater of His Glory: Nature and the Natural Order in the Thought of John Calvin* (Durham: Labyrinth Press, 1991), pp. 7, 8. The same is exemplified by H. Henry Meeter, *The Basic Ideas of Calvinism* (Grand Rapids: Baker, 1939), chapter 1. The overview of Reformed theology which follows is based upon these titles, especially that of Schreiner, which is most apt for the particular concerns of this piece; also upon the works of McNeill and Bouwsma cited above; and upon E. Harris Harbison, *The Christian Scholar in the Age of the Reformation* (New York: Scribner's, 1956), pp. 137-164; John H. Leith, *An Introduction to the Reformed Tradition* (Atlanta: John Knox, 1977); M. Eugene Osterhaven, *The Spirit of the Reformed Tradition* (Grand Rapids: Eerdmans, 1971); David F. Wells, ed.,

nation or total depravity for that honor, not least because these cast a putative insult to humanity over the system as a whole. Some defenders of Calvinism sought (however wisely) to fight on this ground, but others favored more positive principles such as divine sovereignty or holy activism. The quest as such might have been faulty, exaggerating the degree to which Calvin was systematic in the first place, but it is tempting, nonetheless, to locate a central defining principle, since an account of any school of thought must start somewhere. Without attempting to use it as a logical axiom, then, we might treat the concept of divine majesty or glory as the canopy under which Calvinism's various tenets may be clustered.

The Glory of God and Creation

"Majesty" suffused Calvin's references to God in his *Institutes* and biblical commentaries; it was also the image of kingship that the European monarchs of the time were assiduously cultivating. Calvin's God can thus be seen as the ultimate Renaissance prince, the most absolute of monarchs, bearing all power, honor, and rule — and more besides. For if the Sun King would claim *"l'etat c'est moi,"* Calvinists would put Yahweh's declaration of "I am" as *"etre c'est moi."* On this view everything comes from God and exists by God, yet not for its own sake but to refer back to God the more to magnify divine glory.

So pristine an end might wrap people up in sequestered mysticism but for its means, for in Reformed theology God ordained creation as the proper arena of human praise. In Calvin's own words, "God created the world . . . that it might be the theater of his glory."[5] The Reformed have often turned in this connection to the hymn to Christ in Colossians (1:15-17):

> He is the image of the invisible God, the firstborn over all creation. For by him all things were created: things in heaven and on earth, visible and invisible, whether thrones or powers or rulers or authorities; all things were created by him and for him. He is before all things and in him all things hold together.

Two points are of immense importance here for education. First, for Calvinists religion is not long a matter of inwardness. Jesus is not just a savior of

---

Reformed Theology in America: A History of Its Modern Development (Grand Rapids: Eerdmans, 1985); and the classic of Abraham Kuyper, *Lectures on Calvinism* (Grand Rapids: Eerdmans, 1961 [1898]).

5. Quoted in Schreiner, *Theater,* p. 5. The role of creation in Reformed theology is well explicated in Albert M. Wolters, *Creation Regained: Biblical Basics for a Reformed Worldview* (Grand Rapids: Eerdmans, 1985).

souls but a cosmic Lord, wanting his "crown rights" restored, so salvation does not take place only within but pushes the redeemed out into the world. This kind of Christianity has public purchase, expansive scope, from the start. Second, joining comprehensiveness to transcendence in this way makes education a high calling. Searching out every domain of being, plumbing its beauties and mystery, means no less than serving the Most High God with the due honor of delight, awe, and gratitude.

Sin and Common Grace

Calvinists are not known for basking in such bliss, however, but rather for their busy anxiety. The reason lies in creation's fall into corruption, centered on the human fall into sin. By this event both the object and the seeker of God's revelation became perverted and disordered. Nothing looks right anymore because nothing, simply, is right, and even if it were, no one could see it aright. Such is the colloquial meaning of the Reformed doctrines of sin and total depravity. No "higher" realm of being remains unaffected by corruption in the "lower" parts; reason and spirit in the human person are just as twisted as body and passion. This means that being as it is, life as it happens, and people as they are insult God instead of rendering honor. God's creatures have lost sight of their end: they lie instead of giving back a true reflection of their Maker's will, they hurt instead of finding and affording each other their due place.

This stance has mixed implications for education. Sin does not negate the mandate for learning but does engender a distrust *in the midst of* learning. Nothing can be taken as it seems to be "by nature," nor can innate human capacity — *any* human('s) capacity — for knowledge be finally relied upon. Learning among Calvinists thus becomes an edgy business, mandatory but tentative, yearning for a finality or purity it knows will not obtain this side of eternity.

Such a posture invites jokes about the scruples of guilt-ridden conscience, but in fact it is raising a warning against self-righteousness. The contrast Reformed people posit between divine perfection and human evil is so great as to tempt them to believe that their redemption puts them on God's plane and, consequently, in possession of a purity of life and knowledge that far surpasses, that finally trashes, the works and wisdom of "the world." Against such arrogance Calvinism teaches (even though Calvinists have not always remembered) that the redeemed never attain perfect righteousness on this earth, nor — by virtue of their salvation — any intellectual superiority to the "unregenerate."

Furthermore, owing to God's *common* grace, real virtue and knowledge live on among peoples who dwell outside his *special* saving grace. Just as all people have a religious sense that makes them seek a god, so they all have a "relic" of the original image of God that gives them a sense of justice and rectitude. Before the face of God, human nature is totally depraved, but on the face of the earth it is still competent to run life on a fairly respectable level.[6] To invoke Tertullian's terms, the Reformed Jerusalem thus will have considerable to do with Athens — also with Mecca and Benares, New York and St. Petersburg — searching out the gold from the dross, not least for purposes of learning how to discern the dross within its own gold.

Law and Redemption

Still, salvation counts for more than this call to humility alone would allow. Reformed thinkers have often argued that redemption does offer the faithful a package of intellectual advantages: a special revelation, namely, the Word of God in Christ and in Scripture, that corrects their vision so that they can start to see creation aright; the promptings of the Holy Spirit who is promised to lead into all truth; and a sense of the right paradigms, an apprehension by faith of the deep patterns of divine action which will prompt believers to at least ask the right questions.

A key distinction between Calvinism and other Protestant lines with respect to the law supplies vital material here. From the start Reformed theology did not treat the law simply as that proof of human insufficiency which goads people toward grace, nor just as that restraint on desire which makes civil society possible. Rather, the law has a more positive "third use." God's original creation ran according to law, God intended human society to run according to law, and God gave Old Testament Israel a special revelation of the law as proof of their mutual covenant love. And none of these intentions or operations are suspended by sin or superseded by salvation. Law may not be the means *to* salvation, but it is a means of grace *around* salvation — the fabric that holds all being in order, that still holds (however unseen) societies together, that constitutes Christians' "guide for grateful living," the ideal patterns for the life that they should work to restore.[7]

The educational implications of this construct are momentous, though they took some time to unfold. Calvin himself usually conceived of God as

6. Schreiner, *Theater,* cites the "relic" terminology on p. 94; cf. p. 72. The common grace theme was most thoroughly revived in Abraham Kuyper, *De Gemeene Gratie,* 3 vols. (Amsterdam: Hoeveker & Wormser, 1902-1904).

7. I. John Hesselink, *Calvin's Concept of the Law* (Allison Park, PA: Pickwick, 1992; originally University of Basel Ph.D. dissertation, 1961).

direct and dynamic, defined by will more than by reason and preferring to work by unmediated operations. At the same time Calvin recognized natural law and social institutions as secondary causes or modes by which God kept life from falling into chaos.[8] This emphasis grew among his heirs over the subsequent centuries. In coming to terms with the Scientific Revolution and the Enlightenment, Calvinists could take natural law as the will of God and rational exploration thereof as divine service by which even unbelievers inadvertently gave praise to the Master as upholder and sustainer of the world. The distortions wrought by sin in the observed and the observer tended to be minimized on this score, and Calvin's notion that cosmos and society no longer have the "inherent element of stability and order" with which they were created went toward the wall.[9] But this mental adaptability certainly encouraged education. The emerging sciences and explosion of learning in these centuries, to the considerable extent that they found or sought regularity in life, could register on Calvinist ears as a psalm of praise to be taught and sung. The Reformed thus were not only thrust out into the world but were confident they would find it intelligible.

At this point Calvinism's motive for learning became resolutely practical. If the original face of creation has been obscured, making delighted observation in the Lord's theater difficult, the standard of the law makes the corruptions of sin obvious, inviting their correction; furthermore, it makes the will of the Lord plain, compelling the redeemed to be the agents of that correction. Their notion of the law has made Calvinists knights of King Jesus or caretakers in the ruined temple, commissioned to scout out error or polish the mirrors of glory. They would use learning to harness the agonizing clash between divine intent and earthly woe, making education the bit and bridle by which to guide the world in the paths of righteousness. Schooling thus becomes both an invitation — no, a mandate — to action and the means by which to develop the leadership corps to direct that action in a sustained and coordinated manner.

Perhaps the famous Reformed stress on predestination makes most sense at this point; for however it functioned as an issue of controversy in theological speculation, the doctrine mattered existentially as an assurance amid persecution and chaos that the good order of God still held in the external realm, as did God's effectual calling to the elect to be agents of redemption. Education was worthwhile for the long run, whatever one's current commotion, because God had ordained that there would be a long run on a sure plan toward a safe destiny.

8. Schreiner, *Theater*, pp. 30-37.
9. Quotation from Schreiner, *Theater*, p. 3.

Order and Public Life

Indeed, the assurance of order may have played as central a role for Calvinists down through history as the assurance of pardon has for Lutherans. One line of biographers sees "a passion for order" as the mainspring in Calvin himself, as he reacted to the collapse of the medieval world.[10] Certainly this trait in his thought would carry over into that of his heirs. Calvin pictured the fall into sin not as changing the substance of the world so much as making it chaotic and confused. To him God's image in humanity consisted primarily in its "ordered soul" which sin had scrambled; sanctification amounted to the gradual restoration of the same, which would also better illumine the remaining order in creation.[11]

Calvinists therefore have perennially aspired to see — and restore — unity and harmony within the whole. They have thus shown strong proclivities for organic thinking which drive them, in educational terms, to rise above collecting piecemeal knowledge to grasp the big picture, to bring different domains together, and to try to fashion a whole person for a whole world.

Notable as the final fruit on this theological tree is the concern for the public domain as such. The restoration of order in nature the Reformed have deemed to be largely God's business, beyond the scope of their own contribution. The redemption of society is a different matter: it depends more directly on human agency and is all the more urgent because society shows less of the steadying regularity of divine constraints than does nature.[12] If sin from the outset radiated out of human perversity, so must restoration begin from human regeneration. If God's elect are called out of themselves into the society of the church, then the church is called as agent of renewal for all humanity.[13] If God spoke specially to Old Testament Israel in a law for their nation and bequeathed that example as special revelation to his New Testament people, then those people are mandated to institute its principles of justice and charity among themselves and among their neighbors so as to restore as much as possible God's will for earthly life. Calvinists, in short, feel called to be social and cultural leaders and therefore turn to education to teach that knowledge and wisdom, social and historical, theological and political, that are required to make leadership obedient to heaven and effective on earth.

For Calvinists this constitutes the supreme religious service, the true wor-

---

10. Schreiner summarizes this discussion in *Theater*, p. 3. Its best exemplification is Bouwsma, *John Calvin*, chapters 2, 3, and 5.

11. Schreiner, *Theater*, pp. 36, 72, 101, 106, 112.

12. Schreiner, *Theater*, pp. 110-112.

13. This theme is especially strong in Nicholas Wolterstorff's reflections upon the Reformed tradition, *Until Justice and Peace Embrace* (Grand Rapids: Eerdmans, 1983).

ship of God. To return to our beginning, God would have due honor and proven glory; He would have them by "reclaiming all of his creation: the cosmos, human nature, and society"; and He would have his elect lead the way in this project.[14] The divine saga thus becomes a huge conversion narrative, one that does not take the human soul as its end but as a means to a far more majestic destiny. Significantly, the key term in Calvin's own conversion account is "teachableness."[15] So also for God's calling to the church and the church's calling in the world: both are projects in education.

Applications

These theological convictions can be deployed and recombined in any number of ways, and a good number of them were tried in the various local circumstances in which Calvinism took root. We shall sketch here three different educational applications that are the most pertinent to the case studies in this volume: the model of Princeton, which is applicable to Whitworth College, the model of the Free University of Amsterdam, which shapes Calvin College, and the model of Harvard, which has influenced American education as a whole.

Harvard

Whether the Puritans of Massachusetts Bay intended their colony to be a city on a hill or a city of refuge is still in dispute, but in either case they had a fair chance of designing a society consistent with Reformed principles.[16] They also had the talent for the job in the 100-plus university graduates who were among them by 1640. In their transplantation these men were carrying on a dynamic that Michael Walzer argues drove Puritanism from the start: they were an elite of the Word, history's first cadre of "advanced" intellectuals determined to remake society according to an abstract ideal.[17] In the case of Massachusetts

14. Quotation from Schreiner, *Theater*, p. 111.

15. Bouwsma, *John Calvin*, pp. 10-11, 227. See also Richard R. Osmer, *A Teachable Spirit: Recovering the Teaching Office in the Church* (Louisville: Westminster/John Knox, 1990).

16. Perry Miller laid out the first option in the title essay of *Errand Into the Wilderness* (Cambridge, MA: Harvard University Press, 1956); T. Dwight Bozeman, *To Live Ancient Lives: The Primitivist Dimension in Puritanism* (Chapel Hill: University of North Carolina Press, 1988), argues the opposite. For a still different view, see Andrew Delbanco, *The Puritan Ordeal* (Cambridge, MA: Harvard University Press, 1989).

17. Michael Walzer, *The Revolution of the Saints* (Cambridge, MA: Harvard University Press, 1965).

Bay that ideal was righteousness coupled with unity. The collision between these two drove the plot, for which the college founded just six years after the colony itself provided a key setting.

The early organization of Harvard confirms the Calvinist passion for education, especially considering the 85 years it took Anglican Virginia and the 175 years it took the Quakers in Pennsylvania to do likewise. Harvard's mission was also predictable. The Reformed demand for a ministry able to handle Scripture and the body of Christian theology in the original languages lay behind the colony's famous injunction that the college "advance *learning* and perpetuate it to Posterity; dreading to leave an illiterate Ministry to the Churches, when our present Ministers shall lie in the dust." But Harvard was also to produce "masters for grammar schools and educated gentlemen for the magistracy."[18] Magistrate and schoolmaster, in fact, were taken as equally important as the minister for the right ordering of the commonwealth. Piety by itself was inadequate to that purpose, the Puritans thought; so also the state or bare politics; so also the school or mere knowledge. The three were to lean against each other to form a tripod capable of upholding the whole society. Harvard College's importance to the commonwealth thus lay in its being the site where future leaders in all offices would be nurtured together, disciplined by a curriculum that formed a common base for their subsequent specializations. The revelation of the minister, the experience of the magistrate, and the reason of the schoolmaster could be made to work together to display the full counsel of God if they were informed by common principles and practiced in a common conversation.

Harvard's curriculum hardly seemed a model of such unity, however. Students there encountered a scholastic emphasis upon philosophy, a Christian humanist regard for history and ancient languages, the Renaissance's retooled model of medieval rhetoric, and Petrus Ramus's alternative to Aristotelian logic. The mixture reflected the different layers of loyalty and purpose in Puritanism itself. It would cut through corrupt accumulations, it would honor the eternal standards of truth, it would overhaul society, it would maintain order, it would attend to the painstaking harvest of human experience, it would abandon all for the vision of God. The disparities were not fatal because the Puritans saw a deeper coherence lying beneath them. As Perry Miller put it, Massachusetts Bay believed in "the unity of all knowledge," "the divine authorship of every particle in it," and the perfect fit of the same into a "coherent

18. Samuel Eliot Morison, *The Founding of Harvard College* (Cambridge, MA: Harvard University Press, 1935), pp. 247, 250. My treatment of Harvard's history relies on this volume as well as Morison's *Three Centuries of Harvard, 1636-1936* (Cambridge, MA: Harvard University Press, 1936), and Perry Miller, *The New England Mind: The Seventeenth Century* (Boston: Beacon, 1961 [1939]).

organon."[19] All true knowledge conformed to a pre-existing pattern because that pattern lay as the foundation of all being. The pattern was suffused with divine purpose and prescribed all human duty. It also prescribed a model of society as integrated as that of science. The Puritans would be a holy *commonwealth*, founded by covenant, suppressing dissent, and confirmed in town meetings where unanimity was the goal. Their organicism grew out of the thick kinship networks that crisscrossed the New England countryside and out of the shared public norms that suffused the region's culture. These norms were taught in an educational system that the rank and file would support because it held all classes accountable to a set of transcendent standards. In short, Harvard was a public school for a public order.[20]

Long after its original theological dye had faded, the impress of this Puritan stamp remained. That much is clear from E. Digby Baltzell's comparison of *Puritan Boston and Quaker Philadelphia,* especially with regard to the different sorts of intellectual work that the two cities favored. Puritans wrote systematic theology, history, and political theory; Quakers published personal journals. Eighteenth-century Boston majored in law, Philadelphia in medicine. When nineteenth-century Philadelphia became a byword for law, it was the law of "the bar" — cunning advocacy of a particular case. Boston's law remained of "the bench," a line of juridical theory spooled out from James Kent to Joseph Story to Oliver Wendell Holmes, Jr. Harvard set its mainsail to the humanities, Penn to the sciences; but here too, Philadelphia's science was nominalistic — cataloguing, experimenting, observing in the life sciences — while Harvard's was realistic, working at theoretical physics.

In sum, New England aimed at architectonic knowledge, designing big systems that could be communicated by a trained leadership to a unified community. Philadelphians worked piecemeal, seeking incremental additions to personal happiness. Ben Franklin truly was that city's avatar, and the opening lines of Jefferson's Declaration were well suited to their first Philadelphia audience. The Quakers' goal was the pursuit of happiness; Puritan happiness came by the pursuit of goals.

In short, the Puritans' deepest lesson trumped their original intention: the quest for unity undid the demands for godliness. In New England at large divergent convictions required room for dissent; at Harvard in particular, the rise of the new science seemed to marginalize theological demands with respect to both epistemological foundations and social applications. "The basis of moral authority," concludes one study of Harvard at the mid-eighteenth century, "shifted slowly to 'reason' and 'nature' from Scripture and

19. Miller, *New England Mind,* p. 176.
20. My presentation in this and the following paragraph relies on Baltzell, *Puritan Boston and Quaker Philadelphia,* chs. 6-9, 14, 17.

revelation."[21] That makes all the more remarkable the simultaneous emergence of a new strategy of Christianization at Harvard's institutional grandchild, the College of New Jersey at Princeton.

Princeton

The evangelical Presbyterians and transplanted New Englanders who founded this college did not have the burden of trying to steer a whole society from the top. Rather theirs was a network of the likeminded, spread across the colonies and eager for a new supply of ministers to sustain the recent revival of religion that historians call the Great Awakening. Their dream was no sooner institutionalized than it broadened, partly from the accidents of time and Princeton's strategic location, partly because Presbyterianism proved a true heir to the Calvinist desire for public sway. Under the leadership of John Witherspoon, imported to its presidency from Scotland in 1768, Princeton became a — arguably *the* — breeding ground of revolutionary political leadership. It also defined the Christian Enlightenment. By these strokes Princeton claimed science and society in the name of Christ at the very time that Harvard found it impossible to do so.[22]

This feat turned upon a single premise, a magnification of the law side of the Reformed tradition to the near eclipse of its teachings about grace. God had instituted laws for nature and for the nations, Witherspoon enjoined, and it was the calling of Christian minds to find and "improve" these. To be sure, both sets of law were authorized by Scripture and had a transcendent source and meaning, but for practical purposes one worked with them by the rational observation of empirical phenomena. Christian belief as such would have no impact upon that observation or its secular prescriptions, even though enlarging knowledge promised such remarkable improvements in human life as to comprise a signal service to God.

Thus Princeton met the Enlightenment by baptizing it — at least the moderate, "didactic" type of Enlightenment that Witherspoon brought along from Scotland.[23] Its Common Sense philosophy held that knowledge was innocent of any bias or framing functions, that human modes of understanding were

---

21. Norman Fiering, *Moral Philosophy at Seventeenth Century Harvard* (Chapel Hill: University of North Carolina Press, 1981), p. 62.

22. My tour of Princeton's history follows Mark A. Noll, *Princeton and the Republic, 1768-1822* (Princeton: Princeton University Press, 1989) and borrows in part from my review essay, "Christian Ideals and Democratic Faith," *Books & Religion* 17/2 (Summer 1990), pp. 9, 35.

23. Henry F. May, *The Enlightenment in America* (New York: Oxford, 1976), pp. 307-362.

tailor-made for the world as it is, and that simple induction from empirical observation would merit universal rational assent. It hoped to build social ethics upon an innate moral sense into a science analogous to Newton's physics. It thought that education could so imbue this rationality and morality as to produce upright behavior without necessity of spiritual regeneration. Finally, it anticipated broad benefit from its formulas so long as society stayed in the hands of a rational, restrained elite dedicated to the national weal.

Just that circumstance appeared providentially appointed in the growing American resistance to, then revolution against British "tyranny." Witherspoon devoted more of his time to politics than to his presidency and became the only clergyman — and academic — to sign the Declaration of Independence. Liberty *and* order, new nation *and* eternal verities, reason *and* faith: in its first generations Princeton felt no need of hard choices. And so a college founded in evangelical Calvinism could operate educationally without much reference to sin, salvation, or revelation.[24]

This faultline was exposed when the night of national emergency lifted. Witherspoon's successor, Samuel Stanhope Smith, was presiding when the earthquake hit; all the more cruelly, he was enacting what Witherspoon had merely proposed. Smith did not just call for but produced scholarship, and was criticized — with some justice — for not mediating science with Scripture. He produced civic leaders, and heard complaints about a dearth of ministers. He put on the role of elegant gentleman, and his critics sighed for Witherspoon's common touch.

But above all he fell to events that betrayed Princeton's key assumptions. If education, not regeneration, fostered right behavior, why did the students riot in 1807, closing down the school? If cultivated leadership promised national success, why did the election of the educated Jefferson spell doom, as Princeton swore it did, for a righteous nation? Tellingly, Smith left office in 1812, the same year that Princeton B.A. James Madison led the nation into a war that the college's Federalists deemed a calamity. With that, "the organic union of political and religious aspirations" that revolutionary Princeton embodied began to unravel.[25] "Religion" went to the seminary founded next door that year; "politics" would stay at the college on a more secular basis.

Yet the model of the earlier Princeton would long endure along the rolling frontier of EuroAmerican expansion, where "civilization" needed to be built up on the basis of school and store, courthouse and church. (The story of Whitworth College that follows exemplifies this pattern, not least for the similarities between its founder, George Whitworth, and John Witherspoon.) The model was often carried by graduates of Princeton Seminary, an institu-

24. Noll, *Princeton*, especially chapters 3 and 10.
25. Noll, *Princeton*, p. 243.

tion that not only excelled all others in producing educated local community leaders in the nineteenth century, but that also held on longest to Scottish Common Sense philosophy and the identity of rational with religious ethics. Wherever society was less segmented, wherever culture, decency, and Christianity seemed mutually dependent or synonymous, there the Princeton model of the righteous and rational republic would reappear — only to be tested in time again as the ligaments between these loyalties stretched and snapped.

The model might be said to have met its terminal test in the last third of the nineteenth century when three challenges afflicted it at once. Darwinism cast doubt on its rational-religious synthesis; Romantic or Idealist epistemologies undermined its Realism; and immigration and urbanization overwhelmed its British individualist sociology. Put in other terms, Princeton's rationalist voluntarism had for a century and a quarter overcome Harvard's homogeneity but had still posited universals to get a purchase on public order. The need now was to establish such purchase in full view of social and intellectual-religious pluralism. That need was addressed by some unlikely people in another country.

The Free University of Amsterdam

The German poet Heinrich Heine once said that when the world ended he hoped to be in the Netherlands because everything happens there 50 years later. For Dutch society in 1880 this was true: industrialization was just underway. But in high culture, the opposite was true: by comparison to the United States, secularization was well advanced. Dutch Calvinists had responded in one of three ways: by claiming that religion involved ethics, not intellect, so that secularism did not matter; by hunkering down in sectarian clusters, giving up claims to public life; or by identifying God with country and working to roll back pluralism. The genius of the Free University founded that year in Amsterdam was to reject all these solutions and to craft a new one. More accurately, this was the genius of Abraham Kuyper (1837-1920), leader of the Neo-Calvinist movement that lay behind the university.[26]

Kuyper had been raised in a manse of the national Reformed Church, an heir to its establishmentarian heritage. But his contempt for its fatigue —

---

26. The most thorough contextualization of Kuyper's emergence and proposals is Dirk Th. Kuiper, *De Voormannen: Een Sociaal-Wetenschappelijke Studie over Ideologie, Konflikt en Kerngroepvorming binnen de Gereformeerde Wereld in Nederland tussen 1820 en 1930* (Meppel: Boom, 1972). The most concise overview in English is James D. Bratt, *Dutch Calvinism in Modern America: A History of a Conservative Subculture* (Grand Rapids: Eerdmans, 1984), ch. 2.

expressed first in his dalliance with theological liberalism, then in conversion back to a stricter orthodoxy than ever — together with the start of industrialization prompted him to discard that model and propose a twofold pluralism instead. Socially, he would free people from the old unitary hierarchy to live according to their more natural group loyalties. Intellectually, he rejected the pretensions of objectivity and legitimated different groups seeing the world in different ways. These differences Kuyper attributed sometimes to class or ethnicity but usually to religion (secular postures and ideologies being understood as replacement religions). Kuyper thus envisioned a world in which people of different confessions would live in institutionally complete and social-psychologically discrete "pillars," as the Dutch labelled them. Each could make proportionally equitable claims upon public space, but none might coerce another. Each might try to persuade the others of its own merits, but everyone would recognize the particularist provenance of this, and any other, advocacy.[27]

The Free University was founded to be the school of the Reformed pillar. As such it had two principal functions. It was to train leaders to take the group's claims into the public arena, there to negotiate, repel, or sustain as need be. It was also to develop or unfold the implications of Reformed confessional commitments across the curriculum. Since this was the distinctive claim of the Free University and its institutional heirs (see the study of Calvin College that follows), the premises of this position require some attention.

First, Kuyper and his followers down to the present have been truly Calvinist in saying that all the world belongs to God. Thus, not just theology and philosophy but *all* the academic disciplines — being but reflection upon the different domains of creation — are part of *Christian* education. Second, Kuyperians insist that perception and cognition are never value-free but rooted in, shaped and colored by, one's worldview. Worldview, in turn, is built upon what Kuyper called one's "life-principle" which is simply the existential engine of one's (unavoidable) religious commitment. Therefore, the work Christians do in the context of an academic discipline might well differ from that done there by people of other commitments. (Hard-core Kuyperians would insist that it *must* differ.) At the same time academic work is truly a Christian vocation, of equal (the adamant would imply "superior") merit to the pastoral or evangelistic roles the church customarily esteems.

This formula could be most attractive, particularly among the sectarian, economically straitened clientele to whom Kuyper appealed. They recovered

27. The previous paragraph and those that follow draw upon my expanded treatment of the Free University heritage: " 'Big Ideas, Little People': Theological Education in the Dutch Neo-Calvinist Tradition," in D. G. Hart, ed., *Theological Education in the Evangelical Tradition* (forthcoming).

education as a holy calling and creation as God's domain. They could reclaim a public role, yet maintain their separate identity. They could grasp the brass ring of status mobility, yet devote all their ambitions to the Lord. With Princeton, Amsterdam could talk law and reason, yet take grace and revelation as fundamental, comprehend divergent points of view, and win space for its own constructions. With Harvard, the Free University could speak of and to a whole people, but a people defined by voluntary commitment rather than by coercion or accommodationism.

In America, Kuyper's descendants could offer a standard of Christian higher education that, by their estimate of the more familiar models, moved from the periphery to the core of the enterprise. Not required chapel or Bible courses, not opportunities for extracurricular "service," not the cultivation of "character" or "citizenship," not the baptism of middle-class decency with Christian rhetoric or the frosting of Christian conviction with cultural refinement, not the promotion of piety alongside of scholarship or professional preparation; but the classroom as a chapel, scholarship as devotion, Christianity at the base of the curriculum and suffusing all studies, the norms of faith guiding professional development — *that* was the essence of Christian education, honoring the integrity of learning and the faith alike and promoting their genuine integration.

This model, with all its virtues, depended on one key element, namely, Calvinism's old commitment to the organic. Epistemologically, Kuyperians posited a golden chain from commitment to principle to worldview to elaboration and conclusion, with integrality and control guaranteed all the way down. Sociologically, Dutch Neo-Calvinism was at least as tribal as Massachusetts Bay; "pillarization" demanded it. This stance guaranteed the predictable sins of witch-hunting and self-righteousness, but it lay open to more subtle challenges as well. What happened when distinctive premises did not lead on to distinctive conclusions? When the Calvinist professoriate seemed more defined by profession than by confession? A particular difficulty in the Free University heritage has been distinguishing the epistemology from the sociology, the contributions — and limitations — of worldview from those of the network. Thus worldview has not only been underpredictive of conclusions but susceptible to dilution out of democratic and multicultural concerns.

But the greatest challenge of all, not to the Kuyperian model alone but to any venture in Reformed higher education, may be the erosion of organicism or integrality as such. The Free University cut its teeth a century ago on secularism, but it did not anticipate secularization arriving at the complete fragmentation it has achieved today. Kuyper's proposal that worldview compete with worldview does not avail when worldview has given way to lifestyle, conviction to preference, the schoolmaster to MTV.

To put it in terms of Massachusetts Bay, Harvard cannot thrive when the whole nation has become Philadelphia: piecemeal and materialist, antinomian and erratic, therapeutic and medicinal. Christianity can survive by spooling out theology by the week and by "ministering" to people's hurts and needs. Education can proceed by enhancing technical skills and personal sensitivity. But Reformed education cannot feel faithful unless it is aiming to see the world whole, and holy, once again. Transcendent standards fostering coherent knowledge and personal *dis*content — that Reformed trinity is unwelcome on the current scene, perhaps more than ever. Then again, perhaps not. Calvinists know their salvation only out of the depths of their sin, so they have ever entered the world knowing it to be a lost but goodly place that God would bless, even through efforts like their own.

Piety and Progress:
A History of Calvin College

James D. Bratt
and Ronald A. Wells

On 18 February 1876 the Rev. Gerrit E. Boer formally opened the institution from which Calvin College would be born, the theological school of the True Dutch Reformed Church at Grand Rapids, Michigan. The occasion presented Boer with ample challenges. His class of seven students featured varying ages and levels of academic preparation. He faced competition and distraction from noises within and without: from within, because his classroom occupied the second floor (the "upper room" it was soon called) above the parochial grade school sponsored by Boer's 1,300-member congregation; from without, because the building stood hard by Grand Rapids's main railroad yards, lending his instruction the accompaniment of switch engines rumbling, shrieking, and clanging about.

But Boer's most daunting challenge doubtless lay in the 17-subject curriculum he had to teach entirely on his own. The list included typical seminary subjects — isogogics and exegetics, dogmatics and hermeneutics — but also a compressed combination of high school and college courses, the most notable of which were the languages that his farm-boys and shop-hands were expected to master: German, Latin, Greek, and Hebrew.[1]

Nearly a quarter century would pass before Calvin College emerged as an

1. John J. Timmerman, *Promises to Keep: A Centennial History of Calvin College* (Grand Rapids: Eerdmans, 1975), pp. 13-18. Timmerman's is the most accessible of the college's histories, but we rely as well on Henry J. Ryskamp, "The History of Calvin College and Seminary" (unpublished MS in Calvin College and Seminary archives [1967]) upon which Timmerman often depended and which contains much additional information. Another valuable study is George Stob, "The Christian Reformed Church and Her Schools" (hereafter "CRC Schools"; unpublished Th.D. dissertation, Princeton Theological Seminary, 1955), chs. 8-13.

institution in its own right, and 20 years more before it would be granting baccalaureate degrees. The seminary spun off a college preparatory "Literary Department" in 1900; this developed into a two-year junior college by 1906 and a full four-year college in 1920. But most of the salient features of the college's history were present in that upper room in 1876.

The college, first and foremost, belonged to a church, whose name — True, Dutch, and Reformed — testified to its sectarian tenacity, its ethnic identity, and its comprehensive theology. The denomination was born in 1857 among recent Dutch immigrants to western Michigan as a breakaway from the Reformed Church in America (RCA), an institution dating back to colonial New Netherlands. The split was legitimated on grounds of orthodoxy, as a "return to the standpoint of the fathers." This standpoint had been asserted once before, and in these same words, already back in the Netherlands in the 1834 "Secession" *(Afscheiding)* of dozens of congregations from that country's established church. Since Seceders were present not only among the True Reformed but equally among the RCA loyalists in 1857, Calvin College's forebears might be said to qualify as sectarians twice over, a remnant within a remnant, a posture not usually associated with broad and generous liberal arts education.[2]

That form has often held true. Calvin's professors from Boer's time onward have had to deal with suspicions, complaints, and charges of heresy on issues ranging from the fundamental to the trivial. More difficult still for an *academic* institution, the complaints have involved behavior as well as ideas, or behavior as sure token of ideas, with faculty and students being held to strict tests on both. In the earliest instances Boer was called to account for speaking at the funeral of an RCA minister, while the school's first professor with a doctorate, Geerhardus Vos, was harassed for teaching the minority, supralapsarian position on divine election.[3] In years ahead the regulation of student conduct particularly with respect to movie attendance would be the greatest burden the faculty felt, and their greatest shortcoming in the eyes of ecclesiastical monitors. In short, the sectarian tradition placed tight constraints on educational maneuvering. For disruptive "noises within," Boer's heirs might have preferred the commotion of schoolchildren.

If the True (after 1890, "Christian") Reformed had the soul of a sect, however, they had the memory of a national church. The "standpoint" which they upheld was that of the Synod of Dort, an international gathering of no

---

2. For the denomination's history, see James D. Bratt, *Dutch Calvinism in Modern America: A History of a Conservative Subculture* (Grand Rapids: Eerdmans, 1984), pp. 3-13, 37-40; and more thoroughly, Diedrich H. Kromminga, *The Christian Reformed Tradition: From the Reformation to the Present* (Grand Rapids: Eerdmans, 1943).

3. Stob, "CRC Schools," pp. 191-193, 213-217.

mean talent, and Dort meant not only five-point Calvinism but a polity that made the church custodian and critic of national culture. To fulfill this role pastors needed to be educated in the liberal arts; to faithfully exegete Scripture and propound Reformed theology, they had to know the biblical and scholarly languages. Hence Rev. Boer's comprehensive and language-heavy curriculum. Christian Reformed laymen and women before 1900 might not have been well educated themselves but they insisted that their pastors be. Orthodoxy demanded it.

Their cultural mandate gained great vigor under the Neo-Calvinist movement that arose in the Netherlands after 1870 under the leadership of Abraham Kuyper.[4] Kuyper's career was inspiration enough for the most ambitious youth: conversant in many disciplines, a writer of near infinite capacities, an institution-founder par excellence, he served successively as pastor, politician, professor, and eventually prime minister of the Netherlands. More inspiring still was the mission he gave his followers, to renew Dutch society and culture by dint of their Calvinistic critique and constructions. Indeed, Kuyper opened the whole world for Christian participation; as his most famous dictum put it: "There is not a square inch on the whole plain of human existence over which Christ, who is Lord over all, does not proclaim: 'This is Mine!' "[5] Notably, this statement came in an address (1880) opening the Neo-Calvinists' new Free University, which Kuyper founded to develop leadership for his movement and which he placed in Amsterdam, the nation's capital.

"Kuyperianism," then, meant broad and fresh cultural engagement — windows open to the world. But it also meant persistent argument, sometimes a shouting match, through those windows. Kuyper wanted to take on the reigning mentalities of modern culture at the level of fundamental principle. He demanded that Christians build a comprehensive worldview and pit it in full battle against those of secularism, humanism, and naturalism. Appropriately for a modern anti-modernist, Kuyper left a double legacy. Some of his followers, the "Positive" Calvinists, listened most to his lessons on "common grace," the heritage of divine blessing that allowed people of all faiths and none to achieve moral and intellectual good. On that basis Christians were to seek out and harvest all the world's treasures, redeeming them to the glory of God. But others — we might call them "Antithetical" Calvinists — harkened more to Kuyper's insistence that an "antithesis" lay between the fundamental commitments of the regenerate and the worldly, that Christians ought therefore to go their own way in all things and stay

4. For the most convenient English-language overview of Kuyper, see Bratt, *Dutch Calvinism,* pp. 14-33, and the annotated bibliography, pp. 313-314.
5. Abraham Kuyper, "Souvereiniteit in Eigen Kring" (Amsterdam: Kruyt, 1880), p. 32.

critical of opposing systems.[6] Bringing together all these camps, the two sorts of Neo-Calvinists as well as the pietist Seceders, thus added to the noise within Calvin College but also endowed it with a truly creative tension. The tensions were kept in harness by the "noise without," by the clamoring engines of modernity that Boer heard literally and his descendants figuratively. Some at Calvin would try to sort these out, others to drown them out; and a few hoped to take the throttle. But no one could ignore the traffic. The world without fixed the college within.

All this noise should not obscure some of the plainer virtues in the upper room that proved essential to the college's character. First of all, the enterprise has exacted enormous labor from all involved, especially from the faculty. Rev. Boer not only had to teach his 17 subjects but pastor a huge congregation and edit the denomination's magazine. The students caught their share of the load, too; the one item besides its solid curriculum and Christian stance that has regularly won notice from outside observers has been the work ethic, the seriousness of Calvin's students.

Second, almost any student who has felt the call to take on these labors has been permitted to try. Calvin's admissions policy has been as anti-elitist as its curricular standards have been rigorous. These traits together bespeak an egalitarian culture, the fairer fruit of the sectarian tree. From the start and well past World War II, Calvin was known among the Christian Reformed as "our school"; it was the product and pride of a community. Every plausible candidate from that community was entitled to attend but then held to tough measure. Every faculty member was susceptible to a draft for additional, extramural labors. Every member of the denomination was taxed (by the denomination's quota system) the same amount to support the college, and every college-aged person was expected to give Calvin serious — in many cases, sole — consideration.

Calvin's history cannot be understood apart from the benefits and constraints that come with a communal sociology; nor can its philosophical hallmark, Christian worldview construction and teaching within those parameters, be understood apart from the cycle of reinforcement it gave and received from communal solidarity.

The history of the college proper divides into four eras, each of which recast, yet also recycled, these themes. Between 1894 and 1920 the school slowly emerged from the shadow of the seminary with glimpses of bright promise for the future. From 1920 to 1945 that promise was tested by the cultural upheaval, economic depression, and wartime constraints of the outside world.

6. Bratt, *Dutch Calvinism*, pp. 18-20, 50-54; Henry Zwaanstra, *Reformed Thought and Experience in a New World: A Study of the Christian Reformed Church and Its American Environment, 1890-1918* (Kampen: Kok, 1973), pp. 95-131.

Between 1945 and 1970 the college passed through two enormous expansions, a campus relocation, and a curricular overhaul, but all within its traditional parameters of vision and constituency. Since 1970 the communal walls have become notably more porous. Calvin's vision has attracted considerable outside attention, while its own house and supporting community now register far more external influences than ever before.

The Early Years

The movement toward a separate college began in 1894 when the CRC Synod first authorized the admission of other than pre-seminarians into the preparatory program.[7] But such students started to enroll in number only after 1900 when new curricular paths ("classical" and "scientific") were installed along with the faculty to teach them. Three of these faculty would define the college for years to come. Albertus Rooks served as principal of the Literary Department and as dean of the college from his appointment in 1894 until his retirement in 1941. He knew his constituency well and offered the calm practicality necessary to win their trust. Jacob G. Vanden Bosch presided over the English department from 1900 to 1945 from a pedestal of Victorian values that made literature safe for the college. But it was Barend Klaas Kuiper, the college's first history professor, who gave the most public direction.

Kuiper began his turbulent career on a high note in 1903 by writing a booklet to mobilize CRC support for a college of its own.[8] His tract sounded all the Kuyperian themes. He had grand visions of institution building. He insisted that no existing school (including, by name and at length, the RCA's Hope College) taught that thoroughgoing Calvinism which alone was adequate to stem the cultural tides of unbelief. But he then added another note, congruent with Vanden Bosch's gentility and long to endure even, perhaps especially, in the "progressive" circle on campus. He insisted that the CRC needed a college also to rescue "our people" from the materialism they had learned all too well from their immigrant struggles and from the models of success that America offered. The physical was a necessary but lower realm, Kuiper intoned; the spiritual was higher and led on to better ends, i.e., a cultivation of "culture" in its own right, and the development of that wisdom

7. This era is covered in Timmerman, *Promises,* ch. 2; Stob, "CRC Schools," ch. 10; Ryskamp, "History," chs. 4-9; and by a principal architect-observer, Albertus J. Rooks, in "A History of Calvin College 1894-1926," *Semi-Centennial Volume: Theological School and Calvin College, 1876-1926* (Grand Rapids: Semi-Centennial Committee, 1926), pp. 49-90.

8. B[arend K.] Kuiper, *The Proposed Calvinistic College at Grand Rapids* (Grand Rapids: Sevensma, 1903).

which the church and nation so desperately needed. Calvin graduates should enter America to save the nation from its worst instincts; perhaps they might enter its more polished precincts at greater ease.

The voice of Seceder piety did not agree. Jacob Vanden Bosch noted that the college had grown precisely on a parallel cultural track with the CRC's Christian day-school movement, the former providing teachers for the latter and the two together rising along with Dutch-American social standing on the one hand and over against the secularization of the public schools on the other. Prosperity and impiety, perversely, would be the making of the college — but only if kept "out there." The need for a safe place to send their children was the one consistent note in all apologias for the fledgling school. Such a sanctuary would save "our youth" for the faith, train leaders for the church, and allow the group to glean just the untainted fruit from the American horn of plenty.[9]

These two visions clashed at the dawn of Calvin's next era. The immediate source of the conflict lay in World War I, a cause that the Positive Calvinists had championed but which turned into a trauma of forced acculturation for the CRC.[10] Now the set-upon took revenge, ousting the leading progressive from the Calvin Seminary faculty and giving the college's new president, the Rev. J. J. Hiemenga, a cold shower of suspicion. Barely had the first graduating class of the full four-year college marched across the stage in 1921 than the complaint was sounded across the denomination: Had Calvin lost its distinctiveness? Was it not emphasizing physical plant over principle, pursuing worldly eminence instead of simple faithfulness? The plaintiffs' evidence ran from the Glee Club's programming Catholic songs to the pride everyone took in the sparkling new (1917) campus. The watchdogs also sniffed at the words of Hiemenga himself. The president wanted Calvin to rate as "one of the most efficient . . . complete . . . [and] thorough" colleges in the land, "able to compete with any institution of its kind. . . . [Its] policy must be to compete and surpass, not to knock and criticize."[11] Hiemenga added that the school should maintain its "uniqueness" by standing on "the principles of Calvinism," but his hearers thought his heart lay more with the former than with the latter sentiments. He brought to office a go-getter spirit that irked the faculty and

9. Jacob Vanden Bosch, "The School and Christian Education" in *Semi-Centennial Volume*, pp. 147-148. See also Louis Berkhof, "Our School's Reason for Existence and the Preservation Thereof," in *Semi-Centennial Volume*, pp. 127-129.

10. The war and its aftermath are covered in Bratt, *Dutch Calvinism*, pp. 83-104. On the controversy discussed in this paragraph, see Stob, "CRC Schools," pp. 351-370; and Timmerman, *Promises*, pp. 46-52.

11. Quotations from John J. Hiemenga, "Our Own Calvin," *Calvin Annual, 1920* (Grand Rapids: Calvin College, 1920), p. 30. Hiemenga's larger statement of purpose appears in "A Proposed Educational Program," *Banner* 54 (November 13, 1919): 711.

launched a campaign for a $1 million endowment that left the constituency cold. When only $90,000 of new money came in, Hiemenga went back to the pastorate in 1925.

The Christian Reformed were not being tight, only scared. Having been force-marched into American life, they were determined to maintain some sort of distance from the world. They accomplished this through the synodical excision of three forms of heresy in the early 1920s and through the synodical prohibition of three forms of worldly amusements in 1928.[12] In other words Calvin College had the ill fate — or Providence — to be launched simultaneously with the 1920s' moral revolution. Well past that decade its students would be closely monitored for signs of "flaming youth." The faculty were drafted to be enforcers, and the movies (one of the fatalities of 1928) were made the moral boundary. No issue provoked more student dissent, constituent worry, or faculty fatigue from 1920 to 1965 than the prohibition on movie attendance. And no one paid a higher price than B. K. Kuiper, who lost his faculty position in 1928 for apologizing with too many words and too little contrition for having gone to shows.[13]

Under pietist winds the college hugged the shore. Its students were taught solid skills, basic science, and the Western classics under the careful guidance of careful teachers. Their time outside of class divided between working for room and board and participating in the myriad clubs that functioned like nineteenth-century college literary societies — enhancing student initiative, intensive research, public rhetoric, and cultural breadth. Little time went into intercollegiate athletics. The faculty grudgingly permitted a basketball team in 1920 but drew the line at football and fraternities. Calvin would never have either. The graduates of this era went out into the world — or more often, back into the denominational loop — as decent professionals and respectable citizens, stronger on ethical probity than stirring vision.[14]

In the area of curriculum, Calvin's main additions in this era occurred in the natural sciences. Yet the three key faculty appointments came elsewhere and provided whatever boldness of leadership the college had. Henry J. Ryskamp joined the faculty in 1918 as its first bona fide social scientist; he replaced Rooks as dean in 1941 and proved his prowess by flourishing despite a reputation for liberal politics. Seymour Swets, founder of the music program in 1923, won Calvin more respect from more people than did anyone else through his public direction of high classical repertoire. But the most momentous appointment was that of William Harry Jellema in 1921. The philosophy department that he founded won Calvin a national academic reputation and

12. Bratt, *Dutch Calvinism,* pp. 93-119.
13. Stob, "CRC Schools," pp. 370-381; Timmerman, *Promises,* pp. 37-38.
14. Ryskamp, "History," pp. 116-132; Timmerman, *Promises,* pp. 61-66, 76.

produced its first figures of international renown. Jellema himself introduced hundreds of students from other disciplines to the exhilaration of good Socratic method, to the possibility that truth was not a catechism to be memorized but a challenge to be sought out and humbly served.[15]

If this was stimulating to students, it was worrisome to critics. As Professor of Classics, Ralph Stob had found Jellema's Christianity too close to Greek Idealism; made president in 1933, he encouraged Jellema's departure for Indiana University in 1936. But Stob's repetition of the rhetoric of distinctive Calvinism did not assure the pious that its substance was in place. Stob went back to Greek in 1939, leaving the way open for an extraordinary Board of Trustees inquisition into faculty instruction and student behavior. The former yielded up their syllabi for examination, the latter signed pledge cards promising conformity, the Board deliberated to its satisfaction.[16] Then all parties joined to watch the world descend into war.

From World War II to the 1960s

World War II knocked Calvin's enrollment back almost 20 percent, from 520 in 1941 to 420 in 1944. The slump triggered memories of the Depression-era trough (340 in 1933), but the reality never got that bad. Rather, Calvin soared with the postwar education boom into a new epoch in its history. Enrollment tripled in two years, from 420 in 1944 to 1,245 in 1946, and rose steadily thereafter to peak at 3,575 in 1968.[17] This expansion bespoke some fundamental changes but also hid some remarkable continuities and required a combination of daring and sense of tradition that was personified by William Spoelhof. His presidency (1951-1976) more than any other shaped the character and destiny of the college.

Most notable among the continuities would be the ethnoreligious composition of the student body: 90 percent would still be coming from Christian Reformed congregations in 1970, at which date the CRC remained heavily

15. Bratt, *Dutch Calvinism,* pp. 150-151; Timmerman, *Promises,* pp. 64, 81-82; Ryskamp, "History," pp. 142-143, 176-178, 327-328. Some indication of Jellema's impact in particular and the college's in general is evident in the reflections of Alvin Plantinga and Nicholas Wolterstorff in Kelly J. Clark, ed., *Philosophers Who Believe: The Spiritual Journey of Eleven Leading Thinkers* (Downers Grove: InterVarsity Press, 1993), pp. 50-59, 268-271. Notably, Frederick Manfred, one of the "renegade" novelists Calvin produced in this era, dedicated his barely fictionalized memoir of the place to Jellema (Feike Feikema, *The Primitive* [Garden City: Doubleday, 1949]).

16. Ryskamp, "History," pp. 158-159, 174-188; Stob, "CRC Schools," pp. 392-394; Timmerman, *Promises,* pp. 80-87.

17. Ryskamp, "History," p. 191; Timmerman, *Promises,* pp. 92, 161.

Dutch in ethnic background and permitted but modest latitude in doctrine and liturgy. As for the faculty, all 200 of them would still belong to the CRC and send their children to Christian schools as custom and contract required. On the side of change, the most obvious were a new campus and a new curriculum, but the more momentous probably lay in new expectations on either side of the podium. College education became less an entree into than a privilege of middle-class status for Calvin students in this period, while the Ph.D. changed from being a distant goal to being a terminal expectation on the part of faculty.

The first scene in this act, however, featured a new round in the old debate over the purpose and character of Christian college education. From his experience as Calvin's wartime president, Henry Schultze worried about the technical, pragmatic emphases that would come with governmental aid to education, but the war veteran and new faculty star, Henry Zylstra of the English department, thought the threat lay closer to home. It was Christian Reformed people themselves who hungered for the practical, who would indulge a prettified version of mass culture, who wished to join good pay with inner piety and call it a Christian life. B. K. Kuiper's old charge of sanctified materialism was here reborn, and so were both his solutions. On the one hand Zylstra sounded the themes of integrative Calvinism, of world- and life-views lending coherence to education, substance to religion, and glory to God. On the other hand he pitched the contest as mind over nature, art over technique, and elite over popular culture. Not that he endorsed high culture as such; no, every work was to be scrutinized for its motive-mind and tested by Christian measure. But the works worth the scrutiny were the classics. In wrestling with these, students would develop a worthier Christianity than Seceder squeamishness and a worthier mind than pop sentimentality. Zylstra's targets, the pious tract and pulp fiction, he deemed to be soul mates. So also his icons, Christianity and "mind." Kuyperianism and Idealism embraced.[18]

The monitors out in the denomination had nothing against good taste but they did worry about entangling alliances. The one they first suspected was political, namely, the protest of a dozen Calvin faculty members against the denominational magazine's endorsement of Red-baiting and, implicitly (the year was 1951), McCarthyism. The paper's editor, the Rev. Henry J. Kuiper, had led the attack on the college in 1921, had pushed the investigation of 1939, and now once more had the pleasure of exacting a penitent apology from the faculty as a body.[19] The theological winds were up, too. In 1951 virtually the whole Calvin Seminary faculty was replaced for having quarreled themselves to an impasse. One of the temporary replacements was Cornelius Van Til, a

18. Henry Zylstra, *Testament of Vision* (Grand Rapids: Eerdmans, 1958).
19. Stob, "CRC Schools," pp. 394-395; Timmerman, *Promises,* pp. 110-111, 185-193.

former student of Jellema, who had exchanged his teacher's Positive Calvinism for the Antithetical sort. The same year H. Evan Runner, converted to Kuyperianism while a student of Van Til at Westminster Theological Seminary, was hired in the college's philosophy department.[20]

For the first time in 30 years Antithetical Calvinists had a central place in the Calvin circle, and they enjoyed it. They railed against Jellema's "synthesis" of Christianity with Plato, against Zylstra's "confusion" of theology with aesthetics, against the "dualistic" positing of spirit over nature, instead of spirit against spirit, as the essential contest of culture. They scorned dull conformity and flaccid materialism fully as much as did their opponents, only with cutting invective. If their style attracted few among the in-crowd, it thrilled the marginal and outcast — first of all, youth from the postwar Dutch immigration to Canada, but also the native-born raised on and revolting against American culture religion.[21] Those it did not attract were often stimulated to work toward an adequate retort. Thus, the divisions of the early 1950s stimulated intellectual intensity and recommitted all parties involved to the common heritage over which they were quarreling. No one could get away with *just* good taste, scholarly excellence, Christian dogma, or American patriotism. Everyone scouted secularism despite its brilliant mind and Fundamentalism despite its Christian warmth. Everyone could join Harry Jellema in renewing Calvin's quest for a third way, for "education and scholarship that shall be wholly and vitally expressive of the Christian faith, that shall be of the highest academic quality, and that shall be *both at once.*" Or as Henry Zylstra put it amid the battles of 1951: "Our schools must be schools — that for one thing. And then they must be Christian — that for another thing. And in making these two points I shall want to insist, of course, that they must be both at once."[22]

The quarreling also dimmed because two new ventures were demanding attention. In the CRC's centennial year, 1957-58, when questions of "whence and whither" were thick in the air, the college administration began unveiling plans for a huge new campus on the edge of town, and Harry Jellema published a detailed critique of the college curriculum and a proposal for its replacement. The physical relocation began in 1962 and took ten years; the curricular reform went into planning in 1963 and was accomplished in five.[23] Thus, Calvin overhauled its two fundamental structures at the same time — simultaneously

---

20. Timmerman, *Promises,* pp. 189-191; Bratt, *Dutch Calvinism,* pp. 190-196.

21. Bratt, *Dutch Calvinism,* pp. 195-196, 208-210.

22. William Harry Jellema, quoted in Ryskamp, "History," p. 334; Zylstra, *Testament,* p. 90.

23. Jellema, "The Curriculum in a Liberal Arts College" (Grand Rapids: Calvin College, 1958); Timmerman, *Promises,* pp. 144, 164.

with the greatest decade of campus upheaval in American history. The providence that attended the college's fledging in the 1920s now returned for its revamping.

The need for more space was the main reason Calvin moved its campus. College expansion after World War II had tapped all the capacity of the Franklin Street site but had still proved inadequate; the new site was some twenty times larger than the old. An unintended consequence became clear when the long-contemplated move took place during a time of increased racial turmoil. Leaving the section of the city that was rapidly becoming predominantly African-American lent apparent plausibility to accusation of "white flight." Even though this was not true as to motive, some people associated with the college did feel relief at getting out of what was called "a changing neighborhood." And so it happened, English Professor John J. Timmerman recounted, that just as the inner city heated up and students cried for involvement, just when 1960s passions flamed and students demanded relevance, Calvin students found themselves transplanted to the pastoral isolation of Knollcrest Farm.[24] As wheezing buses shuttled students back and forth between the two campuses, the college itself seemed in suspension, trying to transplant a history that had fought to maintain a Dutch Calvinism in America into a future where Christianity, they hoped, would transform America.

To change the world, Calvin decided first to change its own curriculum. The reform owed something to the academic climate of the time, as was evident from the new plan's provision of a pass-fail January Interim term for experimental courses. But the change owed far more to the college's own tradition. From the start Calvin had insisted it would not be a regular college with chapel and Bible courses added on, but in fact the curriculum it had adopted in 1921 was imported en bloc from the University of Michigan — with Bible and theology courses added on. Even worse, Harry Jellema noted, Michigan had then just finished remodeling its curriculum to the fashion set by Charles Eliot at Harvard, meaning that Calvin's curricular structure derived from the dictates of scientific, evolutionary naturalism.[25] Thus the reformers of the 1960s could make fundamental changes in radical times by invoking orthodoxy.

The new plan, published as *Christian Liberal Arts Education (CLAE)*, clearly articulated how a college curriculum might be structured from Reformed premises about the integrality of all life, learning, and faith. *CLAE* instituted a "disciplinary" model of education in which "teachers and students together [would] engag[e] in the various scholarly disciplines, directed and enlightened in their inquiries by the Word of God." This education was still to have a clear liberal arts purpose of "disinterested" study rather than immediately usable

24. Timmerman, *Promises,* pp. 144-148.
25. Jellema, "Curriculum," p. 5.

knowledge; the college's historic rejection of pragmatism continued. But *CLAE* also rejected "classical" curricular models as overemphasizing intellectual history and elite culture.[26] Instead it valorized each discipline as equal in dignity or possibility, consonant with Kuyper's reminder that Christ was Lord over *all* and quite in contrast to Harry Jellema's 1958 proposal which would have made the sciences handmaids to the humanities. *CLAE*, further, resisted the tides of academic specialization by requiring a large core and relatively fewer courses in the major, a breadth-over-depth approach that accorded well with Kuyperian worldview construction. This was also evident in the expectation that both the core course in each discipline and every major as a whole reflect upon their grounds and procedures in light of Christian beliefs and norms. Attention to disciplinary practices, in turn, pointed to the keystone of the new curriculum. Learning was not to take place for its own sake but in order to serve the Lord by prompting action in the world. Here, neither Abraham Kuyper nor John Calvin was the real inspiration so much as H. Richard Niebuhr. His *Christ and Culture* served as scripture for "Christian Perspectives on Learning," a first-year inter-disciplinary course deemed vital to the new curriculum; and his fifth category, "Christ transforming culture," effectively became the college's new motto.

Curricular reform went on without much outside interest, but by the time of its implementation in the late 1960s, the watchmen on the walls of the CRC Zion could only wonder what was transforming what. Better, they did not wonder at all but were certain — and appalled. In this they were one with millions across the land, only with a distinctive twist. There were no riots at Calvin, though some demonstrations; no obstruction of the campus, though a few faculty-approved moratoria to mark Earth Day or allow antiwar protests. Students did not always behave like ladies and gentlemen, though some faculty deemed them, in retrospect, the most inquisitive they have encountered in their entire careers.

To part of the CRC constituency, however, all these considerations, good or ill, paled next to the issue of movie-going. As late as 1962-63 the editors of *Chimes*, the student newspaper, had been censured for reviewing Ingmar Bergman films shown at a local theater. Although feeling compelled to enforce the rules, Calvin President William Spoelhof noted that the editors had been motivated by a Calvinist mandate, the "concern about our broad cultural obligations as Christians living in the world."[27] Then, the 1966 Synod reversed

26. Calvin College Curriculum Study Committee, *Christian Liberal Arts Education* (Grand Rapids: Calvin College/Eerdmans, 1970), pp. 40-47; quotation at p. 47.

27. Board of Trustees minutes, "Student Publications," Article 43R, May 23, 1963, Calvin College Archives; quoted in David Larsen, "Evangelical Christian Higher Education, Culture and Social Conflict" (unpublished Ph.D. dissertation, Loyola University of Chicago, 1992), p. 91. The part of this dissertation pertaining to Calvin College was of considerable help in mapping (changes in) student life there since 1960.

the CRC's historic position by stating that "the film arts are a legitimate cultural medium to be used by the Christian in the same way that every cultural medium is to be used."[28] The next year a student-faculty committee was constituted as the Calvin Film Council and began a regular program of showing movies on campus.

In all this maneuvering the putative cultural qualities of film were obscured by its symbolic status to all parties. To conservative constituents, *the* moral boundary between holiness and worldliness had been erased. The college administration thought that moderation was now to rule. Student reformers-turned-radicals were determined that it would not. Paul Schrader, later a premier film director and screen writer (*Taxi Driver, Last Temptation of Christ*), was, as a student, rejected four times in his applications to serve on the film program. He went on to full martyrdom when he and the rest of the *Chimes* staff lost their positions in 1968 on allegations of bad taste, insubordination, and misuse of funds. Perhaps the film issue *was* an apt symbol after all, for over the next two years protests against dorm hours, mandatory chapel, the Vietnam war, American racism, environmental degradation, and more all swirled around the buildings where movies now were shown and on the *Chimes* pages where Schrader had ruled.

The tumult came to a head in April 1970. On the heels of the United States's invasion of Cambodia, the college gave students place to picket and speak at the Spring convocation, observed the first Earth Day, and witnessed the greatest crisis of William Spoelhof's 25-year presidency. But this third commotion had nothing to do with the first or the second. Perhaps pathetically, perhaps absurdly, but in any case tellingly, the crisis occurred over the *Chimes's* annual mock issue, which that year targeted not campus foibles but the CRC's weekly magazine, the *Banner.* That the student editors' disciplinary hearing was interrupted by news of the shootings at Kent State University demonstrated how great was the distance, still, between Calvin's world and the one outside.

The Recent Past

Administrators and constituents may have feared, and student leaders anticipated, the 1970-71 academic year as the dawn of further radicalism and disruption. Yet that year was one of almost eerie calm. Student leaders turned to new interests, and the college as a whole returned to face historic questions in its markedly changed environment. The 1970s was a time when Calvin sought to replace faltering formulas, structurally and ideologically.

28. *Acts of Synod of the Christian Reformed Church, 1966* (Grand Rapids: Christian Reformed Publishing House, 1966), p. 200.

The first revision came in the student recruitment system. For its entire history Calvin had relied upon denominational mechanisms to deliver it students, and the system had worked. Each year the college could expect a fixed yield of the CRC's age-eligible youth. But the system and the demographic pool slipped simultaneously in the early 1970s: enrollment fell from 3,575 in 1968 to 3,185 in 1972. After straining to build the new campus, the college now faced a prospect of empty desks. Both out of necessity and of the conviction that it had much to offer Christians beyond the CRC, Calvin undertook its first venture outside the ethnic-denominational fold by recruiting in evangelical Protestant circles. By and large the initiative worked. Enrollments broke the 4,000 mark in 1980 and peaked at 4,505 in 1988, with the percentages coming from CRC background (still around 90 in 1970) dipping to 72 and 65 respectively.

This success had its costs, of course. One has been the increased level of uncertainty regarding each year's enrollment, a particularly acute concern at an institution whose budget is 85 percent tuition-driven and where refusing to cap the size of entering classes is an article of faith. Faculty, facility, and budget planning have therefore been chained to the roller-coaster of enrollment vagaries: 4,108 in 1980 became 3,828 in 1982; 4,505 in 1988 fell to 3,725 in 1992. Another cost has come in increased pressure for student retention. Calvin's tradition of virtually open admissions had always been balanced by a process of honest or heartless (depending on the source) excisions, typically exercised on first-year students by self-appointed faculty commissars of quality control. Any tilt toward toleration or second chances could threaten the college's academic quality, just as any perceived tilt could lower faculty morale. Finally, recruitment and retention have required more staff, more faculty energies, and continuous nuancing of the campus image.

Nor did administration grow only on these counts. Along with other colleges and universities, Calvin saw staff numbers increase over the 1970s and 1980s at a rate far higher than the faculty's, with the result that by the late 1980s the latter fell below the former for the first time in the college's history. It is noteworthy that the college's administration building, named after William Spoelhof, was dubbed the "college center." On the original campus design that title belonged to the trinity of library-classroom building, chapel, and college-denominational archive clustered together on Knollcrest's high ground to symbolize past and future, faith and reason, intersecting in the present.[29] The elevation of the administrative "center" in their place might be taken as a sad tale of bureaucratization except that, in architectural fact, the college has no center. The campus is rather a tasteful arrangement of pods quite reflective of the department-centric curriculum and the divisionally-directed co-

29. Ryskamp, "History," p. 309.

curriculum that define how the college actually functions. Two rhetorical sinews tie all these together: positively, the dedication of all parties to solid Christian higher education; negatively, the complaint that faculty rarely see members of other departments nor administrators of any division nor students outside of class. The integrity of the positive bond has always depended on Calvin's being an integral community. Worry about the contrary bespeaks a significant challenge.

Increased differentiation is thus one hallmark of Calvin's past quarter century. Another is suggested by the transit from "professorial" to "professional" as the overriding tone of college life. While teaching undergraduates remains their primary work, the faculty over the last twenty-five years have shown a marked increase in commitment to research, publication, and related artistic and professional endeavors. Under the leadership of President Anthony Diekema, more funding for research was provided, especially in a program called Calvin Research Fellowships. Coupled with a strong sabbatical program, this initiative distinguishes Calvin in terms of support for research. At the same time, the expectation of scholarship has left many faculty feeling significant tension between the investments in time and energy required for research and the continuing demands of teaching, advising, and community service. Department and discipline have come to rival college in defining primary loyalties. This became especially noteworthy in the 1980s as Calvin had to compete, with only modest success, with major research universities for the services of its best-known scholars.

The trend toward professionalization affected governance as well. A new policy-making structure heavy on faculty committees was instituted in the late 1960s on the heels of campus and curricular changes, but its impact took longer to play out. In theory the FOSCO (Faculty Organization Study Committee) plan installed broader and more effective power in the faculty by subdividing responsibilities that formerly had preoccupied the body as a whole and by subjecting administrative fiat to regular faculty review. In practice the reorganization vitiated the faculty meeting as a deliberative body, turning it into a virtual rubber stamp for committee decisions. And increased complexity within the administration submerged effective decision-making on some issues of long-term community significance in the toils of divisional structures. In short, the more concrete detail the faculty have had to deal with in committee, the less philosophical discussion they have been able to carry on as a body. This development has meshed with the style that Anthony Diekema brought to the college presidency in 1976. While Spoelhof was caricatured as a benevolent monarch, Diekema was viewed by many as a manager whose favorite word was "process." He frankly told the college at his arrival that he was not a visionary but one to implement the vision of others, particularly the faculty. Through no necessary fault of his, however, the coherence of faculty vision and the mechanisms for its expression have lessened in the past twenty years.

Professionalization was also a key ingredient in the main curricular change of the Diekema administration. In the early 1970s a special faculty committee produced a report that suggested moving the college from "liberal arts monism" to "liberal arts centrism." To die-hards of such "monism" the notion had all the charm of the report's acronym: *PECLAC (Professional Education and the Christian Liberal Arts College)*.[30] The report self-consciously stood on the shoulders of the previous decade's *Christian Liberal Arts Education* and, at the hands of its principal writer, philosophy professor Richard Mouw, aimed to flesh out the neo-Kuyperian concerns of that document. Theologically, *PECLAC* argued that since all of life is corrupted by sin and so needs to be redeemed, there is no subject unworthy of study in a Christian college. Historically, it noted that Calvin was not just now beginning professional programs but had offered these from the start, in fact had taken two of these — pre-seminary and teacher education — as its original *raison d'être*. Qualitatively, the report did not open the door to any and every field but set forward criteria compatible with liberal arts interests for determining acceptability.

The ensuing years brought success down this track, and unease around it. Students voted with their feet for new programs in accountancy, social work, criminal justice, recreation, and nursing, while already extant programs in engineering and especially business expanded greatly. By the late 1980s the numbers of students graduating in professional programs would outnumber those in traditional liberal arts disciplines. The *PECLAC* curriculum thus probably equalled the new recruiting strategy in bolstering enrollment. But many wondered about the cost. Preparing preachers and teachers — the old pre-professionalism — clearly carried on the usual purposes of liberal arts education; the new programs were more ambiguous on that score. *PECLAC* had advocated a curricular move from "liberal arts monism" to "liberal arts centrism." Upon the eve of his departure for Fuller Seminary, *PECLAC* author Richard Mouw warned that the many new programs threatened precisely that liberal arts center and with it the vitality of the collegiate enterprise.[31]

If the liberal arts classroom has felt rivaled in this era, so has the classroom as such. The student-affairs division has grown in staff and confidence to claim a mission of providing the "co-curriculum" of college life. This venture, too, claims Kuyperian warrant. If "all of life" falls under Christ's lordship, then surely the majority of their time that Calvin students spend outside the classroom must be claimed and redeemed. Besides, recruitment and retention

30. Calvin College Professional Programs Committee, "Professional Education and the Christian Liberal Arts College," February 9, 1973.

31. Comments by Mouw in a meeting of the Calvin faculty, heard by the authors.

imperatives demanded programming congruent with this effort, as did student perceptions that college is now an entitlement — as before 1970 it was a privilege — of middle-class status. Dorm room and classroom, gymnasium and library on this view can all become feeding stations in the smorgasbord of the college "experience" that one passes through between parental home and finding a job.

Managing these mandates required another, equally innovative professionalization. The oversight of student life on Calvin's campus had usually been left to sanctified amateurs. There was no counseling center and only lately a chaplain. Authority figures in the residence halls were not trained specifically for the job, and many qualified because they were widowed mothers. This too changed around 1970. The Broene Counseling Center now has five professionally trained staff; the vice-president and the deans of student life are well credentialed in human services delivery. The chaplain carries on a wideranging ministry, and residence hall directors have replaced the widowed moms, bringing along concepts of community building learned in graduate schools. Indeed, a lovely paradox is the genuine concern that many of the student-affairs staff have for "the whole person," a clear echo of the Kuyperian notions of the faculty who sometimes look dourly on their doings. At the same time the campus religious ethos, set less by the voluntary (since 1970) chapel program than by dorm and interest-group Bible studies, indicates some drift towards a piety that drafts off both the old Seceder impulses and movements in the CRC toward models of fundamentalistic evangelicalism.

This account of structural changes indicates a ready, if at times ironic, consensus in place around Kuyperian ideology. Such a consensus was never complete nor quickly achieved, nor have its notions been as clearly directive as its proponents had hoped. Yet since 1975 a Kuyperianism at once chastened and cheerful has held sway over the college's rhetoric and action, put there by the same person who designed the new curriculum, Nicholas Wolterstorff. His triumph was all the more notable for being announced in what had been the den of the enemy. Ever since the early 1950s battles between philosophers Evan Runner and Cornelius Van Til on the one hand and Harry Jellema and Henry Stob on the other, the Kuyperian cause had been divided — sometimes with real animosity — between the "antitheticals" and the "progressives." It was as heir to the latter that Wolterstorff in 1975 ventured into the bastion of the former, the Institute for Christian Studies in Toronto, to offer an accord.[32]

The offer exacted a high price. The antitheticals (or Dooyeweerdians, as they called themselves after the Dutch legal philosopher Herman Dooyeweerd) first had to give up their claims that God's "law-word," embedded in the

32. Nicholas Wolterstorff, "The AACS in the CRC: Will It Guide Us or Divide us?" *The Banner* 110 (January 3, 1975): 13-15; (January 10, 1975): 18-20.

structures of creation, constituted a revelation equal to Scripture. "This understanding of the Word of God," Wolterstorff concluded, was "unacceptable as Christian theology." Secondly, he demystified the Dooyeweerdians' social philosophy of "sphere sovereignty." What was original in it, Wolterstorff insisted, came from Kuyper; what was ornate, from Dooyeweerd; what was true and useful — and much of it was, the speaker allowed — was to be so credited from experience, not from Scripture. What credit, then, belonged to the Dooyeweerdian party? A most important role, Wolterstorff answered: it had kept the CRC and Calvin College from a likely fall into Fundamentalism; it had cultivated the Reformed heritage, pressing its claims against a flaccid accommodation to Americanism; and it stood ready to bring its zeal to the reinvigoration of the Kuyperian progressive wing.

Wolterstorff's lecture marked a fundamental turning point in Calvin's post-war history. At one stroke he resolved the historic tensions between *all* the parties in the church. The pietists were glad to hear his affirmation that the definitive speech of God was in the Bible, not in creation. Those interested in Christian cultural critique now had the Kuyperian tradition accessible to them without the complex system of Dooyeweerd. Here was an insight, even a motto, that could be appropriated for the academic calling at Calvin College. Its integral view of all of life as response to God made plausible the assertion that chemistry, physics, biology, and mathematics have as much a place in the curriculum as theology, history, philosophy, and literature. Moreover, the guiding methodology for all these undertakings would be the desire to integrate Christian faith with learning in a particular discipline.

Later on, the Christian College Coalition (now the Coalition for Christian Colleges and Universities) would also take up these notions as its reason for being. While other traditions — most notably the Anglo-American neo-evangelicals associated with Wheaton College and Fuller Seminary — contributed to the Coalition's ideology, it is this line in the Reformed tradition that has given the approach its real appeal to evangelicals. On the other hand, while closely associated with Calvin College, this approach came to dominance there only a little before its spread elsewhere. Put another way, the ideology had been around in Dutch Reformed thinking for about a century but surely as a minority view. Only after 1975 did it become a vision for all seasons.

Yet, this story of ideological development is not complete without mentioning an alternative mission statement that has gone largely unheeded. While the Kuyperian "worldview" approach was still rising in evangelical circles, a number of critics emerged, especially amid Wesleyan/Holiness and Mennonite circles, complaining of its static and all-too-academic character. On this view Reformed ideology is too long on principles and too short on practice. The same critique emerged at Calvin College itself, once again from Nicholas Wolterstorff. This time, however, Calvin gave the local prophet only the honor of a polite hearing, and that second-hand, for this critique was first offered at the 1982 inauguration of Richard Chase as president of Wheaton College.[33] However much cited at other institutions, Wolterstorff's proposal for a "third stage" in Christian higher education has been little heeded on his home ground.

Wolterstorff's points were both easy to comprehend and difficult to make operational. There were two stages, the author suggested, that characterized Wheaton's history, and a third stage toward which it should aspire. Stage I was characterized by the evangelical withdrawal from culture and society following the loss of face in the fundamentalist-modernist controversy. Stage II was characterized by the re-emergence of confidence in the years after World War II, when neo-evangelicalism rose from fundamentalism's ashes. Its main theme was engagement with culture, not withdrawal from it, a theme whose touchstone phrase was "the integration of faith and learning." Wolterstorff was gracious enough not to stress the Reformed roots of integrative educational theories. He nevertheless noted that "Christ and culture" issues had become the staple products of the Christian College Coalition.

For Stage III Wolterstorff asked Wheaton — and other leading Christian colleges — to move from a consideration of Christ and culture to the church in society. Just as there was no disembodied "Christ" outside the real life of the churches, so "culture" devoid of its social location was at least feckless, and probably sterile. What Wolterstorff called for was a collegiate commitment to social transformation. This would, the author insisted, require Christian colleges to change both ethos and curriculum; ethos insofar as it invoked a sense of holy unease with society as it was disordered by, e.g., nationalism and capitalism; curriculum insofar as it needed to change from the disciplinary structures that the same author had advocated in *Christian Liberal Arts Education* to programs in "peace and war, nationalism, poverty, urban ugliness, ecology, crime and punishment."[34] Calvin College has made some new efforts in off-campus programs in this direction but otherwise has shown little inclination to move much beyond the "faith and learning" consensus of Stage II.

Conclusions

Internally, then, Calvin over the past twenty-five years has felt the conundrum of quantitative growth on every count set off by diffusion in organization and ethos. The paradox mounts in light of Calvin's unprecedented visibility on the

33. Nicholas Wolterstorff, "The Mission of the Christian College at the End of the 20th Century," *Reformed Journal* 33 (June 1983): 14-18.
34. Wolterstorff, "Mission," p. 18.

national scene during these same years as a model of Christian higher education. *U.S. News & World Report* rates it high for students, the secular academy notes its distinctive angle, and the Christian College Coalition follows its example of faith-learning integration. Calvin has won these roles, particularly the latter, because, just as the CRC has opened up to the evangelical Protestant world, so the evangelical world has arrived historically at the point that Dutch Neo-Calvinism might have been the first to discern. If one takes just Abraham Kuyper's dicta about perspectival scholarship, he sounds postmodern. And if one takes his dicta about the continuing salience of creation and the universal Lordship of Christ, he legitimates for Christians the study of every person, place, and thing on earth — and he warrants study, the academic life, as fully as good a Christian calling as the "full-time Christian service" American evangelicals have ritually praised. Taking seriously his combined stress upon principle and pluralism, Calvin College has become fit for articulating credible Christian conviction in a postmodern world. In earnestly applying principle across all domains of campus life while blending and intertwining these with Dutch, or immigrant, hard-headed practicality, Calvin has become a proven, workable enterprise.

This enterprise has not only proven workable but has gained a recognition in North American religious and academic culture that was nearly unimaginable two generations ago. In the whole growth of evangelical scholarship, Calvin College has exercised a leadership disproportionate to its size and history. For example, the Calvin Center for Christian Scholarship (CCCS) was founded in 1977 under the lead of President Diekema with provisions for an ample endowment. The CCCS has sponsored some thirty research teams (a majority of whose members have come from outside of Calvin) in producing books and articles which have signaled not only the possibility but the desirability of perspectival scholarship. Several of the CCCS books have had considerable impact. Indeed, the entire question of how to work out a Christian perspective in a given discipline was new to most evangelicals, thus allowing Calvin people the opportunity of being given the lead. This can be most pointedly seen in the perspectival series "Through the Eyes of Faith," sponsored by the Christian College Coalition and published by HarperCollins. The series offers accessible supplementary texts to be used in beginning courses in the various liberal arts disciplines. When the Coalition wanted a person to head the series, they chose Nicholas Wolterstorff. When writers were needed, the Coalition again went disproportionally to Calvin people, e.g., Susan Gallagher for the literature volume, Shirley Roels for the business book, and Ronald Wells for the history volume. Further, when Christian organizations within academic disciplines were formed (e.g., the Society of Christian Philosophers, the Conference on Faith and History, the Conference on Christianity and Literature, Christians in Political Science), Calvin College professors were once more in the lead. In sum this remarkable record of leadership, though sometimes arousing resentment among evangelical institutions, was a natural outreach for scholars in a college committed to Kuyperian-principled learning and scholarship. If others wish to emulate Calvin in this regard, the college will take it as a sign of divine blessing.

Providence is still deft enough, however, to keep the college from pure joy. Calvin College is perennially as anxious as was its namesake, and with good reason. The historical record shows that Calvinism, despite or because of claiming all the world so insistently for God, has been one of the West's great engines of secularization. In academic life in particular, as former Calvin history professor George Marsden has written, secularization occurs not necessarily when religion becomes too little but when it becomes so much and so broad that it is robbed of content.[35] It was not craven atheists who engineered the secularization of the major American universities but those purveyors of religion whose parameters were so broad that, like Holmes' "Wonderful One Hoss Shay," they just broke one day, for reasons that no one could fully explain. In Calvin's case, setting all aspects of campus life under Kuyperian principle may also have made that principle flaccid, while teaching and writing from a distinctively Christian slant does not always produce as distinctive or as predictable a result as had been imagined.

Yet at the end of 120 years, with all the shifts of scene and slant, Calvin finds itself close to where it started under Gerrit Boer. It is still *"onze school,"* a CRC venture; only the denomination is now filled with prosperous members who cannot regard themselves as despised of the world, or who reject it in return. The college still looks out at nearby traffic, though today, not at the railroad but at a major highway which runs right past the campus. Along that road to the north lie mega-churches, one Christian Reformed in title but little distinguishable from the other, undenominational fundamentalist giant it emulates. Over against evangelicalism's recent rise in numbers and public visibility, the distinctives of Calvinism that have given the CRC its glue and the college its edge seem less compelling to maintain. A mile south, the highway runs between two shopping malls, one West Michigan's largest. These were built simultaneously with the Knollcrest campus and provide Calvin with its greatest challenge. For they represent the kind of world that even pietist Seceders had a hard time resisting, as B. K. Kuiper and Henry Zylstra noted. Their proximity represents a magnetism more likely to transform the church and the college according to the culture than the opposite flow idealized by Kuyper and Niebuhr.

35. George M. Marsden, *The Soul of the American University* (New York: Oxford University Press, 1994).

In 1995, Anthony Diekema honorably completed his twenty-year presidency. Chief on the agenda of his successor, Gaylen Byker, will be assessing the current status of Calvin's historic struggles: the first between two Christian attitudes toward culture, flight or transformation; the other between the commitments of Christianity and the culture of American materialism. It would be a cruel irony if the whole enterprise wound up halfway between the first pair as a mode of avoiding the second choice; that is, if Calvin turns out world-affirming enough to remain respectably middle class, world-denying enough to keep religion private, and worldly-American enough to shop the mall without the guilt or anxiety that Calvinism has always thought the anteroom of conversion.

Whitworth College: Evangelical in the Reformed Tradition

Dale E. Soden
and Arlin Migliazzo[1]

Whitworth College, affiliated with the Presbyterian Church from its beginning in 1890, has emerged as the denomination's most self-consciously Christian institution in the Western United States. This article traces the evolution of that religious identity for over one hundred years and specifically focuses on the tension created by its standing within both the Reformed and evangelical traditions. This tension has been evident in varying ways throughout the college's history and has at times caused moments of difficulty both internally and externally. Whitworth's distinctiveness results from its requirement that all full-time faculty be Christian while providing great latitude relative to the varying expressions of that Christianity. More recently, the college appears to be gaining confidence in its Christian identity, and its faculty have assumed more regional and national leadership relative to the issue of the integration of faith and learning.

As Whitworth College celebrated its centennial in 1990, it could look back on a hundred years of Christian education in the Pacific Northwest. The college had been born in the mind of its founder as a non-sectarian, Presbyterian-affiliated college dedicated to the advancement of Christian civilization in the

1. The authors wish to express their thanks to past and present administrators, faculty, and students of Whitworth College for their assistance in the preparation of this essay. The skills of Ms. Barbara Brodrick, Ms. Anna Kenney, and Ms. Terry Mitchell have expedited the completion of this project.

hinterlands of the Pacific Northwest. Early enthusiasm gave way to hard economic realities. The college moved from Puget Sound to eastern Washington in 1914, lured by the promise of land from Spokane land developer and Presbyterian layman Jay P. Graves. But the move did not spare the tiny school further hardships, including temporary closure and a major fire, both of which threatened to end its existence. Small graduating classes, jack-of-all-trades faculty members, and shoestring budgets characterized Whitworth until the postwar GI bill days. From the 1940s through the mid-1970s, enrollments increased and facilities and faculty expanded to meet the needs of a growing student body. The 1980s brought declining numbers which led to severe retrenchment by the decade's end. The opening years of the 1990s saw computerization, further facility enhancement, and increasing evidence of teaching and scholarly excellence among faculty members; a burgeoning regional reputation contributed to a massive upsurge in student numbers and the quality of applicants.

There is much about this historical trajectory which links Whitworth College to numerous other church-related institutions around the country. But perhaps Whitworth's most significant contribution to Christian higher education over the past hundred years is the model it provides for analyzing the nature of the church-relatedness of Christian colleges and universities born and nurtured in a frontier environment on the West Coast. While many other colleges have severed their linkages with their founding denominations, Whitworth has, by and large, remained faithful to its Presbyterian heritage.

Few would deny that Presbyterians have always been serious about education. Presbyterians and others in the Reformed tradition were among the leaders in establishing colleges throughout the country in the nineteenth century.[2] And while there is much that these colleges share in terms of the intellectual and social forces that shaped them, it is clear that each represents a different story.

While Whitworth College has emerged among the institutions most intentionally connected to the Presbyterian Church in the USA, it is hardly a typical Presbyterian college. In fact, it has consistently and with few exceptions affirmed its relationship with the Presbyterian tradition while concurrently choosing to travel down a more evangelical path than its sponsoring denom-

2. Citing earlier research on Presbyterians and higher education, Bradley J. Longfield and George M. Marsden note that prior to the Civil War, Presbyterians had established more than a quarter of the 180 church-related colleges in the country and that they played leading roles in numerous other institutions, both public and private, not directly founded by the denomination. See Bradley J. Longfield and George M. Marsden, "Presbyterian Colleges in Twentieth Century America," pp. 99-125 in Milton J. Coalter, John M. Mulder, and Louis B. Weeks, eds., *The Pluralistic Vision: Presbyterians and Mainstream Protestant Education and Leadership* (Louisville: Westminster/John Knox Press, 1992), p. 99.

ination. Yet, Whitworth is not prototypically evangelical. While Whitworth requires that all faculty be professing Christians, there are no formal faith statements to be signed as at Wheaton College, no requirement for church membership as at Calvin College, and few restrictions on lifestyle such as pertain at Seattle Pacific University.

It is our conviction that this dual heritage — both Presbyterian and evangelical — had its genesis in the geographical, denominational, sociological, and personal contexts of its founding and maturation on the Pacific Northwestern frontier. It will be our contention that Whitworth's non-sectarian evangelicalism and its concurrent identification with the Presbyterian Church saved its Christian distinctiveness to the present day, but meant that the college has never quite fallen completely into either camp.

Three Defining Eras

From our vantage point as historians of the American experience, we would argue that the dynamic tension involved in being both Reformed and evangelical is best understood in the context of three different eras in the college's history. In all three eras, the tension between these two strands is clearly evident and clearly a shaping intellectual and spiritual force for the college. However, in all three eras it takes a different shape, has a different life, and responds to different forces in the external environment of American culture and specifically American higher education. Nevertheless, it helps explain why Whitworth's identity is so deeply rooted in a dynamic that is best described as both evangelical and Reformed.

The first era ran from the founding of the college in 1890 until 1929 when President Ward Sullivan (1929-38) came to the college. Whitworth's distance from the Presbyterian "home office" allowed it to be formed in an environment where doctrinal distinctiveness was less important than it was back east. Survival demanded that the college expand its appeal by becoming broadly evangelical while relying on its Reformed tradition to maintain a Presbyterian identity. The second era began with Sullivan's tenure as president and extended through 1980 and the presidency of Edward Lindaman (1970-80). In this era, the Reformed tradition expressed itself in efforts to make the college more academically respectable, and yet it was with the presidencies of Frank Warren (1940-63) and Mark Koehler (1964-69) that the evangelical identity of the college was firmly established. The third era began with the presidency of Robert Mounce (1981-87) and continues through the present. Through the mid-1980s, Whitworth was strongly influenced by an evangelical ethos that in fact created some tension with the national Presbyterian Church, but in the recent past, under presidents Arthur De Jong (1988-92), interim president Phil

Eaton (1992-93), and Bill Robinson (1993–), there has been a conscious effort to be *both* evangelical and Reformed.

George Whitworth and the Birth of a College

Whitworth's peculiar quality of being broadly evangelical yet nondogmatic originated with the vision of its founder, George Whitworth, and in the particular contexts in which the college came into existence. Although George Whitworth was born in England in 1816, his formative experience came in Ohio and Indiana. At the relatively advanced age of 28, he enrolled in seminary. He was ordained four years later, and then began serving churches in Indiana and Kentucky. Measured by the indices of church membership, pastoral leadership, or missionary activity, Presbyterianism in antebellum Indiana fought a losing battle with the Methodists and Baptists.[3] Yet this is the vineyard in which Whitworth chose to begin his labors. We have little of his own writings, and so his motives are not entirely clear, but it seems probable that Whitworth was enamored with civilizing the West, and for him Protestantism was a key element of what it meant to be civilized.

The unchurched Pacific Northwest soon proved an attractive lure. No doubt having heard of the exploits of Dr. Marcus and Narcissa Prentice Whitman and Henry and Eliza Hart Spaulding, pioneer missionaries sent to the Pacific Northwest by the American Board of Commissioners for Foreign Missions in 1836, Whitworth went west to Puget Sound on the Oregon Trail after his appointment by the Presbyterian Board of Home Missions as missionary. Whitworth spent the next thirty years establishing some twenty Presbyterian churches in Oregon and Washington. But he was also a lawyer, a farmer, a businessman, and a public servant, holding the post of chief clerk of the Indian Department of Washington Territory. He was elected superintendent of common schools for Thurston County in 1854, and served as president of the young University of Washington for two short terms in the 1870s. His career embodies the nineteenth-century ideal of a civilizing evangelical Protestantism. All of this is to suggest that George Whitworth was less concerned about theological rigor on the frontier than he was about the broad sense in which religion served society by

---

3. L. C. Rudolph, *Hoosier Zion: The Presbyterians in Early Indiana* (New Haven: Yale University Press, 1963), pp. 14-36. Rudolph also notes the insurmountable gulf between a more educated Presbyterian clergy and the uneducated inhabitants of early Indiana and Kentucky. Doctrinal disputes, clerical criticism of frontier patterns of worship, and lay charges of social elitism skewed the relationship between pastors and congregations. Similar animosity appears to have been generated from the non-Presbyterians.

providing a moral outlook and by developing in young people a sense of citizenship.

His commitment to civilize the region by promoting a broadly evangelical Protestant worldview meant that the dream of an educational institution affiliated with the Presbyterian Church was never far from his mind. Finally, in 1883 Whitworth convinced several other Presbyterian clergy and laity that an academy might be started in the small town of Sumner, some ten miles southeast of Tacoma, Washington. Although there are no surviving records to indicate the specifics, it is probable that the decision that same year by the General Assembly of the Presbyterian Church, U.S.A. to support its schools was the key factor in the establishment of the academy at Sumner, as it was for many other Presbyterian institutions. The General Assembly argued that Presbyterians needed a college education because the church's "doctrines are such that they require intelligence for their grasp and retention."[4] But if the home office thought that doctrines needed to be explicated, in the Pacific Northwest the situation was far less complicated: students needed education and character needed to be developed. For that first generation, the phrase "an education of heart and mind" entered into the descriptions of educational purpose. By 1890, the trustees decided to incorporate into a college, naming the institution after Whitworth.

In those early days, students lived primarily in the surrounding hills of the Puyallup Valley near Sumner. Most traveled on horseback, although some came by train. The 1893 Depression, however, nearly destroyed the college, as enrollment dropped from 91 to 56 students. The drop in prices for the region's agricultural products crippled the young college even further. Trustees began to entertain offers to relocate and finally, in 1899, decided to move to Tacoma where they had purchased a mansion and several other buildings. Overlooking Commencement Bay and the Olympic Mountains, the campus was situated on a spectacular site.[5]

The Early Years

Christian colleges in the nineteenth century were marked by several common characteristics, ranging from the Christian identity of their faculty, administrators, and trustees to a Bible-centered, classical curriculum and carefully orchestrated extracurricular activities. Whitworth certainly fit the larger pat-

4. *Minutes of the General Assembly, Presbyterian Church U.S.A., 1883*, p. 582.
5. Alfred O. Gray, *Not By Might: The Story of Whitworth College, 1890-1965* (Spokane: Whitworth College, 1965), pp. 23-56; Dale E. Soden, *A Venture of Mind and Spirit: An Illustrated History of Whitworth College* (Spokane: Whitworth College, 1990), pp. 13-33.

tern of Presbyterian colleges in regard to all of these characteristics. Clergy served both as presidents and as lower-level administrators between 1890 and 1920, and in the first thirty years of the college's history, approximately half of the faculty who taught in the humanities and in the natural and social sciences at any one time were seminary trained.

Not surprisingly, Presbyterian institutions as well as other Christian colleges utilized the Scripture as a key textbook in many subject areas. Early catalogues at Whitworth reveal the role the Bible played in the curriculum. The 1891 catalogue stated:

> The Bible is used as a text book for regular recitations throughout the course in each department of the College. . . . In Political Philosophy reference is made to the Hebrew Commonwealth. The truths taught in the Bible in relation to the character, powers, and duties of man are inculcated as fundamental in Mental and Moral Philosophy, and Philosophy of History is identified with the History of Redemption. It is designed to make the Bible the central object of study in the whole College course.[6]

Through the first two decades of the college's history, all students were required to attend daily chapel. Like other colleges, Whitworth also required its students to attend religious services every Sunday morning as a body, although non-Presbyterians could be excused "for denominational reasons" by parents or pastors.

The development in each student of a Christian worldview and a concept of public service constituted the major curricular goals for Whitworth and other church-related colleges. Unlike their later counterparts in the twentieth century, these earlier institutions made it clear that the acquisition of knowledge and expertise in a particular area was not the primary purpose of an education. Emphasis was repeatedly placed on the development of character and citizenship — education was to be for life.[7] Again, an early Whitworth catalogue reflects the ways in which college officials affirmed the importance of character rather than expert knowledge:

> It must be kept in mind that knowledge is not the highest value sought, but culture, the discipline of the powers, the vitalizing of the faculties and the developing of self-activity. . . . But above all this the dominant principle in education and in the preparation for active life is the supreme

6. *Whitworth College Catalogue, 1891-92*, pp. 22-23.

7. As noted by Longfield and Marsden, this notion of "Christian" higher education drew as much from classical, humanistic non-Christian antecedents as from more modern Christian educational theory. See Longfield and Marsden, "Presbyterian Colleges," in *Pluralistic Vision*, p. 100.

importance of character. Christian education means the utilization of the best years of acquisition for founding deep broad principles of conduct. Expertness, capacity, knowledge, culture, all are valueless without character. There can be no true success, no real honor, no permanent good without character.[8]

Early faculty, if they were not members of the clergy, were still expected to be mentors in the broadest sense and not simply experts in their fields. For example, David Guy not only taught mathematics and civil engineering but participated in most activities on campus. The student newspaper described him as the one "who coached all athletics, managed all teams and served as math instructor, campus surveyor, dean of men, dormitory head, second tenor in the quartet, and adviser of his male fussers."[9]

College presidents, usually ordained ministers, were typically responsible for teaching an integrative seminar each year to the graduating class. The seminar was based not on specialized knowledge learned in one's major but on a holistic view of Christian citizenship.[10]

Nevertheless, while biblical principles and a church experience were thought essential to a Whitworth education, early Whitworth presidents, and most specifically Franklin Gault, emphasized the importance of a thorough classical education. The college gained distinction in 1908 when it was awarded a Rhodes Scholarship for one of its students, Frederic Metzger.[11]

Yet even the attractions of a beautiful campus, combined with academic respectability, could not overcome the ongoing financial problems of the college. In 1912, the Spokane Presbytery began voicing the need for a college of its own in the Inland Northwest. With the aid of a substantial land grant from Spokane developer Jay P. Graves, and financial assistance from the city of Spokane and the Synod of Washington, Whitworth moved to north Spokane in 1914. By the fall of that year, two new buildings had been constructed and although there were plans for more, these two buildings would serve as the college's primary facilities for the next thirty-five years.

Moving to Spokane did not solve the financial difficulties, however. The college closed in 1919 as a result of the First World War. Once reopened, Whitworth faced enormous financial problems in the 1920s. One student

8. *Whitworth College Catalogue, 1902-03*, p. 12.
9. Gray, *Not By Might*, p. 93.
10. The senior seminar in Christian ethics and citizenship was very common among church-related institutions. The president normally taught this course to graduating seniors; see Mark A. Noll, "The University Arrives in America, 1870-1930: Christian Traditionalism During the Academic Revolution," in Joel Carpenter and Kenneth Shipps, eds., *Making Higher Education Christian*, (Grand Rapids: Eerdmans, 1987), pp. 98-109.
11. Gray, *Not By Might*, p. 67.

graduated in 1924 and two students in 1926. Fire destroyed one of only two substantial buildings on campus in 1927 (it was rebuilt within a year). Presidential leadership throughout this decade was virtually non-existent.[12] Talk of a possible merger with other Christian colleges in Spokane occupied the trustee meetings. In fact, it was only due to the dogged determination of one Presbyterian trustee during the 1920s that Whitworth remained Presbyterian. However, theological distinctiveness was not the highest priority. Financial resources were. The dire economic straits faced by the college, along with the Fundamentalist-Modernist controversy raging within the Presbyterian Church, left the college relatively untethered to its sponsoring denomination, both financially and theologically.

By the end of this period, Whitworth College was exhibiting broadly evangelical traits in the sense that its commitment to the development of character and citizenship placed less emphasis on particular doctrinal understanding than on the disposition of the heart. At the same time, college officials remained doggedly determined to maintain Presbyterian affiliation.

Whitworth Comes of Age

Beginning in the 1930s, the tension between Reformed and evangelical perspectives took a different shape. While survival remained in doubt and the attention paid to doctrinal and theological issues was therefore less prominent than in places like Calvin College, Whitworth nonetheless felt the impact of the changes that were taking place in research institutions across the country. Higher education increasingly valued the trained expert in a given academic field over the generalist who could embody good citizenship and teach the moral virtues in the context of the liberal arts. The M.A. and Ph.D. soon supplanted the degree in divinity held by the earlier generation of faculty members. In the leading institutions in the country, not only were religious perspectives found to be inappropriate for the scholarly process, but the whole question of whether pre-existing values were anything more than subjective tastes was thrown into question.[13]

12. Gray, *Not By Might*, pp. 105-132.

13. The impetus for the professionalization and specialization of academia came from a variety of disparate sources. One of these sources, Scottish Common Sense Realism, had driven much of Christian (especially Reformed) higher educational theory since the eighteenth century, but its vitality was badly eroded by the time the challenge from objectivists was fully mounted in the 1930s. Under the influence of Scottish Realism, Whitworth — like other Reformed Christian institutions — had assumed for decades the almost Thomistic nature of free inquiry. When the challenges from Freud, Dewey, Wittgenstein, and others against the revealed and revealing nature of inquiry were fully

The new breed of social scientists found concepts like character and citizenship to be too value-laden. Many of the newly trained social scientists believed that such things as "values" were not observable and therefore not verifiable or objective. The scientific model and radical empiricism influenced all disciplines, including religious studies, philosophy, and the other humanities. To argue a particular perspective relative to knowledge, or consciously to advocate "higher truths" or specific behavioral values or societal norms, made an educational institution vulnerable to the charge that these were inappropriate positions from the standpoint of research. The secular academy argued that colleges and universities were places where all ideas should have equal currency. Academics valued freedom of expression only in the context of objective empirical research into all areas of life.[14]

Although all of this had little immediate effect at places like Whitworth, it was to have enormous effect over the course of the century.[15] Gradually an older generation of faculty was replaced by a younger group of scholars and teachers who were trained not at the seminary, but at these burgeoning secular

---

mounted by the 1930s, Christian institutions had no other model on which to base their commitment to free inquiry. Since they had already accepted the professionalization of higher education, hiring more university-trained specialists, they soon found themselves coping with specialists whose values and educational theoretical assumptions were sharply at odds with traditional Christian notions of inquiry. On the impact of Scottish Common Sense Realism upon Presbyterianism see Thomas A. Askew and Peter W. Spellman, *The Churches and the American Experience: Ideals and Institutions* (Grand Rapids: Baker Book House, 1984), p. 72.

14. On this point, see Edward Purcell, *The Crisis of Democratic Theory: Scientific Naturalism and the Problem of Value* (Lexington: University of Kentucky Press, 1973); George Marsden, "The Soul of the American University: An Historical Overview," *First Things* (January 1991): 34-47; Richard Hofstadter and Walter P. Metzger, the *Development of Academic Freedom in the United States* (New York: Columbia University Press, 1955); Laurence Veysey, *The Emergence of the American University* (Chicago: University of Chicago Press, 1965); Thomas Haskell, *The Emergence of Professional Social Science* (Urbana: University of Illinois Press, 1977); David Hollinger, "Justification by Verification: The Scientific Challenge to the Moral Authority of Christianity in Modern America," in Michael J. Lacey, ed., *Religion and Twentieth-Century American Intellectual Life* (Cambridge: Cambridge University Press, 1989), pp. 116-134.

15. Whitworth's adoption of the standards of the new research universities should come as no surprise. From its founding the college had adopted the educational "norms" of the broader academic culture. The only difference was that in the early years, those norms were more amenable to Christian assumptions. For example, the classics were part of a Whitworth education from the beginning because it was assumed, much like it had been since the scholastic period, that a truly educated person knew Latin and studied the trivium and quadrivium as a matter of course. No further rationale for their inclusion in the curriculum of any church-related institution was necessary.

graduate schools. Both methodologically and ideologically, secularization began to have a greater impact on the way subjects were taught.[16]

Ward Sullivan, who assumed the office of President at Whitworth in 1930, was not an ordained clergyman but a Ph.D. from the University of Illinois who had taught history at the University of Kansas. Sullivan did not abandon the religious emphasis of the college, and in fact valued the traditional Presbyterian and Reformed commitment to the pursuit of truth wherever it led. However, subtle changes in Whitworth's religious ethos became increasingly evident. For example, by the end of the decade Whitworth attempted to appeal to a widening circle of students: "Whitworth College, while primarily a college of the Arts and Sciences, has also wider outlooks and aims. It offers opportunities for culture, but does not neglect the fact that many students desire courses which lead to earning a living or pre-professional preparation."[17] During the 1930s Whitworth therefore added courses and departments to the curriculum in order to meet the demand for more specialized education.

At the same time, Whitworth reduced its statement regarding religion to the following: "Whitworth College provides courses in the Bible as a foundation for the Christian faith and an environment designed to stimulate growth in Christian living."[18] The college required chapel on a daily basis but dropped the stipulation that students had to attend Sunday services. Sullivan hired faculty if they were qualified academically, but increasingly put the religious issue on the back burner.[19] In all of this Whitworth was following the pattern established by her sister Presbyterian and church-related colleges, broadening the curriculum and hiring faculty according to predominantly academic considerations.

The traditional Reformed commitment to the nurturing of the mind provided the strength of purpose for Sullivan to try and make the college more academically respectable. Sullivan wanted the college to become fully accredited, a goal which was achieved in 1933. In effect, the college found itself in the 1930s accepting the "rules" of the educational game as played by the public and private research universities which had already jettisoned the notion that religious issues were appropriate subjects of inquiry for a modern

16. Robert Sandin expresses the dilemma most succinctly: "Lacking adequate operational models of their own design, they (Christian colleges and universities) have often resorted to imitation of educational patterns which serve them badly." See Robert T. Sandin, *The Search for Excellence: The Christian College in an Age of Educational Competition* (Macon: Mercer University Press, 1982), p. 11.

17. *Whitworth College Catalogue, 1939-40*, p. 14.

18. *Whitworth College Catalogue, 1939-40*, p. 14.

19. Letter from former Whitworth College president Mark Koehler to Dale Soden, February 15, 1991.

student.[20] Simultaneously, the Presbyterian Church rent itself over the impact of scientific objectivism, thus proving incapable of offering Whitworth any viable alternative to the secularization which was affecting the church itself as much as its institutions of higher learning.

Holding Fast

If subtle pressures were beginning to change the nature of the intellectual environment at the college, the typical student of the 1930s would barely have noticed. Of course, the overwhelming memory for most students was the impact of the Depression. Like students all over the country, Whitworth students struggled to make ends meet. They found a marvelous array of part-time jobs to put themselves through school. One student reported that she picked and canned 742 quarts of fruit during one summer to pay for her first year's tuition. But students and faculty from that era speak nostalgically of school spirit, college traditions, and their sense that collectively they had made it together through difficult times.[21]

By the 1940s, the religious identity of Presbyterian colleges continued to emerge as an issue for denominational leaders as well as for college administrators. As a partial result of the continuing fallout from the evolution controversy of the 1920s, many Christians regarded both academic quality and academic research with considerable suspicion. In turn, the presidents of many institutions seemed less and less inclined to hire prospective faculty who pointedly identified themselves as Christian.

However, just when other institutions drifted more noticeably away from their denominational heritage, Whitworth turned in a different direction. In 1940, Frank Warren assumed the presidency of the college, a position he would retain until his death in 1963. Warren came out of a Free Methodist tradition and had been dean of the department of religion at Seattle Pacific College. But he was also strongly considered to succeed Mark Matthews as the pastor of Seattle's First Presbyterian Church, at that time the largest congregation in the denomination. As president of Whitworth, Warren pushed the college to reaffirm much more strongly its ties to the Presbyterian Church and its identity as an evangelical institution. If other colleges were becoming more nervous about hiring Christian faculty, Warren made sure that Whitworth's professors

20. One of the central arguments of George Marsden's recent study of American higher education concerns the marginalization of religious issues on the university campus by the mid-twentieth century. See George M. Marsden, *The Soul of the American University: From Protestant Establishment to Established Unbelief* (New York: Oxford University Press, 1994).

21. Dale E. Soden, *A Venture of Mind and Spirit,* pp. 62-63.

professed a commitment to Christianity. Before the end of Warren's first decade as president, the catalogue included a statement about the hiring of faculty:

> The administration is frank to admit that only those teachers are appointed who give clear evidence that they possess a genuine Christian faith and are actively related to some evangelical church. It believes also that its teachers must be leaders in their chosen fields of teaching. The College can adequately serve the youth of America only to the degree that its faculty is scholarly and Christian.[22]

The same year that statement appeared, 1948-49, Warren placed in the catalogue a more specific doctrinal statement about the religious identity of the college.

> Whitworth College accedes to the historic faith of Protestantism and stands unequivocally for its fundamental principles. We believe the Scriptures of the Old and New Testaments to be the inspired Word of God and the only infallible rule of faith and practice. We believe in the sovereignty of redemption on the cross, and in the Holy Spirit who dwells in every believer as the Spirit of Truth, of Holiness, and of Comfort.[23]

College trustees from the Warren era repeatedly assert that Frank Warren exercised enormous influence over the religious environment of the college as well as over faculty hiring, although he imposed no specific statement of faith.

After World War II, Whitworth was, like most colleges and universities, flooded with returning veterans seeking a college education. Whitworth grew into a substantially larger operation during those years. Enrollment broke all records and climbed from 223 in 1940 to 755 in 1950. This swelling enrollment forced the college to replace the surplus hospital buildings that served as makeshift quarters with new permanent facilities: a gymnasium, an auditorium, new classroom buildings, a library, and dormitories. By 1965, the undergraduate population strained even these facilities with a total enrollment of 1,147.

Two faculty members provided intellectual leadership for Whitworth during the Warren years: Clarence Simpson in English and Fenton Duvall in history. Simpson earned his Ph.D. from Stanford; Duvall received his from the University of Pennsylvania. They symbolized Warren's efforts to build the college around a community of professing Christians who were trained at the nation's best graduate schools. Again, broadly evangelical (Simpson and Duvall

22. *Whitworth College Catalogue, 1948-49*, p. 13.
23. *Whitworth College Catalogue, 1948-49*, p. 13.

were Wesleyan in background), they were committed to academic excellence and rejected efforts to define religious identity at the college more rigidly.

Frank Warren died in 1963, precisely when the challenge to the notion of *in loco parentis* began to be felt at virtually all church-related or Christian colleges in the country. Leaders of many of these schools took steps to relax or eliminate altogether dress codes along with rules that prohibited dancing and smoking. Most schools made chapel voluntary by the end of the decade. Pressures began to mount on the Whitworth administration to relax its rules in all of these areas. Warren's successor, Mark Koehler, retained the requirement that faculty be Christian although there was no insistence that they should be members of an evangelical church. Koehler, the only alumnus to serve Whitworth as president, had attended the college during the thirties and returned to the college to head the Bible Department in 1942. Eventually Koehler served under Warren as executive vice-president. His presidency insured the general continuity of Warren's vision.

However, the practice of hiring only Christian faculty — while probably the single most important factor in maintaining the college's close relationship with the Presbyterian Church — did not solve the problem of what kind of Christian or Presbyterian college Whitworth would be. Pressures continued to mount both from inside and outside the church to relax the college's level of control over the lives of its students. Throughout much of the 1960s, Whitworth continued to resist many of the challenges to its restrictions on student choices. By the end of the 1960s, women under the age of 21 were still "not permitted to travel by car beyond the boundaries of Washington and North Idaho except upon receipt of written permission from parent or guardian."[24] However, by the end of the decade, the Board of Trustees finally allowed dancing and movies on campus and implemented a relaxed dress code. Mandatory chapel ended in 1970.

The Challenge of Turbulent Times

By the late 1960s and early 1970s, Presbyterian and other denominational colleges were faced with significant political and social pressures. From the civil rights movement and the war in Vietnam to the demands of a baby-boom generation of students for greater control of their educational experience, the challenges confronting Whitworth faculty and administrators were enormous. In this context, the Reformed heritage, taking seriously the call to "transform" culture on the basis of biblical principles, began to make itself felt at Whitworth College as never before.

24. *Whitworth College Catalogue, 1969-70*, p. 14.

Some faculty point to John Kennedy's visit during the presidential campaign of 1960 as the beginning of a heightened political consciousness on campus. Other visits from civil rights activists James Farmer and Julian Bond galvanized increasing numbers of students. Activist-theologian William Stringfellow wielded perhaps the greatest influence of any campus visitor. He pointed especially to the absence of African American students, staff, and faculty on the Whitworth campus. As a result, students pressured the administration and officials responded by aggressively recruiting African American students from as close as Seattle and from as far away as Harlem. Frustrations from both sides eventually surfaced: students claimed that too little financial aid and no adequate support system were available for black students on campus, and many professors were simply unprepared for the increasingly militant approach of many black students. Within a few years, the numbers of black students decreased. But the events of those years provide an excellent example of the way in which Reformed impulses mesh with the spirit of the times in an attempt to transform the culture along biblical principles.

By the 1970s, Whitworth trustees, administrators, and faculty began to want to define the college's relationship to the church in a new way. Under president Edward Lindaman, who took office in 1970, Whitworth continued to identify itself as a Christian institution affiliated with the Presbyterian Church. But under Lindaman the nature of that Christian context began to take on a different cast. While Lindaman remained committed to hiring a Christian faculty, his new approach reflected a more liberal theology.

First, Lindaman insisted that faculty make every effort to apply their Christianity to the social and political problems facing society. He embraced experimentalism in almost every arena including religious expression. "A shared enthusiasm for Jesus Christ binds the youngest Ph.D. with the most senior member of the faculty," stated the 1978 catalogue. "They express this enthusiasm in many different ways — membership in a whole spectrum of Christian denominations (including the 'underground' church based in homes), by varied political affiliations, and contrasting lifestyles and cultures."[25] In fact, prospective faculty were asked whether they had this "enthusiasm" for Christ but were not asked about membership in a particular church. Lindaman encouraged faculty members to integrate issues of faith and learning wherever and whenever they felt such integration was appropriate. As a result, Christian values and Christian perspectives on public policy issues found their way into classroom discussions. At the same time, stressing toleration as a Christian virtue, the administration encouraged faculty to be tolerant of non-Christian points of view.

Second, Whitworth committed resources to expanding the chaplaincy pro-

25. *Whitworth College Catalogue, 1978-79*, p. 14.

gram. Fostering small groups, Bible studies, "dialogues, growth groups, and action groups," the chaplain's office also established mission programs in London, Mississippi, Newark, and San Francisco. Student volunteers organized through the chaplain's office met local social concerns in Spokane. By the end of the decade, the college constructed a new chapel on campus.

Third, Whitworth remained proactive regarding the dormitory experience of its students. While Whitworth still prohibited drinking, premarital sex, and drugs in the 1970s, administrators also introduced the notion of student development. The student-life arm of the college grew significantly during this decade, incorporating programs to help students "mature" into adulthood. The college established co-educational dormitories and increased hours of visitation between members of the opposite sex. From community building and an awareness of non-western cultures, to theme dorms ranging from those housing black students to those devoted to foreign languages, the administration and faculty endorsed a whole range of new policies which it deemed to be consistent with Whitworth's mission as a Christian college. "We believe that Jesus Christ is the model of the fully developed whole person," wrote one administrator in 1978, "the One who was able to give and receive love most fully, perceive people and the world most clearly, and welcome rather than resist change."[26]

In several ways it is possible to see the presidencies of Sullivan and Lindaman as the Reformed bookends to the more evangelical tendencies of Warren and Koehler. Sullivan reflected the Reformed commitment to increasing the reputation of the faculty; he believed that truth was not to be feared in any form. Lindaman represented the more transformational side of the Reformed tradition. He clearly believed that Christians should be about the business of shaping the present and the future on the basis of Christian principles. In between were thirty years of leadership that focused on the importance of hiring a Christian faculty and developing a "committed student body." This combination continues to provide the underlying ethos for the college today.

Curricular Changes in the 1960s and 1970s

The desire to maintain a Christian identity and yet be academically respectable led to significant changes in the curriculum, beginning in the late 1960s and early 1970s. Most revealing were the changes regarding, first, the religion requirement and, second, the civilization requirement — both Western and non-Western. Until 1967, Whitworth maintained a rather stringent Bible requirement. Since the 1930s, the college had mandated that each student take eight semester hours

26. *Whitworth College Catalogue, 1978-79*, p. 66.

of Bible courses. These generally consisted of two semester hours during the freshman year or first year of transfer, and three hours in each of the following two years of residency. In 1967 the faculty agreed to reduce this requirement to six semester hours (two hours in each of three years).

The most significant change occurred in 1969 when the college moved away from the formal semester system and approved what was known as the 4-1-4 calendar. That same year, the college reduced its Bible requirement to three semester hours, including one course in Old Testament, one in New Testament, and one on any book of the Bible. The college jettisoned a required course entitled, "Fundamentals of the Christian Faith," which was a study of the basic doctrines of Protestant Christianity.[27] In its place the new curriculum included courses called Core 150, Core 250, and Core 350. Core 150, entitled "The Judeo-Christian Tradition," focused attention on the historic roots of Christianity and presented the religious culture and values of the Judeo-Christian tradition with the idea that the student would be "challenged to decide what these insights mean for him in assuming a constructive and satisfying role in society today."[28] The course did not attempt to inculcate religious doctrine; rather it focused on the history and culture of Judaism and an overview of the history of the Christian church, and attempted to articulate a Judeo-Christian perspective regarding contemporary political and social problems.

Core 250, entitled "The Rationalist Tradition," focused on the development of Western civilization through an analysis of great thinkers. Faculty teaching in this course stressed the differences of opinion among these thinkers regarding issues of epistemology, metaphysics, ethics, and politics. Presenting each thinker as objectively as possible, faculty sought to avoid highlighting their own "preferences."

Core 350, entitled "Science and Civilization," focused on the impact of science and technology on Western civilization. This course died after only a couple of years in the 1970s, then was revived in almost identical form in 1988. Essentially, the course examined the underlying assumptions and values of technology and science in contemporary society.

These courses, forming the cornerstone of Whitworth's liberal arts curriculum, were designed with the assumption that the values of Western civilization ought to be identified and studied. In most cases the faculty, all trained at secular institutions, attempted to teach these values "objectively." Faculty

27. One might argue that with the reduction of the religion requirement, the end of required chapel attendance, the termination of "Fundamentals of the Christian Faith" as a course required for all students, and the redefinition of the formerly *in loco parentis* model of residence life, Whitworth had effectively terminated any understanding of itself as a Christian college by way of specific programmatic institutional support for religious issues.

28. *Whitworth College Catalogue, 1973-74*, p. 23.

described the core program in the catalogue as "inter-disciplinary, thematic courses [which] confront the student with the social forces which help shape our patterns of thinking, define our standards of values, and create options of behavior which are open to us today."[29]

Yet on more than one occasion during the last twenty years, Whitworth's faculty has struggled with the question of how these courses differ from those offered at Stanford, Harvard, or any first-rate secular institution. Faculty ask, for example, what is distinctively Christian about these courses. More recently, particularly in Core 250, C. S. Lewis has emerged as the principal Christian thinker to have dealt most thoughtfully with the challenges posed by the rationalist tradition. Whitworth's philosophy department has also offered a very popular course on the thought of C. S. Lewis. This emphasis on Lewis occurs in spite of the fact that, in some ways, Lewis shares more with the Thomistic tradition of Roman Catholicism than he does with the Reformed tradition of the Protestant Reformation.

Broader Visions

Throughout the 1980s and into the 1990s, Whitworth sought to refine its Christian identity while searching to find that delicate balance between its dual affinity with American Presbyterianism and American evangelicalism. The selection of Conservative Baptist Robert Mounce to succeed Lindaman as President in 1980 signaled a return to the more broadly pietistic distinctives of the Warren years. While Mounce strengthened the evangelical identity of the college, conscious linkage with the founding denomination languished. The college tended not to hire tenure-track faculty unless they professed a belief in Jesus Christ. Mounce himself interviewed prospective faculty members and, in addition to assessing academic qualifications, sought to determine the interviewee's faith perspectives.[30] To insure a certain measure of orthodoxy, even in the initial stages of a faculty search, Mounce instituted the requirement that each applicant for a faculty position submit in writing a personal faith statement — a requirement that remained in force in 1995.[31]

29. *Whitworth College Catalogue, 1973-74,* p. 22.

30. Many of those hired under Mounce's presidency have been involved in revivifying the religious ethos of the college in a more broadly evangelical tradition, even though they themselves may be personally committed to the Reformed expression of the Christian faith.

31. Compare the centrality of the faith question at Whitworth in the 1990s with the controversy regarding the role of orthodoxy at a sister Reformed institution of the upper Midwest. For a brief summary of this debate see Mary Crystal Cage, "Hope College Is Urged' to Clarify Policy of Hiring Christians," *The Chronicle of Higher Education* 41 (September 7, 1994): A31.

Mounce's swing toward evangelicalism pleased some but dismayed others. With the appointment of Darrell Guder as vice-president for academic affairs in 1986, the Reformed expression of faith regained a champion at Whitworth. In some ways, Mounce and Guder embodied the larger college identity in their respective emphasis on evangelicalism and the Reformed tradition. Guder continually reminded faculty of the college's ties to the Reformed tradition. He also helped strengthen the Presbyterian connection through such programs as the Ecclesia Project, a college-wide effort designed to encourage students systematically to consider church membership in the present and church leadership in the future, as well as to help faculty develop into spiritual mentors. Guder's personal scholarship further demonstrated his commitment to the Reformed perspective. Whitworth retained the curriculum that had developed in the late 1960s and 1970s and the college continued to support its Office of Student Development. However, Lindaman's emphasis on connecting Whitworth with the Spokane community diminished under Mounce.

The retirement of President Mounce just prior to the centennial celebration in 1990 led to an even stronger revival of the Reformed perspective on campus with the appointment of Arthur De Jong as his successor. De Jong had lifelong ties with the Dutch Reformed church and in concert with Dean Guder sought stronger ties to the Presbyterian church. These ties, however, threatened at certain points the school's close association with the more evangelical wing of the Christian higher educational community.[32]

Guder's departure in 1991 and De Jong's in 1992 appeared to leave the question of Whitworth's future direction up in the air. Yet Whitworth's dual identity appears to have achieved a balance at the college. In Whitworth's recent past, Bible study groups and mission service organizations have existed side by side with very active chapters of Habitat for Humanity and Amnesty International. Racial, sexual, and women's awareness events, environmental programs, and anti-apartheid days — reflecting concerns emphasized by the Presbyterian Church as part of its mission to be an agency of justice and reconciliation — have marked the school calendar as much as have programs from a more conservative or evangelical perspective — the Staley lectures featuring in recent years speakers such as Tony Campolo and John Fischer, Young Life ministry training, and student-generated ministries to the homeless of Spokane. Weekly contemporary praise-worship services with a charismatic flavor are held in the same facility which houses the newly appointed Dean of the Chapel who is responsible for heightening the Reformed worship style of west coast Presbyterianism at the college. Less creedal and confessionally oriented than pertains in Presbyterian

32. For example, when the college ran into funding problems in the late 1980s, senior administrators seriously considered pulling the college out of the Christian College Coalition and attempting to form a smaller network of more like-minded Reformed institutions.

settings elsewhere in the country, the style and liturgy are still distinctly Presbyterian in nature. Students and faculty come together in spiritual mentoring groups where denominational loyalties are not a consideration.

More recently, Provost Kenneth Shipps routinely encouraged faculty to integrate Christian (not necessarily Reformed) perspectives with the content of their classes and to struggle with the relationship between faith and learning. A national intellectual climate, radically different from the climate that has prevailed throughout most of the twentieth century, made possible the kind of leadership Provost Shipps provided. Indeed, the radical empiricism of the twentieth century academic community had worn itself out even in its own arena — the public research university. With the advent of postmodernism and its affirmation of perspectival thinking and knowing, a new generation of Christian scholars and students stood ready to challenge the old objectivist goals of education and the notion that scholarship could be divorced from presuppositions. Highly qualified faculty and well motivated students have demonstrated the possibility of fusing unabashedly Christian faith perspectives with high academic achievement and a deep concern for humanity.

Over the past decade many Whitworth faculty members and administrators have contributed to national dialogue on the issue of faith and learning.[33]

33. A partial listing of such contributions by Whitworth administrators would include former President Arthur J. De Jong's *Reclaiming a Mission: New Directions for the Church-Related College* (Grand Rapids: Eerdmans, 1990); former provost Kenneth Shipps' "Church-Related Colleges and Academics" in David S. Guthrie and Richard Nofzger, Jr., eds., *Agendas for Church-Related Colleges and Universities, New Directions for Higher Education Series* 20 (San Francisco: Jossey-Bass, Inc., 1992); and Shipps with J. A. Carpenter, eds., *Making Higher Education Christian* (Grand Rapids: Eerdmans, 1987).

Whitworth faculty members have also been quite active in this field. Psychology professor James Waller and a colleague from Asbury College received a sizable grant from the Pew Charitable Trusts to study pedagogy and values acquisition in the early 1990s. Waller, philosophy professor Forrest E. Baird, English professor Leonard Oakland, and historians Dale E. Soden and Arlin Migliazzo participated in the public presentation of the funded research. Most of the presentations were collected and published in *Faculty Dialogue* 19 (Winter 1993). Migliazzo has also published two articles on the topic: "Teaching History as an Act of Faith," *Fides et Historia* 23 (Winter/Spring 1991): 6-19; and "Cultural Mimesis and Christian Higher Education: A Personal Reconnaissance," *Fides et Historia* 25 (Fall 1993): 102-108. Biologist Jean L. Bertlesen Pond's article "Catholic Frogs" won the Howard Vollum Writing Award as the best essay on the "horizons of science and the Christian faith." It appeared in *Faculty Dialogue* 18 (Fall 1992): 83-90. Philosopher of science Steve Meyer engages in the debate regarding intelligent design on numerous fronts, speaking to both academic and lay audiences.

Perhaps most prolific in his quest to bring Christian perspectives to bear on his discipline is sociologist Robert A. Clark. Dating back to his years at Gordon College, professor Clark has been instrumental in the faith-learning dialogue. During the 1980s he co-chaired

Whitworth is among the charter members of a national group of church-related institutions brought together to discuss such issues. Funded by the Lilly Endowment in 1991 and hosted by Valparaiso University, this project has stimulated on-going conversation on the Whitworth campus itself. In 1994 Whitworth launched an annual regional conference to address such issues. In addition, throughout the 1980s and early 1990s, the Christian College Coalition has sponsored workshops hosted by Whitworth. The faculty have also made significant contributions to their respective disciplines, resulting in national or regional scholarly recognition.[34]

Like its more secular counterparts, Whitworth prides itself on the number of national merit scholars enrolled, the variety of scholarships earned by its students, and the placement of its students in the top medical, law, and graduate schools in the country. Over the past decade Whitworth students have won Fulbright and NEH grants and a Mellon Fellowship. International History and Psychology Honor Societies have had active chapters on the Whitworth campus since the 1980s. Whitworth was chosen in 1994 to participate in a highly selective program sponsored by the Pew Charitable Trusts to identify Christian college students who hold great promise for graduate study. Three appearances on the much-touted *U.S. News & World Report* ranking of the best colleges and universities in the country (1983, 1994, and 1995) have bolstered its academic reputation. A recent front page article in the regional press praised the college's music department for its impressive graduates.[35]

Current president Bill Robinson, with roots in both the Reformed *and* evangelical traditions,[36] openly celebrates Whitworth's twin commitment to evangelicalism and the Reformed tradition. He fully supports the notion that the college should be unapologetically Christian while not requiring a specific faith statement or church membership. Robinson often refers to George Whitworth's original desire to educate both the mind and the heart as a testimony to the consistency of mission and the general sense in which Whitworth continues to

---

sessions, read papers, and served as panel discussant at meetings of the Association of Christians Teaching Sociology, and in 1989 Clark was a panelist on "Teaching Sociology in the Religiously Affiliated Liberal Arts College" at the annual meeting of the American Sociological Association. He has published "Thinking About Culture: Theirs and Ours," in M. Leming, R. DeVries, and B. Furnish, eds., *The Sociological Perspective: A Value-Committed Approach* (Grand Rapids: Zondervan, 1989), and with S. D. Gaede, "Knowing Together: Reflections of a Wholistic Sociology of Knowledge," in H. Heie and D. Wolfe, eds., *The Reality of Christian Learning* (Grand Rapids: Eerdmans, 1987).

34. See Dale E. Soden, *A Venture of Mind and Spirit,* pp. 135-149.

35. Mike Prager, "School of Note: Whitworth Builds Reputation for Musical Excellence," *The Spokesman-Review* (February 27, 1995), A1.

36. President Robinson's own educational background illumines his dual commitment. He attended Wheaton College, Moody Bible Institute, and Princeton Seminary.

be evangelical in the Reformed tradition without being doctrinaire or pedantic.[37] Current strategic planning initiatives which should take Whitworth well into the next century reiterate the need to be true to the Reformed perspective of the Presbyterian Church and to a broad evangelicalism, characteristic of so many of its students, faculty, and administrators, past and present.[38]

A Healthy Tension

While the historic connection of Whitworth College to the Presbyterian Church has remained relatively strong, particularly when compared to many other denominationally-sponsored institutions, the future relationship is not without its challenges. The decline in membership and the concomitant decrease in financial resources of the national Presbyterian Church make it unrealistic to expect an increase in church support for Whitworth College. Unlike a century ago, when the church took a more proactive role in the establishment and nurturing of its colleges and universities, the church today allows each institution to define the relationship to the denomination. This decentralizing tendency highlights the precarious nature of Presbyterian higher education at the end of the twentieth century.[39] Whitworth's geographic distance from the headquarters of the church

37. A series of interviews conducted with students, faculty, and administrators specifically for this article bear out the importance of these twin perspectives. The interviews were conducted on October 25, 1994.

38. Bill Robinson, "Whitworth College in Year 2000," unpublished vision statement, September 1994; "Strategic Plan for Whitworth College," draft, Whitworth College Institutional Planning Group, February 1995.

39. The Presbyterian Church has had an equivocal relationship with its related colleges in the latter half of the twentieth century. While all judicatories theoretically share in the higher educational mission of the church, such support had become so tenuous that in March 1990 the presidents of the then sixty-nine Presbyterian colleges and universities voiced their alarm about the future of their institutions. This note of deep concern has moved the church to think more intentionally again with regard to its mission in higher education. Among other recommendations in its report to the 206th General Assembly (1994), the Higher Education Program Team of the church urged (1) a serious study at all governing levels "to identify and implement sustainable models for ministry in higher education" and to report to the 208th General Assembly (1996) "how, if at all, and at what governing levels, the PC(USA) should be involved," and (2) that 1998 "be designated the Year of Emphasis on Education, focusing on the church as a educating institution and on the church's mission in and through education." See "A Statement of the Association of Presbyterian Colleges and Universities," March 25, 1990, quoted in Robert Wood Lynn, " 'The Survival of Recognizably Protestant Colleges': Reflections on Old-Line Protestantism, 1950-1990," pp. 170-194, in George M. Marsden and Bradley J. Longfield, eds., *The Secularization of the Academy* (New York: Oxford University Press, 1992), p. 170. The quotations

in Louisville, Kentucky renders this condition even more problematic. In his book on the future of Christian higher education, Robert Sandin warns:

> the viability of the Christian college as an instrument of the church's witness and nurture depends not on the material help of Washington, but on the clarity and firmness of the church's own faith in the enterprise of Christian higher education.[40]

Sandin's call for a clear vision and strong commitment on the part of the church to Christian education is an important message. The future health of the denomination may depend on strengthening its support for its colleges. For the moment, however, Whitworth College will continue to depend less on the commitment of the national church and more on the choices made by its president, faculty, and board of trustees to retain and invigorate the college's historic identity as a Presbyterian institution. The strength of that commitment will be tested by the fact that the Pacific Northwest remains the least churched region in the country.[41]

As we have suggested, the Reformed and evangelical roots run deep in this institution. Though they have intertwined in different ways throughout the last century, they nevertheless are clearly identifiable keys to understanding the specific ethos of the college. While it will be difficult to predict in what exact ways the Reformed and evangelical traditions will be expressed in the future, it is likely that Whitworth College will continue to be identified by those twin strands as it seeks to advance the vision of George Whitworth for providing a Christian education of both the mind and heart.

---

above are from *On Being Faithful: The Continuing Mission of the Presbyterian Church (U.S.A.) in Higher Education* (Louisville: Higher Education Program Team, 1995), p. 65.

These "in-house" concerns mirror some of the findings Mennonite scholar Victor Stoltzfus noted in his recent comparative case-study look at church-related higher education. See Stoltzfus, *Church-Affiliated Higher Education: Exploratory Case Studies of Presbyterian, Roman Catholic, and Wesleyan Colleges* (Goshen: Pinchpenny Press, 1992). Ten years earlier Robert Sandin voiced his concern regarding the future viability of the entire enterprise of Christian higher education in his previously cited monograph, *The Search for Excellence.*

40. Sandin, *The Search for Excellence,* p. 7.

41. According to statistics cited by Stark and Bainbridge, Washington is the least churched state in the union. Of 215 Standard Metropolitan Statistical Areas identified by the U.S. Census Bureau, Spokane ranks 184th with an average of 388 church members for every thousand inhabitants. See Rodney Stark and William Sims Bainbridge, *The Future of Religion: Secularization, Revival, and Cult Formation* (Berkeley: University of California Press, 1985), pp. 70-71, 75-76. Utilizing comparison data from 1906 Stark and Bainbridge note the same tendencies toward lower church involvement in the far West in the early years of the century. See Stark and Bainbridge, *Future of Religion,* p. 94. For a more detailed description of the impact of this phenomenon on the Spokane area see "Change of Faith," *The Spokesman-Review* (December 15, 1991), A1.

THE MENNONITE TRADITION

What Can the Mennonite Tradition Contribute to Christian Higher Education?

Rodney J. Sawatsky

In North America today, twenty-four post-secondary institutions are Mennonite affiliated. Of these, five are Bible schools, five are Bible colleges, one is a junior college, eight are liberal arts colleges or universities, two are liberal arts affiliates of provincial universities, and three are seminaries. All of these are sponsored by a total community of fewer than 600,000 people. In addition, this small Christian tradition operates numerous elementary and secondary schools and assists in funding Mennonite schools, colleges, and seminaries abroad.

These Mennonite institutions represent not only a major investment in higher education but also a considerable variety of educational models and, to a lesser extent, varied philosophies of Christian post-secondary education. Yet several common motifs are shared by virtually all these schools — motifs which are fundamentally Anabaptist in inspiration and orientation. This Anabaptist perspective is best summarized as incarnational. The Word made flesh is the pervasive theological foundation. Before characterizing this Anabaptist educational perspective, two brief excurses are necessary to provide context.

Mennonite Attitudes Toward Higher Education

Despite the apparent unreserved commitment to the cause evidenced by its many schools, the Mennonite community as a whole remains ambivalent toward higher education. Interestingly, ambivalence is felt even by those Mennonites at the more progressive end of the continuum. A growing percentage of Mennonites are attending schools and universities that are not Mennonite affiliated. Many of these are students pursuing undergraduate and graduate programs unavailable in Mennonite colleges and seminaries. Others, however, make alternative choices apparently because the Mennonite options are considered too sectarian or insufficiently evangelical or lacking in quality and prestige. Stewards of Mennonite distinctiveness are concerned about this dynamic, since graduates of Mennonite schools tend to score higher in surveys on such variables as Anabaptism, pacifism, church participation, and communalism.[1] Ambivalence towards specifically Mennonite higher education can be considered, therefore, a correlate of acculturation.

Ambivalence is most readily identified, however, with the "old order" segment of Mennonite tradition and most accurately reflects the old order position. Even secondary — not to speak of tertiary — education is deemed unnecessary and even dangerous by most in the conservative end of the spectrum. From the conservative Mennonite perspective, advanced education is closely associated with worldly conformity and pride, primary marks of Christian unfaithfulness. While it may not have a high public profile, this anti-intellectualism of the Mennonite "visible minority" is not disappearing and cannot easily be dismissed. Indeed, demographic projections indicate that early in the twenty-first century the old order/conservative faction will be in the majority.[2] At that point, to characterize the Mennonite attitude toward higher education as ambivalent would be to understate the matter.

Such attitudes are deeply rooted in Mennonite history, residing in the very Anabaptist genes of Mennonitism. Sixteenth-century Anabaptist leaders repeatedly castigated the learned of the day — the Protestant and Roman Catholic theologians who obscured and distorted the simple yet demanding gospel of Christ. For the Anabaptists, "truth was found in living, not in abstract reasoning."[3] Truly following the way of Christ, even if this meant martyrdom, required obedience rather than intellectual or creedal precision. Anabaptists claimed that intellectual sophistry, advanced by the learned, was a primary mechanism to avoid radical obedience.

Yet theirs was not an unambiguous "no" to education. Many of the Anabaptist leaders were themselves learned and sometimes seem almost to have voiced their protestations against education disingeniously. Menno Simons explained on one occasion that John a Lasco

> accuses me saying . . . that I despised learning and proficiency in language, disdainfully called them philosophies; referred to myself as a humble theologian, a matter with which to ensnare the untutored and simple folk, and

1. J. Howard Kauffman and Leo Driedger, *The Mennonite Mosaic: Identity and Modernization* (Scottdale: Herald Press, 1991), pp. 134, 135.

2. Steven Nolt, "The Mennonite Eclipse," *Festival Quarterly* 19 (Summer 1992): 8-12.

3. Walter Klaassen, *Anabaptism: Neither Catholic nor Protestant* (Waterloo, Ontario: Conrad Press, 1977), p. 45.

make myself a reputation. . . . Understand correctly dear readers, learnedness and proficiency in languages I have never disdained, but have honored and coveted them from my youth. . . . I am not so bereft of my senses that I should disdain and despise the knowledge of languages whereby the precious Word of divine grace has come to us. I could wish that I and all pious hearts were at home in them if only we would employ them in genuine humility and to the glory of God and the service of our fellows.[4]

Menno's position: education is legitimate but only if it is exercised in genuine humility — to the glory of God and the service of humanity.

Anabaptist ecclesiology, in fact, required that all believers, not only the leaders, understand and communicate the gospel. The Bible was the book of the people. All should read it for themselves. The theological defenses of relatively untutored men, women, and even children accused of heresy, as recorded in the *Martyrs Mirrors*, evidence surprising knowledge of the Scriptures and sophistication in interpretation. The Mennonites' *Gemeindetheologie*[5] — congregation theology — was a democratized theology which implicitly, if not always explicitly, encouraged all Christians to be educated.

Anabaptist apprehension concerning higher education, however, prevailed and continues among Mennonites to this day. Few educated Mennonites will not have been warned sometime during their careers: "the more learned, the more confused." Persecution, migration, ruralization, and related dynamics for centuries discouraged higher education in favor of humility, simplicity, and obedience — basic Anabaptist themes. To be sure, schools marked every Mennonite community, with time even excellent secondary and specialized schools, but post-secondary schools awaited the late nineteenth and even the twentieth century.

Only the Mennonites of Holland are an exception. They very early parted company with separatistic tendencies characteristic of most other Mennonites in favor of urban life, business, culture, higher education, and an educated ministry. While they never established a college or university, they did establish a seminary in 1735 in association with the University of Amsterdam. One wonders what difference it might have made to the *Doopsgezinde* church in Holland had they established colleges as did their Roman Catholic and some of their Reformed compatriots. Given the declining *Doopsgezinde* membership in Holland, the question is of particular interest in North America where apologists argue that Mennonite post-secondary schools are essential to the health and strength of the Mennonite churches.

---

4. Menno Simons, "The Incarnation of Our Lord," *The Complete Writings of Menno Simons* (Scottdale: Herald Press, 1966), p. 790.

5. Klassen, *Anabaptism: Neither Catholic nor Protestant*, p. 42.

Patterns in Mennonite Higher Education

A new chapter in Mennonite education began with the founding of Wadsworth Institute in Wadsworth, Ohio, in 1868. Although it closed after only ten years due to conflicting visions and inadequate support, Wadsworth was the first of the many post-secondary institutions the North American Mennonites established in the next century. An early project of a new Mennonite conference — the General Conference Mennonite Church — Wadsworth represented the "awakening" of Mennonite interest in missions, evangelism, and publications at the heart of this new conference. Wadsworth's mission was to train young people for this new activism, including pastors for congregations now eager for more educated and professional clergy.

Most of the major actors in this new conference and its new college had recently arrived from south Germany where their cultural environment, including pietism, encouraged pursuit of higher education. Those Mennonites who immigrated from Switzerland and neighboring countries in earlier decades and centuries were less prone to the innovations symbolized by Wadsworth. However, a major new immigration in the 1870s, this time from Russia, brought Mennonites to the United States and Canada who were ready to embrace the General Conference and its interest in higher education. Those who formed the Mennonite Brethren in Russia — a pietist inspired reform movement like the General Conference in the United States — had a similar, more positive attitude toward higher education, while maintaining a separate denominational structure.

But Wadsworth was too far to the east. These new immigrants established their colleges in the midst of their prairie settlements. Bethel College, the oldest continuing Mennonite college, was founded by those associated with the General Conference Mennonites in 1882 in Halstead, Kansas, before moving to Newton, and the Mennonite Brethren community founded Tabor College in Hillsboro, Kansas, in 1908. Freeman College in Freeman, South Dakota, and Bluffton College in Bluffton, Ohio, were also General Conference related. Freeman, founded in 1903, served as a junior college for many years but closed in 1967. Bluffton, originally named Central, in a sense picked up in 1900 where Wadsworth left off several decades before.

A progressive faction within the "old" Mennonite church by this time was also advocating less separatism and more activism, including college education. Goshen College in Goshen, Indiana, was the result. Founded in a neighboring town as Elkhart Institute in 1894, Goshen before long led in the "modernization" of the oldest and largest of North American Mennonite communities, which embraced most of the eighteenth- and early nineteenth-century immigrants of Swiss descent. This same community established Hesston College in Hesston, Kansas, in 1909 and Eastern Mennonite School (renamed College, and now

University) in Harrisonburg, Virginia, in 1917 — the latter designed to be a more conservative counterforce to Goshen.

In 1909 the Brethren in Christ established Messiah Bible School and Missionary Training Home in Grantham, Pennsylvania. In time Messiah became Messiah Bible College and then Messiah College. Today, with an enrollment of some 2400 students, it is much the largest post-secondary institution within the Council of Mennonite Colleges. The Brethren in Christ denomination is not technically Mennonite. It is, however, Anabaptist and identifies with the Mennonites especially through participation in organizations such as Mennonite Central Committee and the Mennonite World Conference. To complete the Brethren in Christ story, its Upland College in Upland, California, which closed its doors several decades ago, should also be noted.

Scholars recognize the changes in the Mennonite community that resulted in and from the new colleges. Some interpreters emphasize the shift towards "Americanism" and "Protestantism" resulting from the "awakening" and "quickening" which spawned the colleges.[6] Others focus more on what was gained than lost, for example, rebalancing the competing themes of separation and mission to the world.[7] From this perspective James Juhnke summarized the first decades of Mennonite college history in this way:

> The colleges had some imposing flaws, yet they successfully established both religious mission and social control. Religious mission meant not only joining the Protestant world missionary crusade but also working within American society to propagate Mennonite values. The main effort at social control was to stem the loss of American-educated youth from the church and to equip new leaders for guiding congregations as they moved out of rural isolation. Achievement was far from complete, yet working at religious mission and social control put new life into the Mennonite denomination, particularly its progressive wings![8]

Mennonite colleges moved in two directions simultaneously: they both liberated and conserved. They aided the Mennonites in becoming successful mainstream Americans and they articulated a distinctive vision — for most an "Anabaptist vision" — for remaining uniquely Mennonite. In turn, the colleges were at the center of most controversies in the Mennonite communi-

6. See Theron F. Schlabach, *Peace, Faith, Nation: Mennonites and Amish in Nineteenth-Century America* (Scottdale: Herald Press, 1988), pp. 295-321.

7. See Leland Harder, "The Quest for Equilibrium in our Established Sect: A Study of Sacred Change in the General Conference Mennonite Church" (unpublished Ph.D. dissertation, Northwestern University, 1962).

8. James C. Juhnke, *Vision, Doctrines, War: Mennonite Identity and Organizations in America, 1890-1930* (Scottdale: Herald Press, 1989), p. 164.

ties, including the fundamentalist-liberal conflict. And the college leaders, prominent champions of bridging both worlds by embracing aspects of the "outside" and maintaining the "inside," were typically highly visible and articulate denominational personalities. Yet, they also always remained somewhat suspect and were typically unable to resolve these inherent tensions even for themselves. "Contradictions between orthodox Mennonites and progressive American education were large, but Mennonite educators lived and worked within them." Most interestingly, "none of the early college leaders set forth a truly coherent philosophy of Mennonite education."[9]

A coherent philosophy of Mennonite higher education still waits to be written. However, the absence of such a philosophy has not deterred the establishment of new and the development of older Mennonite post-secondary schools. World War II pressed the Mennonites as pacifists to fortify their identities, even as it encouraged Mennonites anew to a larger social engagement. In response, existing colleges were strengthened and new colleges founded. In 1944 Fresno Pacific College in Fresno, California, began as Fresno Bible Institute. The Mennonite Brethren also opened Mennonite Brethren Bible College that same year in Winnipeg, Manitoba — a college which recently moved closer toward liberal arts college ranks with the new name, Concord College. The General Conference Mennonites followed suit in 1947 with Canadian Mennonite Bible College, also in Winnipeg.

The same post-war context produced several Mennonite seminaries. The Mennonite Biblical Seminary (MBS) was founded in 1945 in Chicago as a General Conference school. It replaced the Witmarsum Theological Seminary, which operated during the 1920s in Bluffton, Ohio. In 1958 MBS moved to Elkhart, Indiana, to join forces with Goshen Biblical Seminary, an "old" Mennonite institution which became a separate entity from Goshen College in 1946. Together they formed the Associated Mennonite Biblical Seminary. The Mennonite Brethren Biblical Seminary opened its doors in 1955 in Fresno, California, and Eastern Mennonite College (now University) introduced a seminary division which became Eastern Mennonite Seminary in 1965.

Two other types of educational institutions complete the Mennonite panoply of post-secondary options. Almost innumerable Bible schools or Bible institutes dotted the Mennonite landscape at one time or another. One survey identified forty-one such schools in Canada alone. Today only five of these schools remain as Bible schools and all are in Canada: Aylmer Bible School, Aylmer, Ontario; Bethany Bible Institute, Hepburn, Saskatchewan; Institute Biblique Laval, St. Laurent, Quebec; Swift Current Bible Institute, Swift Current, Saskatchewan (recently renamed Marpeck School of Discipleship); and Winkler Bible Institute, Winkler, Manitoba. Three others have upgraded into

9. Juhnke, *Vision, Doctrines, War*, p. 165.

Bible colleges: Columbia Bible College, Clearbrook, B.C.; Rosedale Bible College, Irwin, Ohio; and Steinbach Bible College, Steinbach, Manitoba. These institutions, although not nearly always functioning at a post-secondary education level, enrolled students after at least some secondary education and provided a major educational service to those who attended and, in turn, to their Mennonite communities. They asserted a strong separatist theme even as they prepared young people to serve in their churches and in the larger culture.[10]

Conrad Grebel College in Waterloo, Ontario, is unique among North American Mennonite post-secondary educational institutions. On the model of the British constituent college system, Conrad Grebel College is an affiliate of the University of Waterloo, alongside sister Roman Catholic, Anglican, and United Church of Canada colleges. Students register with and receive their degrees from the university but live at the college and take some of their courses through the college.

Menno Simons College in Winnipeg, Manitoba, on the University of Winnipeg campus, is the most recent arrival on the Mennonite college scene. Gradually taking form in the last decade, Menno Simons College is structured approximately on the Conrad Grebel model but without government funding and its own residential community. Concord College, also affiliated with the University of Winnipeg, is becoming another variant of the same approach. Menno Simons College, Concord College, and Canadian Mennonite Bible College are currently considering joining to form a new Mennonite university in Winnipeg — the city with the largest concentration of Mennonites in the world.

Mennonite post-secondary education in Canada and in the United States represents somewhat contrasting assumptions. In the United States, at least at the undergraduate level, Mennonite college education is designed to serve as an alternative to other available programs. In Canada, Mennonite post-secondary studies pursued at a Bible school, Bible college, or a university college are usually considered as complementary rather than as an alternative to public university education. The reasons for this are complex and relate to the differences in church-state relations between these two countries. Here it must suffice simply to note the contrast.

Besides representing various approaches to post-secondary education, these twenty-four institutions in the United States and Canada also have varied governance structures. Many if not most of these schools were initiated by creative leaders who saw a need and had a vision — and sometimes financial resources. Others were more the product of congregational or conference

10. Walter Unger, "Bible Colleges and Institutes," *Mennonite Encyclopedia* 5 (Scottdale: Herald Press, 1990), p. 74.

decisions. Origins frequently influenced the shape of governance; however, in summary, the church is today always involved in governance. Sometimes congregations, groups of congregations, or conferences are entirely in control. At other times they represent only one voice within membership associations and/or self-perpetuating boards of committed individuals. Debate continues as to the best or the most faithfully Mennonite approach to governance. No uniform governance structure has yet or likely will soon prevail throughout Mennonite post-secondary schools.

Governance is frequently correlated with adherence to the tradition. Many assume that the more control the church has, the more faithful to the church the college will be.[11] Undoubtedly this premise has validity in many settings. Mennonite post-secondary institutions, however, no matter what their particular governance structure, have remained remarkably true to the Christian vision of their founders. They are all changing in various ways, but they are not "secularizing" into colleges which have lost either their Christian or their Mennonite soul. True, they do not all agree on the details and nuances as to what makes a college truly Mennonite, yet despite all their variety, Mennonite post-secondary institutions in North America today share a remarkably common theological perspective which influences who they are and what they do.

Theological Foundations for Mennonite Higher Education

An Anabaptist ecclesiology is a fundamental dynamic shaping a distinctively Mennonite post-secondary educational perspective. The church in Anabaptist-Mennonite thought is the body of Christ defined by the life and teaching of Jesus, transformed by the death and resurrection of Jesus the Christ, and empowered by the Holy Spirit. As the primary vehicle through which God today works His will in the world, the church is to be separated from and nonconformed to the world, yet is also salt and light in the world and the agency of God's reconciling love in the world. The church, accordingly, is visible and tangible for it embraces all those who are baptized as adults upon confession of faith in Christ and who commit themselves to follow the way of Christ in fellowship.[12]

Which is the controlling variable in Anabaptist thought, this view of the church or a vision of discipleship? Among a previous generation of scholars

11. See for example, Victor Stoltzfus, *Church-Affiliated Higher Education: Exploratory Case Studies of Presbyterian, Roman Catholic and Wesleyan Colleges* (Goshen: Pinchpenny Press, 1992).

12. C. J. Dyck, "Doctrine of Church," *Mennonite Encyclopedia* 5, pp. 150-154.

who debated this question, Franklin H. Littell[13] maintained that ecclesiology was paramount, while Harold S. Bender[14] insisted that discipleship came prior to their view of the church. We need not take sides in that debate but rather acknowledge the centrality of both of these theological concepts to Anabaptist thought. However, it is my contention that in the area of education, Mennonite ecclesiology is the more fundamental dynamic but that it, too, is derivative.

The church, as already indicated, is premised on a particular reading of Jesus. The church is after all the body of Christ, and therefore the understanding of Christ, the head, surely determines the nature of the body. From the Anabaptist-Mennonite perspective, Jesus as the Word made flesh reveals God's will for His disciples, His church. The church, accordingly, is also called to incarnate the Word, to represent — that is, to re-present — the Word in the midst of the world. So, too, the Mennonite college is to be incarnational, even as the church is incarnational.

Six perspectives flowing from this premise help to define Mennonite postsecondary education. Mennonite colleges, first, reflect a sociological consequence of Anabaptist-Mennonite incarnationalism. Because the church is the visible community of the redeemed separated from the world, a primary task of the church college is to nurture loyalty to this separate or alternative community. The public schools in any society are by definition mandated to socialize the next generation into the values and mores of that society. Loyal citizenship is their purpose. Teaching the young their history — that is, the history of their nation with all its heroes and virtues — is a pervasive mechanism to this end. Similarly the church, if it is to be a nonconformed community, must socialize its young into its ethic and ethos. Mennonite colleges thus are called upon to nurture citizens of God's kingdom rather than of the nation. Not surprisingly, teaching Mennonite college students Mennonite history, especially the Anabaptist story, is a frequent means to reproduce a separated church.

This ecclesiology implies some degree of church-world dualism. For some Mennonites the dualism is radical, whereas for others it is relatively modest. The degree of acculturation is obviously a determinative factor in the type of dualism operative. While typically established to defend some form of dualism, by their very nature the colleges relativized and modified the dualism they were meant to sustain. Using H. Richard Niebuhr's categories, if "Christ against culture" characterizes the more radical dualism of the old order, especially from the 1960s onward, a "transformation of culture" approach became increasingly operative in the colleges as service, peace, and justice emphases

13. Franklin H. Littell, *The Origins of Sectarian Protestantism: A Study of the Anabaptist View of the Church* (New York: Macmillan, 1964).

14. Harold S. Bender, "The Anabaptist Vision," *Church History* 13 (March 1994): 3-24.

became central.[15] In turn, Mennonite academics found it increasingly difficult to define everything outside of the church as fallen.

Nonetheless, the theme of redemption — and its correlate of separation — has remained primary in Mennonite popular theology. Largely because of a weak doctrine of creation and a latent but implicit dualism, Mennonites argue that God works primarily in and through the redeemed community and only in limited ways in and through the larger created orders. The world outside the church with its cultures and societies — while studied, even appreciated and frequently enjoyed — is only rarely engaged theologically in helpful ways. This dualism and the lack of a meaningful theology of creation has militated against a systematic philosophy of Mennonite liberal arts education.

Mennonite dualism has often shaped decidedly ethnic or sectarian communities. In turn, Mennonite schools were frequently called upon to maintain the German language, particular cultural patterns, or dress restrictions. These were means to reinforce loyalty to the in-group and to assist students in finding marriage mates within the clan. Boundary maintenance and denominational identity were identified as the rationale. More recently, this same dynamic has meant for some that to be truly faithful to the church, a Mennonite college must have a particular percentage of Mennonite faculty and/or students. In this scenario, "Mennonite" is identified with membership in the denomination, and a college, to be truly Mennonite, requires the same membership identification of its central populations.[16] Denominational membership, perhaps even rather than defined theological commitments, becomes the determinative dynamic. To be sure, some Mennonite colleges reject this strategy but have not always offered a compelling alternative explanation as to how they may be identified as Mennonite. Whatever the strategy, all Mennonite colleges hire only Christian faculty, not necessarily for ecclesiological reasons but definitely because of their incarnational assumptions. The professors are both to teach and to model their Christian faith.

At its best, the ethos propelling the church as a distinctive sociological entity and the church college as its servant is an ethic — the ethic of Jesus. Ethics or Christian discipleship is the second dynamic shaping Mennonite colleges. Like the visible church, ethics gives body to the Word. Mennonite christology understands the death and resurrection of Christ as an extension of His life and teachings. Soteriology, in turn, is synergistic, combining God's gracious acts and our response in obedience. Because the Sermon on the Mount is foundational, obedience requires nonresistant love even of the enemy, rather than retribution. Because the state by definition will periodically use the sword to pursue its agenda, the Christian will necessarily sustain an

---

15. H. Richard Niebuhr, *Christ and Culture* (New York: Harper and Row, 1951).
16. Dennis Martin, "Theology of Creation," *Mennonite Encyclopedia* 5, pp. 210-211.

ambiguous relationship to the state. Indeed, critique of the state and of all coercive systems has become a dominant motif of Mennonite colleges.

Discipleship of Christ translates into service and peace-making in Mennonite colleges, which usually emphasize majors which prepare students for careers of service such as teaching, nursing, and ministry. All careers, indeed, are considered as opportunities for service. More recently programs in peace-making and conflict resolution have become commonplace in most Mennonite colleges. Preparation for a life of intelligent and compassionate discipleship is of great importance to these schools.

The church as the incarnate body of Christ living according to Jesus' ethics is also a global community. Internationalism is therefore the third educational perspective flowing from the Anabaptist incarnational ecclesiology operative in Mennonite colleges. National walls ought not to divide the church; rather, nationalism is frequently considered destructive of both the church and the larger society. The church is an international community, including all tongues and races. The "neighbors" which Christians are to love are found everywhere, frequently the victims of legitimated state violence. World citizenship and compassion for all people are thus goals of a Mennonite college education.

Historically Mennonite colleges pursued the international agenda primarily by preparing missionaries and service workers for "foreign" assignments. Recently more emphasis is being placed on the social, cultural, political, and economic environments in pursuit of justice and peace around the world. Understanding of and identification with peoples in other cultures is of concern to all Mennonite colleges. In turn, they all provide for students various opportunities for study, service, and ministry in various settings abroad. Goshen College operates the most extensive study-service program, but all other Mennonite colleges provide some variant of this concern to teach an international perspective, when possible within international settings.

Because the Bible is the authoritative text of the church, the Bible is the primary source of all Mennonite theological reflection. It is the word which reveals the Word. Biblical authority, accordingly, is the fourth Mennonite educational perspective. Mennonites are sometimes considered to be biblicists, people of the book. Mennonites have Bible schools, Bible colleges, and biblical seminaries. Religious studies departments in Mennonite colleges typically include the title "biblical studies" and are heavily oriented toward courses in the Bible. Because Mennonites tend to consider themselves to be less creedal than biblical, theology is often relatively weak in Mennonite colleges. Rather than developing a theology of education, Mennonite colleges are more likely to appeal to biblical injunctions to legitimate their existence and mission.

A fifth educational perspective is omnipresent in Mennonite higher education, namely, the importance of music. Although this perspective functions differently from the first four, it too is derivative from Mennonite incarnational ecclesiology. Music serves as a primary vehicle through which the Mennonite community both worships and celebrates. Every Mennonite school of higher education teaches music, especially choral music. Virtually every Mennonite college boasts a strong choral tradition. While culture and creativity historically have lacked a considered theological foundation and frequently have been suspect, choral music has not only been accepted but even granted a priority status.

A stronger emphasis on creation would serve Mennonite higher education very well. A fully developed doctrine of creation is important not only for the areas of culture and the arts but also to enable Mennonites to respond appropriately to nature and the environment and, in turn, to have a more balanced appraisal of history and human activity. A stronger balance toward creation would also place the Mennonite emphasis on redemption and church into perspective and thus modify the hubris of sectarianism which tempts Mennonites toward pride in their humility.

Finally, the sixth Mennonite educational perspective premised upon the Word becoming the body of Christ is Mennonite communitarianism. Anabaptism was in some ways a "lay monastic" movement and a movement of the common people. With time this has come to mean that Christian faithfulness belongs equally to everyone in the community. Sometimes anti-intellectualism results when the life of the mind and an educated leadership are considered unnecessary, are not highly regarded, and may even be suspect. A more positive consequence is the belief that everyone needs to be educated to use their gifts fully in the service of God and the community. Mennonite colleges, in turn, tend not to emphasize individual achievement very strongly but rather to speak of responsibility and service. Leadership training is for "servant leadership." Education seeks to build a communitarian spirit.

The Mennonite college seeks to model the Christian notion of community. Not only does it speak about community; it is committed to *being* a community. What this means can vary, yet most everyone agrees that the faculty, staff, and students are concerned for each other's well-being not only academically but also personally and socially. Relationships are of central importance to Mennonite colleges because Christian faith is considered to be relational. Worship services, social events, and other formal and informal programming are designed to nurture this sense of being a community. The Mennonite college achieves its mission in no small part when it serves the church by advocating and modeling an incarnational theology — the Word made flesh within the world, serving the world in the name of Christ.

Conclusions

Mennonite colleges represent a distinctive model of Christian post-secondary education. Despite historical ambivalence toward higher education, Mennonites today are heavily invested in colleges, universities, and seminaries. These various schools share a common theological model, namely, the Incarnation, the Word made flesh. In this model, the Christian college as a servant of the church — the body of Christ — nurtures men and women to become agents of the Incarnation through their various disciplines and majors, vocations and avocations.

This model promises great potential well beyond its present realization. Nevertheless, Mennonite colleges do successfully nurture loyalty to the kingdom rather than to the nation, emphasize the ethical life and Christian discipleship, encourage an internationalist perspective, teach the Bible as the authoritative text of the church, enjoy choral music especially as a means to build and express faith and community, and instill a communitarian ethos. All of this is premised on Jesus the Christ, the Incarnate Word.

Goshen College and Its Church Relations: History and Reflections

Theron F. Schlabach

Begun in 1894 by freelancing Mennonites as a kind of private commercial high school at Elkhart, Indiana, the institution began quickly to evolve toward being a fully church-related liberal arts college. In 1903 it moved to nearby Goshen, took on its permanent name, and began anew with a young, Northwestern- and Harvard-trained, liberal-arts-minded president; in 1905 it came fully under the control of a board of the largest Mennonite denomination in North America, the "MC" Mennonite Church. By 1933 it shed its high-school-level academy; in 1941 it received North Central accreditation as a four-year liberal arts college. A strong purpose well into the post–World War II period (though less prominent today) was to train leaders and workers for the Mennonite Church, and in 1946 it opened a graduate-level "Goshen Biblical Seminary" (which later became an independent institution and is now a part of the Associated Mennonite Biblical Seminary, on another campus). Since 1968 the college regularly has operated international "Study-Service" units in a number of foreign countries and 70-80 percent of Goshen students take a semester abroad in those units. They do so in order to meet a requirement that every graduating student must have done a semester's worth of international education. Full-time-equivalent enrollment in the fall of 1994-95 was 938 students.

To this day, Goshen College has kept "conclusive" marks of "a full-bodied, unapologetic church relationship": governance through church boards; a majority of the faculty being Goshen graduates; all tenured faculty having to be Mennonite "or share the spirit of Mennonites"; a rule that 65 percent of the students be Mennonite; and an ethnic feel about the campus. But rather than having a "fortress mentality," Goshen's people "are open and at ease with a visitor." Neither are they by any means "all of one mind"; one visitor-observer remarked that they are "more diverse than Amherst students." They reach out to "the world at large"; their "program in international education is one of their gems, and around 90 percent of the faculty have lived abroad. . . . Mennonite as it proudly is, Goshen is not divorced from the life of society at large. . . ." Yet the "apparent homogeneity" of Goshen's student body offers "little chance to tackle the unbelievers." To a visitor-observer, some students spoke of choosing Goshen so "they would be supported rather than beleaguered in their faith." And one "opined, 'Goshen doesn't preach Christianity enough; it only practices it.'" Some of the more evangelical students said that "'the faculty are not confessional enough.'" Nonetheless, Goshen has made specific efforts to tie "'the college and the churches together. . . .'"

Paraphrased and quoted from
Merrimon Cuninggim, 1978[1]

"It takes a strong church to have strong church schools."

Albert J. Meyer, Mennonite Board
of Education, 1992[2]

Goshen College began at Elkhart, Indiana, in 1894 as the "Elkhart Institute of Science, Industry, and the Arts." In the next decade it became more clearly collegiate and centered on the liberal arts, and in 1903 it moved to nearby Goshen and took its present name. That same decade ushered in the Progressive Era in American history, with its great faith that Americans could overcome the problems that new industry and burgeoning cities were bringing — and could live humanely.

Goshen College was not isolated; both Elkhart and Goshen were and are in the main communication corridor running from the eastern cities to Chicago. The college began with much of the nation's mood of progressive optimism. In 1896 its main early shaper, an irenic and pastoral revivalist and church leader named John S. Coffman, favored the new school with a historic, ethos-breathing address he called "The Spirit of Progress."[3] In 1903, as Elkhart Institute's princi-

---

1. From Merrimon Cuninggim, "Varieties of Church-Relatedness in Higher Education," Section I of Robert Rue Parsonage, ed., *Church Related Higher Education: Perceptions and Perspectives* (Valley Forge: Judson Press, 1978), pp. 52-54.

2. Albert J. Meyer, "Mennonite Colleges and the Changing Educational Environment" (unpublished paper, 1992), 26. Context: that the denomination should let its schools help keep it abreast of the church's mission.

3. J[ohn]. S. Coffman, *The Spirit of Progress: A Lecture, Delivered at the Opening of the*

pal, Noah Byers, was inaugurated as president of the new, reconstituted Goshen College, Byers caught much the same mood in a speech entitled "Culture for Service" — a phrase that caught on and became the college's enduring motto.

For Byers and for the early Goshen College, the service idea was much informed by the then-current Protestant Student Volunteer Movement, with its slogan "the evangelization of the world in this generation."[4] A strong motif was training missionaries and other workers for the Mennonite Church. The service idea also had overtones of the social gospel, Protestantism's version of progressivism, as sounded, for instance, by Goshen College leadership in forming an Intercollegiate Peace Society which held its first convention on the campus in 1905.[5]

Yet even if affected by national moods, the new institution was a Mennonite college. By 1905 it became officially so, as the "old" or "MC" Mennonite branch formed a Board of Education and brought the school fully under denominational control. The Goshen story hardly fits standard analyses based on colleges and universities rooted in Calvinism and the Calvinist-informed national educational culture of New England. Nor, in the case of Goshen, are the paradigms of tension between historic Christian commitments and those of the eighteenth-century's so-called Enlightenment quite apt.[6] Goshen did

---

First School Building of the "Elkhart Institute," Elkhart, Ind., Feb. 11, 1896 (booklet in Mennonite Historical Library, Goshen College [hereafter MHL]), 21 pp. Coffman was the Mennonite Church's leading revivalist; at the time of the speech he was about to become president of the new school's governing board. Not only the speech's title but much of its content fit the rhetoric of the times.

4. Susan Fisher Miller, Culture for Service: A History of Goshen College, 1894-1994 (Goshen: Goshen College, 1994), pp. 44, 24-25. Miller noted (p. 44) that Byers gave his "Culture for Service" speech and coined the motto soon after Columbia University's President Nicholas Murray Butler had given a speech on "Scholarship for Service," but suggested that Byers put his own meaning into the words. In 1896 Woodrow Wilson, future president of Princeton University, gave a major address entitled "Princeton in the Nation's Service"; see Richard Hofstadter and Wilson Smith, American Higher Education: A Documentary History (Chicago: University of Chicago Press, 1961), vol. 2, pp. 684-695. The service idea is a main theme of a book by Mark Noll on Princeton University's early history (Princeton and the Republic, 1768-1822: The Search for a Christian Enlightenment in the Era of Samuel Stanhope Smith [Princeton: Princeton University Press, 1989]); that fact and the Woodrow Wilson reference are reported in George Marsden, "The Soul of the American University: A Historical Overview" in Marsden and Bradley J. Longfield, eds., The Secularization of the Academy (New York: Oxford University Press, 1992), pp. 19, 43n.17.

5. John Sylvanus Umble, Goshen College, 1894-1954: A Venture in Christian Higher Education (Goshen: Goshen College, 1955), 45-46.

6. A framework suggested, e.g., in Richard Hughes, "Models for Christian Higher Education: Strategies for Survival and Success in the 21st Century" (unpublished grant proposal to the Lilly Endowment, underlying this study), p. 1.

not pass through stages which historian George Marsden has proposed for America's previously Protestant or Protestant-dominated universities. By Marsden's reckoning, the time of Goshen's founding was one in which a moral philosophy-oriented and culturally-established Protestantism was losing dominance over higher education. In its place was coming a fusion of scientism and loose, eclectic Protestant liberalism.[7]

Mennonites' outlook transitions were different. In the eighteenth century, instead of fusing an establishment version of Christianity with Enlightenment rationalism, Mennonites were fusing a dissenting version of Christianity with a highly devotional, quietly experiential, and somewhat world-denying German Pietism.[8] And except within the wombs of Pennsylvania-German enclaves, Pietism reinforced an already strong over-against-culture sectarianism which Mennonites had inherited from their spiritual ancestors' persecution and suffering. Nor does Marsden's chronology apply to Mennonites. In the late nineteenth century the "old" (later called "MC") Mennonites and the (non-Old Order) Amish Mennonites[9] were interacting not so much with scientism and modernism as with American revivalism.[10] Goshen College was a product of transition to greater revivalist evangelical activism, not of the stages which Marsden identified for American universities.

From Goshen's beginning, Mennonites have seen their educational enterprise as standing largely over against American thought and culture, not as a transmitter of that culture. To be sure, Mennonite educators have often looked to culture-dominating Protestantism for some of their educational models; and modestly, they have of course interacted with the Enlightenment,

7. Marsden, "The Soul," pp. 9-45.

8. See esp. ch. 6 of Richard K. McMaster, *Land, Piety, Peoplehood: The Making of Mennonite Communities in America, 1683-1790,* The Mennonite Experience in America no. 1 (Scottdale: Herald Press, 1985).

9. The statement does not refer to the Old Order Amish, but instead to a much larger number of Amish who were more progressive, worked closely with the "old" Mennonite church, and then in the 1910s and 1920s merged into the latter and lost the Amish name; see Steven M. Nolt, *A History of the Amish* (Intercourse, PA: Good Books, 1992), chs. 7-8.

10. This transition has been a major subject of my own studies, e.g., in articles in *The Mennonite Quarterly Review* (hereafter *MQR*) [see 51 (July 1977): 213-226; 52 (April 1978): 113-126] and in my *Gospel Versus Gospel: Mission and the Mennonite Church, 1863-1944,* Studies in Anabaptist and Mennonite History no. 21 (Scottdale: Herald Press, 1980), ch. 1 and passim. For the ethos of Mennonitism in decades leading up to acceptance of revivalist activism, see esp.: Joseph C. Liechty, "Humility: The Foundation of Mennonite Religious Outlook in the 1860s," *MQR* 54 (January 1980): 5-31; and my *Peace, Faith, Nation: Mennonites and Amish in Nineteenth-Century America,* The Mennonite Experience in America no. 2 (Scottdale: Herald Press, 1988), esp. chs. 1 and 4 (and for the new activism, ch. 11).

science, and other themes of modern thought. But they have not embraced what Marsden identified as a common assumption in nineteenth-century universities: "that there should be a unified national culture in which the Protestant religion ought to play a major supportive part."[11] Instead, a strong theme of Mennonite intellectuals and college-builders has been that of counter-values and counterculture. In 1991, apparently as a warning to all church-related colleges, Notre Dame University theologian James Tunstead Burtchaell published an analysis of Vanderbilt University's gradual alienation from its founding Southern Methodist church. Along the way he observed that Vanderbilt's late-nineteenth-century "youthful years" were precisely "a time when most Protestants lost conviction about the particularities" of their own respective denominations and reduced their Christianity to mere good citizenship and other hazy notions.[12] But Mennonites have remembered their particularities. In his "Spirit of Progress" speech John S. Coffman connected themes such as progress, peace, and moral character not to national culture but to a tradition of, in his words, "dissenters from state churches." The dissenters he had in mind were sixteenth-century Anabaptists and a string of earlier break-away groups.[13] Since Coffman's day Mennonites and their educators have restated, even redefined their counterculturism; but running throughout Goshen's history is a continuous sense of distinct peoplehood, peculiar and dissenting.

Marsden closed one key article with the observation: "Perhaps . . . it is time for Christians in the post-modern age to recognize that they are part of an unpopular sect."[14] Apparently the point was an afterthought. Perhaps it should not have been. Perhaps Goshen's story could illumine the larger national story after all.

Key Moments, Ideas, and Themes in Goshen College History

Goshen's history, and to an extent the history of its church in the twentieth century, is a tale of some high hopes, strong disappointments, but also stimuli — even some as unfortunate as global war — that in the end seemed to "work together for good to those who love the Lord."

11. Marsden, "The Soul," p. 30.
12. James Tunstead Burtchaell, "The Decline and Fall of the Christian College," *First Things* (April-May 1991): 28.
13. Coffman, *The Spirit of Progress,* p. 9.
14. Marsden, "The Soul," p. 41; see also Burtchaell, "Decline and Fall," p. 38.

1. Beginning to about 1918: a campus mood that was optimistic, oriented toward Christian activism.

In its early years Goshen was imbued with a progressive, Protestant activist outlook. That combination seems to have attracted a good bevy of young people remarkable both in intellectual ability and in idealism.[15] As one had put it privately in 1893, such newly vitalized, progressive Mennonite youth were hoping to be "just the stuff."[16] In later years, quite a few erstwhile students of this optimistic era would look back upon the "old Goshen" as a kind of lost Eden.[17]

2. 1918-1924: a growing distance between academics and ecclesiastics, creating a crisis.

By 1923-24 the Eden had withered; indeed, the college closed for one academic year. When it reopened it had a new administration, on the whole a new faculty, and, since quite a few "old Goshen" students refused to return, a somewhat altered student body. Powerful church leaders (as well as many ordinary Mennonites) had lost confidence in the college over issues of overexpansion, financial mismanagement, and, not least, fear of theological and cultural modernism. (It was, of course, the time when Protestant fundamentalism's first wave was cresting. Once again, larger national and Protestant moods were affecting Mennonites — although with Mennonites the quarrels were as often about cultural matters, such as attire, as about doctrine.) On their side, a number of prominent faculty members, including President Byers and then his successor John E. Hartzler, moved — or, in the minds of many "old" Mennonites, defected — to the more flexible General Conference Mennonite branch and its colleges, Bluffton in Ohio and Bethel in Kansas.[18] Still, strong elements of the "old" Goshen pursued further acculturation and progressivism. College and church, "academics" and "ecclesiastics,"[19] were on diverg-

---

15. I write from a background of researching, writing, and teaching the history of Mennonites in the United States, and also with a debt to Susan Fisher Miller's new *Culture for Service,* cited above; Miller skillfully communicates campus ethos in different eras.

16. George (G. L.) Bender, quoted in Schlabach, *Gospel Versus Gospel,* p. 43.

17. Susan Fisher Miller, in conversation with author on 28 December 1994, used the term "lost Eden" or something close to it.

18. Miller, *Culture for Service,* chs. 3 and 4, esp. pp. 51, 61, 69, 74-81; James C. Juhnke, *Vision, Doctrine, War: Mennonite Identity and Organization in America, 1890-1930,* The Mennonite Experience in America no. 3 (Scottdale: Herald Press, 1989), 264-65; A. Warkentin and Melvin Gingerich, *Who's Who Among the Mennonites* (N. Newton, KS: A. Warkentin, 1943), pp. 37, 44, 99, 224, 272.

19. The analysis of "academics" versus "ecclesiastics" is from Miller, *Culture for Service,* ch. 4.

ing tracks. In that situation the college's form of government — control by a denomination-appointed board[20] — allowed the church to respond accordingly. The Board of Education acted, and for a year the college closed.

The situation was full of unforgettable tragedy: careers were interrupted; all too many students, including some highly able ones, were alienated from the "old" church and in some cases from Mennonitism of any kind (thankfully, some of the brightest and best eventually overcame this sense of alienation); scholarly freedom was compromised;[21] much faculty talent was lost to the church; and many relationships were broken. Nonetheless, from the perspective of bringing college and church back together and of maintaining church-related higher education, out of tragedy came considerable renewal.

3. 1924-1941: a "new" Goshen which was decidedly different, yet remained a liberal arts college with considerable intellectual vigor.

Despite all its tragedy, the 1923-24 closing brought renewal, mainly from three sources: (1) strong and wise leaders in the college after the purge, especially the new president, Sanford C. Yoder, and the new dean, Noah Oyer; (2) a governing structure that simply would not let the college drift too far from its church connection; and (3) not least, underlying the first two sources, a church whose sense of distinctiveness and peoplehood was so strong that persons on both sides of the college-versus-church divide decided that, whatever the problems, they would stick together.

Sanford (S. C.) Yoder, an Iowan with a colorful background of homesteading in Washington state and earlier aspirations of being a lawyer (he was known to intrigue students with the admission that he had earlier used tobacco and still enjoyed the smell of a good cigar),[22] represented the best tradition of the Amish Mennonite bishop as old-style elder and folk leader with shrewd understanding of the tribe's sociology and behaviors. During Goshen's earlier closing, Yoder had been president of the college's governing board. Yet he was not a radical for the ecclesiastical side and after the reopening he quickly built confidence on campus — at least among persons loyal enough to return, including some with deep misgivings. At the time he became Goshen's presi-

20. Not, however, control by central denominational officers. In the "old" Mennonite church, major power and sovereignty lay with district conferences. The district conferences, both "old" Mennonite and Amish Mennonite, appointed members of the Mennonite Board of Education. For a quick review of the history of governance in American church-affiliated higher education, see Victor Stoltzfus, *Church-Affiliated Higher Education: Exploratory Case Studies of Presbyterian, Roman Catholic and Wesleyan Colleges* (Goshen: Pinchpenny Press, 1992), pp. 39-46.

21. Miller, *Culture for Service*, p. 117.

22. Miller, *Culture for Service*, pp. 177-178.

dent, he did not possess even a bachelor's degree. Yet he kept the institution academically respectable, as struggling young colleges go. Oyer, the new dean in 1924, had studied at Princeton Seminary before becoming a Bible teacher in another Mennonite institution. For such intellectual strength, Yoder was willing to take some risks — for instance, hiring in 1924 a youthful Harold S. Bender whose "soundness" was still in some doubt. Bender had studied at Goshen, Garrett, Princeton, and the University of Tübingen. In a few years he would became world Mennonitism's foremost intellectual leader.[23]

Yoder served as president through the rebuilding and then through the Great Depression, until 1940. At first he often felt forced to use temporary teachers, and when he did, he seemed willing to engage non-Mennonites ahead of Mennonites whose intellectual qualifications or ultimate loyalty to church seemed doubtful.[24] By present standards the college suffered shaky finances. It also made heavy demands for orthodoxy and orthopraxis, for instance asking prospective faculty, "Would you be willing to conform to the teaching and the practices of the Church in the matters of plainness of attire and general separation from the world?"[25] In 1931 the faculty and the board adopted — then put in every regular college catalog until 1970 — a firmly written, semi-fundamentalistic, ten-point statement of doctrine.[26] Nonetheless, in Yoder's years Goshen advanced academically to the point that in 1941 the North Central Association approved it for accreditation.

Indeed, Goshen's intellectual climate was vigorous. In the mid-to-latter 1920s Harold S. Bender and several of his closest colleagues revived a Mennonite Historical Society, began what quickly became the respected international journal *The Mennonite Quarterly Review*, and inaugurated a scholarly, enduring book series, "Studies in Anabaptist and Mennonite History." Most notably of all (building somewhat on groundwork laid by others),[27] they developed the "Anabaptist-vision" or "Goshen school" interpretation of the

23. On how fortunate were the choices of Oyer and Bender, see Miller, *Culture for Service,* esp. pp. 128-129, 133-134, 136-137, and 147-150.

24. Miller, *Culture for Service,* pp. 131-132.

25. Quoted in Miller, *Culture for Service,* p. 126.

26. Goshen College catalogs, formerly with the title *Goshen College Bulletin*, 1931-1970. In structure and some content, the statement certainly smacked of Protestant fundamentalist creeds (scriptural inerrancy as its first point, Christ's death as a "substitutionary sacrifice," literal resurrection not only of Jesus Christ but also "of all men," etc.). Yet it omitted some code words, e.g., "plenary and verbal," and it did not specify premillennialism. It incorporated special Mennonite emphases, notably "discipleship," "non-resistance to evil by carnal means," and "nonconformity to the world in life and conduct" (but surprisingly did not specify nonconformity in attire).

27. See Al Keim, "The Anabaptist Vision: The History of a New Paradigm," *The Conrad Grebel Review* 12 (Fall 1994): 243-245, 247-249, and 252.

sixteenth-century Protestant Reformation — an interpretation so well accepted beyond Mennonite circles that by 1943 the American Society of Church History honored Bender with its presidency. Others who added to Goshen's vigorous intellectual climate included Bender's wife Elizabeth Horsch Bender, a German teacher and fine linguist and historian in her own right,[28] and Olive Wyse. Wyse, who in 1925 began a 50-year teaching career at Goshen, mainly in home economics, won high intellectual respect from male colleagues — not automatic in those days — and later, in 1949, was a key writer of a new faculty statement of Goshen's educational philosophy.[29] Not least in the Yoder years (and following) was Guy F. Hershberger, a historian and sociologist who became, from the late 1930s to the 1960s, a (if not *the*) foremost interpreter of Mennonites' position on peace and other questions of church and society. By World War II Bender and Hershberger, with various fellow Mennonites and other historic peace church intellectuals, were key players in developing a national plan of alternative service for conscientious objectors to war.

In 1924 the "new" Goshen's governors had insisted on loyalty to the church. Perhaps they had carried loyalty to a fault; but clearly, the faculty they chose served their church well intellectually. And not only their church: by interpreting the history and sociology of a small dissenting group, and by helping formulate a plan by which government recognized conscientious objection far better than it had in World War I, they served the causes of humane tolerance, national pluralism, and human freedom.

4. World War II and following, to 1968: landmark writings on peace and Anabaptism, response to a global crisis, new ideology, and practice of service.

World War II, of course, deeply impacted almost all Americans, individually and corporately. For Mennonites a considerable part of the impact came via the government-established but largely church-operated alternative service system for conscientious objectors, known as Civilian Public Service or "CPS." The system was a labyrinth that included forestry and other camps, agricultural extension assignments, mental hospital work, guinea-pig roles for medical research, and more. Some CPS draftees and some faculty members at Goshen and elsewhere helped administer it or conducted various educational programs in the various units. Meanwhile Mennonite leaders, including Goshen's new president, "old" Goshen graduate Ernest E. Miller, began to plan for vastly expanded wartime and postwar relief programs. Ideas for various church-sponsored programs of voluntary service were also growing. As a

28. See a special issue of the *MQR* honoring her: 60 (July 1986).
29. Miller, *Culture for Service,* p. 138; author's conversation with Wyse's colleague Robert C. Buschert, December 26, 1994.

result of such thinking, in 1943 the Goshen campus became the site of a Relief Workers Training School.[30] Goshen College's historian Susan Fisher Miller has detected in such wartime activities not only a strong interest in very specific forms of service but also some seeds of Goshen's later, widely recognized program of international education.[31]

In mid–World War II, as president of the American Society of Church History, Harold S. Bender delivered a historic address entitled "The Anabaptist Vision." Its main ideas were that the Mennonites' religious forebears, the Anabaptists, had taken the lead in modern church-state separation; that they had carried the Protestant Reformation on to its logical conclusion; and that the essence of Anabaptism lay in three principles: believers' church, practical discipleship, and pacifistic love in human relations. Bender wrote the address hastily and for non-Mennonite scholars more than for his church, yet for Mennonites it somehow became a kind of manifesto for a postwar identity. In time "Anabaptist" identity became a kind of Mennonite folk myth. Perhaps its power was that it allowed Mennonites to continue a strong sense of people-hood and distinctiveness even as many began shedding older boundary-markers such as plain attire.

Orientation toward service remained strong, so that in the late 1940s and early 1950s the campus still honored students who chose missionary careers, and some students did, including very talented ones.[32] In the county around Goshen the campus Young People's Christian Association (later "Student Christian Association") carried on evangelistic work that spawned a half-dozen new Mennonite congregations. For many Mennonites, not least the faculty and students at Goshen, the Anabaptist vision formula, by calling individuals to practical discipleship and love, reinforced the new war-stimulated emphasis on concrete forms of service. Also fueling that emphasis were the peace advocacy and social commentary of Guy F. Hershberger, culminating in two major books: *War, Peace and Nonresistance* (1944) and *The Way of the Cross in Human Relations* (1958).[33] One strong theme in the writing of Hershberger and others was preservation of the Mennonite community, and for a few years, beginning in 1947, a Mennonite Community Association published a *Mennonite Community* magazine.

30. Miller, *Culture for Service*, pp. 168, 172.

31. Miller, *Culture for Service*, p. 168.

32. Reminiscences on various occasions of Robert C. Buschert, student and then instructor at Goshen during that era, in personal conversation with the author. Singling out names is risky, but there are ample examples of extremely talented persons choosing mission work.

33. For a handy sketch of Hershberger and his thought and activity, see Theron F. Schlabach, "To Focus a Mennonite Vision" in John Richard Burkholder and Calvin Redekop, eds., *Kingdom, Cross and Community: Essays on Mennonite Themes in Honor of Guy F. Hershberger* (Scottdale: Herald Press, 1976), pp. 15-50.

"Anabaptist vision," new service emphasis, internationalism, community language, and theoretical rearticulations of Mennonitism and of at least one version of Mennonite pacifism: all these enriched Goshen's educational environment immeasurably. By the 1950s so many faculty members and spouses had done postwar relief service abroad that such experience seemed commonplace; by 1970, half of Goshen's faculty had served abroad (and not in military service).[34] Meanwhile a group of second-generation interpreters of the "Anabaptist vision" — most of whom had been students at Goshen or its related biblical seminary (including the eventually well known scholar John Howard Yoder) — added highly sophisticated critique and rigor to Mennonite thought and self-understanding. But the impact was felt more widely: a core group of young Mennonite intellectuals held various conferences with World Council of Churches leaders, Eastern European Marxists, and others, trying to bring a pacifist Christian perspective to the modern world's crises.[35] Meanwhile at Goshen and other Mennonite campuses in the 1950s, well before U.S. President John F. Kennedy's Peace Corps, it became common for a student to put in a summer or perhaps two or three years of church-related voluntary service, either breaking into one's college years or doing a term immediately after graduation. A church that had demanded loyalty of its college was now reaping ample benefits.

On campus, ideas clustered around terms and slogans such as "Anabaptist vision," "service," "community," and "peace." These themes ran through various courses not only in religion, ethics, and philosophy (some of which students had to take to meet general education requirements) but in others such as history or literature as well. By the late 1950s a new watchword, "justice," also began to emerge in a prominent way, especially on the lips and in the writings of philosophy professor and future Goshen president J. Lawrence Burkholder.[36] Goshen's service idealism found many forms, including: a pioneer liberal arts based nursing program with strong Christian service emphasis;[37] and an athletic program built around a conviction that sport should be for

34. *Goshen College Bulletin* (March 1969), p. 4.

35. See Beulah Stauffer Hostetler, "Nonresistance and Social Responsibility: Mennonites and the Mainline Peace Emphasis, ca. 1950 to 1985," *MQR* 64 (January 1990): 49-73, esp. 49-58; and Donald F. Durnbaugh, ed., *On Earth Peace: Discussions on War/Peace Issues Between Friends, Mennonites, Brethren and European Churches, 1935-1975* (Elgin: The Brethren Press, 1978).

36. One could cite various articles by Burkholder; his fullest statement is J. Lawrence Burkholder, *The Problem of Social Responsibility from the Perspective of the Mennonite Church* (Elkhart: Institute of Mennonite Studies, 1989), originally written as the author's 1958 Th.D. dissertation at Princeton Theological Seminary.

37. See esp. "Forty Years of Nursing Education at Goshen College" (extended brochure of the Goshen College Department of Nursing [ca. 1993]).

fun and fitness, with modest intra- and inter-varsity activity (eventually including soccer as a pacifist form of football!), rather than an enterprise with win-at-any-cost values.[38] The music faculty, especially Professor Mary Oyer, contributed to church music by active leadership in compiling two major new hymnals produced cooperatively with other Anabaptist-derived groups, and by helping Mennonites make a transition to some use of instruments in worship while, at best, still preserving a strong a cappella tradition.[39] With a much-heralded fine-arts course and by other means, Oyer and colleagues also helped Mennonites immeasurably to expand their limited appreciation for drama and the visual arts.[40]

The most thorough application of Goshen's core values to formal curricula came in 1968, when the college community began its now well-known program of sending the great majority of its students abroad, each for a full trimester, in a program soon labelled "SST," for "Study Service Term." College historian Miller believed she found various roots of the SST idea: the early "Culture for Service" idea and motto; World War II and postwar service, including service abroad; a council of Mennonite college presidents' sponsorship of summer seminars abroad, some led by Goshen faculty members (beginning in 1963, a time of Peace Corps and other service idealism in national life); a milieu of expanding enrollments and general affluence; on campus, the work of a "Future of the College Committee" which President Paul Mininger and Provost Henry Weaver Jr. were challenging to dream new dreams; and not least, a visit in 1965 of a North Central Association accreditation team whose members asked why Goshen was not using its faculty's extensive international experience more effectively for its students' education.[41] Also, by this time Mennonites had a strong tradition of church-sponsored voluntary service, much of it abroad either under denominational agencies or under the leading interMennonite organization, Mennonite Central Committee (MCC). At the risk of making a false dichotomy it seems fair to say that Goshen's SST resulted more from the kind of church that sponsored the college than from the college itself.

38. See *Goshen College Bulletin* (March 1972).

39. Some material of this paragraph comes simply from my own memories: I was a student at Goshen from 1956 to 1960, kept in close touch during my graduate studies from 1960 to 1965, and since 1965 have been on Goshen's faculty. Various faculty members, some with long histories at Goshen, read and commented on an earlier draft of this chapter.

40. Conversation between the author and Goshen faculty member Anne Hershberger, 2 March 1994. See esp. two volumes of reproductions from notable 1975 and 1980 visual arts exhibitions of works by Mennonite visual artists: Abner Hershberger, comp., *Mennonite Artists Contemporary 1975* and *Mennonite Artists Contemporary 1980* (Goshen: Goshen College; 1975, 1980).

41. Miller, *Culture for Service*, pp. 168, 246-247.

In any case, since 1968 virtually every Goshen student has had to take, as part of the general education requirement, one trimester's worth of international studies. For some 80 percent[42] of the students, that has meant a trimester or semester abroad in a unit of twelve to twenty-five fellow-students led by a Goshen faculty team (typically, but not always, a faculty member and spouse). The most notable features of the program are: inclusion of international study and experience in the regular curriculum without large extra fees; organization around cross-cultural understanding and service even more than around language-learning; eschewing the world's centers of political, economic, and cultural power, locating instead in areas such as the Caribbean and Central America, or a far-inland province of mainland China, or recently on the Ivory Coast of Africa; units run by Goshen faculty instead of simply attaching students to foreign universities with their special university cultures; and getting students to experience grass roots local culture by placing them with community agencies (schools, clinics, recreation programs, etc.), often in remote places, for half the term. Over time, the SST rationale of learning, relating, and functioning cross-culturally has probably surpassed the service idea per se.[43] Still, the service idea remains part of the program.

A sizable percentage of the faculty has led units abroad, usually for one year (three student groups). Student participation has gradually declined to about 70 percent,[44] yet students still obviously see the term abroad as a highlight. Some careful research strongly suggests that the program, along with the aura surrounding it, is effective pedagogically.[45] Goshen's identity and national reputation have become so tied to its international program that a few faculty members have asked whether, in the college's communal self-identity and values, international education has not moved above the Mennonite church connection. It is a fair question.

---

42. Estimate by Goshen's Director of International Education, Wilbur Birky, who said also that the mid-1990s figure is more like 70 percent, but that both figures would be higher if one counted all persons not specifically in SST but recognized for other academic activities abroad.

43. Probably a false dichotomy: increasingly, Mennonite "service" leaders see cross-cultural relating and functioning as themselves a form of service.

44. See n. 42.

45. See Norman L. Kauffmann, "The Impact of Study Abroad on Personality Change," Ed.D. dissertation, Indiana University, 1983. A book using data from several institutions is Norman L. Kauffmann, Judith N. Martin, Henry D. Weaver, with Judy Weaver, *Students Abroad, Strangers at Home: Education for a Global Society* (Yarmouth, MA: Intercultural Press, 1992).

*5. The generation since about 1970: various innovations, including new formu-
lations of belief and goals; continued academic strength; continued strong relations
with the Mennonite Church; but no ethos-changing developments.*

Since the beginning of SST some innovations at Goshen have been imaginative
enough, but quite a few have been generated mainly just to keep abreast of
what the times demanded. Certainly, Goshen College has retained or even
increased some of its traditional strengths. As a teaching institution it is
currently well-mentioned in guides such as *Barron's Best Buys in College Education, U.S. News & World Report*'s list of "America's best colleges," and Erlene
Wilson's *100 Best Colleges for African-American Students.* Of the 1,565 students
who graduated from 1980 to 1985, 30 percent have reported receiving advanced degrees (36 percent if the calculations exclude certain vocational majors);[46] and of 30 persons of the classes of 1988-1991 who applied to enter
medical school, 83.3 percent were accepted. In keeping with the times, there
is now a Women's Studies minor; some other notable minors are Peace Studies
and Intercultural Studies. At present Goshen is the only Indiana college
selected for the Pew Science Program in Undergraduate Education. Some of
the institution's scholarly facilities have world reputations, especially the Mennonite Historical Library, *The Mennonite Quarterly Review,* and the "Basil S.
Turner Precision X-Ray Measurements Laboratory" built up by Professor
Robert C. Buschert, who clearly chose to be at Goshen because of core values.[47]
Some other outstanding facilities and activities include: an extensive nature
preserve with a vigorous program of environmental studies and demonstra-
tion, as well as continued leadership in peace-related theory and, of course,
international education.

On campus, the college has surely worked — although perhaps not hard
enough — at more inclusion and better cross-cultural relations. It attracts
quite a few international students (in 1994-95, 71 other than Canadian, in a
student body of about 1000). Since 1979 it has hosted a special church-sponsored program to train leaders for Hispanic congregations. It has been somewhat less successful at incorporating American minorities into its regular
program and at improving cross-cultural relations on campus, but in 1992
various earlier efforts metamorphosed into a new Multicultural Affairs Office,
which provides vigorous leadership toward those ends.[48]

On quite a different subject, teaching about sexuality in both campus and

46. Accounting, Business, Elementary or Middle School Education, Hispanic Ministries,
Nursing, and Social Work.

47. Deep personal acquaintance with Buschert; "Physicist Finds a Niche at Goshen
College," *The Elkhart* (Ind.) *Truth,* "Goshen This Week" (December 5, 1994), A2.

48. See Chandron Fernando, "GC Looks Back: Intercultural Efforts Grow, Adapt over
Time," *Goshen College Multicultural Affairs Newsletter* 3 (Fall 1994): 8.

church contexts has had strong leadership from Willard S. Kraybill, college physician and health teacher (now retired); and since 1989 the college's Student Development Division has furnished each student with a set of documents making up a "sexuality packet." Sexuality issues sometimes strain college-church relations (but hardly more than relations within each entity); yet surely the packet is a creative effort to articulate standards and to effect them by education, by counseling, and by instilling inner values, rather than by legalism. Any lack of clarity about sexuality is an ambiguity the college shares with its church.

Goshen College is not resting on its laurels. Nonetheless, since the early 1970s much creative energy has gone into just "keeping up." Enrollments are somewhat below previous peaks, and, rightly or wrongly, the college has not chosen to attract students by offering an overtly aggressive evangelical or other high-profile religious program. (The college's 1980-82 catalog, trying to communicate a purely noncoercive and service-oriented approach to faith, even noted that Goshen College dormitories did *not* have "officially sponsored Bible studies or sharing times.") Nor has the institution tried to sell itself as a culturally safe haven.[49] Meanwhile modern financial demands plus the costs of operating SST have strained the efforts to stay abreast; even a donor's $26 million endowment gift in 1993 has proved no magic solution, especially with anemic enrollments keeping tuition revenues down. Recent expenditures such as putting an up-to-date computer on every faculty desk or providing large,

49. Quotation is from *Goshen College Catalog 1980-82*, p. 10 — quite a remarkable page for expressing the college's idea of religious emphasis. The college has supported pursuit of faith in quite a number of ways; Appendix I offers information on requirements of Bible and religion courses and chapel-convocation attendance, although certainly Goshen College would not want such requirements to be taken as the essence of faith-promotion. Especially in the last generation, most other explicit faith-promoting efforts are low-key and rest quite heavily on student initiative: pastoral counseling services, encouragement to choose from the local smorgasbord of Mennonite and other church congregations, and quiet support of students' own worship services or fellowship groups. As for a cultural "safe haven," since about 1970 a statement of "Standards for the Guidance of Our Life Together," which every student must sign as if entering a personal and voluntary covenant with the larger community, has been the basis for promoting responsible behavior and for bringing sanctions against substance abuse and sexual and other deviances. Substance violations include any possession or use not only of illegal drugs but also of alcohol, either on campus or in other college-approved group settings. They also include use of tobacco anywhere on campus or loitering elsewhere (esp. the campus perimeter) in order to smoke. Since the mid-1970s Goshen has had extensive hours for inter-gender dormitory visits and has introduced some inter-gender housing; its cable connection pipes in MTV for any student who chooses it. Conscientious students appreciate an atmosphere that clearly proscribes or strongly discourages various behaviors; but Goshen does not, and honestly could not, tout itself strongly as a culturally safe haven.

Theron F. Schlabach

well-paved parking lots for resident students may be in some sense "necessary," yet they hardly improve *quality* of education. Some other changes such as excellent computer laboratories, or a multi-million-dollar recreational-and-fitness center opened in 1994, surely do relate to improving education. Yet a strong motive is "just keeping up."

As for the church connection, since 1970 there have been efforts to renew the church's sense of ownership of the college and to restate the essence of what Goshen College aims to be. One fruit of the early years of the administration of J. Lawrence Burkholder, president from 1971 to 1984, was a plan, quite widely accepted in the denomination, whereby congregations subsidized the tuition of their youths who chose a Mennonite institution. As for the essence of what Goshen College aims to be, in the early 1970s the college replaced its 1931 doctrinal statement. Already in 1949 the faculty had formulated a "Concept of Christian Education at Goshen College" expressed very much in early-postwar "Anabaptist-vision" and service language.[50] For a time in the 1970s the college catalog offered a five- or six-point statement that, while still quite doctrinal, reflected a more "Anabaptist vision" idiom.[51] Since 1970, catalog statements have been less doctrinal and more like conversations around certain concepts. Typical concepts include "peace," "discipleship," and "service," plus "community," "caring," and wholistic education.

Since the 1970s Goshen's faculty and its board have applied considerable creativity to producing new statements of mission and objectives. In its short form, the current mission statement states,

> Goshen College is a four-year liberal arts college dedicated to the development of informed, articulate, sensitive, responsible Christians. As a ministry of the Mennonite Church, we seek to integrate Christian values with educational and professional life. As a community of faith and learning, we strive to foster personal, intellectual, spiritual and social growth. We view education as a moral activity that produces servant-leaders for the church and the world.

A longer form of the mission statement includes some more church-related language, such as "encouraging active participation and leadership in congregations" and accepting "Jesus Christ as Son of God, as Lord of Life, and as Savior from the bondage of sin." It also uses some more distinctly Anabaptist/Mennonite language; and it affirms the Mennonite Church statements of faith. There are other documents, including a major 1994 statement whose subheadings include "a vital community of learning"; "Christian faith"; "service and peacemaking"; and "diversity and global awareness." The "Christian

50. *Goshen College Bulletin: Catalog for 1950-51,* 44 (March 1950).
51. *Goshen College Catalog 1976-78.*

215

faith" section is not creedal. Along with its mission statements the college designates ten "desired outcomes."[52]

In all, the several statements do not emphasize the kind of orthodoxy under which the early "new Goshen" regrouped. For instance, the 1994 statement mentions "Spirit" but not Scripture. One might ask, is Goshen College presently in a mode much like one of George Marsden's stages after all — the "Liberal Protestant" stage?[53] Whatever the answer, even the mission and outcomes statements have a strong element of "keeping abreast" — abreast of "management by objective" methods and of the approach demanded by the college's accrediting agency.

Since the beginning of the SST program, then, there have been some worthwhile innovations but none of these has established a new ethos for the coming decades.

Reflections

Goshen's church relationship has remained strong. With the governing pattern established in 1905, the college simply would not be left to itself. More fundamentally, the explanation for Goshen's strong church ties lies not so much with the college itself as with the kind of church to which Goshen College relates. The crux is a church with a strong enough sense of its own place in God's scheme, and a strong enough sense of peoplehood, that its various members, including its academics, hang together, "for better or for worse," to fulfill that place.

52. They are: "faith that is active and reflective"; "intercultural openness with the ability to function effectively with people of other world views"; "the ability to communicate effectively in a variety of sign systems"; "the ability to think actively and strategically"; "an understanding of the transcendent reality of aesthetic and spiritual experience"; "personal integrity that fosters ability to resolve conflict and to promote justice"; "leadership ability that empowers self and others"; "an understanding of responsible stewardship for human systems and the environment"; "a sense of vocational direction"; and "a healthy understanding of self and others that is reflected in social relationships of interdependence and mutual accountability."

53. No doubt if Marsden, Burtchaell, and some others were to compare Goshen's earlier with its more recent statements they would see "secularization." However, the current language probably would cause no alarm with authors of the Parsonage-edited 1978 National Council of Churches' *Church Related Higher Education*. That document sets up an eight-point test of church-relatedness (pp. 74-84); but in the spirit of modern American pluralism it celebrates the many ways colleges may express their church-relatedness and, esp. in chapter one, sees mythology in use of doctrinal tests. Hence the positive tone of Cuninggim's quotation at this chapter's outset.

If one seeks to understand Goshen College, one must understand several other dimensions as well.

1. Goshen's place in higher education rests more on what it and its people have *done* than on *words* or *theory*. Running through Goshen's documents there are indeed some persistent words, having to do with building "character," teaching a faith to permeate all of life, educating the whole person, fostering personal development and growth, and of course educating in the context of faith. But Goshen has been spare with words. A persistent theme of J. Lawrence Burkholder during his presidency was that Goshen College has tended to make its case by understatement and that the college was "authentic."[54] Mennonites tend to search for truth far less in words or abstract systems than in practice.[55] Perhaps for that reason the college and its church have not produced many notable statements of educational theory.

In 1992 Goshen's president, Victor Stoltzfus, used a three-month sabbatical to probe the literature and several key examples of church-related colleges, and wrote a small book on the subject. In sum he offered five points which offer something of an educational philosophy: "the church-affiliated college should serve the students and parents of the founding denomination . . ."; it also should offer "ecumenical sensitivity" for other students; it should teach the liberal arts as "classic wisdom tested by the centuries"; it "should be a 'salt and light' model institution, credible to nation and world" and "intellectually engaged with the cutting edge of intellectual and policy issues of the secular society . . ."; and, "in gratitude for the indirect public support which it enjoys from the state and nation," it should engage in "public service."[56] There have been other statements: catalog statements, a 121-page "Religious Welfare Survey Report"[57] compiled by Goshen faculty in 1947-49,[58] faculty attempts to integrate faith and particular disciplines,[59] and the like. But in 1968 historian

---

54. E.g., Burkholder statements in *Goshen College Catalog 1978-80* and *Goshen College Bulletin* (July 1979).

55. To a degree extensive Mennonite flirtation with Protestant fundamentalism in this century is an exception; but even there, Mennonite fundamentalism strongly emphasized practical nonconformity, nonresistance, and other evidences in life. One might argue that the "Anabaptist vision" school set forth a verbal formula, and indeed its founders took pains to declare their Christian orthodoxy. Yet their message was an interpretation of actual history, not systematic theology.

56. Stoltzfus, *Church-Affiliated Higher Education*, pp. 112-113.

57. Goshen College "Religious Welfare Survey Report" (multilithed, n.d. [1949]; copies in MHL).

58. Paton Yoder, "Toward a Mennonite Philosophy of Higher Education Since 1890" (Hesston, KS; multilithed "Philosophy of Christian Education Study for the Mennonite Church: Workshop Paper C, September 13-16, 1968"), p. 50.

59. Yoder, "Toward a Mennonite Philosophy of Higher Education," p. 48.

Paton Yoder, charged by MC Mennonite leaders with reviewing their denomination's educational philosophy, found none of the attempts very impressive.[60] The same seems true for most of the period since he wrote. For instance, a 1971 booklet with the subtitle *A Philosophy of Education for the Mennonite Church* was replete with code words such as "community" and with good common sense ("the *values taught to the young must be practiced by adults*"); but while it faithfully expressed the general Mennonite approach, it hardly offered the sustained, systematic reasoning implied in the word "philosophy."[61]

2. Despite the 1923-24 closing, Goshen has *not* faced a church or a governing board that was (as Burtchaell found in Vanderbilt's case) "unrelievedly negative."[62] Even during the 1923-24 closing, by keeping Sanford Yoder as chair of the governing board the Mennonite Church showed that it was interested in reconstructing the college, not destroying it. And current figures on contributions from the church to the college show considerable support. Of all contributions to Goshen College in 1993-1994, almost exactly 20 percent were from the Mennonite Church as church. Much of the other 80 percent, including that from alumni, business, and industry, was also from Mennonites. This 80 percent also reflects strong church-college connections; according to Mennonite understandings of church, however, "church support" must mean considerable support from the church corporately, not only individual-by-individual.

3. Neither has the college ever moved into one stage that Marsden and Burtchaell found typical in higher education's "secularization," that of cutting denominational ties while still claiming to be generically Christian — indeed claiming, as Burtchaell paraphrased, to be more "authentically" and "wisely" Christian than before.[63] Goshen has not gone that route. If it did, it would probably become a "generic peace college." Goshen's public rhetoric has indeed changed, and writers such as Marsden and Burtchaell would certainly find a "blurring of nomenclature"[64] or "rhetorical slide."[65] Especially since 1970 the college's catalogs have become more breezy and more oriented to language of personal and relational development when compared to earlier crisper state-

---

60. Yoder, "Toward a Mennonite Philosophy of Higher Education," passim.

61. Daniel Hertzler and others, *Mennonite Education: Why and How? A Philosophy of Education for the Mennonite Church* (Scottdale: Herald Press, 1971), p. 19.

62. Burtchaell, "Decline and Fall," p. 26.

63. Burtchaell, "Decline and Fall," p. 24; see also Marsden, "The Soul," p. 27.

64. Phrase in Burtchaell, "Decline and Fall," p. 27.

65. Phrase in Meyer, "Mennonite Colleges and . . . ," p. 16. In using the phrase, Meyer (the Mennonite Board of Education's former top executive and leading theorist) was paraphrasing Burtchaell, not referring to Mennonite colleges; but he was warning Mennonite educators against "a gradually-increasing vagueness and lack of specificity" in their religious-commitment language.

ments of commitment and belief.[66] Increasingly, Goshen fits a label which Stoltzfus applied to certain Catholic schools: "Humane Values colleges."[67] However good that character, Goshen's people might do well to ponder a point which Marsden strongly implied and Burtchaell stated forthrightly: that *"it has been active Christians, not hostile secularists, who were most effective in alienating the colleges and universities from their communities of faith."*[68]

The change in Goshen's idiom, if it might seem to reflect Marsden's "Liberal Protestant" stage, has not led to that stage's typically devastating effect on church-college relations. Indeed, by the definitions of strong college-church relatedness which come from another quarter, namely those put forward by Merrimon Cuninggim in a 1978 National Council of Churches study, Goshen's change in public rhetoric does not necessarily imply a weakening of relationship to the church; it may actually reflect parallel developments within leading elements of the Mennonite Church itself. Some commentators may think that the case is one of downward slide for both college and church; others may think not. In either case, college and church seem to be moving hand-in-hand.

4. One way that Goshen has maintained its relationship to the church is by having board members 100 percent Mennonite; permanent faculty either Mennonite or highly sympathetic; and at least 65 percent of the students Mennonite. Some faculty and other interested parties are apt to think that relaxing the Mennonite student percentage might help Goshen's enrollment. Others have pointed to losses in Mennonite recruitment: since 1980, "MC" Mennonite students entering Mennonite colleges have declined from about 1750 to 1350 per year, while those in non-Mennonite institutions have increased from about 1750 to 2900. Why, some ask, are Goshen and other Mennonite colleges not attracting so many of their own? Has the 65 percent rule actually depressed enrollment? Viewed individual-by-individual, the enrollment criterion certainly seems arbitrary.[69] Mennonites themselves are diverse, and the presence of other students clearly enriches the educational climate. Why make Mennonite-relatedness a criterion?

A college's students — not only its faculty, administration, boards, and philosophy — do much to set the educational climate. The percentage rule rests on a logic of thresholds, or "critical mass." For present-day Mennonites the practical question seems to be how to find the optimum (and biblical) mix of both "distinctive community" and inclusivism. For Goshen College the specific question seems to be, Where is the threshold beyond which diversity

---

66. Generalization based on survey of the college's catalogs, 1896-1992.

67. Stoltzfus, *Church-Affiliated Higher Education,* p. 21.

68. Burtchaell, "Decline and Fall," p. 29.

69. The last two sentences echo discussions in Goshen faculty meetings in the fall and winter of 1994-95.

brings a loss of the institution's purposes and character? In the aggregate, to assume no correlation between being Mennonite and fostering an educational climate that fits the church's and the college's values is to say that Mennonite rearing or membership means nothing. If that is true, then why any relationship of college and church at all?

Similarly, in choosing faculty, Goshen College does not now impose, or want, rigid uniformity. Mennonite faculty themselves by no means all think alike, and at present a sprinkling of faculty who are other than Mennonite are well-integrated into campus life, enriching it. But again, individual-by-individual thinking is not adequate for policy. Goshen College's policy is that "all faculty members" are "expected to be active participants and members of Mennonite or other Christian congregation[s] and in full sympathy with the doctrines and practices of the Mennonite Church."[70] In recent years, former president Victor Stoltzfus strengthened the steps and requirements for faculty candidates to express their faith and its meaning for the positions they seek.[71] Burtchaell observed that at some point Vanderbilt University "lost the ability to affirm in the first person plural that it was Methodist."[72] Quite apart from governance, the student quota, faculty composition, and other formalities, what does it take for Goshen's people to "affirm in the first person plural" that we are Mennonite?

5. Finally, the subtle issue of commitment versus relativism needs to be addressed. Do Goshen's embracing of pluralism and its promotion of cross-cultural understanding imply a relativism of a kind that can undermine real faith commitment? The intent of the question certainly is not to diminish appreciation for the intrinsic values of pluralism and cross-culturalism; and as led by its director Zenebe Abebe, Goshen's Multicultural Affairs Office clearly works from faith commitment, not relativism. As with Jesus' choice of disciples, the bringing of different people together across various divides is itself a strong Christian value. On this matter, too, college and church seem to be moving together, if one can judge by recent language coming out of the Mennonite Church. The question's intent is only to ask whether pursuing one set of excellent goals might have a side-effect which deserves more attention: temptation toward a faith-corroding relativism. Most notably: Is Goshen communicating well enough to students and others that its heralded SST program rests on faith commitments? Is the message clearly to invite faith commitment, rather than a relativism that might make all faith commitments seem like mere cultural expression?

70. "Goshen College Faculty Handbook" (November 1993), section 7.1.

71. Author's conversation with Goshen's President Victor Stoltzfus, 25 January 1995. See the form he used when interviewing candidates for full- and part-time faculty positions.

72. Burtchaell, "Decline and Fall," p. 27.

Theron F. Schlabach

Conclusion

Much in the "failure" literature of church-college relations — the literature analyzing increasing "secularization" — does not apply well to Goshen. Goshen has not identified fundamentally with national culture, nor has it developed mainly out of struggles with Enlightenment thinking or with a scientific worldview. Yet the main strength of its Mennonite Church relationship rests not on that negative, but on a positive: thus far, both the Mennonite Church and Goshen College have maintained a strong enough sense of purpose and peoplehood to keep their church-college relationship intact. Underlying such purpose and peoplehood have been Mennonites' traditions of countercultural dissent. Still, Goshen's church and faith connections deserve constant reflection. Far from being set over against one another, Goshen College and its church still seem able to ask the questions together. For the two to continue asking the questions together seems to depend as much on what kind of church the Mennonite Church will continue to be as it does on the college itself. "It takes a strong church to have strong church schools."

Religious Idealism and Academic Vocation at Fresno Pacific College

Paul Toews

Pacific Bible Institute (PBI) was established in 1944 in Fresno, California as a school of the Mennonite Brethren Church. In the 1950s it began a metamorphosis that turned it successively into a junior college and a four-year liberal arts college. In 1975 the renamed Fresno Pacific College began offering graduate degrees, primarily in education. This essay focuses mainly on the Bible institute and undergraduate liberal arts dimensions of the college story.

During the 1994-95 academic year, Fresno Pacific College celebrated its fiftieth anniversary. In the history of American colleges that is a short history. Yet the college in five decades has experienced more fundamental shifts than many schools with a longer history: from a Bible institute to a junior college, to a senior college, to a graduate school; from ownership by the Pacific District Conference of Mennonite Brethren Churches to ownership by the United States National Conference and then back to the Pacific District; from training people primarily for "churchly" vocations to educating them primarily for "worldly" vocations; and from a college designed to foster distinctive Mennonite Brethren (MB) patterns of piety to one that is religiously ecumenical.

These transitions might reflect the instability of Western culture, the California syndrome, or the changing fortunes of the Mennonite Brethren on the West Coast. They also reflect fundamental paradoxes and even contradictions in the story of the Mennonite Brethren.

The Mennonite Brethren, since their 1860 origin in the Russian empire as a separate denomination within the larger Mennonite family, have been many things. Born out of multiple impulses, the denomination historically has been diverse rather than singular and frequently fragmented rather than integrated. Present at the creation of the denomination and influencing its early trajectory were historic Anabaptism, Continental Pietism, and British Evangelicalism. Cultural progressives seeking greater liberation from the constraints of a closed community and cultural conservatives seeking a tighter morality worked together to fashion the new religious movement. For some of the founders history was to be normative; for others religious experience was to be the guide.[1]

This incipient theological pluralism was soon matched by a geographical scattering. Given the difficulty of carving out a new religious community within the context of the Mennonite Commonwealth in Ukrainian Russia, many of the early Mennonite Brethren scattered to newer settlements across Asiatic and Siberian Russia. And in 1874, fourteen years after the MB beginnings, the initial migration of Russian Mennonites to North America began. Among the 18,000 migrants of the 1870s were some 200 Mennonite Brethren families who settled in Kansas, Nebraska, South Dakota, and Minnesota. From these fledgling settlements they fanned out across the western United States and Canada. Thus, those Mennonites who first came into California's San Joaquin Valley in the early years of the twentieth century were mostly migrants twice over. Between 1905 and 1915 they established a series of congregations in small towns of the valley.[2]

1. The historiography on the origins of the Mennonite Brethren is extensive. Selected important works include Peter M. Friesen, *The Mennonite Brotherhood in Russia (1789-1910)*, J. B. Toews, Abraham Friesen, Peter J. Klassen, and Harry Loewen, Translation and Editorial Committee (Fresno: Board of Christian Literature, General Conference of Mennonite Brethren Churches 1978); John A. Toews, *A History of the Mennonite Brethren Church: Pilgrims and Pioneers*, ed. A. J. Klassen (Fresno: Board of Christian Literature, General Conference of Mennonite Brethren Churches, 1975); David G. Rempel, "The Mennonite Colonies in New Russia: A Study of their Settlement and Economic Development from 1789-1914" (Ph.D. dissertation, Stanford University, 1933); John B. Toews, *Perilous Journey: The Mennonite Brethren in Nineteenth Century Russia, 1860-1910* (Hillsboro: Kindred Press, 1988); James Urry, "The Social Background to the Emergence of the Mennonite Brethren in Nineteenth Century Russia," *Journal of Mennonite Studies* 6 (October 1988): 8-35; Frank C. Peters, "The Early Mennonite Brethren Church: Baptist or Anabaptist?" *Mennonite Life* 25 (October 1959): 176-178; Victor Adrian, "Born of Anabaptism and Pietism," *Mennonite Brethren Herald* (March 26, 1965 [special insert]). Two pieces assessing this historiography are Peter J. Klassen, "The Historiography of the Birth of the Mennonite Brethren Church: An Introduction" in Abraham Friesen, ed., *P. M. Friesen and His History: Understanding Mennonite Brethren Beginnings* (Fresno: Center for Mennonite Brethren Studies, 1979), pp. 115-127; Paul Toews, "Differing Historical Imaginations and the Changing Identity of the Mennonite Brethren" in Walter Klassen, ed., *Anabaptism Revisited: Essays on Anabaptist/Mennonite Studies in Honor of C. J. Dyck* (Scottdale: Herald Press, 1992), 155-172.

2. See Kevin Enns-Rempel, "A New Life in the West: Settlement and Colonization on the Pacific Coast" in Esther Jost, ed., *75 Years of Fellowship: Pacific District Conference of the Mennonite Brethren Churches, 1912-1987* (Fresno: Pacific District Conference of the Men-

Virtually parallel with the development of Mennonite Brethren congregations across North America was the establishment of schools of various kinds. Among the elements present in the formation of the new denomination in Russia were people yearning for greater educational and cultural freedom than was practiced within the authoritarian structure of Russian colony life. A disproportionate number of young teachers eager to explore how Western European learning and culture might reinvigorate the Russian Mennonite religious life were part of the Brethren movement. Thus it was not surprising that establishment of a new settlement required immediate attention to schooling and the articulation of the inherited religious and cultural values. By 1916 the Pacific District Conference, consisting of churches in California and Oregon, was seeking to establish its own conference-wide school.

For a variety of reasons that school was not established until 1944 with the founding of Pacific Bible Institute (PBI). The intervening years witnessed political and economic stresses that alone were sufficient to explain the delay: the trauma of being Germanic through two world wars; and the economics of coping with the depression and absorbing countless additional migrants from the Midwest.[3] But the more serious reasons for the delay were theological.

Pietistic Beginnings (1944-1960)

The impulse to build a school was rooted in the need to insure that Mennonite Brethren young people would receive appropriate denominational understandings. Denominational schools are typically nurseries of denominational piety. They shelter people from the corrosive impact of alien ways. But the question of what is to be mediated to the next generation sometimes can become unclear.

The period from the 1920s to the 1940s was such a time of uncertainty for West Coast Mennonite Brethren. Some Mennonite Brethren were drawn to the Bible Institute of Los Angeles (Biola) with its brand of vigorous fundamentalism. During the 1920s and 1930s, as the fundamentalist-modernist debate polarized American Protestants, most Mennonites instinctively leaned into the conservative camp. Other MBs found a new freedom and expres-

nonite Brethren Churches, 1987), pp. 9-23; and John A. Toews, *A History of the Mennonite Brethren Church,* pp. 146-149.

3. On the educational efforts of the Mennonite Brethren in California before the 1944 establishment of Pacific Bible Institute see Paul Toews, "'A Shelter In a Time of Storm': The Establishment of Schools in the Pacific District," in Jost, ed., *75 Years of Fellowship,* pp. 57-70.

siveness in the Pentecostal-Holiness movement that contrasted with their own restrained and codified piety.

The leaders who, during the 1920s and 1930s, pushed for the establishment of a school in California were trusted and recognized persons who had grown up within the Mennonite Brethren world and were attuned to historic Anabaptist theological interests. In the early 1940s the leadership passed to a new generation significantly nurtured by pietism and American fundamentalism. This new group of leaders felt comfortable with more expressive and personal forms of piety. They also shared an inclination toward greater precision in theological formulation than had traditionally been the case among the Mennonite Brethren.

While the emphases of pietism and fundamentalism historically had been part of the Mennonite Brethren tradition, they were now highlighted as being more important than before. Some Mennonite Brethren in the West were uneasy about the shift and about the leadership of the school movement passing to this generation. One observer wrote that "many of the old standbys are not at all in sympathy with what these men are trying to feed us. . . . They constantly speak of having a school in which we instruct our young people in the ways and beliefs of our fathers, but if our fathers would arise from the dead and observe, I am sure they would not recognize some of our ways."[4]

Pacific Bible Institute's opening on September 18, 1944, while culminating discussions that began in 1916, did not resolve the uncertainty about what kinds of theology would best nurture Mennonite Brethren youth. The story of the college is that of working with this diverse inheritance. Denominational particularity and generic conservative Christianity have been interwoven. Fundamentalism/evangelicalism, Anabaptism, pietism, and ecumenicism have been dialectically linked, and the college has been pulled and pushed in differing directions at the same time.

The first extended academic catalog, published for its second year of operation in 1945-46, embodied the plurality. It declared that the school was "not sectarian in its program of instruction" but simultaneously noted that it "earnestly contends for the faith once delivered unto the saints." From the very start, students of differing denominational communities were welcomed and assured that the school would not "in any way enforce our views upon them." But that generosity was circumscribed by the necessity that the students "adhere to the fundamental doctrines of the Christian faith, and are zealous in the promotion of His cause."[5] The spirit of tolerance and openness perhaps

4. Robert C. Seibel to Henry W. Lohrenz, July 3, 1944, Henry W. Lohrenz Papers, Correspondence Series, Box 5, Seibel folder, Center for Mennonite Brethren Studies-Fresno (hereafter CMBS-F).

5. "Our Policy Towards Students of Other Denominations," *Pacific Bible Institute Catalog, 1945-1946.*

reflected the Anabaptist commitment to noncoercive faith, but the substance of what was acceptable reflected the strictures of American fundamentalism. Denominational openness notwithstanding, only Mennonite Brethren students enrolled in the first year.

Pacific Bible Institute, like other such schools, articulated the function of education almost entirely as service to the church. Throughout the 1940s the intent of the school was to train people for churchly vocations: pastors, missionaries, Sunday school teachers, and people serving in related church ministries. In contrast to the language of "education," which became more prominent in the subsequent incarnations of the college, the Bible Institute catalogs and course descriptions consistently used the language of "training." The school had specific vocational aims in mind. Preparation for those vocations took precedence over expansion of the mind. The aims of education were articulated in a sevenfold statement:[6]

1. To uphold a positive interpretation of the Scriptures.
2. To strive constantly to maintain a spiritual atmosphere which will tend to lead students into a fully consecrated life.
3. To develop a sincere love for mankind and an intense desire for their salvation.
4. To help each student acquire a skill in practical Christian work through a supervised program of personal work.
5. To uphold the principles of peace, separation from the world, simplicity of life, sanctity of the home, and diligent habits of industry.
6. To train and equip students for pastors, evangelists, Sunday School workers, missionaries and personal soul winners.
7. To instruct men and women in Christian thought, life and service and to hold in high regard the sacredness of the family institution.

There was denominational particularity, preeminently in the fifth statement, but the aims were also sufficiently generic to be part of the catalog of any number of similar institutions. During the 1950s revisions in the statement progressively deleted the specific Mennonite qualities and introduced more militant language like "fortify them [students] against the various unscriptural philosophies of life." And the motto of the early years — "Earnestly contend-

6. "The Aims of the School," *Pacific Bible Institute Catalog, 1945-1946.* These early mission statements are more fully analyzed in Dalton Reimer, "The Origins of the Fresno Pacific College Idea" in Paul Toews, ed., *Mennonite Idealism and Higher Education: The Story of the Fresno Pacific College Idea* (Fresno: Center for Mennonite Brethren Studies, 1995), pp. 24-39. John Yoder, "From Monastery to Marketplace: Idea and Mission in Graduate and Professional Programs at Fresno Pacific College," in Toews, ed., *Mennonite Idealism,* pp. 133-134, notes this distinction between "training" and "education."

ing for the faith" (Jude 3) — could have been the guiding inscription of many explicitly fundamentalist schools.[7]

The embodiment of these aims during the early years of PBI is best revealed in the student practical work: Sunday school teaching, jail visitation, conducting services in old folks homes (as they were called), and street evangelistic services. All evidenced a high degree of spirituality. All evidenced a high commitment to evangelism. It was, however, a spirituality defined largely in terms of personal piety and personal witnessing. The integration of faith and learning was understood as commitment to a particular kind of Christian ministry. If measured by the forty-six students alone who between 1945 and 1959 went into overseas missionary service, then the integration took hold.[8]

The Bible school ideal functioned well for the first decade. Enrollments grew and financial support from Mennonite congregations was forthcoming. From a beginning enrollment of 28 students in 1944 the school grew rapidly to 178 students by 1949. But that support was short-lived. After peaking at 178, the enrollment began a decline that reached a low of 57 students in 1958-1959. A Bible institute education had lost its appeal for Mennonite Brethren people.

The decline was related to fundamental shifts occurring among Mennonites during the postwar era. If one segment in the church yearned for the insulation that an education limited to training church workers brought, another equally strong segment felt a growing level of comfort with American society. The cultural separatism that bounded Mennonite communities in California into the 1940s eroded very quickly following the war. The transition from German to English language, begun already during the 1930s, was completed with the beginning of the war. Under the patriotic fever of the "good war," pacifism long a characteristic distinguishing Mennonites from the larger population — gave way among many California Mennonite Brethren.

After the war Mennonites were positioned to ride the post-war economic boom with its unprecedented opportunities. By the late 1940s they had acquired sufficient investment and status to become important partners in the political process. San Joaquin Valley Mennonites engaged in new political activity, fraternized in civic and community service clubs like Kiwanis and Rotary, and branched out into new entrepreneurial activity.[9] As the cultural

7. See for example *Pacific Bible Institute of Fresno Annual Catalog, 1954-1955,* p. 10. See also Reimer, "The Origins of the Fresno Pacific College Idea," in Toews, ed., *Mennonite Idealism,* pp. 24-39.

8. Joel A. Wiebe, *Remembering . . . Reaching, A vision for Service: A Fifty Year History of Fresno Pacific College* (Fresno: Fresno Pacific College, 1994), p. 41.

9. The best illustration of this new political activism and entrepreneurial activity would be Reedley, California, the valley town with the largest Mennonite Brethren population. In the immediate post-war years the town elected a Mennonite Brethren mayor, others were elected to the city council, and the Brethren gained control of the public education system

barriers between the immigrant ethno-religious folks and the dominant society diminished, students increasingly needed a more diversified educational program. The liberal arts ideal was more appropriate to a people less withdrawn and more ready to enter into many "worldly" vocations.

Anabaptist Reorientation (1960-1975)

In 1956, with the decision to add a junior college curriculum to the Bible institute program, the metamorphosis into a liberal arts college began. By 1965 the college earned full accreditation as a baccalaureate institution and ten years later, in 1975, it was authorized to offer master's degrees. The speed of the transition may have been surprising. But even more surprising was the ideational reorientation that accompanied the liberal arts development.

Arthur Wiebe's installation in 1960 as the new president was symptomatic of the change. He came with no seminary training, but with a doctorate in mathematics education from Stanford University. His profile was that of the educator-churchman rather than the pastor-churchman which had been the case for all the presidents who preceded him.

The decline of the Bible institute program and the necessity of moving toward a liberal arts institution created possibilities of many kinds. It was a time for asking fundamental questions. What kind of college should emerge? What kinds of philosophical, religious, and educational ideals should shape the transformed institution? To answer these questions Wiebe recruited a new generation. Most of those who joined the faculty in the decade of the 1960s were in their late twenties and early thirties. Wiebe picked them out of graduate schools and seminaries, in many cases with terminal degrees still unfinished. It was indeed a propitious moment — one given to few generations — when the future is open, when the dominant institutions and values of the past are clearly on the skids but the shape of the new is not yet clear.

Wiebe, together with this new generation, not only fashioned a liberal arts college but also fashioned a new ideation that would reshape the churchly and academic understandings of what a Mennonite Brethren college could be. The young faculty came with the idealism of the early 1960s. But more important, they came with an awareness of the mid-twentieth-century intellectual reconstruction that had already taken place among other Mennonite groups in North America.

---

even while running their own private high school. The entrepreneurial activity is suggested in the number of main street businesses that now came into Mennonite ownership. See Esther Jost, *The Church Alive In Its 75th Year: Reedley Mennonite Brethren, 1905-1980* (Reedley: Mennonite Brethren Church, 1980) and the *Reedley Exponent,* October 27, 1988 (a special issue commemorating the Reedley centennial).

John Higham, historian at Johns Hopkins University, has argued that ethnic or ethno-religious communities living within democratic societies have only two strategies for group survival: boundary maintenance or nuclei revitalization.[10] Some Mennonite groups faced with the intrusiveness of a national culture consciously choose boundary maintenance. The socially progressive groups, like the Mennonite Brethren, choose revitalization. The revitalization that the young intellectuals at Fresno Pacific wished to emulate was already taking place among the two largest Mennonite denominations in North America — the Mennonite Church and the General Conference Mennonite Church. Those groups, faced with the same erosion of the cultural barriers, had moved toward an ideological redefinition of their identity. Harold S. Bender, the Goshen College historian and Mennonite churchman, provided the most important moment in this ideological redefinition. His presidential address to the American Society of Church History in 1944, entitled "The Anabaptist Vision," articulated a usable past that could also become a means for defining the present and shaping the future. As outlined by Bender the meaning of Anabaptism turned on three ideas: an understanding of discipleship as the essence of Christianity; a gathering together of the faithful in voluntary church communities that practiced mutuality and accountability; and an ethic of love and nonresistance that governed all relationships, civil and religious. The "Anabaptist Vision" soon became the identifying incantation for many Mennonites. It seemed to offer new possibilities for fashioning an alternative community, for creating solidarity, and for a prophetic witness.[11]

These ideas soon surfaced as President Wiebe began an institutional master planning process. At the core of this new institutional visioning was the 1966 drafting of a new institutional mission statement — "The Fresno Pacific College Idea." In its original form the Idea articulated seven principle themes:[12]

Pacific College is a Christian College
Pacific College is a Community

10. See John Higham, *Send These To Me: Immigrants in Urban America* (Baltimore: The Johns Hopkins University Press, 1984), chapter 1; Higham, "Divergent Unities in American History," *Journal of American History* 61 (June 1974): 5-28.

11. See Harold S. Bender, "The Anabaptist Vision," *Church History* 13 (March 1944): 3-23. The literature on the impact of Bender's formulation of Mennonite identity is vast. For starters see Guy F. Hershberger, ed., *The Recovery of the Anabaptist Vision: A Sixtieth Anniversary Tribute to Harold S. Bender* (Scottdale: Herald Press, 1957); *Conrad Grebel Review* 12 (Fall 1994) has a series of articles assessing Bender on the fiftieth anniversary of the publication of the famous address. See also a forthcoming biography of Harold S. Bender by Albert N. Keim.

12. The document is reprinted in Wiebe, *Remembering . . . Reaching,* pp. 94-97, and as the appendix in Toews, ed., *Mennonite Idealism and Higher Education,* pp. 155-162.

Pacific College is a Liberal Arts College
Pacific College is an Experimental College
Pacific College is an Anabaptist-Mennonite College
Pacific College is a Non-Sectarian College
Pacific College is a Prophetic College

Internally the document quickly came to function as a "charter" statement and since 1966 has been at the core of the institution's search for self-understanding. It was a clear statement that what made an institution Mennonite was its ideation rather than the demographics of its student body, faculty, or even board of trustees. Providing an ideational center in one sense was a pragmatic move. There were insufficient Mennonite Brethren on the West Coast to populate, staff, and fund a sizable college. But the driving force behind the "Idea" statement was the idealism of the young faculty. With time, every program and sector of the college would have to legitimate itself before the Idea. Working out the meaning of the Idea to this day remains a process of continuous discussion.

Some elements of the Idea were congruent with the institution's past and with similar statements of other Christian colleges. The definition of the college as Christian borrowed the language of many institutions — the college "accepts as the ultimate authority for life God's self-disclosure of himself to man in Jesus Christ and the record of Scripture . . . , believes in the unity of all knowledge under God, [and] sees no ultimate contradiction between the truth of revelation and of scholarly investigation." The conception of the liberal arts, while hardly articulating the classical concern for the emancipation of the individual from parochial constraints, did utilize language generic to Christian colleges: a richer understanding of "God, man and the world through the disciplines, . . . wholeness of personality, . . . [and] a more perceptive and creative relationship with God and the world."

The distinctive elements of the Idea were the ways it committed the college to the notion of community, to the Anabaptist-Mennonite heritage, and to a prophetic stance. These three elements provide what Dalton Reimer, one of the framers of the Idea, has termed the "interpretative center of the institution."[13] All three elements in some fashion drew from the particularistic theological tradition of the college.

Fresno Pacific College as Community

Mennonite colleges, like their supporting congregations, have typically affirmed the importance of community. Anabaptist/Mennonite ecclesiology has

13. Reimer, "The Origins of the Fresno Pacific College Idea," p. 35.

long rejected the distinction between the clergy and the laity. What is frequently called the "hermeneutic of community" has been a cherished description of how Mennonites arrive at understandings. The congregation makes decisions about important matters of theology and practice. Ideas and persons are to be judged by the collective insight of the community. Mennonite colleges have typically also sought to function as a community. That means more than teaching about the history of communities or the sociology of community formation. The congregation, or in this case the college as an entity, was to be the testing ground for shaping and refining ideas. Martin Buber's image of truth "unfolding" rather than being "imposed" became the preferred style for student-faculty interaction and institutional governance.[14]

The decade following the articulation of the "Idea" statement saw the introduction of a series of programs designed to implement this idealism. A core class that has gone through various name and conceptual changes was introduced in 1972.[15] Initially all entering freshman took the course, and in the past decade it became a requirement for all entering students. Over the years the course has reflected the communitarian commitments of the Idea. It is taught by a team of faculty members from various disciplines. The Biblical Studies faculty provide the anchor and the core lectures but other faculty along with student assistants conduct much of the discussion and work of the course. All students when they arrive at the college are divided into mentor groups or "collegiums." Faculty involved in the core course are also the mentors and work together collaboratively with mentor assistants (students who have previously taken the course) to insure that new students experience the sense of community in this class, if not elsewhere, in their first year at the school. A weekend mountain retreat designed to facilitate friendship within the collegium as well as a public service project are requirements of the course. These components help build community, sustain service, and encourage students to experience the relationship between the two.

Other programs designed to facilitate community included the introduction of a peer-counseling and peer-disciplinary process and a four-day academic calendar that kept Wednesdays open for community activities and special all-campus symposia. To facilitate the Idea's statement that "learning involves the interaction between people and ideas," institutional monies have encouraged student/faculty social interactions and collaborative academic work.

Since the 1960s the college has eschewed the use of academic titles. To this day persons on the campus, including the president, generally are addressed

14. Quoted in Reimer, "The Origins of the Fresno Pacific College Idea," p. 32.
15. "Directions for Learning" file, Academic Vice President's Records, Box 3, Fresno Pacific College Archives, CMBS-F.

by their first names. If unorthodox to academe, it was an adaptation of the traditional designation of "brothers and sisters" in the life of Mennonite congregations. The decision to forego the use of normal academic titles was also part of a larger attempt, flowing out of the "Idea" statement, to create more egalitarian and participatory governance structures. Traditional faculty rank was set aside in favor of a common designation of "Faculty Fellows." In 1974 a new governance structure incorporated students, faculty, staff, and administrators into the chief campus legislative body. Adoption of a comparatively compressed scale between the lowest and highest faculty salaries was a further expression of the community idealism.

Fresno Pacific College as an Anabaptist-Mennonite and Prophetic College

The outworkings of the Anabaptist and prophetic elements of the Idea into the pedagogical and institutional fabric were perhaps less visible than the prominent structural innovations designed to achieve community, but were no less significant for the student educational experience. The Idea was much more than a statement of educational philosophy. It was a new charter for how Mennonite Brethren Christians should function in the world. At the center of the Anabaptist/Mennonite tradition is the question of the relationship between the people of God and the people of the world. The prophetic ideal suggested that Christian education was to educate for social transformation as much as for personal righteousness. Humanity suffered alienation from God, but also alienation from the social world. The political and economic structures that divide people into rich and poor, liberated and oppressed, nourished and malnourished, were also in need of redemption.

As these ideals filtered into the student consciousness, an alteration took place in their patterns of volunteer activity. Engagement shifted from evangelistic street services and jail testimonies to working with agencies offering material assistance to the poor and to providing academic tutorial programs and other allied forms of social reconstruction. The witness of deed came to be seen as a correlate — if not a more adequate representation — of the Christian gospel than the verbal witness.

The Idea articulated a relationship to American culture that included an interesting mixture of both engagement and withdrawal. This neo-Anabaptism proclaimed the relevance of the Mennonite community as the preserver of a higher ideal than offered by the compromised mainstream religious traditions. Thus it had social relevance. Yet its social relevance was hinged to a strong current of critique that fostered a continuing sense of separateness. This idealism could simultaneously engage a new generation in the tasks of social reconstruction and critique and substantive identification with the larger society.

This critical stance toward culture also reshaped academic understandings. The starting point for the nonconformist intellectual tradition became what Paul Ricoeur called the "hermeneutic of suspicion." The young intellectuals now also turned that suspicion on the reigning assumptions about the "integration of faith and learning" rhetoric of American Christian colleges. At the heart of much modern theology has been the project that Stanley Hauerwas and William Willimon recently described as "making the gospel credible to the modern world."[16] Facing the German philosopher Gotthold Lessing's "ugly wide ditch" that separated the ancient faith from modern science, much of recent American and European theologizing sought to translate the faith into modern philosophical categories. Mark Noll, the Wheaton College historian, includes this preoccupation as part of the "scandal of the evangelical mind." But the scandal was not limited to evangelicals. American liberalism also understood the explicit task of theology and the implicit role of the church as demanding adaptation to dominant cultural values.[17]

From the stance of the Radical Reformation and from the vantage point of the young intellectuals at Fresno Pacific College, that entire venture was misguided. The theology of translation assumed an intellectual essence that could be preserved and integrated into changing scientific world views. The Mennonite approach to faith has always begun at a different place. Christian faith is meeting Jesus and joining up, becoming part of the movement, working toward the establishment of the kingdom.[18]

Integration came to be seen as too limited and perhaps even an inadequate metaphor for Mennonites to use. Integration was too closely identified with the Constantinian tradition. Like so much of that tradition it meant absorption of faith into the cultural system. Transformationist language offered a more viable descriptor of the intended relationship of faith to knowledge and of faith to culture. Transformation suggested the creation of an alternative order that by the power of its witness and example would have relevance beyond its borders. This transformationist understanding did not reject an appropriation of high culture and the importance of learning for enriching the faith, but it sought to direct it into the creation of new orders.[19]

16. Stanley Hauerwas and William H. Willimon, *Resident Aliens: Life in the Christian Colony* (Nashville: Abingdon Press, 1989), p. 19.

17. See Mark A. Noll, *The Scandal of the Evangelical Mind* (Grand Rapids: Eerdmans, 1994); and Hauerwas and Willimon, *Resident Aliens*, chapter 1.

18. *Resident Aliens*, p. 21 makes this point as well as any Mennonite author.

19. One quickly detects this transformative notion from perusing course syllabi in the "Curriculum Files," Academic Vice President's Records, Fresno Pacific College Archives, CMBS-F.

Creative as the 1960s and 1970s were in working out the meaning of the Pacific College Idea, other indices of institutional development were not as favorable. Undergraduate enrollment, after steadily rising between 1960 and 1972, leveled off and, for the next decade, fluctuated without any significant increase. By the late 1970s an accumulated deficit in the operational fund hovered between $150,000 and $200,000 in an annual budget of between two and three million. The stagnation called for some kind of institutional alteration in order to achieve sustained growth and maturation.

Broadening the Base (1975-1985)

During the decade from 1975 to 1985 a series of developments did converge to reshape the institution: (1) the expansion of teacher-education-related programs; (2) the transfer of ownership from the United States National Conference to the regional Pacific District Conference; (3) a revision of the "Idea" statement; (4) a new more ecumenical strategy known as "Broadening the Base"; (5) and the inauguration in 1985 of both a new president and an academic vice president from outside the Mennonite Brethren denomination.

One of the distinctive accomplishments of the decade of the 1970s was the development of professional teacher education programs at both the undergraduate and graduate levels. The movement toward professional teacher preparation really began already with the commencement of Arthur Wiebe's presidency in 1960. He came with a distinguished career in secondary education administration and had authored a mathematics textbook widely adopted in high schools across the country. Elias Wiebe, the first academic dean hired by Arthur Wiebe, also had a long career in both elementary teaching and administration and in college teacher preparation programs. Already in 1965 the Board of Trustees approved a proposal for the development of a teacher education program.[20] Beginning in 1970, when Silas Bartsch, another successful local public school administrator, joined the faculty, the college moved toward the development of "in-service education" programs for teachers already in the field. In 1974 the college approved a Master of Arts in Education degree and in 1975 the regional accrediting association approved the new degree programs.

The graduate programs grew rapidly. Beginning in 1975 with seven students, these programs enrolled 246 by 1980, and in 1985, a decade after their inception, 527 individuals were enrolled in various masters degree or advanced educational credential programs. By the late 1970s the enrollment for in-service education courses, frequently offered in collaboration with local school

20. Minutes of the Pacific College Board of Trustees, 26-28 October 1965, Fresno Pacific College Archives, CMBS-F.

234

districts, numbered nearly 5000.[21] In both the in-service and graduate courses the religious affiliation of students has never been tracked. But all knowledgeable sources have consistently placed the Mennonite Brethren enrollment at less than five percent in both categories. The college was clearly reaching a new clientele with these new programs. And they did generate substantial relief for a hard-pressed institutional budget.

Accompanying the enactment of these programs was a considerable discussion as to whether they were congruent with the past and an expansion of the institution's central mission or merely a pragmatic response to financial needs. Teacher preparation was certainly in keeping with the service motifs present in both the pietist phase and the Anabaptist redefinition of the college. There is also a long history of teaching as one of the preferred vocations of Mennonites, and teacher preparation has been central to Mennonite colleges. But in the 1970s none of the other Mennonite colleges, all of them much older than Fresno Pacific, had yet entered into professional teacher preparation to the extent that Pacific now had.

Faculty more interested in the traditional liberal arts curriculum were frequently prone, as current Graduate Dean John Yoder has written, to "interpret the more professional enterprises as selling out the institution's soul for the sake of expediency."[22] Others thought they were legitimate responses to the visible needs of public education. For them the transformationist gospel of Anabaptism could find no more appropriate location for testing than the public education system. Training educators to become personally compassionate and caring, professionally more oriented to the ideals of servant-leadership, and more committed to dialogical pedagogies was entirely consonant with the center of the institution's self-identity.

The discussion reached into the Board of Trustees. When discussing these graduate programs in 1970, the trustees characterized them as "a major fund raising and recruiting tool."[23] But the trustees' discussion in 1973 about establishing the Master of Arts degree noted that a "Christian view of life and knowledge" needed to be central to the new programs.[24] The minutes of the Graduate Council, the administrative body working toward implementation, reflected the difficulty of incorporating into the curriculum the values and commitments of the institution, but also reflected concern that the personal and professional conduct of the graduate faculty model institutional values.[25]

21. Wiebe, *Remembering . . . Reaching*, p. 199.
22. Yoder, "From the Monastery to the Marketplace," p. 135.
23. Quoted in Yoder, "From the Monastery to the Marketplace," p. 139.
24. Quoted in Yoder, "From the Monastery to the Marketplace," p. 139.
25. Graduate Council Minutes, 18 January 1984, Academic Vice President's Records, Fresno Pacific College Archives, CMBS-F.

One change introduced by these new programs was a heavy reliance on adjunct faculty, most of whom had no historic connection to the Mennonite Brethren Church. Into the mid-1970s the number of full-time faculty with religious affiliation other than Mennonite Brethren were few. These teacher preparation programs were the first significant infusion of a religiously diverse faculty. Most of the persons teaching in these programs were practitioners in the field, selected because of their educational expertise. Though not working at cross-purposes with the values as identified in the Fresno Pacific College Idea, they had not been socialized by the same intellectual currents. In 1974, 97 percent of the full-time faculty was Mennonite. Ten years later in 1984 the number was 70 percent.

Pacific Bible Institute began under the auspices of the Pacific District Conference of Mennonite Brethren Churches. Between 1954 and 1979 it was governed by the Board of Education of the United States Conference of Mennonite Brethren Churches. The unified program, for twenty-five years, brought Fresno Pacific and Tabor, a sister college in Kansas, under the same governance structure. A 1979 national conference to regionalize the ownership of the two schools meant that Fresno Pacific returned to the control of the Pacific District Conference.

This new Board of Trustees brought increasing pressures for standardization. Both the public sector and other more mainstream Christian colleges were held up as worthy of emulation. The operative word for the new ideal was to make the college more "market responsive." The stress was on efficiency, the rational allocation of resources, and success. While these were worthy objectives in their own right, the new order eschewed idealism and moralism. Masked by the language of management for success was the benign technocratic ideal of expertise and pragmatism.

In 1979, on the heels of the governance transfer, then President Edmund Janzen called for a review of the "Idea" statement. The change in ownership and the addition of the graduate programs were indeed important structural changes that needed to be reflected in an institutional mission statement. But there were added pressures for review. Significant elements within the Pacific District Conference had concerns about the college's ideological posture. The recovery of the Anabaptist-Mennonite tradition, while important in reshaping the college, was less visible in certain parts of the church constituency. To some congregations the emphases of the "Idea" statement could be understood not as recovery of a partially lost tradition but as a foreign import. Furthermore, coming just when some Mennonite Brethren were pleased with the loss of cultural boundaries that had fenced them off from American society, here was a young faculty at the college offering a new set of ideological boundaries to again impede an easy association with American culture. While the revival of Mennonite history might bring nostalgic memories, the revival of Anabaptist theology challenged the acculturation process with its embrace of the American order. To some, this neo-Anabaptism seemed like the reemergence of older sectarian curbs. Others in the church found this neo-Anabaptism unacceptable because it seemed like a disguised secularity. Its categories were too political. The mystical Jesus of pietism was replaced by a more political Jesus. Furthermore the political Jesus calling for the church to be transformationist and prophetic could easily sound like the political and cultural critics of the 1960s.[26]

The new board members asking for changes in the document felt more comfortable with a more openly defined evangelicalism than with the particularistic elements of the "Idea" statement. The college should remake itself and take counsel from the more nondenominational postures of places like Biola and Messiah College, a Brethren in Christ college that successfully navigated into the mainstream of evangelical colleges.

The revised "Idea" statement contained three sections instead of the original seven. Fresno Pacific College was to be identified as a Christian College, a Liberal Arts College, and a Community. The liberal arts and the community sections retained the essential meanings of the 1966 document. The Christian college section was revised to incorporate some of the language from the original Anabaptist-Mennonite and non-sectarian sections. The sections on Fresno Pacific as a prophetic and experimental college were deleted in their entirety. The revisions clearly diminished the distinctive elements and pushed the college toward becoming a more generic evangelical college.[27]

In 1983, immediately on the heels of the revision of the "Idea" statement, President Janzen wrote a paper outlining his goals for the future. Under the catchy title of "Broadening the Base: My Vision for FPC," it seemed to offer a new direction. In reality the paper was a ringing defense of the Anabaptist-Mennonite ideation of the college. At the same time, Janzen's intent clearly was to broaden the base for the existing program. But the title caught the fancy of numerous folks by hinting at a future more expansive than the Anabaptist/Mennonite past. In an age of sound bites, the title became the slogan for the 1980s. The intent to broaden was rooted in real and critical needs. For some important constituent supporters the accumulated budget deficit and a continuing plateau in undergraduate student enrollment even raised questions of institutional viability. The college certainly needed to broaden its financial and student base. The Mennonite Brethren community in the West did not possess sufficient intellectual, financial, or student resources to sustain a vibrant college.

---

26. Nothing more symbolized the arrival of the "political Jesus" in Mennonite theology than the publication of John Howard Yoder, *The Politics of Jesus* (Grand Rapids: Eerdmans, 1972).

27. Wilfred Martens, "Revision of the FPC Idea, 1979-1982: A Contextual and Linguistic Interpretation" in Toews, ed., *Mennonite Idealism,* pp. 119-131.

In 1985 the broadening momentum took Fresno Pacific in a direction that few denominational institutions have taken. The college turned to people with no history in the denomination for its two top leadership positions. Long-time Wheaton College administrators became the new president and academic vice president. Richard Kriegbaum, incoming president, came out of the Grace Brethren denomination, which had roots, though somewhat removed, in the Church of the Brethren, a long-time denominational ally of Mennonites. While academically nurtured in the non-denominational setting of Wheaton, he came with a strong sense of the college's vital relationship to the Mennonite Brethren Church and with an appreciation for continuing denominational particularity. William Henning, the new academic vice president, was more attuned to the nondenominational and trans-evangelical style of Wheaton. Both brought an articulate evangelical language and a more expressive piety than typified the restrained style of the Mennonite Brethren. This reach to outside leadership, together with the other developments of the 1975-1985 decade, all suggested the future would be more generically evangelical and less distinctively Anabaptist.

Broadening the Base and Gaining Particularity (1985-1995)

The decade since 1985, under new leadership, has in many ways paralleled the explosive period of the 1960s. Total enrollment has risen dramatically, under-graduate enrollment by 45 percent. The physical appearance of the campus has changed significantly with the addition of three new buildings. Broadening is evident in both the financial support for the new physical expansion and in the composition of the students and faculty. With the rapid student popu-lation growth the Mennonite percentage dwindled further. Whereas the num-ber of Mennonite students actually increased in the late 1980s, by 1994 they constituted only 15 percent of the undergraduate students and a much smaller percentage of the graduate and in-service students.

By 1994 the number of Mennonite and Baptist students was virtually equal. Students from nondenominational and Catholic churches constituted the third and fourth largest group. Increasing numbers of students were also drawn from charismatic denominations (Foursquare, Assembly of God, Pente-costal) and other more Methodistic-related denominations. Whether denom-inationally affiliated or not, the mix was clearly more evangelical than Ana-baptist. The faculty underwent a similar transition as the percentage of Mennonite faculty continued to decline. In 1984, 70 percent of the full-time faculty were Mennonite and in the decade following they dropped to 60 percent.

At the demographic level Fresno Pacific clearly was becoming a different kind of institution than the one it had been in the early 1970s. Transformative as the changes were in some ways, in other ways they have not substantially altered the ideation that continues to define institutional identity and shape the curriculum. The academic program was clearly enhanced by the growing faculty ranks. The influx of faculty from different backgrounds required a more explicit dialogue as to what constituted that ideation. The conversations carried on in various forums about how the religious tradition can flavor the curriculum have intensified rather than diminished. The curriculum today is formally more "Anabaptist" than at any other time in the school's history. And it is those Anabaptist emphases that shape the integration of faith and learning.

At the undergraduate level a reworking of the core curriculum around a four-course series entitled "The Stories of Peoples and Cultures" has brought the "narrative" approach to the center of the curriculum. For the past decade a biblical studies course — "Jesus and the Christian Community" — is the one course that all students at Fresno Pacific College are required to take during their first year at the college. The other three courses connect the Christian story with the stories of other peoples around the world.

Mennonites as a people have been informed by the narrative approach. It is not accidental that the intellectual reconstruction of Mennonite identity came through history. When discipleship is at the center of faith, then the story of faithfulness becomes the paramount approach for understanding God. The narrative paradigm begins with God who speaks and acts, and so creates stories that must be recounted. The story of God's actions becomes the primary data of faith around which we understand our stories and all other stories.[28]

At the graduate level the consensual development of a constructivist epistemology has, perhaps somewhat serendipitously, moved graduate education in similar directions. While not as explicitly developed out of Anabaptist thought, it now functions in an analogous way. Constructivism values the

---

28. The Faculty Workshop on 23 October 1987 was devoted to exploring the possibilities of a "narrative framework" for the General Studies curriculum. In addition to materials prepared for circulation by Dalton Reimer, a series of texts that reflect on the possibilities of the narrative approach were read and utilized. Included were Elie Wiesel, *Messengers of God: Biblical Portraits and Legends* (repr. New York: Summit Books, 1976); Michael Novak, *Ascent of the Mountain, Flight of the Dove: An Invitation to Religious Studies* (San Francisco: Harper & Row, 1978); Thomas H. Groome, *Christian Religious Education: Sharing our Story and Vision* (San Francisco: Harper & Row, 1980); Stanley Hauerwas, *A Community of Character: Toward a Constructive Christian Social Ethic* (Notre Dame: University of Notre Dame Press, 1981); Stanley Hauerwas, Richard Bondi, and David B. Burrell, *Truthfulness and Tragedy: Further Investigations in Christian Ethics* (Notre Dame: University of Notre Dame Press, 1977); James William McClendon, *Biography as Theology: How Life Stories Can Remake Today's Theology* (Nashville: Abingdon Press, 1974); and James William McClendon, *Ethics: Systematic Theology* (Nashville: Abingdon Press, 1986).

plurality that is central to Anabaptist pedagogical approaches. It locates all learning in the social environment and emphasizes the logic of discovery and inquiry.[29] The "hermeneutic of community" is replicated in cooperative pedagogies and interdisciplinary approaches and integrations. Through the AIMS (Activities Integrating Math and Science) Foundation, an educational research institute affiliated with the college, those approaches are carried to classrooms literally around the world.

The graduate faculty also conceptualize their role very much in terms of preparing teachers to be agents of change and transformation in the public education system of the country. Paulo Freire's *Pedagogy of the Oppressed* and Neil Postman's and Charles Weingartner's *Teaching as a Subversive Activity* have long been required reading in various courses.[30] Education for empowerment, change, and reconciliation are themes that dominate and integrate religious conviction with specific disciplinary programs.

The 1990 creation of a Center for Conflict Studies and Peacemaking impacted both the undergraduate and graduate curriculums. At the undergraduate level a minor was introduced in 1990. In 1995 a Master of Arts in Conflict Management and Peacemaking was inaugurated. Both programs self-consciously bring perspectives informed by Anabaptist-Mennonite theology to the study of interpersonal, intercultural, and international conflict and conflict resolution.

Conclusion

From its pietist beginnings Fresno Pacific College has transformed itself successively into an Anabaptist and an ecumenical college. Along the way it has achieved notable success. During the early 1990s *U.S. News & World Report* regularly ranked it among the "up and coming" or "best" colleges in the West. In many ways this is a success story.

That very history has forced the college to think about the particular and ecumenical nature of Christian faith. It required the Mennonite Brethren to think seriously about the way in which their tradition interfaces with other religious communities. It moved the discussion of Mennonite Brethren identity from a largely diachronic analysis to a synchronic one. For immigrant

29. For an introduction to constructivism see Jacqueline Grennon Brooks and Martin G. Brooks, *In Search of Understanding: The Case for Constructivist Classrooms* (Alexandria, VA: Association for Supervision and Curriculum Development, 1993).

30. See Paulo Freire, *Pedagogy of the Oppressed* (repr. New York: Continuum, 1993); Neil Postman and Charles Weingartner, *Teaching as a Subversive Activity* (New York: Delacorte Press, 1969).

churches like the Mennonite Brethren, acculturation needs can increasingly create embarrassment about distinctives. Conversation with others can facilitate the development of a sense of the rich pluralism of American religiosity. "Broadening the Base" brought a recognition that others who came to more fully participate in the life of Fresno Pacific College also brought along their particularity.[31] In this more intensified dialogue with other American religious groups the Anabaptist-Mennonite tradition could be reaffirmed as one variety of evangelicalism with its own strength and legitimacy.[32] Authentic religious ecumenicism could only be achieved by respecting religious particularity. The survival of the two are interlinked.

The common story of American church-related colleges is that the church nurtures the colleges, and with time the colleges become secularized and then contribute to the secularity of the church. The Fresno Pacific College story suggests a different pattern. In 1968, roughly simultaneously with the college seeking to advance its particularity, Christopher Jencks and David Riesman argued that distinctive colleges were possible only if distinctive denominations continued to exist.

> The survival of recognizably Protestant colleges . . . seems to depend on the survival within the larger society of Protestant enclaves whose members believe passionately in a way of life radically different from that of the majority, and who are both willing and able to pay for a brand of higher education that embodies their vision. Such enclaves still exist, but they are few in number.[33]

31. The meaning of "Broadening the Base" did provide contentious points of discussion at the 1987 fall faculty meetings and at the Board of Trustees September 19, 1987 meetings. The polar positions were articulated by William Henning, "Ethno-Religious Considerations in Faculty Selection," and a response by Paul Toews, "Broadening the Base: An Alternative Response." At stake were the issues of whether the broadening transition should move toward nondenominationalism or toward multidenominationalism. Papers are in the Minutes of the Academic Commission, Pacific College Board of Trustees Minutes, September 19, 1987, Fresno Pacific College Archives, CMBS-F.

32. The growing appreciation of evangelical pluralism that developed during the 1970s and 1980s no doubt helped to legitimate the sense among Mennonite Brethren that they were a distinctive yet acceptable member of the larger evangelical fraternity. For literature that reflects on the diversity of the American evangelical world see David E. Harrell, Jr., *Varieties of Southern Evangelicalism* (Macon: Mercer University Press, 1982); Cullen Murphy, "Protestantism and the Evangelicals," *The Wilson Quarterly* 5 (August 1981): 105-116; Richard Quebedeaux, *The Worldly Evangelicals* (San Francisco: Harper & Row, 1978); and Leonard I. Sweet, ed., *The Evangelical Tradition in America* (Macon: Mercer University Press, 1984).

33. Christopher Jencks and David Riesman, *The Academic Revolution* (Garden City: Doubleday, 1968), p. 330.

The Mennonite Brethren church born out of plural and even contradictory currents has had an uncertain and frayed identity. In the United States, it has for a long time struggled to find a theological center. The college's history and identity has reflected those divergent theologies and pressures. But the college more than the denomination has sought to root itself in the historical patterns of the Anabaptist-Mennonite traditions. Its ability to survive with that distinctive approach to education will be possible only so long as the denomination wishes to retain those distinctive elements.

THE EVANGELICAL/
INTERDENOMINATIONAL
TRADITION

What Can the Evangelical/Interdenominational Tradition Contribute to Christian Higher Education?

Harold Heie

I hope to initiate a conversation. My overarching proposal is that Christians working out of different Christian traditions in the context of higher education need to create forums for conversation that will enable us to talk to each other so that we can learn from the strengths and distinctive emphases of each tradition. I will challenge the evangelical/interdenominational tradition to begin this conversation. Such a conversation will require, however, that we be honest about the limitations of our respective traditions and open to the possibility that other Christian traditions can help us address these limitations.

My call for conversation will emerge from some preliminary reflections. After clarifying what I take to be the three distinctive emphases of evangelical expressions of the Christian faith, I will summarize what I understand to be the strengths and weaknesses of each of these distinctives as they pertain to the task of Christian higher education. I will then speak on behalf of several Christian traditions often not designated "evangelical," exploring the ways they have enriched my own evangelical faith, leading me to embrace what I will call "chastened" forms of the evangelical distinctives. I will then explore ways in which a chastened evangelicalism might improve existing expressions of evangelical Christian higher education.

After this fragmentary simulated "conversation," I will conclude this essay with reflections on why an evangelical Christian college that is interdenominational in nature may be an ideal setting in theory, if not yet in practice, for continuing this conversation and for creating further forums for conversation

245

that will enable us all to learn from the distinctive emphases of each Christian tradition.

Who Is an Evangelical Christian?

My task is considerably complicated by lack of agreement as to what it means to be an "evangelical Christian." As William Abraham has pointed out, the term "evangelical" is a "contested concept," the "proper use of which inevitably involves endless disputes about their proper uses on the part of their users."[1] But one may even consider the meaning of the word "Christian" to be contestable. I am using the word "Christian" to refer to any person whose beliefs, attitudes, and practices are rooted in the "Christian story," with its major motifs of creation, fall, redemption, church as witness, and consummation.[2]

But, then, which Christians are "evangelicals"? Various attempts at defining "evangelical" are fraught with shortcomings. One approach is to go back to the etymology of the word, and propose that an evangelical is one who is committed to the "evangel" (the "gospel" or "good news"), which can be stated as follows: God has manifested unconditional love and grace in and through Jesus Christ to reconcile humanity to God's self and to redeem all of the created order. But commitment to the "evangel" is not peculiar to "evangelical" Christians; commitment to the redemption kernel of the Christian story is embraced by all Christians.

Donald Dayton takes an historical approach to defining the word. He points out that the term "evangelical" has been applied to any religious tradition rooted in one of the following three movements: (1) the sixteenth-century Protestant Reformation; (2) the revivalist movements in America in the eighteenth and nineteenth centuries, which were in turn rooted in English Puritanism and Continental Lutheran Pietism; and (3) the twentieth-century postfundamentalist, neo-evangelical movement emerging after the modernist-fundamentalist controversy.[3]

---

1. William J. Abraham, quoting W. B. Gallie, in *The Coming Great Revival: Recovering the Full Evangelical Tradition* (San Francisco: Harper & Row, 1984), p. 73.

2. I have argued elsewhere that our articulations of these motifs need to capture "first-order beliefs" that all Christians can share, while allowing for diversity in related "second-order beliefs." For example, the belief that "God created the world" is first-order. The question of "how" God created the world is a second-order issue. See Harold Heie, "Wanted: Christian Colleges for a Dynamic Evangelicalism," *Christian Scholar's Review* 21 (March 1992): 264-268.

3. See Donald W. Dayton and Robert K. Johnston, *The Variety of American Evangelicalism* (Downers Grove: InterVarsity Press, 1991), pp. 47, 48, and 245; and Stanley J. Grenz, *Revisioning Evangelical Theology* (Downers Grove: InterVarsity Press, 1993), pp. 22-27.

But when many in the Dutch Reformed tradition learn that Dayton's definition would classify them as "evangelical," they are uncomfortable with that designation, at best. For many Dutch Reformed, the word "evangelical" conjures up the idea of the necessity of a "crisis conversion," which is contrary to their emphasis on the baptism of children who are then nurtured to grow gradually into maturity as Christians. And there is good reason for that concern, since a distinctive emphasis in the evangelical tradition has been on a "conversion experience."

In light of this example, the best approach for understanding the word "evangelical," at least for purposes of this essay, may be sociological. I therefore will attempt to identify certain "distinctive emphases" that are typically associated with the word "evangelical" at the present time.

I draw here on a proposal made by David Bebbington that three distinctive emphases of evangelicalism are biblicism, conversionism, and evangelistic activism.[4] I will argue that a Christian is evangelical if his or her beliefs, attitudes, and practices emphasize some version of these distinctives (albeit, possibly in some "chastened" form, as in my case). I am using the word "evangelical," therefore, to apply to a Christian institution of higher education when that institution expects (explicitly or implicitly) all or most of its faculty and administrators to emphasize some version of these distinctives.

Biblicism

Bebbington uses the word *biblicism* to refer to "a particular regard for the Bible" or, as Mark Noll has stated, "a reliance on the Bible as ultimate religious authority."[5] This distinctive points to the centrality that evangelicals accord to the biblical record. Evangelicals do not view the Bible as just one great book among many. Rather, they view it as the primary vehicle for God's revelation of the nature of Christian faith and practice. This seems most appropriate since it is the biblical narrative that unfolds the "Christian story" that is central to all Christian traditions. Although we as Christians often disagree in our interpretations of the biblical record, it remains the primary source for helping

---

4. David Bebbington, *Evangelicalism in Modern Britain: A History from the 1730s to the 1980s* (London: Unwin Hyman, 1989), pp. 2-14. Bebbington actually proposes a fourth distinctive of crucicentrism which emphasizes that the reconciliation of humanity to God is "achieved by Christ on the cross" (p. 14). I do not include this in my analysis since, based on my judgment, many Christians besides evangelicals share this focus since it is the redemption kernel of the Christian story.

5. Bebbington, *Evangelicalism,* p. 3; and Mark Noll, *The Scandal of the Evangelical Mind* (Grand Rapids: Eerdmans, 1994), p. 8.

us to understand the Christian faith. Evangelicals serve all of Christendom well by emphasizing this point.

Evangelical Christian colleges typically express in a programmatic way this emphasis on the authority and centrality of the biblical record by including study of the biblical text in the undergraduate curriculum. Most if not all evangelical Christian colleges require biblical studies as a part of their general education requirements,[6] and most make attempts to uncover ways in which biblical understanding can illumine and enrich understandings gained from study in the various academic disciplines.

However, there are some tendencies of biblicism that place limitations on the Christian faith and on Christian higher education. One is a tendency to undervalue sources of knowledge about Christian faith and living other than the Bible, sometimes to the point of extending the insight that the Bible is the ultimate authority and primary source for our understanding to the questionable view that the Bible is the "sole" source for our understanding. This tendency is sometimes aggravated by a questionable intuitionist epistemology which holds that the Bible is self-interpreting and, therefore, Christian believers can always directly apprehend the spiritual truths to be found in the biblical text. This view of the Bible as the "sole" source of understanding can at times manifest itself in a lack of commitment to serious study in the academic disciplines within the humanities, fine arts, social sciences, and natural sciences. In addition, the intuitionist epistemology that sometimes accompanies this view can lead to devaluation of the serious study of theology that ought to complement biblical studies, and to the neglect of the contributions that tradition, pronouncements of the church, experience, and reason can make as we seek to interpret the Bible adequately.

A second limitation of biblicism is a tendency toward too narrow a view of the meaning and significance of the biblical record. As Mark Noll points out, "Evangelicals have . . . been distinctive for the shape of their belief in the

---

6. With some exceptions, the magnitude of this biblical studies requirement has generally decreased over the past quarter of a century, as a result of the intense academic departmental competition for those precious general education credits (which also seem to be shrinking due to the perceived need for students to accumulate more credits in their academic specializations). Whereas the biblical studies requirement at a number of evangelical Christian colleges used to comprise as much as a full "second major," or at least a "minor" (approximately 18 semester credits), the present requirement is more likely to fall in the range of four to twelve semester credits. There are some good reasons for this reduction in specific biblical studies requirements (see n. 9), but it is also ironic in light of the fact that the level of biblical literacy on the part of students enrolling in such colleges is generally on the decline. Nevertheless, some level of biblical studies is still considered important at evangelical Christian colleges.

Bible — that is, for a literal hermeneutic, for a 'scientific' approach to the verses of Scripture that was molded by the eighteenth-century Enlightenment, for keen preoccupation with the doctrine of biblical inerrancy, and for fascination with details of the apocalypse."[7] Making a crucial distinction between what is "distinctive" to evangelicalism and what is "essential to Christianity," Noll points to a larger meaning of a proper emphasis on the Bible: "What is essential to Christianity . . . is a profound trust in the Bible as pointing us to the Savior and for orienting our entire existence to the service of God." Noll notes that even the classic internal witness of 2 Timothy 3 "emphasizes the saving and orienting purposes of the Bible much more than the Bible's potential to serve as an immediate source of detailed knowledge."[8]

The Reformed tradition has helped me understand how one might overcome the limitations of excessive manifestations of biblicism and intuitionism. It has instilled in me a comprehensive view of God's sovereignty that makes the intended rule of Jesus Christ extend to all aspects of creation. Therefore, scholarly work in the academic disciplines is an important area of investigation of God's activity, for God has been active, not only redemptively in the history of Israel and the life, death, and resurrection of Jesus Christ, but also in nature, human life, and history.

As central as the biblical record is, it is not the only source of my understanding about Christian faith and practice.[9] I have also learned correctives to an extreme form of biblicism from Christian believers who speak of pronouncements of the church as important sources of Christian understanding (as in Roman Catholicism or Eastern Orthodoxy), or of reason and experience as sources of understanding that complement the Bible and tradition (as in Methodism's Wesleyan quadrilateral). As I come to the task of interpreting the Bible, I need to benefit from these other sources of Christian understanding, and I can do so without compromising my belief that the Bible is my primary source and ultimate authority.

In light of what we can learn from these other Christian voices, evangelicals might do well to embrace a "chastened" form of biblicism that I call "biblical centrality."

7. Noll, *Scandal,* pp. 243, 244.
8. Noll, *Scandal,* p. 244.
9. It is fortunate for evangelical colleges that over the years they have attracted faculty committed to this Reformed emphasis. The positive curricular result has been an increase in general education requirements in the various academic disciplines and, sometimes, in theology, as a complement to biblical studies. Of course, in light of the increasing biblical illiteracy of students noted in n. 6, this broadening of general education expectations creates some strong faculty disagreements regarding the appropriate balance between these various areas of study.

Biblical Centrality: The biblical record is the primary source and ultimate authority for our understanding of the Christian faith and the implications of that faith for our lives. Such biblical understanding needs to be complemented and enriched by theological reflection and by understanding gained from study in other academic disciplines, and from the gifts of Christian tradition, reason, and experience.

This view of biblical centrality has important implications for current expressions of evangelical Christian higher education. Foremost, it calls us to greater seriousness about the "integration of knowledge" rhetoric typically presented in the first few pages of our evangelical college catalogs. Our rhetoric has far outdistanced our actual practice of integrating knowledge.

In brief, it is not sufficient to separately value two important spheres of knowledge that empirically overlap: the sphere of biblical and theological understanding and the sphere of knowledge claims in other academic disciplines. To try to separate these into two side-by-side spheres is co-existence, a form of intellectual dualism, not integration. Such dualism is commonplace among evangelical Christians. As an antidote to this dualism, a fundamental assumption of evangelical Christian higher education should be that the interaction of these two spheres of knowledge must be intentionally explored. Fully recognizing the tensions that can exist between knowledge claims in these two spheres, the evangelical Christian scholar must nevertheless seek for interrelationships between the two spheres, and for ways in which knowledge claims in each sphere can illumine, enrich, and complement claims in the others. Whereas evangelicals generally embrace the view that biblical and theological understanding can inform knowledge in other academic disciplines, they need more fully to embrace the "second direction" for integration of knowledge: knowledge in other academic disciplines can inform our biblical and theological understanding. Based on the assumption that there is unity of truth, the goal is to develop a unifying conceptual framework informed by Christian ideas for interpreting and acting in the world.

This "biblical centrality" thesis also points to the need for evangelical institutions of higher education to reaffirm the importance of both biblical studies and theological reflection. But how is that practically possible, given the meager level of basic biblical literacy that many of our students bring to college? It is foolish for us to think that we can adequately compensate for years of pre-college neglect by providing comprehensive instruction in biblical studies. We need to be much more creative.

Our rhetoric about the integration of the sphere of biblical and theological understanding with the knowledge claims in other academic disciplines suggests the possibility of an "across the curriculum" approach to biblical and theological understanding, rather than viewing such understanding as the primary responsibility of the "Biblical and Religious Studies Department." Of course, students need to gain some significant knowledge in the two spheres before they can effectively begin integration. Therefore, there remains a significant need for biblical studies during the underclass years, but possibly more emphasis could be placed on developing a "thematic framework" and then establishing expectations for students to take more responsibility for their own biblical learning within that framework.

But the greatest changes may need to occur in the upper-class years, when students have the maturity needed seriously to pursue the integrative quest. Students need some introduction to theological reflection in the upper-class years. But again, that should not be viewed as the responsibility of one department. A more integrative strategy would be to increase the offering of integrative seminars in the various academic disciplines during the upper-class years (not a new idea), but with a greater intentional focus on integrating relevant aspects of biblical studies and theological reflection. However, it can not be assumed that all faculty are well prepared for such an intentional focus on integrating biblical and theological understanding. More attention must therefore be given to faculty development programs that provide faculty with adequate resources and time to pursue their own integrative quest.

Conversionism

Bebbington uses the word *conversionism* to refer to the "belief that lives need to be changed," that persons need to "turn away from their sins in repentance and to Christ in faith."[10] Some evangelicals emphasize the "deep feeling" that is experienced when such a conversion takes place. Some evangelicals also emphasize the view that the tell-tale signs that such a transformation has taken place are a deep desire to immerse oneself in the spiritual disciplines, such as personal prayer and Bible study, and a renunciation of certain lifestyle habits deemed incompatible with the Christian faith.

These emphases have made some very positive contributions to the church and to Christian higher education. They point to the truth that being a Christian is not just a matter of giving intellectual assent to a set of beliefs. Rather, it involves a commitment of the whole person that should be life changing. And although there have surely been some excesses of emotionalism in evangelicalism, it is important for all Christians to be reminded of the truth that to "feel deeply" is an indispensable aspect of our humanness.

These emphases are expressed in a variety of ways at evangelical Christian colleges. First, although evangelical Christian colleges are not churches, they

10. Bebbington, *Evangelicalism,* pp. 3, 5.

251

do typically conduct regular chapel services for students and faculty, with attendance often required of students. Although chapel programming is varied, it will generally include themes related to spiritual transformation and growth, even including, at times, evangelistic efforts aimed toward the conversion of students. Although it is difficult to generalize, it may be fair to say that such chapel programs often reinforce the importance of deeply felt religious experience.

The evangelical emphasis on the spiritual disciplines also finds healthy expression at evangelical Christian colleges through such means as residence hall Bible studies and prayer groups. The evangelical emphasis on personal lifestyle habits consistent with Christian commitment is also expressed at our colleges. Many evangelical Christian colleges have tended toward an *in loco parentis* model, accompanied by attempts to define meaningful limits for student behavior. A positive contribution of this concern has been a general avoidance of campus student behavior that is judged to be inimical to the Christian faith (e.g., fraternity binge drinking, although what goes on off campus could be a different matter).

The evangelical emphasis on spiritual transformation and growth is related to an emphasis on "holistic" student development at evangelical Christian colleges. Students are not disembodied intellects. Rather, they are persons who think, feel, act, worship, play, relate to others, and have bodies that need caring for. Our colleges typically believe that each student should learn about and develop each of these aspects of his or her being, and we often provide extensive student development programming toward that end.

Yet, there is also a dark side to some of these conversionist emphases. The emphasis on feeling can degenerate into a mindless emotionalism that denigrates the importance of adequately reflecting on the meaning of what one is feeling. By failing to recognize that our feelings are not self-interpreting and that they gain meaning as we interpret them in the light of our current framework of thought, such anti-intellectualism enslaves us to our emotions. And in those collegiate settings where there is an overemphasis on deeply-felt religious experience, the intellectual task of "integrating knowledge" takes a back seat, despite our common college catalog claim that this is Christian higher education's most fundamental distinctive.

One limitation of the view that the transformed life brought about by conversion finds expression primarily in terms of the spiritual disciplines and sanctified lifestyle habits is a tendency toward privatization of one's religious commitment. In its most extreme form, this becomes a subjective individualism bordering on a "spiritual narcissism" in which a person is so concerned about "personal holiness" and "feeling good about oneself" that he or she is of no earthly good to anyone. Surely the meaning of a "transformed life" must be big enough to capture the corporate nature of the Body of Christ and to

252

embrace our Christian responsibilities to other human beings and the rest of God's created order.

A related liability of legitimate concern for student lifestyle habits occurs when this concern is manifested in an extreme *in loco parentis* model that suffocates students by making too many choices for them, thereby robbing them of the development of "ethical discernment" that should be a major goal of Christian higher education. Of course, this issue immerses us in the perennial tension between law and Christian liberty. It is appropriate for evangelical Christian colleges to proscribe student behavior (at least on campus) that is inimical to the Christian faith (recognizing legitimate disagreements as to what behaviors fall into this category). At the same time, evangelical Christian colleges have too often erred on the side of being too proscriptive, thereby stunting the development of discernment that is essential to growth toward Christian maturity.

Once again, Christians from other traditions have had much to say about overcoming the liabilities of excessive conversionist emphases. The Reformed and Lutheran traditions can teach us that the gradual coming to Christian maturity experienced by baptized children is fully as redemptive as is crisis conversion experience. It is one thing to say that a crisis conversion experience is one way to come to Christian faith. But it is surely going too far to say that it is the only path to faith. We need to allow for a diversity of personal stories in this regard. Here again, Mark Noll provides us with a "larger meaning" when he contrasts evangelical distinctives with distinctives that are essential to Christianity: "Evangelicals have been distinctive in featuring the crisis conversion. But what is essential to Christianity is the whole life committed to God, from the beginning of faith until death. Some individuals may report being drawn to faith through a crisis conversion; other believers may have a different story to tell."[11]

The Reformed tradition especially can provide us with a corrective to an excessive preoccupation with "feeling" through its commitment to the life of the mind as an expression of worship of God. Of course, it may at times be necessary to remind some Reformed Christians that an arid, lifeless intellectualism is as unworthy as a mindless emotionalism. The ideal is both to feel deeply and think deeply.

Finally, Christians in the Lutheran, Reformed, Episcopal, Catholic, and Eastern Orthodox traditions can help evangelicals to see that an excessive preoccupation with "private spirituality" (which often mimics the extremes of individualism in American culture) can cause one to lose sight of the corporate nature of the church and of worship. As one Episcopal friend recalls, he was uncomfortable with "an evangelical spirituality which seemed to set the self

11. Noll, *Scandal*, p. 244.

center-stage," where "an act of individual or corporate devotion seemed to depend on the fervor we brought to it as individuals."[12] Instead, he found himself attracted to a "liturgical worship in which one enters into an act larger than oneself, prior to oneself, and not experientially dependent on oneself and the fervor one brings to it," where he could "forget [himself] . . . in a corporate action not contingent on [his] . . . own feelings at the moment for its efficacy."[13]

In light of these correctives provided by other Christian voices, evangelicals might do well to embrace a "chastened" form of conversionism best captured by the word "commitment."

> *Commitment:* A Christian personally appropriates the "good news" of the Gospel through a commitment of her or his entire being, whatever the means of that commitment may be. Such commitment should be celebrated with other Christian believers and should be expressed in a personal integration of one's thinking, feeling, and acting.

This focus on commitment expressed through personal integration has an important implication for current expressions of evangelical Christian higher education. Despite our stated emphasis on the holistic development of students, there is still an insidious tendency toward bifurcation, where an emphasis on the life of the mind and an emphasis on deeply felt religious experience and other "non-intellectual" aspects of personal growth coexist at best, or at worst create considerable tensions between "teaching faculty" and student development staff. Such tensions may be due to an excessive "student services" model for student development that places meager emphasis on learning, as if a college were a health spa, a church, or a counseling center.

Since colleges exist primarily for learning, a corrective to excessive preoccupation with student services is a model that places the focus for both "teaching faculty" and student development staff on student learning. The only difference should be that "teaching faculty" foster student learning inside the classroom, while student development staff foster student learning outside the classroom.

It is unfortunate that student development staffs generally have not attained parity with "teaching faculty" as educators at evangelical Christian colleges. A partial explanation for this situation may be an overemphasis on "student services" by some student development staff. But some "teaching

12. John Edward Skillen, "Religious Crisis During My College Years: Notes for a Spiritual Autobiography" in Bruce G. Webb, ed., *Christianity, Character and Liberal Arts* (Acton: Tapestry Press, 1994), p. 103.

13. Skillen, "Religious Crisis," p. 104.

faculty" also contribute to this disparity by their belief that all student learning takes place inside the classroom, including related out-of-class assignments, despite considerable empirical evidence to the contrary. A true partnership between "teaching faculty" and student development staff will be possible only if both groups commit themselves to being "educators," helping students to learn whatever will foster holistic development.

This focus on commitment also suggests that some evangelical institutions of higher education could do more to encourage students to examine their fundamental "worldview" commitments which often are tacit and inarticulate. It is not unusual for students to come to our colleges having been deeply immersed in evangelical institutions since childhood, sometimes leading to their adoption of a set of "hand-me-down" beliefs that they have never critically examined toward the goal of appropriating their own set of beliefs. Some evangelical Christian colleges could do more to create a supportive environment where Christian students are encouraged to examine and potentially refine their beliefs, in conversation with other Christian believers and those students who have other faith commitments.

The suggestion that a student's faith commitment needs to be expressed in actions, not just in thinking and feeling, leads to consideration of a third evangelical distinctive.

Evangelistic Activism

Bebbington uses the word *activism* to refer to "the expression of the gospel in effort," with such effort focused on the conversion of others.[14] Evangelicals are activist in their concern for sharing the Christian faith and for passionately communicating the gospel. As a result of this evangelistic activism, there is a strong tendency to emphasize immediacy of results: the gospel must be spread as soon as possible throughout the world so that many may be "saved" before the consummation.

This evangelistic activism has made some valuable contributions to the church and to Christian higher education. Because "good news" ought to be shared, it is commendable to have a sense of urgency about sharing the gospel with others. Furthermore, the biblical concept of "truth" points to a need for some activism, for it embraces the Hebraic rather than Hellenistic view that "knowing" and "doing" ought to be two sides of the same coin. The "truth" is not something strictly cognitive to "carry around in one's head." Rather, the "truth" is something to be acted on, to be lived out. This important insight has often found expression at evangelical colleges through co-curricular pro-

14. Bebbington, *Evangelicalism*, pp. 3, 10.

grams that provide students and faculty the opportunity to "share the gospel" with others.

Yet, an emphasis on evangelistic activism also has its limitations. First is the tendency of many evangelicals to define appropriate activism almost exclusively in terms of outreach geared toward the redemption of individual people. But the biblical record suggests that all of the created order needs redemption. The biblical record also calls Christians to work toward the redemption of social and political structures and to redeem the "good earth" that God created. Some pockets of evangelicalism have adequately embraced this larger view of creation and redemption, but we still have a long way to go. And as we travel that path, other Christian traditions have much to teach us.

Once again, the Reformed tradition, with its comprehensive view of God as sovereign over all aspects of creation and its commitment to the transformation of all creation, can help us better to understand the nature of our creation-wide responsibilities. We can also learn from Christians in the Anabaptist/Mennonite tradition. Evangelicals would do well to emulate their commitment to serving all the needs of people, not just those labeled "spiritual;" their social concern for justice for the poor and disenfranchised of this world; and their commitment to "peacemaking" in a world torn apart by conflict.

Another limitation of evangelistic activism results from its pragmatic emphasis on immediate results. This emphasis does not create an environment conducive to rigorous Christian scholarship on evangelical Christian college campuses, for the results of serious scholarship are not necessarily immediate. What is lost in this preoccupation with immediate results is the flourishing of Christian thinking about the nature of all of God's creation. In turn, this loss cripples dissemination of "Christian voices" within the larger academy and within a culture that needs to hear Christian perspectives. This latter task of doing and disseminating Christian scholarship is often long-term arduous work without immediacy of results. But, as so many Christians from the Reformed tradition have emphasized, doing Christian scholarship is a vital Christian calling. If Christian academics do not energetically pursue that calling, we will abandon our culture to non-Christian ways of thinking.

This tendency to undervalue Christian scholarship because it often lacks immediate results is further aggravated by the self designation of most evangelical Christian colleges as "teaching institutions," where faculty are hired primarily to teach students, not to do research. In theory, scholarship — integrative or otherwise — is *said* to be important, but scholarly work is clearly a secondary responsibility relative to the primary responsibility of teaching. And because teaching loads are typically high at such institutions, there simply isn't much time left for serious scholarly work during the academic year.

In light of these reflections on some limitations of activism and some correctives provided by other Christian voices, evangelicals might do well to embrace a "chastened" form of activism that I call "comprehensive gospel activism."

> *Comprehensive Gospel Activism:* The gospel message that needs to be communicated passionately is that all aspects of the creation of God and humans need redemption, including the natural world and societal structures. The work of Jesus Christ is decisive for that full scope of redemption, and Christians are called to act as faithful agents for that redemption.

This focus on the comprehensive nature of Christian activism has some major implications for refining current expressions of evangelical Christian higher education. First, evangelical Christian colleges need to exhibit greater commitment to public expressions of service that reflect a broad view of redemption, including the quest for peace and justice for all people.

Although there are promising signs that some programs involving students at some evangelical Christian colleges have embraced this broader scope of redemption, much more needs to be done in the area of faculty scholarship. In brief, there needs to be greater emphasis on praxis-oriented scholarship, wherein faculty members do research related to solving pressing human problems, particularly those evident in the communities in which these Christian colleges are located, without succumbing to the truncated view that all praxis-oriented scholarship should lead to immediate results. Here we can learn from colleges in the Anabaptist/Mennonite tradition, for these colleges have generally embraced the view that service and reconciliation should be central to the collegiate mission.

A related implication is that evangelical Christian colleges need to evidence a much greater commitment to faculty scholarship informed by Christian perspectives. A particular task of Christians called to the academy is to bring Christian perspectives to bear on scholarship about all of God's creation, as carried out in the various academic disciplines. Part of the "witness" of the Christian scholar called to be "salt and light" in the world is to share scholarship informed by Christian perspectives with other scholars who do not share those perspectives. The work of Christian scholars is to penetrate the highest levels of cultural thought with Christian thinking.

To make this possible, evangelical Christian colleges must modify their typical self-designation as "teaching institutions," where scholarly work is generally a secondary responsibility relative to the primary responsibility of teaching. This is not to deny that within the broad spectrum of American higher education, an emphasis on effective teaching is exemplary and ought to be emulated, up to a point, by those research universities where an extraordinary focus on teaching is a sure road to academic oblivion, since scholarly results are what lead to faculty advancement. But "teaching institutions" may invite their own form of abuse. In the past thirty-plus years, I have seen a number of potential Christian scholars "dry up" because they came to work at Christian colleges. The insidious bifurcation between teaching and scholarship needs to be demolished. It must be "both/and," not "either/or." To view a faculty member at an evangelical Christian institution of higher education as "only" a teacher truncates the calling of a Christian academic. Because integrative Christian scholarship is central to the task of being a Christian college teacher, administrators and board members at Christian colleges make a serious mistake if they treat scholarship as an "add-on" if a given faculty member can find the time after heavy teaching responsibilities. It will be a formidable challenge for evangelical Christian colleges to create structures for faculty responsibilities that will enable faculty members to flourish as both effective teachers and productive Christian scholars.

A third implication is that evangelical Christian colleges need to face squarely the sensitive issue of academic freedom. As we encourage our faculty toward higher levels of scholarship dealing with the whole range of complex issues facing our world and difficult questions within our academic disciplines, what limits, if any, should be placed on scholarly inquiry and expression?

Because evangelicalism is largely a populist movement, evangelical Christian colleges are very sensitive to the theological boundaries that appear operative among their church and alumni constituencies, especially those constituencies who send their sons and daughters — along with their tuition dollars — to study at these colleges. Because an increasing number of students come from a very conservative Christian constituency, many evangelical colleges feel pressure to define theological boundaries in terms of a detailed doctrinal statement to which all faculty must agree. This pressure needs to be resisted, for these kinds of detailed statements leave minimal room for doctrinal differences among equally committed Christians, and therefore provide little motivation or space for serious conversation about theological issues and their implications for the academic disciplines and for all of life.

I am not arguing that an evangelical Christian college should take no doctrinal position regarding the "essentials" of the Christian faith, for without some agreed-upon understanding of these "essentials," there is little that will distinguish Christian colleges from other institutions of higher education. But as already suggested, these "essentials" should be defined broadly in terms of the major motifs of the Christian story — creation, fall, redemption, church as witness, and consummation — while leaving considerable room for doctrinal differences in elaboration of these grand themes.[15]

---

15. See Heie, "Wanted," p. 267, for my related proposal for appropriate "theological boundaries."

Conclusion: Evangelical/Interdenominational Christian Colleges as Communities of Conversation

By now, the reader should detect my gratitude to various Christian traditions that have helped me to refine my understanding of what I mean when I profess to be an evangelical Christian. But for the most part, I have limited myself in this essay to those few Christian traditions that I have had the good fortune to be immersed in at various times in my career as an educator. There are many other Christian traditions from which I still need to learn. The entire contents of this book should provide further grist for a more extended conversation between Christian educators from many traditions, one that will enable all conversants to learn from the distinctive emphases and limitations of each tradition.

This brings me, at long last, to the distinctive contribution to Christian higher education of the evangelical Christian college that is intentionally interdenominational (in contrast to evangelical colleges whose identity is primarily tied to one Christian tradition or denomination). The empirical reality about evangelicalism is that it *is* interdenominational. There are believers in many Christian traditions and denominations who embrace various forms of the three evangelical distinctives I have elaborated in this essay. Therefore, an interdenominational evangelical Christian college has a unique opportunity to gather together for conversation faculty and students who are evangelical representatives of many Christian traditions or denominations. But that conversation is still too narrowly defined. In the spirit of this book, that conversation should be opened up to include Christians from all traditions, evangelical or otherwise. I therefore pose a challenge to evangelical/interdenominational Christian colleges to create such communities of conversation.

Of course, my call for conversation is easier said than done in an era when civil discourse in on the decline, even within — or especially across — different Christian sub-cultures. One would think that the conversation for which I call is already in place at evangelical/interdenominational Christian colleges, given their interdenominational nature, but that has not been my experience. In my eighteen years at two evangelical/interdenominational Christian colleges, I have seen very few conversations across a broad spectrum of faith traditions regarding theological differences and the implications of those differences for the academic disciplines and for living well.

I've often wondered why this has been the case. It may partially reflect the fact that our own theological sophistication as faculty members outside the field of theology often does not exceed the advanced Sunday school level. But I think there are two deeper reasons: a fear of where such "controversial" conversation may lead (will the results cross agreed-upon theological boundaries?), and the fact that Christians, not to mention others, have not learned how to disagree with each other with kindness, sharing our differing partial glimpses of God's truth in love. This fact reinforces the need for a *broad* definition of "theological boundaries," as well as a need for the humility and charity necessary for authentic human conversation to flourish. The humility of which I speak is open to the possibility that some of my present beliefs are false, and I can correct a false belief by listening to someone who disagrees with me. The charity of which I speak means I should put the best construction on what another person says by trying to see things from his or her perspective. And I should always express disagreement with kindness. Possibly the reason we experience such meager authentic conversation is that we often lack these qualities.

If my analysis of our tendencies toward non-conversation are correct, then it will be a formidable challenge to create communities of conversation like those called for in this essay. Such communities will not emerge by themselves; intentional strategies must be implemented. I have argued elsewhere that such strategies must include broad, community-wide commitment to aspire to conversational ideals including humility and charity, the intentional orchestration of a plurality of differing "Christian voices" regarding the issue at hand, and curricular and co-curricular means for "teaching disagreements" rather than ignoring or camouflaging them.[16]

If interdenominational evangelical Christian colleges can create and maintain such communities of conversation across Christian theological traditions, then these colleges can make a profound contribution to Christian higher education and, then, to all of higher education by inviting all scholars to "join the conversation." That ideal is the ultimate educational challenge as we move toward the end of this century.

16. For further elaboration, see Harold Heie, "The Postmodern Opportunity: Christians in the Academy," *Christian Scholar's Review,* forthcoming.

Faith and Learning
at Wheaton College

Michael S. Hamilton
and James A. Mathisen

Wheaton College, located in Chicago's western suburb of Wheaton, dates its origin to 1860, although it existed previously as the Illinois Institute. For the first half of its history, Wheaton had only two presidents, the father and son team of Jonathan and Charles Blanchard, who provided remarkably stable leadership. By the time of Charles Blanchard's death in 1925, Wheaton had emerged as a leader among fundamentalist colleges with a student body of about 300. Today it remains a quality, primarily undergraduate Christian liberal arts college, while offering several graduate programs. Wheaton consistently attracts a highly motivated student body from diverse, although generally conservative Protestant, backgrounds who also seek to relate their faith commitments to their educational experiences in a setting intended to enhance both their faith and their learning.

Are religion and education natural antagonists? "Faith is belief without reason," wrote essayist Roger Rosenblatt in *Time* magazine a few years ago. "Fundamentally, religions oppose rational processes."[1] The American version of this idea traces back to Andrew Dickson White, the founding president of Cornell University, whose *A History of the Warfare of Science with Theology in Christendom* first appeared in 1869 and is still in print today. White's conceptual world was moralistic, even melodramatic, peopled with courageous heroes of science struggling against the base villains of Christian dogmatism. Today

1. Roger Rosenblatt, "Defenders of the Faith," *Time* (November 12, 1984): 112.

the work still is widely regarded as one of sound history, despite its prosecutorial zeal and wholesale distortions. It is really more of a polemical tract, a weapon in the late-nineteenth-century battle by university reformers to push traditional Christianity out to the fringes of intellectual life.[2]

The historical demerits of White's work aside, the book has been quite successful in establishing its thesis among the learned. This can be seen in the reactions of journalists who visit Wheaton College, the Illinois liberal arts institution that one reporter tagged "The Harvard of the Bible Belt." Some reporters have interpreted Wheaton as an anomaly. In 1960, and again in 1980, *Time* expressed surprise at finding a "dramatic exception" to the prevailing rule that science and Scripture are separated by an intellectual Grand Canyon. Other reporters have insisted that Wheaton is an impossibility. They simply have refused to believe that the college is anything more than a training center for evangelism, or a place where students go to escape "the real world that Wheaton rejects" in order "to ponder the pieties of the past."[3]

As a matter of fact, Wheaton is one of dozens of collegiate examples, though perhaps one of the most dramatic, of the inadequacy of White's thesis. For Wheaton embodies extremes of faith and learning that White would have believed to be about as compatible as fire and water. Wheaton annually enrolls more National Merit Scholars and sends more students on to prestigious Ph.D. programs than all but a handful of the very best liberal arts colleges in the country.[4] It does so despite being firmly rooted in the American religious tradition generally regarded as the most antagonistic to modern learning — the fundamentalist variant of Protestant evangelicalism.[5]

---

2. The final expanded version of White's book appeared in 1896 as a two-volume work. See David C. Lindberg and Ronald L. Numbers, "Beyond War and Peace: A Reappraisal of the Encounter between Christianity and Science," *Church History* 55 (September 1986): 338-354; and George M. Marsden, *The Soul of the American University: From Protestant Establishment to Established Nonbelief* (New York: Oxford University Press, 1994), 113-122.

3. "Revelation and Education," *Time* (February 1, 1960): 37; Richard N. Ostling, "All That and Billy Graham Too," *Time* (September 22, 1980): 83; Bruce Wexler, "Village of the Saved," *Reader: Chicago's Free Weekly* (May 23, 1980): 1, 34-40; Sharon Johnson, "The Harvard of the Bible Belt," *Change* 6 (March 1974): 20.

4. Ostling, "All That," 83; Franklin and Marshall College, *Baccalaureate Origins of Doctorate Recipients,* 7th ed. (Lancaster: Franklin and Marshall, 1993), 7; National Merit Scholarship Corporation, *Annual Report* (1993-94).

5. *Evangelicalism,* in this essay, consists of those forms of Protestant Christianity that are rooted in the Reformation's emphasis on the Bible as the ultimate religious authority, that highlight the importance of personal conversion as a condition of true Christian faith, and that actively seek to spread their versions of Christianity to non-evangelicals (see Bebbington).

Fundamentalism is a particular form of evangelicalism, one which defies easy characterization. The best definitions to date have focused on the movement's most prominent

Wheaton has been able to nurture both evangelical faith and the liberal arts because it is a true hybrid, a two-cultures institution. Throughout the twentieth century, Wheaton has participated fully in both the cultural networks of fundamentalist evangelicalism and the cultural networks of the American liberal arts college. The college has therefore become both a repository of evangelical beliefs and values and an embodiment of American cultural attitudes toward higher education.

This essay is concerned with the patterns of Wheaton's unlikely mixture of evangelicalism and liberal arts. In the nineteenth century, Wheaton shared the consensus of other educational institutions that faith and learning always converged. This conviction, long after it had faded away at other institutions, lived on at Wheaton through the first quarter of the twentieth century. However, in the second quarter of this century, a changed intellectual climate forced the college to work out new ways of relating faith and learning. In response, Wheatonites developed three new strategies — the triumphalist model, the value-added model, and the integration model. In order to understand these alternatives for yoking evangelicalism and higher education, we need first to

---

doctrinal beliefs (dispensational premillennialism and inerrancy of the Bible — see Sandeen), the forces that galvanized it into a discrete movement (militant opposition to theological modernism — see Marsden), or its institutional base (independent parachurch organizations with a common revivalist ethos, such as evangelistic agencies, missionary groups, publishing houses, and especially Bible institutes — see Carpenter). For the purposes of this essay, fundamentalism is that form of evangelicalism that was *centered* in a loose coalition of interdenominational parachurch organizations; that *always* promoted evangelism, missions, Bible study, prayer, spiritual revival, and Keswick-style ("higher life") holiness; that *often* promoted the doctrines of inerrancy of the Bible, premillennial dispensationalism, and opposition to modernist theology; and that *seldom* promoted the distinctive doctrines of the two other major trans-denominational evangelical movements (the Wesleyan-holiness movement's teachings about a definite second experience of grace and the Pentecostals' teachings about speaking in tongues and divine healing).

The matter of definition is almost hopelessly confused by the fact that fundamentalism split into two parties in the late 1950s. The separatist party retained the name "fundamentalist," while the inclusivist party (which Timothy Smith aptly labeled "postfundamentalists") began calling themselves "evangelicals." David Bebbington, *Evangelicalism in Modern Britain: A History from the 1730s to the 1980s* (London: Unwin Hyman/Routledge, 1989), pp. 2-17; George Marsden, "Introduction: The Evangelical Denomination," in Marsden, ed., *Evangelicalism in Modern America* (Grand Rapids: Eerdmans, 1984), pp. vii-xix; Marsden, *Fundamentalism and American Culture: The Shaping of Twentieth-Century Evangelicalism: 1870-1925* (New York: Oxford University Press, 1980), pp. 4, 231n.4; Ernest R. Sandeen, *The Roots of Fundamentalism: British and American Millenarianism, 1800-1930* (Chicago: University of Chicago Press, 1970), p. 103; Joel A. Carpenter, "The Renewal of American Fundamentalism, 1930-1945" (Ph.D. diss., Johns Hopkins University, 1984), pp. 3-7; and Timothy Smith, "The Postfundamentalist Party," *The Christian Century* 93 (February 4-11, 1976): 125-127.

get a sense of the interdenominational context of the fundamentalism in which they were worked out.

Wheaton College and its Interdenominational Character

Wheaton College, located thirty miles west of Chicago, officially dates its founding to 1860 when the fire-breathing abolitionist Jonathan Blanchard assumed the presidency. Blanchard, of whom it was justly said, "It is his nature to wage war . . . to fight the institutions of the world as he found them," dedicated the school to two ideals — the classical curriculum and radical social reform, evangelical-Republican style. Like Charles Finney's Oberlin College, Blanchard's Wheaton was determinedly coeducational, defiantly integrationist, and tirelessly opposed to secret societies. Women usually comprised the better part of the student body and African-American students who attended the college often boarded in Blanchard's home. Anti-lodge commitments meant that the college frequently knocked heads with nearby Masons; it also meant that students were never allowed to establish fraternities or sororities.[6]

Blanchard was a Congregationalist, but more out of convenience than conviction. His true allegiance was to the "Church of Radical Reform," and Congregationalism's doctrine of local autonomy gave him the elbow-room he needed to agitate against the social order. He welcomed other reform-minded Protestants from whatever denomination as co-laborers in the work of the college, so from the beginning of the Blanchard era interdenominational cooperation ranked among the highest of the college's values.

Jonathan Blanchard was succeeded as president by his son Charles in 1882. Charles never repudiated his father's radical commitments, but was in many ways more at home in the Victorian middle-class world into which he was born than his father ever was. Toward the end of his life, however, Charles and his college were, in a sense, made homeless anew, as the world of higher education rushed headlong to abandon its evangelical heritage. Jonathan had been an eager nonconformist; Charles, a more reluctant one. But nonconformist he was, as he gradually adopted the theological beliefs that set fundamentalists apart. Between 1900 and his death in 1925, and especially after World War I, Charles linked the college to the other leading institutions in the coalescing fundamentalist movement. He remained, like his father, a Congregationalist of convenience, for the doctrine of local autonomy allowed him and his college to remain committed to fundamentalist ideas. And like his

---

6. On Jonathan Blanchard, see Clyde S. Kilby, *Minority of One: The Biography of Jonathan Blanchard* (Grand Rapids: Eerdmans, 1959), quotation on pp. 140-141.

father, he welcomed to the college co-workers from across the spectrum of Protestant denominations.

When Charles died, the trustees cemented Wheaton's ties to emergent fundamentalism by adopting the college's first official creed — a nine-point affirmation that Charles had helped draft for the World's Christian Fundamentals Association. The trustees also hired as the new president an up-and-coming fundamentalist pastor from Brooklyn, J. Oliver Buswell Jr. These actions marked the college's transition from a Blanchard family proprietorship to a public institution within the growing network of independent fundamentalist ministry organizations, which included Moody Bible Institute and a host of other organizations.[7]

The college was one of the fastest-growing in the nation during Buswell's fifteen-year presidency, increasing from just over 300 to around 1,100 students. Buswell was a Presbyterian, as were a quarter of Wheaton's students during his presidency. A second quarter were Baptists of various stripes, and thirty percent were more or less evenly divided among independents, members of European immigrant denominations, and Methodists. The remaining twenty percent came from a wide variety of other traditions, including a sizable number of students who listed themselves as having no denominational preference.[8] Most of the Presbyterians, Methodists, and Congregationalists, and many of the Baptists, belonged to churches that remained affiliated with denominations that tolerated theological liberalism. In the mid-1930s, fundamentalists fought several internal battles over whether or not to separate from these denominations. When the mainline Presbyterian Church U.S.A. publicly tried Buswell and others for insubordination, and then stripped them of their ministerial credentials, Buswell's attitude hardened. He urged fundamentalists to leave the mainline denominations and criticized those who would not. This created an enormous public relations headache for the college. Buswell's intransigence weakened his grip on the presidency, and contributed to the trustees' decision to fire him in 1940.[9]

The trustees replaced the pugnacious Buswell with peace-loving V. Raymond Edman, who reaffirmed Wheaton's tradition of evangelical cooperation across denominational lines. Converted at an interdenominational revival service while still in high school, he later attended the Christian and Missionary Alliance training institute at Nyack, New York. This commenced his lifelong connection to the Alliance and its vision of interdenominational fellowship

7. Joel A. Carpenter, "Fundamentalist Institutions and the Rise of Evangelical Protestantism, 1929-1942," *Church History* 49 (March 1980): 62-75.

8. Figures computed from "Registrar's Report" for 1937.

9. Paul M. Bechtel, *Wheaton College: A Heritage Remembered* (Wheaton: Harold Shaw, 1984), pp. 144-152.

for missions and personal holiness.[10] Like the Blanchards, Edman cared little about denominations, and he made common cause with evangelical revivalists, missionaries, and spiritual teachers from across the ecclesiastical spectrum.

When Edman retired in 1965, enrollment had reached 1,900 students and the college was quite prosperous. The denominational mosaic had altered, but it remained as diverse as ever. A third of the students in 1965 were Baptists and a sixth called themselves independent. Another fourth were split between members of immigrant churches and Presbyterians, with the remaining fourth being scattered all over the denominational map.[11] By this time, the battle between the ecclesiastical separatists and the inclusivists that had sent Buswell packing had produced a major schism in fundamentalism. The smaller, sectarian party retained the name "fundamentalist." The larger inclusivist party, led by Wheaton graduate and Edman protégé Billy Graham, took for itself the broader name of "evangelical." Though Wheaton had internal divisions on the issue, it gradually drifted into alignment with the inclusivist party and retained its position as the preeminent college in this post-fundamentalist "evangelicalism."

Edman was succeeded in 1965 by his provost, Hudson Armerding, a Wheaton alumnus ('41). Armerding came from strong Plymouth Brethren stock, and his father Carl was an itinerant Brethren Bible teacher who also taught at Wheaton. Upon Armerding's retirement in 1982, Richard Chase became Wheaton's sixth president. Chase had been ordained by the American Baptist Convention in California, and served as president of Biola College (later University) before coming to Wheaton. Chase was succeeded in 1993 by Duane Litfin, a self-described "dispensationalist without charts" who pastored a large non-denominational church in Memphis. Throughout the tenures of Armerding, Chase, and Litfin, Wheaton continued to be thoroughly interdenominational in fact and in purpose. By 1994, one-third of Wheaton's students identified themselves as "other," "independent," or "non-denominational." A fifth called themselves Baptist, with another fifth split evenly between Presbyterians and members of the Evangelical Free Church. The remainder were spread out among any number of other Protestant denominations. By the early 1980s, a few Roman Catholic students were attending Wheaton, and in the 1990s several students converted to Orthodoxy during their time at the college.

But interdenominationalism is only part of the story of Wheaton's religious diversity. Students arrived at Wheaton not only to encounter in their

10. Bechtel, *Wheaton College,* pp. 154-275; Earle E. Cairns, *V. Raymond Edman: In the Presence of the King* (Chicago: Moody Press, 1972); and V. Raymond Edman, *Out of My Life* (Grand Rapids: Zondervan, 1961).

11. Figures computed from "Registrar's Report" for 1966.

classmates a variety of denominations, but also a variety of spiritual emphases that crisscrossed the denominational lines. Thomas Howard ('57) was the son of Philip E. Howard Jr., a Wheaton trustee and the editor of the influential *The Sunday School Times.* Thomas recalled one group of students dedicated to colorful, crowd-pleasing evangelism; another to modeling an ethic of success as the ideal testimony to God's power; another to the Keswick holiness ideal of steadfast tranquillity and simplicity in spiritual life; another to cultivating a spirit of personal humility and brokenness; another to the Pentecostal experience of the Holy Spirit flashing across the space between earthbound humanity and a transcendent God; another to the primitivist quest for the apostolic order in worship; and yet another to aesthetically lush sacramentalism of the liturgical traditions.[12] Wheaton's fundamentalism was a lavish spiritual banquet-table, and it was common for Wheaton students to sample different spiritual traditions during their undergraduate years. This caused many anxious moments for parents whose religious convictions were more or less settled, but it also created an overarching sense that the different denominations and spiritual traditions could be harnessed together in service for the greater goal of propagating Christian faith.

No Wheaton graduate better exemplifies this attitude than Billy Graham ('43). Coming to Wheaton in 1940 as a doctrinaire Southern Baptist with separatist tendencies, Graham was greatly influenced by Edman's interdenominational vision. His ecclesiastical universe was also expanded by his future wife Ruth Bell, daughter of a prominent southern Presbyterian missionary surgeon. One of Graham's biographers writes that "Ruth and her family eased Billy Graham from his unspoken conviction that a vigorous scriptural faith could not dwell within the great denominations. The Bells underlined the lesson of Wheaton College that any minister who was a strong evangelical should focus his vision on the entire horizon of American Christianity."[13]

The imperative for interdenominational and intertraditional cooperation required that, to be successful, fundamentalist leaders had to find a common theological ground that excluded theological liberalism but at the same time included a wide range of evangelical Protestants. This meant boiling evangelical theology down to its essentials and laying aside potentially divisive theological peculiarities — denominational and otherwise. Fundamentalism and postfundamentalist evangelicalism, more than other evangelical tradi-

12. Thomas Howard, *Christ the Tiger: A Postscript to Dogma* (Philadelphia: J. B. Lippincott, 1967), pp. 30-41.

13. John Pollock, *Billy Graham: The Authorized Biography* (Grand Rapids: Zondervan 1967 [1966]), p. 26.

tions like the holiness movement and Pentecostalism, were able to organize their communal discourses around widely-held ideas about biblical literalism, personal conversion, and spiritual life. Because they did so, they were able to encompass to some degree large segments of theologically conservative Protestants from Pentecostals to mainline Protestant evangelicals. This impulse kept the vital center of pre-1950s fundamentalism and post-1950s "evangelicalism" from devolving into denominational forms or a sectarian mentality and thrust the movement into a leadership role for many varieties of evangelical Protestants. It is important to remember that the constituencies of the fundamentalist institution-builders were always far larger than fundamentalism proper; the same is true of postfundamentalist evangelicalism. Wheaton College, like other independent fundamentalist institutions, was eager to take on this leadership role. In its case, it became an example for other evangelical colleges trying to sort out how to meld their faith commitments with higher education. However, Wheaton was a complex example, for it harbored internal differences on just how this might best be done.

Faith and Learning in Theory: Four Models

Throughout its history, Wheaton's attempt both to teach the liberal arts and to remain fundamentalist brought numerous troubles and conflicts. Despite these difficulties, however, Wheaton's leadership, faculty, and constituents have always agreed that the college ought to maintain its dual citizenship in the evangelical world and the world of higher education. They have not, however, agreed on the best way to reconcile Wheaton's two loyalties. Over the years, Wheatonites have employed four basic models in their attempt to keep the two together.

The Convergence Model

The convergence model assumes that evangelical Protestantism and higher learning necessarily lead to the same conclusions. In other words, Christianity and education are in no need of reconciliation for they present no real disjunctions. The system of discovered (or natural) knowledge and the system of revealed (or divine) knowledge are thought to be complete in themselves, yet mutually confirming. This model prevailed in American higher education throughout most of the nineteenth century. It depended heavily on the belief that Joseph Butler and William Paley had proven that the natural world and (by implication) the study of the natural world always testify to the truth of the Christian religion.[14] The convergence model had its consummate expression in the year-long moral philosophy course that was taught by most college presidents and required of seniors as the unifying capstone of their formal education. One part ethics, one part psychology, and one part natural theology, the mixture was served up in a broth of evangelical Protestantism that sought to confirm Christian teachings and find theological meaning in all branches of learning.[15]

The great beauty of the convergence model was the unity and coherence it gave to all areas of learning. However, its assumption that the study of the natural world always confirmed the truths of Christianity proved to be the model's fatal flaw. When, in the late nineteenth century, science seemed to lead to naturalistic rather than Christian conclusions, the convergence model collapsed under the weight of its now untenable assumptions.[16]

The Triumphalist Model

The shattering of the nineteenth-century synthesis of faith and learning produced a highly polarized intellectual culture in America, in which secular thinking took a triumphalist form. The operative assumption in the new dispensation was the belief that secular forms of knowing (modeled on the empirical sciences) were superior to religious ways of knowing and had therefore rendered religious ways of knowing irrelevant.[17] The mirror opposite of this scientific triumphalism was a triumphalist form of Christian thinking, which abandoned the nineteenth-century belief that education and Christianity are but different roads to the same mountain top. The basic assumption of the new Christian triumphalism was that the prevailing intellectual culture was hopelessly flawed by nature of its secular assumptions. Its naturalistic materialism, being fundamentally erroneous, would eventually lead to its self-destruction. Christianity, however, being true, would endure and triumph. In this way of relating religion and education, faith always trumps learning. In this model, religious ways of knowing are by definition always superior to secular ways of knowing; secular ways of knowing become, by definition, more or less irrelevant.

14. The two best-known and most influential books making this argument were Joseph [Bishop] Butler, *The Analogy of Religion, Natural and Revealed, to the Constitution and Course of Nature* (London, 1736); and William Paley, *Natural Theology; or Evidences of the Existence and Attributes of the Deity* (London, 1802).

15. Allen Guelzo, "Moral Philosophy as Science," paper given at a conference on "The Evangelical Engagement with Science," Wheaton College, Wheaton, Illinois, March 31, 1995.

16. James Turner, *Without God, Without Creed: The Origins of Unbelief in America* (Baltimore: Johns Hopkins University Press, 1985), p. 187.

17. Turner, *Without God, Without Creed*, p. 199.

Properly speaking, this model was less an attempt to bring faith and learning together than it was an attempt to put learning in subjection to faith. Triumphalist ways of thinking, whether secular or religious, not only accepted the new radical disjuncture between faith and learning, they gloried in it. This was not at all satisfactory to evangelical educators who believed that faith and learning could still be part of a shared educational enterprise. Over against the secular and Christian triumphalists, they developed two alternative models of relating faith to learning.

The Value-Added Model

The first alternative might be called the "value-added" model. This view is neutral toward the prevailing intellectual culture. It assumes that secular knowledge and sacred knowledge do not conflict because they occupy different spheres. The two kinds of knowledge do not change each other in fundamental ways, but they can enrich each other. Thus faith can bring to learning an ethical dimension, an appreciation for the transcendent, and answers to the questions of meaning. Learning can also enrich faith — helping one to understand how God and his creatures have responded to each other in the past, filling in the details of God's creative handiwork, and so forth.

This model is marked by its practical approach to higher education. American higher education attempts two overarching purposes. One, centered around the liberal arts, is concerned with questions of value and meaning. Its primary concern is affecting how students think, how they view themselves and the world. The other purpose, centered around the sciences, is concerned with questions of fact and training. Its primary concern is imparting to students specialized knowledge and skills that will enable them to take their places in the various professions into which our society and its economy are organized. The value-added model is most congenial to this second, more pragmatic, purpose of higher education. Questions of value and meaning are dealt with through religious ways of knowing, but they are not seen as an integral part of the academic disciplines themselves.

Above all else, this model treats the academic disciplines as unchanged in their essence by whatever contact with Christianity they might sustain. Therefore, Christians and non-Christians do geology the same way; likewise with sociology, literature, and so forth. Similarly, Christianity remains unchanged by contact with learning. In this model, there is no distinctive way to undertake the study of any academic discipline, and no academic discipline can alter the fundamental outlines of Christianity. Academic disciplines, properly pursued, are by themselves value-neutral; their methodologies are the same regardless of one's values.

The Integration Model

The second alternative to the two triumphalisms is commonly called the "integration of faith and learning" model. This model begins with the assumption that all academic inquiry starts with a set of assumptions, or presuppositions, rooted in the student's worldview or philosophy of life. These presuppositions unavoidably affect the way academic inquiry proceeds. This model holds that the scholarship of the modern academy, far from being neutral, is shot through with secular assumptions that often, though not always, distort its outcomes. However, these distorting assumptions do not discredit the disciplines themselves nor their methodologies, as the Christian triumphalist model would contend. Rather, academic inquiries are in need of better — that is, Christian — assumptions so that their outcomes are not distorted.

In comparison to the convergence model, the distinguishing feature of integration is the belief that systems of discovered knowledge and revealed knowledge are, by themselves, incomplete. They are both needed for full understanding; they have areas of overlap and are each informed by the other. The mix, however, is a volatile one. When Christian knowledge and natural knowledge conflict, one must be revised to conform to the other. This keeps proponents of integration continually subject to criticism both from defenders of the divine prerogatives and defenders of the disciplines' prerogatives. The distinguishing feature of the integration model is the conviction that Christian scholarship differs from non-Christian scholarship in fundamental ways because it begins at a different starting place. Philosophy, sociology, literature, history, and perhaps even physics and mathematics will be done differently if undertaken with Christian presuppositions. The integration model tends to value liberal arts education with its emphasis on ideas and the training of the mind. In the internal debate common to all higher education, advocates of the integration model tend to take the side of the anti-pragmatists against vocationally-oriented education. Those who have shaped the integration model have tended to concentrate on questions of meaning and the way in which higher education has the obligation to reshape how students think.

Faith and Learning in Practice, 1860-1994

Jonathan Blanchard apparently experienced no difficulty linking faith and learning during his days as Wheaton's president. Virtually all liberal arts colleges in the 1860s and 1870s believed that Christianity and higher education converged on common truths and understandings. This was a congenial view for Jonathan, and its general acceptance in American higher education left him free to fight other battles.

271

Charles, however, found it trying to maintain the convergence model in the first quarter of the twentieth century. He did his best, continuing to teach the old-fashioned year-long moral philosophy course to every one of Wheaton's seniors up until the year before his death. Blanchard taught moral philosophy in the 1920s virtually as it was taught in the 1840s — his reading list for students included Butler's *Analogy of Religion* and Drymond's *Essays on the Principles of Morality.*[18] But as the intellectual world changed, the convergence model simply could not be sustained. Charles Blanchard could only interpret the new thinking as a wave of collective insanity rolling over the modern intellectual world.[19]

In the vacuum left behind by the collapse of the convergence model — and in the shadow of the hegemonic scientific triumphalism that secular scholars established at the universities — Wheaton faculty, students, and trustees developed their alternative ways of relating faith to learning. In the fifteen years following Blanchard's death (that is, during the Buswell presidency) all three models first received expression; and all three continued thereafter to find voices on campus.

The value-added model provided the path of least resistance, for like the convergence model it was able to affirm the independent value of both learning and faith. Much of Wheaton's twentieth-century character came from an uncritical assumption that contemporary collegiate forms ought to be normal for Wheaton. When the North Central Association began accrediting, and therefore standardizing, colleges in 1916, Wheaton worked hard to establish and keep its accreditation by conforming to the NCA standards. College officials also made sure that Wheaton met the accreditation standards of individual professional organizations. When Wheaton contemplated curricular changes, it always surveyed practices at other colleges and universities, both religious and secular. As other colleges added professional preparatory programs such as business administration, health education, and journalism, so did Wheaton. Some Wheaton professors kept religion out of their teaching. Both Orrin Tiffany, a Phi Beta Kappa historian with a Ph.D. from the University of Michigan, and James B. Mack, a zoologist with an Ohio State Ph.D., deliberately limited the amount of religion in their coursework so students would be better prepared for graduate school.[20]

18. Butler, *Analogy of Religion;* Jonathan Drymond, *Essays on the Principles of Morality and on the Private and Political Rights and Obligations of Mankind* (London, 1829). Blanchard's reading list is in *Wheaton College Catalog* (1919-20), p. 28.

19. Marsden, *Fundamentalism and American Culture,* pp. 212-221.

20. Calvin Olin Davis, *A History of the North Central Association of Colleges and Secondary Schools 1895-1945* (Ann Arbor: North Central Association, 1945), pp. 3-64; Herbert Moule, "Department of History and Social Science," and James B. Mack, "Department of Biology," *Faculty Bulletin of Wheaton College,* vol. 4-7 (1940-1944): 232, 243.

In general, students conceptualized the links between higher education and their faith in value-added ways. Student surveys show that one of Wheaton's best recruiting tools in this period was *The Silver Trumpet,* a novel that remained in print for forty years. The book told the story of a worldly young musician who became infatuated with a beautiful young gospel singer, followed her back to Wheaton, and there found true love, salvation, and a vocation of full-time Christian service. In this novel the curricular aspects of Wheaton are presumed to be indistinct from those of other colleges — it is the extracurricular Christian faith, piety, and service that makes Wheaton distinctive and effective.[21] In the mid-1930s, over 80 percent of Wheaton's students participated in extracurricular Christian service activities — traveling Gospel Teams, hospital and prison visitation, and the like. These rarely had any connection to what went on in the classrooms. Many students, upon later reflection, felt that service activities were the most important aspect of their Wheaton education because of the spiritual development and practical skills they provided.[22]

When the Wheaton trustees hired the thirty-one-year-old Buswell to succeed Charles Blanchard in 1925, they thought they were getting an energetic fundamentalist pastor who would steer the college clear of the shoals of modernism and apostasy. This they got, but they also got a leader with true scholarly sensibilities, a man who valued intellectual exploration, academic freedom, full disclosure in the classroom, and open debate. He set Wheaton on the path to academic respectability by upgrading accreditation levels, inviting outside evaluators to campus, and by insisting that new professors have earned doctorates whenever possible. He supported the trustees' decision to require all faculty members to assent to a nine-point fundamentalist doctrinal statement, but was fearless about using in the classroom books written from perspectives hostile to fundamentalist — and even Christian — viewpoints.

In addition to improving Wheaton's academic quality, Buswell also began the school's first efforts to truly integrate faith and learning. He transformed Blanchard's old-fashioned moral philosophy course into required sequential courses on ethics and theism. The theism course used as its text James Orr's *The Christian View of God and the World,* a well-articulated exposition of a Christian worldview that could encompass all of learning. The book and the

---

21. J. Wesley Ingles, *The Silver Trumpet* (Philadelphia: Union Press, 1930); see also Ingles, "*The Silver Trumpet* and How It Blew," *Christian Herald* 93 (March 1970): 36-40.

22. John Charles Swanson, "The Graduates of a Midwestern Liberal Arts College Evaluate Their College Experiences" (Ph.D. diss., Northwestern University, 1957), pp. 148-150. All American colleges and universities developed student subcultures marked by peer-oriented values that at many points opposed those of their faculties. See Helen Lefkowitz Horowitz, *Campus Life: Underground Cultures from the End of the Eighteenth Century to the Present* (New York: Alfred A. Knopf, 1987).

course had its desired effect on at least a few students. Carl F. H. Henry, perhaps the most prominent post-fundamentalist theologian, later wrote that of his entire college experience Orr's book "did the most to give me a cogently comprehensive view of reality and life in a Christian context."[23]

Toward the end of the Buswell era, two men who were to become the leading exponents of the integration model joined the Wheaton faculty. Philosopher Gordon Clark arrived in 1936; political scientist S. Richey Kamm came to Wheaton in 1940. Theologically the two men could not have been more different. Clark was a hard-shelled rationalist, a predestinarian Presbyterian of the most rigid type. In contrast, Kamm was an Arminian Free Methodist with deep sympathies for pietism. But both believed passionately in the life of the mind and in the integration model's proposition that Christianity made, or at least ought to make, a difference in all academic inquiry. Clark was only at Wheaton for seven years, but during that time he helped inspire the first generation of fundamentalist intellectuals, including Henry, Edward Carnell, and several others. Kamm's Wheaton career stretched over a much longer period, from 1940 through 1973. His impact was primarily on the college itself, as he continually prodded his colleagues and his students — several of whom later became Wheaton faculty members — to think more deeply about how their faith influenced their scholarship in ways that made it different from secular models of scholarship.[24]

The triumphalist model also prospered during the Buswell presidency. In 1940 Robert L. Cooke, a professor of education at Wheaton from 1935 through 1955, published *Philosophy, Education, and Certainty.* The book is a breathtakingly ill-informed attempt to assay the entire history of Western philosophy in order to show why modern educational theorists were making such a hash of their work. Cooke's thesis was that every major thinker after Jesus had made seminal blunders that had led them astray. Cooke loftily dismissed the sum of Augustine's thought in three pages (it used Platonic ideas), Calvin's in three pages (it employed humanist ideas), and Luther's in two pages (it depended on Melanchthon, who used Aristotelian ideas). Cooke concluded with the confident assertion that Jesus the master teacher personified the perfect educational philosophy, although Cooke never really explained anything about what that philosophy might look like.[25]

23. Carl F. H. Henry, *Confessions of a Theologian: An Autobiography* (Waco: Word, 1986), p. 75.

24. Clark's expositions of the integration model are found in *A Christian Philosophy of Education* (Grand Rapids: Eerdmans, 1946) and *A Christian View of Men and Things* (Grand Rapids: Eerdmans, 1952). Kamm's ideas are in "Report of the Faculty Planning Committee, 1944-46: The Educational Program" (Wheaton College Archives), and in Hudson T. Armerding, ed., *Christianity and the World of Thought* (Chicago: Moody, 1968).

25. Robert L. Cooke, *Philosophy, Education, and Certainty* (Grand Rapids: Zondervan, 1940), pp. 85-88, 110-111, 112-114, 376.

Buswell's narrowing vision of appropriate interdenominational cooperation, combined with his growing reputation for being too argumentative in
temperament and too intellectual in his approach to Christianity, led to his
abrupt firing in 1940. His replacement, V. Raymond Edman, cared most deeply
about students' spiritual lives and sought to foster expressions of campus piety.
The campus revival of February 1950 was one of his happiest moments, while
dealing with the deaths of three alumni missionaries — Jim Elliot, Nate Saint,
and Ed McCully — in Ecuador in 1956 constituted one of the more sobering
times in Edman's tenure.

Despite his overriding interest in personal piety, the relationship of faith
to learning was not inconsequential for Edman. During the 1950s he had
both an intellectual and a spiritual concern with the spread of communism.
He invited anti-communism lecturer Fred Schwarz to the campus to speak
on "the Red Menace," and wrote regularly of his own distress with the
communist threat. Edman was, however, sufficiently moderate in his anti-
communism that an alumnus reeling under the influence of the John Birch
society publicly accused him of being an unwitting dupe of the communist
conspiracy.[26]

His more general view toward learning was that it played an important,
but instrumental, role in support of individual Christians' witness as well as
of the collective programs of the church. When Edman referred to having been
"demoted" from a life of missionary service to that of Christian college president, many inferred he intended a sincere comparison that also expressed an
underlying but deeply felt anti-intellectual sentiment. He was no triumphalist,
for he wanted Wheaton to remain a full-fledged liberal arts college. His version
of the value-added model stressed the study of the liberal arts with a thick
overlay of evangelical Christianity. His major curricular change was to double
the number of Bible credits required to graduate. This meant that Wheaton
students took a virtual minor in Bible, with all courses being taught from a
dispensationalist perspective.

Edman was ambivalent about the integration of faith and learning. One
of his first actions as president was to shut down Gordon Clark's project. Clark
nettled the dispensationalists with his strict Calvinism and annoyed the pietists
with his sharp rationalism. He disdained popular fundamentalism, and re-
lished teaching his students logic by having them analyze the fallacies of that
day's evangelistic chapel speaker. In response, Edman hamstrung the discipline
of philosophy, remaining forever convinced that it was dangerous to the Christian faith. He then maneuvered to have Gordon Clark fired. Edman thought
the place of "reinforcing values" in Wheaton's curriculum should be examined,

26. Wilhelm E. Schmitt, *Steps Toward Apostasy at Wheaton College* (Wheaton: published
by author, 1966), pp. 75, 148.

and he was not above resolving specific curricular issues such as which secular novels should be taught.

However, Edman also permitted the activities of key faculty members who sought, in a more diplomatic fashion than Clark, to work at integrating faith with learning. He assigned Richey Kamm a major role in Wheaton's self-study report of 1944, and he gave Earle Cairns a year's sabbatical in the early 1950s to work on his *Blueprint for Christian Higher Education.* The former document contained a ringing call for Wheaton to teach the liberal arts in distinctively Christian fashion, which included a revolutionary call for the college to take the lead in promoting social reform. The latter document proposed that Christianity could be the solution to the curricular chaos that plagued all of higher education. The social science chapter — for all intents and purposes written by Kamm — argued that a Christian social science would involve a strong regard for human agency and individuality, an awareness of the moral nature of social problems, and a circumscribed valuation of social institutions, which were necessary for restraining anarchy but ultimately unable to solve social problems apart from the supernatural moral reformation of individuals.[27] Near the end of his tenure, Edman supported tacitly, if not actively, the interests of key faculty members in creating a "Centennial Honors" program during the college's 1959-60 centennial observance year. The curriculum was enhanced with the addition of numerous honors courses, some of which remained in place for a decade or more.

On the other flank, triumphalism still exerted a measurable force upon the college's direction. Some students regarded Christian service activities as the only appropriate activity for evangelical Christians, and they would occasionally criticize students who placed more importance on the classroom or on traditional kinds of extracurricular activities. The trustees, ever worried that Wheaton would follow Harvard and Yale down the path of secularization, regarded the faculty as the greatest threat to the college's religious character. As a result, despite Wheaton's growing prosperity, Wheaton's faculty were among the most poorly-paid in America during the Edman era. Chairman of the trustees Herman Fischer believed that demanding "sacrificial service" of Wheaton's professors would weed out of the faculty all but the most spiritually dedicated men and women, thus preventing the kind of secularizing "decay" that inhered in intellectual life.[28] The triumphalist model had its most impor-

27. Kamm, "Report"; Earle E. Cairns, *A Blueprint for Christian Higher Education* (Wheaton: Wheaton College, 1953).

28. Quotations from Herman Fischer Jr. to Carl F. H. Henry, 8 March 1947, Trustees Papers, Wheaton College Archives. On the relatively low pay of Wheaton faculty, compare the figures in Bechtel, *Wheaton College,* p. 252, to those in U.S. Dept. of Health, Education, and Welfare, Office of Education, *Higher Education Salaries 1961-62* (Washington, D.C.: 1962), p. 26.

tant symbolic victory in 1961 when the trustees added a literalistic human origins clause to Wheaton's doctrinal statement, otherwise unchanged since its institution in 1925. In the addendum, Adam and Eve were affirmed to be real historical persons created "not from previously existing forms of life."[29] Back of the addendum was the conviction of a few trustees — notably David Otis Fuller, a prominent pastor in the fundamentalist General Association of Regular Baptist Churches — that modern science failed to take the Bible seriously. What bothered him was the way the faculty regarded scientific discovery as a source of truth independent of the Bible. Fuller wanted the Bible to provide the limiting framework within which all other knowledge would be pursued.[30]

By and large, however, the value-added model, where faith and learning exist separately but enrich each other, prevailed at Wheaton throughout Edman's presidency. Admissions policies were very similar to those of any other college, heavily skewed toward the academic promise of applicants as measured by class standing and standardized tests. Students for the most part came to Wheaton because it gave them a quality liberal arts education — as measured by secular standards — in an "atmosphere" of evangelical Christianity. Ever higher percentages of students participated in Christian service activities that remained divorced from what went on in the classroom. Alumni evaluations stressed the need for Wheaton's education to be even more "practical" than it was, although a significant minority (mostly those who had gone on to graduate school) complained that their Wheaton education had been insufficiently intellectual.[31] Unlike Buswell, who had been fearless about exposing students to non-fundamentalist ideas, Edman thought it best simply to bathe students in accepted fundamentalist ways of thinking.

Hudson Armerding became Wheaton's fifth president in 1966. He had served in the Navy after his 1941 graduation from Wheaton and then earned his Ph.D. at Chicago in 1948, specializing in Asian history and institutions. Following two years as provost under Edman, Armerding succeeded him as president in early 1966, beginning by literally announcing his own new position to the college community in an awkward, hastily-called faculty meeting.

In contrast to Edman's devotional and experiential approaches to Christian living and learning, Armerding was a Plymouth Brethren-reared intellectual who stressed biblical exposition and theological affirmation. One of his early initiatives as president was instructing Wheaton's admissions office to ascertain

29. Quoted in Bechtel, *Wheaton College*, p. 213.

30. The origin of Wheaton's "Addendum" is discussed more fully in Michael S. Hamilton, "The Fundamentalist Harvard: Wheaton College and the Continuing Vitality of American Evangelicalism, 1919-1965" (Ph.D. diss., University of Notre Dame, 1995), pp. 228-233.

31. Swanson, "The Graduates of a Midwestern Liberal Arts College," pp. 90-94, 148-150.

more closely the faith positions of student applicants and admit only those who professed themselves convincingly as Christians. He also made certain that faculty annually affirmed their agreement with the college's doctrinal statement. In part Armerding's concerns were prompted by external perceptions of the college and its responses to changes in the larger student culture of the 1960s. To the evangelical community, however, Armerding was singularly presidential — the "captain of the ship" — when expressing his own conservative views as worthy of their confidence in the college.

Under Armerding, learning was taken more seriously than under Edman, and therein lay the rub. Armerding's own experience as a Wheaton student, including coursework with Gordon Clark and Richey Kamm, plus his studies at Chicago, had provided him with a foundation for approaching seriously the life of the mind. Those experiences also raised some significant defenses against secular wisdom. On the one hand, Armerding supported curricular and extra-curricular expansion that Edman had resisted, notably by authorizing Arthur Holmes to emerge from the Bible department to chair a department of philosophy, by energizing Edwin Hollatz to develop a full-scale program in drama, and by hiring more faculty trained in the social sciences. On the other hand, Armerding worried that faith and learning were locked in a zero-sum relationship. He feared that some intellectual issues were necessarily off-limits for Christian inquiry and should best be avoided or left untouched. For instance, he strongly discouraged discussion of any Christian responses toward the Vietnam War that might deviate from support of governmental policies.

Armerding also became concerned over the perceived growing laxness in student and faculty attitudes and behavior. The decorum, discipline, and demeanor he had internalized from his Brethren and naval contexts did not fit well with America's changing social mores of the mid-1960s, including those that inevitably intruded onto Christian college campuses via the baby boomers and the Jesus people. Symbolic changes in dress and lifestyle preferences upset Armerding's sensibilities of how Christians ought to look and act, with the implication that such changes also interfered with their ability to think Christianly. For many the crowning symbol of Armerding's concern was his final talk each year with students and their parents at Wheaton's baccalaureate service. As sermons, these talks were superbly crafted and brilliantly delivered. But the talks are also remembered as combinations of a final challenge to pious living plus a warning of the hostile reception the graduates-to-be should expect in the alien world they were entering. Inevitably, some wondered whether and where faith and learning fit into such a worldview.

Amid increasing faculty activism in professional affairs and college governance, Armerding made perhaps his best administrative decision when he appointed Robert Baptista dean of faculty in 1966. Initially the faculty was skeptical about the former soccer coach, but Baptista achieved more for faith and learning than anyone anticipated. His interpersonal style as an encourager and enabler, perfected as a winning coach, easily transferred to work wonders in supporting faculty research and curricular initiatives. Although Armerding approved of faculty involvement in research and professional activities, Baptista was the positive facilitator who helped faculty realize many of their aspirations. He also routinized and stabilized the faculty contract process and set up an equitable salary schedule which proved of particular benefit to women faculty. Baptista's initiatives were particularly well-timed, for this was when Arthur Holmes was articulating more precisely his ideas of how a Christian college should pursue the distinctive task of relating faith, learning, and living. As Holmes was supplying the faculty with a vision for how a Christian world view could affect their vocation as Christian servant-scholars, Baptista was putting the faculty in position to realize the vision.

Armerding often spoke of the importance of "the integration of the biblical text with the academic disciplines," and in 1968 he edited *Christianity and the World of Thought.* The book consisted of sixteen essays — many of them authored by Wheaton faculty and alumni — that Armerding hoped would lead "to a deeper, more thoroughgoing analysis of Scripture and its relationship to the world of thought."[32] Holmes wrote the essay on philosophy and used the collaboration as an occasion to tell Armerding of his vision for a faculty seminar on faith, thinking, and teaching. About that time, Armerding received an offer from a Chicago-area businessman to fund such an endeavor. The first faculty faith and learning seminar was convened in 1969 and directed by Frank Gaebelein, one of evangelicalism's leading educators.[33] Gaebelein repeated the seminar several times, was succeeded by Vernon Grounds, and then by Holmes himself for over a decade. Faculty members participating in the summer seminar wrote papers demonstrating their ability to conceptualize and relate their understanding of Scripture and theology to their disciplinary work.

After twenty years at Wheaton, Holmes had established himself as one of the campus's intellectual and political forces when he assumed the seminar's leadership in 1975. For the next fifteen years Holmes exercised significant influence over the diffusion of the integrative model throughout the college as "Integration of Faith and Learning" and "All Truth is God's Truth" became campus watchwords under his tutelage.[34] Eventually, completing the seminar

32. Armerding, ed., *Christianity and the World of Thought,* p. 7.

33. Gaebelein was the author of a pioneering book on the question, *The Pattern of God's Truth: Problems of Integration in Christian Education* (New York: Oxford University Press, 1954).

34. Holmes's most succinct statements of the integration ideal are *The Idea of a Christian College* (Grand Rapids: Eerdmans, 1975), and *All Truth is God's Truth* (Downers Grove: InterVarsity, 1977).

paper became a prerequisite for tenure and promotion at Wheaton, and Holmes exercised a tacit "approval authority" in those decisions. In so doing, he also fixed the integrative model as normative, while allowing that for some disciplines — especially those in the natural sciences or more applied areas — the value-added approach was acceptable and helpful. Holmes went on to share his distinctive vision for integrating faith, learning, and living in his writing and with literally hundreds of professors from other Christian colleges in similar seminars sponsored by the Coalition for Christian Colleges and Universities.

However, the campus sometimes vacillated on its approach to faith and learning, with the value-added and integration models coexisting uneasily. In 1976 physics professor Howard Claassen persuaded the administration to fund an experimental Human Needs and Global Resources (HNGR) program. HNGR sent students abroad for six-month internships to study and help with "the needs of the developing nations." This alone did not set HNGR apart — students already had ample opportunities for summer missions work abroad. What made HNGR different was its commitment to rigorous academic work integrated into whatever "helping" service the students performed abroad. A 1979 review of the program affirmed that the program not only gave students a chance to serve others, it encouraged "students who participate in the internship to experience and understand firsthand the complexities of human need in developing countries" through the lenses of the academic disciplines.

In the years since, HNGR has developed as an academic program distinctive to Wheaton among Christian colleges. Now supported on an ongoing basis, HNGR lists over 250 alumni interns, including a high of thirty in 1995. But the value-added ethos that pervades much of the campus now locates HNGR's significance less as an integrative, academically-oriented experience than as an opportunity for students' spiritual growth and personal reassessment while serving in a Third World setting. By most criteria, HNGR is a success story, but the persisting ambivalence it symbolizes suggests the campus remains unclear when interpreting both HNGR's *raison d'être* and the reasons for its success.

Richard Chase arrived as president on Wheaton's campus in 1982 with Arthur Holmes's seminars, the HNGR program, and more well in place. While Chase was as conservative theologically as Armerding, he had not lived through the fundamentalist-modernist controversy as Armerding had. More irenic in disposition, he exhibited a spirit of openness toward both the academy and the larger Christian community. A Californian by birth and upbringing, Chase earned his Ph.D. from Cornell in rhetoric and public address. He moved upward quickly through teaching and administrative posts at his alma mater Biola College, becoming president there in 1970 and expanding its student body and academic programs and reputation dramatically in the 1970s.

Chase's refreshing new style stimulated much of the campus community. Chase exuded more confidence in Wheaton's tradition to keep it on line, without emphasizing a sense of urgency over the need to chart a strict course theologically. The campus ethos relaxed, and students and faculty gradually rallied around Chase and his casual and trusting demeanor.

Chase's contribution to the continuities in both the value-added and integrative approaches to faith and learning was simply to accept both as valid understandings of the college's mission. Given his more open approach to Christian higher education and its governance, a more diverse faculty and student body also appeared in the following decade, some of whom knew little firsthand about the subculture of evangelicalism. For both Wheaton students and faculty then, "integrating faith and learning" has become a symbolic means of their socialization to the college, to its distinctive version of Christian higher education, and to its role in the larger subculture.

When Wheaton college celebrated its 125th anniversary in early 1985, Holmes edited a volume entitled *The Making of a Christian Mind* to mark the occasion. Subtitled "A Christian World View and the Academic Enterprise," it consisted of five chapel talks he and four faculty colleagues gave that year. Chase wrote the preface to the volume, declaring in an obviously integrative fashion that Wheaton's "Christian professors seek to integrate their knowledge of God and his Word with both their academic disciplines and their lives. While this is a continuing process, there are also times when it is fitting that we reaffirm our distinctive mission."[35] Several years later, a Chase-mandated review of the general education curriculum brought forth a new "Freshman Experience" course required of all entering freshmen in conjunction with their first-semester "Theology of Culture" course in the Bible department. The "Freshman Experience" course was designed to present new students with the idea of Christian liberal arts; the combination of the two was intended to stimulate their thinking about integrating liberal arts with their faith. On their own initiative, the faculty added required capstone courses for seniors in each department in order to reinforce the importance of the integrative task and to survey the state of integrative thinking in each discipline.

While Chase supported these integrative endeavors, he also championed Wheaton's development of a Doctor of Psychology (Psy.D.) program in the graduate school. Given the more applied orientation of the graduate programs in general and psychology in particular, it might appear that his motivation to add the Psy.D. at Wheaton was a sign of his value-added proclivities. Alternatively, he articulated from the first day of planning that the curriculum of the new program really be integrative in asking first-order theological

35. J. Richard Chase, "Preface," in Arthur Holmes, ed., *The Making of a Christian Mind* (Downers Grove: InterVarsity, 1985), pp. 9-10.

questions about psychological assumptions and methodologies. Ironically, because the college further sought approval of the program from the American Psychological Association, it had to develop a rationale that also satisfied the totally secular expectations of that body, while remaining true to its own Christian worldview orientation.

Chase's nonconfrontational style, which sought to expand the college's programs and ideas of faith and learning into new constituencies, was perhaps best illustrated by his efforts to revise Wheaton's statement of faith. Originally formulated at the height of the fundamentalist-modernist controversy in 1925, Wheaton's statement had committed the college's faculty, administrators, and trustees to premillennialism. However, popular evangelical theology had changed a good deal in the ensuing years, and premillennialism was less important to Wheaton's constituency as a sign of orthodoxy in the 1990s than in the 1920s. After working for months with a faculty committee, Chase presented to the trustees a revised statement of faith. Approved in 1992, the new statement no longer insisted upon premillennialism as a Wheaton touchstone. Symbolically, Chase's actions broadened "faith" considerably, so that faith and learning — whether conceptualized as a value-added or an integrative exercise — might include a larger portion of the Christian church than the college had recognized for the second half of its history. While his actions did not necessarily signal a return to the postmillennialist convergence model of the Blanchard eras, it did mean that Wheaton was making peace with broader audiences in both the church and the larger culture.

Conclusion: The Outcomes of a Dual Identity

It seems fair to say that Wheaton College has successfully held together faith and learning — no mean achievement, given the widespread belief that the two are fundamentally incompatible. By any comparative standard, Wheaton has been a very good liberal arts college at least since the 1930s. It has been so precisely because it has tried to honor both parents at the same time — the culture of higher education and the culture of fundamentalism. Values drawn from the well of higher education kept the school up-to-date, while its evangelical religious commitments kept it supplied with gifted students and devoted faculty who desired an alternative to what they perceived as the established irreligion and moral limpness of most of American higher education. If Wheaton has failed to honor either parent perfectly, perhaps it may be excused on the ground that it is not easy to satisfy both parents when they no longer get along very well.

However, Wheaton is divided about how best to link its dual commitment. Most trustees and most students remain satisfied with the value-added model, while a significant minority of students and most faculty remain committed to promoting the integration model. For the most part these outlooks have been able to coexist, but occasionally the division has erupted into conflict. To further complicate matters, the triumphalist approach still has considerable strength in the world of popular evangelicalism that makes up Wheaton's constituency — witness the resurgence of belief in young-earth creationism since 1961.[36] And there is a strong possibility that some of those who talk about the integration of faith and learning actually think in terms more akin to the convergence model.

Whatever the difficulties, Wheaton has been remarkably successful in holding together its disparate intellectual and religious cultures. Arguably, seeking to negotiate between those cultures, and simultaneously among its multiple visions of faith and learning, has provided it with a vitality that, more often than not, it has harnessed and utilized to good advantage. Furthermore, without its intending, perhaps some of that same vitality has infused Wheaton with the energy that periodically has confounded its critics, surprised to find a Christian college populated by individuals continuing to ask thoughtful questions about both the discovered and the revealed dimensions of reality.

36. Ronald L. Numbers, *The Creationists: The Evolution of Scientific Creationism* (New York: Alfred A. Knopf, 1992).

Clarity through Ambiguity: Transforming Tensions at Seattle Pacific University

Steven Moore
and William Woodward

Founded by Free Methodists as Seattle Seminary in 1891, Seattle Pacific was at first an academy offering college preparatory work. In 1913 the institution became Seattle Seminary and College, and two years later, Seattle Pacific College, an undergraduate college. On June 5, 1977, the name was changed to Seattle Pacific University, appropriate for a comprehensive institution with selected graduate and professional studies. Building on well established master's programs in education, business, nursing, and marriage and family therapy, doctoral programs were added in the 1990s. At its 35-acre campus in the residential neighborhood of north Queen Anne Hill (augmented by two extension campuses on islands in the Puget Sound), Seattle Pacific now annually educates 2,500 undergraduates, nearly 1,000 graduate students, and 12,000 students in various continuing education, summer, and other extension programs.[1]

With the driving of the obligatory golden spike in 1883 near a creek bed in the Western Montana hills, a transcontinental railroad link finally ended the

1. The basic reference for Seattle Pacific's history, to which we are greatly indebted, is Donald McNichols, *Seattle Pacific University: A Growing Vision, 1891-1991* (Seattle: Seattle Pacific University, 1989). McNichols, emeritus professor of English, prepared this official history for the institution's centennial commemoration.

frontier isolation of the Pacific Northwest. The expansive years that followed witnessed the founding of many institutions of learning in the state of Washington, among them the school now known as Seattle Pacific University. The fruit of the grand dreams of recently arrived Free Methodist pioneers, Seattle Pacific opened in the depression year of 1893 as a private academy for elementary and (soon) secondary students.

For the founders, the venture began far from home. It also began . . . and developed, as we shall see, with an amalgam of earnest vision and ambivalent direction. Clarity of identity emerged out of, perhaps because of, ambiguity — in a place far from the heartland of Free Methodism.

From its founding, Seattle Pacific has not enjoyed the luxury — or the temptation — of a settled sense of what it is and what it should be. Rather its unfolding story has been a continuing conversation, indeed a contest, among various centers of interest and vision: trustees, presidents, church leaders, key faculty, alumni, even staff and students. Yet remarkably, the ambiguity and dynamic tension has forged an energetic, identifiable learning community with a powerful commitment to an educational experience that is both academically vigorous and solidly Christian.

In his essay "The Idea of a University," Michael Oakeshott comments that "the world of learning needs no extraneous cement to hold it together, its parts move in a single magnetic field, and the need for go-betweens arises only when the current is gratuitously cut off. The pursuit of learning is not a race in which competitors jockey for the best place, it is not even an argument or a symposium, it is a conversation."[2]

What ultimately matters at Seattle Pacific — what the conversation is about — is what, and how, to teach. For any educator committed to a distinctively Christian dimension to learning, the question of what to teach takes on increased depth and urgency. For Seattle Pacific University, the question has also been an enduring institutional quandary. For most of its history, Seattle Pacific has pondered, indeed often contested, what should be taught. It has done so in an atmosphere of dynamic tension and fruitful ambiguity, certain that it wishes to be Christian, unsettled on the curricular particulars.

Thus Seattle Pacific's story is one of a lively conversation around the course, character, and identity of the institution. It is a story of generations of students, faculty, and staff revisiting basic questions of curriculum, organization, religious ethos, and community life. Yet, as this chapter seeks to demonstrate, it is finally a story of clarity of purpose and dynamic campus culture — in spite of (perhaps even because of) tension and am-

2. Quoted in Timothy Fuller, *The Voice of Liberal Learning* (New Haven: Yale University Press, 1989), p. 29.

biguity.[3] An assertive (some might say fractious) faculty, an active (some might say intrusive) board of trustees, and dedicated (some might say long-suffering) administrators in between have vectored a distinctive if uncharted course. Above all, an emerging identity as an evangelical/inter-denominational institution rooted in the Wesleyan tradition has served as an institutional gyroscope amid successive struggles over the question of what to teach.

Wesley's Educational Legacy

"What to teach" was the first and central item of business at the first Annual Conference of the American followers of John Wesley in 1773. They knew that service flows from substance; that the mission is fueled by the message. They realized content is the superstructure which upholds and gives form to conduct. Accordingly, they selected certain doctrines — distinctives, if you will — which they believed needed fresh and bold proclamation in their day. Annually thereafter, they gathered to reflect, to reaffirm, and to inspire their quest to regenerate the unconverted, renew the church, and reform the nation.[4]

"What to teach" thus became a cornerstone of the Wesleyan imperative that connected faith to life in ways that echoed the words of Charles Wesley's hymn, "to serve the present age, my calling to fulfill." "What to teach" reflects a long-standing commitment to unite "sound learning and vital piety." For Wesley and his followers, personal holiness must lead to transformation of the social order.[5]

Into the next century, American Methodists vigorously pursued their vision to reform the nation. At first, formal education took a back seat to church planting. Theology and moral philosophy seemed lower priorities for a preacher called to persuade the lost to "flee from the wrath to come." However, John Wesley's influence created a concern for the nourishment of the whole person, in mind as well as in body and spirit, bequeathing a commitment to education understood to be more than "religious indoctrination" or "value-centered learning." Wesley made his preachers responsible for the training of children; out of necessity, reading, writing, and arithmetic became the essential curriculum. Soon a familiar

3. As we use the term, *ambiguity* reflects neither intellectual laziness nor lack of moral conviction, but rather unresolved tensions, especially over the question of "what to teach." It is not passion that is lacking in either leaders or faculty, but rather clear and enduring focus.

4. Howard Snyder, *The Radical Wesley* (Downers Grove: InterVarsity Press, 1980), pp. 143-153.

5. Thomas Oden, *John Wesley's Scriptural Christianity* (Grand Rapids: Zondervan, 1994), pp. 55-100.

pattern developed: a Sunday school was established, then a preparatory academy and a course of study for ministry. Few denominations could claim such a strong commitment to the needs of primary and secondary education.

Eventually, the Methodists became activists in higher education as well. By 1880, the Methodist Episcopal Church alone had forty-four colleges and universities and eleven theological seminaries, as well as 130 secondary schools. Such ventures into higher learning met resistance, however. Methodists had long disdained the fancy pretensions of the Presbyterian clergyman or the Episcopal rector. "Give me the evangelist and the revivalist rather than the erudite brother who goes into the pulpit to interpret modern science instead of preaching repentance and faith," cried one leading bishop of the church. Such a challenge reflected a growing tension among Methodists: critics feared that in flourishing, Methodism had lost its zeal for saving souls and bringing in the kingdom of God.

By the mid-1800s, some church leaders — like the charismatic Benjamin Titus Roberts — began to call the church "back" to its early commitments. For some that meant institutional renewal within; for others it meant leaving the old institutions behind. For Roberts it meant criticism of institutionalism, recovery of Wesley's doctrine of perfect love, and, on the eve of the Civil War, condemnation of slavery. It also meant, as a symbol of compassion for the poor, rejecting rented pews. Roberts organized one faction of dissidents into a brand of Methodism which became known as "Free Methodists." Blending the strains of pietism, evangelical revivalism, and the "Holiness movement," their renewal crusade quickly stretched westward after the Civil War in what they called their "march across America."[6] In the process those Free Methodist pioneers would reinvigorate the Wesleyan zeal for education in a burgeoning bayside mill town called Seattle.

The Seattle Pacific Story

Far from its birthplace in upstate New York, Free Methodism in the Pacific Northwest began as a mission enterprise. The fledgling denomination's Susquehanna Conference dispatched the Rev. George Edwards to Washington Territory in 1873. Accompanied by a businessman named Hiram Pease,

6. "Free" Methodists thus variously affirmed freedom for slaves, free pews for all, and free election of bishops. The story will be found most fully in David L. McKenna, *Future with a History* (Indianapolis: Light and Life Press, 1995). See also Leslie R. Marston, *From Age to Age A Living Witness: Historical Interpretations of Free Methodism's First Century* (Winona Lake: Light and Life Press, 1960); and for Roberts, Benson Howard Roberts, *Benjamin Titus Roberts* (North Chili, NY: "The Earnest Christian," 1900). The specific affirmations are codified in The Free Methodist Church of North America, *The Book of Discipline* (Winona Lake: Free Methodist Publishing House, 1980).

Edwards held his first camp meeting in 1875. A decade later, an official "Oregon and Washington Territory Conference" was organized, boasting twelve congregations totalling 112 members. Meanwhile, Pease constructed Seattle's first Free Methodist church building (the city's eighth house of worship) and began promoting his adopted town of 3,500 residents in Free Methodist publications.[7]

Those were heady days for all Seattle citizens. Energetically rebuilding the city after a devastating fire and consumed with a zeal for education, they founded myriad new schools, both public and private. Catching this booster spirit and imbued with the Wesleyan vision for training children, the few Free Methodists in the region boldly began discussing the creation of a Christian school. Chartered in 1891, Seattle Seminary opened two years later with a dozen students.[8] During its first decade the school was housed in a single brick building near the outlying neighborhood at the foot of Queen Anne Hill. (Today that structure, now listed on the Historic Register, bears the name of the school's first president, Alexander Beers. The building is not called "Beers Hall," however — not at a Free Methodist institution which remains alcohol-free — but *Alexander* Hall.)[9]

By 1915 the school was renamed Seattle Pacific College, reflecting the gradual introduction of a collegiate curriculum. The college division grew slowly in both size and academic quality. In 1936, when the college received accreditation, a handful of faculty, four with doctorates, offered three majors to 240 students.[10]

Under the long and stabilizing presidency (1926-1959) of C. Hoyt Watson, the little college achieved a measure of respectability and solvency, especially with the influx of GI Bill veterans in the later 1940s. By Watson's retirement, enrollment stood at 1,200. A building spree in the 1960s accommodated the baby boomers, pushing the school to the brink financially but creating a modern campus. Boomer generation men and women began arriving as fully trained, productive scholars in the 1970s, constituting a strengthened faculty that bolstered both the range and quality of the curriculum. In 1977, the comprehensive college became Seattle Pacific University, reflecting expansion into graduate, professional, and off-campus continuing education programs and reorganization into seven academic schools.[11]

7. Norma G. Cathey, ed., *Free Methodist Church Centennial: Pacific Northwest Conference, 1895-1995* (n.p.: Pacific Northwest Conference of the Free Methodist Church of North America, 1995), pp. 11-12; McNichols, *Growing Vision*, pp. 9-11.

8. McNichols, *Growing Vision*, pp. 9-18.

9. McNichols wryly notes that Beers' surname could not adorn a campus "where the program in the closing day exercises of the first term featured children singing 'Saloons Must Go' . . . ," *Growing Vision*, p. 15.

10. McNichols, *Growing Vision*, pp. 76-77.

11. McNichols, *Growing Vision*, pp. 66-154.

Through the decades, the university has held to its affiliation with the Free Methodist denomination, with direct support and involvement coming from the four Free Methodist "conferences" (regional associations) in the Pacific Northwest and northern California. To this day, the school affirms its adherence to historic orthodox Christianity, requires all full-time faculty and staff to be professing and practicing evangelical Christians,[12] and strives to stamp its identification as a Wesleyan and evangelical university on its curriculum.

This resolve to keep faith with its religious traditions faced legal questions in the 1970s and 1980s, illustrating the dynamic tension among the institution's internal and external constituencies. In 1984 the Washington State Human Rights Commission targeted SPU as a test case on religious discrimination. This occurred at a time when Seattle Pacific was religiously more pluralistic than ever, yet was consciously striving to focus its Christian identity.

After 16 months of legal wrangling, the Commission suddenly dropped its complaint in response to a U.S. Supreme Court ruling which affirmed that "a religious community must enjoy the right to 'self-definition' of its religious character, or it could be chilled in its Free Exercise activity." The decision confirmed the institution's prerogative in hiring and strengthened Seattle Pacific's resolve to exercise its distinctives.[13]

Paradoxically, in the 1970s, the university had had to make an almost inverse argument — that it was *not* a sectarian (i.e. proselytizing) institution — in order for its students to qualify for state financial aid. Several buildings, constructed in part with federal funds, ostensibly could not house religion classes or religious services, though everyone knew that Christian perspectives would be set forth as readily in a psychology class or a committee meeting as in a theology course.

Though these matters were favorably resolved, some found the lines of reasoning disquieting. Certain observers feared that the institution was drifting down the road to secularization. Given James Burtchaell's tests for institutional fidelity,[14] Seattle Pacific, they felt, had failed the criterion that in each of its chief components — trustees, administrators, faculty, staff, and students —

12. Students are not so required.

13. The case and its potentially threatening implications are discussed by attorneys Alexander D. Hill and Chi-Dooh Li, "Discrimination and Religious Institutions," *This World* (Fall 1988), pp. 81-90. Hill is a Seattle Pacific University faculty member, Li one of the university's lawyers in the case. In a sense, the case fulfilled a prophecy of President David McKenna, who once remarked that government intrusions might one day force the institution into a position of civil disobedience for the sake of holding to its distinctives as a Christian university.

14. James Burtchaell, "The Decline and Fall of the Christian College," *First Things* (April 1991): 16-29; and "The Decline and Fall of the Christian College (II)," *First Things* (May 1991): 30-38.

the institution must have a predominance of committed and articulate communicants of its mother church. With the exception of trustees, required by university by-laws to maintain a Free Methodist majority, there were few evidences of denominational "predominance." By the 1980s faculty and staff came from a wide range of Christian traditions: Roman Catholic to Reformed, Baptist to Brethren, Mennonites to Methodists, and numerous other expressions of Wesleyanism. Though a majority of students have been Christians (from an equally wide variety of Christian backgrounds), no faith commitment has been required for admission to undergraduate or graduate programs.

Others simply argued that Seattle Pacific, though "Christian," was hardly a "Free Methodist" university. The relationship with the denomination had become more fraternal than parental. Still others suggested that Seattle Pacific's diversity stemmed, in fact, from its Wesleyan roots. Wesleyan institutions, whether hospitals, orphanages, soup kitchens, or schools, historically were begun with the spirit to serve all people and to transform society. In broadening its sphere of influence, Seattle Pacific was keeping faith with Wesley's plea to "show tenderness [and serve] all people in all things spiritual and temporal."[15] The university's position — as difficult as it was to articulate in the context of judicial interpretation — was therefore not inappropriate. The institution has maintained its founding commitment to historic Christianity, defined in Wesleyan, evangelical terms — a posture that is denominationally particular but also inevitably pluralistic. That Seattle Pacific has been forced in recent years to reject a sectarian identity on the one hand, then to affirm its right to discriminate under the federal constitution on the other, illustrates the ambiguities as well as the kinds of affirmations that pervade the Seattle Pacific story.

These questions of legal standing and constituent perception also point to how the character of Seattle Pacific University has developed within the uniquely uncongenial religious culture of the urban Pacific Northwest, a region notorious as the "least churched" in America. Moreover, the constraints of financial dependence on a fairly narrow base of support have sometimes skewed the university's identity in the public mind. And, as will be explained, the institution's leadership has had a mixed record in instilling an identity and direction for the institution. Yet through it all, SPU has determined to hold to its founding character as a distinctively Christian institution, even while growing beyond its Free Methodist origins.

Reflecting both its history and its geography, Seattle Pacific's story thus demonstrates a distinctive if somewhat diffuse academic heritage evolving from Wesleyan roots and influenced by its location in an urban center in the Pacific Northwest, a place not always hospitable to religious institutions.

15. E. H. Sugden, ed., *The Standard Sermons of John Wesley* (3rd ed.; London: Epworth, 1951), pp. 145-146.

To delineate more precisely the character of this institution, at least four particular defining threads of change and continuity must be analyzed in turn. First, Seattle Pacific has continually struggled to specify its curricular focus. Second, the impact of leadership has been similarly ambiguous; no single personality or group imprinted a clear vision of what the institution would be, nor have successive academic reorganizations brought clarity and coherence. Third, an evolving but unmistakably Christian ethos or culture has characterized the campus community, even in the midst of wrenching change. Finally, these ambiguities and uncertainties have added up, remarkably, to a lively, cohesive, crystallizing educational vision.

An Ambiguous Curriculum

The thrust of the academic program at Seattle Pacific has reflected an uneasy compromise among three distinct visions. All were embodied in the three men who took the lead in founding "Seattle Seminary." Seattle real estate investor Hiram Pease, who had journeyed west with Free Methodist missionary George Edwards, was one. When the Free Methodists' Oregon and Washington Conference at its 1891 meeting recommended establishing a school, Pease rose to endorse the proposal, volunteering a $2,500 donation and his services as chief fundraiser. The second, also present at that meeting, was an immigrant homesteader from the outskirts north of downtown, Nils Peterson, who offered his five-acre garden plot for a site. Apart from their enthusiasm for a religious school, the two had markedly different ideas in mind. Pease envisioned a school that would focus on hygiene and naturopathic medicine; Peterson dreamed of an institute to train foreign missionaries.

A third and broader vision was soon added. The founder and presiding bishop of the Free Methodist movement, Benjamin Titus Roberts, who had established the first denominational institution near Rochester, New York, in 1866, envisioned a typical liberal arts college, open to those outside the denomination and competitive with public schools. Thus, as Seattle Pacific's recent commemorative history delicately admits, these three notions, embedded in the charter documents, "provided the possibility of organizing the school with more than singularity of purpose. . . ."[16]

Moreover, due to its academic eclecticism, heritage, location, and financial stringencies, the school has wrestled with what might be called its institutional self-esteem. Several factors may explain this insecurity. Earnest Free Methodists, first of all, are inclined toward humility and service, not self-promotion. Was it

16. McNichols, *Growing Vision*, pp. 10-11.

truly realistic, many must have wondered, for a tiny denomination to sponsor half a dozen colleges across the country?

The university's location in the midst of the region's largest metropolis — indeed, one that boasted the state's flagship university — has also been a bit intimidating. East of the Rocky Mountains, private higher education preceded or paralleled public colleges. By contrast, in the Puget Sound region the largest public university, the University of Washington, was well established by the time Seattle Pacific dared to offer a baccalaureate degree. One still hears half-embarrassed recollections of days when even those on Seattle Pacific's campus referred to the fledgling institution as the "little Sunday School by the canal."[17] Such was the burden of a location within the orbit of *the* University (of Washington, that is). Additionally, aspirations to academic excellence, at least within the lower and middle class circles where the Holiness movement found its strength, were always faintly suspect. And finally, recurring financial crises only deepened the self-doubts. The hold of such a mentality is persistent; the school cultivated an insular posture for years, only in recent decades emerging into conscious engagement with the city, with other universities in the region, and with the larger world of scholarship.

This flowering of Seattle Pacific as a place of academic distinction has not come from a conscious or coherent program of academic development. Rather pockets of creativity and initiative from time to time produced demonstrated achievement. Now the University points to a faculty that regularly writes books and articles, earns grants, wins consultant contracts, aids native American tribes and other groups in need, testifies before Congress or state agencies, accepts church and conference bookings, and does media appearances. And many of them pursue their scholarship and service in settings around the world.

While the stories are too numerous to tell, even the casual observer would observe the continuing pattern of creative initiative, passion for service, distinguished achievement in teaching and writing, and a broad spectrum of definitions of what it means to be Christian, scholar, teacher, and servant of others. Also evident is the founding mix of three visions: a zeal to extend the Christian enterprise around the world; a wide array of applied and professional programs undergirded by both academic excellence and a vision for service; and, solidly at the core, a commitment to liberal learning.

Not all faculty would articulate those three impulses alike. The result is a

---

17. McNichols, *Growing Vision*, pp. 76-77, 86. At the foot of the north slope of Seattle's Queen Anne Hill, Seattle Pacific's campus abuts the Lake Washington Ship Canal, constructed in the pre–World War I era to permit seagoing vessels to reach a large inland lake from Puget Sound. The University of Washington campus is located north of the canal just three miles to the east.

bracing brew — a distinguished academic enterprise marked not by orderly planning and clear cohesion but by kaleidoscopic variety and often competing claims. Where then is the guiding gyroscope? It might seem that if not to a central academic focus, then to leadership might fall the task of harnessing it all. But here too one finds ambiguity and tension.

Ambiguities of Leadership

Seattle Pacific does not bear the unmistakable stamp of one or two dominant leaders. Indeed, part of the explanation for the ambiguities of curricular design and the uncertainties of institutional self-image may stem from this fact. Presidents usually could articulate a clear sense of what they believed Seattle Pacific should be. But they often could not rally the whole community to their vision. Their legacy was thus one of moving the institution forward, but without forging a consensus on its focus and direction. Nor were they consistently able to achieve the financial stability that might have made such uncertainties more palatable.[18]

Alexander Beers, the first president, shepherded the small academy through its earliest years, constructing two more buildings and encouraging the introduction of a college curriculum when there were hardly resources for the elementary and high schools. However, he managed — innocently, it seems — to mingle his own finances with an increasingly precarious and indebted college treasury, and found it prudent to submit his resignation in 1916.[19]

Successor Orrin Tiffany worked to restore financial solvency, bolstered academics — both in liberal and applied disciplines — and tried to reach out to the city. But a personality clash with the head of the education department, a program Tiffany had worked aggressively to initiate, led to trustee intervention, and Tiffany's appointment was not renewed in 1926.[20]

Remembered as an autocrat of sorts, C. Hoyt Watson followed with three decades of dramatic growth, decisive visibility on campus, an assortment of capital and curricular initiatives — and a rather mixed sense of purpose; the University's chronicler describes his retirement in terms of a "clouded" vision. He shunned risk, explains one who worked for him. He seemed uncomfortable in the city, recalls another.[21]

18. As current SPU president Phil Eaton observes, this financial pattern "is more normal among our type of institutions than it is negative." See also Frederick Rudolph, *The American College and University* (New York: Vintage Books, 1962).

19. McNichols, *Growing Vision*, pp. 180-183.

20. McNichols, *Growing Vision*, pp. 64-65.

21. McNichols, *Growing Vision*, pp. 90-91, 103-105, and interviews.

Watson's successors were bolder. C. Dorr Demaray in the 1960s and David McKenna in the 1970s both presided over even more startling expansion, yet financial strain followed Demaray's retirement, and McKenna moved on to head Asbury Theological Seminary amid murmuring from a few external constituents that Seattle Pacific was drifting away from its denominational, if not its spiritual, moorings. David Le Shana brought a warm pastoral style that eventually proved incongruent with the demands and complexities of a growing institution.[22] Curtis Martin, long-time administrator and Le Shana's executive vice-president, stepped in to provide a stabilizing hand during a three-year term, striving under trustee mandate to lay a foundation for a more focused future. As we shall see, he oversaw the adoption of a formal mission statement as well as substantial plant improvements. Following Martin's retirement, his successor, self-described entrepreneur E. Arthur Self, resigned after only ten months when differences with the trustees over leadership style and an inadequate appreciation for the institution's history and mission became evident. Somehow, Self's aggressive new "vision" for the institution didn't seem to fit. The Board and Self had to agree that "his leadership style, philosophy of governance, and ideas of direction for the university" were incompatible with what the trustees had in mind.[23] Once again, a clear and enduring vision — about which all would say, "This is Seattle Pacific" — failed to emerge.

To an outside observer, it might seem that the university could not decide on the kind of leadership it wanted. In some respects, recent presidents followed an alternating pattern: from relatively assertive to relatively consensual styles, from more corporate to more pastoral personalities. The ideal balance between decisiveness and prudence, between inclusive discussion and independent action has not been resolved.

As for the presidential role in mobilizing financial resources, ambitious capital expansion campaigns in the earlier years periodically transformed the campus, but pushed the school to the brink financially, undermining any vision a president might have advanced. It has always been difficult to keep pace with educational needs. Beers, Watson, and Demaray all oversaw significant building programs. Each time, they left a legacy of improved facilities — and a cash crisis. Each time, the institution was forced to fall back on expanding the student body to increase tuition revenues, which in turn put renewed pressure on capacity.

The record has improved in recent decades. McKenna brought three major projects to debt-free completion: a bank/bookstore complex, a science building,

22. McNichols, *Growing Vision*, pp. 144-148, 196-197, and interviews.
23. Minutes, Board of Trustees, May 1995; subsequently issued as a press release dated May 23, 1995.

and a home for the new School of Business and Economics. But he admits he did not have time to fulfill his goal of building a strong endowment. However, he did create an organization for major donors, the "Fellows," and later set Martin, then vice-president for university advancement, to the task of instituting a Seattle Pacific Foundation.[24] Later, on assuming the president's chair, Martin was able to oversee several major refurbishings or improvements of buildings and grounds. Most notably, the campus's largest building, a new library, opened in 1994 — the result of prudent planning, record corporate financial involvement, and fundraising sufficient to preclude any financial crisis.

Perhaps the most intriguing possibility for breaking this cycle came early on, in 1913, when Alexander Beers secured a challenge gift from no less than James J. Hill, the builder of the Great Northern Railroad. But the stipulation to raise four times the proffered $40,000 within two years proved a hopeless task.[25] The promise of a significant endowment died, and Seattle Pacific College (or what might have been Hill College or Great Northern University) struggled along, relatively impoverished, while some other educational and cultural institutions in the region found benefactors (and still others closed their doors). Seattle Pacific has rarely secured that substantial endowment gift that would ease the dependence on day-to-day tuition revenue, continuing to rely instead on the broad-based support of loyal alumni and committed friends.

If Seattle Pacific's presidents seem neither to come from a common mold nor to articulate a sustained vision, individually they have made their mark. Demaray and McKenna probably had the most lasting impact. Demaray, though a former pastor of Seattle's First Free Methodist church, preferred to be known as a former English professor and president of Los Angeles Pacific College. According to some long-time members of the Seattle Pacific community, it was Demaray who instituted two decisive transformations: an enhanced attention to the academic enterprise, and what one of his successors termed a "much more sophisticated and catholic view of Christianity."

The ethos changed under Demaray, but McKenna transformed the organization. To an institution in the throes of a million-dollar budgetary shortfall, he brought financial stability. To a "company-owned store" (as one observer put it) he brought a corporate style and structure, reflected most vividly in the name change to Seattle Pacific University. McKenna argued that in its academic organization and curricular offerings, the institution already fit the label. Despite faculty qualms about appearing pretentious and student fears that "university" meant a loss of the personal touch and teaching emphasis, the transition went relatively smoothly.[26]

24. McNichols, *Growing Vision*, pp. 180-183, and interviews.
25. McNichols, *Growing Vision*, pp. 42-43.
26. McNichols, *Growing Vision*, pp. 106-195, and interviews.

A veteran trustee looks back proudly and appreciatively at "a sequence of committed presidents who would not roll over amid adversity." Leadership certainly has played a key role in weathering crises and upholding the religious character of the school. As we shall see, these men contributed to an emerging sense of identity and purpose. But from the standpoint of the university's full-time community, the creative ferment of the campus culture itself rather than the impact of senior leadership has been just as influential in shaping what Seattle Pacific has become.

Transformations in Campus Culture

In at least three profound ways, the character of campus life has altered in recent decades. First, campus demographics — that is, the makeup of faculty, staff, and student communities and their relation to each other — have changed radically. Second, the chapel program plays a far different role. And, third, for better or worse, the religion department carries a different image both on and off campus. Mitigating the impact of these factors, however, two emerging trends have recently converged: the quest for a more explicit statement of mission and purpose, and the adoption of a developmental frame of reference for student nurture.

Transformations of campus demographics reflect institutional growth as well as broader regional and national cultural change. Senior faculty members point out that the faculty's role within the Seattle Pacific community has changed since the 1970s. Both faculty size and the spectrum of academic specialties have grown. Obligations to keep current and contribute to one's discipline have intensified as has the temptation to shift one's loyalty from the institution to the guild. Fewer faculty were alumni or indeed had any experience at all in Christian higher education. Perhaps most significantly, a major generational shift occurred from the mid-1970s to the mid-1980s as many long-time faculty members retired.

But there are more pragmatic reasons why faculty involvement on campus has changed. In the late 1970s and again in the late 1980s, real estate inflation, already rampant in California, bludgeoned Seattle. Once most of the faculty lived within blocks of campus. Now new arrivals had to buy far from the city center. Spouses, if employed, had traditionally worked on campus; now they found jobs elsewhere. Accordingly, no longer were substantial numbers of faculty families worshipping at First Free Methodist Church or participating in school and civic groups on Queen Anne Hill. Thus for many new faculty families, three crucial ties to campus had been severed. Moreover, many of the opportunities for out-of-class relationships between faculty and students disappeared as co-curricular responsibilities were delegated to a growing professional student life staff.

Changes in student demographics likewise radically altered the character of the campus community by the end of the 1960s. An increasing fraction of the student body commuted to classes (at present, only half the undergraduate population lives in campus housing). More older adults ("non-traditional learners," as they were aptly but awkwardly called) joined the student body, especially in the expanding graduate programs. Senior citizens took advantage of a space-available tuition-free invitation. International students, some channeled through the autonomous Intensive English Language Institute (IELI) adjacent to campus, brought both cultural and religious diversity. The relatively homogeneous, identifiably Free Methodist student body of the 1950s was no more.

Perhaps the most significant factor shaping changes in the student profile has been changes in strategies for student recruitment and selection. Reactions to the "baby boom," the "baby bust," and now the impending "baby boom echo" have profoundly influenced the campus character. Seattle Pacific has moved from a policy of relatively open enrollment toward greater selectivity.

Seattle Pacific long prided itself on offering its distinctive education to whomever wished it, making no real effort to screen out applicants with lower records of academic achievement. On the other hand, the college's Free Methodist ethos automatically filtered the prospect pool, although some non-Christians matriculated even in the early years. The flagship program for several decades was the teacher training program. Since by law the University of Washington could not offer an elementary certification program, Seattle Pacific filled the void, of necessity attracting students outside the Free Methodist orbit. In the 1960s this openness widened until by the 1970s Free Methodist students were a distinct minority, although professing Christians still constituted a majority of the student body.

The admissions process began to receive increasing emphasis as the pool of high school graduates began to shrink with the close of the baby boom era. Non-traditional learners could not make up the shortfall. Yet the university consciously sought to upgrade its standards. Three strategies ensued. First, the most marginal new students were programmed into a special "Developmental Assistance Program" (now called "ACCESS"). Then, by the late 1980s, the university increased merit-based financial aid in an attempt to attract the top-flight student. National Merit Scholars, once nonexistent on campus, now come in significant numbers. Most recently, the university has shifted to a moderately selective admissions policy. Rising SAT scores and grade point averages and other measures of improved academic capability now characterize the current student population.[27]

---

27. Twenty-six National Merit scholars were enrolled in 1994-95. The entering class had an average entering GPA of 3.4; average SAT score was 1006. "The Facts About Seattle Pacific University," University Relations brochure, 1994.

To academic selectivity has now been added a new kind of religious selectivity based on institutional mission. The question of students' *spiritual* preparation and nurture has returned to the forefront in the last several years. Recruitment efforts target students with a record of faith, leadership, service, and academic preparation with particular aid packages reserved for students who are a "mission match." Yet this approach does not mean a return to the past. Compared to thirty years ago, a very different faculty instructs a very different student body.

One might assume that some unifying experience would be needed for an institution to retain a core character and culture in the face of so many changes in its two main constituent populations: faculty and students. Traditions might bind a campus culture, perhaps, or certain policies, or explicit market positioning, or alumni pressure, or intentional activities — else the center could not hold. At a religiously affiliated institution, one would logically look for more.

In his book, *Uneasy Partners*, Merrimon Cuninggim suggests that "the church related college that recognizes its rootage in more than mere words will give tangible evidence of that fact by offering courses in religion in the regular curriculum, providing opportunities for worship . . . and giving encouragement to a life of service. . . ."[28] At Seattle Pacific, however, neither drift nor centeredness accurately describes the religion curriculum or campus worship. More particularly, neither the chapel program nor the religion curriculum have proven the source of continuity and cohesion.

For much of the history of religious colleges, the chapel stood at the literal and functional center. And, as many authors have noted, few programs at church-related colleges have weathered as much criticism and discussion as chapel. Seattle Pacific has been no exception.

Among those whose memories of campus stretch back to the 1950s, most cite the chapel program as the distinguishing mark of a Seattle Pacific experience in those years. It is far different today, they say. Indeed they believe Seattle Pacific's Christian ethos was, until recent decades, a reflection of the chapel program. In the early years chapel was held in a variety of places but always with the guiding purpose of "the community at worship." Older and emeriti faculty recall the holiness revivalism that marked chapel and other religious services. This impact and purpose held until the 1960s when the student population exceeded the capacity of campus facilities.

With the arrival of president David McKenna in 1968 a new strategy developed. McKenna believed that chapel should be, in essence, "the president's course," the place where the sum of the educational experience was brought together in the institution. He moved the chapel service to First Free Methodist

28. Cuninggim, *Uneasy Partners* (Nashville: Abingdon, 1994), pp. 98-101.

Church across the street. His own office took on the planning of the chapel program, and the president himself was a regular speaker. Some faculty resented the change as an intrusion upon faculty control; others supported it as an opportunity for the community to rally around a central vision and a common experience of worship. Faculty participation expanded with a new small-group program called "Cadre" which augmented the corporate worship services.

By the time David Le Shana assumed the presidency in 1982, a new Office of Campus Ministries had taken responsibility for chapel. In 1989 the university sought to acknowledge the diversity of student schedules and preferences while reaffirming the university's commitment to spiritual formation by instituting a new, more diverse chapel program whose purpose had been expanded to "provide opportunities for the integration of faith and learning, . . . for members of the community to worship together and [to] equip members of the community for leadership, service, and world citizenship." In addition to the regular tri-weekly (later bi-weekly) service in the church, students could meet the chapel requirement through faith-learning forums, reflection retreats, special-subject cadres, discipleship groups, and other worship and instructional events.[29] Perhaps the most popular component of this religious buffet is "GROUP," a weekly student-run praise and devotional service that often attracts over a third of the resident students. Citing GROUP and other examples, many believe the current chapel/forum program more faithfully serves the breadth of denominational background and level of understanding of faith among students and is perhaps one of the most enriching co-curricular pieces of the educational experience. Critics suggest it lacks a coherent theme and fails to attract enough faculty involvement. It is fair to say, in any case, that chapel, though vital to the educational experience, no longer stands at the center of every student's SPU experience.

If not to chapel, many church-related institutions may look to their religion departments to help define their campus religious ethos. But once again, Seattle Pacific's story is one of ambiguity and tension. In the 1970s and 1980s, many faculty who came to Seattle Pacific in the Watson era began to retire, to be replaced by faculty who had come of age in the turbulent 1960s. Curiously, nowhere was this transition more extreme than in the School of Religion. In 1973, when — at the age of 29 — the first of a group of new faculty was hired, the next youngest colleague was 58! Retirements followed; within seven years that same newcomer, then in his thirties, was the senior member of the religion faculty. (Similar transitions, though less drastic, were taking place elsewhere in the university; fewer faculty were alumni, or indeed had any experience at all in

---

29. "The Chapel/Forum Programs of SPU," included with minutes, Board of Trustees, February 1990.

Christian higher education.) In spite of many continuities between the two faculty generations, there were transparent differences in political outlook, church membership (Free Methodists were in steady decline), academic philosophy, cultural expression, academic culture, and even academic training (the doctorate had become requisite). A veritable metamorphosis had occurred.

To the extent that religion faculty in Christian schools have been counted on to insure continuity with the past, the new religion professors were, in the words of one of them, "abject failures." In their unstintingly academic approach, commitment to publishing within the canons of critical biblical scholarship, and political activism in the university, the School of Religion seemed to be at the center of campus tension. As one current religion faculty member put it, "For those who coveted the 'old' Seattle Pacific, the religion faculty was not an ally but a foe." In the critics' view, he admitted, "we were complicit not only in changing theology and biblical studies at Seattle Pacific, but were also systematically undermining its coveted cultural heritage."[30]

Most of the new religion faculty elicited sharp criticism on campus and among the larger SPU constituency. One professor was even subjected to an extraordinary examination before tenure was granted. But a second explanation for the controversy, in addition to the generational transformation, is evident. Within the larger evangelical communion during that same period a deep conflict erupted over what author Harold Lindsell called a *Battle for the Bible*. The issue was Scripture, and the specific formulation, long a watchword of the fundamentalist movement in twentieth-century American Protestantism, was Biblical "inerrancy." Evangelicals divided over the concept. Seattle Pacific religion faculty, steeped in a non-creedal Wesleyanism, sought, sometimes combatively, to show how earnest Christians could retain a reverence for Scripture without adopting the inerrantist model.[31] But in the 1970s that

---

30. Frank Spina, "Biblical Scholarship in a Wesleyan Mode: Retrospect and Prospect" (unpublished manuscript, January 1991), p. 6. In hindsight, this traditionalist critique seems overheated at best, although it still can be heard from some quarters. Yet Spina himself demonstrates how religion faculty firmly align themselves with the historic heart of the institution. To new students and their families, he recently affirmed, "As a Christian university, Seattle Pacific's intellectual program . . . means that the content of Christian faith impinges on every single truth claim made by the various academic disciplines. . . . Our attempts to get at that 'more rigorous' aspect are what make the Christian education to which we are committed profoundly rather than superficially Christian." Spina, "Wisdom from a Grizzled Academic Veteran," New Student Convocation address excerpted in SPU's *Response* 18 (November 1995): pp. 10-11.

31. Lindsell, *The Battle for the Bible* (Grand Rapids: Zondervan, 1976). The Free Methodist Book of Discipline does not stipulate inerrancy: Free Methodist Church of North America, *The Book of Discipline* (Winona Lake: Free Methodist Publishing House, 1980), pp. 13-14.

assertive position brought them under attack (from some area pastors and at least one visiting chapel speaker) for a doctrine of Scripture they believed they *shared* with their recently retired predecessors.

By the mid-1980s the tensions had muted somewhat, but the scars remained. Religion faculty felt besieged; some colleagues in turn found them abrasive or defensive. From a trustee standpoint, the controversy reflected a broader change in faculty demeanor and orientation. Some on the board perceived a growing adversarial relationship that at its core threatened a drift from Free Methodist moorings; other trustees believed it to be a departure from the very Christian foundation of the institution. That some faculty would discount those fears, that others would concur, and that still others would agree on the trend but think it a good thing is yet more evidence of the hard reality of differing perspectives at Seattle Pacific.

Hence, in the midst of rapid change, neither the chapel program nor the religion faculty provided an organizing center. Where could a clarifying focus be found?

Toward an Emerging Organizational Focus

During the 1980s, trustees, administrators and faculty increasingly felt the need for a more explicit and comprehensive understanding of Seattle Pacific's direction as it approached its centennial. A formalized mission statement eventually provided one kind of resolution. But more helpful was a growing trend within the community toward understanding all dimensions of life and learning from a developmental perspective.

President David Le Shana attempted to focus the institution's identity. He thought he might crystallize a sense of mission by asserting that Seattle Pacific's primary purpose was "world evangelization." This grandiose claim by the son of Methodist missionaries was misunderstood, and it didn't "take." Rather it elicited a chorus of complaints that "we're a university, not a church." Le Shana simply meant that a Christian university should function as an extension of the church. Critics, some uneasy with the vocabulary, others cynical over motive, saw Le Shana's gentle reaffirmation of the Great Commission as a narrowly pietistic vision that would undervalue academics, especially the liberal arts. Though he created an "Intercultural Institute of Missions" to give structure to the vision, Le Shana could secure neither internal support nor external funding, and the initiative died.

Under pressure from trustees, Le Shana eventually commissioned a task force to draft a mission and vision statement as a means to codify the "case" for Seattle Pacific in advance of a major centennial capital campaign. The group produced a draft, but in this instance, too, momentum seemed to ebb at the end of Le Shana's tenure.[32] When Le Shana departed in 1990, some feared Seattle Pacific's faith tradition would be pushed to the bottom of campus priorities. Quite the opposite occurred.

Curtis Martin, a career administrator at SPU, assumed the presidency for a three-year term. He immediately set about to establish an agenda which would clearly focus the institution as an evangelical university. One of his first actions, at this ambiguous moment, was to finalize the mission statement. He pulled together the essence of what he believed was the core of SPU's mission, and decisively ordered it printed, framed, and nailed to the wall of every building on campus. Suddenly the campus population found phrases it had debated for years staring down at them: "As a community of learners, Seattle Pacific University seeks to educate and prepare students for service and leadership. We are committed to evangelical Christian faith and values and to excellence in teaching and scholarship for the intellectual, personal and spiritual growth of students."

Trustees and denominational leaders "thunderously approved" the statement.[33] On campus, some expressed enthusiasm; some offered modest concurrence; some simply thought it fell flat, like another public relations slogan. For others, process was the issue: not everyone had been consulted, nor had everyone given his or her approval. Still others wondered about nuances of meaning. What does it mean that we are a community? What is evangelical? But Martin demonstrated an openness to continuing dialogue, and the Faculty Senate gave its assent after the fact.[34]

One revealing point of contention was, in fact, the statement's embrace of the "evangelical" label. The increasing use of the term in the popular media since the later 1970s made some people on campus uncomfortable because it threatened to pigeonhole a very diverse and open community as "fundamentalist" in the public mind. Others feared that appropriating an "evangelical" label signified a loss (real or potential) of a distinctive Wesleyan identity. Still others felt it highly appropriate — the culmination of a trend, begun during the Demaray years and promoted under McKenna, toward broadening beyond Free Methodist roots. And certainly there were those who understood the term as a call to draw the line, an explicit repudiation of any drift away from orthodox Christian teaching. Depending on their angle of vision, then, members of the community understood "evangelical" as either widening or narrowing the institution's self-definition.[35]

32. Earlier in Le Shana's tenure, a declaration of Seattle Pacific's "Commitments" had been issued, but had limited impact on the campus. McNichols, *Growing Vision*, pp. 196-199, and interviews.

33. Minutes, Board of Trustees, November 1991. The quoted phrase is Martin's.

34. Minutes, Faculty Senate, December 1991.

35. A faculty member conducted an informal survey of colleagues in 1992 to determine the meaning of "evangelical," eliciting a wide range of responses. See Kathleen Braden, "Some Voices on the Meaning of 'Evangelical,'" unpublished typescript, April 29, 1993.

A less controversial but equally significant commitment contained in the mission statement was its affirmation of a developmental model of learning. The acceptance of this statement on campus was due in part to a quiet reorientation in thinking that had made inroads on campus since the 1970s when theories of human development were introduced. The increasingly pro- fessionalized student life staff, initially more than faculty, redirected their work toward fostering spiritual, social, and intellectual development.

More recently, the two processes — the steps toward a specified mission statement and the developmental perspective — converged in a second initia- tive from president Curtis Martin. Martin appointed a university-wide task force to "examine, evaluate, and recommend ways the university can provide a more intentional pastoral presence encouraging spiritual nurture, commu- nity worship, and volunteer service."

Out of the ensuing discussions came a series of initiatives under the rubric of "spiritual formation," defined as "encouraging members of the community to make Jesus Christ the authentic center and integrating power of their lives." All community members were to be encouraged to grow through cultivating "the spiritual disciplines," through "modeling a community of love, justice, reconciliation, support, authenticity and civility," by developing "an informed and thoughtful faith," and by "advancing faith through service."[36]

To lay a strong foundation for the future, the spiritual formation initiative included a required seminar for new faculty (with a parallel seminar for new staff). The seminar provides an interdisciplinary "opportunity to reflect on the distinctive feature of Christian higher education, namely the combination (or integration) of faith and learning. . . . As Charles Wesley once put it, 'to unite the pair so long disjoined: knowledge and vital piety.'"[37]

As Martin left the presidency in 1994, Seattle Pacific had apparently re- consolidated its sense of purpose and direction after more than a quarter-cen- tury of transforming change. In addition, the university had opened the new library and reorganized the academic units into a unified college of arts and sciences and three professional schools. The future seemed clear and bright. Organizational focus seemed at hand. But when Martin's successor, E. Arthur Self, resigned before completing his first year, change and uncertainty, rather than continuity and clarity, descended upon the campus. Yet this time it was somehow different. This time the vessel seemed on course after all. The board placed the leadership of the institution in the hands of the vice presidents and immediately launched a nation-wide search for a new president. In February 1996, SPU provost Philip Eaton was named the University's ninth president. Eaton, a team builder with a rich family history in Christian higher learning,

36. "Spiritual Formation Task Force Document," 1993.
37. "Spiritual Formation Task Force Document," 1993.

brought a breadth of experience as a former Whitworth College English professor, a businessman, a Presbyterian elder, and a former college trustee.

Toward a Crystallizing Educational Vision

The ambiguities surrounding academics, the erratic pattern of leadership, the changing demographic and religious culture — all these have shaped a place that, ironically and remarkably, has not lost its core character. Almost in spite of itself, it seems, Seattle Pacific has managed to develop an educational identity. Indeed it has found a unifying sense of what Christian higher education ought to be.

The religious commitment that drives the academic program at Seattle Pacific has been articulated in different ways through its history. Vocabularies and boundaries have evolved over time. Yet Seattle Pacific has retained an intentional identification with its evangelical and Wesleyan roots, usually with an open, ecumenical spirit rather than in sectarian terms.

For much of its history, Seattle Pacific defined Christian education more in terms of the personal spirituality of its students and faculty than as a distinctive theological system or curriculum or teaching style. In the beginning, it was "Education for Character." Later, Tiffany yearned for the little college to be "the center of all the deep spiritual movements of the Northwest." For Watson it was "Education Plus" that included an explicit goal of "training for Christian service." Echoing this emphasis, older and emeriti faculty vividly speak of the array of spiritual activities and lifestyle expectations, but do not readily recall ways in which the Christian ethos shaped the academic enterprise.[38]

Official catalog statements similarly suggest that for more than half a century Seattle Pacific College understood its Christian dimension primarily in terms of the formative setting within which courses were taught. The first catalog spoke of "a thorough education under Christian influences." Soon after accreditation a statement referred simply to "scholarship and training in a wholesome spiritual environment."[39] As late as the mid-1950s the emphasis remained firmly on personal spiritual nurture, on "inculcating these [Christian] principles in the lives of students . . . to bring about sound student growth spiritually, professionally, socially and physically." (One notes that but one adverb alludes, obliquely, to the curriculum.) "Spiritual growth,"

38. Various college catalogs, 1930s-1980s; McNichols, *Growing Vision,* pp. 19, 55, 67, 74, 90-91; interviews.

39. *Seattle Pacific College Catalog, 1935-36.* The quotations from the first catalog appeared on the flyleaf of later catalogs, e.g., from 1962-1969.

the 1955 statement continues, "is encouraged through a Christian dynamic which permeates the entire program," meaning chapel and other religious services, and "wholesome standards of life and practice are promoted." And throughout the 1950s and beyond, the cover slogan was "Youth Facing Life with Christ."[40]

It is true that a holistic understanding of education implicitly, and often explicitly, shaped the various statements, beginning at least in the 1950s. The college sought to portray itself as concerned with intellectual, social, and physical (and later cultural and vocational), as well as spiritual development. Such a view carried forward, of course, the fundamental emphasis on moral education that characterized the nineteenth-century college and rested on the bedrock belief of progressive education that environment determines character.

In the turbulent 1960s, faculty and students alike scrutinized the meanings of the historic commitments, but neither fortress fundamentalism nor a muted moralism resulted. Instead, academic excellence became a more central theme, and notions of "a completely integrated Christian life," as the catalog put it, gained greater visibility.[41]

But it was the arrival of President David McKenna in 1968 that produced a more clearly articulated sense of purpose. McKenna proclaimed a "vision of wholeness," arguing that a Christian education ought to be marked by the integration of the various dimensions of personhood. He derived this formulation, he explains, from "the Wesleyan distinctive to integrate faith and learning," to unite being and doing by "bringing together individuals, the community, and the curriculum."[42]

McKenna became the spokesman for this Wesleyan understanding within Christian higher education. He clearly believed that the institution must engage the broader Christian culture — and the city of Seattle as well. "I wanted to make the city our campus," he recalls.[43]

Symbolic of this embrace of a less pietistic, more "evangelical" posture was the redesign of the college seal. An aggressive falcon, perched above the motto "Valiant for the Truth," was replaced with a more stylized and contemplative bird surrounded by the words "Wholeness in Truth."

Preoccupied in his early tenure with the financial crisis he inherited, McKenna had to wait to address the curriculum. But in the later 1970s he encouraged a move to revise general education. In reaction against a lax and undifferentiated list of general requirements, a much more intentional and

40. *Seattle Pacific College Catalog, 1955-56.*

41. *Seattle Pacific College Catalog, 1962-63,* and subsequent years.

42. David McKenna, oral and written comments, June 1995; see catalogs, especially 1971-72 and 1974-76.

43. McKenna, oral and written comments, June 1995.

complex structure of general education was developed.[44] A Seattle Pacific education, proponents felt, ought to strive toward a goal that was at once broadly Christian, distinctively evangelical, and authentically Wesleyan: the ideal of the "Christian scholar-servant." The life of the mind, in this view, was no end in itself, but a means to fulfill the call of God to serve the church and the world. In the words of Wesley, frequently quoted by McKenna, "the world is my parish."

When the college renamed itself Seattle Pacific University, the scholarship side of the ideal took on increasing importance to the faculty, especially by the 1980s. Universities produce original knowledge, it was argued, so the SPU faculty ought to some degree to be engaged in primary research and writing. Though still a "teaching university," the institution therefore encouraged present faculty (and recruited new faculty) to research and publish. If scholarship without service was seen as sterile, service without scholarship would constitute mere earnest ignorance. The output today is impressive.

But neither service nor scholarship should be divorced from spirituality. Thus the most recent emphasis on "spiritual formation" constitutes a key refinement. Now in process of implementation, this latest initiative more clearly focuses the relationship between the religious culture of the campus and the academic enterprise. It also incorporates the greater diversity of faculty, staff, and students now found in Seattle Pacific's extended community, for it focuses on the goal — maturing in all of life — rather than on one prescribed means to that end.

It will be noted that these four steps — character, wholeness, scholarship-for-service, and spiritual formation — represent a progression toward an ever more precisely Christian understanding of the academic task. Indeed, taken as a sequence of objectives, these four may be said to characterize the way SPU now seeks to educate its diverse student body. In sum, then, Seattle Pacific implicitly stands for the following affirmations as a synthesis of its crystallizing educational mission.

SPU seeks to nurture its students as people of *virtue*, people for whom learning leads to godly character and therefore Kingdom-advancing behavior and lifestyle.

SPU seeks to nurture its students as *whole* persons, able to integrate all the dimensions of their lives, and thus to embody the biblical ideal of *shalom*.

SPU seeks to nurture its students as persons *obedient* to the Lord's Great

44. McKenna, oral and written comments, June 1995; and McNichols, *Growing Vision*, pp. 161-162.

Commands, committed to loving God with all their hearts, souls, strength, and especially minds (scholarship); and loving their neighbors as themselves (service).

SPU seeks to nurture its students as persons of *faith, formed in and by the Spirit,* maturing in relationship to the God they serve and the neighbors they love, developing in all the disciplines of thought and belief.

For all students, Christian or non-Christian, there is the hope that a Christian education will produce good character. For most students who will be open to the spiritual dimension, Seattle Pacific's integration of learning and life seeks to instill a recognition that learning and maturing entail more than just intellectual activity. For the substantial number of students who claim sincere Christian faith, a Seattle Pacific education should lead to a lifetime of intellectually-grounded service to God and to others. For those students who embrace the core vision, Seattle Pacific offers the challenge of full, active, lifelong commitment to the unifying of character and intellect in the quest to become conformed to the image of Christ.

That is to say, if there have been entrenched self-doubts or self-deprecation about money and academic mission, there has been no such ambivalence about maintaining an explicitly religious identity. In a uniquely Wesleyan, evangelical spirit, Seattle Pacific has been unashamed to call itself Christian, rejecting the cultural and attitudinal limitations of both fundamentalism and liberalism. And that identity has survived in recent decades as the school has faced great changes while making significant strides academically. It has survived in spite of, perhaps because of, the region's acknowledged "unchurched" character. And it has thrived in spite of, perhaps because of, the institution's own internal tensions and uncertainties.

Conclusion: Clarity Through Ambiguity

Seattle Pacific University, as we have seen, has endured uncertainties in leadership and ambiguities in its curriculum while retaining its traditional religious affirmations. How could an emerging university struggle to define itself, yet enjoy objective indicators of academic success? The answer seems to be related to both people and place. Earnest, often unselfconscious commitments of faculty, staff, and administrators along with conscious interactions with the regional culture of the Pacific Northwest have shaped Seattle Pacific's unique mix of cohesive religious ethos and highly diversified yet strong academic programs.

Let us first consider place. As with Whitworth College, location within the Pacific Northwest region has influenced the character of Seattle Pacific. It is one of a mere handful of enduring Christian organizations in the region, and the only urban evangelical Christian university. Far from the heartland of Free Methodism, squarely located in a religiously pluralistic, unchurched culture, and cherishing an open, Wesleyan style, SPU necessarily developed a broadly Christian rather than sectarian flavor. Conversely, it was founded in a burgeoning metropolis and matured in the shadow of the state's largest and oldest public university. Thus it sustained a sense of purpose in some measure because it was intentionally countercultural. It deliberately retained allegiance to its religious roots in the midst of a regional culture that often was cool to organized religion and its institutions. It might also be surmised that location on the West Coast contributed to a more practical, vocational, or applied orientation in contrast to the classic religiously affiliated liberal arts college back East. Hanging on for sheer survival, the school necessarily became market sensitive. As such, it stressed the practical benefits of the curriculum, whether religiously in terms of Christian citizenship and service, or academically in terms of vocational relevance.

But as influential as place has been, people have had the far greater impact. The people of the community that is Seattle Pacific have demonstrated a commitment to the vocation of teaching for the sake of the Christian imperative. One reads this in the institutional archives; one hears this repeatedly in the reminiscences of emeriti and older faculty, and unmistakably still in the newer arrivals.

Thus there have been two essential components to what the university's centennial chronicler called "a growing vision" — what we have termed a "crystallizing vision." First is the faithfulness to a strong religious heritage — to Wesleyan and evangelical understandings of Christian faith — broadly but earnestly held. Second is the continuing trajectory of academic development and innovation — toward excellence without elitism in the preparation of students for service to church and society.

All this is Seattle Pacific's story — all this, but also a pattern of ambiguity and tension. Virtually oblivious at first to any need to define institutional distinctives, Seattle Pacific has struggled in recent decades to discover some coherence in its heritage and its dreams. In the final analysis, clarity in the midst of ambiguity has come in the continuities and commitments that continue to characterize the institution.

Seattle Pacific, remarked one faculty member, is a "tradition in search of an articulation. It *has* a tradition, it *has* an identity, in spite of itself."[45] As journalist Joel Garreau noted in another context,[46] there are places where, instinctively and beyond explanation, it feels like home.

45. Interview.
46. Garreau, *The Nine Nations of North America* (Boston: Houghton-Mifflin, 1981).

There is today a prejudice in some circles that too staunch a religious commitment can undermine scholarly objectivity, intellectual freedom, and academic excellence. In other circles, the faithful believer might harbor a different prejudice that is the opposite point of view: that deep thought is the subtle seducer of true faith.

In answer to both these prejudices, Seattle Pacific witnesses to the value of joint commitments to both faith and learning. Indeed, such dual allegiances provide mutual correctives to each other: firm faith brings accountability to unchallenged orthodoxies in the academic establishment, just as the search for new knowledge can hold accountable the untested orthodoxies of a faith community.

The interaction produces tension and ambiguity. But it feels like home.

THE WESLEYAN/HOLINESS TRADITION

What Can the Wesleyan/Holiness Tradition Contribute to Christian Higher Education?

John E. and Susie C. Stanley

The Wesleyan/Holiness movement began as an attempt to reclaim traits of the eighteenth-century Wesleyan or Methodist revival which, Wesleyan/Holiness leaders contended, the broad mainstream of Methodism had forsaken. The largest denominations of the tradition are the Salvation Army, the Church of the Nazarene, and the Church of God (Anderson). Smaller denominations include the Free Methodist Church and the Wesleyan Church. These denominations, except for the Salvation Army, emerged from the nineteenth-century holiness movement in the United States.

Major Motifs in the Wesleyan/Holiness Tradition

Despite the separate distinctives of these specific denominations which began as reform movements, three general theological principles nourish the Wesleyan/Holiness tradition: (1) the Wesleyan quadrilateral as a theological method, (2) sanctification of the believer and the call to holy living, and (3) social holiness. Understanding these three essentials not only explains foundational theological impulses but also acquaints one with the spirit of the Wesleyan/Holiness heritage.

The Wesleyan Quadrilateral as Theological Method

The Wesleyan quadrilateral describes the four essential elements in the theological method of the Wesleyan/Holiness movement: Scripture, tradition, reason, and experience.[1] They were the key ingredients of the Anglican theological method inherited by John Wesley. The manner in which the Wesleyan/Holiness tradition implicitly appropriated these Anglican elements from the beginning, and then eventually explicitly adapted and endorsed them as the Wesleyan quadrilateral, illustrates the theological inclusiveness characteristic of the tradition.

The Bible is the primary means of God's revelation to humanity. Foundational as a source of doctrine, inspiration, moral guidance, and spiritual formation, the Bible serves not only as the record of God's revelation through Israel, Jesus, and the church, but also as the controlling boundary by which other theological claims are measured. Second Timothy 3:16 witnesses to Scripture's being "inspired by God" for guidance in doctrine and "training in righteousness," or living.

Tradition refers to the inherited witness, beliefs, and practices of religious bodies. Affirming tradition as a source of truth recognizes that one's religious heritage influences how one receives and perceives the Bible. While the quadrilateral rightly notes the role of tradition in shaping persons and communities, holiness churches which began as reform movements obviously have adapted varied stances toward the role of tradition, as will be illustrated later in this chapter.

Wesley affirmed human reason as a third avenue toward theological understanding. Reason is God's gift to humanity, reflecting the mind of God. Reason inspires human creativity, enables us to think about God and life, and guides moral inquiry. Although sin stained and distorted human reason after the fall, originally the gift of reason was part of what it meant to be created in the image of God. This positive regard for reason generated positive implications for Christian higher education in the Wesleyan/Holiness tradition.

Experience is the validating link which enables persons and groups to know the truth God discloses through Scripture, tradition, and reason. Experience had two dimensions for Wesley. On the one hand, experience was like Old Testament wisdom. It denoted the accumulated reservoir of practical knowledge gleaned from living a God-honoring life. On the other hand, experience connoted the validating presence of the Holy Spirit. Dennis Kinlaw, former president of Asbury College, observes that for Wesley experience was

> a third gift from the Spirit, a personal and immediate authentication that moved Christian truth from information about God and faith in the Gospel to an existential personal apprehension of that truth for oneself.[2]

1. Albert C. Outler coined the term. See his "The Wesleyan Quadrilateral in John Wesley," *Wesleyan Theological Journal* [hereafter *WTJ*] 20 (Spring 1985): 7-18; also Donald A. D. Thorsen, *The Wesleyan Quadrilateral* (Grand Rapids: Zondervan, 1990).

2. Dennis Kinlaw, "The Bible and Theology" in E. E. Carpenter and W. McCown, eds., *Asbury Bible Commentary* (Grand Rapids: Zondervan, 1992), p. 88.

Placing value on experience as the Spirit's confirming role in the inward, subjective life is consistent with Wesley's testimony that his heart was strangely warmed at Aldersgate. According to Wesley, "Revelation is complete, yet we cannot be saved unless Christ be revealed in our hearts, neither unless God cleanses the thoughts of our hearts by the inspiration of His Holy Spirit."[3] Again, in his *Explanatory Notes Upon the New Testament,* Wesley wrote concerning the inspiration of Scripture, "The Spirit of God not only once inspired those who wrote it, but continually inspires, supernaturally, those that read it with earnest prayer."[4] Albert F. Gray, a pastoral theologian and founding president of Pacific Bible College, now Warner Pacific College, wrote a theology in which he entitled the section on biblical inspiration, "It Is The Person That Is Inspired."[5] The role of the Holy Spirit in authenticating experience for Christians means that the Spirit transforms the Bible into God's Word for believers. Truth is relational. The confirming presence of the Spirit enables the realities taught in Scripture, perceived by reason, and delivered via tradition to become the truth necessary for salvation, spiritual formation, and social witness. Because truth is relational and experiential, humility and tolerance should season the believer and the church. The Wesleyan quadrilateral highlights the work of the Holy Spirit and Christian experience. As the song writer D. Otis Teasley phrased it, "I know in my heart what it means."[6]

Sanctification

The second essential theological distinctive is sanctification, which is the defining doctrine and experience of the Wesleyan/Holiness tradition. John Wesley spoke of Christian perfection as a growing love in the believer's life as the Holy Spirit cleansed the human heart. In the Wesleyan/Holiness tradition sanctification came to be understood as a definite second work of grace following justification and salvation. Sanctification purifies the heart of inbred sin and is accomplished by the Spirit who empowers the believer for service. In spite of intramural debates regarding the meaning of sanctifica-

3. John Wesley, *The Letters of the Rev. John Wesley, A.M.,* ed. by John Telford (London: The Epworth Press, 1931), vol. 6, p. 28, as cited by Rob L. Staples, "John Wesley's Doctrine of the Holy Spirit," *WTJ* 21 (Spring/Fall 1986): 100.

4. John Wesley, *Explanatory Notes Upon the New Testament* (London: Epworth, 1966), p. 794.

5. Albert F. Gray, *Christian Theology. Book 1* (Anderson: Warner Press, 1944), p. 80.

6. D. Otis Teasley, "I Know in My heart What It Means," in *Worship the Lord: Hymnal of the Church of God* (Anderson: Warner Press, 1989), #417. Outler notes, "But always, Biblical revelation must be received in the heart by faith: this is the requirement of 'experience' " ("The Wesleyan Quadrilateral," p. 11).

tion, Wesleyan/Holiness scholars concur that the theology of sanctification is the heart of the heritage.

The Wesleyan/Holiness movement was a reform movement combating moral pollution in society and doctrinal dilution in church. Thus, it is easy to understand why early leaders maintained that purity of heart and power for service were two essential aspects of sanctification. Three biblical texts anchored holiness preaching — 1 Thessalonians 5:23, Romans 12:2, and Acts 1:8. First Thessalonians 5:23 and Romans 12:2 called for purity of heart and holy living. According to these passages, the Spirit produces a people whose lives demonstrate a positive change in daily behavior. Moral integrity becomes the intention of holiness Christians. But purity should not be bottled up. Holiness preachers also proclaimed Jesus' promise in Acts 1:8: "but you shall receive power when the Holy Spirit has come upon you; and you will be my witnesses in Jerusalem, in all Judea and Samaria, and to the ends of the earth."

Because of its emphasis on the sanctified life, the Wesleyan/Holiness tradition stresses what the saved self can become rather than what the sinful self has been. The accent falls on what humans can become through the continuing work of the purifying and empowering Holy Spirit. A high estimate of the church prevails because the Spirit calls the church to be a fellowship demonstrating the divine possibilities of life together in the Spirit. Sanctification orients the church toward continual renewal and outreach. The gifts of the Spirit empower the church for service. The Wesleyan/Holiness tradition stands on the left wing of the Protestant Reformation because of its optimistic view of sanctified human potential, its stress upon love as an actualization rather than a mere intention of Christian experience, and its emphasis on spiritual experience. The Spirit's purifying and empowering ministry makes the renewal of persons, the church, and society possible here and now rather than postponing renewal to a future age or dispensation.

Social Holiness

Social holiness, the third characteristic of the tradition, indicates the compassionate ministries and social impulses which emerged within the Wesleyan/Holiness movement. Scholars and lay persons alike often categorize Protestants into two camps: those who are concerned with saving souls and those who focus on transforming the social order.[7] For John Wesley, ministry was not an either/or proposition; he placed one foot firmly in each camp by refusing to separate the two. In addition to preaching to the poor on the streets, Wesley started an employment bureau, a loan fund, a medical dispensary, and

7. Jean Miller Schmidt outlined the two-party system in *Souls or the Social Order: The Two-Party System in American Protestantism* (Brooklyn: Carlson Publishing, 1991), p. 173.

homes for the poor. Wesley's followers continued his emphasis on love. William Booth, cofounder of the Salvation Army, summarized all of religion in the word "love," declaring that love must be put into action.[8] Booth's *In Darkest England and The Way Out* detailed the Salvation Army's social campaign to end poverty, minister to criminal offenders, and rehabilitate persons crippled by drink and prostitution. Booth envisioned his plan as "a scheme for the working out of social salvation."[9]

In the United States, the Wesleyan/Holiness tradition reflected both the social holiness of Wesley and the temporal salvation of Booth. Speaking of "sanctified compassion,"[10] historian Timothy Smith observed:

> all the socially potent doctrines of revivalism reached white heat in the Oberlin and Wesleyan experience of sanctification — ethical seriousness, the call to full personal consecration, the belief in God's immanence, in his readiness to transform the present world through the outpoured Holy Ghost, and the exaltation of Christian love.[11]

Social holiness was especially evident in ministries to the urban poor and women. Also, it spawned a zeal for education. Love fueled holiness outreach to those in need. Holiness churches sponsored missionary homes in cities where newcomers could live while seeking work and permanent housing. Such homes existed in Detroit, Spokane, Denver, Seattle, Cincinnati, and elsewhere. Phineas F. Bresee, a founder of the Church of the Nazarene, planted churches "in the heart of the city . . . where the gospel could be preached to the poor."[12] Bresee wanted church buildings "to be 'plain and cheap' so that everything should say welcome to the poor."[13]

The inclusive ministry of Jesus, the outpouring of the Spirit on men and women at Pentecost, and Galatians 3:28[14] motivated Wesleyan/Holiness

---

8. William Booth, *In Darkest England and The Way Out* (London: International Headquarters of the Salvation Army, 1890), pp. 219-220.

9. Booth, *In Darkest England*, p. 271.

10. Timothy L. Smith, *Revivalism and Social Reform: Revivalism in Mid-Nineteenth-Century America* (New York: Abingdon, 1957); reprinted as *Revivalism and Social Reform: American Revivalism on the Eve of the Civil War* (Baltimore: Johns Hopkins University Press, 1980), p. 176.

11. Smith, *Revivalism and Social Reform*, p. 154. Although Smith described holiness prior to the Civil War, the social holiness activities of the following paragraph continue the emphasis of Wesley and Booth.

12. "Our Social Service Heritage: Unto the Poor," *Herald of Holiness* 72 (October 1, 1983): 18.

13. "Our Social Service Heritage," p. 18.

14. Galatians 3:28 (NIV) says, "There is no longer Jew or Greek, there is no longer slave or free, there is no longer male and female; for all of you are one in Christ Jesus."

leaders to value and ordain women as ministers. Benjamin Titus Roberts, founder of the Free Methodist Church, penned *Ordaining Women*[15] to expound Galatians 3:28 as the key text on women in ministry. Alma White, founding bishop of the Pillar of Fire Church, published *Woman's Chains,* a monthly magazine lobbying for women's rights in church and society. Susie C. Stanley has documented a holiness hermeneutic supporting women's equality and ministries of Wesleyan/Holiness women.[16] In 1908, 20 percent of Nazarene clergy were women, and in 1925 the Church of God (Anderson) reported that 32 percent of its clergy were women, while a majority of Salvation Army officers have always been women.

Wesleyan/Holiness churches founded schools such as Adrian College as early as 1848 and Roberts Wesleyan College in 1866. Several later schools grew out of urban mission homes. Schools often served as regional training centers for churches. Although a strong belief in the imminent return of Christ led people to sing "This World Is Not My Home," a concern for this-worldly obedience prompted them to establish rescue missions and plant colleges to train leaders for future generations.

These ministries of social holiness were the external dimensions of the doctrine and experience of sanctification which was understood as holiness embodied in love. As a social ethic based on the call for moral integrity or purity in persons and society, social holiness is possible — holiness advocates contended — because the Holy Spirit empowers believers to serve in ministries of love and justice.

What Has the Wesleyan/Holiness Tradition Contributed to Christian Higher Education?

Having defined three distinctives of the Wesleyan/Holiness tradition, it is essential to consider how the Wesleyan quadrilateral, the doctrine and experience of sanctification with its call to holy living, and social holiness have influenced Christian higher education both positively and negatively.

15. Benjamin T. Roberts, *Ordaining Women* (Rochester: Earnest Christian Publishing House, 1891).

16. Susie C. Stanley, *Feminist Pillar of Fire* (Cleveland: The Pilgrim Press, 1993), pp. 98-104; also her "Empowered Foremothers: Wesleyan/Holiness Women Speak To Today's Christian Feminists," *WTJ* 24 (1989): 103-116, and " 'Tell Me the Old, Old Story': Analysis of Autobiographies by Holiness Women," *WTJ* 29 (Spring/Fall 1994): 7-22.

John E. and Susie C. Stanley

The Quadrilateral in Wesleyan Higher Education

The Wesleyan quadrilateral fostered a sense of theological tolerance. That tolerance becomes apparent in light of how holiness schools have understood and studied Scripture. Amid the debate on biblical authority between fundamentalism — and its successor, evangelicalism — and liberalism, the Wesleyan/Holiness tradition understands itself as a third alternative. The nineteenth-century Wesleyan/Holiness revival occurred during the period when modernism was embracing historical criticism, along with its tendency to discount the supernatural dimensions of biblical revelation. Fundamentalism was a theological and social response to modernism. In 1919 the World Christian Fundamentals Association insisted upon inerrancy as essential to the doctrine of biblical authority. Fundamentalism, with its doctrine of inerrancy, made inroads into Wesleyan/Holiness schools and churches.[17] However, both fundamentalism and evangelicalism differ from the Wesleyan/Holiness tradition on the three basic issues of social holiness, sanctification, and the understanding and use of the Bible as informed by the Wesleyan quadrilateral.

Fundamentalism seeks renewal in a millennial dispensation at the end of time whereas the Wesleyan/Holiness tradition, with its social holiness emphasis, seeks renewal through compassionate ministries of love and justice in this world while awaiting God's ultimate action. Fundamentalism is pessimistic regarding human nature and the reign of sin whereas the Wesleyan/Holiness tradition's doctrine of sanctification is intrinsically optimistic regarding human renewal. The fatal flaw of fundamentalism and a broad swath of evangelicalism is that the doctrine of inerrancy turns the Bible into a self-authenticating revelation. The Bible is defined as the Word of God rather than being a witness to the Word which became incarnate in Jesus Christ. On the other hand, the Wesleyan/Holiness tradition has insisted that the Spirit gives life and applies Scripture to the needs of the believer and church, as has been indicated in the quotations from John Wesley and A. F. Gray. The Wesleyan/Holiness heritage values the confirming and continuing presence of the Spirit in validating the truth of what the Bible claims, renewing human potential, and empowering and actualizing social holiness.

Despite its intrinsic theological incompatibility, fundamentalism with its doctrine of inerrancy did infiltrate the Wesleyan/Holiness movement. At the same time, the early history of the Wesleyan Theological Society (WTS) reflects both tolerance for diversity and a conscious effort to preserve the Wesleyan/Holiness tradition as a third viable alternative to the contesting claims of fundamentalism/evangelicalism and liberalism. The WTS began in 1965 as

17. See Paul Bassett, "The Fundamentalist Leavening of the Holiness Movement: 1914-1940," *WTJ* 13 (Spring 1978): 65-91.

the academic and theological commission of the National Holiness Association, now known as the Christian Holiness Association. Kenneth Geiger, in a paper at the initial meeting of the WTS, described the inerrancy of the original autographs of Scripture as "the official position of the National Holiness Association and, quite uniformly, the view of Wesleyan-Arminians everywhere."[18] Doctrinal statements in the 1966-69 issues of the *Wesleyan Theological Journal* (WTJ) also affirmed inerrancy. At the 1967 meeting of the WTS, however, a panel on "Biblical Inerrancy" debated the issue. W. Ralph Thompson, secretary-treasurer of the society, ended his 1966-69 annual report with a plea for reconciliation. Thompson stated his own commitment to the doctrine of inerrancy. Then he added:

> Let us be exceedingly careful lest we take any step that will weaken our position with respect to the inspiration and authority of the Scriptures. But if a change in the wording of our doctrinal statement could be made that would protect our position and at the same time respect that of our brethren whose intellectual honesty will not allow them to subscribe to our statement, I recommend that such an action be taken.[19]

Members of the society, all of whom were inerrantists, revised the doctrinal statement in the 1969 meeting by removing the inerrancy clause. That revised statement on Scripture appeared in the 1970 edition of the *WTJ*.

Two recent Wesleyan/Holiness publications reflect the continuing diversity within the tradition. *The Wesley Bible*[20] required "that all participating scholars sign a statement affirming their belief in the verbal and plenary inspiration of Scripture and in the inerrancy of the original autographs."[21] On the other hand, William Cannon in his "General Introduction" to the 1992 *Asbury Bible Commentary* advised,

> Rather than speak of the inerrancy of Scripture or verbal inspiration, it is much better to speak of the defectability of the Bible or its infallibility, the breathing of the Holy Spirit upon its authors to assure their accuracy in presenting God's plan of salvation in its perfection.[22]

18. Kenneth G. Geiger, "The Biblical Basis for the Doctrine of Holiness," *WTJ* 1 (Spring 1966): 43, as quoted in John G. Merritt, "Fellowship In Ferment: A History of the Wesleyan Theological Society, 1965-84," *WTJ* 21 (1986): 189.

19. Secretary-treasurer's report to the annual meeting, Wesleyan Theological Society, November 1967, as quoted in Merritt, "Fellowship ln Ferment," 195.

20. *The Wesley Bible,* ed. by Albert F. Harper (Nashville: Thomas Nelson, 1990). Frank A. Spina pointed out this diversity in "Wesleyan Faith Seeking Biblical Understanding," *WTJ* 30 (Fall 1995): 26-49.

21. "Preface," *The Wesley Bible*, p. xiii.

22. William Cannon, "General Introduction," *Asbury Bible Commentary*, p. 18.

In summary, although the Wesleyan/Holiness tradition is in many ways incompatible with fundamentalism and its inerrancy approach, a minority within the tradition has affirmed and continues to affirm a form of inerrancy while still stressing the confirming, authenticating work of the Spirit. A tolerant willingness to agree to disagree has prevailed.

How has the Bible actually been taught in Wesleyan/Holiness schools? Most institutions have utilized the historical critical method. Robert Traina at Asbury Theological Seminary, for example, used an inductive method of Bible study and related his inductive approach to other contemporary exegetical and hermeneutical methods.[23] During the period from 1920-1945 — the very period when fundamentalists voiced their alarm most loudly over critical study of Scripture — many holiness schools employed the historical critical method with modifications to allow for a belief in biblical miracles and healings.[24]

For all of this, however, the quadrilateral's accent on reason was late blooming in Wesleyan/Holiness schools. Early theologizing, for example, often involved little more than statements of church doctrine. Yet there were exceptions. In 1919, the Church of the Nazarene requested H. Orton Wiley to write a systematic theology, which was eventually published in 1940 by the Nazarene Publishing House. In addition, Russell Byrum produced a systematic theology for the Church of God in 1925.

Likewise, the quadrilateral's notion of tradition received mixed responses in the Wesleyan/Holiness tradition. Schools sponsored by primitivist churches, such as the Church of God (Anderson), initially valued tradition only if the tradition could be traced to the New Testament church. Ironically, some primitivist theologians knew and used church history and systematic theology to argue their case for primitivism.[25]

Because of the emphasis on the Holy Spirit as the guide to and authenticator of truth, Wesleyan/Holiness advocates have understood knowledge as a matter of the heart as well as of the mind. A liability of this posture has been an attitude that says, "trust the Spirit rather than rely on human planning and reasoning."

The Wesleyan quadrilateral's holistic inclusion of Scripture, tradition, experience, and reason implies that all facets of a liberal arts curriculum embody

---

23. Robert Traina, "Inductive Bible Study Reexamined in the Light of Contemporary Hermeneutics" in Wayne McCown and James Earl Massey, eds., *Interpreting God's Word For Today* (Anderson: Warner Press, 1982), pp. 53-109. Essays in the book document the methodological diversity of Wesleyan/Holiness biblical scholars in the early 1980s.

24. For two accounts of how they experienced the Bible being taught at Wesleyan/Holiness schools, see Spina, "Wesleyan Faith Seeking Biblical Understanding," *WTJ* 30 (Fall 1995): 27-29; and John E. Stanley's "Elements of a Postmodern Holiness Hermeneutic Illustrated by Way of the Book of Revelation," *WTJ* 28 (Spring/Fall 1993): 23-43.

25. See John E. Stanley, "Unity Amid Diversity: Interpreting The Book of Revelation In the Church of God (Anderson)," *WTJ* 25 (Fall 1990): 74-98.

God's truth. Ideally, therefore, Christian higher education would involve learning to write, to speak, to read widely, to know how to ask critical questions, to use the scientific method, to appreciate the fine arts, to value physical fitness, and to integrate faith and learning. On this view, the humanities and the sciences would be vital parts of the curricula of liberal arts colleges in the Wesleyan/Holiness tradition.

But this ideal has not always been implemented. Melvin Dieter contends that many in the Wesleyan/Holiness tradition are unclear whether they belong to a church or a revival movement. This ambivalence plays itself out in the educational institutions these people have established. Thus, while supporting the classical liberal arts college, every holiness denomination, according to Dieter, has also established Bible schools to train ministers.[26] Sometimes the Bible school founders felt motivated by an urgent mission to restore a sense of evangelism which they thought dormant in the liberal arts colleges. Some Bible schools do not offer courses in the humanities and sciences because their administrators view them as unnecessary. Sometimes, however, Bible schools have developed into liberal arts colleges. Individual denominations within the Wesleyan/Holines tradition vary in their educational requirements for ministry: some require seminary training; others require no higher education at all.

Sanctification in Wesleyan Higher Education

The emphasis on sanctification and holy living has had positive and negative repercussions on campus life. At times this emphasis has produced a vital worship life. The size and prominence of the chapel buildings at Anderson University and Asbury College, for example, reflect the centrality of a strong chapel ministry. Indeed, some of the calls to commitment and holy living issued in chapel at Anderson College rank for many students as important moments of spiritual formation. Many experience there the full meaning of the Wesleyan quadrilateral with its emphasis on holistically appropriating Scripture, tradition, reason, and experience.[27] In this way, worship integrates faith and learning, links theology to the arts, and issues a call to committed holy living — all an essential outgrowth of the traditional Wesleyan emphasis on sanctification.

---

26. Melvin E. Dieter, "Theological Education in the American Holiness Movement" (unpublished manuscript, December 6, 1993), p. 37. After establishing Nazarene Theological Seminary in 1944, for example, the General Assembly of the Church of the Nazarene in 1964 founded Nazarene Bible College at Colorado Springs.

27. This was the experience of John E. Stanley, one of the authors of this essay, when he was a student at Anderson College (now Anderson University) from 1961 to 1965.

Moreover, sound holiness theology often becomes incarnate in relationships between faculty, staff, and students, and these relationships often shape lives, motivate ministries, and transform shy, social wallflowers into confident leaders. Periodically we meet persons who feel overwhelmed by the pressures of college, work, and family, or feel baffled by vocational indecision. In the belief that the Spirit sustains students in their seasons of preparation, we encourage them to seek staying power from the Spirit who is the heart of the Wesleyan/Holiness legacy. That has been a dynamic asset to higher education in the Wesleyan/Holiness tradition.

On the other hand, the theme of sanctification can sometimes foster legalism and a fanatical "Christ against culture" stance. As a result, extreme separate-from-the-world behavior patterns sometimes exist on campuses aligned with the Wesleyan/Holiness tradition. Dieter suggests that legalism has often "shattered the vitality of the movement's spirituality and its outreach in evangelism and mission."[28] As a result, campus lifestyle codes occasionally convey mistrust of the sanctified student's ability to be a disciplined dresser, dater, or driver. Some colleges and universities in the Wesleyan/Holiness tradition, for example, restricted unchaperoned off-campus dating in the 1950s, prohibited the wearing of shorts to class or chapel in the 1960s, and forbade women to wear slacks to class or chapel in the 1970s. A continuing challenge is the task of implementing the call to holy living in lifestyle agreements which meet the requirements for integrity, as perceived by diverse campus constituencies, without compromising trust in students.

Social Holiness in Wesleyan Higher Education

Social holiness, the third component of this heritage, has also continued to thrive on campuses aligned with the Wesleyan/Holiness tradition. This tradition's historic commitment to the poor manifests itself especially when colleges understand themselves as opportunity schools, willing to accept some students with weak academic backgrounds and to provide them with an opportunity to develop their gifts and talents. Twice in the last twelve years at Warner Pacific College, for instance, the presidential award, annually given to the senior who best exemplifies the college's service values, has gone to a graduate who was admitted on conditional status.

Service through compassionate ministries has also characterized these campuses. At Anderson College, for example, Professor Marie Strong developed a student led Christianity-In-Action program in the 1950s. On a weekly basis, students participated in jail and prison ministries, shut-in visitation,

28. Dieter, "Theological Education," p. 8.

literacy clinics, children's home visitation, mental hospital visitation, a ministry at a home for troubled girls, and a cooperative ministry with clients of the local county's Department of Social Services. By 1963-64, 25 percent of the student body was actively involved in Christianity-In-Action ministries. From 1986 to 1994, Warner Pacific College sponsored the first on-campus shelter in the United States for homeless families. Both Azusa Pacific University and Warner Pacific College sponsor annual spring break mission trips to Mexico which involve social outreach to the poor. Several schools sponsor student summer service projects which plug students into internships or ministries, often of a cross-cultural nature. These ventures incorporate service into the informal curriculum, provide leadership development opportunities, extend the classroom into the hurting world, foster internal reflection and prayer, and preserve the legacy of social holiness. Through compassionate ministries like these, biblical admonitions to social holiness become internalized.

Historically, a commitment to the equality and ordination of women has characterized most Wesleyan/Holiness churches. This commitment declined after World War II, however, except in the Salvation Army, until a renewed concern began to develop in the 1970s for recapturing this Wesleyan/Holiness distinctive. At least 25 students attended the first Wesleyan/Holiness Women Clergy Conference in 1994. Thirteen sponsoring schools subsidized a publication resulting from that conference, *Wesleyan/Holiness Women Clergy: A Preliminary Bibliography*,[29] and covered expenses for at least one of their students.

A disturbing collapse of this tradition, however, occurs each year when outstanding women who graduate from Wesleyan/Holiness colleges discover that the promise of their call and their preparation does not culminate in ministerial placement as readily for them as for some of their less qualified male peers.[30]

Over the years a significant percentage of faculty in Wesleyan/Holiness institutions have been women, and especially in recent years several women have served as academic deans. However, as of 1995, there are fewer than ten women with doctoral degrees in a theological discipline in the Wesleyan/Holiness tradition. Students, therefore, have very few models of women serving as leaders in theological disciplines. Obviously, Wesleyan/Holiness schools in recent years have not lived up to the promise for women that is inherent in their theological heritage.

Likewise, on many Wesleyan/Holiness campuses, a powerful strain of social

---

29. Susie C. Stanley, *Wesleyan/Holiness Women Clergy. A Preliminary Bibliography* (Portland: Western Evangelical Seminary, 1994).

30. C. S. Cowles speaks of this dilemma in *A Woman's Place?: Leadership in the Church* (Kansas City: Nazarene Publishing House, 1993).

and political conservatism currently threatens to smother the theme of social holiness intrinsic to the heritage. Two examples will suffice. First, people who have spoken on gender-related issues at various Wesleyan/Holiness colleges report hostility and intolerance. This was especially the case in the aftermath of the 1992 presidential election. Second, faculty who teach at Wesleyan/Holiness institutions report a growing unwillingness among students to debate political and social issues. Faculty who attend Wesleyan Theological Studies meetings, for example, speak of a growing intolerance on campuses and an insensitivity to human needs which would have been the focus of compassionate ministries in earlier years.

Conclusions

One wonders if the threat to social holiness, and perhaps to the entire Wesleyan/Holiness tradition, stems from a loss of institutional identity. Given the increasing pressure toward uniformity, many find it easier to identify with evangelicalism and the Christian College Coalition than to nurture and sustain their own Wesleyan/Holiness heritage. Further, the cost of institutional survival has made many Wesleyan/Holiness institutions more market-driven than mission-driven. To increase their enrollments, these schools often seek to attract fundamentalist and evangelical students who have little sense of the Wesleyan/Holiness heritage.

One important way to resist absorption into a broad evangelical culture is to revisit one's own institutional identity on a regular basis so that faculty, staff, administrators, and trustees can remember and affirm their heritage. Seattle Pacific University's religion faculty is a case in point. Sensing the possibility of absorption of that school into a broad evangelical ethos, SPU faculty members actively call their school to remember its Wesleyan/Holiness origins.[31] Likewise, in 1994, the administration, faculty, and trustees of Northwest Nazarene College inaugurated the Wesley Center for Applied Theology. The center features three components: the Wesleyan Studies Program, Compassionate Care, and the Church Growth and Ministerial Resource Program. According to Richard Hagood, president of Northwest Nazarene College, the

31. Frank Spina has delivered a series of faculty discussion papers on this topic including "Hiding Our Lamp Under a Bushel: The 'Secret' Wesleyan Factor at Seattle Pacific University" (unpublished manuscript, September 11, 1991), and "*Christianity Today* or *The Christian Century*? Where Is Seattle Pacific University headed?" (unpublished manuscript, no date); also, Robert W. Wall distinguishes Seattle Pacific University's Wesleyan/Holiness identity from that of evangelicalism in his review of *Evangelicalism: The Coming Generation,* by James Davidson Hunter, in *Seattle Pacific University Review* 6 (1989): 44-55. Wall defines six characteristics of Wesleyan/Holiness Christian higher education on pp. 53-55.

center's purpose was to "bring the essentials of the Wesleyan/Holiness tradition into creative and redemptive contact with the contemporary world."[32] Such efforts can preserve and renew the Wesleyan/Holiness tradition.

The lifeblood of the Wesleyan/Holiness tradition flows through the three arteries of the Wesleyan quadrilateral as a theological method, the emphasis on sanctification and holy living, and social holiness. Schools within the tradition must not allow these arteries to become clogged through cultural absorption into the larger movements of evangelicalism or liberalism.

32. Letter from Richard Hagood, president of Northwest Nazarene College, to Susie C. Stanley, January 9, 1994. Subsequently, Point Loma Nazarene College has established the Wesleyan Center for 21st Century Studies.

The History and Character of Messiah College, 1909-1995

Douglas Jacobsen

Messiah College was founded by the Brethren in Christ Church in 1909 as a denominational high school and missions training institute. The school began to offer college-level instruction in 1920, but did not develop a four-year baccalaureate program until 1951. The college remained quite small until the early 1960s when it enrolled just over 200 students. Current enrollment is well over 2300. A strong connection is still maintained between the church and college, a connection that has been defined since 1972 in terms of a covenant relationship. Messiah College is located in south central Pennsylvania near the state capital of Harrisburg on 300 acres of rolling hills bisected by the Yellow Breeches Creek.

The founding denomination of Messiah College, the Brethren in Christ, was born during the late eighteenth century as part of the pietistic awakening that was stirring through the German-speaking community of Pennsylvania. Many of the original members of the new church had been Mennonites; others seem to have been Moravians and Quakers. Near the end of the nineteenth century, the Brethren in Christ would add an explicitly Wesleyan and Holiness understanding of the Christian faith to their religious profile.[1]

1. See Martin H. Schrag, "The Brethren in Christ Attitude Toward the 'World': A Historical Study of the Movement from Separation to an Increasing Acceptance of American Society" (Ph.D. dissertation, Temple University, 1967); and Carlton O. Wittlinger, *Quest for Piety and Obedience: The Story of the Brethren in Christ* (Nappanee, IN: Evangel Press, 1978).

While Messiah College is thus properly classified as a Wesleyan institution in the present study, the history of its founding denomination indicates that the religious identity of the school has always been somewhat eclectic and open to new theological input. Wesleyan emphases at Messiah College have existed in a symbiotic, hybrid relationship with other religious ideas and ideals. The most frequently repeated description of the heritage of the college identifies three religious roots: Anabaptism, Pietism, and Wesleyanism. In more recent years, the evangelical movement has also had a deep impact on both the college and its founding denomination.[2]

Messiah College has been shaped by the culture of the Brethren in Christ as well as by the church's theology. A pattern of intermarriage and communal separatism led the Brethren in Christ to develop a distinctive "ethnicity" early in their history. The overarching configuration of Brethren in Christ faith is perhaps best described as an *"Ordnung"* — an Amish term describing a community's total way of life. Like the Amish (and in contrast to "creedal" Christian churches), the Brethren in Christ never conceived of Christian faith as a set of beliefs amenable to articulation in a single creed. The Brethren in Christ have also eschewed the radical individualism of some American Protestant traditions. Rather, faith is seen as a communal way of life, developed slowly over time, that has guided the faithful in their attempts to live out the gospel.

This "ethnic" identity was characterized by (among other things) simplicity, humility, and the shunning of frivolity. The Brethren in Christ were also a peaceable people who sought to avoid (or sometimes just to ignore) conflict. Finally, they were a spiritual people who strove to be perfect in both their Christian walk and their Christian experience and, as such, they were a spiritually self-confident people, perhaps sometimes to the point of humble arrogance.[3] In addition, there was an earthy, agrarian side to this Brethren in Christ ethnicity that opened their otherwise rather conservative world to innovation in ways that could sometimes be surprising. Enos Hess, one of the early presidents of Messiah, put it this way: "In matters of farming we, as farmers, seem much more liberal than we do in our religious affairs. Our aim in farming is to grow maximum crops at minimum cost. If a self-binder, mower, cultivator, etc. serves our main purpose, we get the new implement and do not give

2. Messiah's complex religious make-up is illustrated in the present volume. Three of the theological pieces included in this book have been written by people associated with the college. Rodney Sawatsky is the current president; Harold Heie was academic dean from 1988 to 1993; and Susie Stanley has just accepted a position in the Biblical and Religious Studies Department.

3. For a more detailed description of the social characteristics of the Brethren in Christ see Owen H. Alderfer, "The Mind of the Brethren in Christ: A Synthesis of Revivalism and the Church as Total Community," Ph.D. dissertation, Claremont Graduate School, 1964.

the question of right and wrong much thought."[4] This capacity for simultaneous conservatism and innovation would also deeply affect the history of the college.

While Messiah College has been shaped by the abiding *Ordnung* of the Brethren in Christ, it is also true that the church itself has had to cope with internal diversity and outside influences throughout its history. Regional differences of opinion and practice have always been visible — differences that were accentuated as members of the church spread out across the country in the late nineteenth century. The influence of Wesleyan/Holiness thinking increased the internal diversity of the denomination as it encouraged a more individualistic understanding of the Christian faith in some members. In the twentieth century, the evangelical movement has had a marked influence within the church, flattening out some of the church's older distinctives and replacing them with a pan-evangelical sense of Christian faith. As a result, many contemporary Brethren in Christ congregations differ only slightly, if at all, from the variety of other more or less evangelical churches that dot the American landscape. Some congregations and individual members of the church, however, continue to stress one or several of the denomination's older religious emphases. It is against this denominational history of communalism, progressive-conservatism, internal diversity, evangelical homogenization, and unevenly retained bits of past identity that the story of Messiah College must be told.

Practical Education for a Suspicious Church, 1909-1934

Messiah Bible School and Missionary Training Home was founded by the Brethren in Christ in 1909. At the time, the denomination had only about 3000 members. Two different groups within the denomination favored the establishment of a school, but for two rather different reasons. One group consisted of those who thought the church needed a school to prepare individuals for the denomination's fair share of the work of evangelism in the world. These Brethren in Christ evangelical "progressives," who had been influenced by the missions fervor of late-nineteenth-century evangelicalism, wanted to use the school to modify the traditional separatism of earlier Brethren in Christ history. Their goal was to get Brethren in Christ young people off the farm and into the work of the gospel.

A second group of Brethren in Christ thought the church needed a school precisely to keep their children down on the farm. Like most turn-of-the-cen-

---

4. "The Sunday-School," *Evangelical Visitor* 19 (March 15, 1905): p. 16, quoted in Wittlinger, *Quest*, pp. 109-110.

tury Americans, they believed that education would be more and more necessary for success in the years ahead. If advanced education was a necessity, then these members of the church felt their only choice was to develop their own denominational schools. Otherwise, they would risk losing their children to other denominations or to mere secularism when they attended non-Brethren in Christ high schools and colleges.[5]

So, Messiah Bible School and Missionary Training Home was launched with a bipolar identity: to provide biblical and ecclesial education for church workers and missionaries and to provide for other Brethren in Christ young people a "secular" program of education that would allow them to enter the general job market "without a handicap as to mental training and moral stamina."[6] Reflecting these mixed goals, Messiah's early curriculum included a variety of general education courses that extended well beyond the limited Bible and ministry training that characterized so many other Bible schools at the turn of the century. The first president, S. R. Smith (1909-16), said Messiah was to be "an institution where the word of God is held up as the main standard of teaching and all secular branches of study are held up and taught as rays emanating from the great center — God."[7]

To some, the "secular" dimension of the school came as a surprise. One Brethren in Christ leader, after seeing a draft of the proposed curriculum, exclaimed,

> For what reason are we to send young people hundreds of miles from home, and at great expense, to engage in secular studies which they could learn more cheaply and effectively in their nearest High School, is more than I can fathom. I may be counted dense, if I fail to find the connection between Bible study and Trigonometry, Geometry, Caesar or Virgil, and the History of the United States.[8]

But other members of the church apparently felt the school was too religious. In 1917, Messiah's Dean Enos Hess (who would serve as president from 1923 to 1934) stated in his report to General Conference that

---

5. For a narrative history of Messiah College including these early years, see E. Morris Sider, *Messiah College: A History* (Nappanee, IN: Evangel Press, 1984), especially ch. 4, "A School Is Launched." See also Wittlinger, *Quest,* ch. 13, "Institutional Beginnings: Education."

6. "Report of the Messiah Bible School and Missionary Training Home," *Minutes of the General Conference of the Brethren in Christ,* May 20-24, 1912, p. 70.

7. "The Messiah Bible School," *Evangelical Visitor* 25 (September 4, 1911): 3, quoted in Wittlinger, *Quest,* p. 299.

8. F. Elliott, "The Bible School Again," *Evangelical Visitor* 21 (November 1, 1907): 6, quoted in Wittlinger, *Quest,* p. 295.

the school carried such a reputation along the line of spiritual emphasis that even brethrens [sic] children are unwilling to attend lest they be caught in the gospel net. It grieves us to think that in some instances the wish of the child has been acquiesced to on the part of the parent.[9]

Numerous other members of the "brotherhood," reflecting the historic anti-intellectualism of the denomination, continued to worry about the very notion of education.[10] All in all, the school enjoyed only moderate support from the denomination.

The institution in its early years constantly had to justify itself to a suspicious church. Several lines of defense were available, but the single most common refrain (and the one that carried the most weight with the practical and hardworking church members) was that the school was training young people successfully for work in church and society. The college's 1928 report to the denomination presented a page of data designed to convince the church of this very fact: 25 percent of recent graduates were in missionary work, 13 percent were teachers, five percent were doing some kind of medical work, and 14 percent were continuing to further their education. The report concluded by stating that "this data gives full proof of the creditable results of a course of study taken under religious influence" and asked parents to reflect on "the difference in probable outcome of the lives of children [had they been] educated under . . . a non-religious, or in many instances, an irreligious environment."[11]

Messiah's close connection with the Brethren in Christ Church was evident throughout the entire structure of the institution, although the school had always welcomed students from outside the denomination. School administrators and faculty were all respected members of the church. Like the church, Messiah stressed the study of the Bible over instruction in doctrine or theology and emphasized pragmatic concerns over philosophic. School "maxims" included in one of the early student handbooks embodied the Brethren in Christ ethos of hard work and community deference:

One should be embarrassed to mention subjects that embarrass others.
While you are putting up with others, remember that they are putting up with you.
Be businesslike; have something to do and be about it.
Do not be caught asking questions about matters that do not necessarily

9. "Report of the Faculty of Messiah Bible School and Missionary Training Home," *Minutes, General Conference of the Brethren in Christ,* May 17-22, 1917, p. 34.

10. See Sider, *Messiah College,* pp. 8-11, and Wittlinger, *Quest,* pp. 120 and 296.

11. "Report of the Board of Trustees, Messiah Bible College," *Minutes of the General Conference of the Brethren in Christ,* June 1, 1928, pp. 41-42.

concern you, the asking of which may prove that you are one of the inquisitive kind.[12]

Students were required to attend daily morning worship (immediately following breakfast), daily chapel, two Sunday worship services, and a mid-week prayer meeting. They also were strongly encouraged to participate in other religious meetings: the missionary circle, the purity association, and the literary society. Revival services were held twice a year, and in connection with the January revival, a denominational Bible conference was run on the college grounds.[13] Messiah Bible College (as the school came to be called in 1924) remained integrally connected to the denomination throughout these early years.

A Policy of Progressive Foot Dragging, 1934-1964

In 1934 Christian Neff Hostetter, Jr., was elected president of the college. (His father had served in the same office from 1917-23.) No dramatic change in the direction of the school was evident that year or for several years to come, but slowly "C. N.," as he was commonly known, began to put his stamp on the institution. That stamp reflected a unique blend of piety and learning that educationally was quite progressive, but that religiously was deeply respectful of the heritage and contemporary life of the Brethren in Christ. Hostetter created and nurtured a kind of family network at the college — one that was almost ready-made, given the familial inter-relatedness of the small Brethren in Christ denomination. It was a patriarchal arrangement, with C. N. as the paterfamilias, but it was also cozy. Students, faculty, and staff all worked together to maintain the campus; they worshipped together both in school chapels and other religious services; and they even canned some of their own food together in the college kitchen. The school was definitely a *"gemeinschaft"* community well rooted in the *Ordnung* of the Brethren in Christ.[14]

Hostetter was concerned about success and envisioned grand plans. (For a while he would even use the phrase "a small school with a great future" as the college's motto.) As early as 1936 Hostetter mused that he was "looking forward to the time when we [would] become an accredited junior college

12. *Student Guide*, 1916, pp. 29-31.

13. For a fuller description of the spiritual life of the campus during these years see Sider, *Messiah College*, ch. 7, "Life in the Spirit," pp. 82-103.

14. For general background on Messiah College during these years see Sider, *Messiah College*, "Part Two: The Middle Years, 1934-1960." For more information on C. N. Hostetter, Jr. see E. Morris Sider, *Messenger of Grace: A Biography of C. N. Hostetter, Jr.* (Nappanee, IN: Evangel Press, 1982).

and eventually a senior college."[15] He also saw the college as the best hope for the future of the Brethren in Christ Church. He believed that the rightful role of the college was to lead the church into the future slowly and carefully — staying far enough ahead of the church truly to lead, but not so far out in front that contact would be lost. Hostetter used to say that the college had to "drag its feet" while it forged ahead so that the church could keep up. But the college also needed the church. Since the school did not have (nor did it want) a creed to keep the school tethered to the gospel, the church acted as a living tether, anchoring the school to its gospel mission. Church and school were thus locked together in a symbiotic relationship of mutual accountability that assigned each its appropriate role.[16]

Messiah also served a constituency that extended beyond the Brethren in Christ church during the C. N. Hostetter years. The 1956 college report to the General Conference meeting of the church, for example, indicates that nineteen denominations (other than the Brethren in Christ) were represented on the campus. Some Brethren thought this diversity was becoming excessive, but the denomination's Board for Schools and Colleges would, in 1957, refer to these non-Brethren students as "tremendous spiritual re-enforcements" for the church and for the work of the gospel in general.[17] School policy regarding non-Christian students seems to have been (somewhat ambiguously) to admit only those unconverted students who expressed a desire to become Christians.[18] Scant data exists regarding the numbers involved, but a poll conducted in 1951 indicated that 166 members of a total student body (college and academy) of 180 identified themselves as Christian believers, five declared themselves not Christian, and nine were unsure of the status of their faith.[19]

Hostetter's educational goals for students brought an enlarged respect for the liberal arts to the campus. He took the ideas and expertise of the larger academy quite seriously, and he recognized that the wisdom of Christian faith needed, at times, to be augmented by the wisdom of mere learning. In "personal reflections" handwritten into his class notes from the Winona Lake School of Theology in 1938, he put it this way:

15. C. N. Hostetter to B. E. Thuma, January 14, 1936, in Sider, *Messiah College,* p. 186.

16. Interview with Kenneth B. Hoover, December 8, 1994. Hoover was a member of the natural science faculty, 1942-77, and dean of students, 1944-56.

17. "Report of the Board for Schools and Colleges, *Minutes, Eighty-Sixth Annual General Conference of the Brethren in Christ,* June 13-18, 1956, p. 100; and "Report of the Board for Schools and Colleges, *Minutes, Eighty-Seventh Annual General Conference of the Brethren in Christ,* June 12-17, 1957, p. 105.

18. The college's 1948 application for accreditation with the Association of Bible Institutes and Bible Colleges states, "We require that our students shall be Christians or express a willingness and desire to become a Christian for admission."

19. Sider, *Messiah College,* pp. 208-209.

To have a clear conception of life in terms of Christianity and a knowledge of God by Christian experience solves the basic problems of life. [But,] a Christian experience and the Christian view do not automatically solve every problem in life.[20]

For Hostetter, faith took care of the big questions, while the more open-ended liberal arts could help mop up the smaller questions that remained.

Later, Hostetter would assign rough percentages to the "faith" versus "knowledge" dimensions of Messiah's curriculum. Responding to an opinion survey distributed to all faculty in the mid-1940s, Hostetter indicated that 65 percent of a student's education should be devoted to "endoctrination" [sic] while only 35 percent should be relegated to student "investigation." Hostetter put "teacher control" of education at 60 percent against 40 percent for "student activity"; "conformity" was scored at 65 percent in contrast to 35 percent for "self-determination"; and "socialized pupils" received an overwhelming 75 percent rating in opposition to the goal of producing "individualized students." But while the school clearly intended to wield a strong educational hand, pure indoctrination was also supposed to be avoided. Hostetter wrote:

We allow initiative but present the basic facts positively from which the student can build a philosophy of life that is Christian and workable. . . . I do not "play up" problems — too great an emphasis of that nature makes pupils "problem conscious" and develops "neurotics." I stress right rela- tionships.[21]

A similar conclusion was expressed at one faculty meeting during this same time period: "We ought not aim to indoctrinate [students], but let them indoctrinate themselves."[22] While the notion of self-indoctrination may make us smile, that is precisely what is always required of "children of the *Ordnung*."

Hostetter wanted the college to be formally recognized as a quality insti- tution within the world of American higher education. As part of this strategy, Hostetter helped found the Pennsylvania Association of Junior Colleges in 1944 and made Messiah a charter member, then completed a University of Chicago master's thesis in 1945 on the topic of the junior college's place in American society. In 1948, Hostetter sought and received approval of Messiah's ministerial training program by the Accrediting Association of Bible Institutes and Colleges. By 1951, Hostetter had changed the school's name (from Messiah

20. Course notes on Philosophy of Christianity taught by H. C. Mason, Winona Lake School of Theology, July 12-19, 1938. C. N. Hostetter Jr. Papers, Messiah College Archives.

21. "Questionnaire" (undated, early 1940s — part of process of writing of philosophy of education for the college). Hostetter Papers, Messiah College Archives.

22. Faculty Meeting, *Minutes*, February 21, 1944.

Bible College to Messiah College), had rewritten its motto ("Christ Preeminent"), and had developed a full-blown four-year baccalaureate program of study, jettisoning the older junior college model he had advocated earlier.

All of this activity produced tension in a school not oriented toward rapid change. In fact, a group of "co-workers" confronted Hostetter on this point in 1950 saying they "would welcome slower progress toward our institutional goals, if this is necessary to insure continuity of policy in reaching them. We must frankly admit that we are laboring under an increasing sense of uneasiness and insecurity."[23] Hostetter, however, diplomatically pushed on and by 1960, he thought the school was ready to apply for accreditation from the Middle States Association.

The result was negative; Messiah was denied accreditation in 1960. In retrospect, this decision is quite understandable. Messiah was still a tiny school. It enrolled only 110 full time students in its four-year programs and the faculty were overworked and underpaid. The school was also still quite parochial — over two-thirds of the students and essentially all the faculty were Brethren in Christ. But, great strides had been made and just three years later, while Arthur Climenhaga was president (1960-64), the college did receive accreditation.

Perhaps even more significant than accreditation as a mark of the school's maturation was the fact that the school no longer had to sell itself purely on pragmatics. Rather than touting the marketability of its graduates for religious and secular employment, the college could (as early as 1951) declare itself a vision-making institution.

> The inclusive aim of the College, then, is to develop a live spirituality, a vigorous intellectuality, a healthy moral tone, a wholesome social attitude, and a strong body — all with the purpose of giving to the individual a vision of the needs of mankind, a realization that he can play a part in meeting those needs, and the power and the willingness to do his part.[24]

The Challenges of Success, 1964-1994

During the thirty years from 1964 to 1994 Messiah College experienced a tremendous spurt of growth and a marked increase in the breadth and quality of education offered at the school. In 1964 the college had less than 250 students; by 1994 the numbers were approaching 2400. The old college campus that contained only a few substantial buildings was expanded and rebuilt into

23. "'Your Co-Workers' to C. N. Hostetter, Jr.," January 26, 1950, Hostetter Papers, Messiah College Archives.

24. *Messiah College Bulletin*, 1951-52, p. 18.

a new spacious and gracious campus with state-of-the-art facilities. In 1968, a branch campus in Philadelphia was added that offered several programs in cooperation with Temple University. Curricular offerings expanded from ten majors in 1964 to over 80 majors today, including several expensive programs such as nursing and engineering. The school now also boasts a reputable intercollegiate athletic program (which was nonexistent in 1964), including nationally recognized soccer and field hockey teams. In almost any way one might measure it, the quality of education has improved dramatically since 1964: the percentage of faculty with earned doctorates has risen from approximately 15 percent to over 60 percent; library holdings have expanded from 16,000 books to over 250,000 catalogued items; and technical and social support services, which were less than minimal in 1964, are now second to none.

Several competing theories exist concerning how to explain this success. The most commonly repeated explanation focuses on the leadership of D. Ray Hostetter (C. N. Hostetter's son), who was president of the college for this entire period. Hostetter was the first president not to enter the office through church leadership. He came to the post through the development office, and as a traditional Brethren in Christ pragmatist he was always concerned about fiscal matters. He knew that any real improvements in the quality of education at Messiah would have to be paid for with real dollars. The question for him was where to get those funds. Hostetter knew that Messiah would be unable to tap into many of the sources of revenue available to other small private colleges such as a wealthy alumni pool or government largesse (the school's religious stance seemed to block this). So he adopted a plan of development based largely on institutional growth which included an implicit understanding that certain areas of budget planning would lag behind that growth.[25] The process of growth itself thus produced additional income for the school as did the economies of scale that resulted from the enlargement of the institution. When this strategy was combined with other fund raising efforts among the Brethren in Christ and the local business community, the school was able to develop a significant financial reserve. Using those resources as a fulcrum, Hostetter was able to leverage the college into the future by improving and expanding the school's physical plant and by developing a new range of academic programs.

Hostetter's thirty-year tenure lends credence to this "presidential leadership" theory, but few think it a sufficient explanation by itself. Some suggest, as an alternate or supplementary thesis, that the real cause of the school's

25. D. Ray Hostetter, "Future Financial Support for Messiah College," memorandum to the Brethren in Christ members of the Board of Trustees and Associates, April 14, 1967. In written correspondence (June 20, 1995) concerning an earlier draft of this chapter, Hostetter indicated that he was here following the lead of what he had been taught by "Dr. Rhoades . . . in Budget Principles and in Funding at Columbia University."

success was a string of strong and very capable academic deans (Carlton Wittlinger, Daniel Chamberlain, H. David Brandt, and Harold Heie). While the president always maintained final authority over the life of the college, these deans ran much of the show during the Hostetter years and a portion of the school's success must be credited to them. A third suggestion is that Messiah's long-term director (later vice president) of admissions, Ron Long, simply did a better job of recruiting students than did admissions officers at competing evangelical Christian colleges. In particular, Long used the networks and publications of the Youth for Christ organization and funneled attention on the growing number of Christian high schools in the region to market the school to a broadened audience of evangelically-inclined youth. Clearly this was part of Messiah's story of success. A fourth hypothesis argues that the school grew almost by chance. During the 1977-78 school year, the college received a large grant (half of a coal mine) that allowed the school to increase its endowment dramatically and subsequently to expand its building program. The newness of the campus, the upbeat sense of progress and growth, and the crime-free safety of the college's rural environment seemed to fill an evangelical market niche in the mid-Atlantic states that no one previously had seemed to notice. Once wittingly or unwittingly ensconced in that niche, Messiah's growth became a self-sustaining cycle.

Doubtless each of these four different theories gets at part of the truth. The point here is not to choose between these interpretations or to try to weave them together into a unified explanation for Messiah's success. The school's progress, like that of almost any successful organization, undoubtedly has been partly intentional and partly serendipitous. The more significant point for this essay is to examine the way Messiah College has handled its success, especially in the areas of church relations, institutional culture, educational philosophy, and identity and market positioning.

The first challenge of success concerned the school's relation to the founding denomination. When Hostetter suggested in 1967 that the college should continue to expand at a rapid rate, he knew that such growth would make "the task of controlling the future of Messiah College as a distinctly Brethren in Christ college . . . more difficult."[26] Because the church could claim only 10,000 members in 1967, it simply could not supply all the new students the college needed. The result was a dramatic percentage decline of Brethren in Christ students at the school. By 1969 Brethren in Christ enrollment had dropped to 38 percent. Four years later it stood at 20 percent (even though almost 60 percent of all Brethren in Christ students enrolled in college were attending Messiah). Today only 6 percent of the student body is drawn from the founding church.

26. D. Ray Hostetter, "Future Financial Support for Messiah College."

These changing numbers were part of a larger pattern that would soon lead Hostetter to suggest that the Brethren in Christ Church and Messiah College needed to develop a new understanding of their relationship. Hostetter argued that broadening the college beyond its Brethren in Christ center was not the same as moving the college away from the church. He further suggested that a new "covenant" relationship could actually improve relations because then "neither the Church nor the College could take each other for granted."[27] His ideas seemed to shock some church leaders, but the realities of the situation were on Hostetter's side. The school was simply becoming too big for the denomination to control or to underwrite the costs of its operation. A formal church-college covenant was drawn up and approved by the church in 1972.[28]

This change in relationship might not have been a problem for many other church schools, but the *Ordnung* form of Brethren in Christ faith had always been based on a communal understanding of Christian discipleship. Individuals were to keep each other faithful in their Christian walk, and on a different level, institutions like the church and the college were to do the same. The new covenant related the church and college in a more formal way that kept communication lines open, but that also made dialogue a matter to be negotiated instead of being simply an institutional fact of life. The warmth, intensity, and ease of the covenant relationship has varied considerably since 1972, but currently the bond between the two institutions seems to be on a significant upswing as evidenced by the 1993 relocation of the denomination's headquarters onto college-owned land adjacent to the campus.

A second challenge that Messiah has had to face falls within the realm of institutional culture. In particular, success seemed to take its toll on the sense of "community" that had previously marked life at the school. As the college staff increased in size, members of the faculty were, of necessity, slowly becoming acquaintances and colleagues rather than close friends. Procedures of decision-making were also impacted. The college was outgrowing the cozy patriarchalism of C. N.'s years, and the bureaucratic patriarchalism that was coming to replace it sometimes produced tensions between faculty and administration — even to the point of raising quasi-moral questions about the way people were acting. For example, a 1973 faculty report states, "Relationships in a community like ours suffer when we deal with each other in 'un-

27. See D. Ray Hostetter to Dr. Owen H. Alderfer, October 27, 1970, and D. Ray Hostetter to Bishop Henry A. Ginder and others, June 22, 1971.

28. For the original text of the covenant agreement see "The Covenant between the Board of Trustees of Messiah College and the General Conference of the Brethren in Christ," *Minutes, 102nd Annual General Conference of the Brethren in Christ Church*, June 28 to July 2, 1972. Various points of the covenant have been re-negotiated over the years since then.

derhanded' ways. It is high time we become more open, more honest, and put 'our cards on the table.' "[29]

It is somewhat difficult to evaluate the actual state of affairs regarding "community" at the college during this time. Numerous off-campus visitors commented on the warm collegiality that existed at the school.[30] If community was on the decline, it was certainly not by intention. But *gemeinschaft* can only be stretched so far, and Messiah was reaching a size at which it was becoming impossible to maintain the previous intimacy of the campus. At a place like Messiah, where C. N. Hostetter had once claimed that "right relationships" were more central to the institution than fine points of religious doctrine, frustrations about community have flourished. In a certain sense this has been an institutional strength. Being a good college — even an excellent one — has never been seen as a sufficient goal; friendliness has always been a necessary additional criterion of success. The school's emphasis on community, however, has sometimes also had a downside — the stifling of debate and the ignoring of real conflict (characteristics that have also been part and parcel of Brethren in Christ ethnic culture). As such, community has sometimes inhibited the free range of inquiry and argument that is so central to the academic enterprise.

A third challenge of success has been to articulate the school's evolving philosophy of education. Earlier, Messiah College had operated out of a modified indoctrinational understanding of the educational process. As the school's student body grew in both numbers and Christian diversity, the denominational-indoctrinational model of education was becoming less appropriate. In 1966, a faculty committee charged with developing a new educational philosophy produced a working draft which argued that the primary goal of Christian education was "to free the mind for redemptive service." In order for this to happen, education at Messiah College would need to "inculcate in the student the spirit of a scholar, impelling him through life in an unending enterprise of adventure toward the liberating light of knowledge." It was further argued that this academic "adventure involves a certain kind of risk . . . [and was] thus improperly conceived as an attempt to 'hold our own young people,' to shelter evangelical youth from the corrupting influences of our age, to inspire them with a personal piety, or to 'defend the faith once delivered to the denominational saints.' "[31]

29. Study Committee on Internal Governance, *Minutes,* February 17, 1973.

30. See, for example, *Research and Action,* the Third Annual Progress Report of the Project on Student Development at Selected Small Colleges, Arthur W. Chickering, director (March 31, 1968); William Hannah, Jack Lindquist, and Charles Stannard, "Interim Report of the Strategies for Change and Knowledge Utilization Project" (January 1973); and the "Report to the Faculty, Administration, [and] Trustees of Messiah College" by the Middle States Association Evaluation Team (November 1972).

31. "Report to the Faculty of Messiah College by the Study Committee on a Philosophy of Christian Higher Education," Faculty Meeting, *Minutes,* January 13, 1966.

Neither the faculty nor the administration were ready for a statement that was this radical and they toned the document down considerably. An alternative statement was developed that defined education as "the process by which the individual's subjective experience and overt behavior are modified by his interaction with his environment. . . . It is the deliberate bringing about of changes in other persons in a general direction which is thought desirable by those who teach." This traditional and hierarchical approach was balanced, however, by a new recognition of the complex tensions that could exist between faith and learning. The school was defined as both a "community of faith" and a "community of learning" and, accordingly, every faculty member needed to be both a "practical theologian and a critical analyst" to help bridge the gap between the two.[32]

The atmosphere of education at the institution was not to be defined only by these philosophic documents, however. Real life intruded into the debate when the dismissal of a controversial new member of the faculty occurred in 1967. One of the reasons for dismissal seems to have been the content of this young professor's classroom teaching. Questions about academic freedom were raised by some members of the faculty, and responses came from Dean Carlton Wittlinger and later from the Dean and President Hostetter together. These administrators worried that many Messiah College students came "from relatively unsophisticated backgrounds" and were not ready for academic "'shock' treatment." Nonetheless, the president and the dean argued against indoctrination in the classroom and on behalf of academic freedom. Their bottom line was that the college could reasonably "expect that students [would] not be 'indoctrinated against' its basic theological affirmations."[33]

This policy of constrained, but encouraged, academic freedom has largely prevailed to the present. Many of the "hot button" issues that have troubled other relatively conservative Christian colleges have not been issues at Messiah. Specific items like evolution and biblical criticism have rarely become points of contention for faculty members who were otherwise generally respectful of the school's religious stance. One could push at the academic edges as long as one remained visibly deferential to the core commitments of the school. A similar range of academic freedom has become available to students as well. In place of the old pattern of teacher control, the 1982 statement of educational philosophy states, "the learner is at the center of the educational process" and ultimately the goal of education is the "integrity and actualization of 'self.'"[34]

32. "The Philosophy of Higher Education at Messiah College," September 1967.
33. See Carlton O. Wittlinger, "The Integrity of the Christian College," Faculty Meeting, *Minutes,* November 20, 1967; and D. Ray Hostetter and Carlton O. Wittlinger, "A Statement of Administrative Position Presented to the Messiah College Faculty," January 8, 1968.
34. See "Messiah College Philosophy," Faculty Meeting, *Minutes,* March 22, 1982.

The final area of challenge facing the college as a result of its growth and success was the overarching issue of identity and "market positioning." American higher education is a competitive endeavor and schools rise and fall largely based on their ability to attract capable students away from other colleges and universities. As long as Messiah College had remained a small, denomination-ally-oriented college, it had rather easily avoided the pressures of the academic market place. With the college's decision to grow, however, those market realities began to make a greater and greater impact on the life of the institution. Along with asking what kind of school Messiah ideally ought to be, the leaders of the college also had to ask what kinds of students the school could reasonably attract. Answers to these pragmatic questions would not necessarily undermine the general ideals of the school, but they would significantly bend the orientation of the college away from the particular Wesleyan and Anabaptist evangelicalism of the Brethren in Christ tradition toward a more homogenized form of evangelical Christianity.

In 1979, the college articulated five "essential values" that were to describe the basic character of the school. A prefatory statement argued that these values were derived from "a synthesis of [the] Pietist, Anabaptist, and Wesleyan traditions" that had informed the founding identity of the school — a claim that was repeated in the college catalog for several years. The five included: the unity of faith and life; the importance of the person; the significance of community; disciplined and purpose-directed living; and service and reconciliation. While these values can sound rather platitudinous when expressed in this shorthand form, the longer explanation that accompanied the original statement provided Messiah College with an important contact point with the school's past — a bridge of identity that seemed capable of carrying much of the pre-1960s character of the school into the 1980s and beyond. These five values tried to restate and update the old *Ordnung* of the school, distilling general principles of behavior but avoiding most of the older parochialism.

This attempt at underscoring the particularity of Messiah's identity as a Christian college was relatively short-lived, however, and was soon overwhelmed by the language of homogeneous American evangelicalism. Nowhere is this more blatantly evident than in how the college's five essential values were reframed in the college *Catalog* in 1986. In that year, the introduction section to these very same five values were given an "evangelical" context. The statement read: "Messiah College is committed to quality higher education within the evangelical Christian college tradition. Within that tradition the curricular and communal values of the College include the following distinctives."[35] This sudden change in language — substituting the phrase "the evangelical Christian college tradition" for "the Pietist, Anabaptist, and Wesleyan traditions" — is

35. *Messiah College Catalog,* 1986-88, p. 5.

symbolic of what was happening to the college at large. Messiah seemed more and more to be trading its particular and historically informed religious identity for a new and largely ahistorical evangelical identity. Various "champions" of the school's particularly Anabaptist and Wesleyan distinctives continued to speak up, but they often expressed frustration that the college seemed to be moving irreversibly beyond its past markers of identity.

It would misrepresent the truth to drive a wedge between Messiah's history and the broader currents of American evangelicalism. The college had always been evangelical in the sense of emphasizing the importance of the Bible as a guide for Christian faith and practice, the centrality of Jesus' atonement for human sin, and evangelism as one of the primary missions of the church. The Brethren in Christ church had joined the National Association of Evangelicals (NAE) in 1950, and C. N. Hostetter attended the annual meetings, holding several leadership positions in the organization. Arthur Climenhaga actually resigned the presidency of Messiah College in 1964 to take over the job of chief executive officer of the NAE. Yet the church and the college had always been a little leery of the total package of evangelicalism. C. N. Hostetter, in fact, was known for his willingness to confront the NAE about its militarism, a position out of sync with his church's historic pacifism. While most people associated with the college would consider themselves "evangelical" in what they saw as the best sense of the term, not everyone wanted to be known as a card-carrying "Evangelical."[36]

The college's shift toward a more homogeneous evangelical posture, however, did facilitate successful student recruitment. Starting in the early 1980s, the college began to target more aggressively the graduates of the many Christian high schools springing up across the country, partly because the parents of these students had already demonstrated their willingness to pay for a Christian education and "some thought that this would make them more likely to pay for college at a place like Messiah — as long as we were in the evangelical mainstream."[37] This strategy helped the college buck the trend at American colleges and universities as it continued to grow throughout the decade despite the declining college-bound student population. The net result was that by the early 1990s the college had a more denominationally diverse student body than ever, but also a student body that was more homogeneously evangelical and more politically conservative than ever before.[38]

36. Interviews with Kenneth B. Hoover, December 8, 1994, and June 12, 1995.

37. Information supplied by James Barnes (vice president for student development, 1980-95) in a written response (June 12, 1995) to an earlier draft of this essay.

38. In recent years more than 90 different denominations have been represented in a student body drawn from 39 states and 21 foreign countries. Recent data from the Cooperative Institutional Research Project supplied by Ronald Burwell, Assistant Dean of the Faculty at Messiah, indicates that in 1993 Messiah students labeled themselves as politically "con-

The story among the faculty members of the college was somewhat different. As the student body grew, more and more faculty also needed to be recruited, and most would come from outside the old Brethren in Christ circles. As a natural result, denominational diversity of the faculty grew at perhaps an even more marked rate than that of the students. These were also a different breed of faculty. As late as 1960, most of the male faculty members had been licensed or ordained Brethren in Christ ministers and many of the women faculty had been missionaries. The younger faculty being hired were not, by and large, former ministers and missionaries; increasingly, they were academic specialists. These younger faculty were also a diverse lot theologically. While most would call themselves evangelicals of one stripe or another, their evangelicalism ranged (and this was the result of a deliberate hiring strategy)[39] throughout the entire breadth of that category.

All in all the situation was ripe, by the end of the 1980s, for a moderate crisis of identity to emerge at the college. The student body diverged (but not far) from the historic center of gravity of the school in one direction, the faculty diverged (but not far) from the school's heritage in a number of different directions, and the paper documents of the college regarding the school's identity were fuzzier than ever before. What is more, the college board decided at this same time to cap enrollment at 2400 students. This meant that the school now had to consider questions of institutional priorities which had not surfaced during the school's period of growth when all the divisions of the school could plan on annual budget increases.

Back to the Future

As D. Ray Hostetter approached his retirement from the presidency of the college, his actions seemed to reflect a growing sense of uneasiness with the possible trajectory of the college. On the one hand, Hostetter was concerned that the college not lock itself into a mode of operation that might hinder its flexibility in the future. But he also expressed on occasion a fear about the danger of "drift" at the college. The primary focus of this concern seemed to

---

servative" (60.7 percent), "middle of the road" (30.6 percent), and "liberal" (6 percent). Comparative national college figures for 1993 were "conservative" (21.4 percent), "middle of the road" (49.9 percent), and "liberal" (24.7 percent).

39. Information supplied by James Barnes, vice-president for student development, 1980-95. Barnes wrote that former academic dean H. David Brandt would often say something along the following lines: "If evangelicalism represents this part of the spectrum of Christianity (and he would hold his hands 2 feet apart like he was measuring a fish), then we try to have all aspects of the spectrum represented on the faculty."

be upon the faculty, and Hostetter and the Board of Trustees began to talk of the need for a college "identity committee" at the same time as they launched a reexamination of tenure policies.

Needless to say, faculty anxiety increased during this period. In an attempt to assuage those fears and turn things in a more conversational direction, the academic dean of the college, Harold Heie, organized a forum where the issue of institutional identity was approached in the style of an academic conference: position papers were written, critical responses were offered, and open discussion followed. A tone of collegiality was set for discussion of the topic.[40] That tone was altered dramatically in the fall of 1993 when D. Ray Hostetter announced the dismissal of Dean Heie for reasons of "lack of deference to the President and Board."[41] Vagueness surrounded the whole process, and the 1993-94 school year dragged on in what can only be called a depressed state.

In the midst of all this, a new trustee-initiated Institutional Identity Committee was, in fact, constituted in the spring of 1994. Some on the campus saw in this new committee the mechanism for what they feared might be a significant narrowing of the theological options allowed at the college. Others saw it as a last chance to turn the school back from incipient "liberalism." As things have turned out, the Institutional Identity Committee has taken upon itself a much more neutral charge. The committee first constituted itself a fact finding body and only subsequently took on the role of trying to help the college consensually to articulate a new statement of institutional identity and mission.

The work of the Institutional Identity Committee is not yet finished (its work is slated for completion by the fall of 1997), but certain things about the future of the school already seem clear. Perhaps most apparent is the fact that Messiah College will need to be more self-conscious in the way it describes its identity and mission in the future. The college can no longer assume that either the bonds of family and friendship, or the vagaries of the student market place, will provide a natural and clear identity for the school. Such self-consciousness of identity ought not to be seen as entailing a necessary narrowing of options or opinions at the college. The current diversity evident in the student body and faculty is rooted in a long trajectory of institutional development and is seen by most people associated with the school as a good thing. Growth in diversity at the college will likely continue in the years ahead. Given this situation, Messiah College needs to develop new ways of affirming both its historically-rooted particularity and its contemporary diversity.

Actually, those developments are already underway. Upon the retirement of D. Ray Hostetter at the end of the 1993-94 academic year, the Board of

40. See Heie's essay in this volume on his understanding of the role of conversation.
41. Interview with Harold Heie, June 21, 1995.

Trustees selected Rodney Sawatsky as the new president of the college. Sawatsky is the first non-Brethren in Christ president of the college. He is a Canadian Mennonite who has an earned Ph.D. in American religious history from Princeton University. When first introduced to the faculty, he described himself as an evangelical Christian who had been deeply steeped in the Anabaptist tradition but as one who had also drunk refreshingly from the wells of mainline Protestant, Catholic, and Orthodox spirituality. In his inaugural lecture he argued,

> The Brethren in Christ who founded Messiah College [had] a holistic vision of the Christian personality and of the Christian Church. This denomination combines the social and cultural critique of the Anabaptists with the personal experience of faith of the Pietists and the disciplines and holy living of the Wesleyans. Christianity for the BIC [i.e., Brethren in Christ] is multi-dimensional. It is a dynamic, daily response to God. It is a non-dogmatic, embracing piety. Messiah College has moved beyond its BIC roots to include a broader faculty and student community. Yet, these historical BIC connections remain strong and need to be strengthened. And in keeping with the BIC tradition, Messiah today represents an ecumenical, evangelical Christian spirit — a spirit which does not erect walls but rather builds bridges between Christian communities and the larger world.[42]

The vision Sawatsky expresses here is one of ecumenical particularity — a blending of specificity and diversity. This seems to be a vision that fits the college's current makeup. It is also in harmony with the long history of the school. The hope is that Messiah College will be able to negotiate this two-lane road with real integrity regarding its heritage and with deep respect for the valid diversity of viewpoints that ought to be present in any genuinely truth-seeking Christian educational institution.

42. Rodney J. Sawatsky, "Renewing Our Minds, Transforming Our World," *Bridge* 86 (December 1994): 6.

Point Loma Nazarene College: Modernization in Christian Higher Education

Ronald Kirkemo

Point Loma Nazarene College is one of eight Nazarene colleges in the continental United States. It is the largest of the eight, currently enrolling 2459 students. They represent 49 denominations. There are 122 full-time faculty in seventeen departments. The college's mission is to provide education in the liberal arts and preparation for service and leadership in selected professions in an environment of vital Christianity in the evangelical and Wesleyan traditions. The 90-acre campus is located in San Diego, California, in the Point Loma neighborhood, on the bluffs overlooking the Pacific Ocean.

The mission of Point Loma Nazarene College is to provide a liberal arts education in an environment of vital Christianity in the evangelical and Wesleyan traditions. The liberal arts ideal is more than breadth in knowledge; it is a state of mind that rejects narrow and set answers. It seeks to impact intrinsic values through moral reflection on the great issues of life. Liberal arts education expects knowledge to expand, paradigms to shift, and interpretations to change; to that end it promotes creativity, exploration, and discovery of new knowledge. It seeks intellectual coherence, but without dogmatism.[1]

One would expect the Wesleyan tradition to be comfortable with liberal arts. Intellectually, its epistemology places high value on reason and experience.

---

1. This definition of liberal arts is developed in my book *For Zion's Sake: History of Pasadena/Point Loma College* (San Diego: Point Loma Press, 1992), pp. 1-4.

Wesley was influenced by Lockean inductive reasoning and by the Eastern Church's emphases on deification or divine transformation. Theologically, two of Wesleyanism's prime categories are freedom and grace. Wesley emphasized the dynamics of prevenient grace rather than static and regulatory common grace. In his view people and constructed social orders can resist and constrict grace to minimal levels if not extinction, and also open up and accept grace in increasing abundance until it transforms lives and societies. Free will means life is not predetermined; God's sovereignty does not overwhelm life, society, and history. Thus, moral reflection, exploration, and creativity can be valuable means of grace in allowing individuals to see beyond themselves and the empirical world.

Further, Wesleyan thought is *conjunctive*, holding together East and West, piety and learning, experience and thought, transcendence and imminence. Wesleyan thought is comfortable with paradox, with a broad understanding, and with diversity and differences within the tradition. At its worst, such an epistemology could be a prescription for confusion; at its best, it puts together a broad-gauged multifaceted understanding of life, the world, and the mind of God.[2]

This tradition also holds that religion involves more than cultural values or creedal orthodoxy; it is a robust relationship with the living Lord. Knowing Christ is existential. Beyond that, Wesleyans believe a Spirit-filled life should have social consequences. Wesley's optimism about the transforming power of grace entailed a belief that society can be reformed and made more just. The mandate was not to rule society but to transform it through ministry and through those structural reforms that open up society to the movement of God's grace.

A Wesleyan liberal arts college, then, should combine intellectual flexibility with personal spiritual nurture and growth, and it should be a Christian community that models the social holiness of justice and respect for people. It should be a prophetic community. More than an educational corporation or a warm moral community, it should be a place of constant challenge to the self-interest and self-sufficiency that can pervade the symbols and practices of the broader church and secular worlds.[3]

A college does not exist in isolation. It is a social system of multiple internal and external components, existing in a broader social/intellectual environ-

2. See Samuel L. Dunn and Joseph Nielson, "The Theology and Practice of Wesleyan Higher Education," *Faculty Dialogue* 7 (Fall/Winter 1986-87): 71-82.

3. I take the concept of a prophetic community from Paul Hanson, *A People Called* (San Francisco: Harper & Row, 1986). Hanson distinguishes a prophetic model, a royal model, and a priestly model of community in ancient Israel. Those models are useful in categorizing both the ethos of a campus and the leadership styles of college presidents.

ment. A college is not just a social system in steady-state. These internal and external forces cause change.

Point Loma Nazarene College was born at the turn of the century and embodied the nineteenth-century vision of a private school inculcating students with absolute and unchanging values. Very quickly, however, Point Loma confronted a new American culture based on constant social and intellectual change, driven by industrialization and the new ideas of Darwin and Freud, Lester Frank Ward, and Albert Einstein. It began as a Bible training school, took the name university, and then became a college. From its beginning the college promoted social mobility, and its success inevitably changed its own campus culture within two generations. Any college so conceived and constituted has to modernize.

Modernization means more than simply expanding the curriculum, adding Ph.D.'s, and using sophisticated scientific equipment. Modernization is a change in institutional culture as a college moves from a point of indoctrination in a simplistic and exclusivist one-factor epistemology to a balanced position of holding the multiple sources of truth together in a conjunctive or integrated coherent relationship. This movement to modernization involves change in a number of areas. There is some secularization — that is, movement away from a tight church subculture and engaging the achievements of the broader social/intellectual world — but not secularism — which is another simplistic and exclusivist one-factor epistemology, the belief that all of life is devoid of any transcendent Christian significance.[4] Secularism can be as dogmatic as any religious fundamentalism in its reductionism.

There is, then, a kind of S-curve that represents the move from one-factor indoctrination up through Bible-centered education, to education with the plus factor of Christianity, to a modernized liberal arts college that embodies the higher stages of reasoning and analysis. The goal for an institution like Point Loma Nazarene College is to move toward the top of the curve and remain there, supported by strong religious faith, experience, perspective, and academic integrity. The task then is to avoid rounding the top of the S-curve which would transform it into a bell curve with the other side being that "slippery slope" to secularism as the institution's faith commitments collapse and are replaced with skepticism, then value neutrality, and finally opposition to Christianity. Reaching and living at the top is risky and requires honesty, integrity, and diligence. This model is simple, unable to represent the multiple factors involved in modernization. It does not necessarily represent time, and certainly does not do so inevitability. It does, however, suggest that there are stages of modernization and secularization, and that modernization is a

4. See William M. Greathouse, *Nazarene Theology in Perspective* (Kansas City: Nazarene Publishing House, 1970), pp. 25-27.

process, one that can be aborted, can loop backwards, can be restarted on a new S-curve, or can reach and remain at a fruitful point of balance.

In a modernized Christian college, primitive biblicism is replaced not with secularized disbelief but with hermeneutical pluralism that allows the biblical messages to be critically examined rather than worshipped. Evidence, analysis, and moral reflection replace Christian or secular indoctrination. Professional expertise becomes the norm for faculty recruitment, a dimension as important as, but not a substitute for, the primary priority of Christian commitment. In its institutional and student cultures the college moves from a sectarian subculture to the more cosmopolitan and open-minded mainstream of American culture without succumbing to the opposite temptation toward a secularized elitist subculture. In governance, the college moves from authoritarianism, particularly clerical, through structural differentiation to a collegiality of expertise.

Modernization is not natural and inevitable, because agreement or acculturation to that modernization must occur in all the components of the college — students, faculty, administration, trustees, denominational hierarchy, and constituents. Ideally, the various aspects of change would occur in harmony, reinforcing each other, as the college moves through the stages of traditionalism, preconditions for maturity, and the drive to modernization led by presidents and deans who are carefully chosen examples and witnesses to a life of sanctity.[5]

Such a coherent, compatible, and linear line of progression, however, was not possible for Point Loma Nazarene College.

Early Years of Struggle and Decline

The nineteenth-century holiness movement, manifested in revivals, sprang up around the country and in various denominations and splinter groups. The movement was diverse in leadership, theology, manifestation, and class. The Church of the Nazarene, organized by Phineas F. Bresee, a leader in the holiness movement, temperance crusade, skid row mission work, and other social reform activities, emerged from a union of some of those groups.

Responding to concern among his parishioners that the church organize its own college so its young people could avoid the more extreme holiness

---

5. I take this model of stages toward modernization from W. W. Rostow, *The Stages of Economic Growth* (London: Cambridge University Press, 1960). Such a model is incomplete for a Christian college, for we want also to know about the quality of leadership. On this, see the fine article by John F. Woolverton, "Crossing Frontiers: Theological Reflections on the Writing of a Parish History," *Anglican Theological Review* 69 (July 1981): esp. pp. 247-256.

groups and also those colleges where "the Bible [was] questioned, and Christianity itself [was] dead and formal," Bresee organized Pacific Bible College in September 1902. It operated for eight years with a typical Bible college orientation of memorization of content and homiletical commentary on the Scriptures. Socially it was a typical Victorian college. The founders wanted to build what they called a Bible culture at the college. Reflecting both the Victorian values of its time and the Wesleyan emphasis on free will, and implicitly acknowledging the opportunity for students to "backslide" into sin, students lived under a strict regime.

Of special note, a Mr. LaFontaine taught the course on holiness, using J. A. Wood's *Purity and Maturity* as a text. Whereas one group within the holiness movement, represented by Bresee's close friend and confident C. W. Ruth, emphasized "entire sanctification" and "perfect love" and tended toward a "perfectionism" that needed no further growth, others like Wood emphasized sanctification as a process that should lead toward maturity.

In 1910 the Bible college moved to Pasadena, added a liberal arts college, and became Nazarene University. Two years later the seventy-four-year-old Bresee stepped down as president, and E. P. Ellyson was elected to take his place. If Bresee founded the college, Ellyson brought to the college a coherent educational philosophy. For Ellyson, the purpose of education was moral character, not merely intellectual prowess; character-building was supreme, intellectual development was "incidental." If science and the Bible did not agree, science was wrong. "Only that Astronomy, that Geology, that Biology, and that Psychology which harmonizes with God's revealed truth can be true."[6] In the Ellysonian tradition in Nazarene higher education, because the Bible was regarded as the only source of truth, education was equated with indoctrination. Ellyson and his allies were the "old intellectuals" who rejected modern thought. Ellyson was succeeded in 1913 by the academic dean, H. Orton Wiley, who had a broader view of academic life.

The new denomination was beset by its own extremists advocating moral and intellectual correctness. The on-campus church at Nazarene University was pastored by the well-known holiness evangelist Seth Rees. A darling of the holiness camp meeting and revival circuit, the stout fifty-six-year-old Rees was forceful, emotional, and intense. Convinced that a permanent spirit of revival was hampered by sin in the church, he purged his church of questionable members. Inevitably, Rees created conflict with other Nazarene pastors and with the college, and a major crisis erupted between Rees the revivalist, President Wiley the academician, and Rev. Andrew Hendricks the organization

6. Ethel Westmark Bailey, *That's Enough for Me: The Story of E. P. Ellyson* (Kansas City: Nazarene Publishing House, 1976), p. 40; and Edgar Painter Ellyson, *The Bible in Education* (Kansas City: Publishing House of the Pentecostal Church of the Nazarene, 1913), p. 144.

man. Hendricks and his allies won. President Wiley left, Rees' church was disbanded, and the college went through ten years of struggle and decline. Bresee's vision died as the name was changed to reflect actual realities, from Nazarene University to Pasadena College; the Board of Trustees was henceforth required to be exclusively Nazarene.

The corpulent and convivial professor C. B. Widmeyer was elected president in 1923. A self-made man with dubious degrees, Widmeyer emphasized defensive education to defend the "old faith" against modern thought. He allied himself with the fundamentalists of the 1920s and was involved in the founding of the Association of Orthodox Colleges of California and the national Conservative Protestant Colleges of America. He supported a local pastor who accused the dean and another professor of heresy, both of whom were fired.[7] Submission to the vocal right-wing of the church did not increase students or contributions, and Widmeyer was asked to resign in 1926. Another presidential search led the Board back to H. Orton Wiley. With his election, years of struggle and decline ended.

After World War I: The Impact of Fundamentalism and Legalism

This was a bad time for the college to experience a period of decline. Industrialization and the social dislocations it spawned in the late nineteenth century gave rise to a series of social-intellectual movements that competed with traditional Christianity. By the 1920s, the forces of traditionalism and modernism were locked in mortal social and intellectual combat. Churches again split as fundamentalists demanded a rejection of evolution in the sciences, "higher criticism" in theology, and social engineering in the social sciences.

In this context, the 1924 Nazarene General Assembly was historic for the church. Led by southern delegates, the assembly adopted a series of behavior rules, moving away from Bresee's flexibility toward a legalistic definition of Christian behavior. This "Christ against culture" stance provided the basis for Nazarenes in the interior American "heartland" to become suspicious of a college located in a major urban center like Los Angeles, so close to Hollywood. Concurrently, the C. W. Ruth understanding of sanctification as a "second crisis experience" that "eradicated" the sinful nature in one's life came to

---

7. On Widmeyer see Samuel E. Deets, "A Tribute to a Fruitful Life," *God's Revivalist and Bible Advocate* 87 (January 23, 1975): 1-3; on his degrees see the correspondence between C. B. Widmeyer, H. P. Thomas, and W. B. Dunken in *Widmeyer Collection: Biographical Materials*, Point Loma Nazarene College Archives [hereafter PLNC Archives]; and on "defensive education" see "Constitution and By-Laws of the Association of Orthodox Colleges of California," *Widmeyer Collection: Biographical Materials*, PLNC Archives.

dominance over J. A. Wood's understanding of the second crisis as the beginning of a process of growth toward maturity. These developments helped institutionalize among Nazarenes of the nineteenth century a revivalistic rather than a Wesleyan understanding of holiness.

Wiley, during his years of exile from Pasadena College, had remained active in the church and was present at that Assembly, doing his best to deflect the inroads of fundamentalists among the Nazarenes. Charged with writing the denomination's statement on inspiration, Wiley declared a position of "plenary" inspiration, a position that rejected inerrancy and a "flat" or uniform view of scriptural inspiration. Plenary inspiration held that the Bible was fully but not literally inspired, and was only without error on matters of salvation and Christian conduct. This position provided what Wiley called "elbow room" for the church to properly adjust to, rather than automatically oppose, modern scientific and social thought.

When Wiley returned to the college in 1926, he broke with the Ellysonian tradition and with Widmeyer's flirtation with the fundamentalists, and established a more Wesleyan intellectual foundation, that is, a biblical hermeneutic more conducive to engagement with modern thought. While the churches emphasized revivals, Wiley made systematic theology dominant at the college. This meant that the college and its theology, at least in theory, could remain in open (though fairly narrowly constricted) dialogue with philosophy, new discoveries in science, and the break with deterministic thought in the social sciences.

But such was not to be the case. Overall, the faculty was weak. Committed to hiring only Nazarenes as faculty, the college inevitably placed academic quality secondary to denominational considerations. Faculty preparation was limited to mid-level degrees, often only A.B.'s and B.D.'s. Widmeyer was still employing Bible school style in his college teaching. So was A. M. Hills, an acrid crusader against Calvinism, evolution, and higher criticism, and an equally fervent promoter of postmillennialism. His postmillennial posture put him out of step with nearly all the conservative church world in America after World War I. Further, none of Hills' issues were articles of faith for the Church of the Nazarene. At Pasadena, Hills provoked criticism for his postmillennialism, but Wiley refused to prevent him from teaching it to resistant students.

Social sciences, such as sociology and history, could still be taught at Pasadena College as fields of academic study. In the 1920s, however, conservative denominations such as the Nazarenes, fearing that the social gospel movement might undermine belief in the doctrines of original sin and redemption, underwent a "great reversal," emphasized personal sin and holiness, and rejected concern with social reform. Accordingly, the college's sociologist declined to teach the new paradigms developing as sociology broke with formalistic thought. At the same time, faculty in the sciences roundly condemned evolution, and Joshua Hoover, who taught astronomy and took students to the Mt. Wilson observatory, refused to accept the findings of the observatory that the universe was older than Hoover wanted to believe it was.

Yet there were exceptions to such insular thinking. In the literature department, Robert White taught that truth could be found in great writers like Shakespeare, and he taught literature as a search for truth. Students who had been raised to believe that only the Bible contained truth found White's teaching disturbing. During a two year period when Wiley was absent from campus in the late 1920s, White was fired. When Wiley returned, he rehired White.

Culturally insular and isolated, the college during this period enveloped students with rules and activities that sheltered them from forces in the broader society and kept them focused on preserving religious fervor. Moral character was defined in terms of repressing natural emotions, a strategy that inevitably worked to make revival emotions more fervent. Relations between genders was guarded and formal, but some students invariably found shadows of large trees and other dark places where they could express affection. Most students accepted the social regulations, especially at the beginning of the decade, for these regulations were not particularly different from the rules they had experienced at home.[8]

Revivals were a continuing part of the college's effort to promote a sanctified life. In a setting as small as Pasadena College, they were campus-side affairs that took on a predictable group dynamic. Faculty and students took them seriously, sometimes devoting whole class periods to special prayer for a "mighty tide of salvation to come over the school." Revivals were most intense and demonstrative at Pasadena College when its financial situation was most desperate, and probably represented a particular campus culture rather than true holiness.[9]

The early loss of Brescc and subsequent internal struggles left the college on the verge of financial collapse. It survived by selling off portions of its campus until only 17 acres remained. The college was in desperate straits, but

8. This material is taken from surveys of 1920s graduates conducted by the author, and located in the College History Project files, PLNC Archives.

9. The "mighty tide" revivals, which ceased characterizing revivals in later years, may be linked to the desperate financial and leadership struggles of the early years. The two styles of revival may reflect Walter Brueggemann's concepts of (1) "salvation theology," a theology for those in desperate straits, and (2) "creation theology" which characterizes those who are established and have assets and who are expected to use those assets responsibly. This sociological explanation for the style of revival typical of different decades is certainly not the only explanation for the causes of revivals. But it is helpful for two reasons. It helps explain why revival styles change over time and why a change in revival style does not constitute a difference in spiritual quality.

if it was going to survive, it would do so on its own terms, a commitment that led Wiley to turn down a major donation from George Pepperdine, the man who would found and endow George Pepperdine College in 1937.

Throughout the Depression, the Nazarenes clung to their personalistic conception of holiness, a commitment that had two consequences. First, Nazarenes opposed social reform. While several of the faculty were interested in Upton Sinclair's "End Poverty in California" program, most Nazarenes believed the Depression would be overcome through individual moral reform. Second, the campus ethos remained narrow. For the most part, chapel speakers and revivalists presented the demands of the faith in fearful terms, telling students to be wary, careful, and diligent in protecting their salvation and sanctification. To combat that danger, one's spiritual life had constantly to be renewed or revived to keep intensity high and the campus a distinct subculture. Such an ethos placed narrow constraints on creativity and openness to new ideas, for too much thoughtfulness was thought to jeopardize the simplicity of faith which was needed to sustain the primacy of personal experience. In those days, intellectual depth and coherence were not high priorities since the world would be saved through personal witness, not by reasoned argument.

Academic ambiguity characterized the 1930s. Wiley hired Dr. Olive Winchester to join him in the religion department. Winchester was truly bright, but she was committed to the "hermeneutic of holiness" and so utilized her skills to defend the doctrine of a second work of grace through proof-texting and grammatical analysis of scripture.[10]

In a break with the past, Wiley hired Dr. Adele Steele in sociology. A founder of the local chapter of the Women's International League for Peace and Freedom, Steele stimulated students to think on their own and to understand the structural arrangements of power and injustice. She opened up the world of social reform to students, particularly in the area of criminal rehabilitation. Wiley also hired Dr. Phil Carlson to teach physics, a man who took the college well beyond Ellysonian science. Carlson brought to his science classes the view that "if something is true, it is true because evidence shows it to be true." For Carlson, truth in science was not eternal but was simply the most accurate understanding possible, based on current data.[11]

The war years brought financial relief. World War II ended the depression, so people could (and did) support college fundraising campaigns which ended the college's burden of debt, insecurity, and limited vision. But the war had other effects as well. The number of male students dropped precipitously in 1942 and

---

10. On the hermeneutic of holiness see Leon O. Hynson, "The Wesleyan Quadrilateral in the American Holiness Tradition," *Wesley Theological Journal* 20 (Spring 1985): 22.

11. Taken from Philip R. Carlson, "Christ and the World of Science" (unpublished address delivered at Pasadena College, in *Biographical Files,* PLNC Archives).

1943, leaving ministerial students to dominate the student body. What little opposition there had been to campus regulations now disappeared, and a generation of church leaders formed their view of a Christian college out of their unique position of ministerial dominance of the student body in these years.

While Southern California's urban population and economy grew and modernized after the war, rural areas remained stagnant, and cultural distinctions within the college grew sharper. Additionally, as the denomination moved to a second generation of leadership, it became more concerned to preserve a holy lifestyle on the basis of law rather than grace.[12] "The background of grace is law," General Superintendent H. V. Miller told the students. "You cannot preach grace until you preach law." Wiley, on the other hand, was more moderate and told students that "grace can do at times more than law can do."[13] These currents defined two tendencies that were embodied both in the college and in the church. Between 1948 and 1952, many defined holiness in terms of tightened and expanded behavior codes, particularly with reference to wedding rings and television. Shortly before his death in 1946, General Superintendent R. T. Williams warned, "If we ever have a division within the Church of the Nazarene, it will be over a question of legalism."[14]

From World War II through the 1960s

This was an unfortunate time for the denomination to succumb to legalism, for the dangers of nuclear weapons and nuclear annihilation forced upon the world a reconsideration of the role of human freedom. In this context, Wesley's perspectives on freedom and grace might well have made the Wesleyan tradition even more relevant to Christian liberal arts education and to the world. Writing just a few years after Auschwitz and Hiroshima, Arnold Toynbee called for a new program of action that would lead to a cumulative increase in the means of grace in the world.[15] Would Pasadena College rise to the challenge and resist legalism, become a prophetic model of Christian liberal arts, and use the Wesleyan tradition to better understand and transform the world?

The victory over debt coincided with Wiley's perception that returning soldiers would not qualify for GI benefits to attend the college if it was not

---

12. Timothy L. Smith, *Called Unto Holiness: The Story of the Nazarenes — The Formative Years* (Kansas City: Nazarene Publishing House, 1962), pp. 289-297.

13. Quoted and referenced in Kirkemo, *For Zion's Sake*, p. 139.

14. See Audrey J. Williamson, *Gideon: An Intimate Portrait* (Kansas City: Beacon Hill Press, 1983), pp. 86-88.

15. See Richard Bauckham, "Theology after Hiroshima," *Scottish Journal of Theology* 38 (March 1985): 583; and Arnold Toynbee, *Civilization on Trial* (New York: Oxford University Press, 1948), p. 262.

accredited. The time was finally right for him to move the college forward: the college should not be allowed to secularize by abandoning the great truths of revelation, Wiley told a church audience, nor should it become a narrow Bible College that would dwarf the students by abandoning the great truths of human culture. The college should continue to improve, Wiley argued, in order to achieve two objectives: to teach the principles of Christianity and morality, and to broaden and deepen the minds of students.[16] Under Wiley's leadership, there were significant changes, some intended, others unforeseen. There would be curricular reform, new faculty with a new definition of professionalism, and students who were more affluent and less tolerant of legalism. The years 1944 to 1956 were a dozen years of progress. Wiley laid the foundations for a move to modernization.

Wiley suffered a heart attack in 1948 and had to give up the presidency. His chosen successor was Westlake T. Purkiser. An alumnus who had majored in literature in order to sit under Robert White, Purkiser earned a Ph.D. in philosophy from the University of Southern California where the doctrine of personalism at that time held sway. The doctrine of personalism held that reality is ultimately personal, that a divine personality pervades the cosmos, and that there is rich, empirical meaning in religious experience. Personalism provided a conducive framework in which Christians like Nazarenes might pursue graduate studies, since it was amenable to the belief that God is real and personal and created humanity in His own image. Personalism therefore served Purkiser and his colleagues in important ways. However, personalism lost credibility in the 1950s, thereby helping to undermine Purkiser's achievements. But that is a story to which we will return later.

In the meantime, Purkiser's inaugural address was reprinted in *Vital Speeches*. His goals were to upgrade the quality of the faculty and to socialize the faculty into a campus value structure that made them both pastoral and professional. In a series of addresses, he and his dean laid out five qualities that should characterize Nazarene professors. First, as always, faculty had to be New Testament Christians who had personally experienced the regenerating and sanctifying grace of Jesus. Second, they should understand the three purposes of the college — to conserve and promote the great spiritual truths, to provide leadership in applying those truths to political and social problems, and to create in every student a sense of Christian vocation. Third, teaching should be a hallowed act of communication. Fourth, professional objectivity and detachment should not lead to habitual neutrality in other areas of life. Fifth, Nazarene faculty should cultivate Christian modes of thinking.[17]

16. H. Orton Wiley, "Educational Address," May 18, 1944, *Wiley Files*, PLNC Archives.
17. These addresses were summarized in 1956 in an unpublished manuscript by Paul Culbertson. See "The Effective Nazarene College Teacher," *Culbertson Files*, PLNC Archives.

Though there was no faculty handbook statement on academic freedom, denominational faculty were trusted to have differing opinions so long as they were circumspect in their presentations.

The American economy boomed after the war, strengthening consumer and middle class values, especially in California. Nazarene families shared in this growing economy and many Nazarenes, especially from the Midwest, migrated to California. Some of these merely attached middle class accoutrements onto thinking patterns that characterized their particular subcultures. Others left their subcultures and entered the American mainstream. As a result, the church's constant warnings about worldliness and its too-easy reliance on legalism as holy living fell into disrepute with many students. Those students, as well as students who had not moved beyond fear and legality, were part of the enrollment surge of the 1950s that democratized higher education. Further, tuition was kept very low to allow nearly any Nazarene student to attend a Nazarene college.

In the early 1950s, the college was able to attract significant new faculty — bright Nazarene men and women with earned degrees, despite the fact the college paid its faculty less than churches paid their preachers and less than Pasadena paid its trash collectors.[18] Charles Browning succeeded Adele Steele in sociology, and led the successful effort to have the denomination denounce racial segregation in 1956. Warren Bryan Martin was a gifted teacher who fearlessly raised issues of critical analysis of the Scriptures and who had difficulty tolerating students who refused to examine their own beliefs.

The religion department declined in status in the 1950s, entering a transitional decade between the prominence associated with Wiley and Winchester in the 1930s and the new faculty of the 1960s. In this period of decline in the religion department, Paul Culbertson rose to a point of high influence on the campus. Dean of the College and professor of psychology, Culbertson struggled with denominational terms like "pure love" and "entire sanctification." He saw no models of those terms; nobody living them out. They were abstractions, absolutes. Life, he claimed, is lived in tension between the natural and supernatural. He also failed to understand why holiness preachers who emphasized the guidance of the Holy Spirit should be so concerned with telling people how they ought to live. The moral law of God was written on the hearts of human beings, not in codes of rules.[19] So he began to redefine and operationalize those concepts in psychological terms. His influence was historic, for he reintroduced the purity and maturity themes of J. A. Wood that were

18. On the salary comparisons see Westlake T. Purkiser, "Report to the Board, February 12, 1952" and "Report of the President to the Board of Trustees of Pasadena College, October 12, 1954" in *Purkiser Files*, PLNC Archives.

19. Paul T. Culbertson, *A Hewer of Windows* (San Diego: Point Loma Press, 1991), pp. 15 and 25.

taught in the earlier years of the college, themes that had been lost in the 1920s and buried by legalism in the 1940s.

In the mid-1950s some of the younger faculty sought to organize a faculty council, an effort that conservative faculty and church members linked to Warren Martin, his provocative style, and his willingness to critically analyze ideas like the virgin birth. When a group of four faculty became identified as a threat to orthodoxy, pastors mobilized against them and called upon key trustees to become involved. Purkiser was unable to heal the breach and resigned. The four faculty were terminated. Sympathizers were cowed. Many students were traumatized. Those who criticized those unfortunate events did not bring a return to normalcy but weakened the legitimacy of the institution and strengthened the forces of personality and the polarization of power. Cautious modernization had persisted for twelve years, but had never become fully institutionalized. Nor had the trustees and constituents become accultu-rated to it. The modernization program now seemed to have ended.

What does a church like the Church of the Nazarene want from its college? Probably foremost, it wants to keep the "fires" of personal spiritual experience real among the students. As a corollary, it wants the faith of its young people not to be shaken. Modern thinking may be tolerated, even modern hermeneu-tics, but only if it does not weaken the faith of the students. Third, it wants the concept of holiness kept alive, for that concept was the very justification for the creation of the denomination. Fourth, the church does not want the college to get too far ahead of the church in ideas and values. Nazarenes place a premium on higher education, and though they intellectually subscribe to the liberal arts, practically they tend to expect essential congruence with the established denominational ethos. Finally, the church expects warm feelings from the faculty for the church and its doctrines, and seeks to remain in effective control of the college, thereby preventing it from moving toward interdenominationalism or separation. All these dynamics were apparent in the mid-1950s when the move toward modernization collapsed.

The Board successively hired two men as president over the next seven years. Russell V. DeLong squandered his great talents in an overbearing autocratic style that smacked of royalism. Loyalty and deference were demanded and dissent repressed. Dialogue became dangerous. The trustees replaced DeLong with one of their own — District Superintendent Oscar J. Finch. Finch told the faculty that Christian education was "quality education with the 'plus' qualities of Christianity." The latter was an open avowal of a Christian commitment, an emphasis on the Bible, Christian thought, and biography in all disciplines, and a commitment to a lifestyle of service and moral standards.[20] Yet, Finch never explained how those qualities related to quality education.

20. Oscar J. Finch, "Loyalty to Christ and the Bible," *Finch Files,* PLNC Archives.

Both presidents reflected a new fear that was growing among the trustees. To understand this fear, one must understand changes that had taken place both in the college and in the larger culture. The concept of a Bible culture, which the college was founded to promote, was now gone. In the larger culture, Victorian themes of a mechanical and purposeful universe, notions of humanity as reasoning and rational beings who can decide for God and become perfectly whole, and visions of a stable society with normative standards defended by intellectuals — all these were under siege in the twentieth century. Further, with the demise of the philosophy of personalism in the late 1940s and 1950s, there were no "safe" graduate schools in the Wesleyan tradition — not Emory, not Boston, not even the University of Southern California. With no viable denominational creed or philosophy of education, the trustees felt the need to contain the college and to restrict its prophetic role.

The 1960s brought many changes to the college. In 1964 the denomination's General Assembly voted to create a Bible college and two new junior colleges. The decision reflected concern within the church over the dangers of modernization. One danger was political, a fear or resentment concerning the emergence of "empire builders" — college presidents who were building successful colleges and who were gaining power within the denomination. The other danger was ideological. The church feared that post-war enrollment growth would dilute the small college homogeneity and the religious fervor that had characterized earlier decades when they had attended very small Nazarene colleges. They feared that a revivalistic atmosphere was unlikely in a student body of more than a thousand, and the college might therefore drift from the revival fires of the old faith. To partially compensate the older colleges that were now losing enrollment to the new colleges, the denomination increased its subsidy to the older institutions.[21]

By the 1960s the faculty at Pasadena College no longer typified the Ellysonian "old intellectual" model since many had been trained in the best graduate schools. In the natural sciences and the social sciences, they were professional and pastoral, but they tended not to relate their faith in an intellectual way to their fields. There was the classroom, and there was chapel, or, in the words of the mission statement, there was education and there was atmosphere. This was a style of Wesleyan education, better than its Ellysonian predecessor, but still incomplete.

In 1964 the Board made an historic decision when it chose District Superintendent W. Shelburne Brown as president. Brown brought an administrator's commitment to financial integrity, a leader's willingness to identify with

21. The budget of each local Nazarene church is assessed an amount by its administrative district, and that district then channels a fixed percentage of its budget to the Nazarene college of its educational zone.

the personal lives and academic drives of faculty, and a statesman's effort to define a vision of the future and a master plan for getting there.

During his tenure, Frank Carver taught biblical theology, a departure both from the descriptive-doctrinaire approach of Ellyson, Widmeyer, and Winchester, and also from the systematic theology approach of H. Orton Wiley. Biblical theology is comfortable with historical and literary analysis. With that approach, Carver could resist the use of the Bible for doctrinal "proof texting" and the reemerging fundamentalist movement, while retaining his belief in divine inspiration. Not surprisingly, Brown made him chairman of the religion department.

Brown appointed Reuben Welch chaplain in 1964. While neoorthodoxy prevailed in the School of Religion at the University of Southern California where Welch studied theology, he never adopted neoorthodoxy as his own since in his view, its radical view of sin was not matched by a radical view of grace. From the Old Testament prophets, however, he did gain a heightened appreciation for God's work in history as well as in the lives of individual believers. From his studies of Emil Brunner, his understanding of the prophets, and his talks with students, Welch preached a clear theme: we are human and subject to sin and failure, yet we are the people of God. We live between what we were and what we want to be. Our spiritual life is a journey, not a state of grace. Sanctification is a journey in which God continues to work in our lives to help us through our failures to fulfill His will and to break the pattern of self-sovereignty in our lives. This represented a break with the more traditional Nazarene view of sanctification as a state of perfection achieved through a once-and-for-all second work of grace. Welch also replaced the term "revival" with a "spiritual emphasis week."

What happens when ideas are modified in the way Carver and Welch redefined the central nomenclature of the church? Many constituents loved the changes, and Welch became one of the most popular speakers in the denomination — at churches, retreats, and other colleges. Yet, many pastors worried. One district superintendent organized a letter writing campaign to President Brown, protesting Welch's preaching. A few pastors canceled speaking invitations they previously had extended to Welch. Welch was making spirituality more relevant to that generation than were those who were still tied to the Nazarene subculture of the 1940s and 1950s. President Brown told Welch to keep up the good work!

This new approach to theology coincided with the arrival of Kenneth Frey in sociology and a new generation of students. A pastor and a vocal Goldwater supporter from New Mexico, Frey intended to get his doctorate and use it to legitimize his role as "a voice on the right within the Church of the Nazarene."[22]

22. Letter from Kenneth O. Frey to the author, in *College History Project Files*, PLNC Archives.

Instead, his doctoral work broadened his thinking and led him to embrace structural reform in society. At the same time many students came to the college convinced of the moral correctness of integration. From these new perspectives grew a new concern at the college with social holiness. A variety of consciousness-raising, dialogue, and action opportunities were established that later bore on the issue of the Vietnam War as faculty and students sought to relate their faith in God's activity and presence to political issues of injustice and war.

The Move to San Diego: Broadening and Modernization

Brown developed a master plan for the campus, envisioning the purchase of surrounding land and construction of new buildings. The cost of land was astronomical, but the college had to grow and improve if it was not to stagnate. Suddenly, the California Western campus of United States International University in San Diego came up for sale. Brown felt a clear leading of the Lord and, in turn, led the Board of Trustees in buying it. The purchase was amazingly complex and the move difficult, but Brown was a leader without equal in the Nazarene denomination, kicking down doors that would not open. In the summer of 1973 Pasadena College moved to a 95-acre site on the bluffs above the Pacific Ocean, and became Point Loma College: An Institution of the Church of the Nazarene.

It is risky to move a college. Books and microscopes are easy to move, but not so a heritage and ethos. Many worried about the fate of the college. The continuities were crucial. Holding firm to a view of "plenary inspiration" and to the flexibility modeled by H. Orton Wiley, the college remained free from any need to find Adam's bones or Noah's Ark, or to repeat Joshua Hoover's refusal to deal with the new ideas of science. The religion department could present a God not bound by the figurative language of Genesis or by its spatial conceptions of matter and time. Herb Prince came to teach theology and brought Process Theology as a way to bridge the gap between a transcendent God and the realities of science and society.

In the first years at San Diego, the college hired numerous new faculty since the college was growing and since several had chosen not to make the move from Pasadena. The number of non-Nazarene faculty rose, provoking recurring concern among trustees that a "critical mass" of non-Nazarene faculty not be established. Trustees emphasized that when faculty were recruited, the administration should seek for qualified Nazarenes first, then Wesleyans, and finally those who are in strong sympathy with the college's doctrine and ethos. As had always been true, the specifics of what a professor taught in class were not an issue so long as he or she identified closely with the denomination.

A Faculty Council was organized and a process-oriented ethos developed on campus. Collegial governance gradually replaced presidential dominance.

Continuities among the students were also important. The college had never required students to be "saved" (though overwhelmingly, most were), but the growing student body produced more numbers of unsaved students, and they seemed more visible, especially to those who had opposed the move. Still, the spiritual tone remained high. Welch continued his strong Bible teachings in required chapel. Yet, that was not enough for many students, who organized a variety of new ministry teams, from puppet ministries for children, to Ocean Beach Ministries to feed the homeless, to Wings of Praise to sing in local churches, to a Christian Resource Center that acquired devotional and Bible study books not available in the library.

But discontinuities were also noteworthy. The college had moved from the Los Angeles area, an urban environment where many church-related colleges competed with one another, to San Diego, an environment where it had no evangelical competition. It moved from an area rich with Nazarene churches and alumni to one with far fewer of both. It was a new market, and many students from many denominations welcomed the college and came to it. Enrollment steadily grew, and the percentage of Nazarene students changed dramatically, falling from 80 percent to less than 40 percent. While this shift worried the trustees, they eventually concluded that the college had a wider ministry than simply the education of Nazarene students.

Students and their parents were wealthier in the 1970s, more diverse, and less deferential. In 1982, church leaders sponsored a poll of students in Nazarene colleges. They found the students were theologically orthodox — 96 percent believed in the full inspiration of the Bible, 90 percent believed in the Trinity, 85 percent believed they were saved, and 55 percent believed they were sanctified. What worried the leaders — and the reason the poll was never published — was the clear divergence of this generation's views from the official 1924 rules regarding such issues as movies and dances. A supermajority of 70 percent thought these issues ought to be regarded as matters of personal decision.[23]

The college had never sought to place supportive alumni in the pastorates of churches on its educational zone, a decision which did not help bridge the natural gulf between pulpit and pew that developed during the course of modernization. Once again, a small group of revivalistic pastors grew alarmed at the direction of the college. Because of the large number of non-Nazarene students from San Diego, some constituents derisively referred to the school as a community college. In 1978 President Brown developed cancer and died the next year. For critics of the college, the time was ripe for a change in direction. A small group of district superintendents within the

23. A copy of this study is located in the College History Project Files, PLNC Archives.

board now built a coalition with colleagues who had been students at Pasadena College during World War II. All parties in this coalition felt some unease about the college and now sought to pull it back to the orbit of the older church culture. They wanted a president who not only would be "God's man for the hour" but who also would rebuild personal, presidential control of key aspects of the college and re-establish a traditional Nazarene subculture. They sought a president with a strong devotion to churchmanship, and through him, a renewed emphasis on denominational loyalty and tradition. They found that man in a midwestern pastor, Rev. Bill Draper, who believed the college needed his kind of midwestern and traditional Nazarene cultural values and denominational loyalty. Draper sought to reestablish presidential control, reverse the declining percentage of Nazarene students, renew Ellysonian-style education, and reinforce the linkage to the denomination by elevating the role of district superintendents in the Board of Trustees. He also relocated San Diego First Church of the Nazarene onto the campus and changed the college name to Point Loma Nazarene College. These changes caused alienation both on and off the campus.

Draper died of cancer in May 1983. The trustees felt secure about continued church control, and an older generation of board leaders retired within a few years. The new president was Rev. Jim L. Bond. Bond was an alumnus of the 1950s, a former pastor and missionary who strongly reaffirmed a commitment to the liberal arts, to the faculty, and to collegial decision-making processes. With an earned doctorate, Bond supported academic progress and placed special emphasis on spiritual development. He created the new position of director of spiritual development, and under Rev. Norman Shoemaker, chapel became more attuned to the youth culture. Shoemaker established multiple ministry projects, especially mission teams destined for Brazil, Albania, and Russia. This emphasis found widespread positive response among a new generation of students, heirs of the disillusionment with social reform that characterized the waning years of the 1970s.

Though most faculty currently feel alienated from what they see as a "Christianity lite" ethos in chapel, students bristle at the suggestion that their generation is spiritually shallow.[24] Eighty-three percent of the entering freshmen report themselves as born again, and over half the students find that chapel contributes most to their spiritual growth, while classroom instruction makes "some contribution."[25] At the same time, President Bond continues to

24. This sentence is based on discussions with faculty and students by the author.

25. PLNC Planning and Institutional Research Office. The data on freshmen comes from an annual survey by the Higher Education Research Institute's 1993 Student Information Form, and the data on chapel comes from the additional questions section of the HERI's 1993 College Student Survey, taken annually at PLNC by graduating seniors.

urge students to remember that a college is an intellectual institution and not to lose belief in the primacy of the classroom.

Conclusions

The faculty increased in size and sophistication in the 1970s and 1980s, a fact represented by a sharp increase in awards, publications, and professional activities. Still, these reflected little overall intellectual vision among them. Then, in the late 1980s and early 1990s, many faculty shifted their interest from being "new intellectuals" to being "Christian intellectuals," to finding new ways to bridge the two cultures of Wesleyan faith and academic expertise. In response to requests from some faculty, Herb Prince taught a voluntary semester course for faculty on Wesleyan theology and perspectives. The next year 20 percent of the faculty participated in a voluntary study of environmental issues from an explicitly Wesleyan perspective. The college also established a Wesleyan Center for 21st Century Studies, designed to fund conferences and faculty study projects that would address specific issues over the next quarter-century from a Wesleyan perspective of grace and freedom. As part of that effort, a new course in "Wesleyan Theology in the 21st Century" was developed primarily for faculty.

The college had moved from salvation theology to creation theology in which it was managing its intellectual assets for greater service to the Kingdom. With these structures, Point Loma Nazarene College had moved to a new plateau, a new balance and relationship between Christian faith and modern academics. It had built strong structures of academics coupled with strong structures of grace. Those structures included denomination-only trustees, a preponderantly Nazarene faculty, required and relevant chapel, a strong spiritual development program, a dynamic or plenary approach to scripture, and a Wesleyan epistemology.

THE BAPTIST AND
RESTORATIONIST TRADITIONS

What Can the Baptist Tradition Contribute to Christian Higher Education?

Bill J. Leonard

Baptists are an unruly lot. Their theology, polity, and overall diversity create the possibility, if not the probability, for continued debate, controversy, and division. Nowhere is this more evident than in the Baptist response to education.

On one hand, Baptists long have affirmed the value of education for clergy and laity alike. Throughout their history they established schools which promoted Christian education among a predominantly Baptist constituency. Early in the American experience, Baptists founded academies and colleges, many of which became prominent liberal arts institutions.

On the other hand, many Baptists have remained suspect of education, or educational institutions, fearing that the "wisdom of this world" would inhibit genuine faith. Some rejected formal education altogether, while others worried that certain kinds of education might undermine personal piety and religious devotion. Some of the most significant controversies in Baptist life have centered around the role of education and educational institutions within a particular faith tradition.

Such debates should not be dismissed as mere conflicts between the forces of intellectualism and anti-intellectualism, however. They raise important questions as to the nature of Christian education itself. It would be far too simplistic to suggest that Baptists were anti-intellectual because they feared learning as such (although some probably did). Rather, throughout their history they have struggled continuously with the relationship between faith and learning, academic integrity and doctrinal orthodoxy, ideology and pragmatism.

Theologically, Baptists reflect a variety of traditions, with influences from both classical and populist dogma. Confessions of faith delineated basic beliefs. Yet a powerful concern for freedom of conscience and the priesthood of all believers made many Baptists hesitant to impose extensive doctrinal require-ments on educators and educational institutions. That concern for freedom of inquiry meant that Baptists often created learning environments which moved beyond stereotypical parochialism, introducing students to a wide range of academic insights and methodologies. Defining and adhering to "Baptist Doctrines," however, often created dilemmas for those who con-fronted multiple constituencies, each claiming to represent the true Baptist orthodoxy. Controversies often erupted as educational institutions moved toward broader instructional programs which introduced issues of religious, literary, or scientific pluralism, challenging traditional dogmas and world views.

At the same time, Baptists, particularly the Southern Baptist variety, were shaped by particular social, political, and economic environments. Throughout much of the nineteenth and early twentieth centuries, Southern Baptists represented something of a *de facto* religious establishment, dominat-ing the religious landscape. That cultural and numerical hegemony meant that Baptist schools had an extensive potential clientele spread across the region, willing to send their young people to a college which bore the Baptist name. This constituency included the "gentlemen theologian-pastors" in the urban centers and the "farmer-preachers" in the rural backwoods. While they agreed on the need for education, they often disagreed as to the content of the curriculum at Baptist schools. Likewise, Southern Baptists were economic and ecclesiastical pragmatists who sought to use education to better their social and financial standing in the broader society. Fiscal realities led them to develop varying pragmatic responses necessary for maintaining institutions.

What, then, is the nature of Baptist higher education? What is the Baptist contribution to American higher education? How does education at a Baptist college or university differ from that offered at any other academic institution? Historian Mark Noll writes, "True, evangelicals have often contrasted the institutions of the Spirit with the mechanics of worldly learning. There may exist, however, a genuinely Christian justification for this contrast that need not lead as directly to intellectually disastrous consequences. . . ."[1] On the threshold of the twenty-first century many Baptists continue to struggle with the meaning of "Christian education" in institutions which claim Baptist identity in one form or another.

This chapter surveys the Baptist tradition of education with particular concentration on the development of institutions of higher learning. It sug-

1. Mark Noll, *The Scandal of the Evangelical Mind* (Grand Rapids: Eerdmans, 1994), p. 12.

gests that many Baptists continue to live in two worlds, at once committed to and suspicious of higher education and its impact on Christian faith. That tension illustrates something of the Baptist contribution to education. While some attention is given to the Baptist tradition in general, primary focus is on the Southern Baptist Convention, the largest Baptist (and Protestant) denomination in the United States.

The Baptist Legacy: A Historical/Theological Overview

Baptists trace their origins to a group of seventeenth-century English Separatists who immigrated to the Netherlands to escape persecution from the Anglican Church. Led by John Smyth (ca. 1565-1612) and Thomas Helwys (ca. 1550-1615), they constituted a church around the year 1609 on the basis of a covenant between God and those believers who claimed faith in Christ. They insisted that baptism be administered only to those (adults) who could testify to an experience of divine grace.

Both Smyth and Helwys were well educated individuals; Smyth received the M.A. from Cambridge in 1593 and Helwys was admitted to Grey's Inn, the British legal society.[2] They produced an extensive collection of writings, many stressing the issue of freedom. Indeed, historian Robert Torbet described Helwys' fourth work, *A Short Declaration of the Mistery of Iniquity,* as "the first claim for freedom of worship to be published in the English language."[3] Smyth, Helwys, and their followers are known as the General Baptists because of their support for Arminian views on free will and the general atonement. They believed that Christ died for the entire race, not merely for a preordained elect.

A second Baptist tradition began in England in the 1630s among the Independent or Congregational Puritans. Known as Particular Baptists because of their Calvinist theology, they insisted that Christ died only for the elect whom God had chosen for salvation before the foundation of the world. Their acceptance of believers' baptism led to the break with the Puritans by 1638. Like their Arminian counterparts, many of these Baptists were well educated with degrees from Cambridge and Oxford.

By the 1630s, Baptists found their way to the American colonies. Roger Williams (ca. 1603-1684), a Puritan teacher and preacher, came to Massachusetts in 1631, only to be exiled in 1636 for his views on religious liberty, freedom of conscience, and the rights of Native Americans. He was instru-

---

2. Robert Torbet, *A History of the Baptists* (Valley Forge: Judson Press, 1978), p. 33; and Bill J. Leonard, ed., *The Dictionary of Baptists in America* (Downers Grove: InterVarsity Press, 1994), p. 143.

3. Torbet, *History of Baptists,* p. 38.

mental in founding the First Baptist Church of Providence in 1639, probably the first Baptist congregation in the colonies.

In 1627 Williams received his B.A. from Pembroke College, Cambridge, but failed to complete the Masters degree, perhaps due to his increasing commitment to religious non-conformity. University records declare "that Roger Williams . . . hath forsaken the Universitye and is become a discontinuer of his studyes."[4] Although Williams' time as a Baptist was brief (he became a Seeker, waiting on a new revelation from God), his legacy significantly shaped Baptist life in the New World.

Persecuted in New England, Baptists flourished in the middle colonies. The first American Baptist association, a gathering of churches for fellowship and encouragement, was established in Philadelphia in 1707. This association later approved a confession of faith, the Philadelphia Confession, in 1742. Its Calvinistic doctrines shaped other statements of faith used in Baptist churches. The New Hampshire Confession of 1833 offered a more modified Calvinistic approach to dogma. Baptists thrived on the frontier and by the mid-nineteenth century were second only to Methodists among America's largest Protestant denominations. Baptist growth in the nineteenth century led to the formation of numerous institutions of higher learning in the North and South.

Baptists and Higher Education

The (Southern) Baptist legacy of higher education in America may be understood in terms of several significant events and issues. These include: (1) the establishment of Baptist institutions of higher learning; (2) the theological orientation of various Baptist groups; (3) the tension between corporate confessionalism and individual freedom informing educational identity and approach; (4) the role of Baptist institutions in shaping a constituency intellectually and socially; and (5) the controversies which arose regarding the nature of education in a Baptist context.

Baptist Institutions Established

Historian William McLoughlin notes that "as early as 1708, they [Baptists] had begun to send some of their young men to Harvard to be educated."[5]

4. Leon McBeth, *The Baptist Heritage: Four Centuries of Baptist Witness* (Nashville: Broadman Press, 1987), p. 125.
5. William G. McLoughlin, *Soul Liberty: The Baptists' Struggle in New England, 1630-1833* (Hanover, MA: Brown University Press, 1991), p. 6.

Waning in number by 1710, Baptists were reinvigorated by the Great Awakening. That movement, McLoughlin believed, influenced the effort to found the College of Rhode Island (later Brown University) in 1764, the first Baptist educational institution in America. Although established to train Baptist ministers, the institution required no religious test of students or faculty and promoted Baptist principles of religious liberty. Jews were admitted by 1770, although Catholics, atheists, and deists were refused admission until the nineteenth century.[6]

In the South, colonial Baptists, like their Methodist and Presbyterian counterparts, sought to establish academies (precollege schools) for training young men. Except for the work of Virginia minister, Robert B. Semple (1769-1831), these were not highly successful.[7]

Following the Revolutionary War, Baptist cooperation flourished and other schools were initiated. Columbian College was founded in 1821 in Washington, D.C. It offered students a classical education while providing Baptists with a sense of national identity. Columbian College endured until 1904 when it became George Washington University and relinquished its Baptist affiliation.[8]

By the early nineteenth century, Baptist academies and colleges appeared throughout the South. Donald Mathews observes that "by the 1830s Methodists and Baptists were energetically establishing educational societies throughout the South in an attempt to broaden the scope and constituency of Evangelical education."[9] He concludes that while the academies (precollege) were significant, "they did not represent Evangelical aspirations and ambitions so well as the fragile 'denominational' colleges which began to spring up in the 1820s and 1830s."[10]

Brooks Holifield notes that in 1820 only about a dozen colleges existed in the southern region. By 1850 that number had expanded to more than a hundred institutions serving a student population of over 9,000 persons.[11] These included several Baptist colleges, among them Georgetown College (Kentucky, 1829), Richmond College (Virginia, 1840), Wake Forest College (North Carolina, 1838), Mercer University (Georgia, 1837), and Howard College (later Samford University, Alabama, 1841).[12] These schools were founded

6. Leonard, *Dictionary of Baptists in America,* p. 67.

7. Donald Mathews, *Religion in the Old South* (Chicago: University of Chicago Press, 1977), p. 86.

8. Leonard, *Dictionary of Baptists in America,* p. 88.

9. Mathews, *Religion in the Old South,* p. 89.

10. Mathews, *Religion in the Old South,* p. 89.

11. Brooks Holifield, *The Gentlemen Theologians: American Theology in Southern Culture, 1795-1860* (Durham: Duke University Press, 1978), p. 45.

12. Mathews, *Religion in the Old South,* p. 90.

by regional, not national, groups, many aligned with Baptist conventions in their respective states.

Theological Orientation and Response to Education

As noted earlier, Baptists did not adhere to one uniform theological or educational tradition. Their doctrines and educational enterprises were informed by ideas which extended across the theological spectrum from classical to populist, from Calvinist to Arminian. While Calvinism was strong, the forces of revivalism, evangelical fervor, and democratic idealism shaped an expanding Arminian approach to free will and human choice. Southern Baptists, for example, often talked like Calvinists but acted like Arminians when it came to evangelism, missions, and philosophies of education.

Nonetheless, most Baptist groups shared certain views concerning the nature and practice of Christian faith. These included commitment to the authority of Holy Scripture, the autonomy of the local church, the liberty of individual conscience, the priesthood of all believers, a regenerate church membership, ordinances of immersion baptism and the Lord's Supper, and a free church in a free state. Their positions on that latter issue created continuing debates regarding academic freedom, the use of state funds by private institutions, and the reaction of institutions to upheavals in the broader culture.

Theological Traditions in the South

Founded in 1845, the Southern Baptist Convention was heir to these basic beliefs as shaped by a variety of theological traditions, many of which appeared in the South long before the Convention itself was organized. The earliest Baptists in the South came from New England to Charleston, South Carolina, establishing the First Baptist Church there by the mid-1690s. These Regular Baptists reflected Calvinist theology and questioned the emotionalism of colonial revivalism. Their preachers were often well-educated, many trained in New England or abroad.[13]

Brooks Holifield numbers Regular Baptist ministers among the "gentlemen theologians" of the antebellum South. Holifield cites James Taylor, a Virginia Baptist minister instrumental in founding Virginia Baptist Seminary (1832), later known as Richmond College (1840). He notes that "Taylor typified an

---

13. Walter B. Shurden, "The Southern Baptist Synthesis: Is it Cracking?" in the 1980-81 Carver Barnes Lectures, published by Southeastern Baptist Theological Seminary, 1981.

influential group of Southern theologians who inherited, modified, and prop-agated 'rational orthodoxy.' "[14] Regular Baptists founded schools which trained generations of Baptist clergy and laity across the South.

The Separate Baptists represent another southern theological and cultural tradition. Arriving in the 1750s, they supported revivalism and its influences. The Separates encouraged religious "enthusiasm," calling on sinners to receive God's overpowering grace. Separate Baptist ministers were self-supporting "farmer-preachers," given to impassioned sermons which often produced sim-ilar outbursts from their hearers. Many were suspicious of education, some even suggesting that if God had chosen to call uneducated ministers, such persons should "abide in the same condition wherein they were called."[15] In 1761, one critic noted that Separate Baptists were guilty of "preaching up the inexpediency of human learning . . . and the great expediency of dreams, visions, and immediate revelations."[16] For many Separates, the Holy Spirit, not any human institution, was the source of true spiritual learning. In the view of many Separates, Baptist higher education involved the founding of what might be termed "peoples' colleges" aimed at offering basic education to young people while nurturing in them the solid principles of the faith and the heart religion of direct experience with the Divine.

Another theological tradition which impacted Baptist views of education is known as Old Landmarkism. Originating in the nineteenth century, Land-markism was a theological and political effort to trace Baptist origins all the way back to the New Testament church. In contrast to those restorationists who claimed to have re-established New Testament Christianity, Old Land-markers insisted that they maintained an unbroken line of succession from Jesus and his baptism by John (the Baptist). Landmarkists rejected infant baptism as well as any "alien immersion" administered outside Baptist churches. They advocated "closed communion," convinced that the Lord's Supper could be given only to members of the specific congregation in which it was celebrated.

Landmarkist attempts to impose their dogmas on all Southern Baptist institutions often brought them into conflict with colleges and seminaries. Some demanded that faculty members be compelled to subscribe to Land-mark definitions of Baptist dogmas. Many urged that educational institutions avoid any action which would undermine the authority of the local Baptist congregation, the primary source of ecclesiastical authority. For example, the Landmarkist insistence that only local congregations had authority to ad-minister the Lord's Supper often prevented many Southern Baptist schools

14. Holifield, *Gentlemen Theologians,* p. 6.
15. Holifield, *Gentlemen Theologians,* p. 230.
16. Holifield, *Gentlemen Theologians,* p. 231.

from serving communion in the campus chapel. During the late nineteenth and twentieth centuries other movements among Baptists influenced the directions of education. These are evident in the ideas and actions of liberal-progressives, conservative-fundamentalists, and centrist-denominationalists. The presence of these diverse theological and regional subgroups illustrate the difficulty which Southern Baptists faced in developing consensus regarding a theory or theology of Christian education for use in the schools they established. To a large extent, consensus was more evident in cultural than theological issues.

At the same time, Southern Baptists demonstrated a basic conservatism in matters theological and social. Their theology was reflected in a commitment to biblical authority and personal heart religion. They sought to fulfill the church's missionary calling through evangelical and missionary endeavors. Socially, they did not hesitate to address matters of personal morality — temperance, gambling, prostitution, dancing, and other ethical concerns. As John Lee Eighmy wrote, when it came to social issues most Southern Baptists "assumed the role of a cultural establishment by sanctifying a secular order devoted to states' rights, white supremacy, laissez faire economics, and property rights."[17] This general social and theological conservatism was one reason the fundamentalist-modernist controversy of the early twentieth century did not cause major divisions in the denomination.

Nonetheless, certain divisions did occur. Some saw themselves as "progressives" who would bring modern social, scientific, and biblical studies into Baptist institutions. Georgia pastor Jesse Mercer (1769-1841) was an early representative of the progressive view of Baptist education. While the Georgia university which now bears his name was established as a "classical and theological school," its broad curriculum apparently created some concern from the Baptist constituency. Thus, Holifield observes, "Mercer tried to assuage anxieties by elaborating the religious import of even the 'secular' curriculum. Each of the academic disciplines, he said, exhibited the truth of God: to study geography, chemistry, history, or philosophy was to study 'the works of God, in creation, and providence, and grace.'"[18] Mercer's ideas no doubt reflected what became the "progressive" response of those Baptists who wanted to broaden university education even if it was threatening to traditional orthodoxy. Not everyone agreed. One of Mercer's contemporaries protested against "the learned gentry of the day, who swarm out of the theological institutions like locusts, and are ready to devour the land."[19] From the begin-

17. John Lee Eighmy, *Churches in Cultural Captivity: A History of the Social Attitudes of Southern Baptists* (Knoxville: University of Tennessee Press, 1972), p. x.

18. Holifield, *Gentlemen Theologians*, p. 47.

19. Holifield, *Gentlemen Theologians*, pp. 47-48.

ning, Baptist schools were subjected to debates over education relative to both religious orthodoxy and social class.

Some Baptists such as William Louis Poteat (1856-1938), president of Wake Forest College, argued that Baptists should not fear new learning but incorporate its best truths into their institutions. In an address to the North Carolina Baptist Convention in 1922, Poteat defended the teaching of evolution and other "modernist" ideas. He urged Baptists to "welcome truth" since Christ himself was the "theme, origin and end of all truth."[20] These progressives desired that their schools be as academically respectable as Brown, Princeton, Harvard, or Yale.

Others such as Texas fundamentalist pastor J. Frank Norris (1887-1952) warned that Baptist schools should not accept an agenda set by secular standards which might easily undermine the faith and doctrine of the churches. Norris attacked the liberalism he believed prevalent at Baylor University and other Baptist schools which tolerated "infidel professors" or invited known liberals to speak on campus. According to C. Allyn Russell, Norris took credit for the ouster of eight "anthropoid apes" (Baylor professors) who taught the doctrine of "animal ancestry" (evolution).[21] Norris left the SBC and founded his own school, one of a number of Bible colleges founded by Independent Baptist churches.

Still other conservatives, such as George W. Truett (1867-1944), longtime pastor of First Baptist Church in Dallas, opposed strident fundamentalism but warned that progressivism could go too far. In an address delivered on the steps of the U.S. capitol in 1920, Truett declared:

> The one transcending inspiring influence in civilization is the Christian religion. By all means, let the teachers and trustees and student bodies of all our Christian schools remember this supremely important fact, that civilization without Christianity is doomed. Let there be no pagan ideals in our Christian schools, and no hesitation or apology for the insistence that the one hope for the individual, the one hope for society, for civilization, is in the Christian religion. If ever the drum beat of duty sounded clearly, it is calling to us now to strengthen and magnify our Christian schools.[22]

Debates over the nature of higher education among progressives, fundamentalists, and denominationalists illustrate the many views evident among Southern Baptists.

20. Leonard, *Dictionary of Baptists in America*, p. 223.
21. C. Allyn Russell, *Voices of American Fundamentalism* (Philadelphia: Westminster Press, 1976), p. 29.
22. Leon McBeth, *A Sourcebook for Baptist Heritage* (Nashville: Broadman Press, 1990), p. 476.

The Purposes of Baptist Higher Education

Baptists in the South, like other nineteenth-century evangelicals, had numerous reasons for establishing institutions of higher learning. Donald Mathews cites Baptist educator William Hooper, president of Wake Forest College, as articulating the rationale for Baptist-oriented education.

First, he suggested that these endeavors were the initial stage of an extended plan. Such efforts, he believed, "may raise our people & our ministry to a point from which our successors may raise them to still greater elevation."[23] Second, Baptists believed that schools would prepare denominational leaders, both clergy and laity. They were bastions of learning founded to eradicate "ignorance and illiteracy" among Baptists.[24] Third, higher education among Baptists offered them opportunity to develop social and economic status in the new American society. It represented a move away from their sectarian stance "against culture" and their willingness to become valuable participants in the progress of the community.[25]

Finally, they wanted schools which would communicate Christian and Baptist beliefs, values, and identity to succeeding generations. Mathews concludes that Baptists and other southern evangelicals

> built colleges to increase educational opportunities, improve the quality of their common life, and enhance their own prestige, but they had a strictly ideological motive as well. They wanted to make sure that the college education received by their children was shaped by Evangelical assumptions and goals. Fearful of a non- or anti-Christian ethos, which, along with an aristocratic bias, seemed to pervade state universities, Evangelicals were relieved when they could find ways to control their own colleges, in which their world view, far from being critically scrutinized, was acclaimed.[26]

Baptist colleges served many purposes. They provided Christian education, inculcated a Baptist ethos, and offered Baptist families the promise of a better life and social status for their children. Generations of Baptist youth were nurtured in churches and sent off to Baptist colleges, many returning to their communities to serve as active citizens and church members. In fact, Southern Baptist schools were part of a network of agencies and institutions which represented and communicated Baptist identity across the South.

From the perspective of the laity, one of the most important contributions

23. Mathews, *Religion in the Old South*, p. 92.
24. Mathews, *Religion in the Old South*, p. 92.
25. Mathews, *Religion in the Old South*, pp. 92-93.
26. Mathews, *Religion in the Old South*, p. 94.

of Baptist education was in improving the social and economic status of an essentially lower-class, rural constituency. John Boles cites nineteenth-century preacher William Fristoe's comment that Baptists were taken from "the common people" who were "low in circumstances [of] the world."[27] He observed that Baptists "have been of the mediocrity, or poorer sort among the people — instances have been very few, of persons being called who were rich in this world."[28] Thus the Baptists who organized small, struggling schools across the South sought to provide education and social status for their constituency. In an era before the growth of public education, Baptists offered inexpensive education for persons who otherwise could not have afforded such an experience. In a sense, the early Baptist colleges were peoples' colleges, providing basic elements of higher education for a new generation and class of Americans. While they were not the only ones to provide such a service, Baptists' egalitarian response was a major contribution of the Baptist tradition to American higher education.

At the same time, Baptist involvement in higher education was not unrelated to their fear of secularism in the public realm. In the post-Civil War era many Southern Baptists expressed strong reservations about public education in the region. During the last three decades of the nineteenth century, some Southern Baptist leaders opposed the use of tax money for public education. One Virginia Baptist wrote: "I indignantly protest against the compulsory payment of a single cent for the education of the children of worthless vagabonds, who are quartered by law upon my labor for support. . . . A tax bill that takes my money to educate another man's children is a wanton and wicked aggression upon my rights. . . ."[29] Others feared that public institutions of higher education would undermine denominational schools. Many agreed with the Alabama Baptist who suggested that liberal arts education should be provided by church schools while state universities would offer graduate studies and teacher training programs.[30] Historian Rufus Spain concluded that these attitudes

> developed into an all-inclusive, four-level school system with the responsibilities of the church and state specifically delineated as follows: common schools for all children through six grades at state expense; college pre-

27. John B. Boles, *The Great Revival, 1787-1805* (Lexington: The University of Kentucky Press, 1972), p. 169, citing William Fristoe, *History of the Ketocton Baptist Association*, pp. 57 and 148.

28. Boles, *Great Revival*, pp. 169-170.

29. Rufus Spain, *At Ease in Zion: Social History of Southern Baptists 1865-1900* (Nashville: Vanderbilt University Press, 1961), p. 39. Spain made extensive use of Baptist state papers in his survey of social attitudes.

30. Spain, *At Ease in Zion*, p. 40.

paratory academies, either state or privately operated; liberal-arts colleges under church control; and, finally state universities. At the first two levels the home was to be responsible for moral training; the church assumed this responsibility at the college level; and, presumably, students at the university level were to look after their own morals.[31]

In time, Southern Baptists came to support public education somewhat grudgingly while insisting that liberal arts education was best offered within the moral and religious context of church-supported schools.

Education and Orthodoxy

Questions regarding theological orthodoxy and the nature of Christian education set the stage for numerous controversies surrounding Baptist schools. Early debates centered on the use of confessional documents as requirements for faculty members. Should faculty members at Baptist schools be required to subscribe to basic statements of theological orthodoxy? While many of the Baptist colleges did not make such a requirement, most of the seminaries did.

The struggle between educational diversity and doctrinal integrity was particularly evident in the debate over evolution which exploded among American evangelicals in the 1920s. Unlike other denominations, Southern Baptists were not polarized by fundamentalist debate. They were not unaffected, however. The need for clarity of doctrine led to the approval of their first denominational confession of faith, *The Baptist Faith and Message*, in 1925. Supporters noted that "the present occasion for a reaffirmation of Christian fundamentals is the prevalence of naturalism in the modern teaching and preaching of religion."[32] Of particular concern was the possible teaching of evolution in Baptist colleges.

A statement condemning evolution was approved the same year as the confession of faith — 1925. It declared, "We protest against the imposition of this theory [evolution] upon the minds of our children in denominational, or public schools, as if it were a definite and established truth of science."[33] The same statement addressed the question of faculty members at Baptist schools, asserting:

Teachers in our schools should be careful to free themselves from any suspicion of disloyalty on this point. In the present period of agitation

31. Spain, *At Ease in Zion*, pp. 41-42.

32. H. Shelton Smith, Robert T. Handy, and Lefferts A. Loetscher, eds., *American Christianity: An Historical Interpretation with Representative Documents*, vol. 2 (New York: Charles Scribner's sons, 1963), p. 354.

33. Smith, Handy, and Loetscher, *American Christianity*, vol. 2, p. 355.

Bill J. Leonard

and unrest they are obligated to make their positions clear. We pledge our support to all schools and teachers who are thus loyal to the facts of Christianity as revealed in the Scriptures.[34]

The controversy over evolution burned hot and quick. By the late 1920s other matters — financial difficulties and prohibition — had claimed the attention of the convention. Nonetheless, debates regarding curriculum and course content at Baptist colleges and universities would characterize most of the twentieth century.

The article on "Education" in the denominational confession of faith, the *Baptist Faith and Message,* approved in 1925 and revised in 1963, illustrates Southern Baptist tensions over higher education throughout the twentieth century. The earlier document affirms that "Christianity is the religion of enlightenment and intelligence. In Jesus Christ are hidden all the treasures of wisdom and knowledge. All sound learning is therefore a part of our Christian heritage."[35] This approach reflects something of a more "progressive" understanding of the nature of Christian education — all truth is God's truth and therefore within the purview of the Baptist institution. No reference is made to the issue of academic freedom.

The 1963 revisions in the statement on "Education" reveal certain changes in Baptist response to the matter. The document affirms the importance of "the cause of education," noting that "an adequate system of Christian schools is necessary to a complete spiritual program for Christ's people."[36] The article calls for a proper balance between freedom and responsibility in academic institutions. It declares that "the freedom of a teacher in a Christian school, college, or seminary is limited by the pre-eminence of Jesus Christ, by the authoritative nature of the Scriptures, and by the distinct purpose for which the school exists."[37] The earlier statements on the nature of Christian learning are not included in the revised confession. Clearly, by 1963 Southern Baptists were more interested in the question of academic freedom and responsibility than in the idea that all truth comes from God. These two views of educational freedom and responsibility illustrate the continuing dilemma which Southern Baptists face regarding the nature of higher education. Clearly, for some, freedom was the primary issue in educational investigation and expression. At the same time, many wanted to insure that the exploration of truth did not undermine, let alone contradict, established dogma. Yet, agreeing on the specifics of such dogma was difficult, given Baptist polity and practice.

34. Smith, Handy, and Loetscher, *American Christianity,* vol. 2, pp. 555-556.
35. McBeth, *A Sourcebook for Baptist Heritage,* p. 514.
36. *The Baptist Faith and Message* (pamphlet) (Nashville: Sunday School Board, 1963), p. 16.
37. *Baptist Faith and Message,* p. 16.

379

Perhaps no controversy affected Southern Baptist higher education more than the struggle between so-called moderates and fundamentalists over control of the denomination itself. Out of that controversy numerous Southern Baptist colleges and universities have redefined their relationship with the Convention. In 1979, SBC fundamentalists, long concerned by what they felt was the leftward drift of denominational agencies, particularly educational institutions, launched an effort to retake the convention. They succeeded in electing a series of convention presidents who used their appointive powers to place fundamentalist majorities on boards of trustees of all convention agencies. Fundamentalists were those who promoted the doctrine of biblical inerrancy — the idea that the Bible is infallible and inerrant in every matter it discusses — and who were committed to pressing those definitions on all convention-owned institutions. They insisted that their views represented the majority of Southern Baptists and that the denominational system had long ignored their concerns.[38]

Moderates, on the other hand, were Southern Baptists who, while accepting the doctrine of biblical authority, did not mandate a doctrine of biblical inerrancy for all true believers. Many moderates claimed to be inerrantists but opposed the fundamentalist methods for gaining control of the convention.

Throughout the debate fundamentalists charged that educational institutions were a major part of the denominational problem. Certain seminaries, colleges, and universities were described as seedbeds of liberalism which undermined doctrines of inerrancy, atonement, original sin, and other orthodox truths. As fundamentalists gained majorities on seminary boards of trustees, several schools were thrown into turmoil with administrators and faculty fired or forced to resign and move to other institutions.[39]

The denominational strife created a dilemma for many of the Baptist colleges and universities. While these schools were not owned by the national convention, many were directly related to specific state Baptist organizations which provided funding and appointed trustees. In the years before the moderate-fundamentalist controversy arose, several Baptist schools — the University of Richmond and Wake Forest University, for example — had redefined their relationship to their respective conventions, retaining greater autonomy. As the denominational controversy gained momentum, several schools moved to distance themselves from the state Baptist conventions, establishing some form of a self-perpetuating trustee board. These included Baylor University (Texas), Furman University (South Carolina), Stetson University (Florida), and Samford University (Ala-

38. Bill J. Leonard, *God's Last and Only Hope: The Fragmentation of the Southern Baptist Convention* (Grand Rapids: Eerdmans, 1990).

39. Walter B. Shurden, ed., *The Struggle for the Soul of the SBC: Moderate Responses to the Fundamentalist Movement* (Macon: Mercer University Press, 1993).

bama). Still other schools, such as the University of Mobile (Alabama) and Southwest Baptist College (Missouri), affirmed their loyalty to the state conventions and their willingness to implement appropriate conservative mandates. Supporters of self-perpetuating trustee boards insisted that their schools were protected from the turmoil which had befallen the SBC seminaries. Critics of such actions warned that the break with the denomination would lead ultimately to a secularization of the academy evident at previously Baptist institutions such as Brown, Chicago, and George Washington universities. Whatever the long-term consequences, the immediate result seems to be a significant reorientation of Baptist educational organization and identity.

Conclusions

This brief study prompts several conclusions regarding the (Southern) Baptist legacy of higher education and its implications for the future. First, a concern for higher education led nineteenth-century Baptists to establish an impressive array of colleges across the American South. Today, many of those schools are among the finest in the region. These schools now reflect varying responses to their denominational identity and heritage. Some continue to promote their Baptist roots while others minimize their relationship to the tradition.

Second, the Baptist system of higher education helped to shape religious identity and denominational consciousness for generations of Southern Baptists. Baptist schools were important elements of an elaborate denominational network which linked constituents to a variety of Southern Baptist programmatic, benevolent, and missionary endeavors. Such regional and ecclesiastical intactness is fast disappearing at every level of denominational life. While some traditional denominational bonds remain intact, new organizational alignments are rapidly taking shape. Regional, local, and ideological alliances are breaking down and re-forming their identities inside and outside the Southern Baptist Convention. Colleges and universities are reshaping their relationships with their respective state Baptist Conventions. Some retain traditional ties with trustees appointed by the parent Baptist body and with faculty drawn primarily from a Baptist constituency. Others retain a Baptist character but have severed official affiliation with their respective state conventions. Still others have distanced themselves both from their conventions and their earlier Baptist identity. Baptist colleges and universities must come to terms with these realities in shaping their own identity as Baptist-related institutions.

Third, Southern Baptist schools significantly impacted the social and economic environment of the South. Baptist institutions of higher learning aided generations of Baptist and other Southern youth in securing educational and economic opportunities which many of their parents had not known. Early in their history, many Baptist colleges and universities cultivated an image of egalitarianism and opportunity for all. Today, rising operating costs and ever-increasing tuition challenge that ideal. Indeed, many contemporary educators acknowledge that they have increasingly "priced themselves" away from some segments of the Baptist communion and toward a more affluent constituency.

Fourth, from the beginning, Southern Baptist efforts in higher education aimed at providing academic instruction within the context of a Christian/Baptist piety. Although this was never easy, it was facilitated by a powerful Protestant and Baptist subculture which spread throughout the South. In earlier eras college religion created its own peculiar ethos involving dormitory regulations, mandatory chapel, particular types of spirituality, and faculty members with strong ecclesiastical, even ministerial, orientation. Even then, however, Baptists worried about the potential conflicts which education might create in the youthful minds of faithful students. Those questions continue to create controversy and division, particularly as some of the old evidences of campus piety have changed or disappeared. While affirming the value of Christian higher education and its significance in an ever-changing world, Baptists continue to debate the impact of education on faith and spiritual formation. Disagreements remain over the relationship of "progressive education" — the search for truth wherever it may be found — to the "unchanging truths" of Christian orthodoxy. Thus Baptist schools confront what seems an endless debate over the nature of academic and Christian community on a Baptist campus. What does it mean to be a "Christian" university? How does a Christian identity shape the academic environment?

Fifth, the unending tension between academic freedom and doctrinal orthodoxy has led to significant organizational fractures and restructuring in Southern Baptist seminaries, colleges, and universities. Some have reaffirmed elaborate doctrinal parameters for faculty and students alike while other institutions have redefined themselves to avoid what they viewed as doctrinal narrowness and political machinations among competing subgroups. This educational development mirrors the institutional fragmentation of the denomination as a whole.

Finally, one of the most crucial questions involves that of identity. As denominational alignments are redefined or minimized, what elements of an historically Baptist identity might be retained? What particular Baptist distinctives will continue to inform higher education? Who will determine the nature of that identity, that is, define what it means to be "historically Baptist"? How will schools identify, indeed, distinguish themselves in the changing environment of the church and the society? In responding to those and other challenges, Baptist educators would do well to act as creatively as their forebears.

Christian Identity and Academic Rigor: The Case of Samford University

Bill J. Leonard

Samford University was founded in 1841 as Howard College in Marion, Alabama. The Baptist-oriented school moved to Birmingham, Alabama, in 1887 and to its present Birmingham location in 1957. The name was changed to Samford University in 1965. Howard College continues as the college of arts and sciences, one of seven schools which include Business, Law, Education, Pharmacy, Nursing, and Divinity. This essay focuses on the Howard/Samford experience with particular attention to the undergraduate college.

Samford University looks like a southern college is supposed to look. Georgian-colonial architecture dominates a well-manicured campus lying just over Birmingham's Red Mountain. The spire of the Reid Chapel and the dome of the Beeson Divinity School Chapel face each other across the quadrangle — two striking landmarks which set Samford's Christian commitments in stone. As the twentieth century draws to a close, Samford University is a school in transition, gaining national recognition for its academic excellence, renegotiating its relationship with its Baptist constituency, and devoting serious attention to its heritage as a Christian institution of higher learning.

Such exercises have not gone unnoticed. In *The Scandal of the Evangelical Mind,* historian Mark Noll writes that, although it has a way to go, Samford is among those "few evangelical colleges" which "have made some progress in the postwar years at promoting scholarship alongside the more general goals of broad learning and basic Christian orientation."[1]

---

1. Mark Noll, *The Scandal of the Evangelical Mind* (Grand Rapids: Eerdmans, 1994), p. 17.

Others are not so convinced. In November 1994, a group of Alabama Baptists circulated a letter lamenting changes in university governance and declaring that "not a single denominational college or university in America that has severed its organic ties to its denomination has even remained distinctively Christian, much less denominational. We must act now so that this same thing won't happen to Samford."[2] They apparently feared that the school would move away from the Baptist heritage to a more secular orientation.

This chapter suggests that Samford is indeed a university in transition. Issues of academic integrity and Christian identity, long bound to a regional and denominational orientation, now require other definitions and strategies for the future. Such a transition makes Samford a good case study for this volume. This brief narrative will focus on three aspects of the Howard/Samford history: its *Christian/Baptist identity* in relation to its *pursuit of academic excellence*, all considered in the context of *significant milestones* in the university's life.

Origins: Baptist and Southern

Samford University began as Howard College, a school founded by and for Alabama Baptists. From the beginning, Samford's identity was formed by both its cultural setting and its denominational affiliation. Throughout most of its history, the school was shaped by the ethos of the American South as well as that of the Southern and Alabama Baptist Conventions. During the last two decades, as those sources of order and identity have experienced significant transition,[3] Samford has been forced to reexamine its own identity. While continuing to rely on Samford's regional reputation and history, the school's leaders now confront new realities of curriculum and constituency. Conscious efforts are underway to extend Samford's academic reputation while remaining intentionally Christian within a changing regional and denominational environment.

The school that is today Samford University was chartered in 1841 in Marion, Alabama, and named for John Howard, an eighteenth-century British social and religious reformer. It retained that appellation until 1965 when it was renamed in honor of Frank Samford, an Alabama business leader and longtime trustee chairman and benefactor. Howard College remained as the name of the undergraduate college of arts and sciences.

2. Letter, "Pastors to Protect Samford," President's Office, Samford University, November 1, 1994.

3. Bill J. Leonard, *God's Last and Only Hope: The Fragmentation of the Southern Baptist Convention* (Grand Rapids: Eerdmans, 1994); and Nancy Ammerman, *Baptist Battles* (New York: Rutgers University Press, 1994).

Howard was one of many Baptist colleges founded in the South during the early 1800s. By approval of the Alabama Legislature, the charter invested trustees with "full power and authority to have and use a common seal, to receive donations and purchase property, . . . to confer such degrees in the Arts and Sciences, . . . [and] to give diplomas or certificates thereof."[4] While the school was organized by persons related to the Alabama Baptist Convention, its original relationship with Alabama Baptists remains a matter of some debate, particularly as concerns the right of the convention to appoint trustees. The nineteenth-century charter and its description of the work of the trustees took on added significance in the latter decades of the twentieth century. That issue is discussed later in this chapter.

The institution began classes January 3, 1842, offering programs in literary and theological studies to nine students.[5] Its primary purpose was to provide educational instruction for Alabama Baptist youth. The resolution encouraging Baptists to found a school recommended "that all indigent young men of approved talents and piety, who shall have been licensed by regular Baptist churches in Alabama to preach the Gospel, have their tuition [provided] in both the literary and [theological departments]."[6]

Howard remained in Marion, Alabama, from 1841 to 1887, when it was moved to the East Lake section of Birmingham. The school occupied that campus until 1957 when it was relocated in the Homewood region of Birmingham where it remains today. Like most American private colleges, Samford's history is colored by a series of financial crises. While in Marion, several fires destroyed campus facilities. The college remained open during the Civil War with only two professors and two students. Its facilities were utilized as wartime hospitals and its finances were devastated. The school endured, but often graduated only one student per year.[7]

The struggle for funds and students was a primary factor in the decision to move the school to Birmingham. The *Birmingham Sunday Chronicle* welcomed the proposed relocation in 1886:

> Birmingham wants Howard College and Howard College needs Birmingham. A new era is upon us and Birmingham is the center of new thought in the South. In the long ago it was considered necessary to isolate the student and also to isolate the school. . . . Now, the theory is to give a utilitarian education to fit a man to live among his fellow men. Howard

4. James F. Sulzby, Jr., *Toward a History of Samford University* (Birmingham: Samford University Press, 1986), vol. 1, p. 5.

5. Clifton J. Allen, ed., *Encyclopedia of Southern Baptists* (Nashville: Broadman Press, 1958), vol. 1, p. 654.

6. Sulzby, *Toward a History of Samford University,* vol. 1, p. 3.

7. *Encyclopedia of Southern Baptists,* vol. 1, p. 654.

College is a college of the present age. Birmingham is a city of today. The two seem to be made for each other.[8]

That optimism was frustrated when the economic panic of 1893 struck the South, again creating a financial imbroglio for the college. In 1896 Howard faced total bankruptcy for failure to maintain mortgage payments. Only after negotiation with the banks, and an emergency appeal to Baptists, did the college avoid collapse. Dean Percy Pratt Burns observed that through their sacrifice "the faculty saved the college as they had saved it in Marion."[9] Former students insist that such sacrifice had long characterized Samford.

By the turn of the century some financial stability was achieved through the work of President A. P. Montague (1902-10), who completed library and dormitory buildings while raising almost $100,000 in endowment.[10] The school's academic reputation also flourished. Women were first enrolled in 1913, and in 1920 Howard became the second Alabama college to be admitted to the Southern Association of Colleges and Secondary Schools. Faculty was expanded and new programs, including a Pharmacy Division (1927), were developed. The Great Depression again created financial problems, but enrollment remained stable and no programs were abolished.[11] Following the Depression the college thrived, still struggling financially but developing a curriculum which paralleled that of other private liberal arts institutions. For over seventy years Howard required Greek and Latin of all its B.A. graduates. In 1945 an innovative core curriculum known as the "Nuclear Curriculum" was adopted as a means of providing interdisciplinary instruction. Throughout these years, Howard's reputation was that of a small Baptist school offering a basic liberal arts education with limited fiscal resources.

In the 1940s some 400 acres were purchased in the Shades Valley (Homewood) section of Birmingham and, with construction of a series of buildings, the school moved to the new campus in 1957. The new campus offered an impressive collection of edifices in Georgian-colonial architectural style. While President Harwell Davis presided over the initial move, his successor, Leslie Wright, devoted his twenty-five year tenure to constructing new facilities and continuing the relationship with Alabama Baptists. In 1983, Thomas Corts assumed the presidency, with the goal of expanding Samford's national academic reputation and its Christian identity. During the first decade of Corts's presidency Samford's endowment increased from 8 million to over 100 million dollars.

8. Sulzby, *Toward a History of Samford University*, vol. 1, pp. 115-116.
9. *Encyclopedia of Southern Baptists*, vol. 1, p. 654.
10. *Encyclopedia of Southern Baptists*, vol. 1, p. 654.
11. *Encyclopedia of Southern Baptists*, vol. 1, p. 654.

Christian Institution

Samford's religious orientation was apparent from the beginning. Founded four years before the Southern Baptist Convention, Howard's institutional identity was closely linked to Baptist denominationalism. Even a brief survey of the school's legacy reveals its Christian and Baptist character. The early supporters of Howard College declared that it was a Baptist school promoting high spiritual and ethical standards. As Reverend E. B. Teague commented in 1874, "No parent need feel the slightest apprehension in regard to the moral influence of this (Howard) College. Young men cannot be safer under parental roof."[12] By the 1880s, students were compelled to attend morning prayers on campus as well as Sunday morning services at the church of their choice.[13] By the 1890s, campus revivals were an annual affair, to be replaced in the mid-twentieth century by Religious Emphasis Week. An 1894 report noted that "Howard (College) should exist to hasten the Kingdom of God, and when sinners are converted under the college's influence, its mission is being fulfilled."[14] For many Alabamians, education and evangelism were inseparable elements of a Baptist education.

This atmosphere continued after the move to Birmingham. President A. D. Smith wrote, "The society of the place is cultured and religious. The students . . . are free from the temptations to immorality which prevail in larger towns . . . and the unwholesome social excitements of such places. It is six miles to Birmingham and students will be allowed to go to that city once a week — from 8 to 12 on Saturday."[15] Apparently, the college was at least six miles from the nearest sin!

Yet some worried that modern philosophies might pollute even the most protected environment. In a 1909 sermon, Howard's president, A. P. Montague, warned:

> We have come upon new things and strange things in American education. The history of our elder years is held up to scorn; traditions long regarded sacred, are derided; fundamental principles of government are pronounced old-fashioned and out of date; orthodox religion is treated with disdain; the Bible is cast aside with a sneer or said to be in need of revision to suit latter-day scholarship. . . . The danger is in colleges in which are found professors who attack the Bible, and assail long-established views and traditions.[16]

12. Sulzby, *Toward a History of Samford University*, vol. 1, p. 82.
13. Sulzby, *Toward a History of Samford University*, vol. 1, p. 110.
14. Sulzby, *Toward a History of Samford University*, vol. 1, p. 181.
15. Sulzby, *Toward a History of Samford University*, vol. 1, p. 207.
16. Sulzby, *Toward a History of Samford University*, vol. 1, pp. 311-312.

Throughout this century, many Alabama Baptists worried that Howard had or could become such a place. Their concerns did not go unanswered. The Howard 1916 trustee report asserted that the college was "an exponent of Baptist principles," and that "it stands for an interpretation of the Bible which is both scholarly and religiously constructive."[17] In 1923, the faculty issued a response to "false rumors" regarding Howard, declaring:

1. That we do not teach, nor do we believe in any doctrine, theory, or philosophy of evolution which is contrary to the Bible or which would tend to undermine Christianity.
2. That we believe and teach the principles of Christianity as enunciated in the New Testament.
3. That we hold to the fundamental Baptist principles.
4. That we recognize that Howard College is a Christian institution, supported and controlled by the Baptists of Alabama, and that it is our duty to so conduct the institution as to meet the approval of the Baptists of Alabama.[18]

Such exchanges reflect the long term suspicion of education among the Baptist constituency as well as the difficulty of promoting scholarly investigation within the parameters of Baptist confessionalism.

This "Christian institution" occasionally utilized non-Christian faculty, however. A report from the fall semester 1914 noted that Dr. Morris Newfield, rabbi of Temple Emanu-El, Birmingham, was also professor of Hebrew at Howard College.[19] He apparently received no salary but his children were given free tuition at the school. His son, John, later taught in the Speech/Drama Department.

The concern for academic freedom and confessional integrity is evident in a 1927 statement from the religion faculty. It affirmed Howard's respect for

the religious convictions of all non-Baptists in its walls. No matter what they are — Jew, Gentile, Catholic, Methodist, Presbyterian or what not — they are allowed to interpret the Bible as they see it, and no effort is made to proselyte any of its students. At the same time Howard was founded and supported by loyal Baptist people and in keeping faith with them, the teaching of the Baptists are upheld on all proper occasions, the Bible being allowed to speak out its full and faithful message from its every page

17. Sulzby, *Toward a History of Samford University,* vol. 1, p. 384.
18. Letter, September 24, 1923; photocopy located in office of the president, Samford University.
19. Sulzby, *Toward a History of Samford University,* vol. 1, p. 358.

without putting any soft pedal on its Baptistic truths and without any evasion of its pointed lessons.[20]

By the 1920s, therefore, Howard College was apparently attracting a religiously diverse student body while assuring Alabama Baptists that their doctrines were "upheld" appropriately.

As the twentieth century progressed, Howard reflected a denominational milieu characteristic of many southern church-related colleges. Like other such schools, it had become one institutional component of an overarching denominational system. Guest preachers and lecturers were drawn from prominent pulpits and educational institutions aligned with the Southern Baptist Convention. Many faculty members held degrees from assorted Baptist colleges and seminaries. Most ministerial students went from Samford to one of the Southern Baptist seminaries. From there they usually moved into the denominational network as pastors, staff members, missionaries, and convention workers. The school's mission was informed by elaborate denominational mechanisms for shaping personal and corporate identity. The Alabama Baptist State Convention elected Samford trustees and provided funds for both general operation and ministerial scholarships.[21]

The insular nature of the southern environment meant that Samford was not strongly impacted by many social and political upheavals which swept other universities in the 1960s and 1970s. Indeed, those years may well represent the beginning of the so-called "Samford bubble," a protected environment disengaged from the broader culture. Longtime Samford faculty remember President Wright's determination that the school would not experience the disruptions evident at other institutions during the era. To that end, the university did not sign the compliance regulation for federal student aid participation nor admit any black students until 1969 when, after much debate, Samford admitted a black student to the law school.

The effort to create a protected environment for Samford students was particularly ironic given the school's location in Birmingham, Alabama, scene of some of the most violent confrontations of the Civil Rights Movement. Graduates from those years recall, however, that professors often raised issues of race, war, and poverty, especially in response to local upheavals. Alumni from the 1970s also remember the religious impact of the so-called "Jesus

---

20. Sulzby, *Toward a History of Samford University,* vol. 1, p. 532.

21. The Alabama Convention elected trustees from 1845 to 1994. Few operational funds came from the Convention until after World War II, and those moderate amounts were primarily for ministerial scholarships. In 1994, Samford received over four million dollars from the Convention, more than any other denominationally related school in the United States.

Movement" on campus religious life. Throughout that period some 70 percent of the student body claimed Baptist affiliation.

Defining the Mission and Governance

When Thomas Corts became president, he instituted programs which would reshape faculty, administration, and curriculum while reaffirming Samford's identity as a Christian and Baptist institution. To facilitate that goal, Corts adopted the use of the Deming method for Total Quality Management (TQM) as a source of university organization. Inaugurated at Samford in 1990, the Deming plan was originally applied to businesses, especially in Japan, with phenomenal success. Corts and Assistant Provost John Harris were at the forefront of those college administrators who sought to apply TQM methods to higher education.

As articulated by Provost William Hull, the "Quality Paradigm" for the university involved three specific imperatives:

> 1) Know your mission. Clarify it for every associate. . . . Let it shape the values and drive the vision which you are seeking to attain. Insist that every leader, starting at the top, infuse the entire organization with a strong sense of purpose. In a word, be *distinctive!* Know and fill your niche in the crowded academic marketplace.[22] 2) Satisfy your customers. Meet or exceed both the needs and the expectations of such client groups as students, parents, alumni and employers.[23] 3) Improve processes from beginning to end. Do not concentrate on how authority flows up and down the vertical reporting relationships on an organizational chart but on how functions flow back and forth across the horizontal terrain where critical tasks are actually accomplished.

Hull concluded that Samford "is committed to build a Quality Culture because it is consonant both with our enduring values over the past 150 years and with the emerging paradigm that is likely to shape our vision over the next 150 years."[24] As Hull and others understood it, TQM was a vehicle for linking Christian identity and academic excellence.

Implementation of TQM required that each academic unit link its specific mission with the overall mission of the university. After extensive revision, the following statement was approved by trustees in 1995. It begins with these affirmations:

22. William E. Hull, "The Quality Culture in Academia" (November 7, 1994, unpublished manuscript), p. 2.
23. Hull, "Quality Culture in Academia," p. 3.
24. Hull, "Quality Culture in Academia," p. 12.

We nurture persons — for God, for learning, forever. The mission of Samford University is to nurture persons, offering learning experiences and relationships within a Christian community, so that each participant may develop personal empowerment, academic and career competency, social and civic responsibility, ethical and spiritual strength; and continuously to improve the effectiveness of the community.

The statement continues with the assertion that at Samford

we expect to develop academic and career competency as we:
  read books, utilize technology, experience the arts, discuss ideas, and develop ideals;
  reason, measure, and research to engage the issues of our time and our world;
  identify and cultivate our talents, develop career goals, and participate in meaningful work.

Likewise, the statement notes that

we expect to develop ethical and spiritual strength as we:
  forge personal integrity in classroom and community life, in relation to God and to persons;
  discern right and wrong, good and evil, the consequences of actions and words, and shape a purpose in life that includes but exceeds "making a living";
  grow in grace and in the knowledge of Jesus Christ.[25]

The mission statement is addressed to all segments of the Samford community — faculty, staff, and students.

Departmental mission statements describe Samford's common purpose and unique contribution to university education. They represent its public commitment to providing higher education in the context of Christian identity. For example, the Department of Religion and Philosophy identifies its mission as nurturing

students intellectually, spiritually, emotionally, and socially through studies in Scripture, theology, philosophy, history, sociology and ministry as well as through personal mentoring relationships so that knowledge gained in the study of religion and philosophy is integrated with other disciplines and applied to their lives; and continuously to improve the content, methods, and resources of our curriculum so that students may serve effectively and compassionately as both professional and lay persons in

25. Samford University Mission Statement, March 19, 1995.

their churches and communities and are valued by those whom they serve.[26]

While Samford remains a Baptist university, the mission declarations are geared to the broader Christian community. Through long-range planning programs, university leaders recognized that the future required expansion of Samford's student base, inside and outside the Baptist constituency. Demographics suggested a substantial decline in potential students from Alabama high schools and the need to look outside the state for additional students. To define the mission too narrowly might discourage some students who preferred a Christian environment but were not necessarily Baptists. Yet to define the mission too broadly might alienate traditional constituents. Likewise, by offering Baptist ministerial students an approximately 40 percent tuition credit, the school sought to nurture a new generation of Christian leaders and, in the words of one administrator, "leaven" the student community.

Turmoil in Southern Baptist life, prompted by fundamentalist attempts to control the national and state conventions, also influenced changes in university governance. In 1994, in a return to what they believed to be the original trustee selection process, Samford trustees voted 30 to 2 to return to the original practice of selecting their own members, while retaining full participation as a school related to the Alabama Baptist State Convention. They asserted that the original charter allowed for a self-perpetuating board. They also insisted that the changes were a response to the fifteen-year controversy between theological fundamentalists and moderates over control of denominational institutions.[27] Samford trustees feared that fundamentalist attempts to gain control of the board would create a climate of instability evident in trustee-faculty conflicts at numerous Southern Baptist seminaries. A public statement declared:

> If the election of Samford trustees . . . is placed in doubt every year, and the threat of "stacking" the Board of Trustees with persons of particular political loyalties is ever-present, and Samford is regularly harassed with minor charges only to be exploited for what appear to be political objectives, then the University's current operations and future progress are jeopardized.[28]

Trustees maintain that Samford will continue to be a Baptist university with board members appointed only from Alabama Baptist churches. Some af-

26. "Team Mission Responses, Department of Religion and Philosophy," 1994.
27. For a discussion of the controversy between fundamentalists and moderates, see Leonard, *God's Last and Only Hope.*
28. "A Report to Alabama Baptists," September 13, 1994; typescript located in office of the president, Samford University.

firmed the action as necessary to prevent a fundamentalist "takeover." Opponents of the move, however, warned that it would lead inevitably to a "secularization of the academy." Trustees contend that their endeavors will preserve Baptist identity and protect academic integrity, nurturing the spirit and the mind. Samford trustees were not alone in their efforts. Similar actions were taken by trustees at Wake Forest, Furman, Baylor, and other Baptist-related colleges and universities.

While some Alabama Baptists protested the change, many saw it as a regrettable but inevitable result of denominational conflicts and fragmentation. University leaders insisted that the religious climate on campus would continue to be a primary element of Samford's identity.

Nurturing Religion on Campus

At Samford University, public religious life is nurtured in formal and informal ways. First, the curriculum requires all undergraduates to take six hours (two courses) of introductory religion. Choices include Old and New Testament, Ethics, or Introduction to Religion. Classes are taught by members of the Department of Religion and Philosophy. That seven-person department also offers courses toward majors in religion, religion and philosophy, and congregational studies. Graduate study in religion is provided through the Beeson Divinity School, founded in 1989 with gifts and promise of further support which amounted to almost $50 million at the death of Presbyterian layman Ralph Waldo Beeson. The final gift was $53.8 million with interest. While all religion department members are Baptists, the Beeson bequest requires that some five members of the fifteen-member divinity faculty come from non-Baptist traditions.

Second, convocation is required of all undergraduate students, with sixty-four "convo credits" necessary for graduation. Convocations offer semi-weekly programs of worship, lectureships, and other presentations. Credit is also given for other university events — music, drama, and special lectures series — as well as for approved service projects.

The convocation requirements are a matter of continuing debate on the campus. Some students resent being compelled to attend religious services while others bemoan the number of credits required. Still others complain that various programs are too liberal, too conservative, or too parochial. For many students and faculty, convocation is a symbol of Samford's public identity as a Christian university and an occasion for introducing students to speakers and ideas they might not otherwise experience. Recent student surveys suggest that a majority (some 60 percent) support the existing requirement.

Third, convocation and other aspects of university religious life are directed by the minister to the university, a position created in 1989. While the school long maintained a part-time chaplain and campus ministry director, the position of minister to the university was initiated, at least in part, to demonstrate Samford's Christian commitment. The minister plans weekly student convocations and a Tuesday morning worship service especially for staff, provides pastoral care to all segments of the university community, and coordinates the ministerial scholarship program.

Another staff member, the director of student ministries, coordinates such activities as a weekly student-led worship service, campus prayer groups, and student mission enterprises. Samford claims the largest group of student summer missionaries sent out annually by any Southern Baptist school. The campus minister also directs Religious Emphasis Week, an annual event aimed at promoting spiritual renewal.

Fourth, significant numbers of Samford students manifest a strong religious enthusiasm in their actions and attitudes. Almost 300 of the 2400 undergraduates are Baptist ministerial students, receiving some 40 percent tuition remission. Religion majors number around 100. Many students demonstrate a high degree of Christian activism, participating in various missionary, evangelistic, or benevolent endeavors. Indeed, an ardent strain of popular religion exists throughout the Samford student body.

Such religious devotion characterizes an evangelical subculture evident on many Christian college campuses in contemporary America. It reflects a highly individualized piety, evidenced in moral rigor and intimacy with the divine. Spirituality is pursued in personal prayer, meditation, and Bible study, along with corporate worship ("praise services") in a charismatic style. A weekly student-led worship service called Quest blends Christian pop music, praise choruses, corporate prayer, and public "sharing" in an informal setting.

While students' theological ideas are far from systematic, they exhibit a decidedly conservative, traditionalist, or fundamentalist orientation regarding biblical authority, the necessity of salvation, the uniqueness of the Christian revelation, and the need to evangelize those who have not "had an experience with Jesus Christ." In classroom discussions and personal interviews, such students are likely to express opposition to abortion, homosexuality, feminism, and "New Age" philosophies that they believe permeate American society. Politically, many identify themselves with the policies of the Republican Party or the Christian Coalition. Some insist that they have chosen Samford because of its Christian/Baptist identity and environment, an atmosphere they would not find at public colleges and universities or more "secularized" private institutions.

Students in this generation also wear their denominational affiliations loosely, many shaped by the ethos of their home congregations. While at least

65 percent of the current undergraduate student body claims to be Baptist, interviews and experience suggest that most do not consider their primary religious identity to be linked to the Baptist tradition. Indeed, they often minimize the role of denominations, sacraments, and traditional rituals for informing Christian identity. Rather, their faith commitments seem shaped by a highly individualized, conservative, generic Christianity and a hesitancy to identify exclusively with any specific Christian tradition, Baptist or otherwise. That student ethos and its impact on the classroom is a matter of extensive discussion within the Samford community.

Academic Environment

The religious context at Samford, official and unofficial, exists within an academic environment which has also undergone considerable change in the last decade. While Howard/Samford administration and faculty have always promoted academic excellence and a strong educational atmosphere, the Corts era witnessed increased efforts to establish Samford's national reputation. In addition to higher ACT scores for freshmen and a higher percentage of Ph.D.s on the faculty, this priority is apparent in a variety of other developments.

First, new educational approaches were established. These included a program of "writing across the curriculum" which promoted writing skills in every discipline. Writing specialists were secured, labs created, and faculty instruction funded. All undergraduate students are now required to take at least two courses designated "w" (writing) courses. A senior seminar program encourages research projects and the preparation of a written thesis in the student's major field.

An experimental curriculum called Cornerstone was developed in 1991 as a replacement for the traditional undergraduate core courses. Initiated as a trial program for a selected group of students, it offers a cross-disciplinary, team-taught approach, linking faculty from diverse academic fields. A three-semester segment called Personal Wholeness incorporates studies in Scripture, spirituality, Christian ethics, and other religious components. Cultural Legacies, another multi-semester module, includes history, literature, art, and music, with some reference to religious issues throughout. Ideally, the Cornerstone curriculum would blend religion and other disciplines through interactive and cross-disciplinary teaching. Students would be introduced to subject matter through multiple lenses of varying academic fields.

To initiate the new curriculum, Samford received grants from the National Endowment for the Humanities and the Fund for the Improvement of Post-secondary Education. In 1994 the faculty voted to replace the existing core curriculum with the Cornerstone-type program. Higher costs of such a program make it uncertain whether that decision can ever be completely implemented. Indeed, in the spring term 1995, the administration proposed that only certain portions of Cornerstone be developed into a multi-semester interdisciplinary course for all undergraduates. The full Cornerstone curriculum would remain optional alongside the traditional core. While Samford invested over a million dollars in the program, the decision for limited implementation illustrates the way in which fiscal realities shape many of Samford's most creative endeavors.

Second, efforts were made to improve faculty hiring and support services. In the past, many faculty received their baccalaureate degrees from Howard/Samford and returned to teach at the school. While that tradition remains, many professors now come from other schools and regions outside the South. Reared outside a Southern Baptist context and unfamiliar with Samford's cultural and religious milieu, some experience a certain culture shock on arrival.

Currently, Samford's employment policies do not mandate the hiring of Christian or religiously oriented faculty members. Deans and search committees, nonetheless, are encouraged to give clear preference to persons of sincere religious commitment. Although employment forms request information regarding religious preference, no precise data is available as to faculty affiliations. Most are presumed to be Baptists, however. Roman Catholics, Jews, and members of various Protestant traditions are also represented in the Samford community. While some faculty would probably describe themselves as religiously non-affiliated, most are practicing churchmen and women.

With the exception of those teaching religion, faculty members are not required to subscribe to a formal confession of faith. Those who teach courses in the religion department or the Beeson Divinity School must affirm the "Baptist Faith and Message," the official confession of faith of the Southern Baptist Convention, a requirement instituted in 1991. This requirement sets Samford apart, since few Southern Baptist-related colleges and universities require a confessional or creedal affirmation of any of their faculty.

Faculty governance was reconfigured in 1983-84 to involve more direct participation in decision-making. Long-time faculty generally acknowledge that the Corts era expanded faculty governance, yet some wonder how effective these procedures are in actually shaping policy.

Support services were expanded to provide faculty with computers and numerous mainframe capabilities. Library resources were also augmented and a new addition to the library was completed in 1994. Tenure policies were reorganized and a more formal process established. Hiring procedures were reformed to provide for greater faculty participation. Twelve to fifteen faculty research grants are approved annually.

Faculty and administration continue to explore several open questions of university life. These include teaching load and faculty research, academic rigor, and student evaluations. Samford teaching load remains high, with the Liberal Arts faculty teaching four to five courses each semester. Some insist that the situation can only be changed by securing more faculty. Others believe that old "turf battles" and departmental intransigence militate against a solution. As yet, no consensus has been reached for dealing with the teaching load question.

Faculty research is closely related to the issue of teaching load. Some suggest that Samford is predominately a "teaching university" which cultivates class-room prowess among its faculty. Others contend that faculty should be en-couraged, if not mandated, to devote significant time to research and writing in their respective fields. Still others want options for both. For many faculty the high teaching load effectively ends the debate.

Student Response

Student assessment of the relationship between academics and Christian iden-tity vary. Many students thrive in the campus religious subculture, participating in opportunities for worship, prayer, Bible study, and religious vocation. Inter-views confirm popular opinion that Samford students (particularly under-graduates) reflect a strong evangelical-conservative approach to Christianity. Other students, however, complain that the religious environment creates the so-called "Samford Bubble," highly paternalistic and separated from the "real world." They worry that student conservatism inhibits classroom discussion and academic rigor. One student reported that after two semesters of being "shot down" by conservative students, he learned "to keep my mouth shut."

Other student interviews reflected positive response to the academic rigor of the university, specifically the religion department. In a random survey of religion majors and minors some 95 percent of those questioned agreed or strongly agreed that religion professors "know their subjects well." Another 85 percent agreed, 41 percent strongly, when asked if courses in the religion department are "relevant to your goals." Eighty-eight percent of students questioned agreed that professors allow sufficient time for student participa-tion in class. Of the twenty students interviewed, six were concerned that religion classes were "too Southern Baptist," "too liberal," or "not theologically diverse" enough. Another recent student evaluatory instrument placed the religion/philosophy and history/political science departments at the top of those departments which offer both academic rigor and intriguing material.[29]

29. The first profile was conducted by sociology of religion professor Penny Marler as a part of the assessment project for SACS accreditation, 1995. The second profile was developed by Dean Rod Davis of the Howard College of Arts and Sciences, also in 1995. It was also used in the college assessment process.

Faculty Response

In 1994-95 Samford claimed 250 full-time faculty in seven schools — Arts and Sciences, Business, Pharmacy, Education, Nursing, Law, and Divinity. Faculty opinions vary as to the nature of Samford as a Christian university. The following observations are taken from numerous dialogues conducted with representative faculty members. They may be divided into several categories.

1. *Toward a Baptist Tradition of Education.* In interviews conducted for this study, many faculty members acknowledged the peculiar difficulty of defining a Christian university from a Baptist perspective. Some suggest that, unlike institutions in the Roman Catholic or Reformed traditions, Baptists have no uniform theology of education. Rather, one administrator suggested, Baptists, like Christian restorationists, are pulled between forces of dogma and sociology, often being overwhelmed by both. That is, they desire schools that reflect a strong doctrinal base but, lacking a clear doctrinal consensus, are shaped by varying regional, pragmatic, or cultural dynamics. Ironically, questions of theology have often consumed segments of a constituency that was unable to establish frameworks for theological and educational unanimity. That fact does not keep Baptists from establishing institutions, however, and attempting to maintain a religious identity.

A law school professor noted that, in his view, the Baptist tradition, unlike the Reformed tradition, lacked a coherent theological perspective and thus as the university community became more diverse, it had limited resources for maintaining doctrinal or theological identity. Lacking a creedal base and appealing to a primitivist approach to Scripture, the Baptist tradition was less helpful in shaping a Christian institutional identity in an increasingly pluralistic university environment. Some faculty agreed that Baptists had never developed a clear-cut theory of Christian education. The challenge, therefore, might be to articulate one at Samford, since there is still opportunity to do so in the changing climate of Baptist denominationalism.

2. *"Customer" Expectations.* One administrator insisted that Samford's Christian ethos attracts many parents and students. He commented that what parents are "buying" is a campus "where the values of home have at least a fighting chance to survive the four years away from home." Samford constituents demand a strong Christian identity. Another administrator observed that the current student generation comes from environments so disjointed that students need a stable place with parameters and more direct guidance. He appealed to the most basic aspect of Samford's mission statement: "our business is nurturing people — for God, for learning, forever." This involves an environment which offers mutual encouragement "to be our optimum selves."

3. *The Learning Environment.* Other faculty worried that the conservative

environment undermined some approaches to education. One professor commented that some students seemed "afraid of certain thoughts" regarding social, political, or theological issues. Some students seemed to think that they had been sent to Samford so that they would not have to confront certain questions. Another teacher wondered about the common student question, "Can you teach that at Samford?" concerning discussion of such issues as abortion, homosexuality, or evolution, as if even raising such issues was out of place in a Christian university. Thus, many faculty wondered about their roles in the learning community at Samford. Were they to reinforce existing beliefs or challenge them?

4. *Defining a Christian University.* Throughout the discussions, faculty and administrators raised numerous questions regarding the nature of a university that declared itself Christian. How could Samford define what it means to be a Christian institution? A dean noted that while most constituents did not want the school to be a fundamentalist school, neither did they want it to be liberal. He expressed hope that it might reflect an evangelical orientation not unlike that at Wheaton or Calvin College. Another administrator wondered whether those traditional categories could adequately inform the university's Christian ethos in a postmodern era. A faculty member responded that much of Alabama culture remains hostile to intellectual inquiry, and thus Samford will always be at odds with that segment of the constituency. While Christian values might be the concern of both faculty and students, therefore, significant differences exist regarding what those values are and how to approach them. Challenging them, even in the name of Christianity, inevitably creates tension. The Samford community should acknowledge that reality and deal with it.

Several faculty noted the tensions created by the issue of language. For example, at a Christian university what kinds of literature would be acceptable? Should students be encouraged to read or experience materials which may be morally questionable among certain Christian groups? Should students insulted by profanity be excused from reading "offensive" literature or be given alternative readings? Such questions led to a 1994 discussion regarding a "language policy" for the school. The matter was tabled because of concerns over censorship, monitoring, and professorial freedom.

5. *Social Expectations.* William Hull, university provost, suggested that Baptist higher education began as a socially marginalized protest movement which became mainstream and dominant in the South. Baptists were a "free people who, in a free land, claimed social mobility without being gentry." The promise of education at a Baptist school was the promise of economic and social mobility. Samford began as such an institution. Later on, public universities made such education cheaper, so Baptist schools had to articulate other reasons for their "value centered" approach to education. Samford is engaged in that process.

6. *Freedom.* Noting the diversity of faculty and students, W. T. Edwards, longtime religion department member, suggested that Samford, like other Baptist schools, was not shaped around one common theory of Christian education. Rather, Samford has struggled with the Baptist legacy of freedom, nurturing an environment which promotes numerous voices, definitions, and approaches within the same academic community. "That is simply who we are," he declared.

Toward the Future

On the threshold of a new century, Samford University seeks to promote academic rigor alongside Christian identity. Clearly, the university has devoted extensive attention to describing its mission and attempting to implement goals compatible with Christian identity and academic integrity. Interviews suggest that this process has raised the consciousness of many faculty, eliciting a variety of responses. As noted, the relationship between Christianity and academics at Samford sparks debates regarding such issues as mandatory convocation, textbooks, and the religious life of the school. Some want a more confessional Christian environment while others believe that religious issues are already too confining. Consensus is elusive but dialogue continues.

All this suggests that Samford University still has a way to go in determining what it wants to be. The fragmentation and realignments of denominational mechanisms mean that Samford must decide if and how it will remain a Baptist institution. What aspects of the Baptist heritage will it retain or, indeed, promote? How will a Baptist perspective inform the increasingly generic Christianity of the student body? Perhaps Samford could affirm its identity as a university that is Christian in perspective and Baptist by tradition, using the Baptist heritage (at least segments of it) as a way of informing the broader Christian experience.

Likewise, in determining what it wants to be, the Samford community must improve methods for prioritizing goals and implementing programs realistically in light of actual resources. In their present mode, school leaders seem adept at proposing new and often prestigious programs and, like leaders at many other institutions, are then forced to implement them on the basis of fiscal reality. This often leads faculty and students to conclude that the school tends to promise beyond its ability to deliver. Administrators and other faculty respond that at a time of institutional downsizing at schools around the country, Samford continues to grow and expand.

Ideologically, in this time of transition, Samford University exists between the perspectives on Christian education reflected in recent books by George Marsden and Mark Noll. Some read Marsden's *The Soul of the American*

University and fear that in expanding its constituency and redefining its relationship to the Baptists, Samford will create a nonsectarianism which, in Marsden's words, "has come to mean the exclusion of all religious concerns."[30] Thus the institution hits the "slippery slope" to liberalism, relinquishing a distinguishable Christian identity. Others warn that in appealing to a generic Christianity and a rightward student body the school may give way, as Mark Noll warns, to the "scandal of evangelical thinking in America" which "often resulted from a way of pursuing knowledge that does not accord with Christianity as it has been an 'anti-intellectual' desire to play the fool for Christ."[31] Most, however, hope for a new identity unashamedly informed by Christian integrity, the best of the Baptist heritage, and an abiding commitment to freedom of inquiry. Time will tell.

30. George M. Marsden, *The Soul of the American University: From Protestant Establishment to Established Nonbelief* (New York: Oxford University Press, 1994), p. 440.

31. Noll, *The Scandal of the Evangelical Mind*, p. 12.

What Can the Church of Christ Tradition Contribute to Christian Higher Education?

Richard T. Hughes

If we wish to ask what Churches of Christ can contribute to Christian higher education, we first must ask about the historic and theological identity of this tradition. We then will explore some of the assets — along with some of the liabilities — that Churches of Christ bring to the task of Christian higher education.

Who Were/Are the Churches of Christ?

While Churches of Christ trace their lineage to two early nineteenth-century leaders, Barton W. Stone and Alexander Campbell, they owe their greatest debt to Campbell, whose influence on this tradition has persisted for almost two centuries. As an ecumenist, Campbell devoted his entire career to the interests of Christian unity. But Campbell was also a primitivist who argued that Christian union could best be achieved if Christians would abandon the creeds and particular doctrines that divided them and unite on those principles of primitive Christianity clearly taught in the New Testament.

Like many in his day, Campbell was also a rationalist, deeply influenced by the British Enlightenment. He stood indebted especially to John Locke and to Scottish Common Sense Realism, often known as "Baconianism." While Francis Bacon defined the scientific method as the basis for scientific inquiry, the eighteenth-century Scottish "Baconians" sought to apply that method to the larger world of things and ideas. Alexander Campbell sought to apply it to the Bible.

As a result, Campbell read the Bible through a scientific lens and often portrayed the Bible as a blueprint for the reconstruction of the forms and structures of the ancient Christian faith. Churches of Christ inherited from Campbell this understanding of the Bible, an understanding that has been pervasive in this tradition ever since.

Moreover, Campbell thought the Bible could be understood — at least in its central teachings — with scientific precision. This assumption provided the epistemological foundation for his conviction that the restoration of primitive Christianity would finally unite all Christians. If all could understand the Bible — at least its central teachings — with scientific precision, then all could understand it alike. The restoration of both form and content of first-century Christianity would therefore be the basis for Christian union.

From his base in Bethany, West Virginia, Campbell developed a sizable following throughout the Midwest and the Upper South.

By the mid-nineteenth century, it became clear to many in this movement that Christians neither read the Bible with scientific precision nor understood it alike. When this problem became apparent, Campbell's movement began to divide, a process aggravated by sectional differences related to the Civil War. Some took their stand on the unity of all Christians and expressed less and less interest in primitive Christianity. This side of the tradition would eventually become the modern, ecumenically oriented denomination, the Disciples of Christ, centered in the old Campbell heartland of the upper Midwest. Others took their stand on the recovery of primitive Christianity and expressed less and less interest in the unity of all Christians. This side of the tradition would eventually become the Churches of Christ which centered in the Upper South, especially in a belt running from Middle Tennessee to West Texas.

Campbell's understanding of primitive Christianity formed the basis for what Churches of Christ in time would call "nondenominational Christianity." They meant by that phrase a Christianity based on allegiance to the Bible, not on allegiance to denominational traditions, even their own.

In the hands of Churches of Christ, the notion of primitive, nondenominational Christianity was a two-edged sword that cut in two very different ways. At its best, this notion meant that members of Churches of Christ aspired to be nothing more and nothing less than Christians, defined by a biblical standard. According to this conception, the nondenominational vision was an ideal that stood in judgment even on Churches of Christ and summoned them to ever greater fidelity to the ancient Christian message and tradition. Those who embraced this understanding readily confessed their shortcomings, not only as individuals, but as a church.

On the other hand, the nondenominational vision at its worst produced an assumption that Churches of Christ were not a denomination like other denominations but, instead, had successfully reproduced primitive Christianity in all its perfections. More often than not, this interpretation of the nondenominational vision prevailed and created a host of illusions which defined this tradition from the mid-nineteenth century until recent years. Churches of Christ, for example, eventually traced their lineage to no history other than the Bible itself, rigorously denied the existence of any human founders (Alexander Campbell and Barton Stone, for example), and expressed virtually no interest in their own history in the United States. To recognize such a history and such a tradition, they imagined, would be tantamount to recognizing that they, too, were a denomination with a human founding. Or again, Churches of Christ claimed to have developed no theology except the message of the Bible, defined in the Bible's own terms. In a word, Churches of Christ often imagined themselves immune to the power of history and culture. For this reason, they grounded their tradition in their conviction that they had no tradition at all.

A corollary of all these notions was the conviction that manifested itself among these people from an early date: they were the true church of the apostolic age, grounded exclusively in the Word of God; others were simply denominations, descending from human history and rooted in human opinion and tradition. As much as any other theme Churches of Christ held dear, this became a fundamental support for Christian higher education in this fellowship. After all, if a college or university community was comprised exclusively of Christians who were members of the one true church, that fact alone was sufficient to validate that institution as a Christian institution. For this reason colleges and universities related to Churches of Christ seldom developed systematic theological understandings of the qualities and characteristics that ideally might characterize Christian higher education.

In all fairness, it should be said that in recent years, many if not most within the mainstream of Churches of Christ — especially the young — have abandoned these exclusivist assumptions, at least intellectually. For many members of Churches of Christ, however, these assumptions are so thoroughly bred in the bone that, though they may well abandon them intellectually, they have great difficulty abandoning them emotionally. For this reason, exclusivist presuppositions continue to define policy and procedure in a variety of ways, even within the most progressive institutions of higher learning related to Churches of Christ. All of this we must understand if we want seriously to ask what the Church of Christ tradition can contribute to Christian higher education.

What Assets Do Churches of Christ Bring to Christian Higher Education?

In spite of their historic denial of history and tradition, Churches of Christ bring to the task of Christian higher education a number of potential assets. Chief among those assets is their own historic vision of nondenominational Christianity, if that vision is understood as ideal and process, not as accomplished fact. This vision can provide strong supports for Christian higher education since it summons believers to question their own traditions and presuppositions and to measure them at every step along the way by the biblical standard. The nondenominational ideal of Churches of Christ can thus help sustain the relentless search for truth that characterizes serious higher education.

A second potential asset that Churches of Christ bring to Christian higher education is their long-standing commitment to the biblical text. It is true that their preoccupation with the biblical text as legal pattern often obscured the Bible's theological core. That preoccupation in turn has prevented Churches of Christ from developing any kind of overarching, theological worldview. Yet, all that is changing. Over the past quarter century, strategically placed professors in several Church of Christ-related colleges have helped raise up a new generation of preachers who have made the great theological motifs of the biblical text the centerpiece of their proclamation. That kind of preaching has helped create within Churches of Christ a climate in which a theological worldview can develop and which can help sustain the enterprise of Christian higher education in ways that were not possible for previous generations.

A third asset which Churches of Christ bring to Christian higher education is their emphasis on rational inquiry. Many who are only slightly acquainted with the Churches of Christ imagine this tradition as fundamentally anti-intellectual. Nothing could be further from the truth. Because of their deep roots in the eighteenth-century Enlightenment, Churches of Christ have a strong intellectual tradition and have consistently prized reason over emotion and logic over speculation. Further, until recent years, Churches of Christ have produced a host of distinguished debaters who learned to use logic with razor-sharp precision. In the mid-nineteenth century, Moses E. Lard described the hard-nosed, jut-jawed reliance on reason that characterized Churches of Christ in that period:

> In no denomination of Christendom, we venture to think, . . . can an equal number of discriminating critics, accomplished logicians, and skillful debatants be found. Indeed, so . . . brilliantly and successfully are these powers displayed when encountering opposition, that those who take part in such discussions are frequently accused of believing in and having only *a religion of the head*.[1]

This emphasis on reason from an early date sustained an interest in inquiry and learning, and in 1836 the people of this movement established their first

1. Moses Lard, "The Reformation for Which We Are Pleading: What Is It?" *Lard's Quarterly* 1 (September 1863): 18.

college and appropriately named it Bacon College, after Francis Bacon, the founder of the scientific method. Walter Scott, the college's first president, centered his inaugural address on Francis Bacon's treatise, *Novum Organum*. Alexander Campbell himself established in 1840 the second college in the movement's history: Bethany College in Bethany, Virginia (now West Virginia), still a strong and viable college belonging to the Disciples of Christ. By 1865 the *Baltimore American* ran an editorial extolling this movement for its devotion "to the interests of education," and noted that, even then, these people had "under their control thirteen first-class colleges and . . . a large number of academies and higher seminaries of learning."[2]

By the twentieth century, colleges spawned by this movement included such institutions as Butler University, Drake University, and Texas Christian University, all connected with the Disciples of Christ; Milligan College, connected with the Independent Christian Churches; and Freed-Hardeman University, David Lipscomb University, Abilene Christian University, Harding University, and Pepperdine University, all connected with the Churches of Christ.

Among the most impressive developments in the twentieth century is the number of scholars from Churches of Christ who hold strategic positions in religion departments in some of the most distinguished colleges and universities in the United States. Standing at the fountainhead of this development was LeMoine G. Lewis, professor of church history at Abilene Christian University from 1949 to 1986. Lewis earned his Ph.D. from Harvard in the 1940s and then fathered a whole multigenerational wave of students who studied religion at Harvard, Yale, Princeton, Chicago, and elsewhere.

This small army of scholars has made a significant impact on scholarship in the field of religion — especially biblical studies — in the United States. These people have held and continue to hold positions in a variety of institutions including Yale, Princeton, Brown, Rice, Emory, Miami University of Ohio, Rhoades College, Cleveland State University, Wellesley, Dartmouth, Johns Hopkins, Erskine College, Miami University of Florida, the University of Georgia, the University of Illinois, and the list goes on.

The point is not to boast of scholars from Churches of Christ in strategic academic positions but to ask why these people pursued scholarship in the first place. The truth is that they were authentic products of Churches of Christ. Many of them inherited the nondenominational understanding of Churches of Christ at its best; that is, they learned that Churches of Christ sought to place themselves under the judgment of the biblical text. That perspective taught them that the search for truth was an important search, and under the influence of mentors like LeMoine G. Lewis, they made that search their life.

2. "The Disciples of Christ," *Baltimore American* (1865), cited in Jerry Rushford, Forrest F. Reed Lectures of the Disciples of Christ Historical Society, 1984.

Richard T. Hughes

What Liabilities Do Churches of Christ Bring to Christian Higher Education?

If Churches of Christ bring several assets to the task of Christian higher education, they also bring several liabilities.

The Anti-Intellectual Tradition of Churches of Christ

While Churches of Christ have sustained an intellectual tradition, they also have sustained a strongly anti-intellectual tradition at the same time. To say that members of the Churches of Christ have been anti-intellectual does not mean that they have demeaned intellectual activity. Rather, their anti-intellectual bias has manifested itself in the way they often have shielded themselves from the implications of their own intellectual work. While they study history and culture, for example, they often fail to see how they themselves are products of the very history they study. Already we have seen how little interest they have expressed over the years in their own particular history in the United States. They have imagined, instead, that they have descended directly from the Bible and the first Christian age, bypassing the power of history and culture altogether. This juxtaposition of Bible and culture underscores the extent to which Churches of Christ have defined their entire identity by the biblical text. They have been, indeed, a "people of the Book." Little else really mattered.

Within the context of Christian higher education, this perspective effectively worked to divide the world into two realms. On the one hand stood the realm of the sacred, defined by the naked and unadorned biblical text. On the other hand stood the realm of secular culture which embraced everything else.

This pattern has prevailed not only with reference to history and culture; it also has prevailed with reference to philosophy, for philosophy inevitably imposed a human (i.e., "secular") lens through which one might read and interpret the sacred biblical text. As Tolbert Fanning, the founder of Franklin College in Nashville, Tennessee, the first institution of higher learning strictly associated with Churches of Christ in the South, complained, "It is impious beyond expression, for a frail worm of earth, to attempt an interpretation of what God has made so plain. . . ." No wonder that Fanning wrote that "all philosophers are, in the true sense, infidels and only infidels."[3]

It is therefore not surprising that most institutions of higher learning

---

3. Tolbert Fanning, "First Principles, Number VI," *Gospel Advocate* 1 (December 1855): 164; and "Sermon Delivered by T. Fanning at Ebenezer Church, October, 1857," in James E. Scobey, ed., *Franklin College and Its Influences* (Nashville: Gospel Advocate Company, 1954), p. 300.

related to Churches of Christ have avoided the study of philosophy. None has ever developed a philosophy department, only one or two have employed trained philosophers, and those few that have offered courses in philosophy typically have done so under the aegis of their Bible departments.[4] Understandably, few among Churches of Christ academics have earned their doctorates in philosophy, and most who have, have had to pursue their philosophical studies outside the boundaries of their own religious heritage, once again underscoring the split Churches of Christ have created between the sacred (biblical) realm and the secular.

The same can be said of theology. Though theology involves systematic thought about God and the way God relates to humankind and the world He created, Churches of Christ for the most part have studiously avoided theological inquiry. The reason is clear: one does not think about God in a systematic way, but rather takes what the biblical text says about God at face value. Until recent years, therefore, colleges and universities related to Churches of Christ seldom offered courses specifically billed as "theology" courses.

Though educators among the Churches of Christ no doubt imagined they were enhancing Christian higher education by focusing their energies entirely on the biblical text to the exclusion of philosophical and theological reflection, in reality this decision undermined the very enterprise they sought to enhance. Without systematic theological reflection, for example, how could those educators bring the study of history, literature, physics, political science, and other "secular" disciplines under the umbrella of a Christian worldview? In the first place, the Bible said nothing about those disciplines. In the second place, by rejecting philosophical and theological reflection, educators among Churches of Christ virtually guaranteed their own inability to construct a Christian worldview which might in some way embrace those otherwise secular disciplines.

Apart from an overarching Christian worldview, Christian higher education in Church of Christ-related institutions typically has meant two things: (1) encouragement and preservation of good moral values and (2) an institutional context in which 100 percent of the faculty and a significant majority of the students were members of Churches of Christ. With a world effectively divided into sacred (biblical) and secular spheres, little else could be done.

So long as most of these institutions maintained student bodies composed largely of members of Churches of Christ, the lack of a systematic, overarching, Christian worldview was seldom noticed. Good and moral behavior, coupled with the institutional allegiance of the vast majority of faculty and students to

4. Pepperdine University is an exception to this pattern, currently employing two trained philosophers in its Humanities Division.

the Churches of Christ, seemed enough to insure a thoroughgoing Christian institution of higher learning. Clearly, many of these institutions also promoted other dimensions like personal piety and a concern for world missions. But the two baseline factors that virtually defined whether an institution was Christian or not were (1) the building of character and morality (2) carried out in the context of an institution dominated by members of Churches of Christ.

"Barren of Imagination"

The way in which Churches of Christ divided the world into sacred and secular domains is perhaps most striking in the realm of aesthetics.[5] Stephen Findley, a musician, painter, actor, and recent M.Div. graduate at Pepperdine University, did a research project on the Reformation and the arts that helped illustrate this point. Part of Findley's paper focused on Ulrich Zwingli, the noted sixteenth-century reformer, who in many ways stands as the spiritual father of Churches of Christ.[6] Though an accomplished musician, Zwingli was also an uncompromising biblical primitivist who sought to conform the church to the biblical model in every way his circumstances permitted.[7] Zwingli therefore banished not only instrumental music but vocal singing from the worship on biblical grounds. He argued that the New Testament offers no precedent or justification for instruments in worship and that Paul virtually prohibited vocal singing when he wrote, "Sing and make music in your heart to the Lord" (Eph. 5:19, NIV). Likewise, Zwingli stripped the great cathedral in Zurich of all works of art and ornamentation and created instead a house of God that was aesthetically barren.

Findley observed that in those acts Zwingli virtually banished aesthetics from the sacred domain. If worship was sacred, artistic creativity of all kinds belonged not to the sacred but to the secular realm. Churches of Christ have to a very great extent perpetuated that dichotomy, and many artists and musicians who belong to Churches of Christ have had to pursue their creative endeavors outside the boundaries of their church relationship.

This does not mean that colleges and universities associated with Churches of Christ have refused to teach and nurture the aesthetic life. Indeed, many of these institutions have boasted outstanding programs in the visual arts, drama, and music. But aesthetics, like theology and philosophy, typically have been pushed outside the bounds of the church and therefore

5. On Churches of Christ and aesthetics, see Dale A. Jorgenson, *Theological and Aesthetic Roots in the Stone-Campbell Movement* (Kirksville: Thomas University Press, 1989).

6. Stephen Findley, "Zwingli, Luther, and the Arts of the Liturgy: Two Theological Views" (unpublished paper, Pepperdine University, 1994).

7. Cf. Charles Garside, *Zwingli and the Arts* (New Haven: Yale University Press, 1966).

outside the sphere of the sacred. This means that fine arts programs in colleges and universities related to Churches of Christ seldom foster artistic creativity in ways that invite serious theological reflection on the creative enterprise itself, or in ways that allow self-conscious integration of artistic creativity with theological imagination.

This continues to be an intensely practical problem for artists of all kinds — painters, sculptors, thespians, and even musicians — who work in institutions related to Churches of Christ. This is less true of choral music than it is of other artistic disciplines, mainly because Churches of Christ historically have utilized a cappella music as a fundamental part of the worship experience. But in the context of many other artistic disciplines — and in the context of at least some of the institutions related to Churches of Christ — artists often find little support for their concern to integrate their passion for aesthetics with their Christian faith. They nurture both, but they often do so on separate tracks.

Not only has the "traditionless tradition" of Churches of Christ separated aesthetics from religious faith, it has failed to provide an intellectual climate hospitable to aesthetic work. While Churches of Christ have produced a host of scholars who excel in fields requiring technical and logical expertise, they have produced relatively few scholars or professionals who excel in fields requiring creativity and imagination — literature, art, and music, for example. Indeed, with their concern for a scientifically precise reading of the biblical text and with their disdain for theological and philosophical reflection, Churches of Christ have never had much interest in nurturing the imagination. David Lipscomb, perhaps the most important leader of Churches of Christ in the second half of the nineteenth century, explained why.

> [Taking the Bible alone] . . . to many seems narrow. [But] it keeps man on safe ground. It ties him to God and his word in all matters of moral and religious duty and all questions of right and wrong. It clips the wings of imagination and speculation and makes the Bible the only and safest teacher of duty to man.[8]

Accordingly, when H. R. Moore eulogized Tolbert Fanning, Lipscomb's mentor, he intended only the highest praise when he flatly declared, "He waved no plumes, wreathed no garlands, but struck from the shoulder and at the vitals. He was destitute of poetry and barren of imagination."[9]

The lack of imagination and theological reflection that has characterized Churches of Christ for most of their history — coupled with a lack of any

8. David Lipscomb, "Tolbert Fanning's Teaching and Influence," in Scobey, ed., *Franklin College and Its Influences*, p. 14.

9. H. R. Moore, "Tolbert Fanning," in Scobey, ed., *Franklin College and Its Influences*, p. 143.

sense of tradition — has created important consequences for Christian higher education in this fellowship. Most of all, imagination and theological reflection, in the context of a particular tradition, are the crucial ingredients for the creation of a theoretical model that might sustain and give long-term direction to Christian higher education. Because Churches of Christ, for the most part, have lacked these ingredients, higher education in this tradition has evolved with no well-defined theoretical model. Instead, Christian higher education among Churches of Christ has rested, as we have seen, on two supports, one institutional and one moral. The institutional support is the intent that all faculty and a large majority of the students be members of Churches of Christ. Simply put, the moral support demands moral behavior.

Conclusion

It is clear that Christian higher education is rendered lame without a sympathetic and numerically strong base of support at every level of the institution — the board, the administration, the faculty, the staff, and the students. At the same time, authentic Christian higher education cannot finally rest on these kinds of supports alone. There must also be well-conceived theoretical supports, rooted deeply in the core message of the biblical text, lived out in a community of faith, and sustained by imaginative theological reflection. Without those theoretical supports — shared, discussed, and debated in the university community from the board level down — it is idle to imagine that sheer numbers of Christians can possibly sustain an institution in the experiment of Christian higher education.

In the case of Churches of Christ, the good news is the wave of renewal that is currently sweeping that tradition. The traditional understanding of the Bible as a blueprint for reproducing ancient forms and structures is slowly giving way to an understanding of the Bible as a theological treatise. And sectarianism, exclusivism, and legalism are slowly giving way to great biblical themes like creation, redemption, and self-giving love — themes that can provide a foundation for Christian higher education at its best.

Most of all, Churches of Christ have two especially rich resources for sustaining their work in the field of Christian higher education. One is their historic allegiance to the biblical text. The other is their commitment to the vision of non-denominational Christianity, if they can define that vision in terms of ideal and process rather than in terms of accomplished fact.

Whether colleges and universities related to the Churches of Christ will weave all these dimensions into strong theoretical supports for the task of Christian higher education is the story that remains to be told.

Faith and Learning
at Pepperdine University

Richard T. Hughes

*Founded in 1937 in Los Angeles, California, George Pepperdine Col-
lege was essentially an undergraduate institution, offering limited
graduate work in a few fields, until the late 1960s and early 1970s.
At that time, Pepperdine expanded into four distinct schools: the
School of Business and Management, the Graduate School of Education and Psychology, the School of Law, and the undergraduate college
which in 1972 opened a shining new campus in Malibu, some twenty
miles northwest of Los Angeles, and which acquired in 1975 the name,
Seaver College. In keeping with the focus of this volume, this essay
will explore the dynamics at work at George Pepperdine College until
the early 1970s. From that point on, it will follow the trajectory of
Seaver College only.*

From its founding, Pepperdine University has been one of the most interesting
of all the American experiments in Christian higher education. In part this is
because Pepperdine has developed a multi-faceted identity, even with respect
to the institution's spiritual commitments, and in turn has created a complex
and diverse constituency.

Spiritually, Pepperdine finds its deepest roots in the school's historic relationship to the Churches of Christ, though that relationship has always been

---

This essay appeared in a slightly different form in the *Restoration Quarterly,* 4th quarter,
1994, pp. 327-339. The author and publisher are grateful to the editor of this journal for
permission to incorporate that material in this volume.

an ambiguous one. On the one hand, Pepperdine carefully nurtures its ties to that religious tradition. Over the years, many leaders of this institution have argued that apart from that relationship, Pepperdine would cease to be a Christian institution altogether. On the other hand, Pepperdine has never defined itself as a typical or traditional Church of Christ-related institution. In fact, Pepperdine's relationship to Churches of Christ has occasioned considerable dispute and controversy within the institution itself.

There are several reasons for this awkward partnership. One is the fact that Churches of Christ have never supported Pepperdine to any significant extent, either with dollars or with students. Many in Churches of Christ, a conservative Bible-based tradition whose heartland spans a belt running from Middle Tennessee to West Texas, have viewed this Southern California school with considerable suspicion, often thinking Pepperdine too "liberal."

Yet, the suspicion runs both ways. Over the years many faculty and administrators have worried that Churches of Christ alone provide an insufficient base to sustain a quality academic institution. Several factors have led them to that conclusion.

First, members of Churches of Christ historically have often defined themselves in highly exclusive terms, contending that they are the only true Christians and comprise the only true church. That position stands in contrast to values intrinsic to the academy, which prizes diversity and fosters exploration of a plurality of perspectives. Pepperdine's location in the Los Angeles area, one of the most culturally and religiously diverse regions in the world, has only magnified this dilemma.

From the time of its founding, in fact, Pepperdine has valued religious diversity. While it has especially nurtured its relation to the Churches of Christ, it has never sought to appeal only to students of that tradition. From 1976 to 1995, for example, the numbers of students attending Seaver College who were members of Churches of Christ never exceeded 15 percent of the total student body.[1] At the same time, Pepperdine has attracted students from a variety of Christian traditions and, especially in more recent years, from non-Christian traditions as well.

The same has been true with respect to faculty. While Pepperdine has sought to maintain a "critical mass" of faculty who are members of Churches of Christ, the institution has regularly employed faculty who belong to other Christian denominations and sometimes faculty who adhere to other religions, especially Islam and Judaism.

Over the years, therefore, the question has nagged: how could the school nurture its relation to the Churches of Christ with their history of exclusivism

---

1. "Seaver College Undergraduate Church of Christ Fall Enrollment," Report of the Office of Institutional Research, January 23, 1995.

and separatism and at the same time cultivate genuine "spiritual diversity"? This was a very practical problem that produced serious tensions in every decade of the institution's history, as we shall see.

Second, Churches of Christ have seldom nurtured systematic theological reflection or an overarching worldview. Instead, they generally have defined themselves in terms of their zeal to restore the primitive church, focusing especially on external ecclesiastical practices rather than on biblical theology. Further, as an American frontier tradition devoted to the democratic ethos, Churches of Christ have always resisted both creeds and confessions of faith. Instead, they have prized the right of the individual believer to interpret scripture for himself or herself, within certain generally accepted boundaries. As a result, Churches of Christ have never generated a coherent theological perspective that might sustain the enterprise of Christian higher education.

Because the heritage of Churches of Christ provides Pepperdine with its principle model for Christian higher education, Pepperdine differs from Protestant confessional institutions like Wheaton College and Calvin College in at least two ways. First, Pepperdine has never required its faculty or students to assent even to the most minimal statement of faith. Indeed, most faculty continue to view the imposition of any creedal standard as an unwarranted infringement both on individual freedom in Christ and on academic freedom. In a survey administered to Seaver College faculty in the spring of 1995, only 17 percent of the responding faculty indicated that they would support any kind of faith statement at Seaver College.[2] And second, if schools like Calvin and Wheaton seek to "integrate faith and learning" around a distinctly "Christian worldview," informed by a deliberate and well-formulated faith perspective, Pepperdine has never defined a theological perspective that might inform such a "Christian worldview."

What, then, does Pepperdine's relation with Churches of Christ finally mean? What of intellectual or spiritual substance do Churches of Christ contribute to the institution? How does that religious tradition nurture critical thinking? Or ethics? Or spiritual formation? Or Christian scholarship? Or diversity? Or academic excellence? Pepperdine's leaders and faculty have seldom explored the possibilities inherent in that relationship beyond the persistent affirmation that apart from its church connection, Pepperdine would lose its Christian identity altogether.

In the absence of a well-articulated theological base, Pepperdine has often defined itself in terms of the ethical and spiritual ideals of the Christian faith. On the one hand, that orientation would sustain morality, character, and Christian behavior. For that reason, Pepperdine often describes itself as a "value centered" institution. On the other hand, Pepperdine's spiritual orien-

2. This survey generated a 65 percent Seaver College faculty response.

tation would allow for genuine diversity. As the University's official statement describing its religious orientation explains:

> Pepperdine University is religiously affiliated with Churches of Christ. It is the purpose of Pepperdine University to pursue the very highest academic standards within a context which celebrates and extends the spiritual and ethical ideals of the Christian faith. Students, faculty, administrators, and members of the Board of Regents represent many religious backgrounds, and people of all races and faiths are welcome to benefit from the University's value centered campus.[3]

When all was said and done, the values Pepperdine affirmed were multifaceted. The school often affirmed specifically Christian values, but it also affirmed broader spiritual values which resisted the empirical spirit of the modern age. As William S. Banowsky, Pepperdine's president from 1971 to 1978, pointed out, "The liberal arts experience, grounded in spiritual values, offers the student a life with meaning and a faith transcending empirical limitations."[4]

Pepperdine also affirmed values that could hardly be distinguished from conservative American values. In part, the school inherited this emphasis from its founder, George Pepperdine, whose life story reads like a Horatio Alger novel. A Kansas farmboy of limited means, Mr. Pepperdine spent five dollars on 500 postage stamps in 1908 in order to launch a small mail-order business, specializing in automobile parts. From that modest beginning, Mr. Pepperdine developed the Western Auto Supply Company, a multi-million dollar chain that did business from coast to coast.

In later years, he extolled what he called "the miracle of the American way of life." He especially praised the "God-inspired disciplines of the free individual" and the free enterprise system which, he argued, "could be harmonized with basic Christian principles."[5] Finally, he argued that those who profit from the American system were obligated to use their wealth for the benefit of others. Accordingly, Mr. Pepperdine adopted as the motto for his school five words in Matthew 10:8: "Freely ye received; freely give."

For the most part, Churches of Christ shared these perspectives. As a Christian tradition born on the American frontier, Churches of Christ have always prized individualism and democracy, along with the virtues of hard

3. "Long Statement of Church Affiliation," distributed June 27, 1995.

4. William S. Banowsky, "The Spiritual Mission of Pepperdine University," *Mission* 10 (September 1976): 6.

5. George Pepperdine, "The Miracle of the American Way of Life" in Richard L. Clark and Jack W. Bates, *Faith Is My Fortune: A Life Story of George Pepperdine* (Los Angeles: Pepperdine College Bookstore, 1962), pp. 241-244.

work, thrift, and strong moral character. It was therefore almost natural for Pepperdine College to extol traditional American values, even as it claimed a relationship with Churches of Christ.

From its beginning, therefore, this college was different from virtually any other Christian institution. It was church-related, but not church-controlled. It affirmed Christian, spiritual, and traditional American values, but resisted any creed, confession of faith, or even a theological definition of its mission. And it sought to combine Christian commitment with openness to genuine diversity.

Finally, Pepperdine has sought to build a strong academic tradition — a dimension that will be considered later in this chapter.

As the years unfolded, therefore, the saga of this university revolved around five distinct dimensions and the way those dimensions intersected with one another: Pepperdine's relation to the Churches of Christ, its affirmation of a Christian and spiritual identity that transcended the bounds of its Church of Christ constituency, its affirmation of traditional American values, its quest for diversity, and its quest for academic excellence. How these five themes intersected with one another over the years is the story we now seek to tell.

The Founding Years

Deeply committed to the Churches of Christ, George Pepperdine embraced the basic doctrinal outlook of that tradition as enthusiastically as anyone of his era.[6] However, he did not grow up in the mainstream of that heritage. Instead, he identified for many years with the Sommerite wing of Churches of Christ, a group of congregations noted for their opposition to church-related colleges. Radically democratic in sentiment, the Sommerites claimed that church-related colleges eventually tend to grow rich and powerful and finally threaten the autonomy of the local church or congregation.[7]

This dimension of Mr. Pepperdine's background is perhaps most responsible for the way he envisioned the religious dimensions of the college he established. In his "Founding Statement," he stipulated that the college "shall be a private enterprise, not connected with any church, and shall not solicit contributions from the churches."

6. See George Pepperdine's tract, "More Than Life," reprinted in Clark and Bates, *Faith Is My Fortune*, pp. 206-228.

7. The Sommerite congregations centered in the Middle West in the late nineteenth century and followed the leadership of Daniel Sommer. On this tradition, see Richard T. Hughes, *Reviving the Ancient Faith: The Story of Churches of Christ in America* (Grand Rapids: Eerdmans, 1996), pp. 228-231.

In truth, because George Pepperdine funded the college so generously in its earliest years, the college was not dependent on any church relationship for financial support. The level of that funding granted Pepperdine a measure of fiscal and spiritual independence that has not characterized any other college or university related to Churches of Christ.

Further, when Mr. Pepperdine defined the religious mission of his college, he avoided any mention of the Church of Christ. He also avoided theological or confessional categories, but spoke instead in very practical terms. This school, he said, would place "special emphasis on Christian living and funda-mental Christian faith." He wanted his college to provide a "wholesome Christian atmosphere." And he wanted the faculty and trustees to be "devout Christian men and women, who will give careful attention to safeguarding and deepening the faith of the students, increasing their loyalty to Jesus and their zeal for saving souls."[8]

The college instituted from the beginning a tradition of daily chapel in which the entire community shared in worship together. In addition, begin-ning in 1943, the college reached out to the Churches of Christ through an annual Bible lectureship that brought to Pepperdine's campus leaders and members of Churches of Christ from far and near. Still, the college jealously guarded its independence from any church controls.[9]

Because Mr. Pepperdine defined his school in terms of character and piety, not in terms of theology or orthodox belief — and certainly not in terms of church control — he created a sizable pocket of ambiguity surrounding the church relationship. In a sense, George Pepperdine College was no different from any other college or university related to Churches of Christ in this regard. But most of the other institutions — Abilene Christian College in Texas, Harding College in Arkansas, and David Lipscomb College in Tennessee, for example — existed in parts of the nation where Churches of Christ were strong. In those cases, the active presence of a strong church constituency helped to assure a strong church relationship. Historically, however, Churches of Christ on the West Coast have been few, small, and weak.

From the time of Pepperdine's founding, ambiguity over the church rela-tionship has invited tension. Some have sought to enhance that relationship and to turn the institution into a more traditional Church of Christ college. Others have sought to weaken the tie with Churches of Christ, arguing that

8. George Pepperdine, *Founding Statement,* reproduced in "Minutes of Regular Quar-terly Meeting of the Board of Trustees of the George Pepperdine College," June 6, 1938, Board Minutes Book, vol. 1, pp. 24-25.

9. With their congregational polity, Churches of Christ have no centralized bureaucracy that is capable of exercising control over any of the colleges. Church control over colleges or other church-related institutions is therefore informal, based on power-factions or consensus within the larger denomination.

Pepperdine could fulfill its religious and academic missions apart from a strong relation with that religious tradition. Moreover, the fortunes of the University in this regard have often correlated with the leadership of key administrators.

A case in point was Batsell Baxter, the first president of George Pepperdine College. Mr. Pepperdine's rather broadly worded "Founder's Statement" appeared in the college bulletin in June of 1937. The very next month, a curious letter from Mr. Pepperdine to President Baxter appeared in the minutes of the Board of Trustees, a letter that sought to qualify the "Founder's Statement" in terms far more specific with respect to the doctrinal positions of Churches of Christ. Because Baxter stood squarely in the heart of the mainline Churches of Christ, having served previously as president of two other Church of Christ-related colleges — David Lipscomb College in Nashville and Abilene Christian College in Texas — it is perhaps safe to assume that Baxter encouraged Mr. Pepperdine to write this letter or that Baxter wrote it over Mr. Pepperdine's name.

In any event, the letter stipulated that members of the faculty and the board should adhere to themes like the deity of Christ, the virgin birth, Jesus' miracles, the atonement, and the inspiration and authority of the Bible. While these themes comprised standard fundamentalist fare for that period, the letter went on to specify other doctrines specific to Churches of Christ. All faculty and board members, for example, should uphold the "plan of salvation" which Churches of Christ commonly taught: belief, repentance, confession, and baptism. Further, all faculty and board members should be "members in good standing" of the Church of Christ. To tighten things down even more, the letter noted that "the New Testament plan of church organization and worship which includes the regular observance of the Lord's Supper and which excludes instrumental music in the worship, shall be the definition of the Church of Christ."[10]

On the other hand, some felt that Pepperdine College could best achieve academic distinction apart from a strong tie to the Churches of Christ. No one better exemplified this tendency in the early years than Earl V. Pullias, the academic dean for seventeen years beginning in 1940. Ironically, Batsell Baxter was responsible for Pullias' association with the institution.

Baxter served as Pepperdine's president for only two years. While he provided strategic academic leadership, securing accreditation for the institution during its first year of operation, E. V. Pullias was the first to bring to the school an unyielding commitment to academic excellence. Further, Pullias was the principle driving force for the institution for most of the years that he served as dean.

10. Letter from George Pepperdine to Batsell Baxter, July 21, 1937, Board Minutes Book, vol. 1, pp. 22-23.

Pullias insisted on a first-class faculty, and because Mr. Pepperdine funded the institution so well, Pullias was able to pay handsome salaries — $3,000 per year for at least some professors[11] — and thereby sought to attract some of the best and the brightest. At the same time, Pullias favored a broader religious vision for Pepperdine than he felt an exclusive relation with Churches of Christ could provide. Accordingly, he hired faculty who represented an array of religious traditions. He hired some members of Churches of Christ, but he also hired many who were not. And he hired as well a number of faculty whose roots were in Churches of Christ but who believed — along with Pullias — that the Church of Christ heritage provided a base too narrow to sustain a first-rate institution of higher learning.[12]

Current Provost Steven Lemley concludes that Pullias helped create "much of the ambiguity with regard to church relationship and Christian dimension that has occupied us for nearly sixty years."[13] It might be more accurate to say that George Pepperdine created the ambiguity which Batsell Baxter exploited on behalf of an exclusive relationship with the Churches of Christ, and which Earl Pullias exploited on behalf of diversity and strong academics.

In this way, Batsell Baxter and Earl V. Pullias served as metaphors for the entire future history of the institution. Their commitments relative to the Churches of Christ defined the tension between faith and learning that has characterized Pepperdine University ever since.

Though Pullias was able to assemble an outstanding faculty, his efforts finally proved abortive in the short run, mainly because Mr. Pepperdine lost much of his fortune through some unfortunate investments. The college fell on hard times, faculty salaries were cut, and the glory days were over — at least for now.

The Norvel Young Era

By the mid-1950s, the board of trustees, composed entirely of members of Churches of Christ, had become alarmed over what they perceived as Pepperdine's continual drift away from a strong church connection. When Hugh Tiner, who had served as president since 1939, resigned in 1957, the board seized the opportunity to hire a man who they believed would bind Pepperdine College closer to the Churches of Christ. That man was M. Norvel Young, a Ph.D. in history from George Peabody College and the preacher for the Broad-

11. "Minutes of Special Meeting of the Board of Trustees," Board Minutes Book, vol. 1, pp. 18-19.

12. Interview with M. Norvel Young, Pepperdine Chancellor Emeritus, April 18, 1995.

13. Steven Lemley, "Remarks to Seaver Faculty," August 23, 1994, p. 2.

way Church of Christ in Lubbock, Texas. At the same time, the board requested and received Earl V. Pullias's resignation from his post as dean.

When Young arrived as Pepperdine's new president in 1957, he faced a mass resignation on the part of the faculty. Some felt that Pullias's departure and Young's arrival signaled a betrayal of academic values for the sake of a church relationship that had little to do with serious intellectual life. Many others left because the institution's fiscal future seemed so shaky. In all, twenty-seven faculty and staff persons left during Young's first year in office, including the business manager, the director of publicity, the director of admissions, the head librarian, the dean of students, and heads of the social science, speech, and education departments.[14]

As Pepperdine's new president, Young faced three daunting challenges. He had to rebuild the faculty. He had to bind Pepperdine more closely to its heritage in the Churches of Christ. And he had to place the school on a firm financial footing. He integrated the first two challenges and addressed them simultaneously. That is, he sought to achieve for Pepperdine a closer relationship with Churches of Christ in part by hiring administrators and faculty who were faithful to that tradition. He also reached out to Churches of Christ by enhancing Pepperdine's Bible lectureship, an annual program designed specifically for members of that communion. In 1967, for example, the lectureship attracted 14,000 people.[15]

Ideally, Young would integrate his fund-raising efforts into his attempt to build bridges to Churches of Christ. By 1957, however, Young found very little support in the churches for Pepperdine College. Pepperdine was far from the heartland of Churches of Christ and, perhaps even more important, had earned during the Pullias years a reputation for "liberalism." Few in Churches of Christ in those days had great wealth, and the few who did chose to invest their contributions in "safer" institutions like Abilene Christian College, Harding College, and David Lipscomb College.

Young therefore did what he felt he had to do. He continued to build bridges to the Churches of Christ, but in his search for funding, he turned to civic leaders and to the business community of Southern California. In this effort, he followed the lead of President Hugh Tiner who had already built strong relations with that community. The civic and business constituency, however, cared little about Pepperdine's relation with Churches of Christ. They cared instead about traditional American values: patriotism, hard work, basic morality, and faith in God. Because those themes were deeply rooted both in

14. Interviews with M. Norvel Young, April 18 and 19, 1995. See also Pepperdine College Bulletins for 1956-58 and 1958-59.

15. M. Norvel Young, *Pepperdine University: A Place, A People, A Purpose* (Princeton: The Newcomen Society, 1982), p. 13.

Pepperdine's founding and even in the ethos of Churches of Christ, Young was able to exploit that dimension of the college to great effect.

Young's efforts to cultivate a civic and business constituency subtly but inevitably redefined the mission of the institution in terms that had little to do with the historic Christian faith. For example, in a speech delivered to the Newcomen Society in 1982, Young described Pepperdine as "a liberal arts college of academic excellence, founded upon the principles of private enterprise and loyalty to God and country." Fourteen years into his presidency, Young explained that Pepperdine's "relationship with the business community has been a great factor in our success. While many businessmen are not concerned with our theology, they do like the fact that we turn out students with a sense of moral responsibility and faith in God."[16]

While Young nurtured a constituency in the business and civic community of Southern California, he did not seek to cultivate a broader Christian constituency that transcended the bounds of Churches of Christ. Because of the entrenched exclusivism in Churches of Christ at that time, had Young turned to a broader Christian community, he would have risked cutting the tie with Churches of Christ altogether.

This point is crucial, for it suggests that Pepperdine had two options at that time. It could define its religious mission in terms of the Churches of Christ, an option that virtually eliminated ties to a broader Christian world; or it could define its mission in the broader, more inclusive terms of morality and traditional values, an option that appealed far beyond the confines of an explicitly Christian constituency and even to a variety of secular constituencies.

As time went on, Pepperdine gradually cultivated two well-defined external constituencies. On the one hand stood a church constituency whose chief concern was that Pepperdine remain faithful to the heritage of that tradition, but this constituency did not pay the bills. On the other hand stood a donor base chiefly interested in traditional American values.

Because of this dual constituency, Pepperdine gradually began to wear two different public faces. To its church constituency, the college portrayed itself as a Christian institution, loyal to the ideals of the Churches of Christ. To the larger public, it projected traditional American values and seldom invoked either its particular church relationship or its explicitly Christian dimensions.[17]

16. Young, *Pepperdine University: A Place, A People, A Purpose*, p. 15; and Jerry Rushford, ed., *Crest of a Golden Wave: A 50th Anniversary Pictorial History* (Malibu: Pepperdine University Press, 1987), p. 118.

17. According to Fred Casmir, communications professor at Pepperdine since 1956, "this double image became very clear perhaps by the early 1960s." Interview with Fred Casmir, November 8, 1994.

At one level, these two persona were not incompatible, especially since the college had embraced both these visions from its founding. So long as the college directed these two images to a single, church constituency, they remained in sync. Yet, once the two images began to serve two different constituencies, neither of which knew much about the other and neither of which was in touch with the other, the two images slowly began to drift apart.

Impact of the 1960s

From its founding in 1937, George Pepperdine College sat on a thirty-four acre tract of land, seventy-eight blocks due south of downtown Los Angeles. By the 1960s, middle-class African Americans occupied most of the homes surrounding the campus for many miles to the north, south, and west. Less than one mile to the east, however, lay an economically depressed African American neighborhood known as Watts. That area exploded into the news when rioting erupted there in August of 1965. From temporary headquarters on the Pepperdine campus, the National Guard now patrolled the streets of South Central Los Angeles

The riots raised questions about Pepperdine's prospects for continuing to attract students from conservative Church of Christ homes in places like Texas and Tennessee. Further, donors were reluctant to fund buildings that might be constructed on that campus.[18] Those concerns, coupled with the fact that Pepperdine was land-locked and perpetually confined to a thirty-four acre campus, prompted the administration and board of trustees to launch a search for a new site for the campus.

In the fall of 1968, the college announced a gift of land, a magnificent 138-acre property in Malibu, situated in the Santa Monica Mountains and overlooking the Pacific Ocean. That site eventually would expand to 830 acres. There Pepperdine built an entirely new campus that opened in the fall of 1972 and that accommodated most of the undergraduate instruction.

It is impossible to overestimate the impact of the Malibu location both on the academic development and on the religious mission of the institution. The Malibu site contributed more perhaps than any other single factor to the academic enhancement of the institution, as we shall see. But Malibu, California — a spectacularly beautiful playground for the rich and the famous — also stood light-years removed from the mainstream values of the traditional, heartland heritage of Churches of Christ.

As Pepperdine laid the groundwork for its new Malibu campus, it also

18. "Pepperdine University Torn by Tragedy, Internal Dissent," *Los Angeles Times* (April 18, 1976), CCII1.

developed three new professional schools to complement its traditional undergraduate programs. In 1969, Pepperdine acquired an Orange County-based law school and created that same year a graduate school of education and a graduate school of business. For the next several years, Pepperdine maintained on the Los Angeles campus a small undergraduate program, a small graduate program in the liberal arts, a school of continuing education, a school of education, and a school of business. In 1971, George Pepperdine College declared itself Pepperdine University, and on April 20, 1975, thanks to historic gifts from Mrs. Frank R. Seaver, Pepperdine named its undergraduate school at Malibu, Seaver College.

With its new professional schools, Pepperdine to a great extent institutionalized the dichotomy between the two constituencies it now had cultivated for several years. The schools of business and education provided substantial revenue that helped underwrite the new Malibu campus,[19] but functioned almost independently of any effort to relate to Churches of Christ. At the same time, the University hoped that the new undergraduate college at Malibu would help the school renew its ties with its Church of Christ constituency. Pepperdine therefore launched a vigorous effort to recruit both faculty and students from this tradition for the Malibu operation, awarding unprecedented amounts of scholarship money to qualified students from that heritage. When the Malibu campus opened in the fall of 1972, 28 percent of the student body and well over three-fourths of the faculty belonged to the Churches of Christ.[20]

The William S. Banowsky Era and the Birth of the Malibu Campus

Since 1963, Pepperdine faculty on the Los Angeles campus, most of whom were members of the Churches of Christ, had taught fourteen credit hours per trimester, three trimesters a year, for a total of forty-two units annually. Salaries were so low that most faculty had to supplement their incomes by various forms of moonlighting. There was little opportunity for these faculty to develop into outstanding scholars, in spite of the fact that several had received first-class doctoral training.[21] Still, many of these faculty accepted

19. Interview with M. Norvel Young, April 19, 1995. Young estimates that these programs generated the equivalent of a $50 million endowment.
20. Information regarding scholarship money came from a telephone interview with Robert Fraley, May 23, 1995. Fraley was Dean of Admissions from 1972-1989. In 1974, 83 percent of the faculty teaching at Pepperdine's Malibu campus belonged to Churches of Christ. See memorandum from Provost Jerry E. Hudson to President William S. Banowsky, December 9, 1974.
21. Interview with James Smythe, November 8, 1994. Smythe chaired the Humanities Division from 1971 to 1994.

these limitations since they had come to Pepperdine, as they often said, to "sacrifice for Christian higher education." For many of those older faculty, however, Christian higher education meant higher education in the service of the Church of Christ.

Initially, the administration viewed the birth of the Malibu campus as an opportunity to move into a whole new league academically. The Malibu program would be small, experimental, rigorous, and interdisciplinary. The administration therefore sought to build that program around a small core of scholars imported from the Los Angeles campus but also around new faculty who were young and only recently out of graduate school, and who could invigorate that program with fresh ideas, creative energy, sound scholarship, and academic leadership. The balance of the faculty on the Los Angeles campus would remain where they were.

With so much money required for development of the campus, however, the administration soon decided to expand the Malibu program into a larger enterprise than had initially been envisioned, a decision that seriously diluted the original vision for a small, experimental, and academically upgraded college. Faculty originally scheduled to remain on the Los Angeles campus now made the trek to Malibu, virtually assuring more continuity with the Los Angeles program than had originally been intended.[22]

The initial decision to build the Malibu program around new and younger faculty created a whole new set of problems for the religious identity of the institution. Many of these faculty, after all, were children of the 1960s. They were deeply committed to the Christian faith, but their understanding of Christianity was often quite different from that of the previous generation. They had learned the values of social justice and of ecumenical cooperation to make a difference in the world. Accordingly, many of these faculty had little interest in "sacrificing for Christian higher education" if that meant Church-of-Christ higher education, defined in narrow, sectarian terms.

In addition, several of these faculty were still in Churches of Christ, but barely. During the 1960s, some had taught at other Church of Christ-related institutions where they had not fit well. Some had been terminated from those positions. Others resigned because of dissatisfaction or discomfort. Still others had been fired from positions with local congregations of Churches of Christ at some point in their careers. Needless to say, for many of these people, Pepperdine was a last stop in the Churches of Christ.[23]

22. Telephone interview with Jerry E. Hudson, provost for Malibu campus, 1972-1975, July 31, 1995.

23. According to retired faculty member Jennings Davis, Pepperdine had always been a last stop in Churches of Christ for many of its faculty and staff. These comments were offered in response to an early draft of this chapter, June 15, 1995.

But they *were* in the Church of Christ and still cared deeply about that tradition, and they were all Ph.D.s with promising academic careers. That combination recommended them strongly for employment in Pepperdine's new undergraduate program at Malibu.

These younger faculty related in complex and interesting ways to the double image that Pepperdine had developed since Norvel Young had become president in 1957. On the one hand, since they cared about Churches of Christ, they supported efforts to relate to that tradition. At the same time, most also supported a broader, value-centered education, rooted in an ecumenical approach to the Christian faith. Most hoped that Pepperdine might integrate these two dimensions so that, on this campus at least, the Church of Christ heritage might stand for a Christian-based education, centering on values and ethics. As children of the 1960s, however, few of these younger faculty shared the institution's commitment to conservative political and economic values.

The presence of two distinct groups on the faculty created a struggle for the soul of the institution that engulfed the Malibu campus in the 1970s. Many of the older faculty thought their younger colleagues uncommitted either to Churches of Christ or to a vision of Christian higher education. On the other hand, most younger faculty viewed at least some of their older colleagues as academically deficient, narrow, and sectarian.[24]

Very quickly, however, it became clear which side would prevail in this struggle. The senior University administration moved several of the younger, more progressive faculty into strategic positions of leadership, both in the larger University and on the Malibu campus. One served as the University's academic vice-president, another as provost for the Malibu campus, another as dean of Seaver College, and others as chairpersons of their academic divisions.

These developments cannot be understood apart from the leadership of William S. Banowsky, fourth president of Pepperdine University from 1971 to 1978. And one cannot understand Banowsky apart from his upbringing in Churches of Christ.

Unlike Norvel Young, who grew up in Tennessee congregations often marked by tolerance and grace, Banowsky grew up in Fort Worth, Texas, where Churches of Christ often were known for their legalism and their claims to be the one true church. In time, Banowsky found such claims repugnant and came to resist any form of sectarianism.

Still, at an early age, he was a golden boy in the Churches of Christ. He was only twenty-two years old, fresh out of school with his B.A. from David Lipscomb College and an M.A. from the University of New Mexico, when

---

24. Interview with John Nicks, March 31, 1995. Nicks served as vice-president for academic affairs, 1976-81.

Norvel Young recruited him to serve as assistant to the president at Pepperdine. Five years later, the influential Broadway Church of Christ in Lubbock, Texas, where Young had preached for thirteen years, invited Banowsky to become its minister. He accepted. Then, in 1968, Young invited Banowsky to return to Pepperdine as his executive vice-president. That was the same year that Pepperdine acquired the Malibu property, and between them, Banowsky and Young raised $40 million to develop the new campus. Then, in 1970, Banowsky was named founding chancellor of the Malibu campus.

Not only was Banowsky a darling of Churches of Christ. He soon became a darling of the Republican Party in Southern California. Winsome and charismatic, he was so highly regarded in those circles that, in 1972, he was appointed Republican National Committeeman from California. That same year, he coordinated Richard Nixon's California campaign for re-election to the presidency. By 1975, the *Los Angeles Times* reported that many California Republicans had urged Banowsky to run for governor.

All these characteristics made Banowsky especially attractive to the University's trustees who installed him as the University's fourth president in 1971. Norvel Young became at that time the institution's chancellor and chairman of the Board of Regents. Even before he became president, Banowsky provided critical guidance for the institution, and it is perhaps fair to say that his vision, more than any other, defined the institution for the all-critical ten-year period, beginning in 1968. His role, therefore, is crucial for understanding the faith/learning nexus as that relationship evolved at Seaver College.

Banowsky was convinced that Churches of Christ — and for that matter, institutional Christianity at large — provided a foundation far too narrow to undergird the major university he hoped to build. Instead, he articulated a vision of "spiritual values," capable of embracing a diversity of religious and philosophical traditions. With that focus, he sought to broaden the University's base at three strategic points.

First, he broadened the religious identity of the institution. In May of 1970, at the dedication ceremonies for Pepperdine's new Malibu campus, Banowsky delivered his inaugural address as the founding chancellor of Pepperdine College at Malibu. He called his address, "A Spirit of Place," and the very next month, Pepperdine published his speech "as a statement of the philosophy of the college." There, Banowsky spoke of Churches of Christ as the college's "closest constituency," and affirmed the school's determination "to strengthen, not loosen" the ties with that community of faith. At the same time, he issued a warning: "We will resist any sectarian spirit."

While Banowsky located Pepperdine in the context of "Christian education," he never in that speech defined Pepperdine as an institution shaped by the Churches of Christ. Instead, in the most crucial paragraph of that address, he argued that "since its founding in 1937, Pepperdine College's deepest con-

426

victions have always centered upon spiritual realities." Based on that broad, spiritual foundation, Banowsky argued that Pepperdine was a "person-centered college" offering a "value-centered education."[25]

Though Banowsky was the first president to define Pepperdine explicitly in terms of "value-centeredness,"[26] he would not be the last. Banowsky understood "Christian," "spiritual realities," and "value-centered" as virtually equivalent terms. Yet, his understanding of the University as "Christian," on the one hand, and "spiritual" and "value-centered," on the other, served well the University's dual constituency. The "Christian" descriptor allowed the institution to pursue its church relationship, while the "value-centered" and "spiritual" descriptors allowed the institution to broaden its base of constituents among potential friends who cared little about the Churches of Christ but a great deal about traditional, conservative values.

Second, in addition to his attempt to broaden the religious identity of Pepperdine, Banowsky also restructured the board of trustees. Banowsky felt that a board composed exclusively of members of Churches of Christ could not provide the financial underpinnings or the breadth of intellectual support for the kind of institution he envisioned.

Banowsky and Norvel Young had vigorously debated this issue for a number of years. Then, in 1975, Young was involved in a serious automobile accident that, for a time, removed him from any significant decision-making role in the University. At that point, Banowsky exerted the leadership that resulted in a major change to Pepperdine's "Articles and By-Laws."

During the previous year, Banowsky had retained a Los Angeles law firm "to assist in the total revision of the University's 'Articles and By-Laws'" which provided for twelve trustees, all of whom had to be members of Churches of Christ.[27] The revised "Articles and By-Laws" provided for a forty-person Board of Regents, a bare majority of whom had to be members of Churches of Christ. This centerpiece of Banowsky's administration enabled him to invite onto the board nineteen people whom he regarded as some "of the most distinguished men and women in western America." With this move, he now recalls, "we reestablished the institution on a strong non-sectarian foundation."[28] Indeed, this move would have critical implications for every phase of the institution's life, including its religious identity.

Jack Scott, a member of Pepperdine's Board of Regents who served as provost and dean of the Los Angeles campus from 1970 to 1973, suggested that while the new, non-Church of Christ regents likely were not offended by the school's

25. Banowsky, "A Spirit of Place," pp. 4-6.
26. Interview with M. Norvel Young, May 2, 1995.
27. Telephone interview with William S. Banowsky, May 23, 1995.
28. Interviews with William S. Banowsky, May 19 and 23, 1995.

Church of Christ connection, they "were attracted to Pepperdine on the basis of
... the political and economic conservatism of Pepperdine's leadership."[29]

Third, the leadership in the Banowsky administration sought to secure
faculty who belonged to Churches of Christ, but they placed an even higher
premium on securing academically qualified faculty regardless of denominational affiliation.

Reflecting on his administration some twenty years later, Banowsky recalled, "In a very real sense, I sought to nourish and expand the larger Christian
vision which Earl Pullias had built into the soul of the school, but which had
been systematically resisted by his opponents."[30]

If Banowsky identified the traditional sectarianism of Churches of Christ as
a fundamental problem at Pepperdine during those years, others thought the
problem was a drift toward secularism, fostered by the president himself. In 1975,
for example, thirty faculty addressed to President Banowsky a letter which
complained, "We are apprehensive about the possibility that Pepperdine may
ultimately become so secularized that all Christian impact will be lost." It called
on the president to launch "a full scale effort to relate meaningfully and as
servants to our constituency in churches of Christ," and concluded, "We feel that
it might be preferable for the institution not to operate at all, than to function
in such a way that Christian convictions are compromised or even denied."[31]

In any event, Banowsky's agenda prompted far-reaching change within
Seaver College. From the fall of 1977 through the fall of 1980, the college hired
approximately forty new faculty, most of whom identified themselves as Christian but many of whom did not share the heritage of Churches of Christ.[32] In
fairness, it must be acknowledged that because of the unusually rapid growth of
the faculty during those years, it was often impossible to hire academically
qualified people who were also members of Churches of Christ. While the Seaver
College faculty almost doubled in size during those years, the percentage affiliated with Churches of Christ dropped from over 75 percent in 1972 to 44
percent in 1981-82. By 1994-95, that figure had climbed to only 55 percent, still
more than 20 percent less than it had been some twenty years before.[33]

29. Interview with Jack Scott, April 17, 1995.
30. Telephone interview with William S. Banowsky, May 23, 1995.
31. Letter to William S. Banowsky from thirty Seaver College faculty, February 28, 1975.
Copy of letter in possession of Richard T. Hughes.
32. Interview with Jere Yates, chairperson of Business Division, April 16, 1995; and John
Nicks, March 31, 1995.
33. In 1976-77, the percentage of Seaver College faculty affiliated with Churches of
Christ stood at sixty-five percent. For this data, see memorandum from Provost Jerry E.
Hudson to President William S. Banowsky, December 9, 1974, and Pepperdine University
Full-Time Instructional Faculty Headcount, Percentage Church of Christ, from Office of
Institutional Research.

At the same time, in spite of a major effort to recruit students who belonged to Churches of Christ, that percentage fell as well. When the Malibu campus opened in the fall of 1972, the undergraduate enrollment included 28 percent members of Churches of Christ. By 1982, that figure had dropped to only 8 percent. While that decline reflected the continued estrangement between Pepperdine and Churches of Christ in spite of massive efforts on the part of the institution to improve that relationship, it also reflected the fact that Pepperdine's rising tuition made it increasingly difficult to attract students from Churches of Christ, most of whom came from middle-class homes, at best.

During those same years, the academic quality of the Malibu undergraduate program increased dramatically. While that improvement owed much to academic leadership within the faculty and especially to the new generation of scholars and academic leaders the administration had recruited for the Malibu program, it was also a function of the Malibu location itself. One could argue that the Malibu campus was to Seaver College what football was to Notre Dame: it created enormous visibility for the institution, and its location and extraordinary beauty attracted students who might never have considered Pepperdine otherwise.

The student body that enrolled at Pepperdine in the fall of 1972, the year the Malibu campus opened, posted the highest scholastic aptitude scores of any student body in the history of the institution up to that time. Twenty percent of the freshman class scored at or above the 93rd percentile nationwide. That same class brought with them an average high school GPA of 3.08, with 20 percent having earned 3.50.[34]

Since that time, the quality of students enrolling in Seaver College has systematically improved. For example, the average GPA for domestic, enrolling freshmen was 3.26 in 1990, 3.33 in 1993, and 3.50 in 1995. Interestingly, the statistics reflect no appreciable difference in academic quality between students who are members of Churches of Christ and those who are not.[35]

During those years, Seaver College also enhanced academic quality in the faculty through several teaching load reductions and a corresponding emphasis on faculty scholarship. From 1963 until 1973, the teaching load for the undergraduate faculty remained unchanged: fourteen units per trimester, three trimesters a year, for a total of forty-two units annually. The load was reduced to 14-14-8 in 1973-74 and to 12-12-8, based on four-unit courses across the board, in 1974-75. In the mid-1980s, the load was reduced to 12-12-4, and in the fall of 1996, to 12-12-0.

34. Rushford, ed., *Crest of a Golden Wave*, p. 163.

35. Statistics supplied by Dean of Admission Paul Long. See especially "Domestic Admission Decision Summary" and "Regularly Admitted/Enrolled Statistics — Comparison: Domestic Only."

By the time Banowsky resigned his presidency in 1978, Seaver College had significantly improved its academic quality. The explicitly Christian dimensions of the institution, on the other hand, lagged behind. There are several reasons for this. First, throughout the Banowsky years, the institution portrayed itself to the general public more as an institution informed by "spiritual values" than as an explicitly Christian university. Today's conventional wisdom suggests that fiscal uncertainty was so severe during those years that if Pepperdine's administration had portrayed the school in explicitly Christian terms, the institution might never have survived.[36] Second, the glamorous Malibu campus increasingly attracted students who had little or no interest in Pepperdine's historic Christian commitment. And third, in the ranks of the faculty, the question of the religious dimensions of the institution had become a bone of contention, not a matter for constructive discussion and planning. Some faculty passionately pled for a stronger relation with Churches of Christ. Others had little or no interest in that option or, in any event, supported a broader base for the institution. In the course of the acrimonious debates that ensued, the explicitly Christian supports for Seaver College fell on hard times.

In that context, few in those years explored the integration of faith and learning at all. Instead, most assumed that faith and learning were inherently juxtaposed and polarized, and that the best one could do was to strike a balance between them. President Banowsky expressed this point of view as well as anyone:

> What we are attempting, then, is to achieve a delicate balance between spiritual intensity and genuine academic distinction. It will not be easy. It would be simpler, philosophically, to be either a Bible college, on the one hand, or an utterly secular university on the other. To combine spiritual commitment with academic openness is to tread the narrow edge of un-relieved intellectual tension. But it is a more exciting path than either the emptiness of mere secularity or the sterility of fundamentalistic simplicity.[37]

The Recent Past

In 1978, Banowsky left Pepperdine to become president of the University of Oklahoma. At that time, the Board of Regents appointed Howard A. White (1978-1985), a former history professor and Banowsky's executive vice-president, to a one-year interim presidency which was renewed for a second year in 1979. In 1980, the Board asked White to serve as president for an extended term.

36. Interviews with David Davenport, April 4, 1995; Steven Lemley, April 16, 1995; and Jere Yates, April 16, 1995.

37. Banowsky, "The Spiritual Mission of Pepperdine University,"p. 6.

Rooted in the academic tradition, White sought to enhance the academic stature of the University. With the campus infrastructure well in place and with greater funding at his disposal, he achieved much. For example, under his presidency, Seaver College erected a new music building which significantly enhanced the fine arts, expanded and equipped science laboratories, equipped many faculty with computers, provided more academic scholarships in order to attract better students, approved an expansion of the faculty relative to the size of the student body, and increased faculty salaries, thereby enabling Seaver College to retain more of its best professors.

White also articulated for the institution a Mission Statement which the Board of Regents approved in 1982 and which emphasized both "spiritual matters" and "Christian values." Within a few years, Seaver College required that all candidates for faculty positions, for promotion, or for tenure express in writing their response to the mission of the University, defined in that statement.

From the perspective of Pepperdine's relation to Churches of Christ, White's presidency was in many respects a reaction against developments over the previous decade. Indeed, White felt that the previous ten years had witnessed considerable secularization of the University, and he determined to reverse those trends. Once appointed to a three-year term as president in 1980, he took decisive steps to shore up Pepperdine's Christian mission as he understood it and to create stronger ties between the University and the Churches of Christ.

From the executive vice-president to the vice-president for academic affairs to the dean of Seaver College, he assembled a whole new administrative team, composed of people especially known for their commitment to that heritage. With those strategic positions filled, White insisted on greater attention to hiring faculty who not only were members of Churches of Christ but who were loyal to that tradition.[38] Faculty who were not members of Churches of Christ and who had been hired during the Banowsky years felt that White's hiring policies created tension between what amounted to two different faculties: those who belonged to Churches of Christ and those who did not.[39] Yet, if one understands Howard White in terms of Pepperdine's larger history, one is forced to view White as part of a long-standing struggle between these two forces, reaching all the way back to Batsell Baxter and E. V. Pullias.

When the Board of Regents selected David Davenport as Pepperdine's sixth president in 1985, they sought to perpetuate the emphases of Howard A.

38. Interviews with Loyd Frashier, chairperson of Natural Science Division, 1970-78, March 16, 1995; Mike O'Neal, vice chancellor, April 18, 1995; and John Watson, vice president for student affairs, 1984-92, April 16, 1995.

39. Telephone interview with Lydia Reineck, professor of English, July 17, 1995.

White, both academically and religiously.[40] Academically, Davenport inherited an institution on the upswing, a fact noted by the annual college and university rankings published in *U.S. News & World Report*. In the very year that Davenport became president, for example, Pepperdine ranked in first place among "comprehensive universities" in the Midwest and Far West. *U.S. News & World Report* subsequently reclassified Pepperdine as a research institution. Even there, however, Pepperdine has done well, placing in the first quartile every year but one.

Several factors have contributed to the enhanced academic quality of Seaver College. William Adrian, University provost from 1985 to 1993, sent an important memo to all University faculties in 1987, noting that "the most significant academic challenge facing the University at the present time is to gain the same respect among our academic and professional colleagues that we have among the general public." He therefore noted that while "care and concern for students" and "stimulating classroom teaching" would continue as "tangible expressions of the Christian mission of the University," one could not progress through the academic ranks without "scholarly activity in support of [one's] teaching functions."[41] While some Seaver College faculty resisted the research implications of this statement,[42] most responded favorably, and Seaver College has made significant academic strides within the past decade.

Much of the impetus for original, creative scholarship, however, has come from within the faculty itself and especially from the faculty's Rank, Tenure, and Promotions (RTP) Committee. Organized in the early 1970s on the Los Angeles campus,[43] that committee chiefly sought to bring equity to the promotion and tenure process. However, because high teaching loads at that time virtually prohibited serious scholarly research and publication, the RTP committee based tenure and promotion decisions on two factors: length of time with the institution and the quality of one's teaching.[44]

By the late 1970s, with teaching loads reduced, evidence of scholarly activity became more and more important for promotion and/or tenure. Even then, however, a professor whose publications were minimal or nonexistent could still win promotion and/or tenure by virtue of outstanding teaching and service to the institution. By the 1990s, however, the RTP Committee, in concert with the administration, tightened requirements even further. It would

40. Telephone interview with Jerry E. Hudson, July 31, 1995.
41. "Teaching and Scholarly Activity," a memo from Provost William Adrian to all Pepperdine University faculty, January 12, 1987.
42. Interview with Thomas H. Olbricht, chairperson of Religion Division, May 15, 1995; and William Adrian, May 4, 1995.
43. Telephone interview with Ken Perrin, May 4, 1995. Perrin chaired the Natural Science Division from 1978 to 1991.
44. Telephone interview with Ken Perrin, May 4, 1995.

now be impossible to earn either tenure or promotion without some evidence of serious scholarship, resulting in publications and/or presentations at professional meetings.[45]

At the same time, Seaver College continues to identify itself primarily as a teaching institution. In the faculty survey mentioned earlier in this essay, only 16 percent of the faculty placed "maximum possible emphasis" on the proposition that Seaver College should "advance knowledge through research." At the same time, 84 percent placed "maximum possible emphasis" on the proposal that the college should "extend knowledge through teaching."

While many Seaver College faculty are active scholars seriously involved in research and publication, some argue that original, creative scholarship is seldom promoted or publicized either among the students or among the University's external constituencies. One senior faculty member, for example, pointed to the various publications the University produces for alumni, parents, friends, and donors. "For our size university," he suggested, "we probably produce as many quality publications aimed at external constituencies as any school in the country. But none of these publications focuses on scholarship, and the message sent to the clientele has almost nothing to do with the academic dimensions of the University."[46]

Not only did President Davenport inherit an institution on the upswing academically, but under his watch, some of the religious polarization that characterized the institution for so long began to recede, at least at certain levels. In the first place, Davenport and Provost William Adrian sought to strengthen Pepperdine's broad Christian base and, at the same time, to improve the relationship between the University and the Churches of Christ. They did this especially through strategic hiring policies aimed at securing faculty primarily from Churches of Christ but also from other Christian traditions. They also fostered conversation about the meaning of Christian higher education in a variety of settings, especially the annual faculty retreats.[47]

Second, in recent years, Davenport has attempted to tie the language of "value-centeredness" more closely to Pepperdine's Christian mission. In a strategic vision speech delivered to the Seaver College faculty in 1990, he argued that "we need to become more broadly, more fully known as a Christian university." He acknowledged that "Pepperdine has for one reason or another stepped back a bit from just saying we're a Christian university." For that reason, he noted, "I hear a lot of people who are surprised to find that we are

45. Interviews with W. Royce Clark, religion professor, April 24, 1995; and Randall Chesnutt, religion professor, May 15, 1995.
46. Interview with Thomas H. Olbricht, April 20, 1995.
47. Written statement by William Adrian, May 18, 1995.

a Christian university. . . . I think one of the reasons is [that] we don't say it . . . a lot."[48]

In recent years, however, Pepperdine has been more explicit on this point. The *1995 Annual Report,* for example, points out that "the University is unashamedly Christian in its values orientation."[49] Still, if there is a single operative term the University routinely employs to describe its mission, that term is "value centered." The term "Christian" is often used to describe the kinds of values the University supports, though that descriptor is not used consistently.

Seaver College, especially, has taken its Christian mission with greater seriousness over the past several years. During the 1994-95 academic year, for example, John F. Wilson, dean of the college since 1983, led the faculty in revising the Seaver College Strategic Plan. One of the most striking characteristics of the new document is its forthright and deliberate emphasis on the Christian character of the institution. For example, the previous Strategic Plan, drafted in 1988, described the faculty's religious commitments in terms of their "devotion to Christian moral and ethical values based upon a personal spiritual commitment."[50] The new plan adds that "the majority of faculty base their commitment to such values, and their daily lives, on a personal faith in Jesus Christ, and live out that faith in their churches and communities."[51]

Wilson also has pressed the questions, What does it mean that Seaver College is a Christian institution and related to the Churches of Christ? What difference should that make for recruiting policies, admissions, the awarding of scholarships, and faculty hiring? What difference should it make in one's teaching or one's scholarship? Wilson recalls that when he first came to Pepperdine, few were asking these questions. Now, he feels, these sorts of questions increasingly characterize the college.[52]

At the very least, Wilson can count on significant faculty support for the ideal of Christian higher education. For example, in the survey mentioned above, almost 80 percent of faculty either agreed or strongly agreed that "Seaver College should provide an academic environment that encourages students to develop a well-thought-out Christian philosophy of life." And 82 percent of the faculty agreed that Seaver College should encourage "students to develop a Christian worldview."

The question remains, how might that commitment best work itself out

---

48. David Davenport, "Strategic Vision Address to Seaver College Faculty," October 16, 1990, pp. 7-8.

49. *Challenge of a New World: 1995 Annual Report of Pepperdine University,* p. 13.

50. Seaver College Strategic Plan, 1988, section II.E.

51. Integrated Strategic Plan: Seaver College, 1995, p. 6.

52. Interview with John F. Wilson, April 20, 1995.

in actual practice? With presidential funding, Seaver College sponsored faculty seminars in the summers of 1992 and 1993 on the theme, "A Christian World-view in the Classroom: What Does It Mean?" Those conversations have continued in a number of ways, though implementation is always left to the discretion of the individual professor.

Because of Pepperdine's Christian orientation, President Davenport has encouraged faculty to focus their scholarship on moral, ethical, and service-oriented issues to every extent possible. He also has argued that, at the very least, Pepperdine should emphasize service to others, with service learning and volunteerism playing a significant role in the life of the institution. The recently established Volunteer Center has given tangible expression to these ideals. Davenport has also urged the Pepperdine community to place the student at the heart of the educational enterprise as a tangible expression of the service motif.[53]

Yet, Pepperdine seldom articulates, in any overarching way, how the Christian faith empowers these dimensions of the common, academic life. How, for example, does the ideal of service, in the context of a Christian university, differ from the ideal of service in the context of corporate America?

For years, Seaver College has maintained three curricular and extra-curricular vehicles that especially lend themselves to the enhancement of the Christian dimensions of the institution. One is convocation, which began in 1937 as required daily chapel. During the Pullias years, the chapel requirement dropped to one day a week. Norvel Young increased that requirement to three days a week in 1957.[54] When the Malibu campus opened in 1972, the requirement dropped again to two days a week, and in 1977, the college scaled the requirement back once again to one day a week.[55] Convocation today is no longer a religious service, though it may sometimes feature a religious theme and always opens with a Scripture reading and a prayer. At the same time, since 1995, students have been able to earn convocation credit by participating in a variety of experiences, including worship.

A second explicitly religious vehicle is the annual lectureship that attracts to the campus each year several thousand members of Churches of Christ for lectures and classes dealing with biblical and related themes. While all colleges and universities related to the Churches of Christ sponsor comparable lectureship programs, Pepperdine's stands on the cutting edge of thought and reflection among Churches of Christ. It surely is among the most popular of all the lecture programs, and draws church members from all over the United

53. Interview with David Davenport, April 4, 1995; and Davenport, "Strategic Vision Address to Seaver College Faculty," October 16, 1990, p. 5.
54. Telephone interview with Norvel Young, June 8, 1995.
55. Telephone interview with Steven Lemley, June 8, 1995.

States and abroad. However, because the University can accommodate such large numbers of visitors only when school is not in session, lectureship is held each year immediately following the spring semester when virtually all the students and many faculty are away from campus. This means that the lectureship, more than anything else, affords the University an opportunity to extend goodwill to the church, but it is not an occasion for interaction between the church and the normal life of the University.

The third vehicle that especially lends itself to the enhancement of the Christian dimensions of the institution is the three-course religion requirement in the general education curriculum: "History and Religion of Israel" (Old Testament), "History and Religion of the Early Church" (New Testament), and "Religion and Culture." The religion faculty is one of the strongest in Seaver College and is committed to providing academically serious courses. At the same time, members of this faculty routinely search for ways to enable questions of faith, ethics, and a Christian perspective on reality to surface, both in their lectures and in their interactions with students. Yet they continue to experience difficulties integrating these two dimensions and, in some ways, their dilemmas symbolize the dilemmas facing the entire Seaver College faculty.

Nurturing Cultural and Religious Diversity

In recent years, Pepperdine's leadership has also emphasized the University's relationship with Churches of Christ. Dean Wilson has placed particular emphasis on hiring faculty from that tradition. At the same time, President Davenport has articulated a vision that makes room for faculty of all religious persuasions and has encouraged all faculty, regardless of religious orientation, to contribute to Pepperdine's Christian mission.[56] Likewise, the Seaver College Plan of 1988, a product of considerable faculty input but finally written by Dean Wilson, notes:

> the makeup of the faculty reflects the university's strong historic relationship to the Churches of Christ while fully recognizing the valuable contributions of those who, while not members of the Churches of Christ, complement and share a commitment to the mission of Seaver College.[57]

Seaver's recent emphasis on diversity of faith commitments cannot be divorced from recent changes in Churches of Christ, themselves, where the old exclusivist perspectives are slowly breaking down.

56. David Davenport, "Strategic Vision Address to Seaver College Faculty," October 16, 1990, pp. 7-9.
57. Seaver College Strategic Plan, 1988, section II.F.

The Seaver College strategic plan also calls for a long-term goal of 20 percent of students from Churches of Christ, and in the fall of 1995, the numbers of Church of Christ students finally climbed to 16 percent, the first time in twenty years that students from that tradition accounted for more than 15 percent of the total student body.[58] At the same time, the strategic plan emphasizes diversity in the context of the Christian faith: "A significant majority of Seaver students should be active Christians from a broad variety of traditions."[59]

It is too soon to tell how deeply the commitment to diversity runs. Yet, at the very least it represents a significant departure from the policies that characterized Seaver College in its early years when Christian students who did not belong to Churches of Christ were not allowed to lead prayer or read Scripture in chapel or convocation. Though that restriction has long since been overturned, the college now seeks to address other, similar kinds of issues.

One of those issues involves the legitimacy of student religious organizations on campus. In recent years, Seaver College has not formally recognized student organizations that are "denominational" in character. One can only read that provision in light of the fact that Churches of Christ have always claimed to be "non-denominational."[60] Campus Ministry, sponsored by the Church of Christ that meets on campus, receives substantial University support since it represents Pepperdine's founding religious tradition, since technically it is not a student organization, and since, according to traditional Church of Christ understandings, it represents no particular denomination. Campus Crusade is also permitted organizational rights, being clearly trans-denominational in character, though it is not permitted to have paid staff members on campus.

On the other hand, when students have attempted to create organizations allied with specific denominational traditions, they typically have been denied. The Catholic student population at Seaver College is a case in point. That population grew quickly from 12 percent in 1972 to over 20 percent, where it has remained relatively constant, outpacing the student population of Churches of Christ for the past ten years.[61] Yet, Seaver College has never recognized any Catholic student organization and, until recently, has made no specific provisions for the spiritual welfare of its Catholic students. Typically, the University has encouraged Catholics, as well as students from other non-

58. Integrated Strategic Plan: Seaver College, 1995, p. 14; and "Influx of Christians Highlight Freshman Class," *The Graphic*, September 14, 1995, 1.

59. Integrated Strategic Plan: Seaver College, 1995, p. 14.

60. Interview with D'Esta Love, April 18, 1995.

61. Analysis of Religious Preference for Los Angeles and Malibu Campus: 1970-1974; data obtained from the registrar's enrollment reports, by university information service, January 8, 1975; and University Fact Book, 5th ed., p. A21.

Church of Christ traditions, to participate in the Church of Christ-sponsored Campus Ministry.

Recognizing Pepperdine's inherent diversity, however, and the school's commitment to become a Christian institution that encourages the spiritual development of *all* faculty, staff, and students, dean of students D'Esta Love has worked over the past several years with students of various religious traditions who have sought to create their own religious organizations. Recently, students have established both a Jewish club and a Catholic club. Though the University has not yet chartered either of these organizations, both have faculty sponsorship and vital student participation.[62]

A comparable issue involves the role of women in University-sponsored, public worship services. In keeping with traditional teachings of Churches of Christ, the University for years did not permit women to pray, preach, read Scripture, or otherwise participate in University-sponsored public worship services, including chapel and convocation. In the late 1980s, however, the University began to reexamine this issue.[63] In 1990, in response to a questionnaire, the Seaver College faculty overwhelmingly registered their lack of sympathy with the University's traditional stand on this question.[64] Then, in March of 1992, on the grounds that the University is not the church, the University reversed its stand and permitted women full participation in all University-sponsored public worship services.

The University has made limited progress with regard to the integration of women into leadership positions in the academic and student affairs divisions of the institution. Within the past few years, for example, the University has appointed women to the positions of dean of the Graduate School of Education and Psychology, dean of students at Seaver College, and dean of academic administration at Seaver College. Of these three, only one is a member of Churches of Christ.

The Role of Church Relationship at Seaver College

In spite of the progress Seaver College has made in defining itself as a Christian institution, the relationship of the institution to the Churches of Christ is still, in many ways, a bone of contention, both among the faculty and within the student body. William Adrian, for example, recalls that when he served as provost, some faculty inevitably saw the selection of a non–Church of Christ

62. Interview with D'Esta Love, April 18, 1995.
63. Interview with John Watson, April 20, 1995.
64. See survey results submitted by Professor Stuart Love to President David Davenport, June 7, 1990.

person for a faculty position as "a diminution of the Christian mission" of the institution. On the other hand, selection of a member of Churches of Christ often prompted "comments about sectarianism winning out over academic quality."[65]

Those tensions continue today. Many faculty continue to feel that the administration places membership in Churches of Christ ahead of academic quality when hiring new faculty.[66] On the other hand, the administration argues that if Seaver College fails to place a priority on faculty who belong to Churches of Christ, a critical mass of faculty from that tradition would soon disappear.

Both faculty and students are divided over this issue. For example, when asked by the questionnaire if "Seaver College should search for and hire faculty who have achieved academic prominence and who are members of Churches of Christ," 13 percent of the faculty either disagreed or strongly disagreed and 18 percent were neutral. Perhaps even more striking, when asked if Seaver College "should seek to admit an increasingly larger number of students who are members of Churches of Christ," over a third of the faculty registered some level of disagreement, while 15 percent were neutral.

At the same time, a sizable number of faculty support the Church of Christ presence at Seaver College. When asked if Seaver should seek to admit additional students who belong to Churches of Christ, exactly 50 percent registered some level of agreement. Further, almost 25 percent of the faculty support the addition of Church of Christ members to the faculty, even if those recruits "may not have achieved academic prominence."

While faculty differ over how desirable it may be to recruit additional faculty and students from the Church of Christ, they basically agree that Seaver College should seek to recruit faculty and students who are Christian, but who come from a variety of Christian traditions. Eighty-three percent of the faculty responding to the questionnaire agreed that Seaver College should seek to hire academically prominent faculty "who are committed Christian believers regardless of denominational affiliation," and almost 80 percent agreed that Seaver should seek to recruit a broad range of Christian students.

The student responses to the same questions were even more striking.[67] When asked whether Seaver College should hire Church of Christ members

65. Written statement by William Adrian, May 18, 1995.

66. Telephone interview with Lydia Reineck, July 17, 1995; interview with Dan Caldwell, political science professor, July 3, 1995.

67. The student questionnaire was similar, though not identical, to the one given the faculty. The student questionnaire was administered in the spring of 1995 through the religion general education courses: Rel. 101 (Old Testament), Rel. 102 (New Testament) and Rel. 301 (Religion and Culture). Six hundred and forty-five students completed the survey.

"who have achieved academic prominence," 37 percent strongly disagreed, another 28 percent disagreed, and only 13 percent expressed any level of agreement at all. When asked if Pepperdine should hire Church of Christ members who have *not* achieved academic prominence, 91 percent registered disapproval, and only two percent concurred. When asked if Seaver College should seek to admit a higher percentage of Church of Christ students, 76 percent either disagreed or strongly disagreed, while less than 9 percent registered any sympathy with that proposal.

If the faculty is divided over Pepperdine's relation with the Churches of Christ, it is obvious that the student body is not: for whatever reasons, an overwhelming majority of the students at Seaver College express little or no sympathy for that tradition. When asked about Pepperdine's relation to Churches of Christ, 55 percent thought that relationship "of no practical consequence," 25 percent viewed it as "a minus," and only 20 percent thought it "a plus."

In truth, however, few students other than those who belong to Churches of Christ have any idea what the Church of Christ tradition is all about, what Churches of Christ stand for, or what this heritage might contribute to the enterprise of higher education. This suggests that if Pepperdine wants its relation with Churches of Christ to be more than a bone of contention within the University community, it must go far beyond simply recruiting faculty and students from that tradition. The institution must begin to explore, with students and faculty alike, what this heritage can contribute to the task of higher education, and then find ways to build on that tradition whenever possible or to supplement it whenever necessary.

Interestingly, however, over 20 percent of the students who participated in the survey quarreled with the proposition that Seaver College should seek to hire academically prominent faculty who are Christians, regardless of denominational affiliation. An even higher percentage — 37 percent — disagreed with the proposal that Seaver should seek to recruit a larger number of Christian students, regardless of denomination.

This suggests that a sizable core of students at Seaver College have little or no interest in Christian higher education at all. Indeed, 43 percent of Seaver College students indicated that Pepperdine's identity as a Christian institution was "of no practical consequence" for their decision to enroll in Seaver College, and 10 percent thought it was "a minus."

The gap between faculty and students regarding the importance of the Christian faith in the college context is not the only gap that yawns between faculty and students at Seaver College. An equally significant gap divides faculty and students on the purposes of higher education. The Seaver College faculty, for the most part, is deeply committed to a broad liberal arts education. On the other hand, 78 percent of the students placed "maximum possible emphasis" on the proposal that Seaver College should "train students for productive careers," and almost 90 percent asked for courses "that provide technical, work-related skills relevant to a successful career."

Finally, from the creation of a Cultural Enrichment Center to summer faculty seminars which have encouraged teaching about a variety of cultures, Seaver College has made cultural diversity a central part of its mission in the 1990s. To a degree, enrollment shifts reflect this commitment. From 1974 to 1994, for example, the percentage of Asian students climbed from 2 percent (27) to 7 percent (205), while the percentage of Hispanic students during that same period increased from 3.5 percent (56) to 8 percent (238). The actual number of African American students climbed only slightly during those same years from eighty-two to ninety-four, though the percentage of African Americans in the total enrollment dropped from 5 to 3 percent.[68]

It remains to be seen how the college will relate its emphasis on cultural diversity to its Christian orientation and especially to its heritage in the Churches of Christ. So far, that relationship remains largely unexplored.

Conclusion

When all is said and done, Pepperdine University preserves a remarkable continuity with the kind of school it was from the beginning. It is still a Christian institution. If anything, that commitment is stronger today than ever before, at least on the part of the faculty and the administration. And Pepperdine is still related to the Churches of Christ. One could argue that that commitment is stronger than ever before as well. Yet, the tension that existed over this relationship in the days of Batsell Baxter and Earl Pullias has never disappeared.

Moreover, Pepperdine is stronger academically than at any other time in its history. The challenge today is to find constructive ways to relate the life of the mind to the Christian faith, and to do so in a way that respects — and even builds upon — the heritage of Churches of Christ, but that also respects the diversity of faith expressions that abounds on Pepperdine's campus.

68. Pepperdine College/Seaver College Historical Data, Office of Institutional Research. The figures on African American students stand in marked contrast to Pepperdine's Los Angeles campus where African Americans made up 17 percent of the overall student body in 1968 (282 out of a total enrollment of 1674).

CONCLUSION

The Christian University: Maintaining Distinctions in a Pluralistic Culture

William B. Adrian Jr.

This volume began with the question, "How is it possible for Christian institutions of higher learning to develop into academic institutions of the first order and, at the same time, to nurture in creative ways the faith commitments that called them into existence in the first place?" The question presumed that dual institutional commitments to both faith and learning were not only compatible, but that examples could be found to demonstrate how they interact in Christian institutions today.

The historical evidence is clear that the large majority of institutions founded on faith commitments have, at some time in their history, given up those commitments. Yet the fourteen institutions in this study, representing at least seven different faith traditions, have a common, distinguishing characteristic: they take seriously their faith traditions and continue to seek ways to make those traditions viable on their campuses.

Each of these institutions has a unique story, which makes it difficult to offer summary statements about the entire group. The uniqueness of each story is related to the historic faith traditions of the school, and in most instances, characteristics of these traditions have shaped the characteristics of the schools. The image of Goshen College, for example, is a clear reflection of the Mennonite traditions of personal discipline, peace, and international service.

In spite of their differences, all these schools face similar pressures as they seek to maintain the viability of their faith traditions in the current environment of higher education. Accordingly, this chapter will summarize the similarities and differences between these institutions, and ask what we can learn from these fourteen schools that have lived simultaneously in Athens and Jerusalem, the two worlds of faith and learning.

CONCLUSION

Broadening the Scope and Vision

The most obvious generalization that can be made about the historical development of these institutions is that their scope and vision have broadened — both academically and religiously. These schools are far different today than they were in their early years. Most were born of meager finances and strong parochial or sectarian visions. Several of the schools began as Bible schools with limited programs designed to train students for service to the church. Often, they viewed the culture around them as alien, if not hostile, to the religious values of the faith tradition. Even the Catholic schools and several belonging to mainstream Protestant traditions (such as Lutherans) initially sought to establish an outpost of faith in the midst of an unbelieving culture. As a result, distinctive doctrinal and denominational characteristics were clearly evident in their early development.

Through the years, however, denominational identities have become less noticeable in school publications, in the curriculum, and in the composition of both students and faculty. Religious expressions which once permeated these institutions are still evident and even thriving in some cases, but typically, required religious observances are fewer in number and less intrusive. There are still many optional religious activities and observances, but they are more like a "religious buffet" where students select what is of particular interest to them, as one narrative observes. In catalogs and other school literature, one finds a diminished emphasis on particular religious doctrines and greater relaxation regarding student dress and behavior. In the Catholic schools, clerical apparel and religious symbols are less evident than was the case in previous years, and leaders of these schools have broadened the denominational emphasis to include a more ecumenical Christian presence. A transplanted visitor from the past might see less *visual* evidence of a Christian presence on most of these campuses, but beyond the visual, our visitor might recognize a Christian dimension of substantial breadth and depth.

Broadening is evident in the curriculum which has expanded in scope and now includes professional courses and programs. There are fewer required religion courses and their nature has changed. In some cases, religion has been integrated into courses in Western civilization, while in others, courses on doctrine have been broadened to include emphases on social issues such as peace, justice, ecology, and crime and punishment. Departments of religion or theology still play an important role on these campuses, but now they must compete with other departments for new faculty, financial resources, and required niches in the general education curriculum. In religion courses, one finds less emphasis on pietistic and scholastic traditions and more focus on critical scholarship. Particular faith traditions are evident, but are often incorporated into a more ecumenical Christian vision.

Several Protestant institutions which were founded on particular faith traditions have tried to find a broader niche as "evangelical" schools. A good case in point is Wheaton College, which has focused on integrating faith and learning through the articulation of a Christian worldview. The Wheaton model has influenced a variety of institutions whose vision has grown beyond sectarian or denominational identities in their search for a broader Christian self-understanding. Other schools have tried to incorporate a broader Christian image in other ways. Instead of expanding in "evangelical" directions, many of these schools have defined themselves in terms like "community," "values," "peace," and "service," and have linked these themes to traditional academic terms like "inquiry" and "critical thinking." In this way, statements of a broader vision may encompass a social and academic orientation in addition to the Christian faith.

Many of these schools have expanded academically into full-blown universities and look more like their counterparts in the larger world of American higher education. Indeed, each of these institutions has been highly motivated to develop academic programs of superior quality, and they now compete for recognition as outstanding institutions of higher learning. They have passed the phase of "survival" to become recognized as respectable, if not strong, academic institutions.

Generally speaking, the academic qualifications of faculty have increased, a development supported by the growing percentage of doctorates and the expanding lists of faculty publications. Many faculty in these colleges have become recognized leaders in their disciplines. Several schools boast Phi Beta Kappa chapters, Rhodes and Fulbright scholars among faculty and students, and other academic distinctions bestowed from outside the institution. Some enroll disproportionate numbers of National Merit Scholars and several have become "selective" institutions as their student SAT scores have increased. Many have been recognized as leading academic institutions in national publications such as *U.S. News & World Report*, and some would be considered institutions of academic distinction.

The drive for academic recognition, however, has not been without costs, and achieving academic status has often made it difficult for these institutions to maintain their religious distinctives. Their motivation to "keep abreast" in higher education has meant that accrediting associations and other leading universities have helped define their direction, perhaps in disproportionate ways. One participant observed that "keeping up" in higher education is a more compelling issue on the campus than maintaining the religious character of the school, while another suggested his institution has been more "market driven than mission driven."

The subtle influences in the drive for excellence may affect the institutions in ways not fully comprehended, especially since academic recognition is more closely related to public perceptions than to genuine academic quality. Recognition is dependent upon resources, and since virtually all of these schools are tuition dependent, their viability depends on tuition-paying students and their families. Maintaining enrollments is essential to long-term survival and explains why one author admitted frankly that financial resources are a higher priority than theological distinctiveness. These schools that struggled financially in their early years simply to keep the doors open each fall now struggle to compete against the well-endowed leaders of American higher education.

In practical terms, SAT scores and other academic qualifications of prospective students have grown increasingly important in the selection of students, and academic credentials such as doctoral degrees and publications have become more important in the selection of faculty. Academic qualifications and religious commitment are not mutually exclusive, but in the marketplace, it is increasingly difficult to attract adequate numbers of students and faculty who share the religious distinctives of the schools.

These schools also are attracting a broader mix of students. This fact is evident in student demographics which show a trend in most of the schools of diminishing percentages of students from the founding faith traditions. And even students who do come from the same religious traditions are increasingly diverse theologically, which suggests the same religious influences affecting the schools are affecting the churches as well. Our modern pluralistic culture poses a major challenge for the founding faith traditions as well as for Christianity itself. One of the more troubling developments in that regard is that the increasing diversity of students is driven as much or more by market forces as by design.

Geography is another major factor in the diversity which exists within these schools. The schools on the West Coast have more diverse students and faculty than those in the Midwest. The cultural environment of the West Coast is more diverse, and the denominations which support these schools tend to be smaller in proportion to the population than in the Midwest. Also, the tradition of church-related higher education has been much more firmly rooted in the Midwest than on the West Coast, where public higher education has always been dominant. Church-supported schools in the West have been smaller and younger than their counterparts in the Midwest. Finally, it is generally assumed that the culture in the West, especially in the large urban areas, is less traditionally religious than in the Midwest. Thus, geographical comparisons of schools provide further evidence that the broadening missions of the schools are often influenced more by culture than by intention. The broadened vision of all the schools may be the result of a convenient marriage of conviction and expediency, but it has presented each of them with a major challenge to maintain a distinctive religious character.

Not only are these schools influenced by their cultural milieus in various ways. They are also shaped by the expectation that they reflect genuine academic quality and distinction. This expectation is driven both by the higher education establishment to which they owe allegiance — and which has its own presuppositions and standards — and also by modern students and parents who are careful and demanding "shoppers" in a consumer environment. To compete effectively in this environment, institutions have become "consumer" colleges, responding to both the needs and whims of an activist clientele. Is it possible for these institutions which are committed to faith and learning to chart their own course and find their own distinctive niche in such an environment?

Engaging the Culture

While a common concern among all the schools in this study is how their historic faith traditions should engage the modern, pluralistic culture in which they live, their approaches to this question reflect widely differing views. Many of the schools were founded with strong "countercultural" characteristics, and in many instances those characteristics are still evident. Generally, however, most of these schools have become more accommodating to the culture as they have matured into respectable academic institutions. Several authors used Reinhold Neibuhr's theological paradigm to describe the historical development of their institutions which moved from a separatist approach which Neibuhr described as "Christ against culture" to a more integrated relationship of "Christ transforming culture." Despite tensions with the culture, most of these schools are still more "at home" in their various cultural milieus than they were in their earlier years. One author admitted frankly that there is a greater likelihood that culture will transform the church and college than vice versa.

One countercultural element remains common to all of the schools — a commitment to the validity and transcendence of the Christian faith. However, beyond that commonality, each has chosen to engage the culture with a different emphasis. Wheaton and Calvin, for example, have been intellectually and philosophically active in challenging common presuppositions of American higher education and articulating an intellectually defensible Christian worldview. These and other evangelical schools have been searching for common theological ground and exploring ways to integrate faith and learning. Further, the strong emphasis on evangelism that persists at Wheaton and many other evangelical institutions suggests a pervading countercultural stance in the schools' relationship to society.

Mennonite schools, on the other hand, emphasize radical discipleship, pacifism, and community building. With their strong biblical focus, the Mennonite schools typically place discipleship ahead of strictly philosophical or theological concerns. Put another way, Mennonites engage the culture at the personal and practical levels while many evangelical schools typically focus on intellectual issues of relating the Christian faith to the culture. While Wheaton and Calvin provide leadership on faith and learning issues through publications and special programs, Mennonite schools like Goshen and Fresno Pacific provide leadership by involving students and faculty in service learning rooted in a radical understanding of the Christian faith. At Goshen, over one-half of the faculty have had experience in international service in countries around the world, particularly Third World countries, and at Fresno Pacific, all new students must take a course entitled "Jesus and the Christian Community" which introduces them to the Mennonite traditions of service and discipleship.

Informed by a sacramental understanding of the Christian faith, Catholic schools typically engage the culture by focusing on social issues like peace and justice and by involving students in community projects related to those kinds of concerns. These schools often focus the curriculum especially on classical literature and the Christian response to great social themes. Christian community, especially in the smaller Catholic schools, is generated through religious orders which often become the center of Christian involvement on those campuses. Two authors wrote of their schools that "Benedictine values are more important than Catholic values," suggesting the strong identification with orders at the personal and practical level. At the same time, orders are shrinking numerically at all the Catholic schools which raises a question about the future of the religious identity of many Catholic institutions.

Defining a coherent response to the culture is especially difficult for schools of churches aligned with democratic movements of American origin such as Baptist or Church of Christ. These traditions tend to be countercultural in their biblical focus on personal morality, but unlike the older, confessional traditions imported from Europe, they have aligned themselves far more closely with the larger culture. Typically, schools spawned by these traditions have followed suit.

Historically, these and many other schools have challenged the generally accepted values of materialism in American culture — especially when these schools were struggling to survive. This challenge has diminished, however, as the schools and their clienteles have "crossed the tracks" economically to become more integrated with the materialistic culture they challenged in the past. This is especially evident in institutions whose church clienteles have realized the American dream and moved into the upper-middle and upper economic levels of American society. One author reflected on the tensions between the "commitments of Christianity and the culture of American materialism" which are played out on the campus.

While different approaches to engaging the culture are not mutually ex-

450

clusive among the schools, differing emphases in the historic faith traditions are evident in the way each school defines its relationship to the larger culture. The schools' different approaches to engaging the culture may also explain why the issue of secularity is perceived differently. Those with a countercultural stance often view secularity as a threat, while those with a more friendly view of culture — Lutherans, for example, as well as Catholics, with their sacramental understanding of the Christian faith — often see culture as a separate "kingdom" from the church but not necessarily as a hostile one.

In the past, the schools have engaged the culture by incorporating their own faith traditions into institutional mission and life. As the schools change, they must struggle again with the question of how to embrace desirable dimensions of the culture of which they are a part, on the one hand, while challenging its pervasive, less desirable characteristics on the other. This is another form of the challenge to live successfully in both worlds of faith and learning.

Within all of the schools in the study there is continuing dialogue on the relation of faith to culture and an openness to try new approaches. Faith traditions on these campuses today are often contemporary and ecumenical, focusing on the commonalities of the Christian faith. At the same time, many of these schools see their particular faith traditions as essential to maintaining a distinctive religious character. As one author concluded, ecumenism and particularity must be linked.

In the curriculum, one often finds an intentional effort to incorporate positive elements of the faith traditions in courses. Yet it is in the extracurriculum where the most dramatic changes are evident. Compulsory religious observances such as chapel services still exist in several of the schools, but they are fewer than in the past, and voluntary activities are popular and growing. Even voluntary chapel programs are well attended on a few campuses. At St. Olaf, for example, voluntary chapel regularly attracts hundreds of students. Carefully planned religious celebrations at various times of the year are also attracting students. The work of the chaplaincy is evident on several of the campuses, and small groups focused on Bible study or current moral or social issues are also active on most campuses. There has also been an increase in voluntary action groups, often initiated by students, which focus on issues of community and broader social concern.

Is there a risk these schools will follow the familiar path of most religiously founded colleges and slowly lose their religious character altogether? The historical record would suggest they are vulnerable. They are successful and thus subject to increased pressures to conform to models provided by schools generally acknowledged as leaders in American higher education, most of which have long since given up their religious affiliations. Yet, to date, the schools involved in this study have maintained their commitment to having a distinctive religious character which virtually all feel is integral to their academic efforts.

A Slippery Slope?

Are the various forces which shape these schools moving them inexorably away from their faith traditions in spite of their commitments and efforts or, to use a current metaphor, are they on a "slippery slope" toward secularization? The question is complex, and those who are uncomfortable with the issue of secularization may have difficulty with the question. Each school has its own pressures and its own expectations of how to chart its course, but the course can change. Because the schools are in such a dynamic environment, uncertainty about the future is inevitable, even at the level of institutional leadership.

The structures which were generally assumed to provide stable supports for the religious dimensions of the schools are not necessarily what they have appeared to be. Church affiliation and support is an example. Many of the denominations from which the schools receive support are themselves in a state of flux, and church affiliation will therefore not necessarily insure a distinctive religious character. Too, the schools tend to be less financially dependent on the churches than they were years ago.

The Mennonite schools provide a case in point. They are both closely affiliated with the church; in the case of Goshen, it would be difficult to find an institution that more agressively cultivates its relation with its founding church. Obviously, therefore, Goshen rejects the "slippery slope" metaphor. However, the author of the Goshen narrative suggests that some might perceive Goshen as a "humane values" college and acknowledges that some would find a "blurring of nomenclature" and a "rhetorical slide" in the language of the college's catalogs. Still, the college and church "seem to be moving hand-in-hand." Similarly, the author of the Fresno Pacific narrative suggests that the college has more roots in the faith traditions of the church than the church does itself.

Churches without strong theological roots and traditions are most vulnerable to instability and lack of identity, and the same identity problem can be seen in their colleges. Even the mainstream churches such as Catholic and Lutheran are vulnerable as they experience the same religious fragmentation that bedevils so many other groups.

"Critical mass" is another "stabilizing" factor which may be more illusory than real. Many assume that schools which have a critical mass of students and faculty from the supporting denomination will be insured of maintaining distinctive faith traditions, but because of the growing diversity and fragmentation within the churches, one must doubt the truth of this assumption.

Further, the percentage of students from the founding or supporting church is declining in most of the schools. If the loss of a critical mass of students from homes of the affiliated church results in a loss of focus on a particular faith tradition, it follows that the loss of a critical mass of "generic" Christian students will likely result in a loss of focus on the Christian faith, and schools which become too diverse will be vulnerable to losing any meaningful Christian character whatsoever.

Yet the slippery slope metaphor is not appropriate when it assumes the schools *must* succumb to outside forces and pressures. The histories of the schools in this project show they have charted unusual and independent courses for themselves and have not been timid in challenging the cultures in which they live. These schools continue to nurture this independence of spirit, and as long as the Christian faith calls the culture to account, there likely will be individual faculty and administrators within these schools to call them to their respective faith traditions.

Sustaining Distinctive Character

Despite the enormous pressures for conformity in American higher education, especially in the common presuppositions of the enterprise, schools can be distinctive. Christian schools can incorporate their faith traditions and enrich the education of students by relating the Christian faith to their experiences in and out of the classroom. But how can this be done, and what factors are necessary to sustain a distinctive religious character?

In reviewing the histories of these fourteen institutions, one factor surfaces clearly, and that is leadership. Starting with the board of trustees, whose most important function is to select a president, the leadership of an institution can make a major difference. Beyond the board, the president is the most important figure for maintaining a school's distinctive religious character. There is a common assumption that presidents have little influence on the schools they head, but that is not true in the case of the schools in this study. Because the schools are small compared to most universities, the influence of the president can be much more pervasive than in a larger school. In this book one finds examples of presidents who, almost singlehandedly, exerted powerful influence on the direction of their institutions.

In addition to personal influence, the president can also select individuals for other key leadership positions, and thereby multiply the effect of those who share his or her basic commmitments. Thus, to the extent that the president and other key leaders are committed to sustaining the religious nature of the school, they can exert a major influence toward that end.

The religious character of a school is ultimately played out through its people, and it is necessary to have faculty and staff who share and support the religious traditions. Hiring a "critical mass" of faculty because they are members of a particular denomination will not necessarily insure a particular religious character, but hiring those who are genuinely supportive of the school's faith commitment is a necessary condition for sustaining distinctiveness. Thus, procedures for recruiting and selecting faculty and staff are critical. Among the schools in this study, a variety of procedures were evident, ranging from requiring prospective faculty to write a faith statement, to hiring only from a particular religious group to hiring only "active" Christians to having no specific religious expectations of prospective faculty or staff. After faculty are hired, programs can be developed to integrate them into the faith traditions of the school. At Seattle Pacific University, for example, all new faculty participate in a seminar focused on the integration of faith and learning.

If presidents and other key leaders are essential to maintaining distinctive character, what happens when leadership changes? Changes of leadership can be critical periods in the historical development of schools since there are no assurances that new leaders will continue the policies of their predecessors. To sustain religious distinctives beyond current leadership, traditions must become embedded in what Burton Clark has referred to as the "saga" of the school.[1] But saga is defined by historical events and personalities and by an internalized identity which becomes ingrained in the mission across space and time. It is a community of spirit which must be evident in faculty dedication to mission, in programs and practices which reinforce the mission, and in a supportive student subculture. Not all of the schools in the study have a clearly identified saga, partly because some are still very young as institutions count time, and partly because some are still struggling with their own identities, particularly those whose church constituencies are in flux. Emergence of a saga which includes a viable religious dimension may insure continuity of the mission and vision, but faith cannot be assured in people or institutions.

In an effort to strengthen institutional mission, many schools in this study foster open discussion and ongoing dialogue among faculty and staff regarding the mission of the school. Contrary to popular opinion, mission statements are important, and continual review, interpretation, and restatement of the mission are ways to engage faculty and staff with an institution's core philosophy. A mission statement also calls the institution back to the basic rationale for its existence and seeks to integrate the mission into the day-to-day activities which consume most people on every campus. Each of the institutions in this study has conducted campus-wide discussions of mission and heritage, resulting in reconsideration and reaffirmation of the distinctive religious character of the school.

1. Burton R. Clark, *The Distinctive College: Antioch, Reed and Swarthmore* (Chicago: Aldine Publishing Co., 1970).

William B. Adrian Jr.

Conclusion

Christian colleges have provided a rich source of diversity in American higher education, and the schools that participated in this study are special within that category. They represent most major Christian denominations, and they are recognized leaders among their peers. Because they are well respected within the higher education enterprise, they offer proof that colleges can become first rate academically and simultaneously maintain viable faith traditions. Indeed, these institutions are dedicated to the proposition that faith and learning are not only compatible, but that they can be mutually reinforcing for the task of understanding God's world. These schools have made a positive impact on the churches and religious groups that support them and on the world of American higher education, but their best years and most profound contributions may still lie in the future.

Notes on Contributors

WILLIAM B. ADRIAN JR. served successively from 1983 to 1993 as dean of the Graduate School of Education and Psychology, executive vice president, and provost of Pepperdine University. From 1978 to 1983, he was associate professor in the Department of Educational Administration and Higher Education, Oklahoma State University, having served from 1973 to 1976 as Associate Director of the Colorado Commission on Higher Education. In 1981 he was a Fulbright Scholar at the Federal University of Ceara, Fortaleza, Brazil, and in 1993 he was a Fulbright Senior Lecturer at Jagiellonian University, Cracow, Poland. He has served as a consultant for numerous institutions of higher education.

JAMES D. BRATT is professor of history and chair of that department at Calvin College. He took his B.A. there in 1971, and received his Ph.D. in American intellectual history from Yale University in 1978. Prior to returning to Calvin in 1987, he taught in the Religious Studies Department at the University of Pittsburgh. He is the author of *Dutch Calvinism in Modern America* (1984) and *Gathered at the River: Grand Rapids, Michigan, and Its People of Faith* (1993).

DAN G. DANNER teaches at the University of Portland, where he was the first non-Catholic professor, having been hired by the Department of Theology at that university in 1969. As the senior member of that department, he focuses his teaching mainly in the history of Christianity. His published articles include "The Later English Calvinists and the Geneva Bible," in *Later Calvinism: International Perspectives*, vol. 22, Sixteenth Century Essays and Studies, 1994. Other articles and reviews by him have appeared in *Church History, Journal of the American Academy of Religion*, and *Sixteenth Century Journal*, and as chapters in a variety of volumes.

MARK GRANQUIST has been assistant professor of religion at St. Olaf College since 1992. A graduate of St. Olaf, he earned his Master of Divinity degree from Yale Divinity School and a Ph.D. from the University of Chicago, where he studied under Professor Martin E. Marty.

MICHAEL S. HAMILTON is coordinator for the Pew Evangelical Scholars Program and the Pew Younger Scholars Program, and concurrent assistant professor of history at the University of Notre Dame. He wrote his dissertation on a topic central to the theme of this book: "The Fundamentalist Harvard: Wheaton College and the Continuing Vitality of American Evangelicalism, 1919-1965" (University of Notre Dame, 1994). His published articles include "Women, Public Ministry, and American Fundamentalism, 1920-1950," *Religion and American Culture* (1993).

HAROLD HEIE is director of the Center for Christian Studies at Gordon College (MA), and previously served as vice president for academic affairs at two different institutions: Messiah College (PA) and Northwestern College (IA). Prior to holding those positions, he taught mathematics at The King's College (NY) and at Gordon College. His publications include *Slogans or Distinctives: Reforming Christian Higher Education* (coauthor, 1993) and *The Reality of Christian Learning: Strategies for Faith-discipline Integration* (coeditor, 1987).

MONIKA K. HELLWIG is Landegger Distinguished University Professor of Theology at Georgetown University. She has been extensively involved in ecumenical and interfaith international conferences, and has served on various consultations for the World Council of Churches and for the U.S. Catholic Bishops' Conference. A past president of the Catholic Theological Society of America, she has written mainly in the area of contemporary Catholic systematics. Her books include *Understanding Catholicism* (1981), *The Eucharist and the Hunger of the World* (1976), and *Gladness Their Escort: Homiletic Reflections for Sundays and Feastdays* (1987).

RICHARD T. HUGHES is distinguished professor of religion at Pepperdine University. He previously taught at Abilene Christian University and Southwest Missouri State University. His publications include *Reviving the Ancient Faith: The Story of Churches of Christ in America* (1996), *Illusions of Innocence: Protestant Primitivism in America, 1630-1875* (coauthor, 1988), and *The Primitive Church in the Modern World* (editor, 1996).

DOUGLAS JACOBSEN is professor of church history and theology at Messiah College. He also serves as cochair of "Re-Forming the Center," a Lilly Endowment–funded project examining the reigning two-party paradigm for understanding American Protestantism. In addition, he cochairs the Evangelical Theology Group of the American Academy of Religion. His publications include *An Unprov'd Experiment: Religious Pluralism in Colonial New Jersey* (1991).

RONALD KIRKEMO chairs the Department of History and Political Science at Point Loma Nazarene College. He is an alumnus of that institution and holds a Ph.D. in international relations from American University. He is the author of *An Introduction to International Law* (1973), *Between the Eagle and the Dove: The Christian and American Foreign Policy* (1976), and *For Zion's Sake: A History of Pasadena/Point Loma College* (1993).

BILL J. LEONARD is dean of the Divinity School, Wake Forest University. He previously served as chair of the Department of Religion and Philosophy at Samford University, having taught church history for sixteen years prior to that appointment at Southern Baptist Theological Seminary. He has written extensively on Baptist and American studies. His books include *God's Last and Only Hope: The Fragmentation of the Southern Baptist Convention* (1990) and *The Nature of the Church* (1986).

JAMES A. MATHISEN is professor of sociology and chair of the Department of Sociology/Anthropology at Wheaton College (IL). Specializing in sociological theory and sociology of religion, he has spent much of his research on civil religion, the institutionalization of religion, and popular evangelicalism since the 1960s. He is completing a book-length study of evangelicals and modern sports and is working on an undergraduate textbook in the sociology of religion.

ARLIN MIGLIAZZO is professor of history and chair of the History/Political and International Studies Department, Whitworth College. He has published articles on the American family and ethnic history, higher education theory and practice, history of the Pacific Northwest, and comparative democracy (Republic of Korea and the United States). In addition, he has promoted initiatives at Whitworth College and elsewhere that emphasize a revitalized academic framework in the wake of postmodernism.

STEVEN MOORE is vice president for student life at Seattle Pacific University. He has written several works pertaining to higher education, including *The Values of the Academy* (1990) and *College Ministry: The Church at the Frontlines of the Culture* (1996). His current research focuses on church-related higher education and will result in a book, *A Transforming Vision*.

SISTER EMMANUEL RENNER, O.S.B., was president of the College of Saint Benedict from 1979 to 1986. Earlier, she served as chair of the history department from 1959 to 1965, as dean of continuing education from 1974 to 1977, and as director of planning and program development from 1978 to 1979. Currently, she teaches history at the College of Saint Benedict and serves on the board of regents of St. John's University. She has published *The Historical Thought of Frederic Ozanam* (1960).

RODNEY J. SAWATSKY is president of Messiah College, Grantham, Pennsylvania. Previously he served as president of Conrad Grebel College, Waterloo, Ontario. He earned a Ph.D. in religion from Princeton University and coedited *The Limits of Perfection: A Conversation with J. Lawrence Burkholder* (1993).

THERON F. SCHLABACH, a professor of history at Goshen College, is currently in residence as senior fellow and acting director of the Young Center for the Study of Anabaptist and Pietist Groups at Elizabethtown College. His published books include *Gospel Versus Gospel: Mission and the Mennonite Church, 1863-1944* (1980); *Peace, Faith, Nation: Mennonites and Amish in Nineteenth-Century America* (1988); and *Proclaim Peace: Christian Pacifism from Unexpected Quarters* (editor, 1997).

DALE E. SODEN is associate professor of history and associate dean at Whitworth College. He previously taught at Pacific Lutheran University and Oklahoma Baptist College. He has published widely on topics related to religion in the Pacific Northwest, as well as on the decline of the Presbyterian Church at the national level. In 1990 he published an illustrated history of Whitworth College on the occasion of the centennial of that institution.

RICHARD W. SOLBERG is a retired Lutheran pastor and educator and author of *Lutheran Higher Education in North America,* the definitive history of that enterprise. From 1973 to 1982 he served as Director for Higher Education for the Lutheran Church in America. During that period he published a church-wide study of Lutheran Church in America colleges, *How Church-Related Are Church-Related Colleges?* (1985). His other books include *God and Caesar in East Germany* (1961) and *Miracle in Ethiopia* (1991). The latter describes the cooperative Lutheran–Roman Catholic emergency relief partnership during the famine of 1982-84. He has taught at St. Olaf College, Augustana College, and Thiel College, where he was also vice president for academic affairs.

JOHN E. STANLEY is part-time professor of biblical studies at Messiah College. From 1983 to 1985 he served as chair of the Department of Religion and Christian Ministries at Warner Pacific College, Portland, after pastoring for twelve years in the Church of God (Anderson). His published articles have appeared in *Wesleyan Theological Journal, Christian Scholars Review, The Christian Ministry,* and in several edited collections.

SUSIE C. STANLEY is professor of historical theology at Messiah College. Previously, she taught church history and women's studies at Western Evangelical Seminary, Portland. Author of *Feminist Pillar of Fire: The Life of Alma White,* she has written numerous articles regarding both social holiness and the involvement of the Wesleyan/Holiness movement in the fundamentalist/modernist controversy. She is past president of the Wesleyan Theological Society and currently serves as convener of the Wesleyan/Holiness Women Clergy Conference.

BYRON R. SWANSON is professor emeritus of religion at California Lutheran University, where he chaired the Department of Religion and continues to teach on a part-time basis. His teaching has focused on theology, church history, Christian ethics, environmental ethics, and peace and justice. He previously taught at Lutheran School of Theology in Chicago (1973-79) and at Midland Lutheran College in Fremont, Nebraska (1968-79).

HILARY D. THIMMESH, O.S.B., has divided the bulk of his professional career between teaching English and serving in various administrative capacities at St. John's University. President of St. John's from 1982 to 1991, he also served as chancellor of St. Martin's College in Olympia, Washington, from 1978 to 1980. He has published numerous articles and reviews and most recently co-translated and edited *The Little Notebook* (1995).

PAUL TOEWS is professor of history at Fresno Pacific College and director of the Center for Mennonite Brethren Studies, Fresno Pacific College and Mennonite Brethren Biblical Seminary. His published books include *Mennonites in America, 1930-1970: Modernity and the Persistence of Religious Culture* (1996), *Bridging Troubled Waters: Mennonite Brethren at Mid-Twentieth Century* (editor, 1995), *Mennonite Idealism and Higher Education: The Story of the Fresno Pacific College Idea* (editor, 1995), and *Mennonites and Baptists: The Continuing Conversation* (editor, 1993).

RONALD A. WELLS is professor of history and director of the Calvin Center for Christian Scholarship at Calvin College. His published books include *History through the Eyes of Faith* (1989), *Alistair Cooke: America Observed* (1987), and *The Wars of America: Christian Views* (1981).

MARGARET BARTH WOLD is professor emeritus at California Lutheran University. In the early 1970s she was director of American Lutheran Church Women. She has also served on the Board of Directors of Pacific Lutheran Theological Seminary, Berkeley, and as president of the board for six of those years. From 1977 to 1984 she was director for Ministry in Changing Communities in the American Lutheran Church, working with congregations in neighborhoods undergoing racial, economic, cultural, and/or sociological changes. Among her nine books are *Bible Readings for Couples* (1980) and *Women of Faith and Spirit* (1984).

WILLIAM WOODWARD is professor of history at Seattle Pacific University. He also serves as official historian of the Washington Army National Guard, chairs the subject area of "War and Peace" for the American Culture Association, and is a past vice president of the Pacific Northwest Historians' Guild. He has published articles in a variety of scholarly journals and books. Most recently, he coauthored a chapter analyzing regional urban development in *The Pacific Northwest: Geographical Perspectives.* His essay "America as a Culture" was cited as the best article published in 1988 in the *Journal of American Culture.*